Copyediting: Deborah Annan
Illustrations: John and Jean Foster
Composition: Carlisle Communications
Cover Design: Diane Beasley Design

Printed in the United States of America
97 96 95 94 93 92 91 90   8 7 6 5 4 3 2 1
Library of Congress Cataloging-in-Publication Data

Hicks, James O.
   Information systems in business : an introduction / James O.
Hicks, Jr. — 2nd ed.
      p.   cm.
   1. Management information systems.   I. Title.
T58.6.H488   1990
658.4'038—dc20   89-28670
                                                                      CIP

      ISBN 0-314-66772-5
      ISBN 0-314-03391-2 (with *Information Systems in Business: Software Applications Manual*, by James O. Hicks, Jr.)
      ISBN 0-314-03192-8 (with *Information Systems in Business: Software Applications Manual*, by James O. Hicks, Jr. and educational software (three 3½" disks))
      ISBN 0-314-03193-6 (with *Information Systems in Business: Software Applications Manual*, by James O. Hicks, Jr. and educational software (four 5¼" disks))

Photo/Figure Credits

Part One Opening Photo (pp. ix, 1) Chris Jones, The Stock Market. **Chapter 1 Opening Photo (p. 3)** M. Gottlieb, FPG International. **Fig. 1–14 (p. 18)** Copyright Lotus Development Corporation 1985. Used with Permission. **Chapter 2 Opening Photo (p. 31)** Antonio Rosario, The Image Bank. **Figs. 2–2 (p. 35), 2–3 (p. 36), 2–7 (p. 39), 2–9 (p. 40)** From "Personal Computers," by H. D. Toong and A. Gupta. Copyright 1982 by Scientific American, Inc. All rights reserved. **Fig. 2–4 (p. 37)** Courtesy of National Semiconductor Company. **Figs. 2–6 (p. 38), 2–8 (p. 40)** Courtesy of International Business Machines Corporation. **Fig. 2–10 (p. 41)** Illustration by Yukio Kondo, reprinted from "Meet the Mouse", by Phil Lopiccola, published in the March 1983 issue of "Popular Computing" magazine, Copyright 1983 by McGraw-Hill, Inc., NY 10020. All rights reserved. **Fig. 2–11 (p. 42)** Photo Courtesy of Hewlett-Packard Company. **Fig. 2–13 (p. 43)** Courtesy of Hayes Microcomputer Products, Inc. **Fig. 2–16 (p. 48)** Courtesy of "InfoWorld" February 11, 1985, p. 28. **Fig. 2–17 (p. 49)** Courtesy Polaroid Corporation. **Fig. 2–18 (p. 50)** Screen shot copyright 1983–1989 Microsoft Corporation, Reprinted with permission from Microsoft Corporation. **Fig. 2–22 (p. 56)** Reprinted with permission of Dunsplus, Inc. **Fig. 2–23 (p. 60)** Reprinted with permission of Price Waterhouse from "MICROCOMPUTERS: Their Use and Misuse in Your Business". Copyright 1983. Price Waterhouse. All rights reserved. **Part Two Opening Photo (pp. x, 75)** Ralph Mercer, Tony Stone Worldwide. **Chapter 3 Opening Photo (p. 77)** Steve Niedorf, The Image Bank. **Chapter 4 Opening Photo (p. 97)** Ken Biggs, The Stock Market. **Chapter 5 Opening Photo (p. 113)** E. Lettau, FPG International. **Fig 5–7**

(Credits are continued following the Index)

INFORMATION SYSTEMS IN BUSINESS: AN INTRODUCTION

Second Edition

James O. Hicks, Jr.
Virginia Polytechnic Institute and State University

West Publishing Company

Saint Paul ■ New York ■ Los Angeles ■ San Francisco

INFORMATION SYSTEMS
IN BUSINESS:
AN INTRODUCTION

Second Edition

To
My Wife Eva
and
My Son Kevin

■ Contents in Brief

PART ONE ■ Information Systems Fundamentals   1

   Chapter 1   An Introduction to Computers   3
   Chapter 2   Personal Computers   31

PART TWO ■ How Managers Use Computers   75

   Chapter 3   Management Information Systems   77
   Chapter 4   Decision-Support Systems   97
   Chapter 5   An Overview of Information System
              Applications   113

PART THREE ■ Developing User Applications   137

   Chapter 6   System Analysis   139
   Chapter 7   System Design and Implementation   165
   Chapter 8   Application Development by End Users   187

PART FOUR ■ Computer Resources   209

   Chapter 9   The Central Processing Unit and Storage
              Devices   211
   Chapter 10   Data Entry and Information Response   237
   Chapter 11   System Software   259
   Chapter 12   Data Storage and Processing   287
   Chapter 13   Data-Base Management Systems   319
   Chapter 14   Distributed Data Processing and Office
              Automation   345

PART FIVE ■ Information Systems, Management, Society,
     and You   385

   Chapter 15   Managing the Information-System
              Resource   387

Chapter 16   Information Systems and Society   403
Chapter 17   Information Systems and You   415

Module A   History of the Computer Industry   432
Module B   Programming Languages   459
Module C   Computer System Evaluation and
             Acquisition   496

 Contents

Preface   xxi

CHAPTER 1 ■ **An Introduction to Computers**   3

Introduction   4

Why Study Information Systems?   4

What is a Computer?   4
*Definition   4   Characteristics and Capabilities   5   Stored
Programs   6*

Overview of a Computer System   7
*Input Devices   8   Central Processing Unit   8   Secondary
Storage   9   Output Devices   9*

How Does a Computer Store Data?   9
The Data Hierarchy   9   Finding Data in a File   12

How Does a Computer Process Data?   12
Batch Processing   12   Immediate Processing   13

How to Put the Computer to Work for You   15
*Putting the Computer to Work Without Programming   16
Putting the Computer to Work by Writing Programs   22*

A Preview of the Remainder of the Text   24

Summing Up   26

Key Terms   27

Review Questions   28

Discussion Questions and Cases   29

CHAPTER 2 ■ **Personal Computers**   31

Introduction   32

The Hardware of a Personal Computer   33
*Types of Personal Computers   33   The System Unit   33
Input/Output Devices   36   Data Communications   42
The Hardware Industry   42*

■ **PART ONE**
**Information
Systems
Fundamentals   1**

The Software of a Personal Computer 46

*General Business Software 46   Special-Interest Software 50
Interacting with Software 50*

Buying Personal-Computer Hardware and Software 53

*Getting Help in Buying a PC System 53   Where to Buy PC
Systems 55*

Personal Computers in the Home 58

Personal-Computer Challenges 58

*Software Piracy 58   Illegal Access 59   Managing Personal
Computers 59*

Future Directions of Personal Computers 60

Summing Up 61

Key Terms 62

Review Questions 63

Discussion Questions and Cases 63

**Appendix: Introduction to the Macintosh Personal
Computer 65**

PART ONE APPLICATION CASE
Users Steering Toward Self-Service 72

■ PART TWO

How Managers Use Computers 75

CHAPTER 3 ■ **Management Information Systems 77**

Introduction 78

What Is a MIS? 78

**What Are the Parts of a Management Information
System? 79**

Objectives, Decisions, and Information 80

Levels of Decision Making 81

Management Uses of Information 84

**Using Information Systems for Competitive
Advantage 85**

Qualitative Characteristics of Information 85

*Relevance 86   Timeliness 86   Accuracy 86
Verifiability 86*

Data or Information Processing? 87

Types of Reports 87

*Scheduled Reports 87   Demand Reports 88   Exception
Reports 88   Predictive Reports 88*

The MIS and Business Functions 88

The MIS and Data-Base Management Systems 89

Decision-Support Systems and the MIS 90

**The Impact of Management Information Systems on
Business 92**

*Easier Business Growth 92   Fewer Clerical Workers 92
Reduced Information-Processing Costs 93   Automation of
Some Decisions 93   More and Better Information 93*

Summing Up 93

Key Terms 95

Review Questions 95

Discussion Questions and Cases 96

CHAPTER 4 ■ **Decision-Support Systems 97**

Introduction 98

What is a Decision-Support System? 98
Definition 98   DSS Software 99

Functions of a Decision-Support System 100
*Model Building 100   Procedural and/or Nonprocedural
Language 100   What-If Analysis 100   Goal Seeking 101
Risk Analysis 101   Statistical Analysis and Management-
Science Models 101   Financial Functions 101
Graphics 101   Hardware Capabilities 101   Data Bases
and External Files 102*

**Why Do Managers Need Decision Support
Systems? 102**

Organization Environment for a Successful DSS 102

Building a Decision-Support System 103
*Predesign 103   Design 105   Implementation 105
Evaluation 105*

Expert Systems 106
*What Is an Expert System? 106   Advantages of Expert
Systems 106   Picking the Right Problem for an Expert
System 107   Components of an Expert System 107
Developing an Expert System 109*

Summing Up 109

Key Terms 110

Review Questions 111

Discussion Questions and Cases 111

CHAPTER 5 ■ **An Overview of Information System
Applications 113**

Introduction 114

The Business Cycle 114

Inventories 116

Computer-Integrated Manufacturing 118

Order Processing 122

Accounts Receivable   123

Accounts Payable   127

Payroll   128

Other Applications   130

Summing Up   131

Key Terms   132

Review Questions   132

Discussion Questions and Cases   133

PART TWO APPLICATION CASE
Executive Info System: Easy, Easier, Easiest   134

■ PART THREE
Developing User
Applications   137

CHAPTER   6 ■ System Analysis   139

Introduction   140

Partitioning of Systems   140

Structured System-Development Life Cycle   141

Angelo's Pizza   142

Feasibility Study   143

Structured System Analysis   144
  *Study the Current System—Process 2.1   146   Model the
  New-System Requirements—Process 2.2   146   Generate
  Alternative Systems—Process 2.3   155   Quantify Each
  Alternative—Process 2.4   156   Select an Alternative
  System—Process 2.5   157   Package the Requirements—
  Process 2.6   157*

Advantages of Structured System Development   157

Computer-Aided Software Engineering   158

System Analysis and Application Development
Without Programming   159

Summing Up   160

Key Terms   161

Review Questions   161

Discussion Questions and Cases   162

CHAPTER   7 ■ System Design and Implementation   165

Introduction   166

Design the System   166
  *Derive Structure Chart—Process 3.1   167   Design Modules—
  Process 3.2   173   Package the Design—Process 3.3   173*

Build the System   176
  Structured Walkthroughs   176   Top-Down Coding   177
  Top-Down Testing   177   Procedure Development   179
  Chief-Programmer Teams   179

Conversion   180

Post-Implementation Audit and Maintenance   181

Summing Up   181

Key Terms   182

Review Questions   182

Discussion Questions and Cases   183

CHAPTER   8 ■ **Application Development by End Users   187**

Introduction   188

**Problems with Conventional Application
Development   188**
  Increasing Labor Cost   188   Long Time Span Required   189
  Slow Implementation of Changes   190   Work Overload   190
  Prespecified versus User-Driven Computing   191

**Methods for User Development of Application
Software   192**
  *Personal-Computer Tools   192   Query Languages and Report
  Generators   192   Graphics Generators   192   Decision-
  Support/Financial-Modeling Tools   193   Application
  Generators   193*

**Blending User Development with Conventional
Development   195**
  *Types of Application Development   195   Data-Base
  Administration   198   End-User Development and
  Computer-Aided Software Engineering (CASE)   199
  Some Cautions about Application Development by End
  Users   199*

Information Centers   200

**Changing Roles of System Analysts and
Programmers   201**

Summing Up   203

Key Terms   204

Review Questions   204

Discussion Questions and Cases   204

PART THREE APPLICATION CASE
Corporate Programmers Lead the Way with CASE   206

■ PART FOUR
Computer Resources   209

CHAPTER 9 ■ **The Central Processing Unit and Storage Devices   211**

Introduction   212

The Central Processing Unit   213
*Primary Storage   213   Arithmetic-Logic Unit   218
Control Unit   218*

Micros, Minis, Mainframes, and Supercomputers   218
*Microcomputers   218   Minicomputers   219   Mainframe
Computers   220   Supercomputers   221*

Parallel Processing   222

Secondary Storage   222
*Primary versus Secondary Storage   222   Magnetic Tape   223
Hard Disks   225   Floppy Disks   226   Laser-Optical
Disks   231   Other Forms of Secondary Storage   232   Cache
Memory   232*

Summing Up   233

Key Terms   234

Review Questions   235

Discussion Questions and Cases   235

CHAPTER 10 ■ **Data Entry and Information Response   237**

Introduction   238

Data Entry   238
*Offline versus Online Data Entry   238   Key-to-Diskette Data
Entry   238   Key-to-Disk Data Entry   239   Interactive Data
Entry   241   Source-Data Automation   242*

Information Response   249
*Visual Display Terminals   249   Printers   250   Computer-
Output Microfiche   253   Laser-Optical Disks   253
Graphics   254   Other Output Media   254*

Summing Up   255

Key Terms   255

Review Questions   256

Discussion Questions and Cases   256

CHAPTER 11 ■ **System Software   259**

Introduction   260

System Software versus Application Software   260
System Software   260   Application Software   262

Types of System Software 262
System Control Software 262   System Support Software 266
System Development Software 266

Types of Operating Systems 268
Batch Systems 268   Interactive Systems 268

Multitasking 269
Advantages of Multitasking 269   Disadvantages of
Multitasking 271

Virtual Storage 271
Advantages of Virtual Storage 272   Disadvantages of Virtual
Storage 273

Timesharing 274

Multiprocessing 274

Summing Up 275

Key Terms 276

Review Questions 277

Discussion Questions and Cases 277

Appendix: OS/2 versus DOS 280

CHAPTER 12 ■ **Data Storage and Processing 287**

Introduction 288

Data Representation 288
True Binary Representation 288   EBCDIC
Representation 290   ASCII Representation 290
Hexadecimal Representation 292   Parity Bits 292

Record-Access Methods 293
Primary and Secondary Keys 293   Sequential Access 294
Random Access 295

File Organization 295
Terminology Used with Files 295   Sequential File
Organization 296   Direct File Organization 299
Indexed File Organization 302   Selecting a File
Organization 304

Information-Processing Modes 306
Batch Processing 307   Immediate Processing 308   Batch-
Sequential 308   Batch-Direct 308   Immediate-Direct 309

Online Direct-Access Systems 310

Real-Time Systems 312

Summing Up 314

Key Terms 315

Review Questions 315

Discussion Questions and Cases 316

CHAPTER 13 ■ **Data-Base Management Systems   319**

Introduction   320

The Traditional Approach to Information Processing   320
*Data Redundancy   320   Lack of Data Integration   320
Program/Data Dependence   321   Lack of Flexibility   322*

The Data-Base Approach to Information Processing   323
*Logical versus Physical Views of Data Storage   324   The Users   325   The Data-Base Management System   326
The Data-Base Administrator   329   The Data Base   329*

Logical Data-Base Structures   331
Tree Structures   332   Network Structures   332   Relational Structures   334

Advantages and Disadvantages of the Data-Base Approach   339
Advantages   339   Disadvantages   339

Summing Up   340

Key Terms   341

Review Questions   341

Discussion Questions and Cases   342

CHAPTER 14 ■ **Distributed Data Processing and Office Automation   345**

Introduction   346

Data Communication   346
Types of Data Communication   346   The Data Transmission Process   350   Communication Hardware   353   Network Systems   356

Distributed Data Processing   359
The Need for Decentralized Processing   359   Hardware Distribution   360   Software Distribution   362   Data Decentralization   364

Office Automation   368
*Word Processing   369   Desktop Publishing   370
Electronic Mail   371   Voice Mail   372   Computer and Video Conferencing   373   Electronic Calendaring   373
Facsimile Transmission   373   Image Storage and Retrieval   373   Forms Processing   374   Integrated Word Processing/Data Processing   374   Office Decentralization and Productivity   376   Human Factors   376*

Summing Up   378

Key Terms 379

Review Questions 380

Discussion Questions and Cases 380

PART FOUR APPLICATION CASE
Fast-Food Distributor Counts on LANs for Swift
Service 382

CHAPTER 15 ■ **Managing the Information-System Resource** 387

Introduction 388

Structure of a MIS Function 388
The Organizational Location of MIS 388 *The Internal Structure of MIS* 390

Managing System Development 391

Managing System Operations 394
System Maintenance 394 *Data-Processing Operations* 395
Physical Security 397

Summing Up 400

Key Terms 400

Review Questions 401

Discussion Questions and Cases 401

CHAPTER 16 ■ **Information Systems and Society** 403

Introduction 404

The Potential Impact of Computer Information Systems 404
The Information Revolution 404 *Working at Home* 405
Control Problems 405

Displacement of Human Beings 406
Automation 406 *Artificial Intelligence* 406

Computers and Individual Privacy 408
Potential Problems 408 *Privacy Legislation* 409

Personal Computers 410

International Data Transfers 410

Computer Crime Cases 411
Equity Funding 411 *Pacific Bell* 412 *Wells Fargo* 412

Summing Up 412

Key Terms 413

Review Questions 413

Discussion Questions and Cases 413

■ **PART FIVE**
Information Systems, Management, Society, and You 385

CHAPTER 17 ■ Information Systems and You   415

Introduction   416
The Effect of Computers on Professional Careers   416
Information-System Careers   417
*Programmer   417   System Analyst   418   EDP
Auditor   419   Data-Processing Operations   420
Data-Base Administrator   420   Knowledge Engineer   420
Information-System Consultant   421   Information-System
Manager   421*

Professional Associations   422
*AFIPS   422   DPMA   422   ACM   422   ASM   423
SIM   423   EDP Auditors Foundation   423*

Professional Certification Programs   423
THE CDP and CCP   424   CISA   424

Information-System Education   424
Summing Up   426
Key Terms   427
Review Questions   427
Discussion Questions and Cases   428

PART FIVE APPLICATION CASE
Microcomputer Managers Need Well-Rounded
Backgrounds   430

MODULE   A ■ History of the Computer Industry   432

Introduction   432
Early Developments in Data Processing   433
*The Abacus   433   Mechanical Calculators   433   Jacquard's
Loom   434   Babbage's Engines and Ada, Countess of
Lovelace   434*

Punched-Card Equipment   436
*Metcalfe's Cards   436   Hollerith's Punched Cards   437
Powers's Punched Cards   437   Mark I Electromechanical
Computer   438*

The First Electronic Computers   439
*The ENIAC   439   The Binary Number System   441   The
EDVAC and EDSAC   441*

First-Generation Computers: 1951–1958   441
UNIVAC-I   441   First-Generation Software   442

Second-Generation Computers: 1959–1964   443
Hardware Advances   443   Software Advances   444

Third-Generation Computers: 1965–1971   445
Hardware Advances   445   Software Advances   445

Fourth-Generation Computers: 1971-Present 446
Hardware Advances 446   Software Advances 447

History of Personal Computers 447
PC Hardware 447   PC Software 450

Future Computers 451

Summing Up 454

Key Terms 456

Review Questions 457

Discussion Questions and Cases 458

MODULE   B ▪ **Programming Languages 459**

Introduction 459

Types of Programming Languages 459
*Machine Language 459   Symbolic Languages 460
Procedural Languages 462   Fourth-Generation
Languages 484*

Language Selection 490

Summing Up 492

Key Terms 493

Review Questions 493

Discussion Questions and Cases 494

MODULE   C ▪ **Computer System Evaluation and
Acquisition 496**

Introduction 496

Conducting an Evaluation of a Computer System 496
*Development of a Request for Proposal 498   Proposal
Evaluation 498   Evaluation of Purchased Software 502
Vendor Selection 503*

Financing Options 503
Purchasing 504   Renting 504   Leasing 505

**Sources of Information-System Equipment and
Services 505**
*Computer Manufacturers 506   Retail Computer Stores 507
Software Vendors 507   Service Bureaus 508   Timesharing
Services 508   Computer Lessors 508   Facilities-
Management Vendor 509   Peripheral-Hardware
Manufacturers 509   Information-System Consultants 509*

Summing Up 509

Key Terms 510

Review Questions 510

Discussion Questions and Cases 511

Glossary G-1
Index I-1

 Preface

TO THE STUDENT

The computer age has become the information age. In my twenty-five year career as a computer operator, system analyst, information systems consultant, and information systems educator, one fact is clear: Business people who successfully apply computers are not primarily interested in computers. They are most concerned with their needs for information and how to build computer-based information systems to meet those needs. A business person who does not have a basic understanding of the tools and techniques for determining his or her information needs and how to transform these needs into computer software will never apply computers successfully. Business people are interested in how to put the computers to work, how to build and use information systems.

Since this text emphasizes how to effectively use computer technology rather than the technology itself, we cover information systems concepts and management's needs for information first. An introduction to information systems concepts early in the text builds a framework for understanding computer information systems and demonstrates the importance of determining business information needs before being concerned with the technical aspects of hardware, data storage, operating systems, and so on. Any good system analyst will tell you that in building information systems it is most important to determine information needs prior to being concerned with computer hardware. Yet, most introductory textbooks cover computer hardware first and then discuss analysis of information needs later in the text. This approach misleads students into believing that computer hardware is the most important part of information systems. The danger of this approach is demonstrated by the large amount of computer hardware, especially personal computers, that is gathering dust through lack of use. The purchasers of this hardware simply did not have a clear understanding of how they would use it before it was purchased. They were more concerned with computer hardware than how to effectively use the hardware.

Many educators have told me that the reason that most textbooks concentrate on hardware first is because it is interesting to students. I think this is true. Full color pictures of hardware and discussions of the speed with which the hardware can operate are certainly interesting. But, how useful will this information be to you once you graduate and attempt to apply this knowledge to business problems? The hardware that you studied will likely be obsolete then.

There is a better way to introduce you to computer hardware, generate interest and to provide you with skills that will be useful to you now and throughout your career. Hands-on use of the personal computer will be more useful to you than looking at color photos of computer hardware. After covering introductory material in Chapter 1, this text covers personal computers in Chapter 2. You can immediately put the personal computer to work learning the disk operating (DOS), word processing, electronic spreadsheets, data-base management systems and/or expert systems. There is more than ample material in the accompanying *Information Systems in Business: Software Applications Manual* and the *Educate-Ability Student Manual* supplements to provide you with hands-on experience on the personal computer.

Hands-on use of the personal computer not only will provide you with the skills to use this most important tool, but it has another equally important contribution in this text: All computers from the largest supercomputers to personal computers have many characteristics in common. As we study these characteristics, we will use personal computers to illustrate them. As you use PCs you will literally be able to see and feel these characteristics of computers.

The text contains 17 chapters divided into five parts. These chapters cover the topics which I consider to be the most important in a first course in information systems. A certainty in the information systems area is that instructors differ on the material that each feels should be covered in this course. Therefore, the text provides three modules that cover topics which some instructors may want to include in the course. In fact, some instructors will not cover all the chapters in the text. This built-in flexibility will allow your instructor to tailor the course to your specific needs.

Part One of the text is designed to give you an overview of information processing and management information systems, including some examples of information processing systems and an introduction to personal computers. This will provide you with a basic understanding of the information systems field and knowledge of that most user-friendly machine, the personal computer. Part Two surveys how managers typically use computers. Part Three is devoted to covering the methods that are used to apply computers to business information needs. You will find that you can understand these approaches to developing applications without an in-depth understanding of computer hardware and software which is covered in Part Four under Computer Resources. Part Five covers how information systems resources are managed and the relationships between information systems, society, and you. The three modules cover the history of the computer industry, programming languages, and computer system evaluation and acquisition.

As you read this text you will see that users must be directly involved in the process of developing information systems. In fact, research has shown that the most successful information systems are those where there is a direct heavy user involvement in development and maintenance of those systems. A business professional simply cannot afford to take the attitude that knowledge of information systems is not necessary and consequently leave application development entirely to information systems professionals. Only you know what information you need from a system. If you do not understand information systems it will be impossible to translate this need for information into an operational information system. I am sure you will find this an enjoyable and useful course. In fact if you master the material in this course and apply it now and when you begin your career, I think that you will find this course to have been the most useful of any taken in your collegiate program.

This text contains several features which will assist you in learning and reinforcing the material contained in the text. Each chapter contains the following:

1. A detailed chapter outline provides an overview of the chapter so that you can see where we are headed as you read the chapter.

2. Definitions of new and unfamiliar terms that are used in the chapter text are placed in the page margins.

3. A point-by-point summary reviews the major topics introduced in the chapter.

4. A list of key terms is included at the end of each chapter. As with many other fields, information systems terminology is different. Thus, learning the terminology is important to understanding information systems. You should review these key terms and for any that you don't understand you should refer back to the chapter or to the comprehensive glossary at the end of the text.

5. Review questions are provided so that you can independently test your knowledge of the chapter.

6. Short discussion questions and cases apply the material of each chapter to real-world situations. Often these cover controversial topics. Your instructor is likely to use these questions and cases for class discussion purposes.

7. An application case that describes state-of-the-art business computer applications concludes each part. They provide unique insights into the applications, problems, and successes of computers in business.

Supplements to the text include a Study Guide authored by Robert M. Brown. This study guide provides study outlines, additional questions, and other materials to assist you in learning the material in the text.

Information Systems in Business: Software Applications Manual is a most important supplement to the text. This manual contains hands-on tutorials for the personal computer software that is most commonly used in business applications. Tutorials are included for the following software:

- MS-DOS (the most widely used operating system for PCs)
- Lotus 1-2-3 and VP Planner (electronic spreadsheets)
- WordPerfect (a word processor)
- dBASE III Plus (a data-base management system)
- VP-Expert (an expert system shell)

Instructional versions of all this software, except for MS-DOS, are available on both 3 1/2 and 5 1/4 inch disks with the manual.

Some instructors will decide to use Ability, or another integrated package, to give you hands-on experience with integrated software. The *Educate-Ability Student Manual* provides a hands-on tutorial for this very easy-to-use integrated package. Ability has word processing, electronic spreadsheet, data base, graphics, and communications capabilities.

■ TO THE INSTRUCTOR

This text takes a user view of information systems. The intent of the text is to provide a business student with the information systems fundamentals necessary to operate effectively in a computerized business environment. In writing the first edition of this text I had several basic objectives:

1. Since most of the students in the introductory course will, in their careers, be users of information systems rather than information systems professionals, the text should approach information systems from a user perspective.

2. The text should take a top-down approach, therefore information systems concepts, management needs for information, and basic computer concepts should be covered first in the text. This provides the student with a fundamental understanding of the subject and provides a basic framework that the student and the instructor can relate to as the course progresses.

3. The text should have substantial coverage of personal computers and their application software. An early introduction to PC concepts in the text can serve as a basis to introduce large computer hardware and software concepts later in the text.

4. The structured system development cycle, including structured analysis using data flow diagrams, should be covered. Although this course is not designed to provide students with an in-depth understanding of large real-world information systems applications, many students are over-whelmed with the apparent sheer complexity of large information systems applications. They can easily leave some introductory courses with the feeling that information systems applications are hopelessly complex black boxes that they would rather not deal with. They can also easily leave other introductory courses with the naive thought that if they understand how to use an electronic spreadsheet and a word processor they have the knowledge to operate in the information intensive business world of tomorrow. Students *should* leave with a knowledge of the structured set of tools that can be employed to understand and develop any business system, from the smallest to the largest. The hierarchical and graphic approach of structured system development is easy to understand. It provides students with a fundamental understanding of how large and complex systems can be analyzed, designed, implemented, and maintained. This knowledge can give students the confidence that there are methods to deal with complexity in information systems. They can see that the fundamentals of structured methods can be applied to any business computer application and to different approaches to development, including CASE and prototyping.

5. New tools are emerging that will assist users in developing their own applications without programmers. This area should be covered along with its relationship to the information center concept, data-base management systems, and decision support systems.

6. Because of the use of personal computers in business, more users will be directly involved in the evaluation and acquisition of hardware and/or software. A module should be devoted to this topic.

The success of the first edition has proven that many information systems instructors agree with these objectives. Thus, I have retained these objectives in the second edition. The major changes that I have made are:

1. All the material has been updated to reflect technological change, especially hardware, communication, and software topics.

2. Coverage of the personal computer has been increased, both in the Personal Computer chapter and by integrating personal computer material in other chapters.

3. The accompanying *Information Systems in Business: Software Applications Manual* has been added to provide a thorough, hands-on introduction to MS-DOS, Lotus 1-2-3, VP Planner, WordPerfect, dBase III Plus, and VP-Expert. These tutorials have been completely rewritten and are greatly expanded over the tutorials that were contained in an appendix to the previous edition. The tutorials have been designed to lead your students through the software with a minimum of instructor assistance. Hands-on exercises at the end of each topic will give students experience in using the personal computer for word processing, spreadsheet, database, graphics and expert systems tasks.

4. The decision support systems module has been converted to a chapter to reflect the increasing importance of these types of systems.

5. A new chapter, An Overview of Information Systems Applications (Chapter 5) has been added to introduce students to typical business applications of computers. The first portion of this chapter is devoted to providing an overview of the cycle that occurs within a business (or how a business operates) from the acquisition of capital, to the purchase of goods and services, to the sale of the product, and finally the collection of accounts receivable. The explanation of this "business cycle" is accompanied by an explanation of the information needed to support the major functions of a business.

6. More business examples of the concepts being presented have been integrated with the text.

7. Review questions, discussion questions, and cases have been added at the end of each chapter and module. These provide the basis for review and class discussions concerning the application of information systems to business needs.

8. There is expanded coverage of computer-integrated manufacturing, the use of information systems to gain competitive advantage, expert systems, and the management of information systems.

9. The text has a more lively, full-color design.

10. The BASIC appendix and the chapter on general systems concepts have been deleted.

11. Each chapter in the text is written as independently as possible so that you may rearrange the sequencing of the material coverage if you prefer.

The teaching and learning tools included in each chapter are as follows:

1. A detailed outline at the beginning of each chapter to provide an overview of the chapter.

2. Margin definitions are provided for new terms that are not the subject of the discussion at that point in the text.

3. A chapter summary provides a point-by-point review of the major topics of the chapter.

4. A list of key terms may be used for review of terminology.

5. A set of review questions may be used by the students on their own or in class to review the chapter.

6. Discussion questions and cases provide sometimes controversial situations related to the chapter material. I find these particularly useful to generate class discussion.

7. An application case concludes each part. These relate text concepts to real-world applications and problems. They can provide unique insights into the thoughts of managers and information systems professionals concerning material presented in the text. If used properly they can help bring the material alive.

The end-of-text materials include a comprehensive glossary. Understanding terminology is essential to understanding information systems. Quite often I have had students purchase a paperback dictionary of information processing terms. This should not be necessary with this text due to the comprehensive nature of the glossary. Furthermore, I think the definitions in the glossary should be standardized. Therefore, where possible I have used American National Standards Institute definitions from the *American National Dictionary for Information Processing.* Also used are definitions from the IBM publication *Dictionary of Computing.*

The supplements to this text include:

1. The *Information Systems in Business: Software Applications Manual.* This manual contains thorough, hands-on tutorials for MS-DOS, Lotus 1-2-3, VP Planner, WordPerfect, dBASE III Plus, and VP-Expert. Instructional versions of all these packages are provided on either 3 1/2 or 5 1/4 inch disks to each student.

2. The *Educate-Ability Student Manual* and Educate-Ability disks. Educate-Ability, the student version of Ability, is an integrated package with word processing, spreadsheet, graphics, database, and communications capabilities.

3. The *Study Guide to Accompany Information Systems in Business: An Introduction,* 2/e, authored by Robert M. Brown. This study guide provides study outlines, additional questions, and other materials to assist students in learning the material in the text.

4. The *Instructor's Resource Manual to Accompany Information Systems in Business: An Introduction.* This manual contains author's notes, chapter overviews, lecture outlines, and suggested answers to the review questions and discussion questions and cases.

5. A disk containing the lecture outlines in ASCII format. You can use these as a starting point to create your own customized lecture outlines.

6. The *Test Bank to Accompany Information Systems in Business: An Introduction* prepared by George Novotny. This text bank contains over 1,500 multiple choice test questions, grouped by topic and about twenty word match questions for each chapter and module.

7. WestTest computerized testing, containing the multiple choice test questions from the test bank.

8. Color acetate and transparency masters.

■ ACKNOWLEDGMENTS

A text of this type is produced not only by the author but by a team of individuals. There are numerous clerical, proofreading, and research tasks necessary to produce a text. Several individuals have made contributions in one or more of these areas including Sanjeev Mathur, Candace Kim, and Mike Gilmore. Some individuals have made more specific contributions to this text. I would like to thank Sanjeev Mathur for his assistance in developing the hands-on software tutorials that accompany the text and Mario Macaluso for his assistance in developing the Macintosh appendix to chapter two. A particularly important person in developing this text has been Phyllis Neece whose typing and word processing skills were indispensable in completing the manuscript and the supplements to the text. I am also thankful for the environment at Virginia Polytechnic Institute and State University that encourages the commitment and provides the support for projects of this duration and size.

Numerous professors at other institutions were most helpful in providing review and criticism of the first edition and the revised manuscript. These include: Joyce L. Abler, Central Michigan University; Warren J. Boe, University of Iowa; Patricia T. Boggs, John Carroll University; Warren Briggs, Suffolk University; O. Maxie Burns, Georgia Southern University; Joyce L. Capen, Central Michigan University; Belford E. Carver, Southeastern Louisiana University; Thomas L. Case, Georgia Southern College; Eli Boyd Cohen, Bradley University; Marilyn J. Correa, Polk Community College; John S. DaPonte, Southern Connecticut State University; Barbara Denison, Wright State University; Howard Eulencamp, Los Angeles Valley College; Virginia R. Gibson, University of Maine; James Gips, Boston College; Thomas Harris, Ball State University; Jack Hogue, University of North Carolina–Charlotte; John Kelder, Cerritos College; Ambrose S. Kodet, Mankato State University; Gary J. Koehler, University of Florida; Wojtek Kozaczynski, The University of Illinois at Chicago; James E. LaBarre, University of Wisconsin–Eau Claire; Murray Levy, West Los Angeles College; Gretchen Marx, Central Connecticut State University; Bruce J. McLaren, Indiana State University; Elizabeth Megalski, Marquette University; John Melrose, University of Wisconsin–Eau Claire; Lawrence McNitt, College of Charleston; Malik M. Nazir, Illinois State University; Leonard Nicholas, Weber State University; George Novotny, Ferris State University; Robert H. Orr, Purdue University; Ronald Pedigo, Emporia State University; Floyd Ploeger, Southwest Texas State University; Theodore C. Robinson, Central Texas College; Jerry D. Sawyer, Kennesaw College; James B. Shannon, New Mexico State University; Patsy C. Smith, Georgia State University; Sandra Stalker, North Shore Community College; David Stetler, Northern Illinois University; Margaret Thomas, Ohio University; Ronald Thompson, University of Vermont. Many of their ideas have been included in the text.

Finally I am grateful to my family for the support and encouragement they gave me in this project. The support of an author's family is crucial during the long hours that are necessary to produce a text of this type. My family has contributed to this project in many ways. These contributions are important and I am grateful.

James O. Hicks, Jr.
October 20, 1989
Blacksburg, Virginia

INFORMATION SYSTEMS IN BUSINESS: AN INTRODUCTION

Second Edition

PART ONE ■ Information Systems Fundamentals

An Introduction to Computers

■ Chapter 1

CHAPTER OUTLINE

Introduction

Why Study Information Systems?

What Is a Computer?
Definition
Characteristics and Capabilities
Stored Programs

Overview of a Computer System
Input Devices
Central Processing Unit
Secondary Storage
Output Devices

How Does a Computer Store Data?
The Data Hierarchy
Finding Data in a File

How Does a Computer Process Data?
Batch Processing
Immediate Processing

How to Put the Computer to Work for You
Putting the Computer to Work Without Programming
Putting the Computer to Work by Writing Programs

A Preview of the Remainder of the Text

Summing Up

Key Terms

Review Questions

Discussion Questions and Cases

■ INTRODUCTION

The premier invention of this century is the computer. In a relatively short time it has affected many areas of our lives. For example, computers help control our automobiles, act as challenging adversaries in electronic games, make possible very sophisticated medical diagnostic tools such as the computerized axial tomography (CAT) scanner, and even act as an ideal matchmaker through computerized dating services. But most important, computers have had a tremendous impact on the way information is processed within organizations. In fact, modern management information systems would not be possible without the computer.

In the first section of the chapter we will explore the capabilities and characteristics of this machine we call a computer. Afterward we will present a brief overview of a computer system and look at how a computer stores and processes data. In the final section of the chapter we will turn our attention to the most practical and important topic: how to put the computer to work for you.

■ WHY STUDY INFORMATION SYSTEMS?

Computer-based information systems are used in most businesses today, and computers are found in many homes. In fact, many firms, even many small ones, could not operate without these systems. Some businesses are applying computer-based information systems to gain advantages over their competitors.

Yet business people who successfully use computers are not computer experts. They understand the basics of computers and how to use them for business purposes, but they are most concerned about their information needs and how to build computer-based information systems to meet those needs.

An **information system** provides information for decision making; today, this is typically an automated system that uses a computer for processing data. Thus, businesses are interested in information systems, not computers per se. In this text we approach the subject of computers in terms of information systems. Basic knowledge of how computers operate is important, but only to the extent that it helps us with the more critical goal of learning how to acquire, build, and use computer-based information systems. Your goal in this course should be to become information-system literate, not just computer literate.

■ WHAT IS A COMPUTER?

Definition

A **computer** is an information processor capable of performing substantial computation, including numerous arithmetic or logical operations, without intervention by a human operator. The term *substantial* in this definition is open to wide interpretation. Is a pocket calculator that performs a series of computations without human intervention a computer? It may or may not be. In recent years the distinction between calculators and computers—particularly programmable calculators—has become quite blurred.

Characteristics and Capabilities

A computer has the following characteristics and capabilities (see Figure 1–1).

Figure 1–1
Capabilities of a Computer

Both the program and data are stored in the machine. The program is executed in order by statement number (starting with statement 10) until a branching statement is encountered. Statement 20 is a branching IF statement. If the type is equal to salary, then statement 30 is performed. If the type is not equal to salary, then statement 40 is performed.

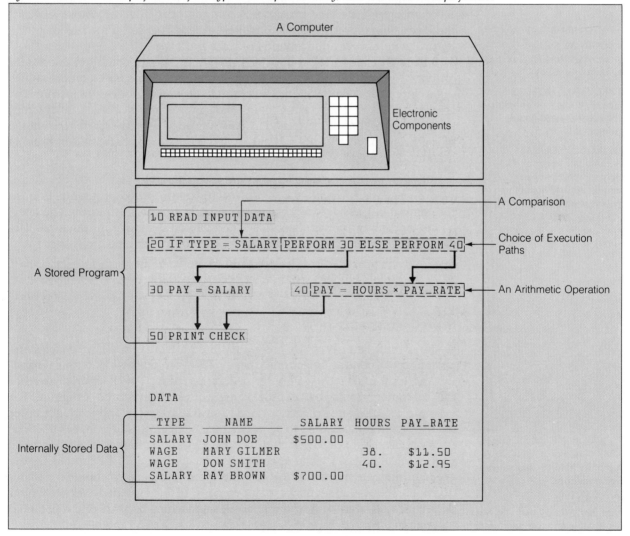

Characteristics of computers

1. It is electronic. A computer operates by the movement of electronic pulses through circuits rather than by the mechanical movement of parts. This characteristic is essential to the speed of modern computers. Electronic pulses flow through the circuits of today's computers at roughly half the speed of light (about six inches in a billionth of a second). This is incredibly fast compared with mechanical movement. Certainly we could build a computer based on mechanical movement; however, such a machine would be useless because of its slow speed.

2. It can perform arithmetic operations. A computer is able to add, subtract, multiply, and divide.

3. It can compare. The ability to compare one piece of information with another (to determine whether they are equal, whether one is less than the other, and so on) is essential to the operation of a computer. Comparison operations are also called logical operations.

✗ RAM **4. It has internal storage and retrieval of data.** Today's computers have vast capabilities for storage and retrieval of data. Some computers can store several million characters of data in internal random access memory (RAM).

5. It can *execute* a stored program. A computer can internally store (or hold) the instructions for operations to be performed. This set of instructions for a particular computer application is called a ***program***.

6. It has a choice of *execution paths* within a program. A computer can choose (or branch) among different sets of program instructions based on the values of the input data. For example, in a *payroll program* one series of instructions is executed if the employee is paid according to hours worked; a different series is executed if the employee is paid a fixed salary. Therefore, the course of execution may vary substantially, based on the input data the computer is examining.

Although all these characteristics are important, the two most crucial are that computers are electronic and they can execute stored programs. Prior to the computer, mechanical calculators were used to perform arithmetic operations, and filing cabinets were used to store and retrieve information. The electronic basis for the computer gives the computer incredible speed and accuracy, and the stored program enables this speed and accuracy to occur without human intervention. Essentially, humans are exceedingly slow compared with the flow of electronic pulses.

Stored Programs

A stored program gives the computer three advantages: (1) it enables the computer to operate at electronic speeds, (2) it provides tremendous reliability, and (3) it makes the computer general-purpose. The electronic speed of the computer would be of little value without the stored program. For example, let's assume an operator had to sit at a computer and manually enter an instruction for each step to be performed, such as an addition, subtraction, or comparison. Obviously, such a machine would be about as useful as a basic pocket calculator, since the speed of the machine would be limited by the speed of the person operating it. Furthermore, the person would be making decisions about the sequence of operations to be executed, which would decrease the *accuracy* and *reliability* of such a machine because of the potential for human error.

EXECUTE
To run a computer program.

PROGRAM
A set of instructions for the computer to follow.

EXECUTION PATH
The specific set of program instructions used by the computer.

PAYROLL PROGRAM
A computer program that prepares checks to pay employees and maintains payment information.

ACCURACY
A quality held by that which is free from error.

RELIABILITY
A quality held by that which is dependable and can be trusted.

Once a computer program has been written to perform a task and has been thoroughly checked so that all errors have been removed, the computer will execute the task with extreme accuracy and reliability—producing results with essentially no error. Many experts would argue that this ability to capture human decision-making and processing capabilities in a computer program is by far the most significant contribution of computers. In essence, once a task that was previously done by humans has been accurately worked out in a computer program, the computer will continuously perform the task with very high accuracy and reliability. In other words, society no longer has to train people to perform that task. Humans are free to perform tasks that computers are not capable of doing. We have long had machines and animals—such as tractors, horses, automobiles, and lawnmowers—that lighten the burden of manual labor. However, the computer is the first machine that relieves us of the intellectual burden of storing, processing, and retrieving data and making decisions based on the data.

The stored-program capability makes the computer general-purpose in that the stored program can be changed. A single computer can be used for many different tasks. These tasks may be as varied as data processing; editing, formatting, and typing this book; and controlling robots that weld automobile parts.

Computers are truly revolutionary machines. Because of the dramatic decrease in their cost, they are being used in many facets of daily life. To function in today's society and especially in the business world you must develop not only a computer literacy, but also the ability to use the vast potential inherent in a computer. It is the primary goal of this text to develop your ability to understand and use computer technology

■ OVERVIEW OF A COMPUTER SYSTEM

In this section we look at the basics of a computer system; the subject will be covered in more depth later. Figure 1–2 shows an overview of a computer

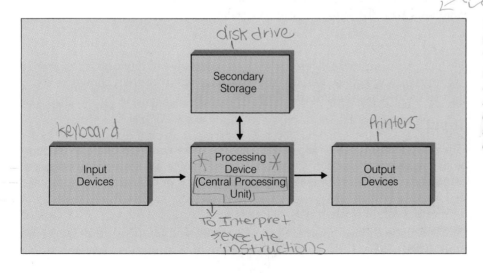

**Figure 1–2
Overview of a
Computer System**

Data and programs are moved back and forth between primary storage (within the central processing unit) and secondary storage, as they are needed for execution of programs.

Figure 1–3
A Personal-Computer System

Although the monitor is sometimes called a cathode-ray tube (CRT), technically the CRT is only a part of the monitor. In fact, monitors on portable PCs use light-emitting diodes (LEDs) or gas plasma rather than CRTs.

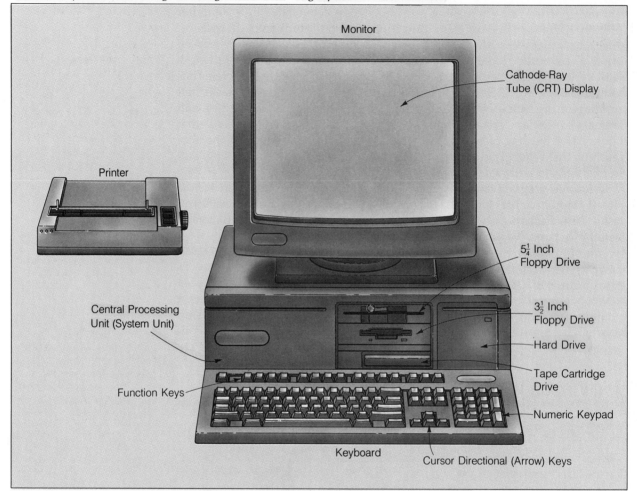

INPUT
Data being received (or to be received) into a device or into a computer program.

PROCESSING
To perform operations on data.

STORAGE
The process of retaining data, program instructions, and output in machine-readable form.

OUTPUT
The information produced by a computer from a specific input.

system. All computer systems have four categories of devices: *input, processing, storage,* and *output.* Refer to the *personal computer* system shown in Figure 1–3 as we discuss these four categories.

Input Devices

There are many types of **input devices**, the most common being a keyboard with an attached *monitor*. Optical scanners, voice-recognition devices, and various devices that read magnetically coded tape or disk are other examples.

Central Processing Unit

The processing in a computer system is performed by the **central processing unit (CPU).** The CPU is the centerpiece of a computer system; strictly speaking, it is the computer. Its function is to interpret and execute the instructions of the program. Thus, the CPU in effect controls the complete computer system. As shown in Figure 1–4 the CPU has three components: the control unit, the arithmetic-logic unit, and primary storage. The **control unit** decodes program instructions and directs other components of the computer to perform the tasks specified in the program instructions. Arithmetic operations such as multiplication, division, subtraction, and addition are performed by the **arithmetic-logic unit**. This unit also performs logical operations, such as comparing the relative magnitude of two pieces of information. **Primary storage** stores the program instructions that are currently being executed and also stores data while they are being processed by the CPU.

Secondary Storage

Secondary storage is used for relatively long-term storage of data. The most widely used secondary-storage media are magnetic disks, such as hard and *floppy disks* used in personal computers, and magnetic tapes. The bulk of information used by a computer application is stored in secondary storage but must be transferred to primary storage before it can be processed by the CPU. Therefore, information is continually being read into and written out of primary storage during the execution of the program. The data not being used by the CPU are stored in secondary storage. The main differences between primary and secondary storage are that primary storage is part of the CPU, allows very fast access to data, is *volatile*, and is more expensive than secondary storage.

PRIMARY — will loose info if the electricity is turned off.
— It is temporary storage

Output Devices

Output devices record data either in forms humans can read, such as printouts, or in machine-readable forms, such as magnetic disks and tapes. Output devices include a wide variety of printers which use different technologies—such as impact, print chains, ink jets, and laser imaging—to produce print. Other examples of output are voice output as well as graphics terminals which display information directly in graphic form, such as bar charts and line graphs. Many input and secondary storage devices (such as magnetic tape, disk, and monitors) also serve as output devices or media. Figure 1–5 illustrates the input, processing, secondary storage, and output devices typically used in a medium-to-large computer system.

■ HOW DOES A COMPUTER STORE DATA?

The Data Hierarchy

Listed here in descending order of complexity are the components of the data hierarchy in an information system:

PERSONAL COMPUTER
A computer small enough to be placed on a desktop and designed to be used by one person who possesses very little, if any, programming knowledge.

MONITOR
A device containing a cathode ray tube (CRT), such as a television picture tube, that can be used to display data or graphic images. This device is also often called a CRT or a video display terminal (VDT).

FLOPPY DISK
A data-storage medium, used in small computers, that is a 3½- or 5¼-disk of polyester film covered with a magnetic coating.

VOLATILE STORAGE
Computer storage that loses the data and/or programs stored in it when the electricity to the computer is turned off, thus it is temporary storage.

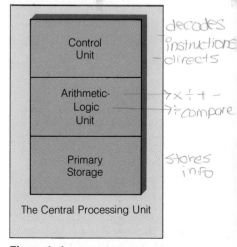

decodes instructions — directs

→ x ÷ + −
→ ? compare

stores info

Figure 1–4
The Central Processing Unit

A central processing unit on a personal computer is often called the system unit.

Figure 1–5
A Medium-to-Large Computer System

There is a large variety of input and output devices for computers (see chapter 10). Only the most common ones are shown here.

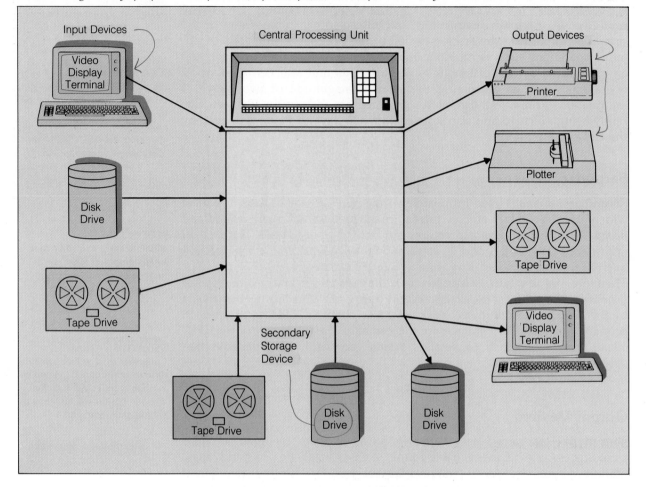

1. Data base   Highest-level storage
2. File or data set
3. Record
4. Field or item
5. Byte
6. Bit   Lowest-level storage

This is called a data hierarchy because data bases are composed of files, files are composed of records, and so on. Figure 1–6 illustrates the relationships among these components of the information-system data hierarchy.

Bit   The term **bit** is short for binary digit. It can assume one of two possible states, representing either a 1 or 0. In secondary storage a bit typically represents data through the positive or negative polarity of an electrical charge on a magnetic recording medium such as tape or disk. In *semiconductor storage,* usually used for primary storage, a bit is represented by an electrical circuit that is either conducting or not conducting electricity.

Figure 1–6
The Data Hierarchy

Data bases contain files, files contain records, records contain fields, fields contain bytes, and bytes contain individual binary digits or bits. Ultimately all data are represented through bits that have values of either 1's or 0's.

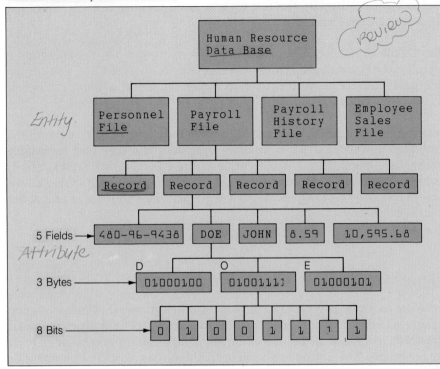

Character	ASCII Bit Pattern
A	01000001
B	01000010
C	01000011
D	01000100
E	01000101
F	01000110
G	01000111
0	00110000
1	00110001
2	00110010
3	00110011
4	00110100
5	00110101
6	00110110
7	00110111
8	00111000
9	00111001

Figure 1–7
Selected Characters in the ASCII Coding Scheme

A coding scheme is a bit pattern that uses bits in specified combinations to represent characters. Only a portion of the ASCII-coding scheme is shown here.

Byte   The ability to represent only binary digits (bits) in a computer system is not sufficient for business information processing. Numeric and alphabetic characters as well as a wide variety of special characters such as dollar signs, question marks, and quotation marks, must be stored. In a computer system, a character of information is called a **byte.** A byte of information is stored by using several bits in specified combinations called **bit patterns.** One widely used bit pattern for personal computers and data communications is the American Standard Code for Information Interchange (ASCII); see Figure 1–7. ASCII uses eight bits to represent one character. Each 1 or 0 corresponds to a single bit.

Field or Item   A **field** or **item** of data is one or more bytes that contain data about an *attribute* of an *entity* in the information system. An entity in a payroll system is an individual employee. Attributes are the employee's name, pay rate, and so on. These attributes are stored in a field or item of data. Figure 1–8 shows a payroll record with typical fields of data.

Record   A **record** is a collection of fields relating to a specific entity. For example, the payroll record shown in Figure 1–6 contains fields of data

ATTRIBUTE
A characteristic or property of an entity.

ENTITY
A subject on which data are kept in an information system.

Payroll Master-File Record
First Name, Middle Initial
Last Name
Street Address
City/State
Zip Code
Social Security Number
Sick Leave Eligibility Date
Effective Date of
Salary Increase
Date of Birth
Department Number
Hourly Rate
Sick Hours
Overtime Earnings
Regular Earnings
Federal Tax Year-to-Date
Marital Status
Number of Dependents
Total Voluntary Deductions
Year-to-Date
FICA Year-to-Date
State Tax Year-to-Date
City Tax Year-to-Date
Net Earnings Year-to-Date

Figure 1–8
Sample Data Fields in a
Payroll Master-File Record

The term master file *often refers to the file that stores relatively permanent data. This payroll master file would be updated whenever employee paychecks are produced or other data fields are changed.*

DATA-BASE MANAGEMENT SYSTEM
A computer program that stores, retrieves, and updates data that are stored in one or more files.

QUERIES
Requests for information from a file.

relating to a specific employee. An analogy can be made between a computer-based record and an individual folder in a manual file (see Figure 1–9). A folder in a payroll file may contain much the same information as a record in a computer-based payroll file. The field that distinguishes a record from all other records in a file is the **primary key.** For example, the primary key in a payroll record is usually the employee's social security number, since it is different for each employee.

File   A **file** is a collection of related records. For example, the collection of payroll records for all employees in a company is a payroll file. The concept of a computer file is very similar to a manual file in a filing cabinet, as illustrated in Figure 1–9.

Data base   A **data base** consists of all the files of an organization, structured and integrated to facilitate update of the files and retrieval of information from them. The term has often been used rather loosely. Technically a data base consists of the files that are part of a *data-base management system*. However, data base is often used to refer to all the files of an organization.

Finding Data in a File

There are basically two types of file organization: those which allow sequential access to the data and those which allow direct access. With a **sequential-access file,** records must be read in the same order as they were written to the storage media. The computer begins searching for a record by examining the first record in the file and then sequentially examining the following records until the required record is located. Certain storage media, such as magnetic tape, allow only sequential access to data. In order for a record to be found on a reel of magnetic tape, the computer must read the tape sequentially, beginning with the first record.

On the other hand, a **direct-access file** allows immediate, direct access to individual records in the file. Several techniques are used to accomplish direct-access file organization; these will be discussed in more depth in chapter 12. Magnetic hard and floppy disks are by far the most commonly used devices for storing direct-access files. Direct-access file organization must be used whenever immediate access to individual records is required.

■ HOW DOES A COMPUTER PROCESS DATA?

Batch Processing

With **batch processing,** changes and *queries* to a file are stored for a period of time. A processing run is made periodically to update the file, produce reports, and produce responses to the queries. Batch runs can be made on a scheduled basis (such as daily, weekly, or monthly) or on an as-required basis.

Figure 1–9
Computer Files and Records Compared to Files in a Manual File

A computer file is analogous to a manual file drawer. Computer records are analogous to individual file folders within a drawer. Computer items of data are analogous to the data items contained in a file folder. Thinking of data storage in this manner will help you remember the way information is stored in a computer system.

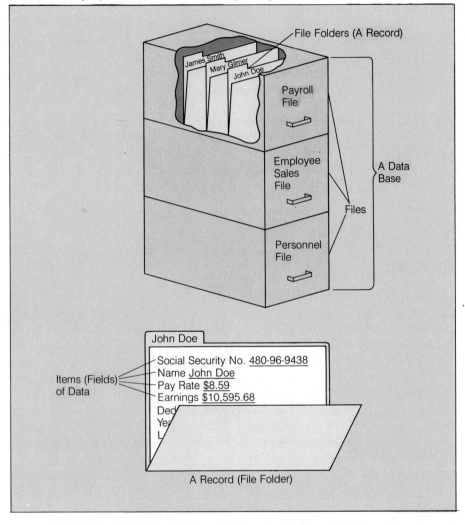

Batch processing with a sequential file stored on magnetic tape is illustrated in Figure 1–10. Figure 1–11 illustrates batch processing with a direct-access file stored on disk.

Immediate Processing

In **immediate processing,** transactions are processed to update the file immediately or shortly after a real-world event occurs (see Figure 1–12 on page 16). Information-processing applications that use immediate processing

Figure 1–10
Batch Processing with Sequential Tape Files

Changes used to update a master file are called transactions. Since the records are stored sequentially on the master file (usually in ascending order by the primary key), the transactions are sorted in this same order prior to updating. In the file-update program, records are read off the old master file simultaneously with changes read off the transaction file. The old master-file records are updated and then written to the new file.

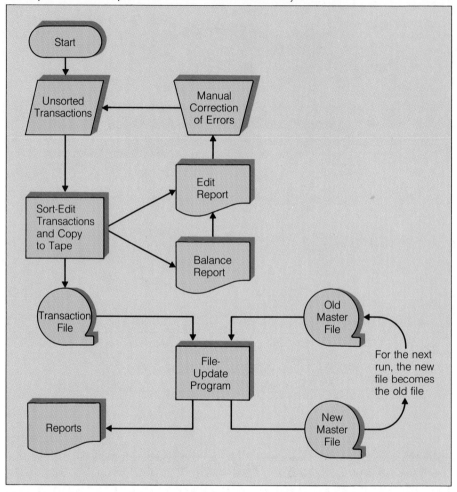

(immediate Processing)

are often called **real-time** or **on-line applications**. A real-time application can immediately capture data about ongoing events or processes and provide the information necessary to manage them. An airline-reservation system is a real-time application. These systems are also called online because the files are directly accessible (online) to the computer.

Real-time systems must have real-time files that are updated immediately after the event occurs. Consequently, at any point in time, the data in real-time files should accurately reflect the status of the real-world variables they represent. For example, when a customer reserves a seat on an airline flight, the travel agent keys in the reservation, and the inventory of available

Figure 1–11
Batch Processing with a Direct-Access File

In this example the master file as well as the transactions used to change the master file are stored on a direct-access file. These changes are held until a periodic file-update is run. During the update run, the records in the master file are read into the file-update program. Each record is changed and then written back to disk.

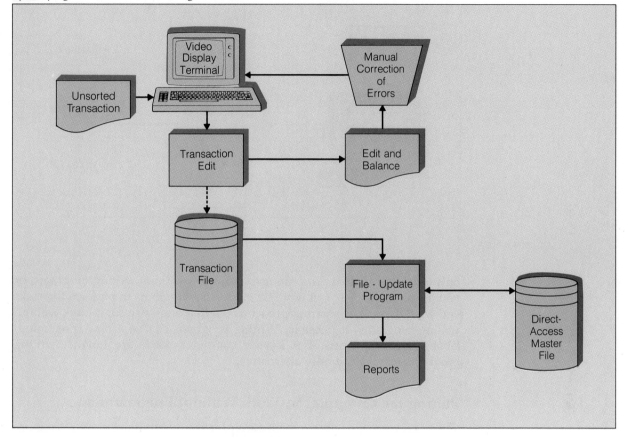

seats on the flight is immediately changed to reflect one less. Immediate processing requires direct-access files—immediate processing with sequential files would be impractical because of the time required to search for individual records. Batch processing, on the other hand, can occur with either sequential- or direct-access files. Chapter 12 will cover these concepts in more depth.

HOW TO PUT THE COMPUTER TO WORK FOR YOU

Now that you have a basic understanding of computers and the ways information is stored and processed, let's look at how you can put the computer to work for you. It is much easier than you may imagine. There are

Figure 1–12
Immediate Processing

As real-world events occur, the real-time master file is updated immediately. When process-ing errors occur, an error message is displayed on the terminal for immediate correction by the terminal operator.

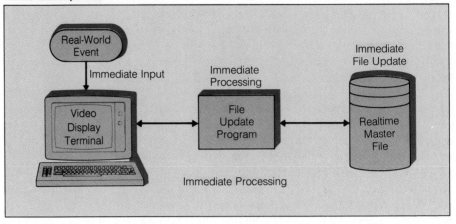

only two ways to do it. You can use computers without writing programs, or you (or someone else) can write the necessary programs to perform the tasks you want done. The smart approach is the first one—use computers without writing programs, if possible. Writing programs can be a time-consuming, labor-intensive process. But if your computer needs are unique, writing programs may be the only alternative.

Putting the Computer to Work Without Programming

There is a very strong movement toward using computers without program-ming. Personal computers (PCs) have been an important contributing factor in this movement. Many people have bought PCs and want them to perform useful work. But no computer performs work without programs. If programs had to be written for all the individual tasks that users wanted done, where would all these programs come from? It has been estimated that if we wrote specific programs for all the tasks performed on computers, by the year 1992 we would need more programmers than the total population of the United States! Fortunately there is a better way. The four most typical ways to apply the computer without programming are word processing, electronic spread-sheets, data-base management systems, and preprogrammed application packages.

Word Processing   In both your academic and professional careers you will continually need to convey your thoughts in writing. Your writing skills will be one of the crucial factors determining your future success. Computers can help you develop these skills. People who teach writing find that students using **word processing** software typically improve their performance by one letter grade.

What can word processing programs do for you? Most important, they store your writing on computer files. This allows you to make extensive revisions with minimal retyping. Any accomplished writer will tell you that refinement through revisions is the secret to good writing.

Excellent word-processing programs are available for PCs. Two of the most popular are **Word** and **WordPerfect**, but there are many other very good ones. Some programs can show when you have made spelling, punctuation, word tense and style errors. Other programs can even tell you when you have used redundant, verbose, unclear, cutesy, or pompous language! We will discuss word processing in more depth in chapter 14.

Electronic Spreadsheets   If a situation calls for little input data but requires complex calculations, an **electronic spreadsheet** is often used. The electronic spreadsheet originated with personal computers, but today almost all kinds of computers support spreadsheets. Some of the widely used spreadsheets are **Lotus 1-2-3, SuperCalc, Excel, Quattro,** and **VP-Planner**. These programs allow users to build a spreadsheet that has **rows** and **columns** on the computer display screen. Figure 1–13 illustrates an electronic spreadsheet. As you can see, each column is labeled by an alphabetic digit and each row by a numeric digit. Any intersection of a row and column on the spreadsheet is called a **cell**. The **cell address** is the column letter and the row number in which the cell is located. For example, the top left cell of a spreadsheet is cell A1.

Think of a spreadsheet as a very large piece of ruled paper on your desk (see Figure 1–14). You can enter data or formulas in cells on this spreadsheet. Each cell has its own address, identifying the row and column in which it is located. Some programs allow users to build very large spreadsheets. For example, Lotus 1-2-3 Version 2.0 allows 256 columns and 8,192 rows. If each cell in such a work-

Figure 1–13
An Electronic Spreadsheet

Electronic spreadsheets have quickly become the most widely used software for personal computers. In fact, they are largely responsible for the personal computer becoming so popular among managers.

A2:						READY
	A	B	C	D	E	F
1	'THIS IS A SAMPLE LOTUS 1-2-3 SPREADSHEET					
2						
3		JAN	FEB	MAR	APR	MAY
4	NET SALES	1000	1100	1210	1331	1464
5						
6	COST OF GOODS SOLD	300	330	363	399	439
7	--					
8	GROSS PROFIT	700	770	847	932	1025
9						
10	RESEARCH 1 DEVELOPMENT	160	176	194	213	234
11	MARKETING	200	224	251	281	315
12	ADMINISTRATIVE	140	151	163	176	190
13	--					
14	TOTAL OPERATING EXPENSES	500	551	608	670	739
15						
16	INCOME BEFORE TAXES	200	219	239	262	286
17						
18	INCOME TAX	80	88	96	105	114
19	--					
20	NET INCOME	120	131	143	157	172
					CAPS	

sheet were ¼-inch high and 1-inch wide, the entire worksheet would be more than 21-feet wide and approximately 170-feet high! Of course, no monitor would show all of that worksheet. Most spreadsheets display about 20 rows and 8 or 9 columns on a screen. The user can move the worksheet around in order to view particular parts of it on the screen, as shown in Figure 1–14.

Any cell within the worksheet may contain alphabetic titles (labels), numeric values, or formulas. For example, in Figure 1–13 the cells in column A contain labels or titles. Cell B4 contains a constant 1,000 and B6 a constant 300. Spreadsheet cells may also contain formulas that calculate a number based on the values contained in other cells in the spreadsheet. For instance, in Figure 1–13 the cell B8 would contain the formula B4-B6. This formula tells the spreadsheet program to subtract the value in B6 from the value in B4 and place the result in B8, where the formula is stored. Formulas in spreadsheet cells can be as complex as a user's courage will allow. Almost any formula using addition, subtraction, multiplication, division, or exponentiation, no matter how complex, can be entered into a spreadsheet cell.

Figure 1–14
Cells in an Electronic Spreadsheet

The computer display screen acts as a window to the spreadsheet, enabling the user to see any part of a very large spreadsheet stored in the computer's memory.

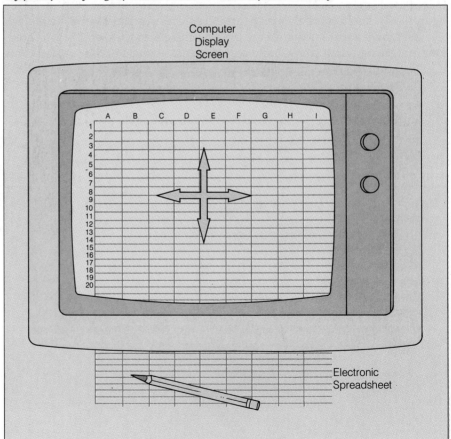

Electronic spreadsheets are most useful when there is relatively little data input but complex calculations are necessary. They are also very handy when a user wants to see how sensitive a final answer is to input data changes (see Figure 1–15). The figure shows a loan-repayment schedule prepared on an electronic spreadsheet. A skilled user of spreadsheets could put this application on a personal computer in less than an hour. The user can input varying values for principal amount of the loan, monthly interest rate, and number of monthly payments. This allows the user to see the impact of changes in these input values on the monthly payment. In addition, the spreadsheet is set up to show the amount of each payment that is applied to the interest and how much is going toward paying off the loan.

Figure 1–15 is a relatively simple spreadsheet application where the user can change only three input variables. Much more complex spreadsheets are being designed today. For example, Figure 1–16 is a spreadsheet used by a

Figure 1–15
Loan-Repayment Schedule on an Electronic Spreadsheet

One of the features that gives a spreadsheet its power is the ability to copy formulas from one part of the spreadsheet to another. For example, in this spreadsheet, after the user entered the formulas in order to calculate the numbers across the row where payment no. 2 appears, these formulas were copied into all cells for payments nos. 3 through 24. Thus all the numbers shown for payments 3 through 24 were automatically calculated without the user having to enter either formulas or numbers.

```
                  LOAN REPAYMENT SCHEDULE
PRINCIPAL AMOUNT OF THE LOAN      $8,000.00    These variables
MONTHLY INTEREST RATE                 1.00%    can be changed
NUMBER OF MONTHLY PAYMENTS               24    by the user
MONTHLY PAYMENT                     $376.59

PAYMENT    REMAINING   BEGINNING    INTEREST    REDUCTION
NUMBER     PAYMENTS      BALANCE     PAYMENT  IN PRINCIPAL

     1          23    $8,000.00      $80.00      $296.59
     2          22    $7,703.41      $77.03      $299.55
     3          21    $7,403.86      $74.04      $302.55
     4          20    $7,101.31      $71.01      $305.57
     5          19    $6,795.73      $67.96      $308.63
     6          18    $6,487.10      $64.87      $311.72
     7          17    $6,175.39      $61.75      $314.83
     8          16    $5,860.55      $58.61      $317.98
     9          15    $5,542.57      $55.43      $321.16
    10          14    $5,221.41      $52.21      $324.37
    11          13    $4,897.04      $48.97      $327.62
    12          12    $4,569.42      $45.69      $330.89
    13          11    $4,238.52      $42.39      $334.20
    14          10    $3,904.32      $39.04      $337.54
    15           9    $3,566.78      $35.67      $340.92
    16           8    $3,225.86      $32.26      $344.33
    17           7    $2,881.53      $28.82      $347.77
    18           6    $2,533.76      $25.34      $351.25
    19           5    $2,182.51      $21.83      $354.76
    20           4    $1,827.74      $18.28      $358.31
    21           3    $1,469.43      $14.69      $361.89
    22           2    $1,107.54      $11.08      $365.51
    23           1      $742.03       $7.42      $369.17
    24           0      $372.86       $3.73      $372.86
```

real-estate company to evaluate whether to invest in the construction of apartment buildings. Figure 1–17 provides a list of values that could be varied to reveal the impact on the after-tax cash flow.

Electronic spreadsheets are an extremely important tool for today's computer users. They are used widely to examine the financial consequences of business decisions.

Data-Base Management Systems Let's now examine how easy it is for a user to implement simple applications in a **data-base management system,** without having to program. If an application consists of keeping records in a file, updating those records periodically, and producing relatively simple

Figure 1–16
A Spreadsheet for Evaluating Apartment Investments

A person who knows the variables involved in apartment investments and also knows how to use an electronic spreadsheet can easily construct a spreadsheet of this type, which could prove invaluable. The spreadsheet shows both the after-tax cash flow and the percentage return on that cash flow. The return is equivalent to interest that would be earned on the money invested in the apartments. Parentheses indicate a negative number.

```
                         APARTMENT CONSTRUCTION SPREADSHEET
                                   22-Apr-89
        SIZE IN SQ. FT.          6000      CONSTRUCTION COST      $240,000
        VACANCY RATE             5.00%     LOT COST                $20,000
        COST/SQ. FT.            $40.00     INT. ON CONSTRUCTION     $9,441
        MARGINAL TAX RATE       40.00%     CLOSING COSTS            $3,000
        APPRECIATION RATE        5.00%     LEGAL FEES               $2,000
        PERCENT DOWN            20.00%     LANDSCAPING COSTS       $15,000
        LOAN INTEREST RATE      14.25%     TOTAL INVESTMENT       $289,441
        MGT. & MAINT. COST      10.00%     DOWN PAYMENT            $57,888
        LOAN TERM (YEARS)          15      NO. OF UNITS                  6
        LOAN PMT. PER MO.   $3,122.67      AVG RENT/UNIT             $462
        RETURN ON CASH FLOW      8.99%     RENT ESCALATION          5.00%
                                           RENT/INVESTMENT         11.50%
```

YEAR	GROSS RENT	CASH OUTFLOW	DEPRECIATION PERCENT	TAX SAVINGS	AFTER TAX CASH FLOW	CASH + EQUITY INCREASE	PROPERTY VALUE
0					($57,888)	($57,888)	
1	$31,621	$40,634	5.56%	$7,802	($1,210)	$18,436	$303,913
2	$33,202	$40,792	5.56%	$6,938	($652)	$20,456	$319,108
3	$34,863	$40,958	5.56%	$6,004	($92)	$22,618	$335,064
4	$36,606	$41,133	5.56%	$4,991	$464	$24,935	$351,817
5	$38,436	$41,316	5.56%	$3,892	$1,013	$27,420	$369,408
6	$40,358	$41,508	5.56%	$2,698	$1,548	$30,091	$387,878
7	$42,376	$41,710	5.56%	$1,397	$2,063	$32,966	$407,272
8	$44,494	$41,921	5.56%	($22)	$2,551	$36,064	$427,636
9	$46,719	$42,144	5.56%	($1,572)	$3,003	$39,408	$449,017
10	$49,055	$42,378	5.56%	($3,269)	$3,408	$43,022	$471,468
11	$51,508	$42,623	5.56%	($5,130)	$3,755	$46,937	$495,042
12	$54,083	$42,880	5.56%	($7,175)	$4,028	$51,183	$519,794
13	$56,787	$43,151	5.56%	($9,426)	$4,211	$55,796	$545,042
14	$59,627	$43,435	5.56%	($11,907)	$4,285	$60,817	$573,073
15	$62,608	$43,733	5.56%	($14,647)	$4,228	$66,292	$601,726
16	$65,739	$6,574	5.56%	($17,678)	$41,486	$71,573	$631,813
17	$69,026	$6,903	5.56%	($18,862)	$43,261	$74,852	$663,403
18	$72,477	$7,248	5.56%	($20,104)	$45,125	$78,295	$696,573
19	$76,101	$7,610	0.00%	($27,396)	$41,094	$75,923	$731,402
20	$79,906	$7,991	0.00%	($28,766)	$43,149	$79,719	$767,972

reports from the data in the file, a nonprogrammer can use a data-base management system to quickly implement the application.

To illustrate this, let's assume a department manager wishes to keep a file containing a record for each employee who works in the department. In the records he wants to store the employees' names, the dates they were hired, their office and home phone numbers, their birthdates, and their spouses' names. He wants to store birthdates because he plans to send birthday cards to employees each year. Also, since he is not very good at remembering names, he wants to store the employees' spouses' names. He would like two reports displaying all the data in the file: one in sequence by employee's last name and a second one in sequence by employee's birthdate. We will use **dBASE III Plus** to show how this application is implemented. First we must enter the structure of the file (see Figure 1–18). We had to give the file a name (employee), give each field a name, indicate whether the field type was *character data* or *numeric data*, and indicate the width of the field. Next, we entered the data to the file. Figure 1–19 illustrates an input screen for entering the employee data. Then, we told dBASE the characteristics of the report we wished to generate. Figure 1–20 on page 24 illustrates the building of a report with dBASE. Once a report form is entered all we have to do is tell dBASE III Plus to generate the report, using the command REPORT FORM EMPBDATE. The report that dBASE III Plus generated is illustrated in Figure 1–21 on page 25.

To generate a report in order by employee last name, we first enter a report form similar to the one in Figure 1–20. In fact the only difference would be the name of the report. We tell dBASE III Plus to sort the file in order by name and then enter the report command again. The report generated is shown in Figure 1–22 on page 26. A skilled user of dBASE III Plus could implement this application in less than an hour, including entering the data shown.

Application Packages   Often users purchase a set of computer programs to implement a particular application. Many businesses, especially those in the same industry, have very similar information requirements. For example, drugstore managers need to keep an inventory of prescription drugs, reorder drugs when the supply gets low, keep records (by customer) of prescriptions filled, and print labels for prescription bottles. A system to meet the needs of drugstore managers can be readily purchased. It often includes not only the software, but also the computer; the system is offered as a complete package. Unless the drugstore has a unique requirement, a manager would find it substantially less expensive to buy the software than to write the programs.

Many accounting applications can be purchased. For example, businesses that sell to customers on a credit basis have a need for accounts receivable. Keeping up with who owes the business money, and how much, is a very standard accounting application. Software packages to perform this application are readily available.

The purpose of this chapter is to inform you of the wide availability of **application packages** that can be purchased. In Module C we discuss evaluation of purchased software in more detail. Evaluation is very important when buying software.

This has been a very brief overview of using computers without programming. We cover this subject in more depth in Chapter 8.

CHARACTER DATA
Data on which arithmetic calculations will not be done.

NUMERIC DATA
Numbers on which arithmetic calculations will be performed.

Size in Square Feet
Vacancy Rate
Cost/Square Foot
Marginal Tax Rate
Appreciation Rate
Percent Down
Loan Interest Rate
Management and
   Maintenance Cost
Loan Term (Years)
Lot Cost
Closing Costs
Legal Fees
Landscaping Costs
Number of Units
Rent Escalation
Rent/Investment

Figure 1–17
Values to Be Varied for Spreadsheet shown in Figure 1–16

Users of the spreadsheet can vary any of these values in order to see the impact that such a change would have on after-tax cash flows and the return on cash flow. This kind of analysis is called what-if analysis. The user is obtaining answers to questions like: what if the vacancy rate were 10 percent instead of 5 percent?

Figure 1–18
Structure of the Employee File

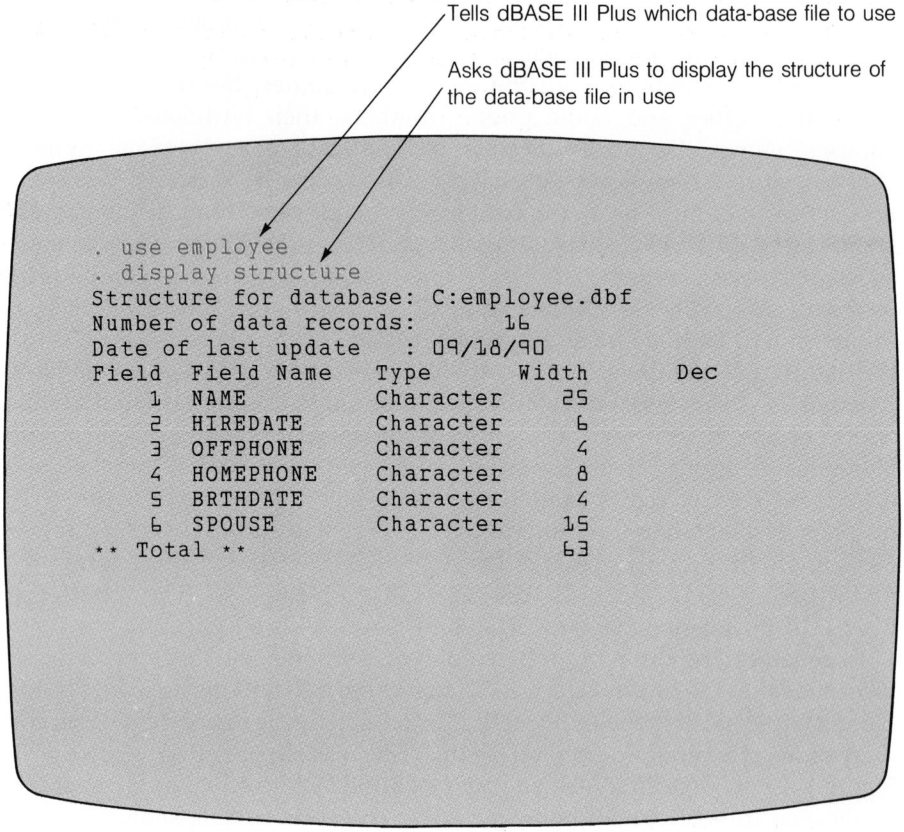

Tells dBASE III Plus which data-base file to use

Asks dBASE III Plus to display the structure of the data-base file in use

```
. use employee
. display structure
Structure for database: C:employee.dbf
Number of data records:        16
Date of last update    : 09/18/90
Field   Field Name   Type        Width        Dec
    1    NAME         Character      25
    2    HIREDATE     Character       6
    3    OFFPHONE     Character       4
    4    HOMEPHONE    Character       8
    5    BRTHDATE     Character       4
    6    SPOUSE       Character      15
** Total **                          63
```

Putting the Computer to Work by Writing Programs

If your computer needs are unique, and many are, you or someone else will have to write tailor-made programs.

Developing computer applications through programming can be time consuming. Furthermore, computer programs are harder to change than, say, electronic spreadsheets. For these reasons it is important to carefully analyze and document your information needs before beginning to write a program.

When your computer processing needs are simple, you may choose to do the *system analysis* and programming yourself. Most users rely on professional system analysts and programmers to develop the more complex programs.

Whether you plan to write programs or not, you should have a general understanding of how programs and information systems are developed. This process, called the **system development life cycle,** is covered in Chapters 6 and 7.

There are a number of reasons the system development life cycle needs to be understood; the most important are as follows:

1. Even when you develop computer applications without programming you have to define your information-processing requirements and decide how to

SYSTEM ANALYSIS
The process of studying an information requirement to determine precisely what must be accomplished and how to accomplish it.

Figure 1–19
dBASE III Plus Input Screen for Entering Employee Data

Each data item is entered between the two colons. Once the last data item is entered, in this case "spouse," dBASE III Plus displays an input screen for record no. 18.

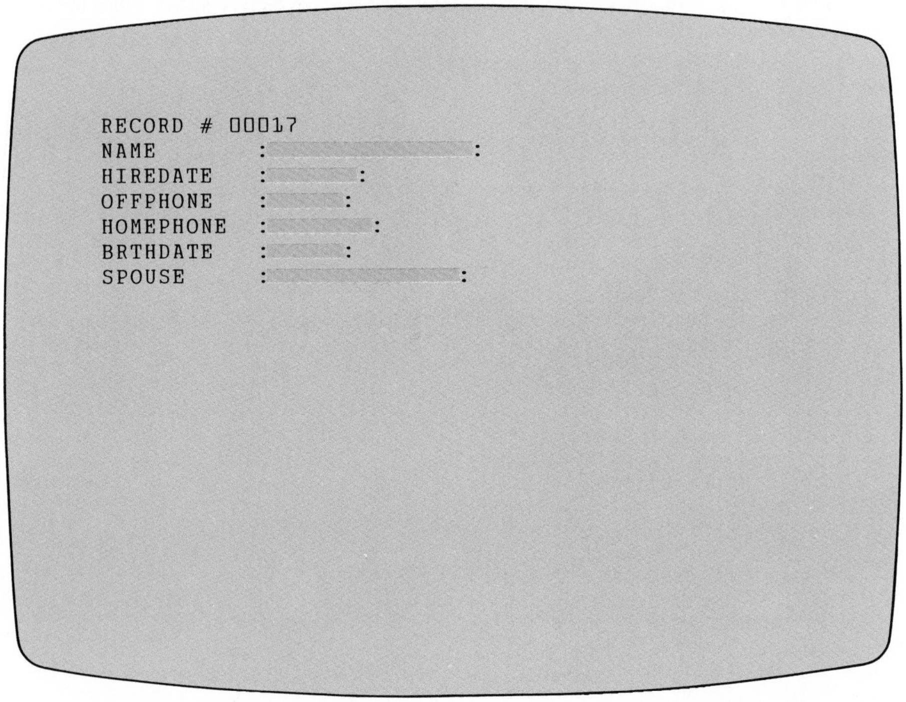

```
RECORD # 00017
NAME       :                     :
HIREDATE   :          :
OFFPHONE   :         :
HOMEPHONE  :           :
BRTHDATE   :       :
SPOUSE     :                  :
```

implement them on the computer. Certain system analysis and design techniques used in developing computer programs can also be helpful in developing applications without programming. For example, good programs are written in separate *modules* that work together. Such programs are much easier for people to understand. Good spreadsheets are also built in modular fashion to improve clarity. Many users with no knowledge of program design concepts have built huge spreadsheets that became useless because no one understood how to use them. Such spreadsheets would be more clear if broken down into modules.

2. A general knowledge of the system development life cycle is valuable when you convey your information requirements to professional system analysts and programmers. You will be much better equipped to decide whether or not the proposed design of your computer system will meet your needs.

Do you, as a user, need to learn to write programs for a computer? Many people say no, arguing that there are several ways to apply the computer without programming. Others argue that to be computer literate, you should have some exposure to programming. Currently there is no clear answer to this question.

The appendices and supplements in this text offer **hands-on exposure** to the most popular methods of using computers without programming—electronic spreadsheets, word processing, and data-base management sys-

PROGRAM MODULE
A small identifiable unit of program statements that performs one program task.

Figure 1–20
Entering a Report Description to dBASE

This is a report form for dBASE II, an earlier version of dBASE. Current versions of dBASE use several menu-driven screens to enter the same report specifications, and thus would be impossible to show here. This figure does illustrate the concept very concisely, since the report specifications are the same.

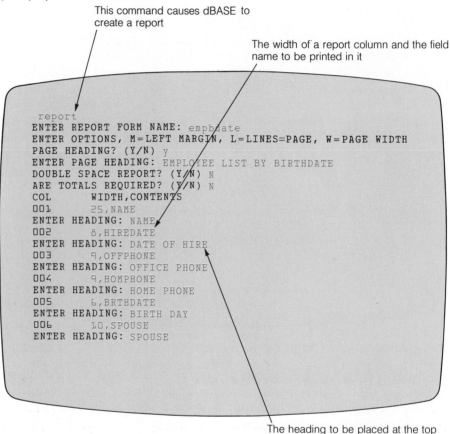

This command causes dBASE to create a report

The width of a report column and the field name to be printed in it

```
   report
ENTER REPORT FORM NAME: empbdate
ENTER OPTIONS, M=LEFT MARGIN, L=LINES=PAGE, W=PAGE WIDTH
PAGE HEADING? (Y/N) y
ENTER PAGE HEADING: EMPLOYEE LIST BY BIRTHDATE
DOUBLE SPACE REPORT? (Y/N) N
ARE TOTALS REQUIRED? (Y/N) N
COL       WIDTH,CONTENTS
001       25,NAME
ENTER HEADING: NAME
002        8,HIREDATE
ENTER HEADING: DATE OF HIRE
003        9,OFFPHONE
ENTER HEADING: OFFICE PHONE
004        9,HOMPHONE
ENTER HEADING: HOME PHONE
005        6,BRTHDATE
ENTER HEADING: BIRTH DAY
006       10,SPOUSE
ENTER HEADING: SPOUSE
```

The heading to be placed at the top of the column

tems. You can be sure that hands-on exposure to the computer—whether it be with or without programming—will be an extremely valuable first step in developing the computer skills needed in your career.

Many people are putting the computer to work by using the personal computer. We will examine this most widely used computer in the next chapter.

■ A PREVIEW OF THE REMAINDER OF THE TEXT

The basic premise of this text has greatly influenced its organization. That premise is that business people are most concerned with their needs for information and how to build computer-based information systems to meet

Figure 1–21
Employee List by Birthdate

```
PAGE NO. 00001
04/22/90
                            EMPLOYEE LIST BY BIRTHDATE

      NAME                 DATE OF   OFFICE   HOME      BIRTH    SPOUSE
                           HIRE      PHONE    PHONE     DAY

   FIRST, I. M.            610101    0001     552-0001  0101     IRMA
   TRESS, MATT             830503    7632     552-9742  0106     ALDA
   CABOODLE, KIT ANNE      720712    9876     552-6789  0201     CURT
   MAID, TAYLOR            820715    1000     552-2000  0209     HARRY
   LIFE, ALMA              850907    3423     552-6775  0309     LARRY
   HIGHWATER, HELEN        540809    0091     552-1907  0406     JOE
   SETTERA, ED             751205    1264     552-6732  0423     MARY
   SHARALIKE, SHARON       850130    9051     552-0382  0501     FRED
   DERHODE, JAUN MOREFORE  831023    5676     552-4385  0607     JANE
   ZON, HANS               841209    5623     552-8791  0717     BARBARA
   ERDBUNS, BUD            760807    1287     552-9845  0924     ELIZABETH
   TOTTLER, T.             780921    1423     552-8294  1005     ALFRED
   WANNAKRACKER, POLLY     690801    4352     552-4938  1115     SAM
   BREAKER, J. L.          840501    8642     552-0978  1209     TOM
   AYRE, CLAIRE D.         860208    9834     552-5683  1223     BOB
   THYME, JUSTIN           790309    9537     552-4973  1231     LISA
```

those needs. They are concerned with how computer systems work only to the extent that it helps them successfully build and use computer-based systems.

In building computer-based systems, systems professionals first analyze and determine the logical information needs for management decision-making. They then design and build the information system using physical devices, such as computers. The process is similar in concept to building a house. First, potential homeowners determine what features in a house will meet their needs. Then, a house is designed to meet those needs. And finally, it is built with physical materials, such as wood, nails, and brick. The potential homeowners are less interested in the details of the housing materials than in their housing needs; business persons, too, are less concerned about the physical devices than in their information needs.

Thus, in Part I we look at the fundamentals of information systems, concentrating on the need for information. This will give you a good top-down overview of information systems. Since it is not necessary to understand computer hardware to understand how to develop applications, we will not examine hardware in depth in Part I. In Part II we will look at how information systems are developed. In Part III we will discuss the computer resources used to physically implement an information system. At this point we will explore computer hardware and software in more depth. Finally, in Part IV we will cover the relationship of information systems to management, society, and you. In this section we will see how information systems are managed, and we'll study the impact of information systems on society and

Figure 1–22
Employee List by Name

```
PAGE NO. 00001
04/22/90

                                    EMPLOYEE LIST

        NAME                DATE OF    OFFICE    HOME      BIRTH    SPOUSE
                            HIRE       PHONE     PHONE     DAY

AYRE, CLAIRE D.             860208     9834      552-5683  1223     BOB
BREAKER, J. L.             840501     8642      552-0978  1209     TOM
CABOODLE, KIT ANNE         720712     9876      552-6789  0201     CURT
DERHODE, JAUN MOREFORE     831023     5676      552-4385  0607     JANE
ERDBUNS,BUD                760807     1287      552-9645  0924     ELIZABETH
FIRST, I. M.               610101     0001      552-0001  0101     IRMA
HIGHWATER, HELEN           540809     0091      552-1907  0406     JOE
LIFE, ALMA                 850907     3423      552-6775  0309     LARRY
MAID, TAYLOR               820715     1000      552-2000  0209     HARRY
SETTERA, ED                751205     1264      552-6732  0423     MARY
SHARALIKE, SHARON          850130     9051      552-0382  0501     FRED
THYME, JUSTIN              790309     9537      552-4973  1231     LISA
TOTTLER, T.                780921     1423      552-8294  1005     ALFRED
TRESS, MATT                830503     7632      552-9742  0106     ALDA
WANNAKRACKER, POLLY        690801     4352      552-4938  1115     SAM
ZON, HANS                  841209     5623      552-8791  0717     BARBARA
```

you. In addition, the text contains three modules that explore specialized areas of computer-based information systems.

If you look at the text's table of contents you will see that we are taking a top-down approach to information systems. This is precisely the approach that managers use. They are first and foremost interested in their needs for information and how to apply a computer to those needs.

We will explore personal computers in depth in Chapter 2. The personal computer is a good model for understanding computers in general, as it is a nonthreatening machine designed to be easy to operate and understand. Furthermore, in many courses your instructor will be introducing you to the personal computer and its software, such as word processing and spreadsheets, concurrent with the remainder of this text.

■ Summing Up

■ The premier invention of this century is the computer. In a relatively short time it has affected many areas of our lives.
■ A computer is a data processor that can perform substantial computation, including numerous arithmetic or comparison operations, without intervention by human operators.
■ The primary capabilities or characteristics of a computer are that it is electronic, it is able to perform arithmetic and comparison operations, it has internal storage and retrieval of data, it has the ability to execute a stored program, and it can modify the execution of a program stream during execution.

■ The electronic basis for the computer gives the computer incredible speed and accuracy, and the stored program enables this speed and accuracy to occur without human intervention.

■ Stored programs have three advantages:

1. They enable the computer to operate at an electronic speed.
2. They provide very high reliability.
3. They make the computer general-purpose.

■ Any computer system has four categories of devices: (1) input devices, (2) processing devices, (3) storage devices, and (4) output devices.

■ The processing role in a computer system is performed by the central processing unit (CPU). Its function is to interpret and execute the instructions of the programmer.

■ A computer system has two types of storage: primary and secondary. Primary storage is contained within the CPU and is used to store programs and the data they use during execution. Secondary storage is used for relatively long-term storage of data outside the CPU.

■ The components of the information-system data hierarchy, in ascending order of complexity, are: (1) bit, (2) byte, (3) field or item, (4) record, (5) file, and (6) data base.

■ In batch processing, changes and queries to a file are stored for a period of time. A processing run is made periodically to update the master file, produce scheduled reports, and produce responses to queries.

■ In immediate processing, transactions are processed to update files immediately or shortly after a real-world event occurs.

■ One type of application that uses immediate processing is a real-time system. A real-time application can immediately capture data about ongoing events or processes and provide the information necessary to manage them. An airline reservation system is a real-time system.

■ Users can apply the computer with or without writing programs.

■ The four most typical ways to apply the computer without programming are word processing, electronic spreadsheets, data-base management systems, and preprogrammed application packages.

■ Word-processing programs allow the user to make extensive revisions with minimal retyping.

■ Electronic spreadsheets allow users to quickly apply the computer to problems that have a small volume of input but involve complex calculations.

■ If an application consists of keeping records in a file, updating those records periodically, and producing relatively simple reports from the data in the file, a data-base management system can be used without programming to quickly implement the application.

■ Many information requirements can be met by application software that is available through purchase.

■ Normally, users write programs when there are unique information requirements; otherwise they rely on software that already exists.

information system	stored program	■ Key Terms
computer	program	

input devices	word processing
central processing unit (CPU)	Word
control unit	WordPerfect
arithmetic-logic unit	electronic spreadsheets
primary storage	Lotus 1-2-3
secondary storage	SuperCalc
output devices	Excel
bit	Quattro
byte	VP-Planner
bit patterns	rows
field *or* item	columns
record	cell
primary key	cell address
file	data-base management system
data base	dBASE III Plus
sequential-access file	character data
direct-access file	numeric data
batch processing	application package
queries	system development life cycle
immediate processing	module
real-time applications	hands-on exposure
on-line applications	

■ Review
▪ Questions

1. Define a computer. What is the difference between a computer and a programmable calculator?

2. What are the two crucial characteristics that a machine must have before it can be called a computer?

3. What are the capabilities and characteristics of a computer?

4. What are the advantages of the computer's ability to store programs?

5. Why are the knowledge of and ability to use a computer important in today's business world?

6. What are the four basic categories of devices in any computer system?

7. What are the functions of the central processing unit?

8. What are the components of the data hierarchy?

9. Compare and relate computer-based files, records, and fields to the contents of manual files.

10. What are the two types of file organization, and how are records retrieved from each?

11. Identify the two methods of processing data.

12. What are the four most typical ways to apply the computer without programing?

13. What are the disadvantages of developing computer applications through programming?

14. What are some reasons business students should understand the system development life cycle?

15. Why would a business buy a software application package rather than develop its own software?

■ **Discussion**
■ **Questions**
and Cases

1. Al's Pharmacy currently operates its business information system manually. Al hires college students to take an inventory each month of his prescription drugs. Al and his wife keep records of their customers' prescriptions, reorder drugs when inventory is low, and greet and assist their customers. Al has recently been approached by one of his student employees about a computer system to help run the business. The college student, a Management Information System (MIS) major, offered to help Al select a computer and some application software for the drugstore business. However, Al thinks it might be better to purchase a computer and hire the student to design and write some software to meet the store's specific needs. What would you advise Al to do?

2. Western University is a large university with a well-respected engineering college. All the departments within engineering and many departments in other colleges do a large amount of funded research. The manager of each research project is called a principal investigator (PI). In addition to assuring that the research is done properly, the PI must be sure that the funds expended do not exceed those allotted for the project. Outside sponsors, such as the National Science Foundation and the Department of Defense, will not cover over-expenditures on these projects. Funds to cover over-expenditures come directly from the university budget. Therefore, before committing to additional expenditures on a project, such as graduate assistants or equipment, the PI must be sure there is enough remaining budget to cover the expenses.

The university has a central accounting system that allows a PI to retrieve the current budget balance through online computer terminals. Many academic departments in the univesity do not trust the central accounting system. Thus they use various methods—from manual ledgers to microcomputer-based systems—to maintain separate accounting systems. Other departments feel that the central system is perfectly adequate and therefore do not expend funds to maintain their own systems. The major complaint of those who do not trust the central system is one of timeliness of data. All commitments to expend resources, such as purchase orders for equipment, are executed through manual forms that are processed through several administrative departments before being entered into the central accounting system on a daily basis. Often it takes four to five days for these expenditure commitments to be reflected in the central-accounting-system files. The vice president of finance of the university is considering a policy that would prohibit departments of the university from maintaining their own accounting systems. Should departments be allowed to maintain their own accounting systems? Does the central system need improvements? If so, what would you suggest? Would a simple policy prohibiting departmental accounting systems be successful?

3. If you are planning a career in the design and implementation of computer-based information systems, is it better to have an educational background in computer science or in management information systems (MIS)? A typical computer-science curriculum emphasizes the technological aspects of computing, whereas a typical MIS curriculum emphasizes business and how computers are used in the business area. Take one side of this argument and support your position.

4. Food Town is a medium-sized grocery chain located in the eastern seaboard states. John Wilson, the chief executive officer of Food Town, has become very concerned about the information he gets from his data-processing system. He knows that a large amount of data is gathered and stored in company disk and tape files. All of the company's accounting systems, such as accounts payable, accounts receivable, and payroll, are computerized. In addition, the company has computer-based inventory-control systems, personnel systems, and sales/marketing systems. Wilson presents his problem as follows: "With all this information being collected and stored, why can't I get better management-information reports? My assistant should be able to sit down at a terminal and pull information from these various systems and integrate it in a way that would be meaningful. Sure I can get information from the personnel system or from the payroll system, but whenever I need information from two or more of these systems, it seems to involve a major undertaking. More often than not, by the time I get the information, a decision has already been made and the information is not used. These computers just don't help me a great deal in my decision making." Does Wilson have a valid point? Is it possible to provide the type of information he is requesting?

Personal Computers ■ Chapter 2

CHAPTER OUTLINE

Introduction

**The Hardware of
a Personal Computer**
Types of Personal Computers
The System Unit
Input/Output Devices
Data Communications
The Hardware Industry

**The Software of
a Personal Computer**
General Business Software
Special-Interest Software
Interacting with Software

**Buying Personal-Computer
Hardware and Software**
*Getting Help in Buying a
PC System*
Where to Buy PC Systems

Personal Computers in the Home

Personal-Computer Challenges
Software Piracy
Illegal Access
Managing Personal Computers

**Future Directions of Personal
Computers**

Summing Up

Key Terms

Review Questions

Discussion Questions and Cases

**Appendix: Introduction to the
Macintosh Personal Computer**

■ INTRODUCTION

Currently, the fastest growing segment of the computer market is personal computers. Just as the industrial revolution of the nineteenth century opened up large markets for inexpensive, mass-produced goods, the personal-computer industry today is broadening the information-processing market through inexpensive and easy-to-use systems. A **personal computer** (PC) is a *microcomputer* designed to be operated by one user possessing very little, if any, programming knowledge. Often PCs are called microcomputers, but the term *personal computer* is more commonly used.

Personal computers make enormous computing power available to people from all walks of life. Consequently, both the number of users and the variety of applications are growing rapidly. Whether the application is mundane, such as balancing a checkbook, or novel, such as composing a symphony, the personal computer effectively serves the needs of the nonprogrammer. This versatility and user-friendliness have made the personal computer the most widely used computer. You are much more likely to use a PC than a *minicomputer* or *mainframe* computer.

The personal computer is a good vehicle for introducing you to computer hardware and software. It is small, nonthreatening, and easily understandable. It may be more than user-friendly—it may be user-seductive!

In this chapter we will explore the hardware components of a typical personal computer. This will be followed by a discussion on software. The software is what makes the personal computer useful, as with all computers; and the software available for PCs is particularly rich and varied. We will then talk about things to consider when buying hardware and software.

Many people have bought personal computers for their homes. However, the market for PCs in homes has not been as large as expected. We will explore some of the reasons for this. Personal computers have not been without their problems and challenges; these challenges will also be discussed. Finally, we will look at some of the future directions of the personal-computer industry.

One of the objectives of this chapter is to introduce you to the vast potential for PC applications. The *Information Systems in Business: Applications Software Manual* which accompanies this book contains software and tutorial for widely used spreadsheet, word-processing, expert systems, and data-base packages. These packages include Lotus 1–2–3, VP–Planner, WordPerfect, VP-Expert, and dBASE. If you have access to a personal computer, you will enhance your knowledge of personal computers by developing applications of your own by using some of these application software packages. That sentence is not strong enough. If I were a student and I did not have access to a personal computer I would find a way to gain access to a personal computer and learn how to apply it in my intended career!

MICROCOMPUTER
The smallest of computers, typically used by one person at a time.

MINICOMPUTER
A midsize computer generally used in midsize or smaller organizations by several users at the same time.

MAINFRAME
The large computer system found in large organizations and used by many people at the same time.

■ THE HARDWARE OF A PERSONAL COMPUTER

Types of Personal Computers

Currently, there are three types of widely used personal computers. They are the IBM PC *standard*, which includes a large variety of compatibles that will execute the same software as the IBM PC; the IBM PS/2 family; and the Apple Macintosh. In addition, several compatible manufacturers have developed their own standard, designed to compete with the IBM PS/2 family. The basic concepts underlying all types of personal computers are the same. In this chapter we will primarily use the IBM PC standard in our illustrations, as you are most likely to be using the IBM PC or a compatible. However, we will cover the PS/2 family where appropriate, and an appendix to the chapter will introduce you to the Macintosh.

STANDARD
One particular design of computer hardware or software. All hardware or software that follows a particular standard will be compatible with one another.

The System Unit

A figure from Chapter 1 has been repeated here to refresh your memory of the components of a personal-computer system (see Figure 2–1). These components are also shown in schematic form in Figure 2–2. Let's take a look inside the *system unit*.

The heart of a personal-computer system is a **microprocessor,** which is a central processing unit (CPU) contained on a semiconductor chip. As you can see from Figure 2–2, a microprocessor, like any computer CPU, contains an arithmetic-logic unit, control units, and various registers (memory) for storing small amounts of data. These microprocessor chips, along with their plastic packages, are about three-quarters of an inch wide and three inches long. The microprocessor, primary memory, disk controller, serial interface, and parallel interface are typically part of the system unit of a personal computer. They are all installed on the main circuit board. Figure 2–3 on page 36 shows a schematic diagram of the main circuit board of a personal computer. This board often is called a system board or mother board.

The speed at which a personal computer operates depends in part on two characteristics of the microprocessor: its **speed** and its **word size.** Microprocessor speed refers to the number of **machine operations** it performs in a second. Within the last few years, microprocessor speeds have increased sevenfold—to about 35 million cycles per second. Although such speeds may seem incredibly high, users are demanding even faster speeds since they do not want to waste time sitting at the keyboard while the microprocessor performs lengthy computations.

The word size of a microprocessor is the amount of information, in terms of bits, processed in one **machine cycle.** The larger the word size, the fewer machine cycles required to do a job. Early microprocessors processed 8-bit words in a single machine cycle. Today, 16-bit and 32-bit microprocessors are the most popular. The IBM PC, IBM PC AT, compatibles, and the PS/2 computers use the Intel 8088, 8086, 80286, 80386, and 80486 microprocessors. These processors operate at speeds of 5 to 35 million cycles per second.

A user can be misled by evaluating the speed of a personal computer solely on the basis of the speed of its microprocessor. Many other factors affect a

SYSTEM UNIT
The part of a personal computer that contains the central processing unit.

Figure 2–1

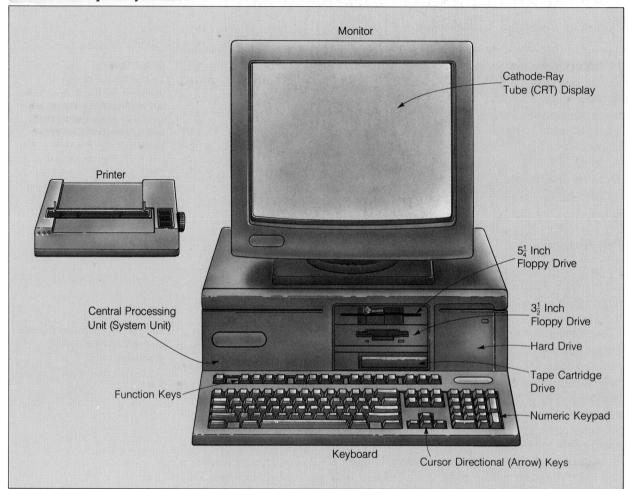

A Personal-Computer System

ROM
Read-only memory, which typically contains programs that can be read and used but cannot be changed.

RAM
Random-access memory, which stores programs and data that can be quickly changed or read in any conceivable (random) order.

personal computer's speed, including the efficiency of programs and whether the operator is using a hard disk or floppy disk. For example, the original PC AT operates two to three times faster than the original IBM PC, even though its microprocessor is only 20 percent faster.

The primary memory of a personal computer consists of some *read-only memory (ROM)* and some *random-access memory (RAM)*. The ROM contains programs that were built into the computer at the factory and cannot be changed by the user. These programs typically are used frequently. For example, some of the programs needed to bring the system up when the power is turned on are often stored in ROM.

Application programs are usually stored in random-access memory while they are being executed. A typical personal computer used for business purposes has 640 *kilobytes* (K) of RAM and may have as much as 16 *megabytes*. The advantage of having a larger memory is that larger and more powerful programs can be executed. Many personal computers are constructed such that their primary storage may be expanded later by adding **memory modules** if the user's needs increase. These modules are simply plugged into the RAM slots (as shown in the lower left corner of Figure 2–3) or are attached to add-on boards.

The disk controller, serial interface, and parallel interface shown in Figure 2–2 are all expansion boards that plug into the main circuit board. The slots for expansion boards are shown at the top left of Figure 2–3. Most personal computers have expansion slots. These enable a user to configure a PC to meet his or her particular needs. Figure 2–2, for example, illustrates a disk controller which allows the machine to use disk drives, a serial interface which is used for telecommunications between two computers, and a parallel

KILOBYTE (K)
1,024 bytes of memory, which will store 1,024 characters of data or programs. Kilobyte is usually abbreviated as K. Therefore, 256K of memory will hold 256 times 1,024, or 262,144, characters of data. In contexts other than computers the word *kilo* or the symbol *K* indicates 1,000. In terms of computers, K is a power of 2 (it is 2^{10} or 1,024) because of the binary nature of computer memory.

Figure 2–2
Hardware of a Personal Computer

The hardware of a personal computer includes devices for processing and storing information and for communicating with the user and other electronic devices. A set of parallel conductors called a bus connects the main components. The microprocessor unit, which generally includes not only the microprocessor chip itself but also various auxiliary chips, carries out essentially all calculations and controls the entire system. Information can be entered into the system through a keyboard. Pressing a key generates a coded signal unique to that key; the code is stored in the display memory and so appears on the cathode-ray-tube display. The primary memory, which consists of semiconductor memory chips, holds programs and data currently in use; it is a random-access memory, meaning that the content of any cell can be examined or changed independently of all the other cells. Disk storage has a larger capacity than the primary memory. The interfaces connect the computer to other devices, such as a printer or a modem (which gives access to other computers through the telephone system). In a serial interface, information is transferred one bit at a time; in a parallel interface, multiple conductors carry several bits (in most instances, eight) at a time.

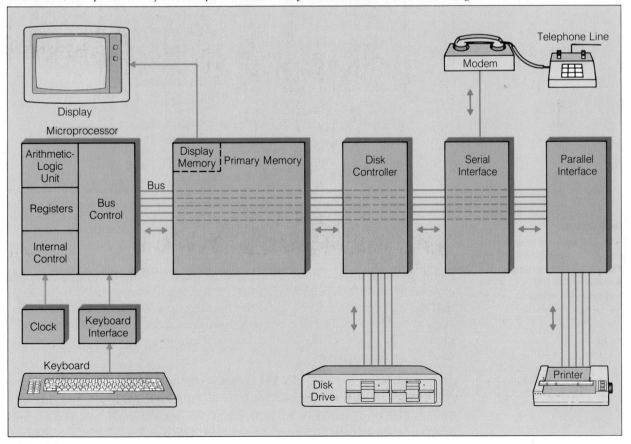

Figure 2–3
Main Circuit Board of a Personal Computer

The major elements of the main circuit board of a personal computer are identified here. A large number of silicon chips carrying integrated circuits are attached to the main circuit board; each chip is about a quarter of an inch square and is encased in a rectangular plastic package fitted with electrodes. The chips and elements, such as resistors and capacitors, are interconnected by conductors printed on the board. "System programs" are stored permanently in the read-only memory (ROM); random-access memory (RAM) stores programs and data that change from time to time.

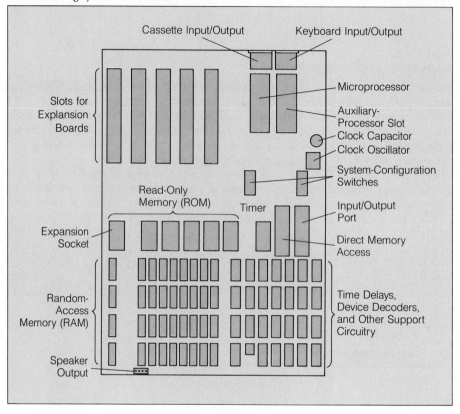

MEGABYTE

1,048,576 bytes of memory. A megabyte is often thought of as 1 million bytes, but more accurately it is 1,048,576 bytes, since it is 2^{20} bytes.

interface which is necessary if a printer is to be used with the personal computer. One of the most widely used expansion boards is the memory expansion board, since the main circuit board of some PCs holds only 256K. Figure 2–4 illustrates a memory expansion board. On the IBM PC, a memory expansion board can hold up to 384K of additional memory. With the 256K that the main circuit board holds, the machine would have 640K. Later PCs, such as the IBM PS/2 family, contain disk controllers, and serial and parallel interfaces as a part of the mother board. Thus their expansion slots can be used for other purposes.

Input/Output Devices

The user usually interacts with a personal computer through a **keyboard** and a **monitor screen** (see Figures 2–5 and 2–6). The user types in menu choices,

Figure 2–4
A Memory Expansion Board

Most memory expansion boards also add other functions, such as a battery operated clock/calendar and additional parallel and serial interfaces (ports).

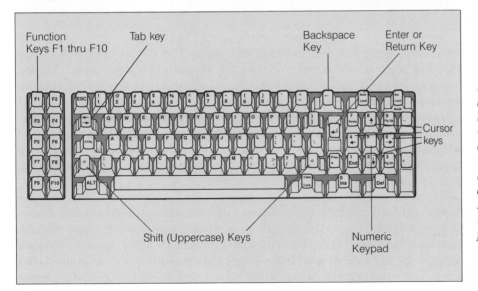

Function
Keys F1 thru F10

Tab key

Backspace
Key

Enter or
Return Key

Cursor
keys

Shift (Uppercase) Keys

Numeric
Keypad

Figure 2–5
A Personal-Computer Keyboard

This particular keyboard has been criticized because it has the arrow directional keys (cursor keys) on the numeric keypad (keys 2, 4, 6, and 8). If the operator uses the cursor and the numeric keypad simultaneously, he or she must use the shift key also. This can be inconvenient. Most new keyboards have directional keys that are separate from the numeric keypad.

Figure 2–6
A Personal Computer Monitor

Personal computer monitors are classified as being either monochrome or color. The mono-
chrome monitor is a single color monitor with the data usually being displayed in either
green or amber with a black background. Color monitors can display a wide variety of colors.
The latest color monitors are the video graphics array monitors (VGA) that were introduced
with the IBM PS/2 computers.

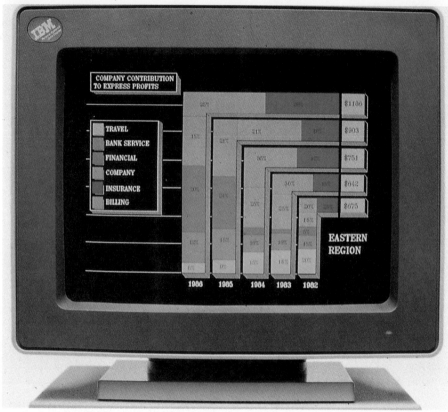

commands, program instructions, and data. The computer echoes these (displays them on the screen) so that the user can check for errors. During execution of a program the computer may display instructions or informative messages on the screen, or prompt the user to key in data items.

Most personal-computer systems support **color monitors.** Color monitors may be used in a wide variety of applications, such as engineering design and business data graphics. Some programmers use bright colors to highlight important information, making it easier to sift through the large quantities of information often generated by a computer.

The most popular secondary-storage media for personal computers are floppy and hard magnetic disks. Often a **diskette (floppy disk)** is used. Earlier PCs used 5¼-inch diskettes, but there is a trend now toward using 3½-inch diskettes, because they can store up to four times as much data as the 5¼-inch diskette. Figure 2–7 shows how a floppy disk is read or written to by a disk drive. The diskette rotates inside the square jacket, and an electromagnetic

Figure 2–7
A Floppy-Disk Drive

The floppy-disk system records large quantities of information on a flexible plastic disk coated with a ferromagnetic material. The disk rotates in a lubricated plastic jacket. An electromagnetic head is moved across the surface of the disk by a stepper motor to a position over one of the concentric tracks where data are stored as a series of reversals in the direction of magnetization. The head can read or write: it can sense the magnetic polarity to retrieve information or impose magnetization to store information. An index mark, whose passage is sensed by a photoelectric device, synchronizes the recording or reading with the rotation of the disk. There are two heads, which read and write information on both sides of the disk. A 5¼ inch disk is illustrated here. The basic characteristics of a 3½ inch disk and drive are the same. Data is recorded in a much denser format on the 3½ inch disk, however, thus, a rigid plastic cover is required to provide additional precision and protection to the disk.

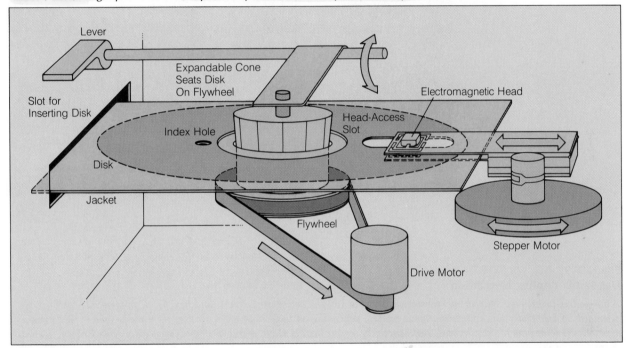

head reads or writes data through the head-access slot. When applications involve large programs or large quantities of data, a **hard disk (Winchester disk)** is used. A typical hard disk stores fifty to a hundred times more data than a floppy disk and it rotates much faster, providing quicker access to data. Refer to chapter 9 for a more in-depth discussion of floppy and hard disks.

Magnetic **tape cartridges** are used for data storage. This tape is similar to the tape used in stereo music recording. Tape is an inexpensive, *nonvolatile* storage medium. But its drawback is that data cannot be accessed at random. The computer has to read every bit of information sequentially until it reaches the desired data. Currently, tape cartridges are used primarily for *backup copies* of data stored on hard disks.

A large variety of printers are available for use with personal computers. Figure 2–8 shows one of the most commonly used types, a **dot-matrix printer.** The printing mechanism of this printer is shown in Figure 2–9. Most dot-matrix printers have either 9- or 24-pin printing mechanisms. A 24-pin printer can produce *letter-quality* print, whereas a 9-pin printer can produce, at best, near letter-quality print. Dot-matrix printers currently cost $200 to $700 and can print 50 to 450 characters per second.

NONVOLATILE
Storage that does not lose the data and programs stored on it when the electricity to the computer is turned off.

BACKUP COPY
A duplicate of data or programs used to restore the original if they are lost or destroyed.

LETTER QUALITY
Printed output that appears to have been typed on a typewriter.

Figure 2–8
Dot-Matrix Printer

Figure 2–9
Dot-Matrix Printing Mechanism

A dot-matrix printer is relatively inexpensive, fast (up to 450 characters per second), and flexible: it can generate compressed, expanded, or bold characters and even graphic images, depending on the commands it receives from the computer. The printing head is a vertical array of pins that are fired selectively, as the head is swept across the paper, to press an inked ribbon against the paper and thereby form a pattern of dots (left). Here each capital letter is a subset of a matrix seven dots high and five dots wide; two more pins are available to form the decenders of lowercase letters such as a p. *The pins are fired by individual electromagnets* (right).

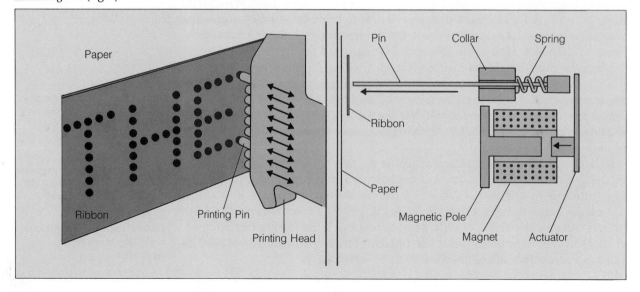

Laser printers that produce very high quality print are also used extensively with PCs, particularly in office environments. These printers use a printing technology very similar to that found in copying machines. The most widely used laser printers cost $1,000 to $3,700 and print four to eight pages per minute. The advantages of laser over dot-matrix printers are that they produce much higher quality print, they are faster, and they produce very little noise. Printers will be covered in more depth in Chapter 10.

There are many specialized input devices. One of the more widely used is a personal-computer **mouse** (see Figure 2–10). A wide variety of output

Figure 2–10
A Personal-Computer Mouse

A mouse is used to move the cursor to an item on the monitor screen. The item is selected (or activated) by pressing a button on the mouse. The mouse is held in your hand and is moved across a desk top in the direction you desire to move the cursor. Inside the mouse we find a ¾-inch stainless-steel ball. (1) As the ball rolls across the desk, it transfers its x and y movements to two small cylindrical drums (2) resting on the ball at a 90-degree angle to one another. The rolling ball turns the cylinders in proportion to the extent and direction of travel. Connected to the ends of the cylinders are small code wheels (3) coated with alternating stripes of conductive and nonconductive material. As these code wheels turn, they deliver electrical pulses for each incremental rotation of the cylinders. Delicate wire fingers (4) resting on the code wheels decode electrical pulses generated by the conductive stripes, and send them to the computer in a digital form it can read to track the mouse's movement. The three buttons (5) on top are used to select from menus on the screen, edit text, and move symbols.

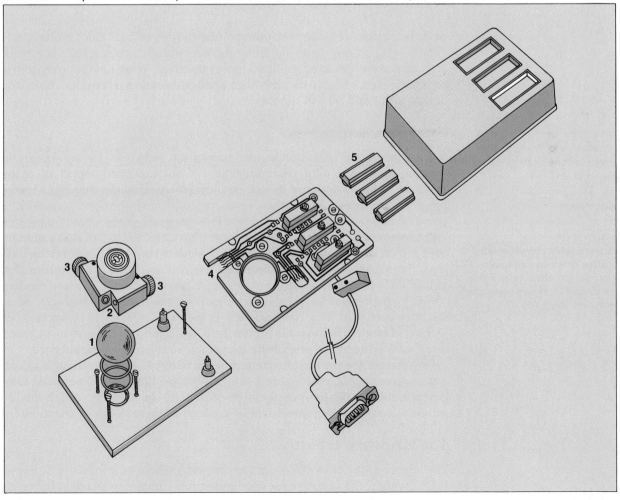

Figure 2–11
A Microcomputer Graphics Plotter

Very high quality graphics can be produced and printed (in color) through the use of a personal computer.

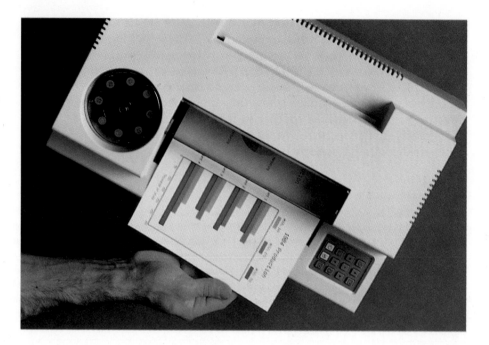

devices are also available, including audio output and graphics plotting (see Figure 2–11). A few years ago these devices would have seemed very exotic and may have required complex programming. With today's easy-to-use software, even a novice can create an application using a complex configuration of input and output devices.

Data Communications

In chapter 14 we will discuss communication networks for computers in general. However, data communication is an important aspect of many personal-computer systems as well. It allows the operator to share data bases, programs, printers, and other resources with many users. Typically, a personal computer has a **communications program** that converts data to a standard *protocol*. The converted data are then transmitted through a modem over private or public telephone lines. A **modem** converts the outgoing data from the digital signals that computers use to the analog sound waves that phone lines transmit. When the computer receives data, the same modem converts analog sound waves into digital signals (see Figure 2–12). Most modems used with PCs transmit data at speeds of 120 or 240 characters per second. A modem is shown in Figure 2–13. A PC modem can also be installed as an internal board in one of the expansion slots on the system board.

Personal computers can also communicate with one another through a local-area network (LAN); see Figure 2–14. LANs also allow several personal computers to share expensive peripheral devices such as hard disks and high-quality printers. Local-area networks will be covered in more depth in chapter 14.

PROTOCOL
A set of rules governing information flow in a communication system. These rules define the format of the message to be sent. See chapter 14.

The Hardware Industry

The advent of the personal computer created a whole new industry. Interestingly enough, the initiative for developing this industry was taken by small,

Figure 2–12
The Conversion of Data with a Modem

Telephone companies are expected to eventually use digital signals to transmit voice. When this occurs, digital computer signals can be transmitted over telephone lines without modems.

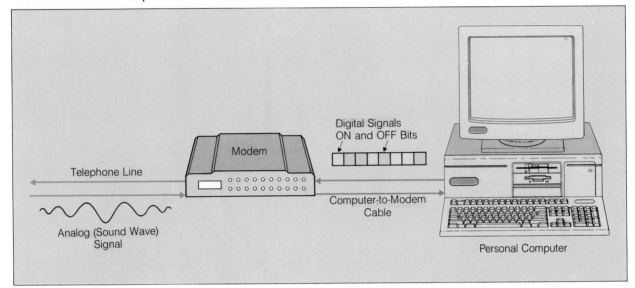

Figure 2–13
A Modem

This is a external modem. The same modem can be purchased as a board to fit into one of the expansion slots of a PC. The advantage of an external modem is that it can be disconnected and used with other PCs. The advantage of the internal modem is that an additional piece of hardware (an external modem) does not have to transported when the computer is being moved around. Internal modems are often used with portable PCs.

Figure 2–14
A Local-Area Network

In the configurations shown, the personal computer to which the hard disk and printer are connected serves as a driver for these devices. This means that the other personal computers communicate with the hard disk and the printer through the driver PC.

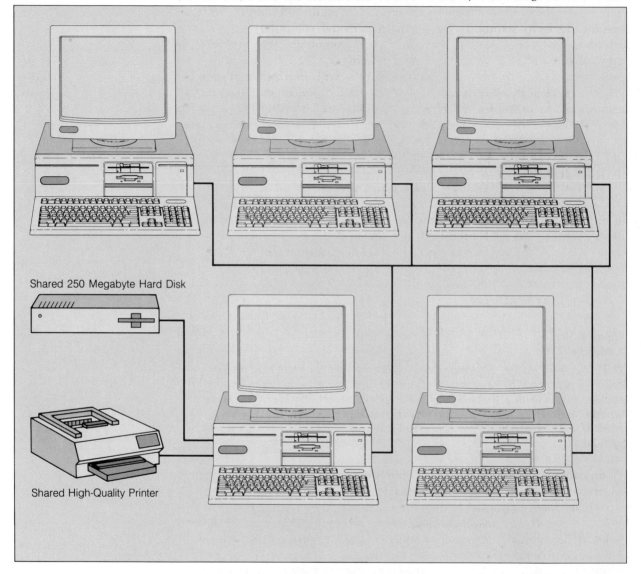

Shared 250 Megabyte Hard Disk

Shared High-Quality Printer

entrepreneurial firms rather than large, established vendors of mainframe computers. The Apple Computer Company produced the first widely used personal computer in 1977. Its founders, two young college students, built the first Apple personal computer in a garage. Despite fierce competition from subsequent entrants in the market, Apple has managed to maintain a position in the industry. Tandy Corporation, a manufacturer and seller of electronic products, has used its extensive network of Radio Shack retail outlets to gain a position in the personal-computer industry. IBM, a latecomer (1981) to the personal-computer business, has become the dominant vendor in the business market for personal computers. The IBM PC and PC AT have become de facto standards for business personal computers. Since their introduction, many vendors have produced computers that are IBM-PC compatible. One of the most successful is Compaq. This firm produces both portable and desktop PCs that compete directly with IBM personal computers. IBM's established reputation as the world's largest manufacturer of computers has certainly helped it achieve dominance in the PC hardware market. Most observers feel that IBM will continue to dominate the business market for personal computers. However, Apple, with its Macintosh computer, is attempting to challenge IBM in the business segment of the personal-computer market.

IBM's PS/2 family has not yet become the standard for the next generation of PCs. It is difficult for compatible manufacturers to sell IBM PS/2 clones at a profit. First, IBM's manufacturing of PS/2s is highly automated and thus these computers can be produced at a low cost. Second, PS/2 compatible makers must pay IBM a royalty because IBM holds patents on the PS/2. In a sense, IBM is playing a delicate balancing act. The firm needs compatibles on the market to make the PS/2 the new standard for business PCs, but it cannot allow compatible makers to freely clone the PS/2 and undercut IBM prices. Meanwhile, the compatible makers have not stood still. Nine of them banded together in September 1988 to develop a new standard PC architecture (or PC design), called the Extended Industry Standard Architecture (EISA). In addition, Steve Jobs, one of the founders of Apple computers, has founded a new company, Next Inc. The Next computer was unveiled in October 1988 and is marketed primarily in educational institutions. But undoubtedly it will be marketed in business firms also, and the company is particularly well financed. Thus, it is likely that we will be able to choose from PCs that are based on at least four different standards: the IBM PC, the Apple Macintosh, the EISA, and the Next Computer.

Stiff competition in the personal-computer business has been beneficial to the consumer. Prices have steadily decreased, while equipment quality and capabilities have continued to improve. Moreover, manufacturers have been forced to standardize many features, such as communication protocols and diskette characteristics, in order to appeal to a wider customer base. As with any competitive market, there have been a number of casualties. Some of the smaller vendors have gone out of business, leaving their customers without maintenance support. A buyer of personal-computer equipment should carefully consider the reputation of the supplier before making a major purchase. Purchasing from an unreliable supplier could cause the user not only to lose an investment in computer hardware and software, but also to lose customers who were dissatisfied with service resulting from computer malfunction. It is also important for the buyer to determine whether a particular component is *plug-compatible* with the equipment he or she has or is likely to acquire.

PLUG-COMPATIBLE
A hardware device that can directly replace units produced by another manufacturer.

■ THE SOFTWARE OF A PERSONAL COMPUTER

Businesses are rapidly adopting the personal computer. Small companies are converting their record-keeping to computerized systems, and both large and small firms are using electronic spreadsheets, data-base management systems, word processing, and graphics. The primary reason for this change is the availability of powerful yet inexpensive software packages for personal computers.

General Business Software

Accounting Applications One of the first systems a business converts to a computer is accounting. Excellent packages are available for general-purpose accounting, including the following: accounts receivable, accounts payable, general ledger, and payroll. These packages are advertised in professional accounting journals. Figure 2–15 shows the output from an accounting software package. Before purchasing such a package, ask the following questions:

1. Are there sufficient accounting controls in the system?
2. Are the various programs integrated so that information which is input once need not be input again for another program?
3. What are the limitations on the number of accounts and transactions the system can process?

Figure 2–15
Sample Printout of an Accounting Package

An aged trial balance provides information about the overdue amounts that customers owe a firm. For example, in this figure Wygant Distributors, Inc. owes the firm $652.19 that is due in the future, $1,125.64 that is currently due, $294.81 that is 1 to 30 days past due, and $108.45 that is 31 to 60 days past due.

```
                                    ACCOUNTS RECEIVABLE
                                  SUMMARY AGED TRIAL BALANCE
                                     D 1 G ENTERPRISES INC.
        REPORT NO AR6315
        RUN DATE 10=31=8X
      COMPANY AA                   FUTURE     CURRENT                              PAST DUE                    OVER   OUTSTANDING
         ACCOUNT         NAME        DUE        DUE        1-30      31-60      61-90     91-120          120   RECEIVABLES
        784612   WYGANT DISTRIBUTORS, INC.  HARTWELL ROAD      JUPITER HILLS  DE       19702-2614
                 MR. W. RAMSDEN
                 AVG. DAYS-36 CR=LMT-3500
        ACCOUNT TOTAL:             652.19    1,125.64      294.81    108.45                                       2,181.09
                                     30%        52%         13%        5%
        799426   ZELLER COMPANY            124 MILLBROOK RD   EAST GALLANT   AL       36902-1157
                 MR. P. GORHAM
                 AVG. DAYS-63 CR=LMT-1000
        ACCOUNT TOTAL:                                       456.24    178.26    312.49                           946.99
                                                              48%       19%       33%
        GRAND TOTAL•••
                 SALES TERRITORY: 01A   1,576.72  16,459.32   9,621.14  1,164.91     447.56   78.60  120.41   29,468.66
                                          5%        56%        32%        3%          2%      1%     1%
                 DISTRICT CR MGR: BB    6,482.19  39,412.80  24,562.44  2,051.23   2,114.86  594.60  403.19   75,621.31
                                          8%        52%        31%        3%          4%      1%     1%
                 REGIONAL CR MGR: WF   10,398.65  98,714.37  52,114.71  5,662.17   3,729.29 1,700.68 1,288.74 173,608.61
                                          6%        57%        30%        3%          2%      1%     1%
                    COMPANY  TOTAL:    26,042.03 256,622.13 107,781.58 12,715.25   7,520.12 3,918.45 2,542.60 417,142.16
                                          6%        62%        25%        3%          2%      1%     1%
```

4. What level of technical expertise (in terms of both the accounting and the computer) is required to operate the system, and is this expertise available to the business?

5. Will the programs produce flexible management reports that can be easily modified to suit changing business needs?

Financial Management Another important application of personal computers is in financial management. Financial-planning packages can be used to project the financial results of alternative management decisions. The projected financial statements produced for the various alternatives allow management to make informed decisions. One such package is Execucom's Integrated Financial Planning System (IFPS). IFPS was originally designed to be used on mainframes but is now available for PCs. Figure 2–16 illustrates the use of IFPS. Other financial programs focus on problems such as stock-portfolio management, stock analysis, capital-project analysis, budgeting, tax planning, and cash management.

Marketing Management Marketing personnel often use programs that generate sales projections. Some packages have powerful **graphics** capabilities such as pie charts, bar graphs, and trend lines (see Figure 2–17). These devices can substantially reduce the paperwork that a marketing manager has to do to prepare for a sales meeting. Software packages written for salespeople remove most of the tedium of booking orders. A well-designed order-processing system will price the order, prepare an invoice, update perpetual inventory records, and produce the shipping authorization document. There are also many personal-computer programs that assist in the warehousing and production management functions. These range from inventory management routines to production scheduling to manpower planning.

Electronic Spreadsheets and Data-Base Management We have covered these two types of software extensively in other parts of the text (chapters 1, 13, and in the accompanying *Information Systems in Business: Application Software Manual*). The first electronic spreadsheet (VisiCalc) and those which followed (Lotus 1–2–3, Quattro, and Excel) have had a primary role in the phenomenal success of the personal computer. For several years electronic spreadsheets and data-base management software have topped the lists of the best-selling PC software. They are both easy to use and most productive. If you plan a career in business, make it a goal to become proficient in the use of software for electronic spreadsheets, data-base management systems, and word processing.

Word Processing One of the most important uses of personal computers in business is **word processing.** When linked to a high-quality printer, a personal computer can produce excellent reports, letters, and other documents. In addition, a user can, with a few keystrokes, store, edit, and neatly format all these documents. Business people, suffering from a heavy load of paperwork, have welcomed this opportunity to improve productivity. Many good word-processing programs, such as WordPerfect and Word, are now on the market. Many are capable of checking the text for spelling and grammatical errors. If your word-processing application involves a large amount of

Figure 2–16
An Income Statement Produced by an IFPS Program

The IFPS instructions to produce the income statement shown in Figure 2–16a are shown in Figure 2–16b. Notice that with IFPS the user is in effect writing a program to produce the income statement. As illustrated in Figure 2–16c this simple income statement could also be produced through the use of an electronic spreadsheet. The numbers and formulas are placed directly in individual cells without the user having to write a separate program. However, IFPS does perform some tasks that electronic spreadsheets are not currently capable of doing.

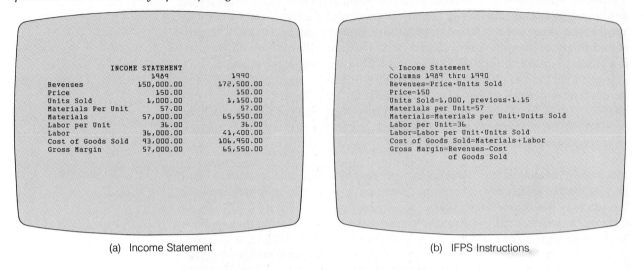

```
              INCOME STATEMENT
                   1989               1990
Revenues         150,000.00         172,500.00
Price                150.00             150.00
Units Sold         1,000.00           1,150.00
Materials Per Unit    57.00              57.00
Materials         57,000.00          65,550.00
Labor per Unit        36.00              36.00
Labor             36,000.00          41,400.00
Cost of Goods Sold 93,000.00         106,950.00
Gross Margin      57,000.00          65,550.00
```

(a)   Income Statement

```
\ Income Statement
Columns 1989 thru 1990
Revenues=Price·Units Sold
Price=150
Units Sold=1,000, previous·1.15
Materials per Unit=57
Materials=Materials per Unit·Units Sold
Labor per Unit=36
Labor=Labor per Unit·Units Sold
Cost of Goods Sold=Materials+Labor
Gross Margin=Revenues-Cost
              of Goods Sold
```

(b)   IFPS Instructions

```
Cell:  Contents:              Cell:  Contents:     Cell:  Contents:
A1     Income Statement       B1                   C1
A2                            B2     1989          C2     1990
A3     Revenues               B3     +B4·B5        C3     +C4·C5
A4     Price                  B4     150.00        C4     150.00
A5     Units Sold             B5     1000.00       C5     +B5·1.15
A6     Materials per Unit     B6     57.00         C6     57.00
A7     Materials              B7     +B6·B5        C7     +C6·C5
A8     Labor per Unit         B8     36.00         C8     36.00
A9     Labor                  B9     +B8·B5        C9     +C8·C5
A10    Cost of Goods Sold     B10    +B7+B9        C10    +C7+C9
A11    Gross Margin           B11    +B3-B10       C11    +C3-C10
```

(c)   Electronic-Spreadsheet Contents

correspondence, be sure to buy a package that includes mailing facilities, such as the printing of address labels.

Integrated Packages   When a business professional is using an electronic spreadsheet, word processor, data-base manager, and graphics program, he or she is often using the same data or text in all of these packages. Moving data from one package to another can sometimes get cumbersome. Consequently, **integrated packages** that combine all four of these functions plus communications software have been developed. Three examples are Migent's Ability, Lotus' Symphony, and Ashton-Tate's Framework. When these pack-

Figure 2–17
Marketing Graphs

A wide variety of graphs can be created on personal computers. They can be printed by color plotters and color laser printers. They can also be transferred directly to 35 mm color photographic slides.

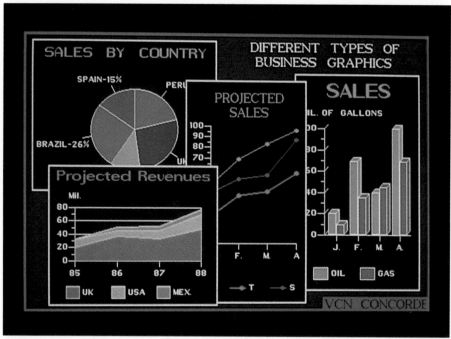

ages were released in the summer of 1984, they were expected to significantly affect the market for *stand-alone* word-processing, electronic-spreadsheet, and data-base packages. The reasoning was that they would give a business person the ability to perform any of these functions on a common set of data and text. For example, a user could produce reports that contained—in an integrated fashion—text, spreadsheets, graphics, and even lists of data. Through the communications package the report could be transmitted to other computers.

Experience has shown that the current integrated packages compromise their functions. For example, the word-processing function of an integrated package may not have all the capabilities of a stand-alone word processor. The same is generally true of the other functions. Therefore, many personal-computer users continue to use their separate stand-alone packages.

Another approach to integration is a package such as Microsoft's Windows. This package runs along with stand-alone electronic spreadsheets, word processors, and so on, allowing the user to transfer data and text between stand-alone packages. The screen of the monitor is split into sections called windows. Each window displays part of each stand-alone package (see Figure 2–18).

The personal computer also plays a central role in implementing *decision-support systems*. Data can be transferred from large, central data bases to personal-computer storage and subsequently be analyzed through the use of tools such as spreadsheets and graphics. The combination of all tools available in a personal computer is often referred to as a personal workstation.

STAND-ALONE
Computer hardware or software that operates in an independent and separate manner.

DECISION-SUPPORT SYSTEM
An integrated set of computer tools that allows a decision maker to interact directly with computers to produce and display information useful in making decisions.

Figure 2–18
Data Displayed in Windows on a Single Computer Screen

Four windows are displayed on this screen. At the top is Microsoft Word, a word processing package. The next two screens below are graphs drawn in Microsoft Chart, a graphics package. The bottom screen is a contacts file, created in Cardfile which is a database package for keeping simple lists. The current trend in PC software is to use windowing to simultaneously show multiple applications on a single screen.

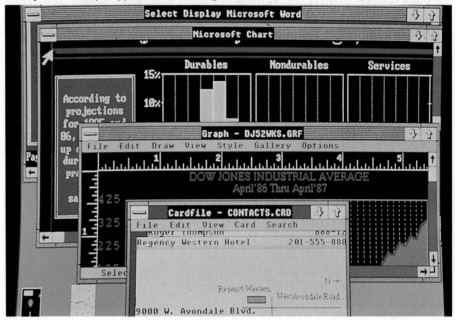

Special-Interest Software

Many industries and professions have very special information-processing requirements. Thus special-purpose software packages have been developed. This software is usually advertised in professional and industrial journals and at conventions and conferences. Users can also find special-interest packages by consulting directories such as *Datapro Reports on Microcomputer Software.*

A major market for specialized software is the medical profession. Faced with increasing government regulation and a rapidly changing medical technology, doctors and pharmacists are finding that the computer is ideal for their record keeping. Applications vary from systems for invoicing patients to data bases for medical-history records. Similarly, lawyers now have their own packages to assist with routine chores such as preparing lengthy legal documents and searching data bases for legal precedents. With the aid of time-keeping and billing programs, accountants and auditors are now able to better manage their practices. There are specialized packages for almost all industries.

Interacting with Software

Computer software has become much more **user-friendly** in recent years. Of course, there are degrees of user-friendliness. In the better software, the methods by which the user communicates with the software are more natural and intuitive and are more likely to be learned without formal training. Also, the user is more likely to remember how to use the software over a long period of time, even though he or she seldom uses it. In this section, we will discuss the following methods of communicating with software: commands, menus, and icons.

The least user-friendly method of communicating with software is commands. A **command** is an instruction that is typed through a keyboard to the computer software. Figure 2–19 shows a series of commands used with the DOS operating system. DOS is a widely used operating system for IBM and compatible PCs.

Some argue that command-driven software is faster for an experienced user, since short commands can be typed quickly and they execute quickly. However, remembering commands can be difficult, even for an experienced user. For example, to exit a particular software package, a user may have to type exit, quit, fin, disc, or qquit or press a function key such as F3 or F10. Imagine the common situation of a person using several software packages that have different commands for the same function. The user will no doubt use the wrong command often.

Many software packages use some form of menu interface. A **menu** is a list of options that appear on the computer screen. Figure 2–20 illustrates a typical set of menus. Choosing an item on a menu causes the software to execute the action chosen. Depending on the software design, a user can

Figure 2–19
DOS Commands

Software that uses a command interface displays a prompt indicating it is ready to accept a command. In DOS, the prompt is the > character. Other software use other characters. For example, dBASE uses a . for its prompt. For a novice user these one-character prompts can be intimidating. There is usually no indication on the screen as to what command the user should type in. Thus, the user must remember the commands.

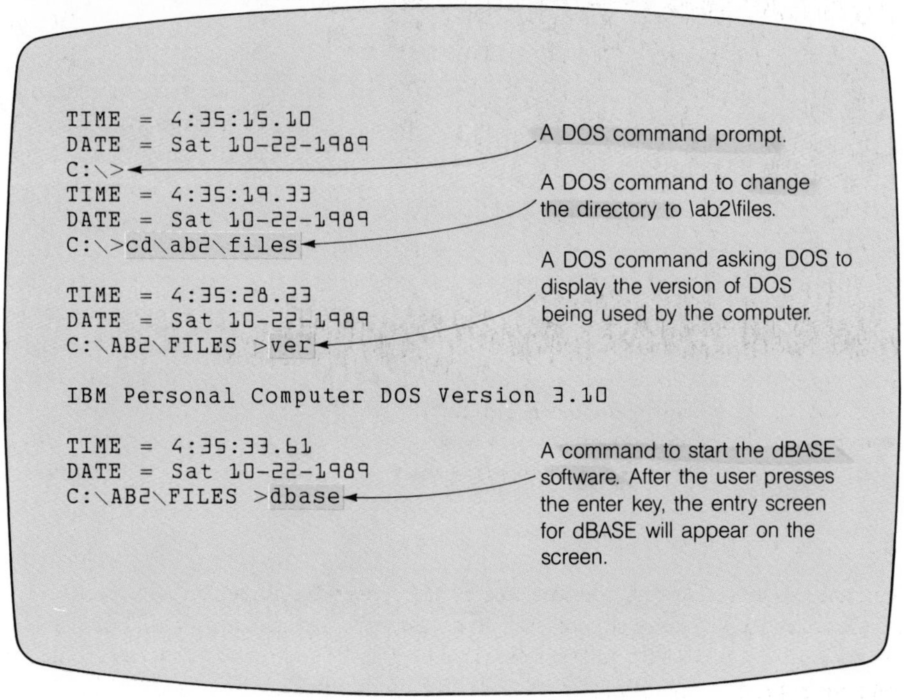

```
TIME = 4:35:15.10
DATE = Sat 10-22-1989          A DOS command prompt.
C:\>
TIME = 4:35:19.33              A DOS command to change
DATE = Sat 10-22-1989          the directory to \ab2\files.
C:\>cd\ab2\files

TIME = 4:35:28.23              A DOS command asking DOS to
DATE = Sat 10-22-1989          display the version of DOS
C:\AB2\FILES >ver              being used by the computer.

IBM Personal Computer DOS Version 3.10

TIME = 4:35:33.61              A command to start the dBASE
DATE = Sat 10-22-1989          software. After the user presses
C:\AB2\FILES >dbase            the enter key, the entry screen
                               for dBASE will appear on the
                               screen.
```

Figure 2–20
A Typical Set of Menus

Choosing item 1 or 2 on the main menu causes the software to display the corresponding menu shown below the main menu.
Choosing 1 on the order-entry menu will cause the customer-information screen to appear, where a user can enter a customer's order.

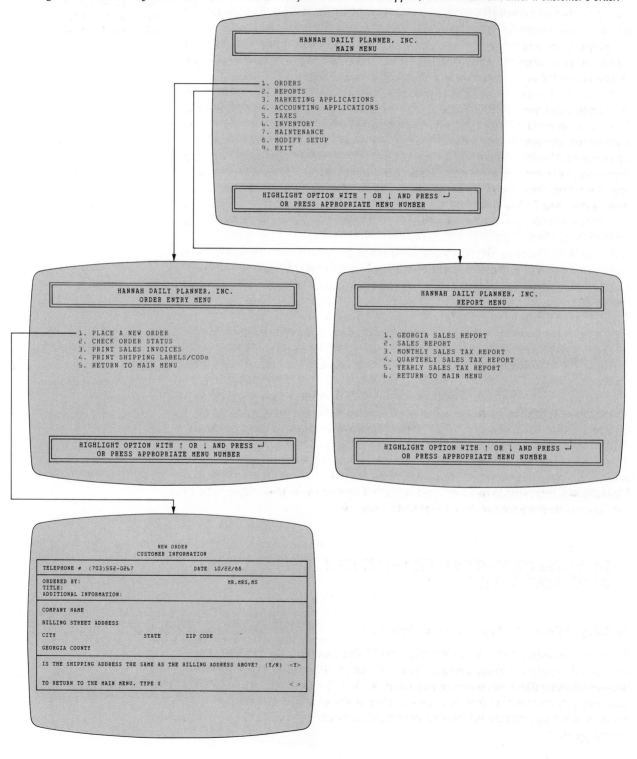

choose a menu item by entering the number associated with the item, by moving the *cursor* to the item and pressing Enter, or by pressing the first letter in the first word of the item. Note that the last technique would not be possible with the main menu in Figure 2–20, since three of the items begin with *M.* The software designer would have to change the wording on two of the menu items for the last technique to work.

CURSOR
A movable spot of light on the screen of a display device, indicating where the next character will be entered or which menu item is selected.

The primary advantage of a menu is that each possible action is displayed on the screen. Thus the user does not have to remember the possible actions or the correctly spelled command that will execute them.

Another form of menu is the **line menu,** as illustrated in Figure 2–21. This is a Lotus 1-2-3 menu, which was one of the first software packages to use the line-menu approach. The second line on screens 1 and 2 display a line menu. Each word represents a different menu choice. A user can choose a menu item by pressing the first letter of the menu word or by moving the cursor to the item and pressing Enter. As the cursor is moved from word to word, the next line (line 3) displays the various actions that can be performed if that menu item is chosen. For example, if menu item File is chosen, the next menu will allow the user to choose among Retrieve, Save, Combine, Xtract, Erase, List, Import, and Directory.

A line menu such as that used in Lotus 1-2-3 can also be used as a command interface. The top-level menu is always invoked by typing a slash (/), and menu items can be selected by pressing the first letter in the word of the item. Thus, to retrieve a file the user merely types /FR. This feature of line menus is very useful. It allows an experienced user who remembers the menu sequence to quickly enter commands without even looking at the menus.

Another way to communicate with software is by using **icons.** Icon interfaces are familiar graphic images that represent certain actions a user may choose. For example, to erase a file the user chooses an icon that resembles a trash can. To choose an icon the user moves the device called a mouse (refer back to Figure 2–10) across the desk to point the cursor to the chosen icon. This type of interface is called a graphics interface.

The major advantage of the icon interface is that it is easy to use. It is very intuitive. The originator of the idea was Xerox, and it is used in the Macintosh, Microsoft Windows, and the OS/2 operating system. This type of interface is likely to be widely used in the future.

■ BUYING PERSONAL-COMPUTER HARDWARE AND SOFTWARE

Getting Help in Buying a PC System

The computer business is sometimes called the information business, and with good reason. Computers not only perform computations, but they also help us manage large volumes of information. But the machine that assists us in coping with information has also caused a flood of information. Books, articles, and magazines related to personal computers have proliferated in recent years.

Figure 2–21
A Lotus 1-2-3 Line Menu

The second line on screens 1 and 2 display a line menu. Each word represents a different menu choice. A user can choose a menu item by pressing the first letter of the menu word or by moving the cursor to the item and pressing Enter.

Screen 1 Level 1 Menu

```
A1: [W18]                                                           MENU
Worksheet  Range  Copy  Move  File  Print  Graph  Data  System  Quit
Retrieve, Save, Combine, Xtract, Erase, List, Import, Directory
              A           B          C          D           E
1
2      YUPPIE CARS INC.
3      INVENTORY OF CARS
4            21-Oct-89
5
6                      QUANTITY     COST       TOTAL        SALES
7      CAR MODEL       ON-HAND      EACH    INVESTMENT      PRICE
8
9      Audi                 5     $12,000     $60,000     $105,000
10     Mercedes             5     $15,000     $75,000     $131,250
11     BMW                  5      $9,000     $45,000      $78,750
12     Porsche              5     $13,000     $65,000     $113,750
13     Volvo               15     $10,000    $150,000     $262,500
14                                         ---------------------------
15     TOTAL                                 $395,000     $691,250
16                                         ===========================
17
18
19
20
22-Oct-88   04:20 AM
```

Screen 2 Level 2 Menu

```
A1: [W18]                                                           MENU
Retrieve  Save  Combine  Xtract  Erase  List  Import  Directory
Erase the current worksheet and display the selected worksheet
              A           B          C          D           E
1
2      YUPPIE CARS INC.
3      INVENTORY OF CARS
4            21-Oct-89
```

Screen 3 Level 3 Menu

```
A1: [W18]                                                           FILES
Name of file to retrieve: C:\LOTUS\*.wk?
COMPARE.WK1    FIDELTY1.WK1    FIDELTY2.WK1    FIDELTY3.WK1    FIDELTY4.WK1
              A           B          C          D           E
1
2      YUPPIE CARS INC.
3      INVENTORY OF CARS
4            21-Oct-89
```

Byte is one of the most widely circulated small-computer magazines. *Infoworld* and *Personal Computing* are also quite popular among users of personal computers. All these magazines carry articles of general interest to business and home users. There are flowcharts and program listings for applications such as managing stock-market investments and playing computer games. The advertisements for software and hardware are an important source of information about products and prices. Magazines that focus mainly on a single, widely used personal computer are also available. For example, *PC Magazine* and *PC Week* cover primarily the IBM PC, PS/2, and their compatibles. Articles related to personal computers can also be found in various professional periodicals. Journals serving professional groups such as engineers, accountants, and bankers often publish articles describing personal-computer applications in their own areas of expertise.

To help the user select equipment and design a system, personal-computer **consultants** are available. Consultants come from a variety of backgrounds, including computer programming, system analysis, marketing, accounting, and engineering. Before selecting a consultant, make sure that he or she has a thorough understanding of your application area. One way of checking the credentials of consultants is to talk to their previous customers about the service received. You can find out about personal-computer consultants either through referrals from professional colleagues or by looking in the *Yellow Pages*. Some consultants give courses in programming and the use of various software packages.

Where to Buy PC Systems

There are several ways to acquire personal-computer hardware and software. Franchised retail chain stores such as Computerland and Entre are major outlets. Owing to their large sales volume they are able to support a staff of technical advisors and maintenance personnel. Specializing in computers, these stores carry a wide variety of products. Many dealers in office equipment offer business-oriented hardware and software. Electronics stores have also entered the personal-computer business.

Many colleges and universities have discount agreements with computer vendors that allow their students, staff, and faculty to purchase PC hardware and software at substantial discounts. If you are a student be sure to check whether your school has such agreements before you purchase PC hardware or software.

There are also many mail-order suppliers of PC systems. A mail-order hardware or software product tends to be less expensive than one bought from a store, but the buyer does assume the extra risk of purchasing a product without testing it. Furthermore, mail-order houses usually offer less personal support than local dealers. It is important that you thoroughly test any computer hardware or software you may buy, and ask questions about anything that is unclear. Figure 2–22 provides a checklist for those interested in buying a personal-computer system. Use this checklist so that you do not miss some important consideration when selecting a PC system. Most buyers will modify this checklist to fit their specific needs.

Figure 2–22
Checklist for Acquiring a Personal-Computer System

Checklists are very valuable to those interested in acquiring a personal computer or any other computer or software. With so many variables involved in the decision, a checklist is the most practical way of assuring that all important factors are considered.

Checklist for Buying a PC

When considering the computer needs of your organization, begin by determining what applications are required. Based on the requirements of the software you choose, you can then make hardware decisions.

The following checklist is intended to aid you in selecting these PC components. First, it provides you with a list of features and capabilities to consider when selecting software. It then goes on to address hardware requirements, including vendor-related considerations.

Software

1. What problem(s) are you trying to solve?

_____
_____
_____
_____
_____
_____

2. What types of application software do you need?
_____ Electronic Spreadsheet
_____ Word Processing
_____ Budgeting
_____ Project Planning
_____ Project Management
_____ Graphics
_____ Data-base Management
_____ Query Languages
_____ Electronic Mail
_____ Scheduling
_____ Statistical
_____ Inventory
_____ Communications
_____ Access to Subscribed-to Data Bases
_____ Industry-Specific Packages
_____ Custom Software
_____ Other_____

3a. Is integrated software, allowing the transfer of data between packages, needed?
_____ Yes
_____ No

3b. If yes, which packages need to be integrated? Check all that apply.
_____ Spreadsheet
_____ Word Processing
_____ Subscribed-to Data-Bases
_____ Data Downloaded from Mainframe
_____ Other

4. Are error-checking capabilities for uploading and downloading data needed?
_____ Yes
_____ No

5. What level of sophistication is the user? The package? (1 = High; 3 = Low)

	User	Package
Package A	_____	_____
Package B	_____	_____
Package C	_____	_____

6. Is hardcopy documentation necessary?
_____ Yes
_____ No

7. Is online help required?
_____ Yes
_____ No

8. What is the development history of the software? (i.e., Have there been several releases, indicating product evolution?)

_____
_____
_____

9a. Is it important that the software be compatible with your existing microcomputer software or with other software of interest?
_____ Yes
_____ No
_____ Doesn't matter

9b. Who will supply the interface programs that may be needed?
_____ Vendor
_____ Corporate staff
_____ Individual user

10. What types of communication support do you need?
_____ PC to PC
_____ Asynch
_____ Bisynch
_____ SDLC
_____ Local Area Network
_____ PC to Dedicated Word Processor
_____ None
_____ Don't know

11a. Is the software installed and guaranteed?
_____ Yes
_____ No

11b. Is it supported through a "hot line"?
_____ Yes
_____ No

12a. Is education available?
_____ Yes
_____ No

12b. Is it provided by the vendor?
_____ Yes
_____ No

13. What operating system does the software require?
_____ OS/2
_____ MS-DOS
_____ PC-DOS
_____ Unix (Xenix, etc.)
_____ UCSD p-System
_____ Vendor Specific
_____ Other_____

Figure 2–22 (continued)

14. What are the hardware requirements of the software?
Memory _____ K
Microprocessor:
_____ Z80/8080/8085
_____ 8086/80286/80386/80486
_____ 6502/6509
_____ 68000/68030
_____ Vendor Specific
_____ Don't know
Diskettes:
_____ 3½
_____ 5¼
Number of disk drives:
_____ One
_____ Two
Hard disks:
_____ Yes
_____ If "Yes", what capacity?
_____
_____ No
Printer:
_____ Dot Matrix
_____ Letter Quality
_____ Laser
_____ Graphics Ink Jet
Terminal:
_____ Alphanumeric
_____ Graphic

Hardware

1. Do you need to be able to expand the memory on your system?
_____ Yes
_____ No

2. Do you need to be able to add peripherals?
_____ Yes
_____ No

3. Do you need a color display?
_____ Yes
_____ No

4a. Do you need graphics capability?
_____ Yes
_____ No

4b. If yes, do you need color graphics?
_____ Yes, immediately
_____ Yes, later
_____ No

5a. Do you need modems?
_____ Yes
_____ No

5b. If yes, what kind?
_____ Direct connection
Speed _____ bps
_____ Acoustic coupler

5c. Will you need intelligent auto-dial capabilities?
_____ Yes
_____ No

6. Will the vendor install the hardware you purchase?
_____ Yes
_____ No

7. Is the hardware maintenance available through the vendor?
_____ Yes
_____ No

8. How long will it take for the system to be delivered?
_____ One to three weeks
_____ Three to six weeks
_____ Over six weeks

Vendor

1. Are you buying hardware from:
_____ A local supplier
_____ A mail-order supplier
_____ Direct sales force

2. How long has the hardware vendor been in the computer business?
_____ Less than one year
_____ One to five years
_____ Five to ten years
_____ More than ten years

3. Is the vendor financially stable?

	Software Vendor	Hardware Vendor	Single Source Vendor
Yes	_____	_____	_____
No	_____	_____	_____

4. Is this a new venture for the hardware vendor?
_____ Yes, first venture in microcomputers
_____ No, part of extensive product line

5. How many hardware service locations are available?
_____ 1
_____ 2 to 10
_____ 11 to 50
_____ 51 to 100
_____ Over 100

6. Is the hardware vendor:
_____ Local
_____ Nationwide

7. How many microcomputer systems has the vendor installed?
_____ None; this is first
_____ Less than 100
_____ 100 to 500
_____ 501 to 1,000
_____ 1,001 to 10,000
_____ More than 10,000

8. Does the vendor supply and support a full line of peripherals?
_____ Yes
_____ No

9. How long will it take to get service?

	Software	Hardware
Less than 24 hours	_____	_____
24 to 48 hours	_____	_____
More than 48 hours	_____	_____

10. How many hours of free consultation time does the vendor provide? _____

▉ PERSONAL COMPUTERS IN THE HOME

Personal computers in the home have a variety of applications, including word processing, entertainment, education, and personal finances. However, the market for home PCs has not been as large as anticipated. It has been found that most people who do not keep financial records will not spend the time to do record keeping on a personal computer. Quite often a task in financial record keeping, such as balancing a checkbook, is easier to do manually than with a personal computer. But for those who keep up with their personal financial planning, a PC can be a great help.

The most likely reason a business person purchases a personal computer for the home is to have the same or compatible hardware and software at home as in the office. Sometimes the home computer is linked to a modem, allowing the user to communicate with office computers. Some companies provide their key employees with portable personal computers so they can use the same machine at home as they use in the office. Portable hard-disk drives are also available that allow the user to move data back and forth from home and office.

▉ PERSONAL-COMPUTER CHALLENGES

Software Piracy

Most personal-computer software costs $20 to $500. Much of this software can be easily copied through the copying facilities of the personal computer. Estimates are that 150 to 200 million dollars in sales are lost to the software industry annually because of this **software piracy.** The federal copyright laws prohibit the copying of software, as it is copyrighted. Such illegal copying harms the PC software industry, since revenues lost to the industry could have been used to develop better software. Some companies, such as Lotus Development Corporation, have actively prosecuted people who illegally copied software.

In the past, many software companies used **copy-protection** schemes to protect their software. These schemes, however, did little to prevent a skilled personal-computer user from copying software. There are programs designed to break the software protection schemes.

Today, most software is not copy-protected. Software companies dropped copy protection because users who had legitimately purchased the software were upset over the difficulties they had in copying the software to hard disks and in making backup copies.

When a company has more than one personal computer, the software license agreements typically require that a particular copy of software be used on only one machine. For example, if a business has ten PCs, then it must purchase ten copies of the software. Many software companies apply discounts when multiple copies are being purchased. There are also license agreements that allow software to be used on more than one computer.

Some software companies actually encourage the user to copy their programs. Their hope is that the user will like the software enough to pay them for a copy of the software manual and for periodic updates to the software. PC Write, a word processor, is marketed with this technique.

There is also quite a bit of **public-domain software** available. Such software is not copyrighted and therefore is available to anyone. It is developed and kept up-to-date by users and is also called shareware.

Illegal Access

Throughout our economy there is much information stored on mainframe computer data bases. These range from public-access data bases (such as the Source and Dow Jones News Retrieval) to private-company data bases, research data bases, and Defense Department data bases. Many of these data bases are linked together through a computer network. A user who gains access to the network has relatively easy access to the various data bases.

Personal computers are an ideal device for a person who wishes to gain illegal access to a data base. Such people are known as **hackers;** they just keep hacking away until they gain the desired access.

Many of the data bases have telephone (dial-up) access. First, the hacker obtains the telephone number needed to access the network or mainframe computer. These numbers are often stored on public-access *electronic bulletin boards* by hackers. Then the hacker simply programs a personal computer to dial the telephone number and systematically try (through trial and error) many password combinations in order to find a valid *password*. Once a password is found, hackers often publicize it among their friends or through an electronic bulletin board. Such a trial and error approach would almost be impossible without a personal computer, since manually inputting many different combinations of passwords would take too much time and effort.

Illegal access to computers, and particularly the subsequent destruction of data, is a crime. The FBI usually gets involved in investigating such crimes. However, comprehensive approaches to the prevention, detection, and prosecution of such acts have not been developed.

ELECTRONIC BULLETIN BOARD
A data base, usually maintained on a single personal computer system, to which other PC users may dial into, and either post messages or read the existing messages.

PASSWORD
A unique string of characters that a user must enter to meet security requirements before gaining access to a data base. The password should be known only to that user.

Managing Personal Computers

Personal computers have certainly brought an increase in productivity to businesses. They allow users to develop, in an efficient and productive manner, applications that fit their particular needs. The laissez-faire (do your own thing) approach to personal computing has kindled the imagination of users; many creative applications have been developed. However, a lack of structure and control in the application of personal computers can result in disasters. For example, a number of top-level executives in an oil firm were fired when the company lost several million dollars after it relied on information produced by an electronic spreadsheet. The spreadsheet, which contained errors, had not been tested properly. It is very easy to introduce errors into electronic spreadsheets, particularly if the spreadsheets are large and complex.

Some people feel that the term *personal computer* is inaccurate. The data contained in a firm's personal computers are often very important to the business as a whole, and therefore they are not "personal" data. Figure 2–23 lists several PC management concerns. The key to managing personal computers is to provide structure and control without stifling innovation. After years of experience with personal computers, most companies recognize that the controls necessary to manage mainframe and minicomputers are often necessary to manage personal computers as well.

■ FUTURE DIRECTIONS OF PERSONAL COMPUTERS

Personal computers of the future will have increased processing power and greater storage capabilities. All of this will be available at a lower cost. At the same time, networking of personal computers with other PCs and with minicomputers and mainframes will become more prevalent. Many experts believe that the economics of computing is tending toward the personal computer and away from minicomputers and mainframes. A counter to this

Figure 2–23
Personal Computer Management Concerns

- Your PC data files and programs are important corporate assets—safeguard them!
- If data entry processing and other applications formerly run on a mainframe or minicomputer are now run on a personal computer, have traditional considerations, such as backup, program changes, cross-training, and balancing procedures, been addressed?
- A diskette is a very portable and fragile medium; the risk of accidental or intentional misuse or destruction of data is very high. Protect the information on a diskette by making a duplicate (backup) copy.
- The proliferation of personal computers means that more and more employees *may* have access to your mainframe's data. More and more computer-literate personnel present a risk. You can't assume employees are unable to access or change centralized data files without permission. Find out!
- Personal computers can be used as sophisticated terminals. They can be programmed to manipulate data received from the centralized computer. Users may also be able to write programs to manipulate data stored in the mainframe. Now, users are programmers.
- Many machines mean many applications, thus increasing the possibility that not all are using the same versions of the information. Are decisions being based on obsolete information? All personal computers that share a common data base should have procedural mechanisms to safeguard integrity of information.
- Don't let the relatively inexpensive nature of PC hardware and software delude you; there is a need to properly plan computerized applications.
- Your implementation plan should be flexible and as nonbureaucratic as possible. Don't destroy the user's imagination just because planning is introduced.
- Document, document, document! Perhaps the most significant weakness of PC applications is the lack of documentation. Address this issue at the start, and stay with it.
- Adequately test systems before committing important applications to them. This may sound obvious, but adequate testing may allow you to avoid time-consuming problems.
- Training and cross-training cannot be ignored. Use your documentation in the training process, and be sure to stress good internal control procedures.

argument is that minis and mainframes will also greatly improve their cost-performance ratio in the future.

In addition, it has been found that the use of personal computers increases the demand for mainframe computers. Individuals who have never used a computer are introduced to computing through user-friendly software on the personal computer. As they become more proficient, they begin to want the capabilities that only the mainframe provides. For example, the mainframe may store large corporate data bases containing information that the PC user would like to periodically *download* to the PC.

DOWNLOAD
To move data from a mainframe or minicomputer to a personal computer.

Once the data are on the personal computer, various analysis tasks using PC software, such as electronic spreadsheets, can be performed. Data can be downloaded from mainframes to personal computers, but to do so requires mainframe computer resources. Certainly, the ability to move data to and from mainframes and personal computers is going to be important in the future. Many experts believe that data shared widely by users throughout a business will continue to be initially collected and stored on mainframe data bases, which provide efficiency and a controlled environment. Personal computers will download these data for decision-support analysis.

The personal computer is relieving business people of much of the paperwork necessary to satisfy accounting, legal, and governmental requirements. This leaves management with much more time and energy for productive work in decision making. The personal computer is providing management with a great deal more analysis and information for decision making than has been available in the past. These trends are going to continue and accelerate in the future.

■ Summing Up

■ Personal computers are the most rapidly growing type of computer system. They are versatile machines that can be used by a person possessing very little computer knowledge.

■ The CPU of a personal computer is basically evaluated in terms of its speed and word size. The major components of a CPU are the control unit, arithmetic-logic unit, and primary memory.

■ A personal computer can support a number of input/output devices, including the following:

Keyboard
Mouse
Monitor screen
Color monitor
Floppy-disk drive
Hard-disk drive
Cartridge-tape drive
Printer

■ Personal computers use both floppy and hard disks for secondary storage.

■ The market for personal-computer hardware is very competitive. Apple, IBM, and Compaq are leading suppliers, but there is a large number of other manufacturers selling high-quality equipment as well.

■ Personal computers communicate over both local-area networks and public telephone lines.

■ A large variety of packaged software is available for personal computers. The most popular software packages are electronic spreadsheets, word processing, data-base management systems, and integrated packages.

■ Sophisticated software packages are available for the major business functions such as accounting, finance, marketing, and production. Also, special-purpose software exists for various professional practices.

■ The typical ways that humans communicate with software (in order of least to most user-friendly) are commands, menus, and icons.

■ In buying a PC, users should assess their needs for information, select the application software, and then choose the hardware.

■ Personal-computer equipment and software can be purchased from a variety of sources, including computer stores, mail-order stores, and office-supply dealers. Numerous periodicals provide information on personal computers.

■ Personal computers can be used in the home for a large number of applications, including personal finances, word processing, and entertainment.

■ The software industry loses more than 100 million dollars per year to illegal copying. Thus far, a satisfactory solution to this problem has not been implemented.

■ The personal computer has become an ideal tool for people attempting to gain illegal access to mainframe computers.

■ Managers must provide structure and control in the PC environment, without stifling innovation.

■ As personal computers become more powerful and more widely used, the ability to move data between personal computers and mainframes will increase in importance.

■ Key Terms

personal computer	hard disk (Winchester disk)
microcomputer	tape cartridge
microprocessor	dot-matrix printer
speed	letter quality
word size	mouse
machine operation	communications program
machine cycle	modem
read-only memory (ROM)	plug-compatible
random-access memory (RAM)	graphics
memory modules	word processing
keyboard	integrated packages
monitor screen	user-friendly
color monitor	command
diskette (floppy disk)	menu

line menu   public-domain software

icon   hacker

consultant   electronic bulletin board

software piracy   download

copy protection

1. How much programming expertise is required to operate a personal computer?

2. Describe the three major parts of a personal-computer CPU.

3. What are the major components of PC hardware?

4. Explain the concepts of speed and word size.

5. Distinguish between RAM and ROM.

6. What are the major input and output devices used by a personal computer?

7. What are the advantages and disadvantages of using a hard disk?

8. What are the functions of serial and parallel ports in a personal computer?

9. Describe the price and quality trends in the PC hardware market.

10. What is the difference between draft quality, near letter quality, and letter quality printing? What types of printers typically produce these three kinds of type?

11. What functions are served by PC magazines?

12. List the categories of general business software.

13. What are the ways that humans communicate with software?

14. What is a modem? What functions does a modem perform?

15. What points would you consider before buying an accounting software package?

16. How does a microcomputer help a professional manage his or her practice?

17. Describe some of the uses of a personal computer in the home.

18. What problems are companies encountering with the proliferation of personal computers?

19. What is a cell in a spreadsheet?

20. Describe the characteristics of applications that are most suited to an electronic spreadsheet.

21. Describe the characteristics of applications that are most suited to a data-base management system running on a personal computer.

1. Why did small, unknown firms assume the leadership in exploiting the personal computer market, while the large, established manufacturers of computers stayed out for years and then decided to follow suit?

2. Will the introduction of personal computers create fundamental changes in the way small firms operate? Will it make them more competitive? Discuss your expectations regarding the role of personal computers in small-business management.

3. Personal computers may be a mixed blessing. Their introduction into the home and office may make some people feel insecure and inadequate. What problems may arise with personal computers? What remedies do you suggest?

4. The typical advice given to a person seeking to buy a personal computer is to choose the software, then the hardware. The rationale is that software is the most important part of the computer system. If hardware is bought first, a company could end up with a restricted choice of software. The Davis Company, however, has been advised to buy hardware first. Its consultant strongly advised the company to buy an IBM compatible, without considering software. The consultant's rationale was that the IBM standard will dominate the personal computer market, the compatible manufacturer is reliable, and the IBM compatible has the widest range of business software available. Evaluate the consultant's advice.

5. The manager of the Jackson Retail Outlet hired a consultant, Jim Lloyd, to establish a personal computer system that would provide inventory and sales information. Jim had recently established his own consulting firm after completing an undergraduate degree at the local university. After waiting four months for his system, the manager of the store approached Jim and wanted to know why the development was taking so long. The manager finally asked Jim what experience he had in consulting. Jim replied that this was his first job, but he had used a spreadsheet package in college. The manager immediately fired Jim, but he had already spent several thousand dollars for Jim to learn (on the company's time) about a new software product. How could the manager have prevented this problem?

Appendix ■ Introduction to the Macintosh Personal Computer

■ INTRODUCTION

Currently, there are two families of microcomputers widely used for business purposes. This chapter has used the IBM PC standard and the IBM PS/2 for the purpose of illustration, because they are the most widely used in business. However, the other standard, the Apple Macintosh (the Mac) is rapidly gaining popularity. In this appendix we will describe the differences between the IBM PC-PS/2 family and the Apple Macintosh. An introduction to the Mac's most popular business applications will also be presented.

■ MAC HARDWARE

In 1982, Apple introduced its first Macintosh machine. It was called the Lisa. It had a graphics-based interface with icons and windows like today's Macintosh, and it used Motorola's 68000 microprocessor. However, because of its $10,000 price tag, Apple sold few Lisas and discontinued the machine in 1985.

Currently, the Macintosh family consists of several computers. Among these are the Mac SE, the Mac II and the Mac Portable. These machines all have similar capabilities, except for the number of expansion boards they will accept. They all have the same microprocessor, the Motorola 68030. Standard versions of these machines come with 1 to 2 megabytes of RAM and they are expandable to 8 megabytes, except for the portable which has a RAM limitation of 2 megabytes. In contrast, most IBM PCs and compatibles come with only 640K bytes of memory, and that is all the DOS operating system will allow the applications to access. However, the OS/2 operating system will allow certain IBM micros to access up to 16 megabytes of main memory. The IBM PS/2 models are shipped with 640 kilobytes to 2 megabytes of memory, and some of the models can be expanded to 16 megabytes of memory. Both the Macintosh and the PS/2s use 3½-inch disk drives, but the disk formats are not compatible. The IBM and compatible machines will not run Macintosh software. However, expansion boards are available that allow the Macintosh to run IBM software. And several software packages, such as Microsoft's electronic spreadsheet Excel, have versions that will run on either machine.

65

■ THE MAC INTERFACE

When Apple introduced the original Macintosh in 1984, it popularized a revolutionary way of using personal computers. The Mac's user interface, which was developed by Xerox at its Palo Alto Research Center, was entirely different from anything that existed at that time. This interface uses graphics-based icons (small pictures) that represent files, applications, and tools. The user employs a pointing device called a mouse to invoke these icons. For any application, all of its functions can be invoked from a menu display of icons on the top line of the screen. The user points to the icon and clicks a button on the mouse to choose a menu item.

A key feature of the Mac interface is its consistency across different applications. Apple publishes specifications for software developers so that all applications for the Macintosh look and feel the same. Certain functions such as loading and saving files, cutting and pasting, and editing are found at the same menu location in different programs for the Mac.

■ FINDER

Another interesting feature of the Mac's interface is a constantly running application called Finder. Finder allows the user to organize and manage documents and to start other applications. The way Finder manages documents and disks is much different from DOS. Programs are represented by icons that depict a function; for example, a picture of a pen represents a word processor, a palette stands for a painting program, and a table of numbers represents a spreadsheet. Figure 2A–1 is the Finder desktop screen showing several icons. The user starts an application by moving the mouse pointer across the desk to the icon and clicking the mouse button twice. Another way of starting an application is to click on a document represented on the screen that was created by the application. Because Macintosh files contain header information telling the operating system which program created the file, Finder is able to find the appropriate application, execute it, and load the document.

Files are arranged and organized by Finder using file folders. These folders can contain application programs, documents, and other file folders. They are used much like directories in PC DOS. The user opens a file folder by double clicking the mouse pointer on it. Then Finder opens a window that displays the folder's contents.

Many file operations can be performed graphically. To copy a document to a folder for example, the user drags the icon to the new folder by moving the mouse while holding down the mouse button. Likewise, the user deletes a file by dragging the icon to the trashcan icon. Most people find this process much easier than typing cryptic commands at a command line.

Finder also gives the user access to desk accessories (DAs). These are utilities the user can invoke from inside most Mac programs. Apple supplies several utilities with Finder, but almost any Mac program can be a DA. Figure 2A–2 shows a Macintosh screen with several DAs. Some common DAs are:

■ *alarm clock*—A compact clock that displays the hour, minute, second, date, and alarm.

Figure 2A–1
The Finder Desktop Screen

This screen shows the icons for tools that are available to the user. This screen is also called a desktop.

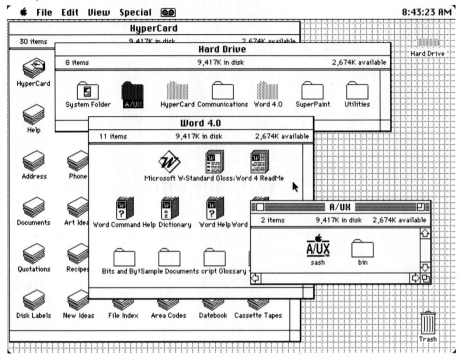

- *calculator*—Looks and works like an ordinary, four-function pocket calculator.
- *chooser*—A program that lets user set preferences for such things as speaker volume, repeating key rate, location of the startup disk, and the background pattern and color of the system.
- *file find*—Helps user locate folders and files on disks.
- *note pad*—Lets user jot down a few notes and keep them separate from the document being worked on.
- *scrapbook*—Contains pictures and text that the user frequently needs. It is also used to cut or copy pictures and text between applications.

Another distinguishing aspect of the Macintosh operating system is that it allows the user to easily cut and paste (move) text and graphics images among all applications. A diagram created with a drafting program or a digitized photograph can be easily included in a word-processing document or spreadsheet. These capabilities in the DOS world are limited at best.

■ BUSINESS SOFTWARE FOR THE MAC

Several applications for Apple's Macintosh line have found their way into business. The most popular Macintosh application is Excel, arguably the

Figure 2A–2
Finder Desk Accessories

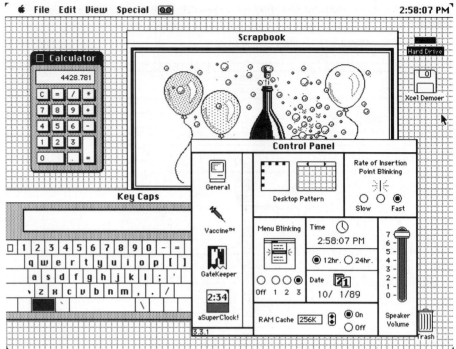
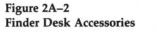

finest spreadsheet available for any microcomputer. Excel has far more functions and programming commands than Lotus 1-2-3 and supports PostScript, a standard, desktop-publishing, page composition language. Also, program routines written in C and FORTRAN (popular third-generation programming languages) can be called from Excel to operate on spreadsheet data. Excel's graphing capabilities are more sophisticated than those of any other spreadsheet, and graphic images can be cut and pasted to and from any other Macintosh application. Figure 2A–3 shows an Excel spreadsheet with three windows. The active window contains the data, the lower right window contains a graph of the data, and the lower left window shows a blank worksheet.

Some very powerful data-base management systems also exist for the Macintosh. The most popular ones are Filemaker Plus, 4th Dimension, and Omnis 3/Plus. All of these are capable of storing graphic images as data. Another powerful feature is their ability to create pointers between related data in the data base by simply drawing lines with the mouse between the fields in the different relations (files). No programming commands are needed.

Several excellent word processors are available for the Macintosh. Two of the better ones are Microsoft Word and Write Now. Macintosh word processors have several distinguishing features over IBM word processors. Most notable is their ability to cut graphic images from other applications into the word-processing document. The word processor wraps text automatically around the imported graphic. Mac word processors are also capable of displaying

Figure 2A–3
An Excel Spreadsheet

Note that the screen is divided into three windows, each showing a different part of the spreadsheet.

many different fonts on the screen exactly as they will appear on the printed page. This feature is known as WYSIWYG (What You See Is What You Get). Figure 2A–4 shows a Word screen with a picture copied from MacPaint.

Another area where the Macintosh has gained inroads into business is with desktop publishing. Applications such as Pagemaker and Ready-Set-Go can be used to create professional-looking documents on Apple's laser printer using the PostScript page-composition language. These documents can contain graphics created with other applications and photographs that have been put into computer form using a scanner. Because the Macintosh is graphics-based, the way the document appears on the screen is identical to the way it will be printed.

■ HYPERCARD

A new type of application development tool became available on the Macintosh in 1987. The program, which comes free with a new purchase of a Macintosh, is called HyperCard, and it is based on a concept called Hyper-Text. The strength of HyperCard is in searching unstructured data and establishing links between seemingly unrelated pieces of data.

Figure 2A–4
A Graphic Image within a Word Processing Screen

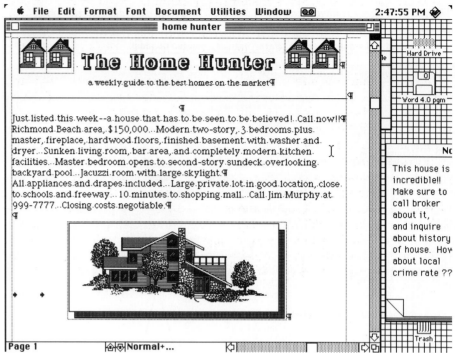

The organization of HyperCard is similar to a library's card catalog. Information is stored on cards, and cards are grouped into stacks. Each stack is a file that serves as a HyperCard application. HyperCard actions are initiated by clicking mouse buttons. Clicking a button may simply bring up the next card in the stack or it may perform a more complex task, such as retrieving exchange rates for one field, converting one currency to another, and putting the result in yet another field. You can also click buttons within graphic images. You would click on a column in a bar chart, for example, to display more detailed information.

In a business environment, HyperCard could be very useful for management information delivery and for interactive training. Also, HyperCard might become a standard interface for CD-ROM (an optical storage media) information retrieval systems on the Macintosh. Because it puts powerful programming tools into the hands of nonprogrammers, HyperCard could inspire a variety of new business applications for the Mac.

■ THE MERGING OF STANDARDS

Although the IBM PC and the Apple Macintosh have many differences, the two standards are gradually coming together. In terms of hardware design, the new versions of Macintosh (the Mac SE and Mac II) come with a bus for adding expansion boards—once an exclusive advantage of the IBM family of microcomputers. On the other side, IBM's new PS/2 line of computers has borrowed many of Mac's features. For example, the IBM PC, XT, and AT require separate expansion boards for displaying graphics. The new PS/2 line has the graphics capabilities built into the motherboard like the Macintosh does. Also, the PS/2 line of computers are more compact, like the Macintosh.

The two standards are also merging in terms of software. IBM and Microsoft's new operating system OS/2 contains a module called Presentation Manager which is very similar to Macintosh's graphics user interface. It provides a common interface for applications running under OS/2 and allows cutting and pasting among applications. Also, commands are executed by pointing to menu choices and icons with a mouse, as on a Macintosh.

Many applications originally written for the Macintosh are appearing on IBM PCs, running under Windows (a forerunner to IBM's Presentation Manager) and OS/2. These applications include the Excel spreadsheet and the Pagemaker desktop publishing software. The Windows and OS/2 versions of these programs look and feel very similar to their Macintosh siblings. Also, many applications originally written for the IBM PC have moved over to the Mac. Some of these are Microsoft Word, Word Perfect, dBASE III, and Turbo Pascal.

PART ONE   ■ APPLICATION CASE

Users Steering Toward Self-Service

By Meghan O'Leary

Developing PC applications is like going to a gas station. You can wait to have your oil checked and your windshield cleaned. Or you can pump your own gas for less money and quickly get back on the road.

As the number of PC users continues to grow, beleaguered systems developers are increasingly pointing their clients toward self-service.

With information systems (IS) departments busy with other concerns, such as software standards and adequate documentation, labor and time constraints seem to have reinstated the PC user as the developer of choice.

"It's the old backlog story," explained Ron Fox, a senior systems analyst for Clintec Nutrition Co., an affiliate of Baxter Healthcare Corp., in Deerfield, Ill. Developing a big application "will take a couple of years and cost a lot of money." Users can avoid "chewing up CPU cycles and manpower," by doing applications themselves, he said.

The ramifications of such time and labor considerations go far beyond the application at hand. "The point is that it's a business decision," said Phillip Gordon, manager of office systems for Charles Schwab & Co., a financial-consulting firm in San Francisco. Department managers, understandably, want to avoid long delays and high development costs.

Another factor pointing toward user-developed applications is quality: Users can help create better programs simply because they know exactly what they need. "I try to point out to people that we're not going to know their business as well as they do," Mr. Gordon said.

Despite the need to control applications standards by some IS departments, most micro managers say that end-user involvement in the development process is desirable.

The level of user involvement will vary according to the needs of the company and the sophistication of the users. In many companies, IS has no involvement at all unless the application under development will be linked to a central mainframe.

Educate Users

The most popular approach to applications development, however, is for the IS or the information center to actively educate users, while retaining some degree of supervision over them.

Since micro managers are accustomed to coming up with ad-hoc solutions to changing demands in the workplace, it's not surprising that they often choose to delegate tasks to users in applications development. And whether the delegation process is formal or informal, incorporating user suggestions in development is usually effective without shocking existing applications-development procedures.

Users' interests "are critical to our relationship with them," said Kevin Cooper, director of customer services for Bekins Van Lines, an interstate shipping company based on Glendale, Calif. Mr. Cooper faces an uncommon challenge in getting input from his 500 users, because they are largely independent owners of moving-and-storage companies who access the Bekins mainframe from individual PCs to enter and trace shipment orders. Their dispersion makes direct involvement in the development of applications impossible. Nevertheless, Mr. Cooper said, the users' diverse and ever-changing business needs makes their input vital.

His solution was to create the Agent Information Systems Committee, a board of 12 agents representing a cross section of their respective industries. Board members meet several times a year to discuss their changing applications needs.

Delegating—moving from centralized to decentralized control—also works well for in-house users, giving them an avenue by which to make their technology needs known without having to shoulder the responsibility of developing applications themselves.

"Usually my users will give me a guide as to what sorts of tools they think are best suited [to the application]," Clintec's Mr. Fox explained. His users are, in his words, "not at all [technically] sophisticated," and they rely on him to translate their verbal suggestions into a working application.

"I have to sit down with them and find out all their requirements. Then I go through corporate IS, which gives guidelines to the environment as well as suggestions for tools."

Mr. Fox explained that he represents his users' interests to corporate IS. The approval of the central com-

PART ONE   ## APPLICATION CASE

puting function is needed to assure access to main-frame information when necessary. IS points users toward the right tools to meet their requirements.

Once central approval becomes part of the formula, however, the process can get murky, warned Barbara Franko, a project manager at Arco Chemical Co. in Philadelphia.

"The real problem is defining the roles and responsibilities of the people involved," Ms. Franko said.

Ideally, she added, the central PC group's role should evolve into a consulting capacity. IS can assign the responsibility for maintaining the application to the department for which it is intended.

"From what I've seen," Ms. Franko explained, "the users just don't have enough time to develop an application, but they're willing to work with us" to learn to maintain it.

Walking a Mile for a Camel

Indeed, it seems some users are willing to go a bit further to get an application that truly meets their needs. "Some users want a choice," said Tom Musante, information center (IC) manager of Drexel Burnham Lambert Inc., a New York investment-banking firm.

"The first thing we do in qualifying [a potential application]," he said, "is to say to the users, 'Are you ready, willing, and able to absorb the responsibility of learning the product and supporting it?' " The answer to this question determines which of his company's three IS tiers, the office-systems group, the IC, or the systems-development group, the user will collaborate with in developing the application, as well as the degree of involvement the user will be allowed.

Although Mr. Musante noted that real development is done only at the IC tier, the company's office-systems group provides basic, off-the-shelf applications packages for users to implement in whatever fashion they choose. "They're the first level of consulting for our users," said Mr. Musante.

Once a department has chosen its software, it has the option of working with the IC to develop a customized application, a process requiring much user input.

The third tier, systems development, serves the user who wants little or no involvement in the development process and who doesn't mind waiting.

"If users are not ready to support the application, it goes to the systems developer and becomes another

project in a queue of projects," Mr. Musante explained. "And it will either prioritize upward or it will remain in the queue. And that's the risk users have to take."

At each level there are different procedures for determining end-user requirements. "The IC, for example, will set up skeletal reports on spec and will instruct the user to change or approve them," Mr. Musante explained. "At the systems-development level, there's a much more structured type of approach. The users have to spec it out completely, and it will be written for them."

Besides user preference, the method of development and level of user input can also hinge on the criticality or timeliness of the project. "If either of the first two tiers feels that it's critical, then they will automatically move this on to the third tier," Mr. Musante said. Thus, in the case of a high-priority application, user input would also take on more importance.

At the third tier of control, the systems-development group takes on the responsibility for maintaining corporate software standards and documentation for an application. In less structured user-development environments, maintaining standards and documenting effectively are the two most often cited problems associated with end-user development.

However, a new breed of problem has arisen in user-driven development areas, one not so easily controlled by a central supervisor. Bob Simon, IC coordinator for CNG Producing Co., a gas and oil company located in New Orleans, said that when he asked a group of employees at the gas and oil company to define their needs for an automated land-lease management system, they couldn't help him.

"It was very frustrating," Mr. Simon said. "They didn't want to be involved, because they didn't think they could define their needs from a business sense, let alone a technical sense. They told us to pick the most popular package. They didn't think they could define their needs as well as someone who had written a best-selling package.

"I think it's a confidence issue," he concluded.

Some users, however, have the opposite problem—overconfidence. Clintec's Mr. Fox described problems with users trying to implement inappropriate applications. With some users, "once they learn one applications package, they try to make it fit everything."

For example, Mr. Fox said, he has had to discourage users from doing word processing and developing

PART ONE   ■ APPLICATION CASE

data bases in Lotus Development Corp.'s 1–2–3 spreadsheet. "I tell them flat out, 'This application is unsuitable, and I will not help you,' " he said. "But it doesn't matter what package you give them. They refuse [to learn it]. They had to fight like hell to learn Lotus and they're not going to give it up."

On the other end of Mr. Fox's experience, he pointed out, some users simply are not interested in development.

Nevertheless, PC coordinators agree that the user is vital to the development process and that the IC should not be solely responsible for it.

"I have always felt that the most efficient use of a support group is in support and not applications development," Mr. Gordon said.

"Control of applications should be with the user," he continued. "Most people of average intelligence can learn to do something if you show them how. The main thing that we should be looking out for is simply . . . that they are aware of the necessary controls."

Reprinted from *PC Week*, March 29, 1988, p. 50. Copyright ©: 1988 Ziff-Davis Publishing Company

DISCUSSION QUESTIONS

1. Given the fact that many end users, such as management, financial, marketing, and accounting personnel, are developing their own PC applications, how important will learning the fundamentals of computer information systems be to your career?
2. What are the advantages and disadvantages of end user development of software?
3. What types of applications are end users most likely to develop successfully?

PART TWO ■ How Managers Use Computers

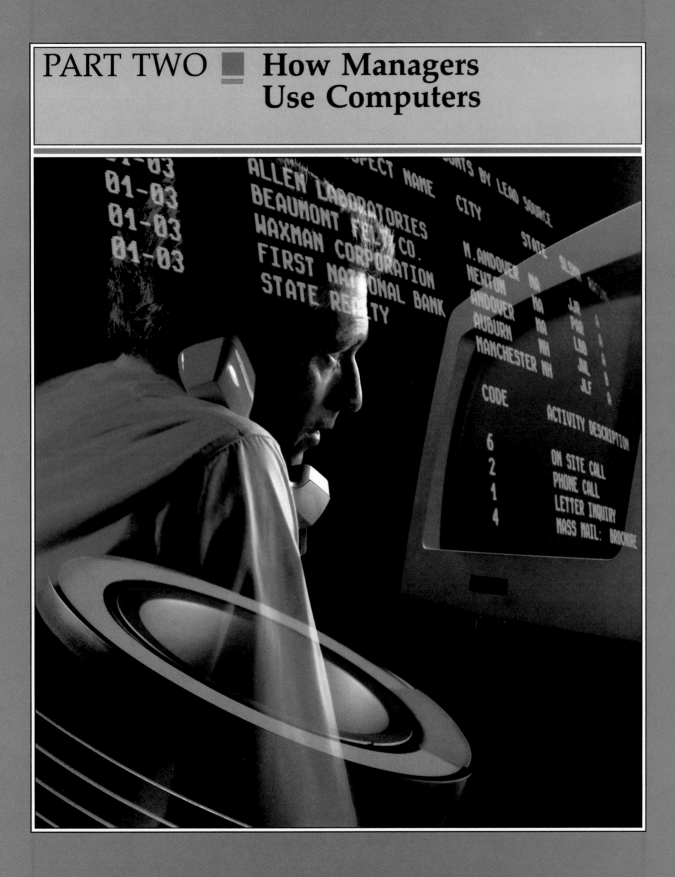

Management Information Systems

Chapter 3

CHAPTER OUTLINE

Introduction

What Is a MIS?

What Are the Parts of a Management Information System?

Objectives, Decisions, and Information

Levels of Decision Making

Management Uses of Information

Using Information Systems for Competitive Advantage

Qualitative Characteristics of Information
Relevance
Timeliness
Accuracy
Verifiability

Data or Information Processing?

Types of Reports
Scheduled Reports
Demand Reports
Exception Reports
Predictive Reports

The MIS and Business Functions

The MIS and Data-Base Management Systems

Decision-Support Systems and the MIS

The Impact of Management Information Systems on Business
Easier Business Growth
Fewer Clerical Workers
Reduced Information-Processing Costs
Automation of Some Decisions
More and Better Information

Summing Up

Key Terms

Review Questions

Discussion Questions and Cases

■ INTRODUCTION

In the last two chapters we developed a basic understanding of the computer and how it processes information. Then we examined that most user-friendly of computer systems, the personal computer.

In this chapter we see how a management information system (MIS) relates to the information needs of management. In Chapter 4 we will examine decision-support systems, which directly support the decision making of management. In Chapter 5 we will look at some typical information system applications. And in Chapters 6 through 8 we will see how information needs are analyzed, how these needs are shaped into information-system designs, and finally how these designs are implemented into a working information system.

This chapter could have been titled "Information Systems from the Viewpoint of Managers," which is the essence of management information systems. An information system is a tool that must fit within the framework of the tasks that managers perform. Managers are interested first in how they can put the computer to work, and then in computer technology.

We first explore the relationship between a management information system and data processing, including the ways that data-processing applications support a MIS. Next we look at the parts of a management information system. Then we examine the close relationship between managerial decisions and the information needs behind these decisions. Fourth, we look at how a MIS produces information through different types of reports. Fifth, we briefly examine the relationship between a MIS and a data-base management system (DBMS). Perhaps the single most important advancement that has made the MIS practical is the software available for data-base management systems. Next, we investigate the relationship between the MIS and decision support systems. And finally, we look at the impact of the MIS on business.

■ WHAT IS A MIS?

TRANSACTION
A business event, such as a sale to a customer. In information systems, the term *transaction* often refers to any change made in a computer file.

DATA BASE
A collection of data fundamental to a system.

A **management information system** is a formalized computer information system that can integrate data from various sources to provide the information necessary for management decision making. Figure 3–1 illustrates the relationship between data processing and management information systems. The data-processing system supports management information systems. Much of the information that the MIS uses is initially captured and stored by the data-processing system. Data processing is oriented toward capturing, processing, and storing data whereas MIS is oriented toward using the data to produce management information. The data-processing system performs *transaction* processing. It is very much involved with processing orders, sales, payments on account, and so on. In the course of processing these transactions, the data-processing system collects and stores a large amount of detailed information. This information is the *data base* for the management information system.

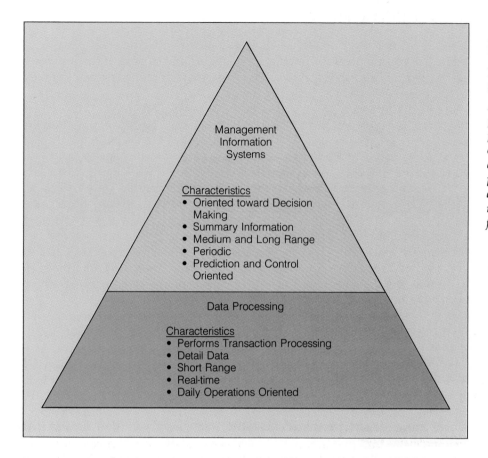

Figure 3–1
The Relationship between Data Processing and Management Information Systems

Most firms implement data-processing systems first since processing of transactions with customers is a necessity. As the data are collected through data processing, they also become available to produce the reports required by a management information system.

Management
Information
Systems

Characteristics
• Oriented toward Decision
  Making
• Summary Information
• Medium and Long Range
• Periodic
• Prediction and Control
  Oriented

Data Processing

Characteristics
• Performs Transaction Processing
• Detail Data
• Short Range
• Real-time
• Daily Operations Oriented

WHAT ARE THE PARTS OF A MANAGEMENT INFORMATION SYSTEM?

Figure 3–2 illustrates the parts of a management information system. A management information system can be broken down into six parts: inputs, processes, data files, outputs, personnel, and hardware. All systems, including management information systems and computer systems, have inputs, processes, and outputs. Processes transform inputs (data) to outputs (management information). Processes can be subdivided into computer programs and procedures. Computer programs are executed by computer hardware, and procedures are executed by people. For example, sometimes data must be collected and checked manually before they are input to the management information system. Manual procedures are still a very important part of a MIS. A MIS also contains data files. These data files can be either computer-based or manual.

Personnel is without a doubt the most important component of a management information system. System analysts and programmers design, implement, and maintain the programs and procedures of a MIS, while computer operators run the computer-based portion of the system. Accounting, finance, marketing, and manufacturing personnel operate other aspects of a MIS, sometimes, in fact, without the use of computer hardware. Further-

Figure 3–2
The Parts of a Management Information System

Note the similarity between this figure and Figure 1–2, Overview of a Computer System. Of course, the portions of a Management Information System that are computer based are executed on a computer system. However, as we will see in this chapter, much of an MIS depends on highly-skilled personnel.

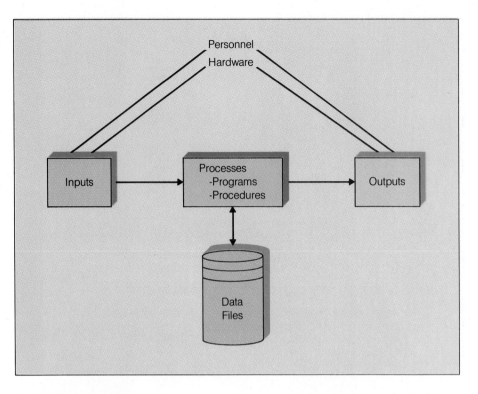

more, management personnel sets the overall policies that govern the operation of a MIS.

In summary, the core of a MIS is made up of inputs, processes, data files, and outputs. These components are executed and controlled by hardware and personnel.

■ OBJECTIVES, DECISIONS, AND INFORMATION

How do we determine what information a manager needs? Information needs are determined by the **decisions** that must be made, which in turn are determined by **objectives.** This relationship between objectives, decisions, and information is illustrated in Figure 3–3.

Assume that a company has an objective of increasing its net profit by 50 percent. Decisions would need to be made about which products should be emphasized in order to reach the desired 50-percent increase in profits. Choosing a certain product might require further decisions about whether to expand a plant or whether to purchase the product from outside. All of these decisions would be based in part on information from the management information system. As the company moves toward the 50-percent increase in net profit, reports showing how well each product is selling would be crucial. These reports could indicate that a decision should be made to emphasize a different product. This approach to determining the information needs of management is very important, as we will see later when we discuss the

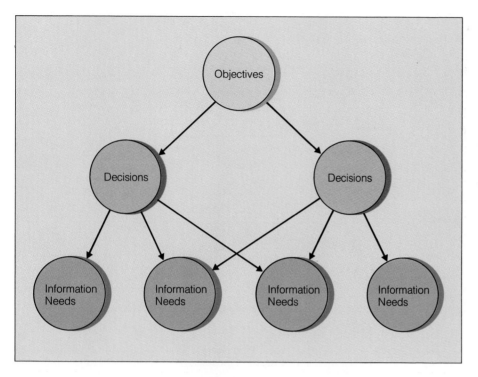

Figure 3–3
The Relationship between Objectives, Decisions, and Information Needs
Sometimes it is tempting to think about information needs without first thinking about business objectives and decisions. Such an approach often results in information systems that do not meet business needs.

development of information systems. The *system analyst* must always keep in mind the decisions and objectives that the MIS supports.

SYSTEM ANALYST
A person whose responsibility is to analyze, design, and develop information systems.

■ LEVELS OF DECISION MAKING

Decisions can be classified as: (1) strategic, (2) tactical, and (3) operational. These levels of decision making correspond to management levels. Strategic decisions are made by top management; tactical decisions by middle management; and operational decisions by lower-level management. As illustrated in Figure 3–4, all three of these levels of decision making rely on data processing for portions of their information.

Strategic decisions are future oriented and include a great deal of uncertainty. **Strategic decision making** involves establishing objectives for the organization and making long-range plans for attaining these objectives. Decisions about the location of plants, about capital sources, and about which products to produce, are examples of strategic decisions.

Tactical decision making involves implementing the decisions made at the strategic level, including allocating resources in order to pursue organizational objectives. Examples of tactical decision making are plant layout, personnel concerns, budget allocation, and production scheduling.

Operational decisions involve executing specific tasks and assuring that they are carried out efficiently and effectively. These decisions are made primarily by lower-level supervisors. *Standards* are usually preset for opera-

STANDARD
An acknowledged guideline or norm against which performance is measured.

Figure 3–4
Levels of Decision Making

Data processing supports these decisions with data that can be further processed to produce information for decision making.

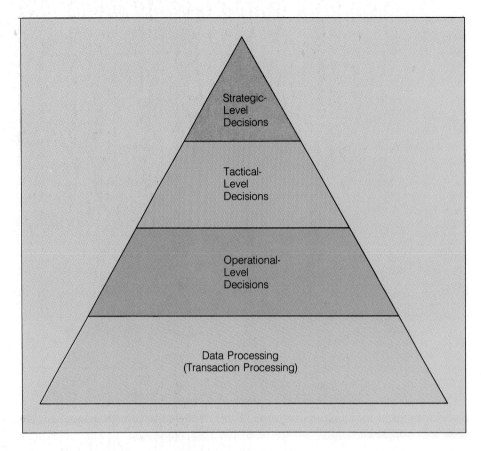

tional decisions. Managers and supervisors at this level are expected to make decisions that keep the operation in line with the predetermined standards. Examples of operational decision making include accepting or rejecting credit, determining inventory reorder times and quantities, and assigning jobs to workers. Table 3–1 summarizes the characteristics of the three levels of decision making.

Table 3–1 ■ Characteristics of the Three Levels of Decision Making

Characteristic	LEVELS OF DECISION MAKING		
	Operational	Tactical	Strategic
Problem Variety	Low	Moderate	High
Degree of Structure	High	Moderate	Low
Degree of Uncertainty	Low	Moderate	High
Degree of Judgment	Low	Moderate	High
Time Horizon	Days	Months	Years
Programmable Decisions	Most	Some	None
Planning Decisions	Few	About half	Most
Control Decisions	Most	About half	Few

Decisions can also be categorized as programmable or nonprogrammable. **Programmable decisions** are decisions for which policy standards or guidelines are already established. For this reason they are often called *structured* decisions. These decisions are routine and can be made by referring to established policy. An example of a programmable decision is whether to grant credit to a person applying for it. Note that programmable decisions do not necessarily have to be made by a computer-based system. Often these decisions are made by lower-level managers or supervisors. **Nonprogrammable decisions** involve ill-defined and unstructured problems. These decisions are future oriented and contain many variables whose impact on the outcome cannot be quantified. These **unstructured decisions** require highly skilled managers. Examples of such decisions are those regarding plant expansion, new products, and mergers.

Table 3–2 summarizes the characteristics of information required at each level of decision making. Note that operational decision making depends heavily on *real-time information*. For example, your school probably uses a real-time system for course registration. The operational decision to allow you to sign up for a particular class depends on the real-time information of whether the class is full. Strategic decision making depends much less on real-time information. For instance, one important type of information used at the strategic level is income statements. These statements identify the profitability of plants, products, and so on. Income statements are usually generated at the end of each month. Therefore, they are not real-time. Strategic decision making also tends to rely heavily on financial information. Decision makers at this level deal with capital requirements and profitability in dollars. On the other hand, a frontline supervisor, at the operational level, is more concerned about the hours worked on a job, the number of orders shipped, the number of defective units produced, and other information of this type.

STRUCTURED
That which is highly organized.

REAL-TIME INFORMATION
Information about ongoing events that reflects the status of these events in a completely up-to-date manner.

Table 3–2 ■ Characteristics of Information Required at Each Level of Decision Making

Information Characteristic	LEVELS OF DECISION MAKING		
	Operational	Tactical	Strategic
Dependence on Computer Information Systems	High	Moderate	Low to Moderate
Dependence on Internal Information	Very High	High	Moderate
Dependence on External Information	Low	Moderate	Very High
Degree of Information Summarization	Very Low	Moderate	High
Need for Online Information	Very High	High	Moderate
Need for Computer Graphics	Low	Moderate	High
Use of Real-Time Information	Very High	High	Moderate
Use of Predictive Information	Low	High	Very High
Use of Historical Information	High	Moderate	Low
Use of What-If Information	Low	High	Very High
Use of Information Stated in Dollars	Low	Moderate	High

■ MANAGEMENT USES OF INFORMATION

Management uses information for two purposes: planning and control. **Planning** occurs prior to the execution of any organizational activity. Objectives are established in the planning process. The activities that must occur to reach the objectives are identified, and the resources (such as money, equipment, and labor) necessary to support these activities are allocated. Although planning takes place at all levels of the organization, most of it occurs at the strategic and tactical levels of decision making. Planning depends to a large degree on predictive and external information. Historic information is useful in planning only in that it helps management predict the future.

Control is the process of comparing actual results with the plans identified in the planning process. Figure 3–5 illustrates management control. Let us assume the system shown in this figure is a factory. Management's plan is for the factory to produce $12 million in profit for the year. Inputs to the factory are the factors of production—land, labor, and capital. Output is a net profit. An income statement that compares actual profit to the planned profit provides feedback to management about the performance of the system (factory). If, during the year, management determines that the factory is not likely to reach the $12-million profit goal, this system is out of control. Management would attempt to get the system back in control by making modifications to the inputs. These changes might include reducing the workforce or buying less expensive raw materials.

A large percentage of the information produced by management information systems is feedback, as shown in Figure 3–5. The information system monitors the system being controlled, compares the system outputs to plans, and provides the feedback information necessary for management control.

Figure 3–5
Management Control

This figure illustrates a system with feedback control. Feedback information about the performance of the system is used by management for control.

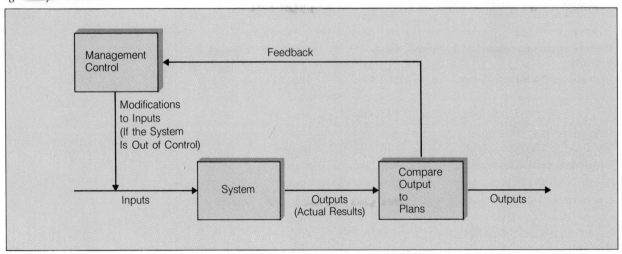

USING INFORMATION SYSTEMS FOR
■ COMPETITIVE ADVANTAGE

In the mid-1980s, many business firms began to view information systems as tools to gain advantages over their competitors. The use of information systems to support management planning and control has always been directed at making business operations more effective and efficient, but the emphasis on using information systems to gain **competitive advantage** is new.

Several major firms have gained significant competitive advantages through the strategic use of information technology. For example, American Airlines' Sabre system and United Airlines' Apollo system are used by reservations agents to book flights on all airlines. Each system is designed to show the owner's (American's or United's) flights first on the computer screen when agents check for available flights. Thus, agents are more likely to book passengers on an American or United flight. These systems have given such a competitive advantage to their owners that competing airlines have appealed to both the courts and the government to change the order in which flights appear on these systems' screens.

Another example of a firm that has used information technology competitively is American Hospital Supply. This firm was the first to install online order-entry terminals in hospitals, thus making it extremely convenient and fast for hospitals to order its supplies. American Hospital Supply now dominates the hospital supply market.

Rackoff, Wiseman, and Ullrich have identified five competitive moves that firms can make to achieve competitive advantage:[1]

■ Differentiate—Distinguish the firm's products or services from competitors, or reduce the differentiation advantage of rivals.
■ Adjust cost—Reduce the firm's costs, the supplier's costs, or the customer's costs, or raise the costs of competitors.
■ Be innovative—Introduce a product or process change that results in a basic change in the way business is conducted in the industry.
■ Improve growth—Increase volume, expand geographically, or integrate with suppliers or customers.
■ Form alliances—Form marketing agreements or joint ventures.

Information technology can be used as the main component or in a supporting role in any of these competitive moves. The technique often used by firms to identify competitive-advantage opportunities is to hold idea-generating sessions among executives and middle managers.

QUALITATIVE CHARACTERISTICS
■ OF INFORMATION

Without quality, information loses its usefulness. A phrase often used to describe the lack of data quality is "garbage in garbage out" (GIGO). This

[1] N. Rackoff, C. Wiseman, and W. A. Ullrich, "Information Systems for Competitive Advantage: Implementation of a Planning Process," *MIS Quarterly* (December 1985), 285–94.

means that unless data meet qualitative characteristics upon input, the information output from the data-processing system will be useless, or garbage. Information must meet four qualitative criteria: relevance, timeliness, accuracy, and verifiability.

Relevance

Information has **relevance** when it is useful in decision making. In other words, if information improves the decision, it is relevant. Obviously, if an airline-reservations agent is making a decision to grant a customer a reservation on a particular flight, the number of empty seats on that flight is relevant information. On the other hand, personal characteristics of the potential customer, such as occupation or sex, generally are not relevant.

Timeliness

The **timeliness** of information is important. In the context of most management information systems, as information becomes older its value decreases. Generally, lower-level decisions in an organization must have more current and timely information, and as we move up the ladder to higher-level decisions the information can be somewhat older. For example, if we are making the very routine and low-level decision of whether to ship a customer the 150 shirts ordered, we must know the number of shirts we have at the moment. The number of shirts available five days or two weeks ago is completely useless information in terms of our decision, so the information is not timely. Conversely, a high-level decision concerning whether to expand a company's capacity for making shirts by building an additional plant depends partly on the history of shirt sales. Information that is several years old is useful in this case.

Accuracy

Accuracy refers to information being free of error. The amount of error that we can tolerate is related to other factors, especially timeliness and the dollar value of the decision to be made. If a decision maker must make a decision quickly, a greater degree of error can be tolerated than if he or she has considerable time and resources available to reduce data error. For example, if you smell smoke in your home you are likely to make a quick decision to call the fire department rather than take the time to establish, without error, the location and actual existence of a fire. On the other hand, if you are reconciling your checkbook to a bank statement, you may want to base your decision to call the bank (and accuse people there of making an error) on information that is accurate to the nearest penny.

Verifiability

Verifiability means that the accuracy of information can be confirmed. Information can be verified through comparison with other information that is known to be accurate. Quite often, though, verification is achieved by tracing information to its original source. The term **audit trail** is often used to describe the means by which summarized information can be traced back to its original source. Without this trail it is usually impossible to determine the accuracy of information, therefore bringing into question the usefulness of such information.

In summary, several variables must be considered when designing a management information system. The designer must keep in mind the objectives of the organization, the decisions that must be made, and whether those decisions are of a planning or control nature. The information must be relevant, timely, accurate, and verifiable. In addition, the type of information required depends heavily on the decision level—whether it is operational, tactical, or strategic. Experience has shown that computer information systems are more successful in providing information for control decisions than for planning decisions. They decrease in success the higher the level of decision making. However, advancements in management information systems are making information systems more applicable to planning and to the higher levels of decision making.

■ DATA OR INFORMATION PROCESSING?

Data processing has traditionally been defined as the capture, storage, and processing of data used to transform the data into information useful in decision making. There is a difference between data and information. **Data** are collected facts that generally are not useful for decision making without further processing. **Information** is directly useful in decision making. It is based on processed data and therefore is the output of a data-processing system. In actual practice, however, this distinction is often difficult to make. One individual's data may be another's information. For example, hours worked by individual employees are certainly information to a frontline supervisor. However, when the decision maker is the president of a company, hours worked by individual employees are simply data that can be further processed and summarized. These summarized data may be information to the president. For these reasons, the trend is to use the term **information processing** rather than data processing.

■ TYPES OF REPORTS

We have thus far discussed management decision making and the need for information to support these decisions. But in what form is this information produced? There are four types of computer reports: scheduled, demand, exception, and predictive *reports*.

REPORT
A printing or display of items of information.

Scheduled Reports

Scheduled reports are produced on a regular basis such as daily, weekly, or monthly. These reports are widely distributed to users and often contain large amounts of information that are not used regularly. As VDTs (video display terminals) have become more widespread, scheduled reports have diminished in importance. Managers do not feel compelled to ask for information on a scheduled listing just in case they may need it in the future—with a VDT the information can be retrieved on demand.

Demand Reports

Demand reports are generated on request. These reports fill irregular needs for information. In the earlier days of computing, the contents of a demand report had to be previously anticipated or there would be a delay of often weeks or months in receiving the data. It simply took time to modify programs to produce information that filled unanticipated demands. Today, largely through the *query languages* of data-base management systems, we can fulfill unanticipated demands for information very quickly, often within minutes. This is possible because users and managers themselves can use the query languages to produce reports. Thus, they can receive reports as needed, rather than receiving regularly scheduled reports that may not be always needed.

QUERY LANGUAGE
A high-level computer language that can be used with minimal training to retrieve specific information from a data base.

Exception Reports

One of the most efficient approaches to management is the management-by-exception approach. **Management by exception** means that managers spend their time dealing with exceptions, or those situations which are out of control. Activities that are proceeding as planned are in control and, therefore, do not need the manager's attention. **Exception reports** notify management when an activity or system is out of control so that corrective action can be taken. A listing that identifies customers having overdue account balances is an exception report. An error report is another type of exception report. **Error reports** identify input or processing errors occurring during the computer's execution of a particular *application*.

APPLICATION
A specific use of a computer to perform a business task.

Predictive Reports

Predictive reports are useful in planning decisions. They often make use of statistical and modeling techniques such as regression, time-series analysis, and simulation. These reports help management personnel answer what-if questions. For example: What if sales increased by 10 percent? What impact would the increase have on net profit? The statistical and modeling techniques that produce predictive reports depend largely on historical data. Such data must be readily accessible by the MIS in a form that can be used by the models; otherwise, these models will be of little use to management. Figure 3–6 shows the types of reports issued by management information systems.

■ THE MIS AND BUSINESS FUNCTIONS

FUNCTIONAL AREA
An organizational unit of a business corresponding to its major duty or activity, such as engineering or finance.

A MIS is a federation of **functional information systems.** This concept is illustrated in Figure 3–7. Specialists within each *functional area* (such as

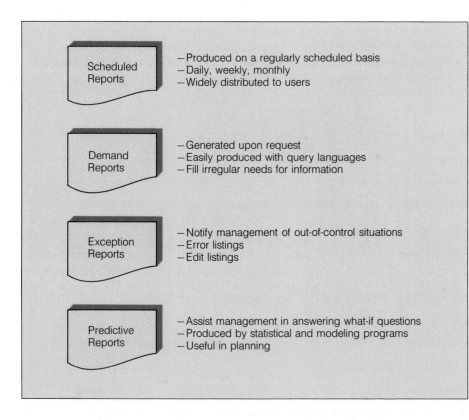

Figure 3–6
Information-System Reports Issued to Management

Although some of these reports are available on video display terminals (VDTs), many managers still prefer that reports be printed out on paper.

finance, production, accounting, and engineering) are much more familiar with the information requirements of that function than anyone else in the firm. These specialists can design systems to produce the information required to manage their function. The functional information systems interact with one another and often share the same data. As we will discuss next, data-base management systems greatly enhance the ability of these functional systems to share data. The important point to remember is that these integrated functional information systems are the MIS.

Each of the functional information systems are, in turn, made up of *application systems*, as shown in Figure 3–7. The accounting information system includes several typical applications. Each application system is also made up of one or more programs. In the payroll system illustrated, there are five programs.

APPLICATION SYSTEMS
Computer programs written to perform specific business tasks.

THE MIS AND DATA-BASE
■ MANAGEMENT SYSTEMS

Data are the central resource of a MIS. Managing this resource is crucial. A **data-base management system** is a collection of programs that serve as an interface between application programs and a set of coordinated and integrated files called a data base. Prior to the DBMS there was little, if any,

Figure 3–7
The MIS as a Federation of Functional Information Systems

Any MIS can be broken down this way into its constituent parts. This hierarchical decomposition of a system is an important tool in understanding complex systems, as we will see in Chapter 6.

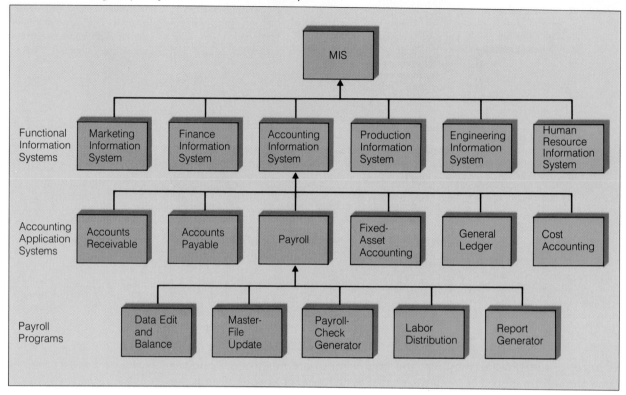

integration or data sharing among the functional information systems. Today there are many opportunities for these systems to share the same data. For instance, the payroll application within the accounting information system could share data with the human resource information system. Examples of data that could be shared are employee names, addresses, and pay rates.

Data-base management systems are, in effect, an interface between the functional applications and the data base, as shown in Figure 3–8. The DBMS allows the various functional systems to access the same data. The DBMS can pool together related data from different files, such as in personnel and payroll files. The DBMS is perhaps the most important tool in making a MIS possible. We will explore data-base management systems in more depth in a later chapter.

■ DECISION-SUPPORT SYSTEMS AND THE MIS

Management information systems in the past have been most successful in providing information for routine, structured, and anticipated types of decisions. In addition, they have been successful in acquiring and storing

Figure 3–8
The Relationship between a DBMS and a MIS

The MIS is made up of individual functional applications such as marketing and finance. These applications in turn use a data-base management system to store and access the data. The data base is stored on disk files.

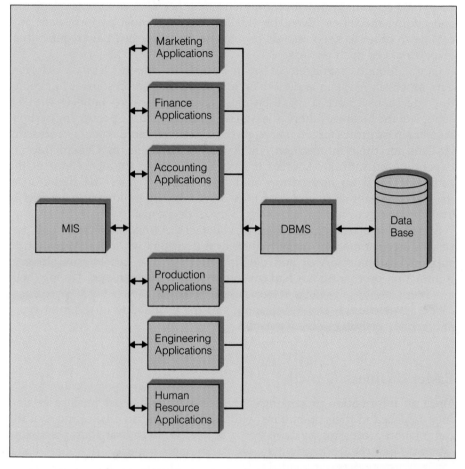

large quantities of detailed data concerning transaction processing. They have been less successful in providing information for semistructured or unstructured decisions, particularly unanticipated ones. A **decision-support system** (DSS) provides a set of integrated computer tools that allow a decision maker to interact directly with computers in order to retrieve information useful for semistructured and unstructured decisions. Such decisions might involve plant expansion, mergers, acquisitions, or new products.

A DSS is an extension of a MIS. It provides user-friendly languages, data retrieval, data processing, and modeling capabilities for the decision maker's direct use. Many decision makers are now using personal computers for decision-support purposes. Integrated software in the form of electronic spreadsheets, data-base management, and graphics allows users to react quickly to the changing information needs that usually go along with unstructured decisions. We will explore the DSS in more depth in Chapter 4.

THE IMPACT OF MANAGEMENT INFORMATION ■ SYSTEMS ON BUSINESS

All businesses, whether large or small, must perform data processing. They do so either manually or with computers and other devices such as calculators and adding machines. Even the smallest business must perform data processing in order to keep records for income-tax purposes. Law requires that taxpayers keep such records.

Often, though, managers of small businesses depend less on a formal data-processing system and more on informal information sources in making their decisions. Since a small-business manager is very familiar with all aspects of the business, there is less need for a formal data-processing system. As a business grows larger, managers depend much more on data-processing systems for their information. Imagine the managers of General Motors depending on informal sources of information about the operations of the company. Such an approach would be a disaster, since the higher-level managers are not close enough to the day-to-day operations to have readily available the information necessary to make decisions.

Information is truly the lifeblood of a business. A business simply could not service its customers or make higher-level decisions without information to support customer service and decision making. The use of computers in information processing has had several impacts on businesses. Among these are easier business growth, fewer clerical workers, reduced data-processing costs, automation of some decisions, and the availability of different types and greater quantities of information.

Easier Business Growth

Once an information-processing system is installed, most businesses find they can expand their operations without making substantial changes in the information-processing system. For example, if the information-processing system is designed correctly it should have excess capacity. Therefore, it can easily accommodate a growth in the number of customers, and only small changes, if any, (such as the addition of a more powerful central processing unit), would be necessary. Furthermore, a significant factor in the growth of today's large businesses is the existence of computer-based information processing which provides managers with the information to control these very large enterprises.

Fewer Clerical Workers

The use of computers has reduced the need for clerical workers, who in the past did the information processing in a manual system. As the demand for clerical workers has decreased, computers have increased the demand for people who are technically oriented, such as system analysts and programmers. The demand for other workers such as accountants, whose discipline is closely linked with information processing, has also increased.

Reduced Information-Processing Costs

Computers can process information at a much lower cost than humans can. Therefore, the cost of processing information in relation to the amount of output generated from the information-processing system has drastically declined.

Automation of Some Decisions

Many businesses have used the computer to automate certain lower-level decisions. Decisions about when to reorder goods to replenish inventory stocks or how much fuel to carry on a specific airline flight are examples of automated decisions.

More and Better Information

Computers have substantially increased the quantity of information available to management. Much of the information now available would have been impossible to obtain with manual systems simply because the amount of calculation necessary to produce the information would have been prohibitive. Examples of this type of information include the output from linear programming, forecasting, and simulation models. Let's consider simulation. With simulation we can build a model (a computer program) of a real-world system (such as an aircraft) through the use of mathematical formulas. The computer, through a large number of manipulations of these mathematical formulas, can simulate the performance of the real-world system, in this case the aircraft. Thus if an aircraft manufacturer is considering developing and producing a new type of passenger aircraft and is thinking about spending millions or billions of dollars to do so, it would be useful to have a simulation of that aircraft prior to investing time and money into the project. Fuel consumption and passenger-load factors in relation to specific airline-route structures could be simulated, for example. The information produced from this simulation would enable the manufacturer to judge how profitable such an aircraft would be.

Large quantities of information are not always useful to managers. Many managers today suffer from information overload. So much information is available that they have difficulty sorting out and using what is truly relevant. The more sophisticated computer users have designed ways for managers to call up the specific information needed for specific decisions.

■ A management information system is a formalized computer information system that can integrate data from various sources to provide the information necessary for management decision making.

■ The parts of a MIS are inputs, processes (programs and procedures), data files, outputs, personnel, and hardware.

■ Information needs are determined by the decisions that must be made, which in turn are determined by objectives.

■ **Summing Up**

- Strategic decision making involves the establishment of objectives for an organization and the long-range plans for attaining these objectives.
- Tactical decision making is concerned with the implementation of the decisions made at the strategic level.
- Operational decisions involve the execution of specific tasks to assure they are carried out efficiently and effectively.
- Programmable decisions are those decisions for which policies, standards, or guidelines are already established.
- Nonprogrammable decisions are those which deal with ill-defined and unstructured problems.
- Management uses information for two purposes: planning and control.
- Planning is the establishment of objectives and the activities that must occur to reach these objectives.
- Control is the process of comparing actual results with the plans identified in the planning process.
- Information systems can be used to give firms competitive advantages.
- Information must meet four qualitative criteria: relevance, timeliness, accuracy, and verifiability.
- Information is relevant when it is useful in decision making. If a piece of information improves the decision, it is relevant.
- Information has time value. In the context of most management information systems, as information becomes older its value decreases.
- Accuracy refers to information being free of error. The amount of error that we can tolerate is related to timeliness and the dollar value of the decision to be made.
- Verifiability means that the accuracy of information can be confirmed.
- Data processing is the capture, storage, and processing of data used to transform the data into information useful to decision makers.
- Data are collected facts that generally are not useful in decision making without further processing. Information is based on processed data and is directly useful in decision making.
- Scheduled listings are produced on a regularly scheduled basis such as daily, weekly, or monthly.
- A demand listing is generated on request.
- Exception reports notify management when an activity or system is out of control.
- Predictive reports assist management in answering what-if questions.
- A MIS is a federation of functional information systems.
- A data-base management system is a program that serves as an interface between application programs and a set of coordinated and integrated files called a data base.
- A decision-support system provides a set of integrated computer tools that allow a decision maker to interact directly with computers in order to retrieve information useful for semistructured and unstructured decisions.
- The use of computers for information processing has had an impact on business in many areas. Computer use has resulted in easier business growth, fewer clerical workers, reduced information processing costs, automation of some decisions, and the availability of different and greater quantities of information.

management information system (MIS)
decisions
objectives
strategic decision making
tactical decision making
operational decision making
programmable decisions
structured decisions
nonprogrammable decisions
unstructured decisions
planning
control
competitive advantage
relevance
timeliness
accuracy

verifiability
audit trail
data processing
data
information
information processing
scheduled reports
demand reports
management by exception
exception reports
error reports
predictive reports
functional information systems
data-base management system
decision-support system

■ Key Terms

■ Review Questions

1. What is the relationship between data processing and management information systems?

2. What are the parts of a management information system?

3. What is the relationship between objectives, decisions, and information?

4. Identify the three levels of decision making, and discuss each.

5. Differentiate between programmable and nonprogrammable decisions.

6. Identify the characteristics of information required at each level of decision making.

7. Identify two purposes for which management uses information, and discuss each.

8. What is the difference between planning and control?

9. What types of information are required for planning and for control?

10. Identify five basic moves that a firm can make to achieve competitive advantage.

11. What are the four qualitative criteria that information must meet?

12. Identify and describe the four types of computer reports.

13. Explain the difference between data and information.

14. What is the relationship between a MIS and functional information systems?

15. Define a DBMS, and discuss how it supports a MIS.

16. What does it mean when information is called the "lifeblood of a business"?

17. Discuss some of the impacts of MIS on business.

18. What is a decision-support system?

■ Discussion
■ Questions
   and Cases

1. Some people argue that a MIS, especially a total MIS, is a myth rather than a reality. Choose one side of this argument and support your position.

2. A typical business college offers undergraduate majors in several areas, including management, marketing, finance, accounting, and management information systems. Many of you have already decided on one of these majors. Justify why knowledge from your chosen major would be necessary preparation for a career in system analysis, which would involve designing and implementing computer-based information systems.

3. John Gilmer is a senior system analyst for Montgomery Furniture Company. John has been assigned the task of developing an information system master plan that would govern the future direction of MIS development for Montgomery Furniture. Bill Harmon is manager of the systems development office. John reports to Bill.

John and Bill discuss the basic approach to developing the master plan. John feels that starting with objectives and deriving the decisions to reach those objectives is a waste of time. He believes the best approach is to conduct interviews with company executives and ask them what information they need to perform their functions. He says to Bill, "Executives just don't think in terms of objectives and decisions. It would be very difficult to get them to think in those terms and to take the logical steps from objectives to decisions to information." Furthermore, he feels that he should not suggest various types of information to the executives. He states, "I want to find out what information they feel they need, and I don't want to contaminate their requirements with my own opinions." Evaluate John's position.

4. Michelle Short, a senior at a large university, will obtain a degree in decision-support systems in June. She has an interview with a representative from a large southwestern oil company. The interviewer asks Michelle what the difference is between a management information system and a decision-support system (DSS). The interviewer then asks how a DSS would aid the oil company. Michelle responds by saying that a decision-support system is an extension of a management information system, DSS uses the information captured by the management information system in a variety of decision models. Michelle states that these models usually are established to evaluate risk, to ask what-if questions, and to provide managers with various alternatives for making a decision that will have an impact on the firm's future. She states that the models are useful for problems such as allocating scarce resources or determining future plant capacity. Would you hire Michelle, based on her answer?

Decision-Support Systems

◼ Chapter 4

CHAPTER OUTLINE

Introduction

What Is a Decision-Support System?
Definition
DSS Software

Functions of a Decision-Support System
Model Building
Procedural and/or Nonprocedural Language
What-If Analysis
Goal Seeking
Risk Analysis
Statistical Analysis and Management-Science Models
Financial Functions
Graphics
Hardware Capabilities
Data Bases and External Files

Why Do Managers Need Decision-Support Systems?

Organization Environment for a Successful DSS

Building a Decision-Support System
Predesign
Design
Implementation
Evaluation

Expert Systems
What Is an Expert System?
Advantages of Expert Systems
Picking the Right Problem for an Expert System
Components of an Expert System
Developing an Expert System

Summing Up

Key Terms

Review Questions

Discussion Questions and Cases

97

■ INTRODUCTION

Computer information systems follow a natural evolution in organizations. Most organizations start with data-processing systems that support transaction processing and evolve to management information systems to support tactical and strategic decision making. In the past few years a new type of system called a decision-support system (DSS) has gained popularity in the information systems field. In this text we view decision-support systems as an evolutionary extension of a management information system.

We will define a decision-support system, identify its functions, and explore the need for such a system. We will also examine some of the organizations where a decision-support system is likely to be successful, and cover the steps in building a decision-support system. Finally, we will explore expert systems.

■ WHAT IS A DECISION-SUPPORT SYSTEM?

Definition

STRUCTURED DECISION
A decision where the methods and rules for making the decision are well defined and known. Examples are when to reorder inventory, and whether or not to grant credit to a customer.

In Chapter 3 we explored the relationship among objectives, decisions, and information. We stressed that the purpose of management information systems is to provide information for decision making. If a management information system supports decision making with information, why is a decision-support system an extension of a MIS? Management information systems in the past have been most successful in providing information for routine, *structured*, and anticipated types of decisions. In addition, they have succeeded in acquiring and storing large quantities of detailed data concerning transaction processing. They have been less successful in providing information for semistructured or unstructured decisions, particularly those which were not anticipated when the computer information system was designed. The basic idea underlying decision-support systems is to provide a set of computer-based tools so that management information systems can produce information to support semistructured and unanticipated decisions.

A **decision-support system** is an integrated set of computer tools that allow a decision maker to interact directly with computers to create information useful in making semistructured and unstructured decisions. These decisions may involve, for example, mergers and acquisitions, plant expansion, new products, stock-portfolio management, or marketing.

It is important that a distinction be made between a decision-support system and the software and hardware tools that make it possible. Electronic spreadsheets, such as Lotus 1–2–3 and Excel, are DSS tools. A particular decision-support system is an application of DSS tools, not the tools themselves.

Decision-support systems and application development by users are closely related. A DSS must be inherently flexible to respond to unanticipated needs for information. This type of flexibility requires that decision makers be directly involved in designing a DSS. Building and using a DSS is a form of application development by users. In fact, many of the hardware and software tools (such as personal computers, electronic spreadsheets, and financial-modeling software) used for application development by users are also used in decision-support systems.

DSS Software

The software components for decision-support systems are illustrated in Figure 4–1. The major components are a **language system** which enables the user to interact with the decision-support system, a **problem-processing system** which is made up of several components that perform various processing tasks, and a **knowledge system** which provides data and artificial-intelligence capabilities to the decision-support system.

The language system may have both procedural and nonprocedural language capabilities. A **procedural language** requires that the user provide the logical steps or procedures to be used in solving a particular problem. Examples of procedural languages are FORTRAN, COBOL, and BASIC. Most decision makers do not use procedural languages; these languages are generally used by professional programmers. However, in a DSS there may be specific problems that the nonprocedural language cannot address; therefore, a procedural language could be useful.

On the other hand, a **nonprocedural language** allows the user to simply specify the characteristics of a problem or information query and lets the DSS determine the logical steps necessary to provide the information. An example of a nonprocedural command is: "Retrieve sales for last year for all stores in the state of New York." This nonprocedural query is very English-like. Nonprocedural languages may be English-like or in other user-friendly forms.

The problem-processing system is the heart of the decision-support system. It should contain several capabilities, including the ability to collect information from data bases through data-base management systems. It should make available a wide variety of management-science models, such as regression, time-series analysis, and goal programming. It also should have a graphics capability and an electronic-spreadsheet feature similar to those offered by packages such as Lotus 1–2–3 and SuperCalc. In fact, many decision-support

Figure 4–1
Components of a Decision-Support System

A DSS typically has several tools, such as an electronic spreadsheet, graphics, etc. Each tool provides one or more of the components illustrated here.

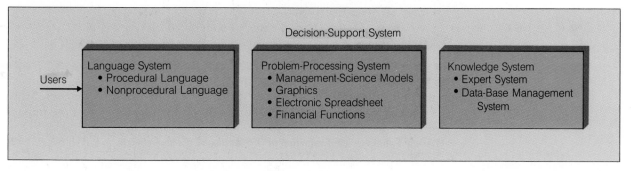

systems are being built with an electronic spreadsheet as the main focus. Most decision-support systems include standard financial functions such as return on investment and net present value.

The knowledge system contains the data-base management system (DBMS) and the associated files stored and managed by the DBMS. These files contain detailed data that have been collected through transaction processing and from other sources. Another type of knowledge that is beginning to be useful in decision-support systems is the **expert system.** It acts much in the same manner as a human expert consultant, providing advice and explaining the advice when necessary. Expert systems are beginning to be applied successfully in several areas, including medicine and prospecting for minerals.

■ FUNCTIONS OF A DECISION-SUPPORT SYSTEM

Briggs has provided a summary of several functions and features that DSS applications should contain.[1]

Model Building

MODEL
An object that represents some real world object. For example, a financial electronic spreadsheet can be used to model the financial state of a business. Models are constructed so that the user can better understand the real world object by manipulating the model.

Building a *model* of the decision-making problem is a central purpose of most decision-support systems. This model is often a two- (or more) dimensional table containing financial numbers and formulas, such as an electronic spreadsheet. The first two dimensions of the table might contain an income statement, the third dimension could represent various products, and the fourth dimension could represent multiple retail outlets. In this case, model development would involve specifying in mathematical terms the relationships among the various sales and expense variables. For example, in building this model, we may assume that sales is a function of advertising expense. In mathematical terms this function might be stated as sales = 20 X advertising expense. This function indicates that for each dollar spent on advertising, sales will increase by twenty dollars.

Procedural and/or Nonprocedural Language

As discussed earlier, these languages allow the user to communicate with the DSS. Most users find nonprocedural languages more convenient to use.

What-If Analysis

The ability to show the impact of changes in data and assumptions is perhaps the most useful feature of a DSS. For example, a DSS could show the impact on profit if sales grew at a rate of 7 to 10 percent instead of 5 percent. Most DSS applications can show instantaneously on the display screen the impact

[1]Warren G. Briggs. "An Evaluation of DSS Packages." *Computer World*, Vol. XVI, No. 9, 1982, p. 31.

of such changes in assumptions. Electronic spreadsheets are especially good for **what-if analysis.**

Goal Seeking

A DSS should be able to show what value a particular *independent variable,* such as advertising expense, would have to be in order to produce a certain target value for the *dependent variable,* such as sales. In effect, the user is asking: "If my goal is $20 million in sales, what must the advertising expense be?" Some electronic spreadsheets for personal computers have this capability. Also, mainframe financial-modeling tools, such as the Integrated Financial Planning System (IFPS), perform **goal seeking.**

Risk Analysis

A very useful piece of information for a decision maker is a probability distribution, which is obtained through **risk analysis.** This provides the probabilities that a particular critical measure, such as profit, will reach a certain level. For example, it would be useful to know the probability that the profit growth rate will be zero, 5 percent, and 10 percent. Such information can be generated using management-science techniques, provided that certain data are available. The necessary data are the probability distributions of the underlying independent variables, such as sales and expenses.

Statistical Analysis and Management-Science Models

A good DSS will be able to provide several useful **management-science models** such as regression and time-series analysis. These two models may be used to project historical data, such as sales, into the future.

Financial Functions

Preprogrammed **financial functions** for commonly used calculations are usually found in DSS packages. These may include corporate tax rates, depreciation methods, and return on investment.

Graphics

An extremely important feature in a decision-support system is a graphics generator. The system should be able to depict any of the data contained in the system in various graphic forms, such as line or pie graphs.

Hardware Capabilities

Decision-support systems in one form or another can be implemented on machines as small as personal computers and as large as mainframes. When a DSS is installed on a PC, the PC should have a large amount of data storage. Mainframes usually have large data storage and processing capacity, so more complex models can be implemented on them. A current trend (expected to continue) is the use of PCs in combination with mainframes for decision-

INDEPENDENT VARIABLE
In a mathematical formula, a variable that can be varied.

DEPENDENT VARIABLE
In a mathematical formula, the variable that is determined by the value of the independent variable(s). For example, in the formula **sales = 20 X advertising expense, sales** is the dependent variable and advertising expense is the independent variable.

support systems. The PC is linked to the mainframe to retrieve data for subsequent processing on the PC if the data volume and processing volumes are relatively small. If, on the other hand, large amounts of data and processing are required, some parts of the DSS may be performed on the mainframe. Many DSS software tools can run on both PCs and mainframes.

Data Bases and External Files

It is crucial that a DSS be able to access data stored in an organization's files. Much of the knowledge-producing data that a DSS uses are stored in these files. This access can be done either through the data-base management system's capabilities or through the DSS's own capability to access external files. In addition, most DSS tools have the capability of maintaining their own internal files once the data are retrieved from other sources.

WHY DO MANAGERS NEED DECISION-SUPPORT SYSTEMS?

There has always been a need for the types of information that a DSS produces. Decision-support systems have become popular primarily because of the hardware and software tools that make them possible. The declining cost of computer hardware has made computer processing and storage relatively inexpensive. In addition, the advent of data-base management systems in the 1970s provided means of storing and managing large amounts of detailed data. These data are now relatively easy to retrieve for use in a decision-support system. Furthermore, there has been a large increase in the number of software packages that incorporate the functions of a DSS. These packages can be used directly to implement DSS applications. And finally, many college graduates trained in analytic techniques are now reaching the middle and upper levels of management where most semistructured and unstructured decisions are made. These individuals know how to use the tools that decision-support systems provide.

ORGANIZATION ENVIRONMENT FOR A SUCCESSFUL DSS

Organizations successful in implementing decision-support systems have many common traits. First, the company has well-controlled and well-structured data-processing systems. Second, the organization has the extra dollars and personnel to maintain a research-and-development focus. Establishing a DSS is a development effort. Therefore, the organization must be willing to commit dollars and personnel to a project whose benefits may be unknown. Third, the *line departments* of the organization have established open communication with the central computer groups. Fourth, the line departments have sufficient confidence to initiate and manage system

LINE DEPARTMENTS
The departments of an organization that are responsible for producing and selling its products or services.

projects. They are continually searching for new ways to use computer-based systems. Fifth, the computer groups act primarily as consultants to assist line departments in implementing systems. Sixth, the computer groups have several people on their staff who either came from line departments or have substantial background in disciplines such as manufacturing, finance, accounting, or marketing. And finally, education and training are used to build understanding between line departments and the computer group.

Many of these characteristics are similar to those of organizations that have adopted application development by users. As mentioned earlier, the subject of application development by users is closely related to DSS.

BUILDING A DECISION-SUPPORT SYSTEM

In Chapter 6 we will present the structured system-development life cycle, which includes the major processes involved in developing either a data-processing or a management information system. Building a DSS is quite different from this life cycle. Design, implementation, and evaluation of decision-support systems tend to be done at the same time. These processes are evolutionary in that upon initial implementation, a decision-support system is likely to be incomplete. Owing to the semistructured and unstructured nature of problems addressed by a DSS, managers change their perceived needs for information, and therefore the DSS must also change. There may be no precise end to implementation. Since decision-support systems are likely to be in a constant state of change, it is most important that users be directly involved in initiating and managing this change.

Predesign

Keen and Morton have outlined the major processes involved in building a decision-support system.[2] Figure 4–2 is a summary of these processes. The first step in the predesign process is to define the objectives for the decision-support effort, which involves laying out the overall goals of the project.

The second step is to identify the available resources that can be applied to the project. Often a firm will already have hardware and software, such as a data-base management system, that can be used in a DSS.

Perhaps the most crucial step in the project is to identify the **key decisions** in the problem area. For example, in a stock-portfolio management system the key decision might be to select the correct stocks for a particular customer's needs. We might conclude that it would be difficult to provide information that would tell a portfolio manager which stock to select, because of the many factors involved, such as different customer needs. Conservative customers might want their money invested in safe stocks; others might prefer high-risk situations because of potential high gains. Two points should be made here. First, the decision-support system is only a tool that provides information to

[2]Peter G. W. Keen and Michael S. Scott Morton. *Decision Support Systems: An Organizational Perspective*. Addison Wesley Publishing Co., Reading, Massachusetts, 1978, pp. 167–225.

the portfolio manager. The portfolio manager makes the final decision as to what stock to select. Second, even though we may find it difficult to provide relevant information for a decision, it is still crucial that we identify the key decision. Providing very relevant information for the wrong decision will get us nowhere. Providing marginally helpful information for the key decision is a useful contribution.

Figure 4–2
Steps in Building a Decision-Support System

Building a DSS is a highly iterative process, with many of these steps operating simultaneously and being repeated. In essence, a DSS is continually being refined.

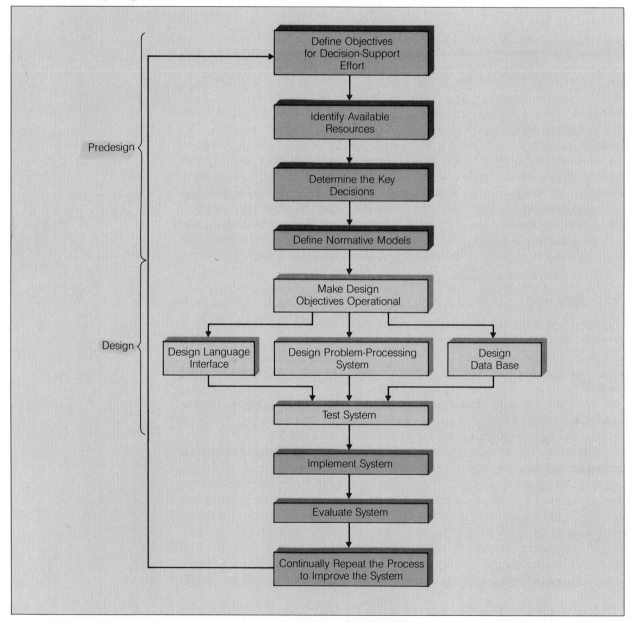

The next step is to define the normative models. A **normative model** is a highly rational approach to providing useful information to the manager making key decisions. The word *normative* means a standard, or what should be. Normative models are likely to be highly idealistic and theoretical. For example, in the stock-portfolio DSS, the ideal information would be the price of stocks at some future date, which is obviously impossible to obtain. It is unlikely that we will attain the level of the normative model in the actual implementation of the DSS. A normative model represents a goal that we attempt to implement in a real-world situation. Although we could not provide the future stock prices to the portfolio manager, we could furnish information to improve the manager's forecast of future stock prices. It may not be practicable or advisable to implement the normative model, but we must keep it in mind when designing the DSS. Normative models become a major part of our design objectives.

Design

The first step in the design process is to make the design objectives operational. In this step we decide what can be done in a real-world implementation of the DSS. The next step is to design the language interface. Ideally, this language interface should be a nonprocedural language, since most users find it easier to communicate a problem to a DSS than to tell the DSS the procedural steps necessary to solve the problem. Designing the problem-solving system is largely a matter of selecting the management-science models (such as regression) and the computer software (such as graphics and electronic spreadsheet) that can be applied to the DSS application. These models and software must be combined in a way that allows the user to readily select and use them in operating the DSS.

Portions of the knowledge system may already be in place. Most companies implementing a DSS already have a great deal of basic data stored in data-base management systems. The final step in design is to thoroughly test the system prior to its implementation.

Implementation

Implementation is a crucial process in building a DSS. Essentially we are asking the user to change from something he or she is doing now and accept a new system. The organization or individual must have a need for the new DSS. There are several ways this need can be created. Obviously, if our boss tells us that we will use the new DSS, this can create a need. However, in the long run this may be counterproductive. Developing user confidence in the need for a system really begins early in the building process. Perhaps one of the most effective ways is to involve the user as much as possible in the development process. As mentioned previously, the ideal situation would be for the user to initiate and manage this process, with the computer specialist acting as a consultant. If this occurs the user will see a system as his or her own and therefore will more likely support and use the DSS.

Evaluation

To evaluate the contributions of a DSS there must be some criteria for evaluation. This is difficult with a DSS since the system is evolutionary and thus does not have a completion date. It is unlikely that a DSS will be justified through reductions in clerical costs. Usually the justification is the provision of more timely and better information. This is a very general benefit and difficult to evaluate. However, it should be possible to measure the impact of this information on better decisions and therefore, better ultimate results. For example, in a portfolio management system used by an investment firm, the ultimate result should be more satisfied customers, and in turn, greater revenue for the firm.

There are three key steps in the evaluation process. First, there should be prior definitions of "improvements." These definitions, or criteria for evaluation, should be established very early in the building process. Second, a means of monitoring the progress toward these improvements must be defined. And finally, a formal review process that periodically measures performance against the definition of improvement should be established.

■ EXPERT SYSTEMS

An expert system is a type of DSS. This section defines expert systems, identifies their advantages, and explains how to pick the correct problem for such systems. It also describes the parts of an expert system and how to develop one.

What Is an Expert System?

An expert system is a computer program that enables a computer to make (or give advice concerning) an unstructured decision normally made by a human with special expertise. Expert systems operate as consulting experts. Examples of decisions that have been made or supported by expert systems are the diagnosis of a disease, loan approvals, the diagnosis of malfunctions in diesel-electric locomotives, and the sizing of computer systems based on a customer's anticipated application work load.

Advantages of Expert Systems

Businesses are interested in applying expert systems for a variety of reasons, the most important being to reduce costs. Expert systems have the following advantages:

■ They reduce the need for highly paid experts, or at least make these experts more productive.
■ They improve the consistency and accuracy of decisions. In their specific area of application, often called a domain, some expert systems have proven that they produce more accurate decisions than do human experts. XCON is such an expert system. It was developed by Digital Equipment Corporation to provide advice in configuring and sizing computer systems.
■ They produce better documentation of the rationale for a decision than many human experts do. One essential feature of an expert system is that it be able to explain the rationale by which it reached a decision. Humans will

not accept advice or a decision from a computer unless the rationale can be explained. Thus, good expert systems have the capability of documenting all the facts and inferences that surround and affect a decision. This capability is particularly valuable when a decision may be challenged in a future lawsuit, as may be the case in medical and financial auditing decisions.

They can be used as training tools for novices. This advantage comes from an expert system's capability of explaining the rationale behind its advice. As novice employees use an expert system, they can learn from the system's explanations of the rationale for specific advice.

Picking the Right Problem for an Expert System

Expert systems are best applied to certain types of problems. The characteristics of suitable problems are as follows:

- Recognized experts work in the problem's field, and they are committed to the idea of developing an expert system. These experts must be better than amateurs at making decisions in the domain of application.
- The task is routinely taught to novices. Thus, the process by which a decision is reached can be explained.
- The problem takes a human expert a few minutes to several hours to perform. This characteristic is desirable because development of an expert system usually requires a high investment of time and resources. Thus, the problem's application must have a high potential payoff.
- No common sense is required to solve the problem; instead, the problem requires facts for its solution. No one has developed a way to give expert systems common sense, but computers are good at sifting through large volumes of facts.
- The domain of the problem's application is limited. Expert system technology has not yet evolved to the point at which it can be applied to wide areas of expertise.

Components of an Expert System

There are two basic types of expert systems—rule-based and frame-based. The rule-based system (RBS) is covered here; this is the most widely used type of expert system. Figure 4–3 shows the components of a rule-based system.

A RBS consists of processing and storage facilities. These are often referred to respectively as an **inference engine** and a **knowledge base.** A knowledge base, as illustrated in the top-right part of Figure 4–3, stores facts and rules. The rules are in the IF-THEN form. For example, a rule in a personal-injury expert system might state

```
If the plaintiff did receive a back injury
    and the injury did require surgery
    and the recovery from the injury was almost
    complete
THEN increase the injury trauma factor by $50,000.
```

These rules specify actions the system should take when certain triggering conditions occur. The conditions correspond to patterns of facts that can arise in the working memory of the system. When the facts that support conditions stated in a rule arise in working memory, that rule is selected and interpreted by the rule interpreter. The combination of selecting and interpreting rules is known as the **firing of rules.**

The output of the rule interpreter can be a request to the user for new inputs, or it can be inferences that are new facts to the system. These inferences are output to the user and are also used to augment (update) working memory's store of facts. Note that new facts change the system's knowledge of conditions, which can in turn cause different rules to be selected and new inferences to be generated. Thus, facts can come from the knowledge base or the inputs, or they can be derived by the system from conditions and rules. An expert system continues cycling through this process of asking for input, firing rules based on conditions that arise in working memory, generating new facts, asking for more input, and so on until a final decision or recommendation is reached.

Figure 4–3
The Components of a Rule-based Expert System

A simple RBS (rule-based system) consists of storage and processing elements, which are often referred to respectively as the knowledge base and the inference engine. The basic cycle of an RBS consists of a select phase and an execute phase. During the execute phase, the system interprets the selected rule to draw inferences that alter the system's dynamic (working) memory. System storage includes components for long-term static data and short-term dynamic data. The long-term store, which is the knowledge base, contains rules and facts. Rules specify actions the system should initiate when certain triggering conditions occur. These conditions define important patterns of data that can arise in working memory. The system represents data in terms of relations, propositions, or equivalent logical expressions. Facts define static, true propositions. In contrast to conventional data-processing systems, most RBSs distribute their logic over numerous independent condition-action rules, monitor dynamic results for triggering patterns of data, determine their sequential behavior by selecting their next activity from a set of candidate-triggered rules, and store their intermediate results exclusively in a global working memory.

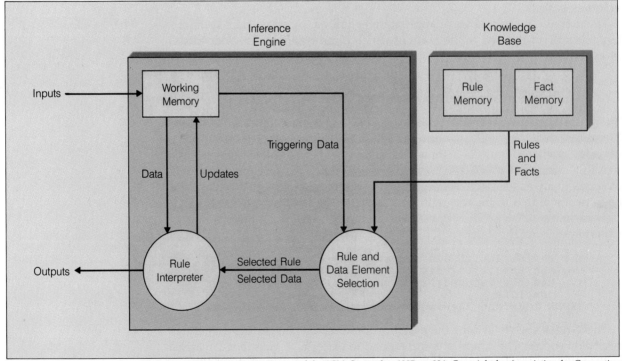

Reprinted with permission from "Rule-based Systems," *Communications of the ACM*, September 1985, p. 924. Copyright by Association for Computing Machinery.

Developing an Expert System

Developing an expert system is a major project. Most useful expert systems have taken at least five employee-years to develop. Certainly, one should select the right kind of problem for an expert system, based on the criteria discussed earlier. But even after the right problem is selected, difficulties can arise.

Typically, a human expert works with a **knowledge engineer** (a person who develops expert systems) to encode into IF-THEN rules the steps a human would use in reaching a decision. But experts often have difficulty explaining the steps they go through in making a decision. Thus, a major difficulty in developing expert systems is the transfer of knowledge from the human expert to the expert system.

There are two basic approaches to developing an expert system. One is to develop it from scratch using one of the two programming languages most widely used for writing expert systems, PROLOG or LISP. Of the two, LISP is more commonly used in the United States. If the system is written from scratch, the knowledge engineer writes all modules of the system, including the inference engine and the knowledge base.

A popular development approach is to create the system through use of a purchased expert system shell. An **expert system shell** already has the inference engine or processing part of the system created. Thus, the knowledge engineer can concentrate on developing the rules and facts for the knowledge base. With the input of rules and facts, the expert system shell becomes an expert system. One widely used shell is VP-Expert.

Expert systems will become an important computer application for business problems. The potential number of applications that have a high payoff will ensure that this occurs.

■ A decision-support system is an integrated set of computer tools that allow a decision maker to interact directly with computers to create information useful in making semistructured and unstructured decisions.

■ The major software components of a decision-support system are the language system, problem-processing system, and knowledge system.

■ The functions of a decision support system include:

Summing Up

1. Model building
2. Procedural and/or nonprocedural languages
3. What-if analysis
4. Goal seeking
5. Risk analysis
6. Statistical analysis and management-science models
7. Financial functions
8. Graphics
9. Ability to run on a wide range of hardware
10. Access to internal and external data bases

■ Organizations successful in implementing decision-support systems have many common traits:

1. A well-controlled and well-structured data-processing system exists.
2. There is a willingness to commit dollars and personnel to the project.

3. There is good communication between line departments and central computer groups.

4. The line departments have sufficient confidence to initiate and manage system projects.

5. The central computer groups act primarily as consultants.

6. The central computer groups have several people on their staff with expertise in the user disciplines.

7. Education and training are used to build understanding between line departments and the computer groups.

■ No precise end exists to the development and implementation of a decision-support system. The major steps in building a DSS are predesign, design, implementation, and evaluation.

■ An expert system is a computer program that enables a computer to make (or give advice concerning) an unstructured decision normally made by a human with special expertise.

■ Expert systems have the following advantages:

1. They reduce the need for highly paid experts.

2. They improve the consistency and accuracy of decisions.

3. They provide better documentation of the rationale for a decision than do many human experts.

4. They can be used as training tools for novices.

■ Suitable problems for an expert system have the following characteristics:

1. Recognized experts work in the problem's field.

2. The steps in solving the problem are routinely taught to novices.

3. The problem takes a human expert a few minutes to several hours to solve.

4. The problem requires facts, rather than common sense, for its solution.

5. The domain of the problem is limited.

■ There are two basic types of expert systems—rule-based and frame-based.

■ A rule-based system consists of processing and storage facilities. These are often referred to respectively as an inference engine and a knowledge base. A knowledge base stores facts and rules. The rules are in the IF-THEN form.

■ An expert system continues cycling through the process of asking for input, firing rules based on conditions that arise in working memory, generating new facts, asking for more input, and so on until a final decision or recommendation is reached.

■ There are two basic approaches to developing an expert system. One is to develop it from scratch using one of the two programming languages most widely used for writing expert systems, PROLOG or LISP. The other is to create the system through use of a purchased expert system shell.

■ Key Terms

decision-support system	procedural language
language system	nonprocedural language
problem-processing system	expert system
knowledge system	what-if analysis

goal seeking	**inference engine**
risk analysis	**knowledge base**
management-science models	**firing of rules**
financial functions	**knowledge engineer**
key decisions	**expert system shell**
normative model	

■ Review
■ Questions

1. What is a decision-support system?
2. What are the major components of a decision-support system?
3. How is a procedural language different from a nonprocedural language?
4. What are some capabilities that should be contained in the problem-processing system?
5. What types of hardware capabilities should a decision-support system have?
6. What are the major functions of a decision-support system?
7. Why is establishing a decision-support system a "development effort"?
8. What are the steps in the predesign phase of building a decision-support system?
9. Why is defining the normative model such an important step in the predesign phase of building a DSS?
10. How does building a decision-support system differ from following the structured system-development life cycle used in building other data-processing or management information systems?
11. What is meant by the phrase "operationalize the design objectives"?
12. How can we help assure that users will use a DSS after it is implemented?
13. Define the key components of the evaluation process.
14. What is an expert system?
15. What are some reasons that firms are interested in applying expert systems?
16. What type of problem is a good candidate for an expert system?
17. What are the two basic types of expert systems?
18. How does a rule-based expert system work?
19. What is a knowledge engineer?
20. How does an expert system shell help in developing an expert system?

■ Discussion
■ Questions
  and Cases

1. What are the relationships among transaction processing systems, management information systems, decision-support systems, and expert systems?
2. If you were ill, which would you rather have to diagnose your illness and prescribe a course of treatment—an expert system, a doctor using an expert system, or a doctor not using an expert system? Why?
3. Some people argue that expert systems are a mirage. They say that experts can always make better decisions than expert systems because experts have common sense. They further argue that it is highly unlikely we will be able to develop computer systems having common sense. What do you think?
4. Are expert systems likely to have a significant impact on the content of education and the methods by which you learn?

5. Bob Lexington is the chief executive officer of Phillips Products, Incorporated. In a recent meeting with his vice president, he expressed the opinion that computer information systems are very valuable for transaction processing and for support of operational-level decision making. He feels, however, that computer information systems are a long way from providing significant support for tactical- and strategic-level decision making, especially for unstructured and unanticipated decisions. He states, "For the type of decisions I make, most of the data and information come from informal and often outside sources. Of course, our computer information systems can provide me with background information. But this is a relatively small percentage of the information I need to make most decisions. The idea of a decision-support system for tactical and strategic decisions is just too new. I think we should wait several years before investing our resources in this untried concept." Do you agree with Mr. Lexington?

6. Wythe Industries is a fast-growing clothing manufacturer in the southeast. Most of Wythe's data-processing applications are computer based. However, none of them are installed on a data-base management system. Each application stands alone, although some applications are linked. Traditionally, central data processing and its system development staff have done all the application development within the company. Most staff members have a computer background, with very little experience in user areas. The management at Wythe is considering a decision-support system. Would you advise Wythe to invest resources in a decision-support system at this time? Support your answer.

7. The Morton Manufacturing Company has recently installed a complete management information system on its mainframe. The next item in Morton's strategic plan for computing is to install a decision-support system. Several analysts have already been assigned to a project team to evaluate decision-support software. Their first task is to interview various user managers to determine what type of decisions the managers make from the data already in the new management information system. Next, the analysts must document their findings and evaluate vendor literature on decision-support software. In addition to being able to answer questions posed by the user managers, what are some specific features that should be in a good decision-support package?

An Overview of Information System Applications

■ Chapter 5

CHAPTER OUTLINE

Introduction

The Business Cycle

Inventories

Computer-Integrated
Manufacturing

Order Processing

Accounts Receivable

Accounts Payable

Payroll

Other Applications

Summing Up

Key Terms

Review Questions

Discussion Questions and Cases

■ INTRODUCTION

As we saw in Chapter 3, a management information system (MIS) can be viewed as a federation of functional information systems. For example, marketing personnel tend to view their part of the MIS as a marketing information system. Personnel in each function (accounting, production, and engineering, for example) engage in activities that support the objectives of the business. In this chapter, we first look at the activities within the business cycle. We then explore the typical information-processing applications that support these activities.

■ THE BUSINESS CYCLE

Figure 5–1 illustrates the **business cycle,** which is a process of converting cash into goods and services for sale and then selling these goods and services in order to convert resources back into cash. A successful business, of course, takes in more cash from selling goods and services than it spends for materials, goods, and/or services. Any business, regardless of whether it sells goods or services, has a business cycle. **Manufacturing firms** produce goods, whereas **merchandising firms** simply purchase goods for resale. An increasingly important business is the service firm. **Service firms** sell the services of their employees to clients. Examples include advertising agencies and accounting firms.

First, a business must raise cash through its **finance activity.** Normally, cash comes from investors, such as stockholders, or the firm's creditors (those who loan money to the business), such as banks. This cash is spent in the **spending activity** in order to acquire the services of employees through the payment of wages and to purchase materials, goods, and services from outside suppliers.

These purchased materials, goods, and services are converted into other goods or services, through the **conversion activity.** In a manufacturing firm, the conversion activity is called production. In a merchandising firm, the conversion activity may consist of receiving goods and placing them in a warehouse so they are ready to be shipped when orders are received.

The **revenue activity** consists of selling the goods or services to customers and collecting from the customers either cash or accounts receivable. The financial activity is responsible for collecting the accounts receivables from customers and paying the accounts payable to the firm's employees and suppliers. During the financial activity, idle cash is invested in short-term securities, such as U.S. Treasury bonds, until the cash is needed in the spending activity. At this point the business cycle begins anew, with the spending of cash for additional purchased materials, goods, and services. In fact, this flow in the business cycle occurs continuously.

Each of the firm's traditional functions, such as accounting/finance, production, and marketing, is involved in these activities. Sometimes a function is involved in more than one activity. For example, accounting/finance is involved in the financial, spending, and revenue activities, whereas production is involved in the spending and conversion activities. Marketing, however, is involved primarily in the revenue activity.

Figure 5–1
The Business Cycle

Note that the four activities—financial, spending, converison, and revenue—form a cycle that converts cash into goods and/or services which are sold and converted back into cash.

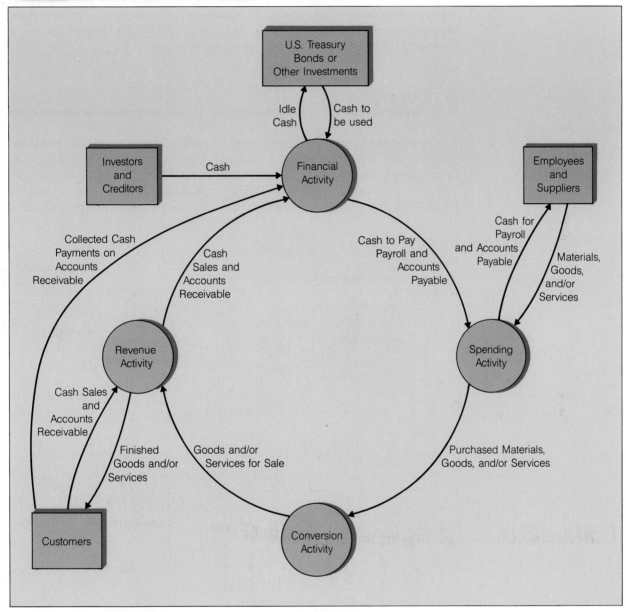

To illustrate typical business information processing applications, we will use a manufacturing firm. Most manufacturing firms have, as a minimum, the systems and applications shown in Figure 5–2. As we shall see in the following section on computer-integrated manufacturing, production systems can be much more pervasive.

Data needed for the multiple applications shown in Figure 5–2 are shared among relevant applications. In most businesses today, these systems are all online; that is, inputs and outputs are processed through computer terminals. Both queries and reports shown in later figures in this chapter can be viewed by management through a terminal (although a significant number of managers still prefer to see reports on paper). Many of these computer systems are also real time, in that their files are updated as soon as real-world events (busines transactions) occur. The remainder of this chapter discusses these and other information processing applications.

■ INVENTORIES

A manufacturing firm has three types of inventory: **raw materials, work-in-process,** and **finished goods.** A merchandising firm has only one type of inventory: finished goods, or **merchandise inventory.** Since a service firm sells services, rather than goods, it does not maintain an inventory system. Regardless of the type of inventory, an **inventory system** has two primary

Figure 5–2
Typical Information-Processing Applications

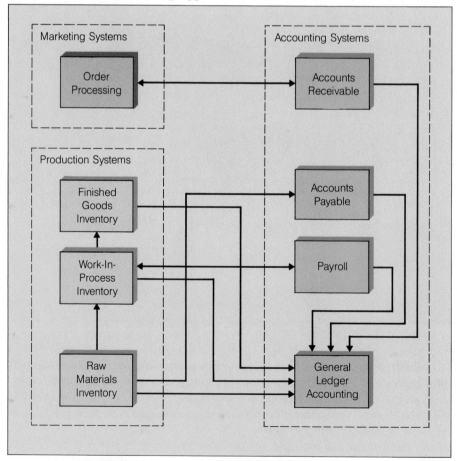

objectives: (1) to minimize costs due to out-of-stock situations, and (2) to minimize inventory carrying costs. The two objectives often conflict.

At the finished-goods level, out-of-stock situations can result in loss of sales; at the raw-materials level, out-of-stock conditions can result in the unnecessary idling of production employees and facilities. However, a company cannot keep large quantities of inventory on hand in order to avoid out-of-stock situations. Such an approach would increase inventory carrying costs beyond acceptable levels. Inventory carrying costs include such things as interest, insurance costs, and warehousing costs. As the amount of inventory increases, carrying costs also increase. Companies could minimize inventory carrying costs by not carrying any inventory; however, out-of-stock costs (loss of sales) might then be unacceptable.

Inventory must be closely monitored to minimize both out-of-stock and inventory costs. Computer-based inventory systems are useful in providing this close monitor. Computers can be programmed to automatically make inventory reorder decisions that minimize these two costs.

Techniques that minimize both out-of-stock and inventory costs are sometimes called **just-in-time inventory systems.** The goal of these systems is to deliver inventory to the firm just-in-time for use. Thus, the inventory on hand is minimal, yet out-of-stock situations are also minimal. With just-in-time inventory systems, a firm shares production information with suppliers through computer links, enabling the suppliers to deliver materials just in time.

The work-in-process inventory system monitors goods while they are being produced. It has two objectives in addition to the ones discussed earlier: (1) to provide scheduling control over individual production jobs so that an accurate prediction of their completion dates can be made; and (2) to accumulate the unit costs of individual products. In large companies, these objectives are often met by two separate applications: a scheduling system and a cost accounting system.

There are many similarities among the three types of inventory systems. The merchandise (or finished goods) inventory system shown in Figure 5–3 illustrates how all three systems operate. This figure provides an overview of the system, which maintains a merchandise inventory master file. Some of the data fields contained in each record in this file are listed in Figure 5–4. At any time, the master file should accurately reflect the quantities stored in the fields indicated in Figure 5–4.

The two primary inputs that update the merchandise inventory master file are quantities of goods shipped (input from the order processing system) and quantities of goods received (input by the receiving department).

The merchandise inventory system produces outputs updating the general ledger system in the areas of current inventory on hand and cost of goods sold. The system also provides the purchasing department with a purchase order notice. This notice identifies the items whose quantities are at or below the reorder level. Many merchandise inventory systems produce a purchase order instead of a purchase order notice. This purchase order, which may be in hard copy or electronic form, is sent to the purchasing department for approval before being sent to a vendor. Figure 5–5 illustrates three typical kinds of inventory management reports. These reports may be printed on paper or displayed on a monitor screen.

Figure 5–3
A Merchandise Inventory System

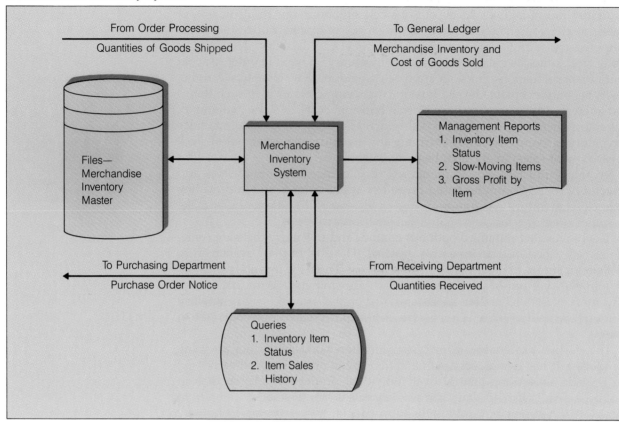

COMPUTER-INTEGRATED MANUFACTURING

Inventory Item Number
Item Description
Location in Warehouse
Current Quantity on Hand
Current Quantity on Order
Quantity Sold—Year-to-Date
Quantity Back-ordered
Standard Cost

Figure 5–4
Typical Fields in a
Merchandise Inventory
Master File Record

The inventory systems, described above, are the minimum systems that a manufacturer uses. Many firms now go much further. Manufacturing is an information-intensive activity. For example, the engineering design of a product must be communicated to manufacturing before the raw materials and parts can be ordered for making the product. Purchase orders must be sent to suppliers. The availability of raw materials in inventory must be known before production can start. Scheduling of materials and labor must be performed. Costs must be accumulated. Often, the same pieces of information flow throughout the production process from engineering to shipment of the final product to customers. Thus, manufacturing firms are viewing the manufacturing process as an information-intensive process that can be managed with an integrated data base. The data base is used in the entire manufacturing process, from engineering, to scheduling, to cost accounting, to marketing of the product, with all the intermediate steps driven by the same data base. This approach is called **computer-integrated manufacturing (CIM).**

Figure 5–5
Typical Inventory Management Reports

```
                                                      PAGE 1
                  GROSS PROFIT BY ITEM
                        REPORT
                  MONTH ENDING 10-31-9X


                                                  QTY
 ITEM    ITEM                       QTY    GROSS  SOLD
 NO      DESCRIPTION        SALES    SOLD   PROFIT  YTD
 ─────────────────────────────────────────────────────
 1003    PAPER.3H.LOOSE LEAF  187.50   250    40.00  3520
 1004    PAPER,TYPING,BOND   7187.50  1250  1000.00  7500
 1005    PAPER,MIMEO,8.5X11   2835.00   750   885.00  6000
 7085    PEN,BALLPOINT        3185.00  3500   385.00 24500
 4106    PENCIL,DRAWING 3H    1425.00   475   209.00  1900
 8165    STAPLER REMOVER       675.00  1500    90.00 16500


                                                  PAGE 1
                    SLOW MOVING ITEMS
                          REPORT
                    AS OF 10-31-9X


                          STD   DAY OF          QTY
 ITEM    ITEM             UNIT  LAST   QTY ON   SOLD
 NO      DESCRIPTION      COST  SALE   HAND     YTD
 ─────────────────────────────────────────────────────
 6405    BOOKCASE,37,5X55X5   133.03  04159X   1000    250
 6408    CHAIR,SWIVEL,ARMS    138.29  06109X     75     20
 8082    CUSION,15X16           5.74  08239X     60     15
 3015    FAN,WINDOW            38.28  05309X     25     10
 6440    TABLE,MULTI-PURPOSE  121.68  07259X     30      7
 6017    TRANSPARENCY,8.5X11   20.93  07239X    550    325


                                                  PAGE 1
                    INVENTORY ITEM
                    STATUS REPORT
                    AS OF 10-31-9X


                                         QTY              STD
 ITEM    ITEM             WAREHOUSE QTY ON QTY ON BACK  QTY SOLD       UNIT
 NO      DESCRIPTION      LOCATION  HAND   ORDER  ORDER  YTD    UNIT   COST
 ──────────────────────────────────────────────────────────────────────────
 6045  BOOKCASE,37.5X55X5  7340   1000   500    0    350   EA  133.03
 3403  CABINET FILE,8"     7340    400     0    0    150   EA  162.15
 8002  CALENDAR,PAD,#SD 170 7428    75    60    0     25   EA     .98
 3403  CLOCK,WALL,8'',ELECT 7428    20    50   30     35   EA   27.88
 9005  FOLDER,MANILA,LETTER 7419    50   750  250    950   BOX   3.78
```

Figure 5–6 illustrates the concept of computer-integrated manufacturing. Engineering personnel use computer-aided design (CAD) software and very high resolution graphics workstations to design a new product and its component parts. As shown in Figure 5–7, these workstations are capable of displaying the design in three-dimensional color, providing a realistic model of the product. Thus, design errors are substantially reduced because the user

Figure 5–6
Computer Integrated Manufacturing (CIM)

CIM systems may also include electronic ties to outside suppliers and customers, enabling suppliers and customers to review designs, schedules, and other production data.

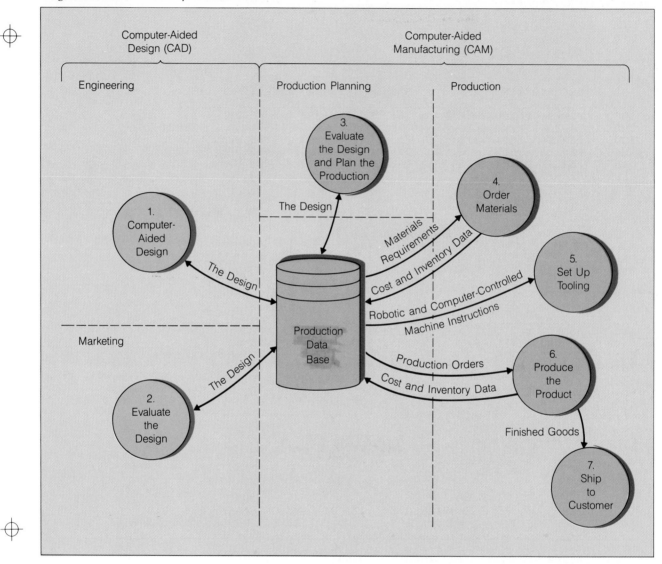

can see and experiment with this realistic model. Marketing and production-planning personnel as well as the customer can view the design, and any changes they make can be quickly incorporated.

A part of the product design is the bill of materials. **The bill of materials** contains quantities and specifications for all the materials necessary to produce one unit of the product. Thus, the bill of materials can be used for ordering materials. Once the product design is complete, the production planning is finalized and materials are ordered.

In factories today, many production machines and tooling are automated. Robots perform fabrication, assembly, and finishing tasks. These automated

Figure 5–7
Computer-Aided Design (CAD)

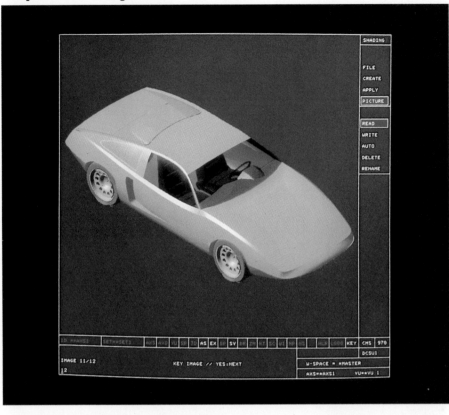

machines are computer controlled, and the computer instructions for specific products are provided by the production data base. In fact, some factories are completely automated. After computer-aided design is complete, the computer orders the materials and feeds the instructions to the automated production machines. Then, the product is produced by these computer-controlled machines and robots. Even the warehousing of the finished product, prior to shipment, is automated.

Here are some of the many advantages of CIM:

1. The labor costs of production are reduced.
2. The time from product conception to product delivery is reduced. This is a major advantage, because beating a competitor to the marketplace almost always results in high sales.
3. Small quantities of a particular product become economical to produce. Such products would not have been produced in the past. The demand was not sufficient to make a profit. This leads to a greater variety of products for the consumer. Thus, small (niche) markets can be exploited.
4. The ability to quickly manipulate and change the product design results in products that have a better design.

CIM is likely to become a must as firms attempt to maintain their competitive advantages. However, implementing CIM is a large undertaking. Most firms buy the necessary software rather than develop it themselves.

Figure 5–8
An Order-Processing System

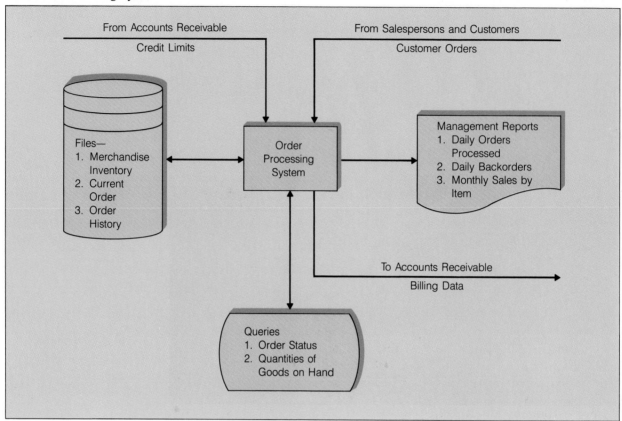

■ ORDER PROCESSING

The **order-processing** system is the place of entry for customer orders, and it initiates the shipping of orders (see Figure 5–8). The system is often called an order entry system. The primary objectives of an order-processing system are (1) to initiate shipping orders, (2) to maintain a record of **back-ordered** items (items that are out of stock and will be shipped later), and (3) to produce sales analysis reports.

A shipping order is illustrated in Figure 5–9. The shipping order is issued in triplicate—a copy is sent to the warehouse to tell employees which goods to ship, a copy is put inside the shipping box, and a copy is kept as a record. Some companies use a fourth copy, which serves as a customer acknowledgment and is sent to the customer when the shipping order is issued.

Before producing a shipping order, most order-processing systems access the merchandise inventory file to determine whether particular goods are on hand. If given items are not on hand, they are placed on back order. The inventory master file is updated to reflect the number of goods shipped. Back orders remain on file, so that when the goods are available, the order-processing system can initiate a shipping order.

Figure 5–9
Typical Shipping Order

```
                                                     PAGE 1
                     SHIPPING ORDER
                  ORDER DATE 10-31-9X

  SHIP TO:

    NAME:  PERDUE PROCESSORS
  ADDRESS:  104 LANDSDOWNE LANE
            BLACKSBURG, VA       24060

  PACKAGE NO:  764290
  SHIPMENT NO:   1721

  ITEM   ITEM                   QTY      QTY              UNIT
  NO     DESCRIPTION            ORDERED  SHIPPED  UNIT    PRICE
  ─────────────────────────────────────────────────────────────
  1003   PAPER,3H,LOOSELEAF     100      100      PKG      .75
  1004   PAPER,TYPING,BOND      500      500      PKG     5.75
  1005   PAPER,MIMEO,8.5x11      30       30      RM      3.65
  9090   PAD,SCRATCH,4x6         12       12      DOZ     1.69
  8039   RUBBER BANDS,1=8x3      10       10      BOX      .79
  1035   STENCIL,8.5x14          12       12      DOZ     3.10
```

In addition to maintaining an inventory file, the order-processing system maintains a current order file and an order history file. These two files are identical in format. The typical fields within a record of these two files contain the same information that is displayed on the shipping order in Figure 5–9.

After a short period of time (for example, three months), records are deleted from the current order file and placed in the order history file. This procedure prevents the current order file from growing too large. The records in the order history file are usually maintained for at least a year to support sales analysis reports that the system produces.

Figure 5–10 illustrates typical order-processing reports. The daily orders processed report is primarily a control report providing daily information about orders processed. Management can use the totals on this report to monitor trends and the number of orders processed. The daily back-order report is also a control report, enabling management to monitor the level of back orders. If the quantity of backorders becomes excessive, customer relations may suffer. The monthly sales-by-item report is an example of the many types of sales analysis reports that can be produced. This particular report enables management to monitor sales trends by following the numbers of individual items sold.

■ ACCOUNTS RECEIVABLE

The objectives of an **accounts receivable** system are (1) to bill customers for orders shipped, (2) to maintain records of the amounts customers owe and pay, and (3) to provide information to assist in the collection of past-due

Figure 5–10
Typical Order-Processing Reports

PAGE 1

```
                          DAILY ORDERS PROCESSED                              PAGE 1
                                  REPORT
                                FOR 10-31-9X


     ORDER        CUSTOMER     CUSTOMER              ITEM       SHIPMENT     SHIPPING
     NO           NO           NAME                  NO         NO           DATE
     ─────────────────────────────────────────────────────────────────────────────
     764290       25190        PERDUE PROCESSORS     1004       1721         12-31-9x
     764290       25190        PERDUE PROCESSORS     1005       1721         12-31-9x
     764290       25190        PERDUE PROCESSORS     9090       1721         12-31-9x
     889233       27300        KINKO'S               1005       2930         12-31-9x
     889233       27300        KINKO'S               1750       2930         12-31-9x
     931240       31790        POLYSCIENTIFIC        9005       3501         12-31-9x



                                                              PAGE 1
                          DAILY BACK-ORDER REPORT
                                FOR 10-31-9x


                                             QTY
     ITEM    ITEM                    QTY      BACK              UNIT
     NO      DESCRIPTION             ORDERED  ORDERED   UNIT    PRICE
     ─────────────────────────────────────────────────────────────────
     3403    CLOCK, WALL,8",ELECT       50       30      EA     27.88
     9005    FOLDER, MANILA, LETTER    750      250      BOX     3.78
     6412    LETTER TRAY, LEGAL         50       20      EA      6.88
     9090    PAD, SCRATCH, 4X6         625      300      DOZ     1.04
     4106    PENCIL, DRAWING 3H        200      150      DOZ     2.56



                                                              PAGE 1
                            SALES-BY-ITEM
                                REPORT
                        MONTH ENDING 10-31-9X


                                                  CURRENT
     ITEM    ITEM                                  MONTHLY       SALES
     NO      DESCRIPTION             QUANTITY      SALES         YTD
     ─────────────────────────────────────────────────────────────────
     1003    PAPER, 3H, LOOSE LEAF      250         187.50      2640.00
     1004    PAPER, TYPING, BOND       1250        7187.50     43125.00
     1005    PAPER, MIMEO, 8.5x11       750        2835.00     22680.00
     7085    PEN, BALLPOINT            3500        3185.00     22295.00
     4106    PENCIL, DRAWING 3H         475        1425.00      4864.00
     8165    STAPLER REMOVER           1500         675.00      6435.00
```

accounts. The billing function is the sending of the initial invoice to the customer. This function can be performed by the order-processing system, by a separate billing system, or by the accounts receivable system.

Figure 5–11 shows an accounts receivable system. The accounts receivable system maintains one file—the accounts receivable master file. Typical fields contained within a record in this file are illustrated in Figure 5–12. This file is

Figure 5–11
An Accounts Receivable System

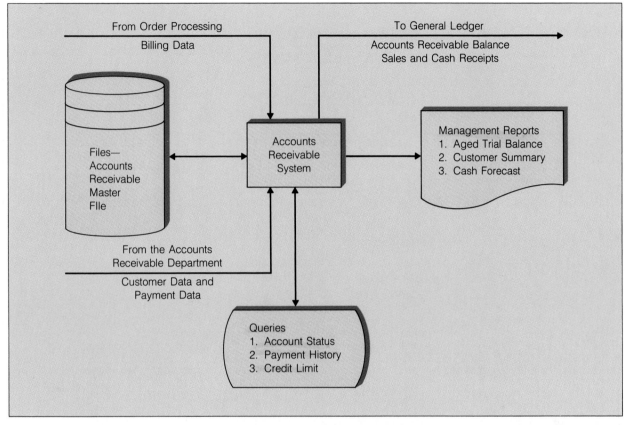

updated with billing data from order processing. All other data in the file are input from the accounts receivable department.

Queries to the accounts receivable system are shown on a monitor screen and include information such as account status and payment history. The account status screen displays unpaid purchases and recent payments; the payment history screen provides detailed information about the payment habits of a particular customer.

Figure 5–13 displays three typical management reports in the accounts receivable system. The aged trial balance is a valuable report for collection purposes, since it indicates the accounts that are past due and how far they are past due—one to thirty days, thirty-one to sixty days, or over sixty days. The customer status report provides detailed information about a specific customer. This information can be valuable to the salesperson assigned a given customer.

Since the accounts receivable system is the primary cash receipt system, it can provide useful cash forecasts. Information in a cash forecast report is usually based on statistics concerning a customer's payment habits, such as the average number of days the customer is late in making payments.

Customer Number
Customer Name
Customer Address
Credit Rating
Average Days Late
Credit Limit
Purchase Date
Purchase Reference
Purchase Amounts
Payment Date
Payment Reference
Payment Amounts
Current Balance

Figure 5–12
Typical Fields in an
Accounts Receivable Master
File Record

Figure 5–13
Typical Accounts Receivable Management Reports

```
                                                                    PAGE 1
                              AGED TRIAL BALANCE
                                   REPORT
                               AS OF 10-31-9X


                       AMOUNT      AMOUNT      AMOUNT    AMOUNT    TOTAL
CUSTOMER   CUSTOMER     NOT         1-30 DAYS   31-60     >60 DAYS  BALANCE
NO         NAME         DUE         OVERDUE     OVERDUE   OVERDUE   DUE
_____
25190      PERDUE PROCESSORS  1000.00   195.00      .00       .00   1195.00
27300      KINKO'S             550.00    25.00      .00       .00    575.00
31790      POLYSCIENTIFIC     1500.00   200.00    90.00       .00   1790.00
51230      BANDY, MW              .00   350.00   400.00       .00    750.00
61359      DORN, HC            195.00    55.00      .00       .00    250.00
73401      JONES, LT              .00    25.00    75.00       .00    100.00


                                                                    PAGE 1

                            ACCOUNTS RECEIVABLE
                              CUSTOMER STATUS
                                   REPORT
                               AS OF 10-31-9X


CUST     CUST              CREDIT    CREDIT      AMNT      AMNT
NO       NAME              RATING    LIMIT       DUE       REC'D     BALANCE
_____
25190    PERDUE PROCESSORS   9      5000.00    2695.50   1500.00   1195.50
27300    KINKO'S             7      3500.00    1325.00    750.00    575.00
31790    POLYSCIENTIFIC     10      7500.00    5290.00   3900.00   1790.00
51230    BANDY,MW            0          .00     750.00       .00    750.00
61359    DORN,HC             6      1000.00     625.00    375.00    250.00
73401    JONES,LT            0          .00     100.00       .00    100.00


                                                                    PAGE 1
                                CASH FORECAST
                                   REPORT
                               AS OF 10-31-9x

PROBABLE
PYMT      DUE      INVOICE    CUSTOMER            PYMT        DISC     AMOUNT
DATE      DATE     NO         NAME                TERMS       AMT      DUE       PYMT
_____
0109x     01159x   23910      PERDUE PROCESSORS   2=10,N=30   10.00    490.00    490.00
01159x    01319x   24920      PERDUE PROCESSORS   2=10,N=30    9.00    441.00    441.00
01319x    02059x   39011      KINKO'S             3=10,N=30    7.50    242.50    242.50
01319x    02059x   39015      KINKO'S             3=10,N=30    2.25     47.75     47.75
01319x    02159x   39120      KINKO'S             3=10,N=30    1.50     38.50     38.50
02059x    02159x   45270      DORN,NH             * * * * *     .00    125.00     75.00
                                                                      _____
                                          TOTAL CASH FORECASTED   $1334.75
```

Figure 5–14
An Accounts Payable System

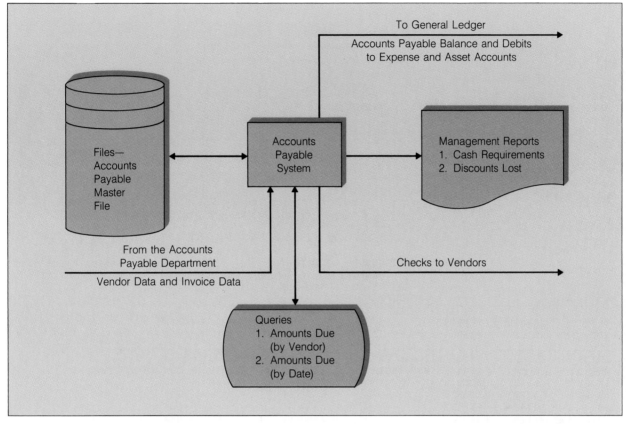

■ ACCOUNTS PAYABLE

Whereas the accounts receivable system keeps records of the amounts owed to the firm, the **accounts payable** system keeps records of amounts owed to suppliers of the firm. The objectives of the accounts payable system are (1) to provide control over payments to vendors of goods and suppliers of services, (2) to issue checks to vendors and suppliers, and (3) to provide information for effective cash management.

Figure 5–14 shows an accounts payable system. The accounts payable system maintains a master file. Typical fields contained in a master file record are illustrated in Figure 5–15. The accounts payable department provides the input to the accounts payable system. The primary types of input are data concerning vendors, such as vendor name and address, and data from new invoices received from vendors and suppliers.

Typical accounts payable management reports are illustrated in Figure 5–16. The cash requirement report is based on amounts owed and the dates those amounts are due. The discounts lost report is a type of cash management report. Many vendors offer customers a discount on payments—say, 2 percent off the

Vendor Number
Vendor Name
Vendor Address
Payment Terms
Amounts Owed by Invoice
Payments—Year-to-Date
Discounts Taken—Year-to-
   Date
Discounts Lost—Year-to-Date

Figure 5–15
Typical Fields in an
Accounts Payable
Master File

Figure 5–16
Typical Accounts Payable Management Reports

```
                                                                    PAGE 1
                          CASH REQUIREMENT
                               REPORT
                           AS OF 10-31-9x


    DUE      VENDOR   VENDOR              PYMT        INVOICE  AMOUNT   DISC     BALANCE
    DATE     NO       NAME                TERMS       NO       DUE      AMOUNT   DUE       PYMT

    01319x   25190    INTERNATIONAL PAPER 2=10,N=30   07519    450.00     9.00  441.00    441.00
    02109x   31723    LLOYD'S MANUFACTURIN ****        21340    652.00      .00  652.00    200.00
    02159x   45310    ABDICK              2=10.N=30    17001    107.50     2.15  105.40    105.00
    02159x   51377    IBM                 3=10,N=30    00910    963.00    28.89  934.11    934.11
    02289x   63784    PENTEL               ****        50003     93.00      .00   93.00     50.00
    03019x   72111    XEROX               1=10,N=30    43000     70.00     7.00   63.00     63.00
                                                                                _____
                                       TOTAL CASH REQUIREMENTS 10-31-9x $1793.51


                                                                    PAGE 1
                          DISCOUNTS LOST
                               REPORT
                           AS OF 10-31-9x


    VOUCHER  VENDOR   VENDOR                  INVOICE    AMOUNT      EFF     DAYS
    NO       NO       NAME                    AMOUNT     LOST        APR     LATE

    15270    25190    INTERNATIONAL PAPER     7500.00    150.00      24%      10
    29563    31723    LLOYD'S MANUFACTURIN    1350.00     13.50      13%       5
    14021    45310    ABDICK                  1080.00     21.60      13%       4
    83910    51377    IBM                     2532.00     75.96      25%       9
    85674    63784    PENTEL                   950.00      9.50      15%       4
    93201    72111    XEROX                   1500.00     30.00      22%       6
```

invoice, if payments are made within ten days. The discounts lost report identifies payables for which discounts were not taken. Such cases are usually deviations from management policy and therefore require investigation.

The accounts payable system also produces checks, which are sent to vendors after review by the accounts payable department. Queries to the system usually involve amounts due to be paid. Management may need to know the amount due a particular vendor or the amount due by a certain date.

■ PAYROLL

Payroll is often the first system a company converts to computer processing because it is a relatively simple operation that does not interface with many other application systems. The primary objectives of the **payroll** system are (1) to pay both hourly and salaried employees on a timely basis, (2) to maintain records of payments to employees and of taxes withheld, and (3) to provide management with the reports needed to manage the payroll function.

Figure 5–17
A Payroll System

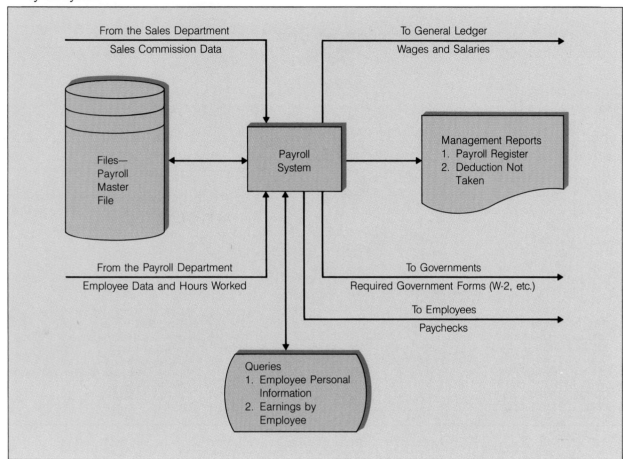

Figure 5–17 shows a payroll system. This system maintains a payroll master file. The contents of a typical payroll master file record are shown in Figure 5–18. The payroll department provides most of the payroll system input in the form of personal employee data, such as name, address, pay rate, and hours worked during a pay period. In some cases, the sales department provides data for commission payments to salespeople. Output from the payroll system includes required government forms, such as the W-2 form used for reporting wages to the Internal Revenue Service. The system also produces paychecks for employees.

Management reports include the deductions-not-taken report and the payroll register (see Figure 5–19). The payroll register is a record of wages paid and amounts withheld for each employee. The deductions-not-taken report lists employees whose deductions were not taken on schedule due to insufficient pay. Queries to the payroll system generally are for information concerning individual employees, such as personal data or earnings.

Employee Number
Employee Name
Employee Address
Department
Occupation
Pay Rate
Vacation Time
Sick Leave Time
Gross Pay Year-to-Date
Federal Income Tax Withheld
State Income Tax Withheld
FICA Tax Withheld
Health Insurance Withheld
Credit Union Savings
 Withheld
Bank Code

Figure 5–18
Contents of a Typical
Payroll Master File Record

Figure 5–19
Typical Payroll Management Reports

```
                                                                    PAGE 1
                         DEDUCTIONS NOT TAKEN
                                REPORT
                           AS OF 10-31-9x


   EMP      EMP               DEDUCTION         AMOUNT    AMOUNT      NOT TAKEN
   NO       NAME              DESC              TAKEN     NOT TAKEN   BALANCE
   ─────────────────────────────────────────────────────────────────────────
   00001    TURNBALL,JW       UNITED   FUND        .00     25.00        25.00
   00001    TURNBALL,JW       CREDIT   UNION     40.00       .00        57.00
   00002    CLARK, TC         HOSPITALIZATION    26.00       .00         5.00
   00003    JONES,  FL        PENSION            45.00       .00        40.00
   00003    JONES,  FL        BONDS                .00     65.00        70.00
   00005    JAMES,  CL        CREDIT UNION       40.00       .00        40.00



                                                                    PAGE 1

                          PAYROLL REGISTER
                               REPORT
                           AS OF 10-31-9X


   EMP      EMP               REG    OT    TOTAL      FEDERAL  FICA   STATE   EARNINGS
   NO       NAME        RATE  HOURS  HOURS EARNINGS   TAX      TAX    TAX     YTD
   ─────────────────────────────────────────────────────────────────────────────────
   00001  TURNBALL,JW   4.51   40    10    248.05     32.20    25.41  13.04   7840.21
   00002  CLARK,TC      5.37   40     0    214.80     16.81    12.10   6.75   8250.00
   00003  JONES,FL      3.35   21     0     70.35      6.91     4.21   2.10   2615.00
   00004  SMITH,AJ      3.35   30     0    100.50      9.22     6.90   4.12   3700.12
   00005  JAMES,CL      5.37   40     5    255.08     41.90    31.76  15.02   9215.91
   00006  FREDERICKSON,JR 4.51 40    0    180.40     12.13    10.91   5.33   7651.00
```

■ OTHER APPLICATIONS

The **general ledger,** a common computer application, maintains the financial accounts of a business. This system is responsible for producing financial statements, such as the income statement, the statement of financial position, and the statement of changes in financial position. This application maintains a record of a firm's assets, liabilities, owner equities, revenues, and expenses.

Most ledger systems can also maintain a budget, especially for revenues and expenses. Reports can be prepared that compare actual revenues and expenses to budgeted amounts. Such reports help maintain control of a business organization. As discussed earlier, a few sales analysis reports can be produced from the order-processing system. A complete **marketing information system** goes far beyond the scope of these reports. In addition to providing information about past sales, the system can assist in estimating future sales, managing the marketing activities, and even help in optimizing the marketing strategy for certain products through a market research approach.

Marketing systems can be used to support account management, direct marketing, lead tracking, mapping, sales forecasting, sales presentations, and telemarketing. Examples of the functions that these systems provide are listed below:

Account Management: Maintains information about customers such as notes, contacts, and sales histories. Produces form letters.

Direct Marketing: Provides mailing list management, finds duplicates, sorts by zip code, produces list analysis and reports.

Lead Tracking: Provides sales lead tracking, auto-dialing, sales scripts, form letters, and labels.

Mapping: Analyzes address, demographic, and spending habits information and provides color graphics maps pin-pointing sales information.

Sales Forecasting: Uses various mathematical techniques to forecast seasonally adjusted sales.

Sales Presentations: Provides visual graphics for use in sales presentations, prepares quotes and formal proposals, and provides training for sales closings.

Telemarketing: Receives calls, plays back prerecorded messages, performs auto-dialing, and transfer to a human telemarketer if there is an answer.

Another application many firms use is a **human-resource information system.** This system maintains data about a firm's employees. Typical data are name, address, birth date, salary, skills, foreign language proficiency, and training courses completed. The information from the human-resource information system is typically used by the personnel department for benefits administration, compensation administration, manpower planning, employee relations, government regulation compliance, and employee profile information. Substantial data are shared between this system and the payroll system.

Several other types of systems are found in specialized industries, such as the reservations systems used by motels and airlines.

■ The business cycle consists of finance, spending, conversion, and revenue activities.

■ The two primary objectives of an inventory system are (1) to minimize costs due to out-of-stock situations, and (2) to minimize inventory carrying costs. The two objectives often conflict.

■ Computer-integrated manufacturing (CIM) systems provide information to manage manufacturing from a single, integrated data base.

■ The primary objectives of an order-processing system are (1) to initiate shipping orders, (2) to maintain a record of back-ordered items, and (3) to produce sales analysis reports.

■ The objectives of an accounts receivable system are (1) to bill customers for orders shipped, (2) to maintain records of the amounts customers owe and pay, and (3) to provide information to assist in the collection of past-due accounts.

■ The objectives of an accounts payable system are (1) to provide control over payments to vendors of goods and suppliers of services, (2) to issue checks to

■ Summing Up

vendors and suppliers, and (3) to provide information for effective cash management.

■ The objectives of the payroll system are (1) to pay both hourly and salaried employees on a timely basis, (2) to maintain records of payments to employees and of taxes withheld, and (3) to provide management with the reports needed to manage the payroll function.

■ The general ledger maintains the financial accounts of the business and produces financial statements. Other typical applications include marketing information systems, human-resource information systems, and specialized applications such as reservations systems.

■ The marketing information system is used to support account management, direct marketing, lead tracking, mapping, sales forecasting, sales presentations, and telemarketing.

■ The human resource system maintains and reports information concerning a firm's employees.

■ Key Terms

business cycle

manufacturing firms

merchandising firms

service firms

finance activity

spending activity

conversion activity

revenue activity

raw materials

work-in-process

finished goods

merchandise inventory

inventory system

just-in-time inventory systems

computer-integrated manufacturing (CIM)

bill of materials

order processing

back order

accounts receivable

accounts payable

payroll

general ledger

marketing information system

human-resource information system

■ Review Questions

1. What is the business cycle?

2. How do merchandising, service, and manufacturing firms differ? Can the basic activities of these three types of firms be depicted by the business cycle?

3. How are the traditional business functions of accounting, manufacturing, and marketing related to the business cycle activities?

4. What are the primary objectives of an inventory system?

5. For the merchandise inventory system, identify the following: primary inputs, typical data maintained on the master file, and some examples of output.

6. What is a computer-integrated manufacturing system?

7. What are the primary objectives of the order-processing system?

8. For the order-processing system, identify the following: primary inputs, typical data maintained on the master file, and some examples of output.

9. What are the primary objectives of the accounts receivable system?

10. For the accounts receivable system, identify the following: primary inputs, typical data maintained on the master file, and some examples of output.

11. What are the primary objectives of the accounts payable system?

12. For the accounts payable system, identify the following: primary inputs, typical data maintained on the master file, and some examples of output.

13. What are the primary objectives of the payroll system?

14. For the payroll system, identify the following: primary inputs, typical data maintained on the master file, and some examples of output.

15. What is a general ledger system?

16. What is a human-resource information system?

1. Of the applications covered in this chapter, which do you think could justify the use of real-time master files? Support your position.

2. Assume a company is installing a computer for the first time. The company plans to eventually computerize all the applications discussed in this chapter. However, its managers think it is impossible to implement all these applications simultaneously and that some applications must have priority over others. Rank the applications in the order you would implement them.

3. Roanoke Power Company, an electrical utility, has a batch accounts-receivable system. The system is updated daily on the night shift. Online terminals allow users to inquire about the status of accounts. Because of the batch update, an account could be out of date as much as a full day. The company is considering installing a real-time accounts receivable system. If you were a consultant to Roanoke Power, what would you say were the advantages and disadvantages of a real-time accounts receivable system, and would you advise the company to install such a system?

4. James River Supply is a medium-sized hardware wholesaler. At any one point, it has approximatey nine hundred retail hardware stores as customers. The vice president of marketing is dissatisfied with the marketing information produced by his staff and computer-based systems. He has initiated a systems development study to figure out the major characteristics of an ideal marketing information system. Outline the characteristics of three or four reports or computer terminal screens that would be most useful in a marketing information system. Where would the data come from to support these reports or screens?

■ Discussion
▬ Questions
and Cases

Executive Info System: Easy, Easier, Easiest

by Jon Pepper

Rainer Paul believes. Mr. Paul sits with restless energy in his office at Avon, high above 57th Street in New York. An athletic-looking, spirited man, he has the sort of evangelistic zeal that could probably inspire the legions of door-to-door sales representatives that made the phrase "Avon calling" famous.

Mr. Paul, vice president of corporate MIS, isn't talking about perfume and cosmetics. He's talking about the company's new Executive Information System (EIS), and his enthusiasm is catching. So far, the top 15 executives at Avon Products, Inc., have caught it; the feeling's going all the way up to the executive suite.

Avon's EIS uses PCs to deliver information that helps executives find potential business problems and spot trends much more quickly than before. The system not only represents a new way of working at Avon, it also reflects changes at the firm.

While Avon is best known for its door-to-door beauty business, the company, which posted sales of almost $3 billion last year, also includes thriving health-care and direct-response divisions. Recent acquisitions include such high-end fragrance manufacturers as Giorgio Inc. and Parfums Stern, which sells the Oscar de la Renta, Perry Ellis, and Valentino designer-fragrance lines.

Avon's corporate MIS department was set up just two years ago; its charter was to better manage the company's continuing metamorphosis into a new, multifaceted corporation.

Mr. Paul and others in the MIS group, notably Frank Giannantonio, director of corporate MIS, engaged in an interview process to uncover the information that would help the executives run the business better. "We asked, for example, 'If you came back from a two-week vacation, what information would you want to see on your desk?' " Mr. Paul said.

The MIS group interviewed executives and staff, gathered information needs from both the top down and the bottom up. Based on the interviews, the group identified over 70 applications of importance,

from human-resource information to business indicators. These were then classified into four basic groups: financial, human resource, competitive and administrative.

With the luxury of the new corporate computing architecture, Mr. Paul urged top management to deliver some of this information electronically, as an Executive Information System. The idea caught on. "People really understood the need for this system," Mr. Paul explained.

The entire development process went quickly, according to Mr. Paul. "We interviewed in April and May, presented the concept in June, got the OK and set up the first prototype in September."

The prototype met with instant approval. "The CEO saw it and immediately said, 'Let's implement it,' " Mr. Paul said.

An unexpected and brief setback in the health-care division helped seal the project. "Our COO [Chief Operating Officer], Jack Chamberlin, said that if he had the EIS in place prior to that, it would have been possible to see the problem and act to head it off before it developed into anything serious," Mr. Paul noted.

The programming team assembled by Mr. Paul and Mr. Giannantonio was a unique aspect of the project. Rather than recruit programmers who understood business, they looked for MBAs who knew or wanted to learn programming. About 12 MBAs were hired as programmers, on the theory they would really understand the needs of the business, Mr. Giannantonio said.

"I think the quality of our product is better because we hired business people, and what we have today reflects that," Mr. Paul explained. "If you bring in good people, they will challenge the functional departments to think differently, and I think it helped us add a lot of value to the project."

The EIS resulting from this effort is a marvel of conciseness, extreme ease of use, and usefulness.

The system resides on the company's IBM mainframes, but service is delivered to executives via either IBM ATs or Compaq 286s, with NEC MultiSync monitors and enhanced graphics adapter (EGA) cards handling the interface and the colorful screen graphics.

All selections from the menu-driven product, which was developed using Pilot, from Pilot Executive Software in Boston, as a front end, are made by pointing and clicking with a mouse. This means busy executives don't have to bother using the keyboard at all.

PART TWO   ■ APPLICATION CASE

When executives log onto the system, they see a menu divided in half; the left side contains internal Avon information, such as financial indicators, while the right side contains external information, such as news and competitive analyses.

Under the theory that less is more, the Avon EIS is heavily graphics oriented, presenting more information concisely. Using a mouse, the user simply moves the cursor over a menu choice, and if there is another level of information behind that selection, it changes color. Clicking the mouse brings up the next level of detail.

For example, under financial indicators, an executive could check the net sales of any one of the companies within Avon. Immediately, a chart showing net sales appears on-screen. All charts and graphs in the system use the following color scheme: actual performance appears in gold, planning in red, and the prior year in blue.

Dropping down to the next level of detail, a user can examine the profit-and-loss statements for each division, then the line items, and so on. Each screen shows a graph on the left side and the actual numbers on the right, so executives can look at the overall picture as well as the numbers on which it is based.

Individuals who want to take a further action based on the information presented can choose a utility icon on the screen, and they can either lay out a report, edit notes, download the figures to Lotus 1–2–3 or print out a hard copy. An electronic-mail function is being added so users can add notes and send the entire screen.

From the beginning, part of the plan was presenting information not only graphically, but also in full color. Consistent with that intent, all hard copy is delivered in color as well. Centrally located output devices give users the option of creating hardcopy reports on a color printer, making 35mm slides or full-color transparencies.

Using color graphics "allows the executives to see the trends and see what has happened from a business point of view much faster than they would by just looking at numbers," according to Mr. Paul. Even though the numbers are presented alongside the graphs on the system, "most users want to see the graphs," he said.

Unlike some systems that are totally preformatted, all analysis on the Avon EIS is done dynamically. Users can customize important views, or set upper and lower limits or variances they want to examine. Other main-menu choices include 30 days worth of business and financial news from the Dow Jones News service and competitive information. The competitive analysis lets users compare the performance of any of Avon's divisions against those of selected competitors.

"An executive could, for example, compare Avon to other companies in the cosmetics industry, looking at financial ratios, with the figures graphed in real time," Mr. Giannantonio said.

Executives can also customize which ratios or companies they want to compare with Avon based on quarterly statements, sales growth, inventory turnover, or a number of other measures. Up to 15 companies can be compared at one time, letting an executive see instantly how Avon stacks up against the competition.

Perhaps the most concise indicator on the system is the Hot Buttons, an addition suggested by Avon CEO Hicks Waldron. He explained that after looking at a demonstration of the system, he wanted to be able to identify major business trends easily.

So the Hot Buttons, which are colored flags on the screen, were added. The top part of the flag represents the current month, and the bottom represents the trend for the last two months.

If the top part of the flag is green, it means the month (or trend) is above plan. If the color is blue, the trend is flat. If it is red, the trend or month is behind. It is, therefore, simple to compare the actual month to the business plan and to the two-month trend. Executives can still point and click on individual flags and see the detailed information behind them.

Response to the system has been extremely positive, and training time is virtually non-existent. Mr. Giannantonio recalled that during an early demo, they were explaining how the system worked to Mr. Waldron. The CEO simply said, "Let me try it," and worked through the system. Help screens, however, are provided. Mr. Chamberlin related how the system let Avon executives quickly see a business downturn in the Avon division.

"One of the indicators helped to show us that we had eliminated some low-priced items from our Christmas line, and that cut our profitability," he said. "So we included those items in our 1987 Christmas line, and the results were much more satisfactory." Mr. Chamberlin felt that without the system, it might not have been possible to correct them for the next season.

PART TWO

APPLICATION CASE

Despite examples of how the system has affected profits, there was never a demand to cost-justify it, because upper management believed it would help executives make better decisions.

This is a trend emerging as corporate computing evolves, according to Mr. Paul. He said he believes that in the early days of computing, computers were installed for direct cost savings such as cutting payroll costs. The next stage saw the use of computers in products.

Now, he sees where businesses in the service sector are looking to differentiate themselves more. "The higher you get in this movement, the less you can cost-justify things," Mr. Paul said. "It's no longer a case of cranking up inventory level, but more in the area of highlighting opportunities or problems in the organization."

Clearly, Avon is counting on EIS. For in the aggressive world of beauty and healthcare products, simply looking good is not enough.

Reprinted from *PC Week*, February 9, 1988 p. 48. Copyright ©: 1988 Ziff-Davis Publishing Company

DISCUSSION QUESTIONS

1. What are some ways Avon's Executive Information System will help Avon gain a competitive advantage over its competitors?

2. Do you think Avon's decision to hire MBAs and train them to be programmers was wise? Why or why not?

PART THREE ■ Developing User Applications

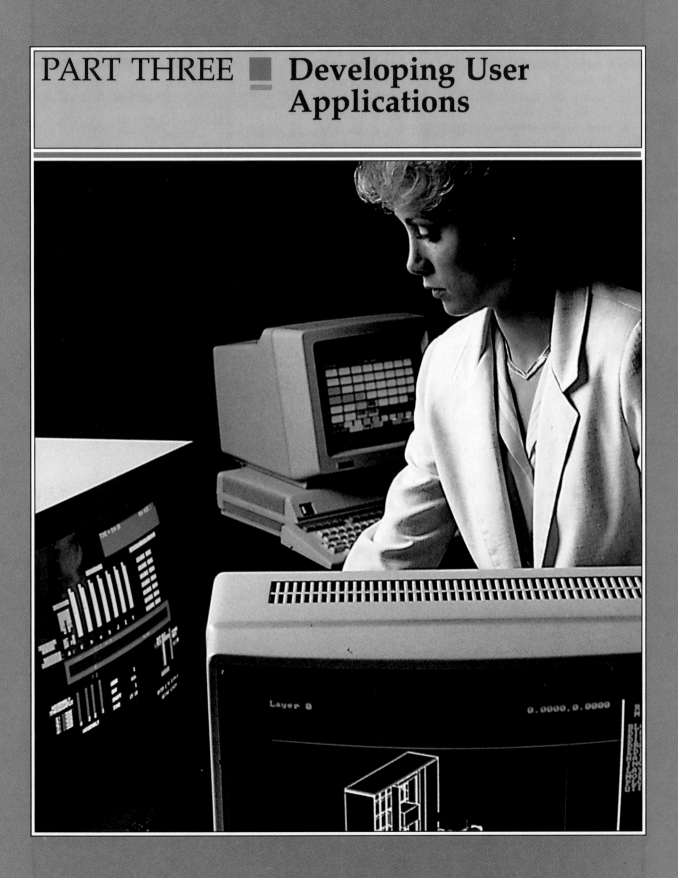

System Analysis ▪ Chapter 6

CHAPTER OUTLINE

Introduction

Partitioning of Systems

**Structured System-Development
Life Cycle**

Angelo's Pizza

Feasibility Study

Structured System Analysis
*Study the Current System—
    Process 2.1*
*Model the New-System
    Requirements—Process 2.2*
*Generate Alternative
    Systems—Process 2.3*
*Quantify Each Alternative—
    Process 2.4*
*Select an Alternative System—
    Process 2.5*
*Package the Requirements—
    Process 2.6*

**Advantages of Structured
System Development**

**Computer-Aided Software
Engineering**

**System Analysis and
Application Development
Without Programming**

Summing Up

Key Terms

Review Questions

Discussion Questions and Cases

■ INTRODUCTION

APPLICATION SOFTWARE
Programs that are written for or by a user and are used in a particular computer application. A payroll program is application software.

SOFTWARE
Computer programs, procedures, and the associated documentation concerned with operating a computer information system.

Acquiring *application software*, whether you purchase it or develop your own, has become the most expensive aspect of information systems. The price of hardware has continued to decline because of technological advances. Unfortunately, software technology has not kept up with hardware advances. In fact, the cost of software continues to increase, primarily because software development is labor-intensive.

However, there have been significant advances in the approaches to developing application software. Chapters 6 through 8 will introduce you to them. These approaches have resulted in significant time and cost savings for many firms. These businesses have avoided some of the perennial problems of application-software development, such as being over-budget and being months, sometimes years, late. There have been some real disasters in application development. Some systems do not produce the output that users want, some systems do not work at all, and some are out of date by the time they are operational.

If you, as a user, are to avoid these pitfalls, you need to be thoroughly familiar with the latest approaches to application-software development or purchase. You must be able to communicate with the system analyst responsible for designing and implementing the system. If a system fails, you as a user will lose, because it is your system that is being developed and you are ultimately responsible. This chapter explores the first major step in system development, system analysis. First, we briefly discuss partitioning of systems upon which good system development is based. This is followed by a discussion of structured system analysis, an approach that has become quite popular in recent years.

■ PARTITIONING OF SYSTEMS

PARTITION
The process of dividing something into parts; for example, dividing systems into subsystems.

System analysis is a method for modeling and understanding complex systems. It is aimed at determining precisely what a new system must accomplish and how to accomplish it. Perhaps the most important concept in system analysis is that any system can be *partitioned* into subsystems (or modules). Figure 6–1 illustrates a **hierarchical partitioning** of a management information system into leveled sets of subsystems. Notice that we have partitioned the accounting information system into its various subsystems and the payroll system into three subsystems. If our system-development project is to modify the reports produced by the payroll system, then we have drawn a boundary around a module. The module that produces output will be our primary interest in the development process. This hierarchical partitioning is the key to structured analysis, design, and programming of computer applications. We will use this concept in one form or another throughout the system-development process.

In fact, the term *structured* is closely related to hierarchical partitioning. The *American Heritage Dictionary* defines *structure* as the interrelation of parts, or the principal organization in a complex entity. In effect, we structure a system

Figure 6–1
Partitioning of a System

In Chapter 7 you will see that we call this chart a structure chart. It shows the hierarchical structure of a system.

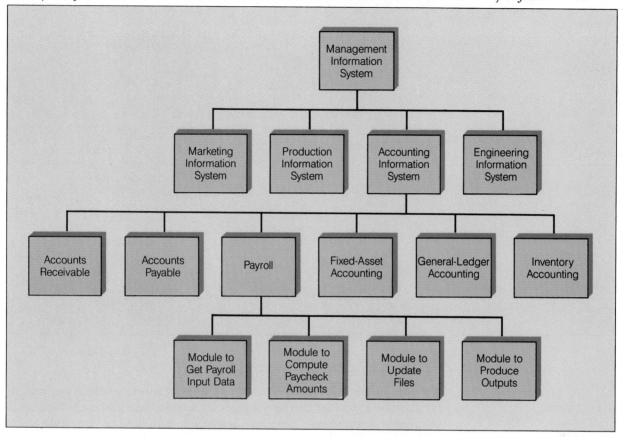

by hierarchically partitioning it. A system is **structured** if it is hierarrchically partitioned into subsystems, and the subsystems' interfaces with one another are defined.

STRUCTURED SYSTEM-DEVELOPMENT
■ **LIFE CYCLE**

The essence of **structured system development** is threefold: (1) we partition complex systems into simple subsystems, (2) we analyze, design, and implement the **interfaces** that exist between subsystems, and (3) we analyze, design, and implement the processes that go on within the subsystems. Think about these three steps; they are most important to your understanding of how information systems are built. Refer to Figure 6–2. The arrows represent the interfaces or data flows between the subsystems, which are illustrated by circles. We analyze, design, and build both the subsystems and

Figure 6–2
The Subsystems (Modules, Programs, or Processes) within the Payroll System

Shown here are the lowest-level modules of Figure 6–1 and the data flows or interfaces between those modules. We have also shown any files the modules use and external entities that interact with this system, in this case an employee who receives a paycheck.

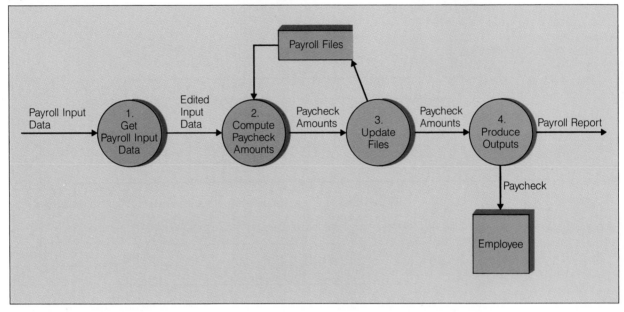

the interfaces between them. Then we combine them to produce a complete payroll system. By first dividing a complex system into understandable and manageable subsystems; then by designing, building, and testing each subsystem; and finally by combining them, we can produce very complex computer information systems.

Figure 6–3 illustrates the structured system-development life cycle. The **system-development life cycle (SDLC)** contains the steps we go through in building a computer information system. In this chapter we discuss the feasibility study and system analysis. Hardware evaluation is covered in Module C, and the remainder of the structured system-development life cycle is presented in Chapter 7.

■ ANGELO'S PIZZA

The structured system-development life cycle is much easier to understand than the older techniques that rely heavily on system and program flow-charts. However, concepts are even easier to learn if you can relate them to real-world situations. We will use the Angelo's Pizza case to illustrate the concepts presented in chapters 6 and 7.

Angelo Patti is the owner and manager of a large restaurant called Angelo's Pizza. Angelo is a very ambitious young man, and he would like to have a

Figure 6-3
Structured System-Development Life Cycle

These steps should occur in any system development whether it is a large complex system or one simple program.

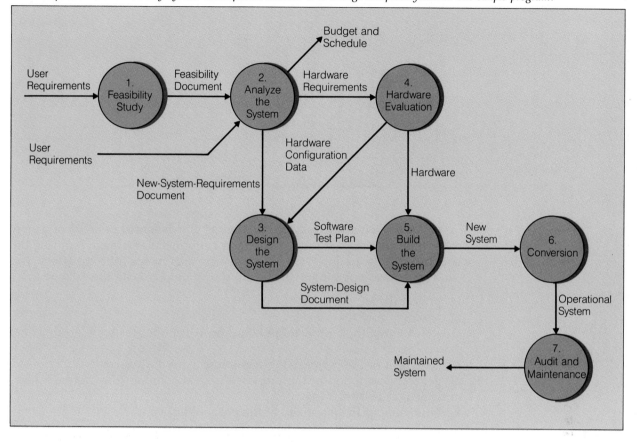

chain of Angelo's Pizza restaurants. He feels that computers could be useful in managing both his current restaurant and a chain of restaurants. Angelo has an old college buddy, Jose Wong, who established a computer consulting business after majoring in management information systems. Angelo hired Jose to help develop the computer information system. After a brief feasibility study, Jose recommended that Angelo start with an information system containing the four subsystems shown in Figure 6-4. To keep the illustration simple, we will use only recipe pricing and order processing.

■ FEASIBILITY STUDY

The **feasibility study** is an abbreviated version of the system-analysis phase. In fact, in this study the system analyst performs many of the same steps that will be performed in the system-analysis phase, but much less thoroughly. The primary purpose of the study is to identify the objectives of the user's

Figure 6–4
Information System for Angelo's Pizza

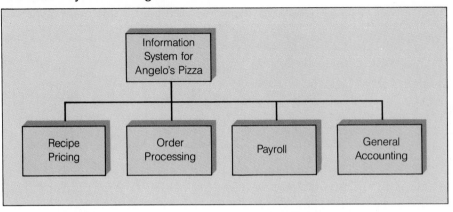

proposed system and to estimate whether the potential benefits of a new system justify the expense of a development project. The major inputs to the feasibility study are interviews and working documents from the users. The study produces a feasibility document that should contain the following:

1. project name
2. description of the problem
3. statement of the critical assumptions on which the feasibility document is based
4. statement of the performance requirements of the system
5. general description of the proposed system solution (this can be a new, modified, or existing system)
6. evaluation of the feasibility of the proposed system
7. possible alternative solutions.

■ STRUCTURED SYSTEM ANALYSIS

Figure 6–5 illustrates the phases within **structured system analysis.** Note that this figure is a partitioning of process 2 in Figure 6–3. In fact, Figures 6–2, 6–3, and 6–5 are all **data-flow diagrams (DFDs).** Data-flow diagrams are the primary tool used in structured system development to graphically depict systems. You probably found that you could understand these figures without an explanation of data-flow diagrams. This is one of their advantages; they are easy to understand because they are not cluttered with a lot of technical symbols. Figure 6–6 illustrates the four symbols used in data-flow diagrams. Contrast the simplicity of these DFD symbols with the **system flowchart** symbols shown in Figure 6–7. Although system flowcharting with this large variety of symbols is still done, many system professionals are using data-flow diagrams. You do not need the complex symbols shown in Figure 6–7! Any information system, no matter how complex, can be graphically depicted using the four symbols of data-flow diagrams. Only three things happen within an information system:

Figure 6–5
Structured System Analysis

System analysis has as its input the user requirements and feasibility documents. Its output includes the hardware requirements, budget and schedule for building the system, and the new-system-requirements document.

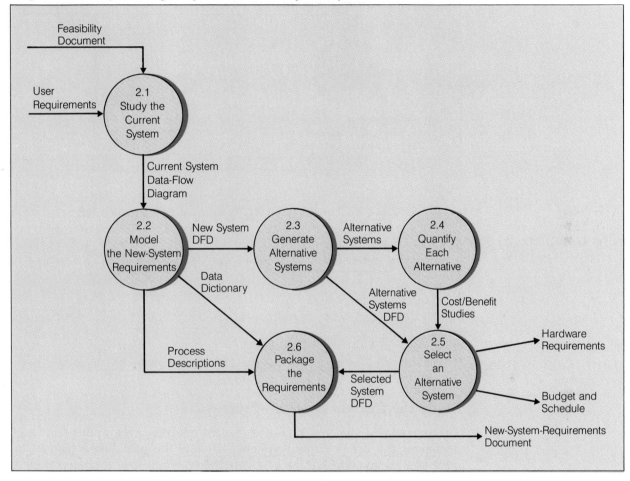

1. Data processing.
2. Data flows (input and output from processes).
3. Data stores.

In addition, the external-entity symbol is needed to depict outside entities that interact with the system.

Note the numbering system used in data-flow diagrams. The fact that the first digit of the numbers of the processes in Figure 6–5 is a 2 indicates that Figure 6–5 is a partitioning of the second process in Figure 6–3. We can carry this partitioning to as many levels as necessary, creating **leveled data-flow diagrams.** In practice it is rarely necessary to exceed five or six levels; they provide enough detail to show what occurs in the most complex systems. We will discuss data-flow diagrams in greater depth in the next section.

Figure 6–6
Symbols Used in Data-Flow Diagrams

Any information system, no matter how complex, can be graphically represented by these symbols. They are widely used by system analysts. Several programs use these symbols to draw data-flow diagrams with computers.

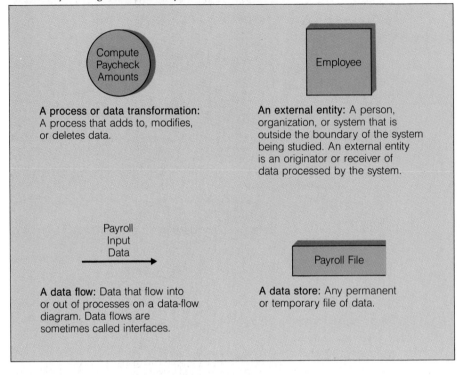

Study the Current System—Process 2.1

The purpose of the first phase of system analysis is to understand and document the user's current system. Usually, the user has a manual or computer information system. Studying the system helps the analyst understand the user's information needs. Many of the processes performed by the current system will have to be performed by the new one also. The study relies on extensive interviews with user personnel, and frequent reviews with users regarding the documentation that the analyst is creating. These reviews are called *walkthroughs*. The primary documentation tool used is a leveled set of data-flow diagrams.

WALKTHROUGH
A step-by-step review of the documentation or other work produced by a system analyst or programmer.

Figure 6–8 and 6–9 are the DFDs that Jose drew for the current order-processing and recipe-pricing systems of Angelo's Pizza. Note that the emphasis of the data-flow diagrams is on the flow of data.

Jose also decided to partition process 3 in Figure 6–8 in order to gain a better understanding of that process. This lower-level DFD is shown in Figure 6–10.

Model the New-System Requirements—Process 2.2

By now the analyst should be thoroughly familiar with the current system. Our goal in defining the new-system requirements is to describe what has to

Figure 6–7
System-Flowchart Symbols

Data-flow diagrams use only four symbols, whereas system flowcharts can use many more. Thus, system flowcharts can provide more information about how a system is physically implemented than data-flow diagrams. For example, we could use the magnetic-disk symbol to indicate that a file is stored on magnetic disk, but this added complexity is totally unnecessary for good system analysis. Good system analysis focuses on what is done in an information system rather than how it is done.

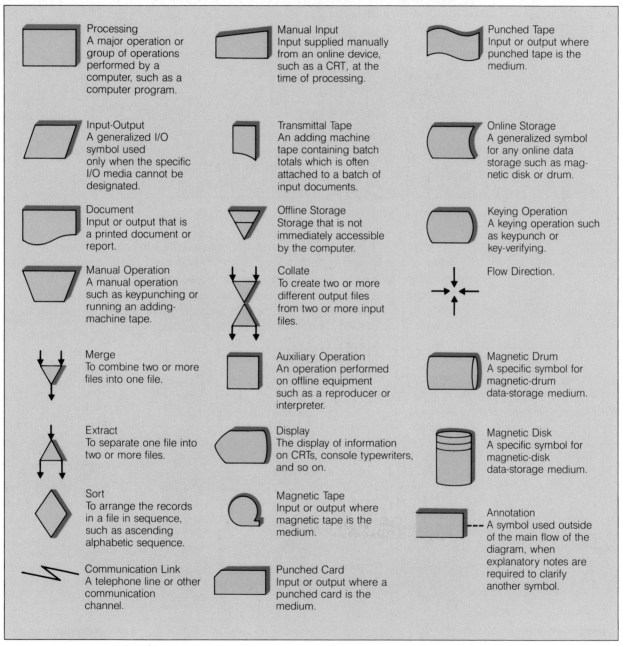

Processing
A major operation or group of operations performed by a computer, such as a computer program.

Manual Input
Input supplied manually from an online device, such as a CRT, at the time of processing.

Punched Tape
Input or output where punched tape is the medium.

Input-Output
A generalized I/O symbol used only when the specific I/O media cannot be designated.

Transmittal Tape
An adding machine tape containing batch totals which is often attached to a batch of input documents.

Online Storage
A generalized symbol for any online data storage such as magnetic disk or drum.

Document
Input or output that is a printed document or report.

Offline Storage
Storage that is not immediately accessible by the computer.

Keying Operation
A keying operation such as keypunch or key-verifying.

Manual Operation
A manual operation such as keypunching or running an adding-machine tape.

Collate
To create two or more different output files from two or more input files.

Flow Direction.

Merge
To combine two or more files into one file.

Auxiliary Operation
An operation performed on offline equipment such as a reproducer or interpreter.

Magnetic Drum
A specific symbol for magnetic-drum data-storage medium.

Extract
To separate one file into two or more files.

Display
The display of information on CRTs, console typewriters, and so on.

Magnetic Disk
A specific symbol for magnetic-disk data-storage medium.

Sort
To arrange the records in a file in sequence, such as ascending alphabetic sequence.

Magnetic Tape
Input or output where magnetic tape is the medium.

Annotation
A symbol used outside of the main flow of the diagram, when explanatory notes are required to clarify another symbol.

Communication Link
A telephone line or other communication channel.

Punched Card
Input or output where a punched card is the medium.

Figure 6–8
Current Order-Processing System, Angelo's Pizza

Notice that this data-flow diagram focuses on what is done rather than how it is done.

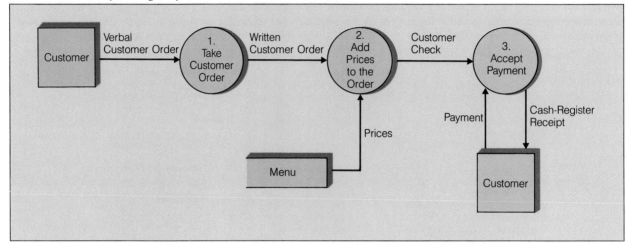

be done, not how it will be done. Of course, the analyst will keep in mind some of the computer technology that could be used in the new system. For example, Jose may feel that an electronic spreadsheet could do Angelo's recipe pricing. But Jose is experienced enough in computer information systems to know that all the computer technology in the world will not help Angelo if he cannot define his information requirements.

Figure 6–9
Current Recipe-Pricing System, Angelo's Pizza

Would you have to know anything about computer hardware to draw this data-flow diagram?

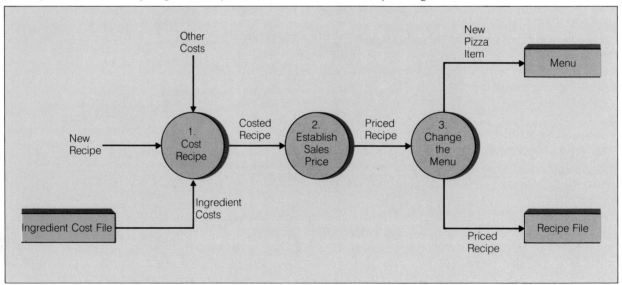

Figure 6–10
A Partitioning of Process 3 in Figure 6–8

Notice that the inputs and outputs here—customer check, payment, and cash-register receipt—are the same as those for process 3 in Figure 6–8.

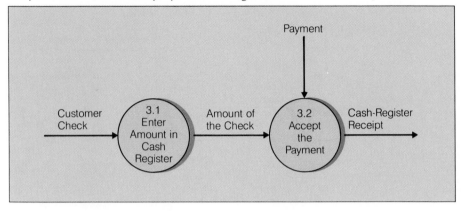

As the first step in defining the information requirements for Angelo's new system, Jose talked at length with Angelo about his needs, particularly about his business expansion plans. In summary, Angelo feels that quick, efficient customer service is important. Most pizza is cooked to the customer's order. Therefore, customers must wait for their orders. Angelo is sure that decreasing the wait time for an order would increase his competitive position. This is particularly true for lunchtime customers. Also, he would like to keep a name and address file on his customers, which would be used for mailing promotional material to them. He may even want to extend credit to selected customers.

After his discussions with Angelo, Jose believes he can define a system that not only would provide better information, but would also improve Angelo's operations in processing customers' orders. In fact, he feels that the system will be so great a competitive tool that Angelo may want to rename the restaurant Angelo's Hi-Tech Pizza!

In further defining Angelo's information requirements, Jose will use data-flow diagrams, a data dictionary, and process descriptions. The **data dictionary** documents files and data flows. **Process** or **transform descriptions** document the internal workings of data processes.

Data-Flow Diagrams   Figures 6–11 and 6–12 are Jose's data-flow diagrams for Angelo's new order-processing and recipe-pricing systems. Note that these DFDs do not differ substantially from the current system's DFDs shown in Figures 6–8 and 6–9. This is typical. Many of the basic information and operational needs are the same regardless of how a system is *physically implemented.*

Another important point about these two DFDs is that neither indicates how the system is to be physically implemented. Either system could be implemented in many different ways on a computer. Or, they could even be performed manually! In fact, at this point it is not even important to think about how the systems will be physically implemented. Decisions about

PHYSICAL IMPLEMENTATION
The way a system is actually performed in the real world. Manual systems and automated systems, using computers, are different types of physical implementation.

Figure 6–11
New Order-Processing System, Angelo's Pizza

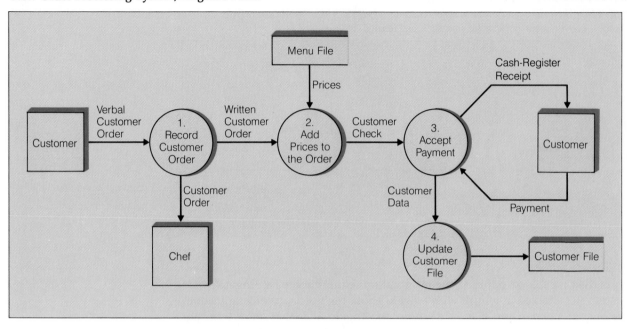

computer hardware are an unnecessary complication here. Angelo's information and operational requirements are the only important considerations. The points made in this paragraph are some of the most crucial to your future success in applying computer information systems. Most failures in computer information systems occur because users buy computer hardware before they have a clear understanding of their information needs. Never buy computer hardware without first knowing how it will help you in meeting your professional, business, or personal objectives.

Data Dictionary   A data dictionary contains definitions of data used in a system. It gives you a single place to look up data definitions you do not understand. In addition, it may contain many other types of information and definitions, depending on the wishes of the analyst. For example, when considering a particular data flow, the analyst may include information such as frequency, volume, affected users, security considerations, and implementation schedule.

For instance, Jose made an entry in his data dictionary that looked like this:

```
Customer_Check = Date + Table_Number + [Item_Ordered +
                 Item_Price] + Sales_Tax + Total_Amount
```

In other words, the data flow called "customer_check" consists of date, table number, one or more items ordered with their item price, as well as sales tax, and the total amount. The (+) signs are not addition symbols. They mean that both data elements must be present. The brackets indicate that there can be multiple items ordered and multiple item prices.

Figure 6–12
New Recipe-Processing System, Angelo's Pizza

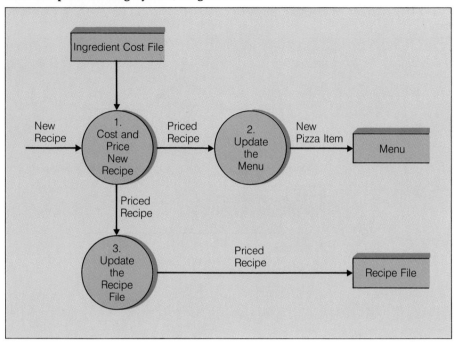

Just as we have partitioned data-flow diagrams, we can also partition data flows. For example, Jose defined *date* in the data dictionary as

$$\text{Date} = \text{Month} + \text{Day} + \text{Year}$$

For our analysis to be complete, every data flow indicated on a leveled set of data-flow diagrams must have a definition entry in the data dictionary. Data dictionaries are also used to define files by specifying the data contained within each individual record.

Many firms use computer-automated data dictionaries. Such dictionaries are a very important part of large and complex information systems.

Process Descriptions   Even though we partition processes in leveled DFDs, at some point we cease to partition. At this most detailed level of the data-flow diagrams the processes are called **functional primitives.** But to be complete we still have to specify the data transformations that go on within these functional primitives. These specifications are called *process* (or *transform*) *descriptions.*

We will examine three ways to describe the data transformations that occur within functional primitives on data-flow diagrams. These are **structured English, decision tables,** and **decision trees.**

Structured English is plain English with a few restrictions. It is often also called pseudocode, because of its similarity to computer *program code.* In fact, the *syntax* of structured English is restricted to the same basic patterns as *structured programming.* Figure 6–13 illustrates the allowable structured-

PROCESS DESCRIPTIONS
A description of the data transformations that occur within the most detailed processes on a data-flow diagram.

PROGRAM CODE
The instructions used in a computer program.

SYNTAX
The structure of expressions in a language.

STRUCTURED PROGRAMMING
An approach to computer programming that restricts the sequence in which the statements are executed to four basic patterns: simple sequence, selection, loop, and case.

Figure 6–13
Allowable Structured-English Control Patterns

These control patterns are useful for describing processes on data-flow diagrams, but as we will see in Chapter 7, they are also useful in writing computer programs.

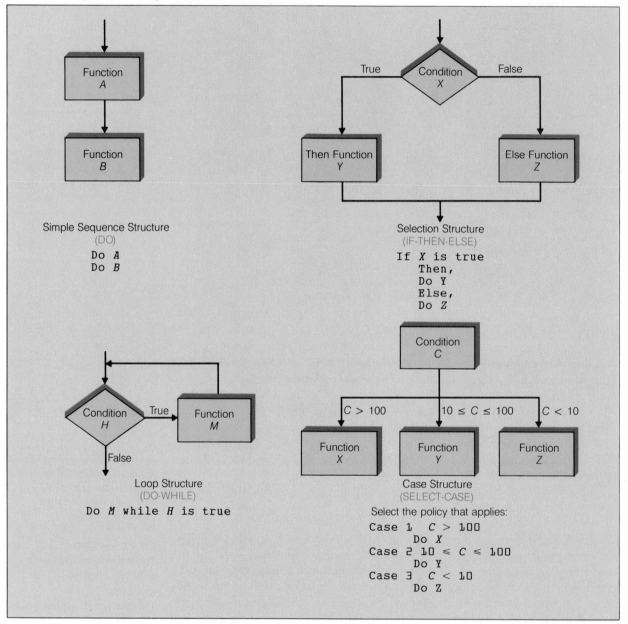

English patterns. When we discuss structured programming in the next chapter, we will use these same control patterns. Structured-English process descriptions are easy to convert to structured computer programs.

Figure 6–14
Structured English for Approval of Customer Credit, Angelo's Pizza

When structured-English process descriptions are done with a word processor, they can be modified and updated quickly.

```
IF the amount of the check exceeds $50,
     IF the customer has any bill more than 60 days overdue,
     THEN
          do not extend credit,
     ELSE (the customer has good credit),
          extend credit.
     ENDIF
ELSE (check is $50 or less),
     IF the customer has any bill more than 60 days overdue,
     THEN
          get manager's approval before extending credit.
     ELSE (the customer has good credit),
          extend credit.
     ENDIF
ENDIF
```

On one of the lower-level DFDs, not shown in the text, Jose had a process called "approve customer credit." The structured English that describes the internal workings of that process is shown in Figure 6–14.

Decision tables allow large numbers of conditions to be concisely documented. Figure 6–15 illustrates a decision table for the same customer credit approval that Jose defined with structured English in Figure 6–14. Decision tables are read from top to bottom. In the example, there are four sets of conditions that can occur. Looking at rule 1, we see that if the check is greater than fifty dollars and a bill is overdue by sixty-plus days, then Angelo refuses credit. The primary advantage of a decision table is that many different combinations of conditions and their appropriate actions can be documented in a compact form.

Figure 6–15
Decision Table for Approval of Customer Credit, Angelo's Pizza

Although this decision table shows only one action for each rule, decision tables can easily document multiple actions for each rule.

	Rules			
Conditions	1	2	3	4
1. Check > $50	Y	N	Y	N
2. Bill Overdue by 60 + days	Y	Y	N	N
Actions				
1. Extend Credit			Y	Y
2. Refuse Credit	Y			
3. Get Manager's Approval		Y		

The credit-approval policy can also be documented with a decision-tree, as shown in Figure 6–16. The decision tree is read from left to right, starting at credit-approval policy. Each branch illustrates a condition that can occur. Combinations of conditions lead to the actions on the right. For example, if the check is greater than fifty dollars and the customer is in good standing, Angelo extends credit (action 2). As you can see, the decision tree is not as compact as a decision table, but most people find a decision tree easier to understand.

Generally, system analysts use structured English for transform descriptions because it is much easier to write program code based on it. Decision tables and decision trees are used in the few situations where there are large numbers of conditions and therefore several different actions that could occur based on the combinations of conditions.

In this phase of the analysis (modeling the new-system requirements), the analyst must have a good understanding of the information needs of the user. He or she develops a model of a system that will take data inputs and transform them into information the user needs. In doing this the analyst relies heavily on the original feasibility study and user interviews. The output

Figure 6–16
Decision Tree for Approval of Customer Credit, Angelo's Pizza

This figure shows two conditions at each node, but decision trees can have more than two conditions at each node.

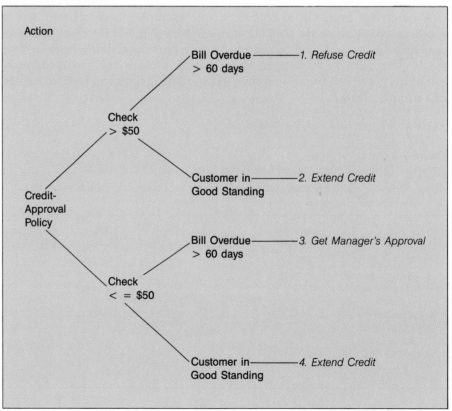

of this phase is a leveled set of data-flow diagrams, process descriptions of functional primitives on the data-flow diagrams, and a data dictionary. These all serve to document the proposed new system.

Generate Alternative Systems—Process 2.3

In this stage of structured system analysis, the analyst develops a number of configurations that will produce the required information. In fact, most managers expect analysts to propose several options.

In developing alternative systems, we are dealing with the how and what of the system; that is, its physical aspects. For each option, some parts of the system may be manual and others automated. In terms of automated parts, there may be several ways to apply the computer. The output of this phase will be several possible physical data-flow diagrams. One method for indicating the alternatives is to simply mark on copies of the new-system DFDs a proposed physical implementation of the system, as shown in Figure 6–17.

Figure 6–17
One Alternative for Implementing the New Recipe-Pricing System for Angelo's Pizza
Circles around the various processes and files show how they will be physically implemented.

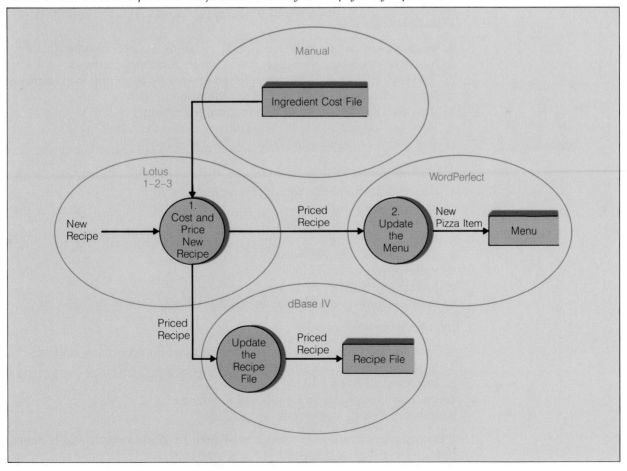

For example, Jose is proposing that Angelo use Lotus 1–2–3 to cost and price new recipes.

Quantify Each Alternative—Process 2.4

Each of the tentative new systems developed in the previous subphase has costs and benefits associated with it. To determine these costs and benefits, we must make a tentative selection of hardware and software, if it is to be purchased. This is only a very general selection. For example, we might decide that the automated system would be executed on a personal computer or minicomputer, or it might be an online system rather than a batch system. We do not want to lock ourselves into a certain set of hardware or software at this point.

Both costs and benefits can be classified as tangible or intangible. Tangible costs include:

1. Maintenance and operating costs.
2. Personnel costs.
3. Training and orientation.
4. Lease or purchase of new hardware and software.
5. Site preparation.
6. Design costs.

Intangible costs include:

1. Negative effects on employee morale, resulting in decreased productivity.
2. Negative effects on customers, resulting in decreased business.
3. Decrease in control of the information system by operating management.
4. Increased centralized control of the information system.
5. Increased specialization in information processing.
6. Increased potential cost for breakdowns or disaster when the information system becomes more centralized.

Tangible benefits include:

1. Reduced maintenance and operating costs.
2. Reduced personnel costs.
3. Reduced investment in hardware and software.
4. Reduced rental costs.
5. Reduced space requirements.
6. Reduced age of accounts receivable.
7. Increased inventory turnover.
8. Reduced investment in inventory.

Intangible benefits include:

1. Freeing operating management from information-processing activities.
2. Improved control over information-processing activities.
3. Improved decision making.
4. Increased emphasis on long-range planning.
5. Improved employee morale.

It is not always possible or necessary to quantify all these costs and benefits. But we should at least identify them if they exist.

Select an Alternative System—Process 2.5

Based on the alternative systems the analyst has developed, and costs and benefits associated with each, management will make a decision on which option to implement. The data-flow diagrams of the new system are very important tools in this phase. Since they are easy to understand, the analyst can readily employ them in presenting the proposed systems to management.

Of course, management does not have to select one of the alternatives presented. It may decide not to proceed, select a combination of the alternatives offered, or select an alternative of its own.

Package the Requirements—Process 2.6

The final output of the structured-analysis phase is integrated into a new system-requirements document, consisting of:

1. An introduction containing the system's goals, objectives, and any useful background information.
2. Data-flow diagrams depicting the major partitioning of functions, and all the interfaces among the parts.
3. A data dictionary documenting each of the interface data flows and data stores (that is, files).
4. Transform descriptions documenting the transformations that occur within each of the most detailed DFD processes through the use of structured English, decision tables, and/or decision trees.
5. Input and output documents.
6. Security, control, and performance requirements.

■ ADVANTAGES OF STRUCTURED
■ SYSTEM DEVELOPMENT

Most system analysts and users are beginning to see that the structured approach has significant advantages over other approaches to system development.

1. Structured analysis requires a complete study of the user area, a study frequently omitted in other approaches.
2. Structured analysis requires that the analyst partition what he or she has specified. The tools of other approaches, system and program flowcharts, are not well suited for partitioning. As we have emphasized, this partitioning is the key to many of the advantages of the structured approach.
3. The structured system specification is very graphic and therefore easy to understand.
4. The other approaches tend to focus on the physical aspects of the system, such as hardware, vendors, and operating procedures. By focusing on the logical aspects of data flows and data processes, the analyst can readily see the essential information flows and processes that are required in the new system.
5. The structured approach produces highly maintainable systems not only from the standpoint of the analysis phase, but, as we will see in the next chapter, also for design and programming purposes.

6. Structured development documentation is cumulative. The documentation developed in any phase builds on the preceeding documentation and serves as the basis for work in subsequent phases. For example, as we will see in the next chapter, the DFDs, process descriptions, and so on developed in the analysis phase will be used heavily in program design and coding.

A system's **maintainability** is the ease with which it can be changed when there is a change in requirements. In the real world, requirements change often. Maintainability problems are responsible for the demise of most systems and thus are very important to consider. The structured approach produces maintainable systems primarily because of its partitioned or modular approach to system design.

■ COMPUTER-AIDED SOFTWARE ENGINEERING

Computer-aided software engineering (CASE) is the application of computers to the task of developing computer software. The term **software engineering** is often used as a synonym for software design and development. CASE tools provide the ability to create and maintain on a computer all the system documentation created during the system-development life cycle. Documents such as data-flow diagrams, data dictionaries, and structured English can be created and maintained by CASE tools. Figure 6–18 shows a data-flow diagram created on Excelerator, one of the most widely used CASE packages. Excelerator and most other CASE packages run on the IBM PC and its compatibles. Since drawings of data flow and other diagrams are a substantial part of system documentation, CASE tools require PCs that have good graphic capabilities.

CASE tools currently have two other important capabilities. First, system analysts can use them to build executable prototypes of input and output screens. This enables users to evaluate these very important human/computer interfaces before computer programs are written. Thus, the programmer can be fairly confident that the screens will meet the users' needs.

Second, some CASE tools are capable of generating executable program code. Thus, CASE tools are becoming application generators that can automatically produce program code, such as COBOL, from the system documentation.

The program code is usually not complete, but it does provide a skeleton for the programs that can be modified and filled in by programmers. This capability certainly reduces the amount of manual coding necessary to produce an operational system.

CASE tools will become increasingly important in software development. They are the application of computers to the task of building software. CASE tools are to system analysts as word processors are to writers. They make the creation, organization, and changing of system documentation much easier. They also offer the capability of automating a significant portion of the programming process.

Figure 6–18
A Data-Flow Diagram Produced by Excelerator (Case)

Note that the file and external-entity symbols are slightly different from those in Figure 6–6. CASE tools and system analysts differ slightly in the shape of the four symbols used for data-flow diagrams.

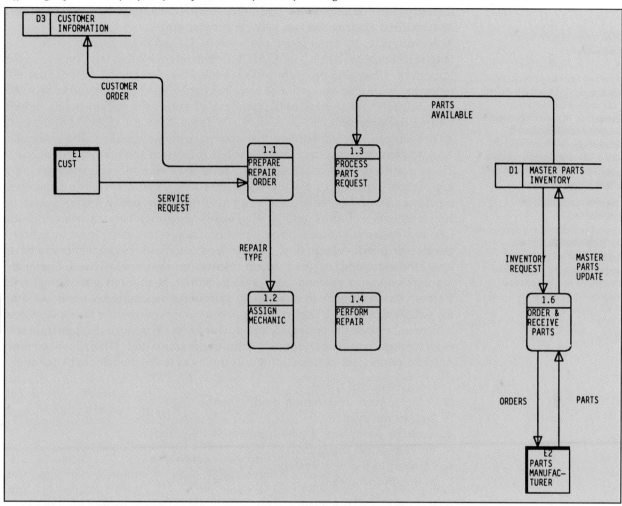

SYSTEM ANALYSIS AND APPLICATION DEVELOPMENT WITHOUT PROGRAMMING

In Chapter 1 we saw that many computer applications can be developed without programming. We will examine the methods for accomplishing this in Chapter 8. However, at this point you may be wondering whether the system-analysis approaches discussed in this chapter are useful for application development without programming. The answer to this question is not clear-cut; it depends on the situation. However, we can give you some guidelines to use in deciding whether a structured system analysis is appropriate in a given situation:

**FOURTH-GENERATION
LANGUAGE**
A flexible application
development tool, such as an
electronic spreadsheet, query
language, or application
generator, that allows you to
develop applications by
describing to the computer
what you want rather than by
programming it in a how-to,
step-by-step fashion.

**THIRD-GENERATION
LANGUAGE**
A programming language, such
as FORTRAN, COBOL,
PASCAL, or BASIC, that
requires you to instruct the
computer in a procedural,
step-by-step fashion.

1. Above all you must understand the inputs, data processes, and information outputs required of the system you are attempting to develop. If you are
having difficulty understanding these, structured system analysis will help
you.

2. As systems become larger and more complex, the partitioning capabilities
of structured system analysis become most useful.

3. If you plan to implement the system by writing program code in a
language such as BASIC or COBOL, structured system analysis is more
important. Changing program code is expensive. Structured system analysis
helps to insure that you will not have to change your program code because
you did not have a clear understanding of your information needs before
writing the programs.

4. If you plan to implement the system with a flexible *fourth-generation
language,* structured system analysis is less important and often not necessary.
These fourth-generation languages, such as electronic spreadsheets and
application generators, usually allow you to change a system much more
quickly and with less expense than if it were programmed in a *third-generation
language,* such as BASIC or COBOL. Fourth-generation languages are tools to
develop systems without programming. They often allow you to quickly
develop an initial version of your system on a computer even when you have
little understanding of your requirements. In effect, you can define your
requirements and develop your system simultaneously in a trial-and-error
fashion. This approach to developing systems is becoming so important that
we will devote all of Chapter 8 to it.

Remember that the system-development life cycle is still a most useful tool,
even for application development without programming. The following steps
must be performed in developing a complex system or a simple program:

1. Do a feasibility study.
2. Analyze your information requirements.
3. Design the system.
4. Evaluate hardware (if new hardware is required).
5. Build and test the system.
6. Convert to the new system.
7. Maintain the system.

It is a question of the degree to which these steps are done and how they are
performed, not whether they are done. For example, if you are developing a
simple electronic spreadsheet you should perform each of these steps. They
may overlap, and some, such as the feasibility study, can be done in your
head. In this case, the analysis, design, building, and testing may occur
simultaneously.

Most difficulties in applying personal computers occur because users omit
some or most of the steps in the system-development life cycle. These steps
have been developed and used over the years by professionals. They are also
useful when people want to develop their own applications.

■ Summing Up

■ Software development is the most expensive part of implementing a
computerized system. A rational approach to system analysis can help to
minimize this expense.

■ System analysis enables us to partition a complex system and focus on the interactions between its parts.

■ The study of a large system is made possible through partitioning it into smaller, manageable parts.

■ Structured analysis begins with a detailed analysis of the current system. Data-flow diagrams are developed that depict the existing system.

■ A new system is designed, based on the review of the current system and new user requirements. The major tools used in this process are data-flow diagrams, data dictionaries, structured English, decision tables, and decision trees.

■ Several alternative ways to implement the system are generated. Since many different combinations may exist, it is necessary to compare the costs and benefits of the various options.

■ Once an alternative is selected, various system specifications are integrated into a complete package called the new-system-requirements document.

■ Structured analysis is superior to other approaches in many respects. Its primary advantage is that it leads to the creation of systems that are easier to understand and maintain.

■ Computer-aided software engineering (CASE) enables system analysts to create and maintain system development documentation with a computer. CASE also can generate program code.

■ The system-development life cycle (SDLC) is useful even when applications are developed without programming. It is a question of the degree to which the steps in the SDLC are applied and how they are applied, rather than whether or not they will be applied.

■ Key Terms

system analysis

hierarchical partitioning

structured

structured system development

interface

system-development life cycle (SDLC)

feasibility study

structured system analysis

data-flow diagrams (DFDs)

system flowchart

leveled data-flow diagrams

data dictionary

process or transform descriptions

functional primitives

structured English

decision tables

decision trees

maintainability

computer-aided software engineering (CASE)

software engineering

■ Review Questions

1. Why does the user need to be familiar with application software development?

2. Define system analysis, and explain how it makes software development a more manageable task.

3. Explain the concept of partitioning.

4. List the elements of a feasibility document.

5. What are the differences in program and system flowcharts?

6. What is the essence of the structured system-development approach?

7. Identify and describe the symbols used in data-flow diagrams.

8. Describe the importance of data-flow diagrams in structured analysis.

9. Differentiate between system flowcharts and data-flow diagrams.

10. Explain the following terms:

  a. Data dictionary
  b. Transform descriptions
  c. Functional primitives
  d. Decision table
  e. Decision tree
  f. Structured English

11. How do walkthroughs aid in the development of systems?

12. List the tangible costs and benefits that should be considered when selecting alternative systems.

13. Describe the components of a new-system-requirements document.

14. Discuss the advantages of the structured approach over other approaches to system development.

15. What is computer-aided software engineering?

■ Discussion Questions and Cases

1. Often managers are reluctant to allow a system analyst to "interfere" with their work. Some common objections are as follows:

■ An outsider cannot understand the nature of the work within a short time period.

■ We have been working like this for years. Why can't we go on indefinitely?

■ Interviews and questionnaires take a lot of time, and our personnel are already overburdened with production work.

How would you respond to these objections?

2. Structured analysis and structured design are superior in many respects to other approaches to analysis and design. They do, however, have drawbacks. Critically review structured techniques, and identify their weaknesses.

3. Jane Montgomery is manager of system development for White Motor Corporation, a large manufacturer of trucks. For the last five years, she has maintained a policy whereby new employees in the system-development group must have an educational background in computer science, math, or industrial engineering. These employees are filling either programming or system analyst positions. Jane believes that computer professionals must first understand hardware and software in order to perform their jobs properly. Furthermore, she feels that the development of application software requires a great deal of logical reasoning and design skill. Therefore, she believes that industrial engineers and mathematicians, as well as those with a computer-science background, make good computer professionals. Several management-level individuals in user organizations suggest to Jane that system development hire more people with backgrounds in user areas, such as marketing, finance, personnel, and accounting. Jane replies that it is the user's responsibility to convey to the system analyst and programmer what he or she needs in an information system. It is the system analyst's and programmer's job to design, code, and

implement the systems. She argues that business and computer information systems are two separate disciplines and that the advantages of specialization support her current hiring policy. Evaluate Jane's position.

4. Sam Jones is vice-president of marketing for Giles Development Corporation, a large developer of condominiums, apartments, and single-family homes. Sam has requested that System Development begin work on a new marketing decision-support system. This system will have the capacity of tracking historical sales, following demographic trends, and projecting sales trends. The primary objective of the system is to provide Giles Development with information that will help it decide what type of housing unit to develop in the future and where the various types of units should be located. System-development personnel estimates that 40 percent of the effort to develop the system will be spent in the analysis phase. Sam is upset with this estimate. He feels that much less time should be spent on analysis and that system development should quickly get into the design and implementation of the system. Do you agree or disagree with Sam? Explain.

5. Frank Jones, a system analyst for Kraco Corporation, a furniture manufacturer, has just completed the analysis phase of a system-development project for the marketing department. In the general design document, he proposed a number of options for implementing the new system. During a review of the design document, the review committee (which consisted of several marketing representatives) asked why he had wasted time developing several alternatives. The marketing vice-president said to Frank, "We need only one system, not three." If you were Frank, how would you respond to the vice-president?

6. Jack Abby has been hired as a system analyst for the Datamax Corporation. His primary job for the coming month is to develop a new computer system that will enable users in the accounting department to perform various payroll and monthly accounting functions. For several weeks, Jack has been conducting an extensive study to gain a thorough understanding of how the current system operates and interacts with its users. He has interviewed users and has spent time working on the current system. Jack feels the study of the current system is a necessary phase in structured system development. Jack's supervisor, however, disagrees with him. The supervisor feels the new system can be developed independently from the current system and has told Jack not to waste any more time. Whom do you agree with? Support your answer.

7. About six months ago, Tony, who owns and manages Tony's Pizza, purchased a personal computer and software to provide information he needs to manage his three pizza restaurants. Shortly after contacting a computer salesperson, he purchased the hardware and software. He did not yet have a clear understanding of his information needs or how a computer would assist in meeting those needs. The computer salesperson reassured him by stating that "these personal computers are so user-friendly and flexible that you will have no difficulty using it. Hundreds of thousands of small-business persons just like you are using them to greatly increase their profits. In today's competitive world you just can't afford to not own one." Tony has become very disillusioned with computers. He has even hired a part-time computer consultant to help him use the computer. Thus far, his computer has been of little practical use to him. How could Tony have avoided this waste of his time and money?

System Design and Implementation

■ Chapter 7

CHAPTER OUTLINE

Introduction

Design the System
*Derive Structure Chart—
Process 3.1*
Design Modules—Process 3.2
Package the Design—Process 3.3

Build the System
Structured Walkthroughs
Top-Down Coding
Top-Down Testing
Procedure Development
Chief-Programmer Teams

Conversion

**Post-Implementation Audit and
Maintenance**

Summing Up

Key Terms

Review Questions

Discussion Questions and Cases

■ INTRODUCTION

In the previous chapter we learned the techniques for structured system analysis of a proposed system. The specifications (data-flow diagrams, process descriptions, and data dictionary) that were developed will be the primary inputs for the structured-design phase. In fact, we will find that designing a new system with these structured specifications is a relatively easy process. For simple programs or programs where the requirements are already known we omit the analysis phase and begin with system design. In Figure 7–1 we have repeated the system-development life cycle so that you can readily see where design (process 3 in Figure 7–1) fits into the picture. This chapter will cover design and building of the new system, as well as conversion to the new system and its audit and maintenance.

■ DESIGN THE SYSTEM

Figure 7–2 shows the structured-design phase. **Structured design** is the process of designing the computer programs that will be used in the system.

Figure 7–1
System-Development Life Cycle

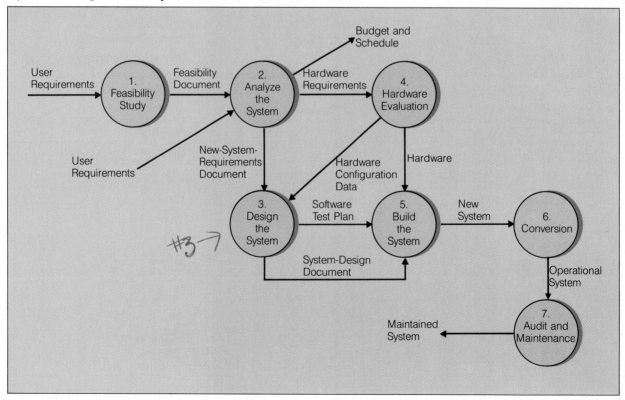

The system-design document produced in the structured-design phase is, in effect, a blueprint that the programmer follows in coding the programs. The system designer is like an architect, whereas the programmer is like a builder. Also, a plan for testing the programs is produced. There are only three activities within structured design. When we use structured analysis, there is relatively less work to be done in the design phase. In fact, a characteristic of structured analysis is that more work is done in planning the system and in the analysis phase than in later stages of the system-development life cycle.

As we shall see, the primary advantages of structured design are that it produces computer programs (1) that are more easily maintained, (2) that can be tested *module* by module in a top-down fashion, and (3) that can be more easily understood. All these advantages occur primarily because the program is broken down into logical modules during the structured-design phase. Usually the system analyst works on the design phase, although in some cases a system designer does it. Sometimes system designers are called programmer analysts, since the process of designing the system requires both analytical and programming skills.

MODULE
A part of a computer program that is separate and identifiable. In a computer program one module can call (cause) another module to be executed. Synonym of *subroutine.*

Derive Structure Chart—Process 3.1

The primary tool used in structured design of computer programs is the structure chart. A **structure chart** is a graphic representation of the hierarchical relationships between modules within a program or system. To create a structure chart, we partition into modules the tasks that a program must perform and tie the modules together in a hierarchical way. Figure 7–3 shows

Figure 7–2
Overview of the Structured-Design Phase
The objective of this phase is to produce a blueprint (the system-design document) that will guide the building of the system. Note that this figure is an explosion of process 3 in Figure 7–1. The inputs and outputs are the same for process 3 in Figure 7–1 as they are in this figure. This is the concept of "explosion of a process" on a data-flow diagram.

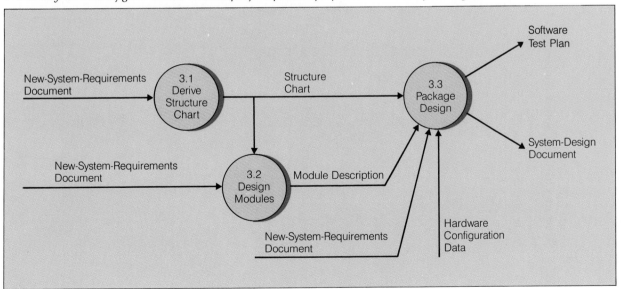

Figure 7–3
Structure Chart for Grocery Shopping

This is a hierarchical partitioning of the tasks that must be performed in shopping for groceries. Tasks performed by computers can be partitioned in similar ways.

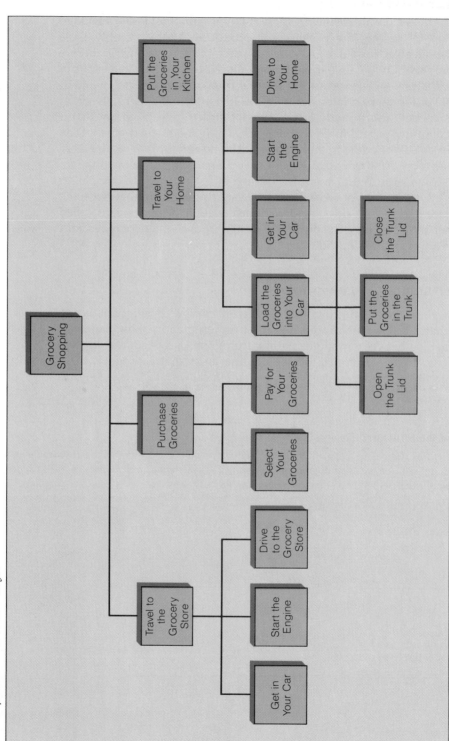

a structure chart that hierarchically partitions the tasks that must be done when you go grocery shopping.

An example of a structure chart used for an information system is shown in Figure 7–4. When a program is designed in a structured way, the approach is often called **top-down design.** The figure shows that the program is broken down into independent modules or *subroutines* from the top down. The module at the top is called a control module which, in Figure 7–4, is the accounts-receivable system. At the appropriate times, this module will *call* the three modules underneath it to get the inputs from files, perform the processing, and write the outputs. To simplify the program structure, we can continue subdividing modules into smaller parts. Ideally, each module should perform a single function.

By now you may have noticed that this structure chart resembles a data-flow diagram (DFD) in concept. Although the two do not look similar, a structure chart is an exercise in hierarchical partitioning just as a data-flow diagram is. In fact, all the advantages we talked about in relation to data-flow diagrams apply to structure charts. There is a very strong correlation between structure charts and data-flow diagrams.

A data-flow diagram documents what has to be accomplished; it is a statement of information-processing requirements. A structure chart, on the

SUBROUTINE
A separate, sequenced set of statements in a computer program. Synonym of *module.*

Figure 7–4
Structure Chart of an Accounts-Receivable System

We can make an analogy between a structure chart and the organization chart of a business. Top managers are at the top and those who do the detailed processing are at the bottom.

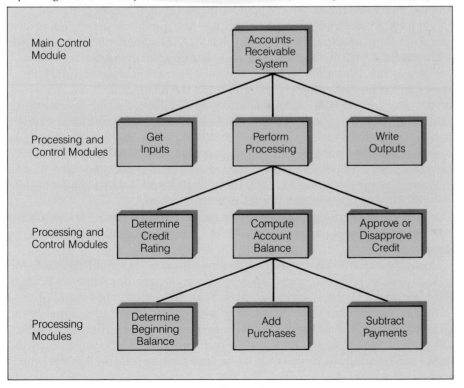

other hand, documents how the requirements will be met in a computer program. The structure chart is the hierarchical partitioning of the programs we will write for the system.

Since there is a close relationship between DFDs and structure charts, we should be able to derive the structure chart directly from the DFD. In the next few paragraphs we will show how this is done. First, let's refine our knowledge of structured design.

As we have stated, a design is structured if it is made up of a logically related hierarchy of modules. However, another highly desirable characteristic of structured design is for each of these modules or subroutines to have a single entry from and a single exit back to its parent module. Each module should be as independent as possible of all other modules, except its parent. For example, in Figure 7–4 there should be no direct exit from the Determine Beginning Balance module to the Add Purchases module. Once the Determine Beginning Balance module has completed its processing, control of execution is passed back to the parent Compute Account Balance module. From there, control of execution can go back up to Perform Processing or back down to any of the fourth-level modules. Control of execution passes along the connecting lines.

A third highly desirable characteristic of structured design is that within each module, the code is to be executed in a top-to-bottom fashion. There should not be any GO TO statements, which cause the program statements to be executed in other than a top-to-bottom manner. Often called **go-to-less programming,** this requirement makes programs much easier to read. For example, how would you like to read a book that had a GO TO statement every few paragraphs, which caused you to go and reread previous paragraphs; then to go forward three pages and read something on that page; then to go back to another page. You can see the problem with reading and understanding a program module that has GO TO statements. Program code with many GO TO statements is often called **spaghetti code.**

There are also certain notational conventions used in structured design, as shown in Figure 7–5. You may recognize that the rectangular box is a module. A **module** is a bounded, named, and contiguous set of program statements often referred to as a **subroutine.** The line joining two modules is called a **connection.** This connection means that the upper module has the capability of calling the lower module. Finally, a couple is represented by a short arrow. A **couple** is a data item that moves from one module to another. For example, in Figure 7–5 the system sends data item *A* to the module labeled Make *A* Into *C*, and then this module sends *C* back to the system.

CALL
To cause a module to begin execution.

Notice the general form of a structure chart. The input modules are on the left, processing modules are in the middle, and output modules are on the right.

Deriving structure charts from data-flow diagrams is straightforward. We will use Jose's DFD of the new order-processing system for Angelo's Pizza to illustrate how it is done (see Figure 7–6). First, we identify the central process in the DFD in Figure 7–6(a). The **central process** must be in the center of the DFD, therefore it is not involved with getting input or generating output. Other than this, it is not important which process we choose; in fact, the choice can be arbitrary. In this case we can use process number 2 as the central process. We make this process, the top module in the structure chart, the

Figure 7–5
Notational Conventions Used in Structured Design

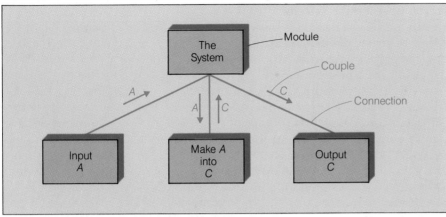

system. Note that the top module in Figure 7–6(b) has the same inputs and outputs as process number 2 in Figure 7–6(a).

At the second level of the structure chart in Figure 7–6(b), we design one module for each input stream to the central module, one module for the central process, and one for each output stream from the central module. We use a similar approach for each of the succeeding lower levels. For example, in terms of the second-level module, Input Written Customer Order, there is one input stream (Get Verbal Customer Order) and the transform of recording the customer order. A **transform** is a process (or module) that changes data into another form or into new data. For example, the module Record Customer Order transforms a verbal customer order into a written customer order. The couples represent the flow of data to and from the various modules.

Note that for each input process on the DFD, there is a two-part substructure (an input module and a transform module) on the structure chart. For each output process on the data-flow diagram, there is a two- (or-more) part substructure (a transform module and one or more output modules) on the structure chart.

Let's look at one of the major advantages of deriving structure charts from DFDs. Note that in Figure 7–6 we isolated the central part of the system (Adding Prices to the Order) from the physical aspects of the input (Get Verbal Customer Order) and the output (Output Cash-Register Receipt and Update Customer File). Changes in systems are very likely to affect inputs and outputs. We hierarchically partitioned the system in such a way that these inputs and outputs are isolated. Therefore, it is very possible that we could make a change in this system by changing just one of these three isolated input or output modules. Remember that one advantage of the structured approach is relatively easy system maintenance. For example, if we change the way prices are computed at Angelo's Pizza, we only have to change the module titled "Add Prices to the Order." Many companies are finding that they spend more money in maintaining existing systems than in designing and implementing new ones. Therefore, ease of maintenance is an extremely important consideration when designing a new system.

Figure 7–6
Deriving a Structure Chart for the New Order-Processing System for Angelo's Pizza

Each module on the structure chart is a separate subroutine in a computer program.

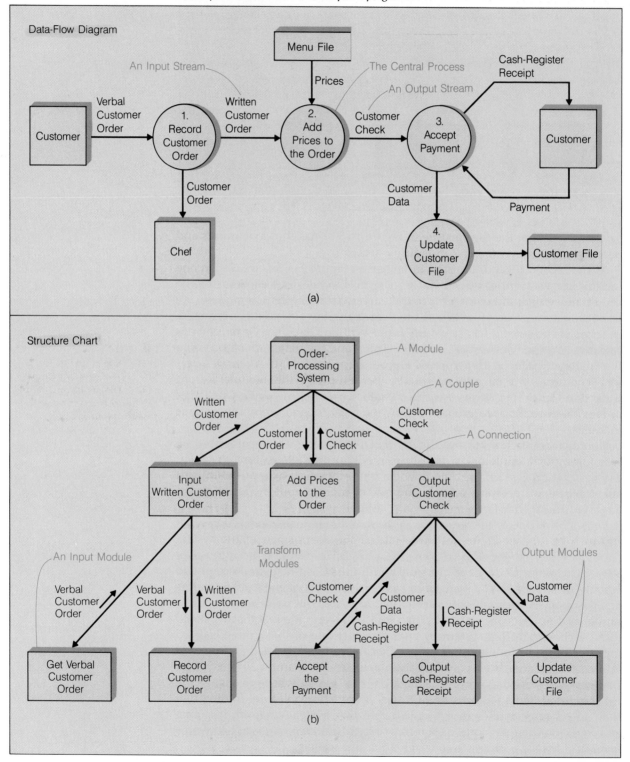

(a)

(b)

In the previous chapter we discussed the emerging importance of computer-aided software engineering (CASE). It is important to remember that CASE tools are used throughout the system-development life cycle. For example, in system design, CASE tools can be used to draw structure charts and to document structured-English descriptions of the internal processing of each program module.

Structure charts are used not only for designing computer programs, but also for application development without programming. When electronic spreadsheets or other fourth-generation languages are applied to complex problems, a structure chart can be used to organize and document the application. Unorganized and undocumented applications developed without programming create just as serious a problem as unorganized and undocumented programs.

We can implement some of the modules in a system by acquiring application software and implement others by coding programs. Recall Jose's plan (in Figure 6–17 of Chapter 6) to implement Angelo's recipe-pricing system by using an electronic spreadsheet for one process (module) within the system.

Design Modules—Process 3.2

In this subphase of the structured-design phase, we design the internal processing within each module. If we did a good job with our structured-English transform description in the analysis phase, and if the structure chart closely resembles the data-flow diagrams, then this subphase will be straightforward. We can convert structured English to *pseudocode* by adding input and output statements as well as control-type statements, such as those which control processing when errors occur. The decision tables and decision trees developed in the analysis phase will be useful in documenting the internal design of the modules.

PSEUDOCODE
English statements that look similar to computer program code. Since the statements are in English they are easier to read than program code.

Some designers prefer to use program flowcharts to document the internal design of modules (see Figure 7–7). If flowcharts are used, they should be structured. In the previous chapter we introduced the allowable control patterns of structured English. (see Figure 6–13). The same control patterns (simple sequence, selection, loop, and case structures) are allowed when we do pseudocode or structured program flowcharts. When drawing a structured flowchart, we should use only these patterns. Note again that we should avoid using a GO TO type of control pattern in structured programming.

Long and complex program flowcharts are often difficult to follow even when drawn in a structured manner. Therefore many designers are adopting the structured-English or pseudocode approach to document the processing that goes on within a module. Figure 7–8 shows a structured program flowchart and the same procedure documented in pseudocode.

Package the Design—Process 3.3

In packaging the design, we modify the design to fit the physical characteristics of the hardware and software configurations on which the system will be implemented. This physical environment can include such things as the program coding language, limitations of disk drives, and time restrictions. Thus far in the structured-design process we have attempted to produce an ideal design, independent of the physical environment in which it will be implemented. In packaging the design, we will modify it to fit the physical environment in such a way as to minimize deviation from the ideal design. We may have to do things like combine modules to produce a system that is efficient in terms of the machine resources (such as execution time and primary-storage usage) it uses. However, in our pursuit of efficiency we do not want to produce a system that compromises modularity and therefore is difficult to modify.

Figure 7–7
Program Flowchart Symbols

Symbols for program flowcharts are much simpler than those used for system flowcharts.

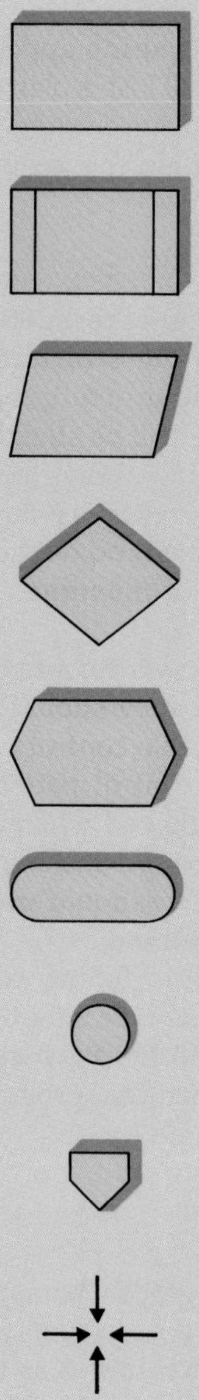

Symbol	Name	Description
	Processing	Instruction or group of program instructions for processing program
	Predefined Process	One or more named operations or program steps specified in a subroutine or another set of flowcharts
	Input-Output	Any function of an input-output device
	Decision	Decision involving branching to alternative points within the program
	Preparation	Instruction or group of instructions that changes the program
	Terminal	Beginning, end, or point of interruption of the program
	Connector	Entry from or exit to another part of flowchart
	Offpage Connector	Designation of entry or exit from a page of flowchart
	Flow Direction (Arrowheads)	Direction of data or processing flow

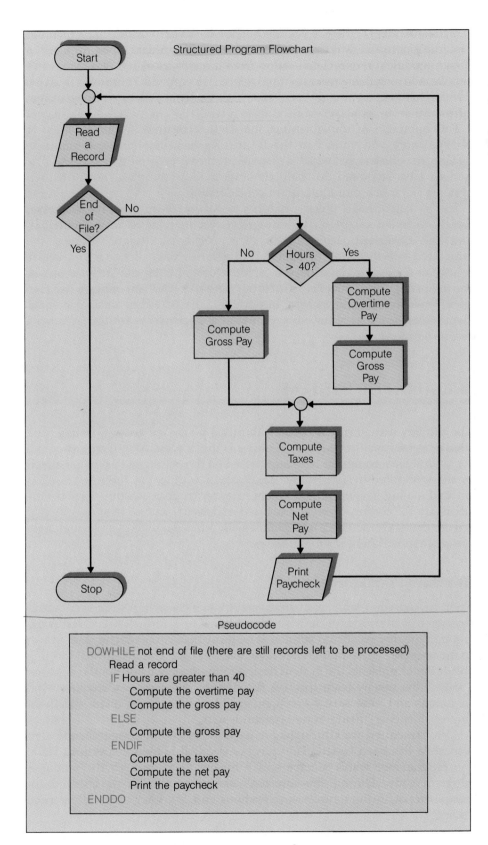

Figure 7–8
A Structured Program
Flowchart and Pseudocode

A program flowchart is a graphical way of representing the logic steps within a computer program. Some people find program flowcharts easier to follow than pseudocode.

Some analysts say that regardless of the physical environment, we should first implement the system based on the ideal design developed back in the design-modules phase. Then, after the system is working, we can worry about modifying the system to improve efficiency. As Ed Yourdon, a systems development expert and author, states, "It is easier to make a working system efficient than to make an efficient system work."

This approach of implementing the ideal structured system is likely to become more widespread in the future. As hardware prices continue to decline, the efficiency at which a system executes is becoming less critical. The human labor required to maintain and modify complex, nonstructured systems is a much more important consideration.

The package-design phase produces two primary outputs: the **test plan**, which documents a plan for testing the system prior to implementation, and the **packaged design** itself. The packaged design includes the structured specifications of data-flow diagrams, data dictionary, structure charts, and module descriptions. Module descriptions can include one of the following: pseudocode, structured English, decision tables, decision trees, and program flowcharts. In addition, the packaged design includes layout sketches that show how inputs and outputs are to appear on the screen or on paper.

■ BUILD THE SYSTEM

The primary activities that occur within this phase are coding, testing, and developing manual procedures. **Coding** is the process of writing a program (or module) in a computer language, based on the packaged design generated in the structured-design phase. The task of coding the modules is often divided among several programmers in order to decrease the elapsed time necessary for coding. A well-structured and well-specified system will help ensure that each module is compatible with other modules even though they are written by different programmers.

Structured Walkthroughs

Prior to coding, many companies are now performing **structured walk-throughs** of the program and system design. In a formal structured walk-through the design documentation is made available to a review team of two to four people. These individuals review the design, and in a formal meeting the designer presents the system design to the review team. As the designer "walks" the review team through the design, questions are clarified. And omissions and necessary corrections are identified. Quite often significant improvements are made in the system design.

Also, structured walkthroughs are used to review the program code after a module has been coded. This process is called a **code inspection.** Here, the programmer walks members of a review team through the module's program code. During this process, the program code is checked for compliance with the module specifications and for other types of errors in coding.

Top-Down Coding

Many firms that use structured programming advocate **top-down coding.** In top-down coding the modules on the structure chart are coded, starting with the top module and going down through the lower levels. The top module is coded and tested, then successively lower levels of modules are coded and tested, going from the top to the bottom of the chart. Many modules are coded concurrently. In fact, sometimes the coding process overlaps with the system-design phase. However, the emphasis is on starting and completing the coding of the top modules first. Certainly, coding of the higher-level modules can begin before the design of the lower-level modules is complete.

Top-Down Testing

After a module is coded, the first test to be performed is a **desk check,** which is a manual review of a module's logic. Both the programmer and the supervisor review the module. Desk checking also includes manual tracing of hypothetical data (both valid and invalid) through the module's logic in order to verify that it will process that data correctly. For example, a payroll check for one million dollars or a requisition for inventory in excess of ten thousand dollars can be evaluated in terms of the logic and controls incorporated in the system.

A structured walkthrough of the program module code can be very useful at this point. Either formal or informal inspections of the code will often identify improvements that can be made in the program code.

After desk checking, modules are *compiled* without execution. The compilation step almost always detects several deviations (*compiler diagnostics*) from the rules and syntax of the particular computer language being used. After these errors are corrected, the module is compiled and executed with test input.

COMPILE
To translate a computer program expressed in a problem-oriented language (such as COBOL or FORTRAN) into machine language.

COMPILER DIAGNOSTICS
Errors detected in a computer program during its compilation.

When programs are structured, this testing can be done in a top-down fashion (see Figure 7–9). Top-down testing is performed when enough modules have been coded (usually the top-level module and some of the second-level ones) to make the testing significant.

Program stubs are used to test these modules. Program stubs are dummy modules that are called by the parent module. They have input/output behavior which is sufficiently similar to the yet-to-be-coded real module that the parent module can be executed. Figure 7–9 illustrates testing with program stubs of the system depicted in Figure 7–6. The top module as well a second-level one, the Input Written Customer Order module, have been coded. All the Program Stub modules perform input and output functions simulating the modules that are yet to be coded.

In addition, the program stubs write out a message, such as "output customer check has been called," every time the particular dummy module is called. The message allows the programmer to trace each program stub being called by the parent module. This makes the debugging task easier. As modules are coded they can be substituted for the program stubs. Then, in turn, if these modules call other modules that are yet to be coded, new program stubs can be inserted.

Figure 7–9
Top-Down Testing

Top-down testing allows a programmer to test a new system, using a module-by-module approach.

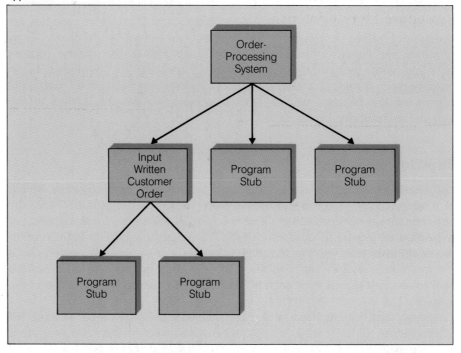

Top-down testing has significant advantages. The testing of the system can proceed in a top-down fashion as each module is coded. This spreads the testing over a longer period of time and avoids "crash" testing in a restricted time period after all the modules have been coded. In addition, errors are likely to relate to the most recently inserted module since all the other modules have been previously tested and corrected. Therefore, errors are much easier to isolate and correct.

Preparation of **test data** is an important step. Inadequate test data can be very costly later on because of undetected errors (*program bugs*). Test data should be comprehensive, covering every possible type of valid and invalid input that could exist when the module is operational. Development of adequate test data usually requires that users participate, since they are most familiar with the various combinations of inputs that may occur. When the test data are used, every statement in the module should be executed, including logic that is seldom used; otherwise the test will not be thorough. Software tools are available to identify the executed and unexecuted module statements. The expected output from the test data input should be determined by means that are independent of the module being tested. In this way the programmer can ascertain whether the module's processing is valid.

After each coded module has been tested in a top-down fashion and then corrected, the modules are tested collectively as a system, using similarly

PROGRAM BUG
An error in a computer program.

comprehensive test data. Once the system has been tested with hypothetical data, the final test prior to implementation should be the processing of real data at the volume levels expected when the system is installed.

Procedure Development

System analysts and user personnel usually develop operating procedures for the system concurrently with module coding and testing. A complete written set of manual procedures must be developed that documents all manual processes to be performed by both user and data-processing personnel in the actual operation of the system. The procedures should cover such items as input preparation, control and balancing, error correction, and computer-operator instructions. Collectively, these procedures form a critical part of the system's documentation.

must make a manual for users.

Documentation is sometimes the most neglected aspect of the system-development life cycle. Firms frequently depend on a key individual or group of individuals to design and operate an information system. If these people rely on their memories for programming, systems, and operating information, and then they find other employment, the firm has to study and document the existing system before work can begin on modifying it or designing a new one. Rarely can anyone remember all the detailed design information of a complex computer information system.

Adequate documentation includes:

1. All the specifications in the system-development life cycle.
2. Data-flow diagrams and structure charts.
3. Data dictionaries.
4. Hardware specifications.
5. Performance specifications.
6. Job descriptions.
7. Procedure manuals.
8. Program and system test documentation.

programmers must document all this

Chief-Programmer Teams

Many firms organize their programming efforts into chief-programmer teams. This team consists of a chief programmer (who in effect supervises the team), one or more programmers, a documentation specialist, and a back-up programmer. The back-up programmer acts as an assistant to the chief programmer, and together they code the more important modules of a system. Other programmers in the team code the remaining modules.

The documentation specialist, is one of the key people on the team. The primary responsibility of the documentation specialist, is to maintain up-to-date documentation for the system the team is working on. Often, programmers do not enjoy doing the clerical and filing tasks necessary to maintain this up-to-date documentation. The documentation is centralized, rather than being under the control of individual programmers, and is available to anyone on the team. The documentation specialist's functions include maintaining copies of program listings, updating test data, picking up computer output, and maintaining up-to-date documentation in a secure file.

■ CONVERSION

In the conversion phase of the system-development life cycle, the user and system personnel must work closely together. Selling the new system to user personnel is an important factor in its future success. Any new system, especially one involving a computer, can be viewed as a threat to the security of some user personnel. Some resistance to change can be overcome if user personnel are meaningfully involved in the system development effort, and this is possible for most phases of development.

A substantial training program may be required if the change in the system is significant. Often employees view training programs as a threat because they believe that evaluations made at the end of the program will be used against them. These people sometimes lack the self-confidence they need to return to school after many years of absence. The analyst must take these reservations into account when planning a training program. There should be an orientation program for all personnel that will have contact with the system in any way.

Two potentially difficult personnel problems are the relocation of displaced employees and adjustments to the organizational structure. If relocation is necessary, the personnel department should be involved in the process as soon as possible, since relocation may require a large adjustment on the part of the employee. Also, employees should be kept fully informed of any changes so that rumors are minimal.

Adjustments to the organizational structure will present human-relations problems also. Changes in supervisory positions or in relationships should be handled in a professional manner. New positions should be meaningful and not created simply to postpone the retirement of an older employee. Job enrichment and other personnel programs are appropriate in these circumstances.

The major physical changes involved in the conversion phase are site preparation and file conversion. Changes in hardware or work flow will require changes in the physical location of the system or the personnel, or both. These must be well planned and coordinated. Inadequate preparation of the site will impair the performance of the system when it begins to operate.

Prior to conversion, files and data bases must be created for the system either through manual inputs (if the old system was manual), or a combination of manual inputs and conversion of data from the old files. Converting files and data bases is often time consuming and costly, and it requires special programs. A critical point in this phase is the control of file conversion. File-conversion programs must be thoroughly tested: new file listings must be manually reviewed for errors, and control totals must be balanced. Until file conversion has taken place, it is not possible to operate the new system.

After personnel and physical changes have been taken care of in the implementation stage, steps must be taken to phase out the old system. Although this may seem obvious, there are numerous instances where new systems have been brought online and the old systems (especially manual ones) have not been terminated.

POST-IMPLEMENTATION AUDIT
AND MAINTENANCE

A frequently overlooked but necessary step in the system-development life cycle is the **post-implementation audit.** Two general areas are reviewed at this point. The performance of the new system is evaluated in terms of the objectives that were stated in the feasibility and analysis phases, and the system-development life cycle is reviewed. The budgets and schedules developed in the feasibility and analysis phases can be used to evaluate the performance of the system-development team.

For example, error rates and processing times can be compared with the rates in the design specifications of the system. User complaints can also be considered. Failure of the system to achieve the design specifications might mean that the expected benefits from the new system will never be realized. It also may mean that the system is not being operated according to the specifications.

Another aspect of evaluating the new system involves comparing the actual operating costs with the estimated costs. Significant deviations over the estimated costs have a negative impact on the cost-benefit ratios of the new system.

Who should conduct the audit? For small projects, the supervisor of the system analysts is generally appropriate. When a large project is reviewed, a team of system personnel and managers who were not part of the project is appropriate. Internal auditors are frequently involved in the post-implementation audit of a large system. Sometimes people outside the firm conduct the audits. Their lack of personal connections, their broader experience, and their view of the organization all contribute to a more objective review. Many companies also have periodic audits of systems in addition to the post-implementation audit.

The life span of an application system can be significantly extended through proper maintenance. Maintenance consists of promptly correcting any additional errors discovered in modules, updating the program modules to meet modified requirements, and maintaining the documentation to reflect system and module program changes.

■ Summing Up

■ The steps in the system-development life cycle are feasibility study, system analysis, hardware evaluation, system design, building the system, conversion, and audit/maintenance.

■ The documents produced during structured analysis are extensively used during system design and implementation.

■ A structure chart is a hierarchical diagram showing the relationship between various program modules. It is derived from data-flow diagrams.

■ The structure chart is used as a guideline for designing the individual modules. The structured-English statements written earlier may be used for documentation at this stage.

■ The design is packaged and then modified to suit the hardware and software environment. In addition to the packaged design, a test plan is produced at this time.

- Structured walkthroughs are often used to review the packaged design as well as the program code.
- Coding and testing are done in a top-down manner. This means that the upper-level control modules are coded and tested before the detailed, lower-level modules are even written.
- Procedure manuals are generally written concurrently with coding and testing. These form a critical part of the final system.
- Programming personnel are often organized into a chief-programmer team. Many firms have found this to be an efficient structure.
- The conversion phase may involve many problems, such as user resistance, personnel relocation, and changes in the organizational structure. Careful planning is a must at this stage.
- After the system has been converted, an audit is done to judge its performance against the original system objectives.
- Maintenance of a system consists of removing any additional program errors and changing the system to meet new information-processing requirements.

■ Key Terms

structured design	packaged design
structure chart	coding
top-down design	structured walkthrough
go-to-less programming	code inspection
spaghetti code	top-down coding
module	desk check
subroutine	program stubs
connection	test data
couple	program bug
central process	documentation
transform	post-implementation audit
pseudocode	
test plan	

■ Review Questions

1. What is a structure chart?
2. What is the difference between a structure chart and a data-flow diagram?
3. Explain the following terms:

    a. Module
    b. Subroutine
    c. Transform
    d. Connection
    e. Couple

4. Is the system-design document analogous to the blueprints an architect produces for a building? If so, how?

5. Why is it important that a module only have a single entry from and a single exit back to its parent module?

6. What is structured programming?

7. How are pseudocode, structured English, and program flowcharts related?

8. What are the outputs of the design packaging subphase?

9. Explain the concept of a structured walkthrough.

10. What is top-down coding?

11. How are program stubs used in testing?

12. What are test data? What qualities should they possess?

13. Why is documentation important to the users and to program maintenance personnel?

14. Describe the composition of a chief-programmer team.

15. List the major problems that may be encountered during system conversion.

16. Why must file conversion be closely controlled?

17. What is the significance of the post-implementation audit?

1. Omega Systems, a management consulting firm, is designing a new inventory control system for Nordener & Mufti, a distributor of petroleum products. The president of Nordener & Mufti feels that costs can be minimized by designing the new system so that it uses most of the existing hardware and software. The project manager at Omega does not agree. She believes that this would unduly restrict the design options and probably lead to the development of an inefficient system. Discuss the merits and demerits of both viewpoints, and give your opinion on the matter.

2. Despite the popularity of the top-down approach, some programmers are skeptical about its usefulness. One common complaint is that the top-level control modules cannot be coded unless the programmer knows exactly what takes place in the lower-level modules. Another problem is the difficulty of creating a simple hierarchy. Since some lower-level modules are called by more than one upper-level routine, the neat, inverted tree structure sometimes cannot exist. Maintenance is not as easy as the proponents of top-down design claim it to be. Most system modifications are never anticipated at the time of original design, and the top-down structure is therefore unable to accommodate these changes. Comment on the validity of these objections. If they are valid, does it mean we should abandon the top-down approach?

3. The system development department for Gatt's Manufacturing Company has a policy whereby computer programs for new systems are written and tested by different programmers. These programs are then put together into various subsystems. Once the subsystems have been written and tested, the whole system is integrated and tested by the user department. In developing an integrated accounts payable/purchasing system, a programmer did not properly code and test an error-checking module used for month-end processing. At the end of the month, the program malfunctioned and brought the whole purchasing system to a halt. It took three weeks to correct the system because several programs had to be changed. A committee was formed to review the company's policies for designing and testing new systems. What design and testing strategy could have been used to prevent this problem?

Discussion Questions and Cases

4. In the past year, the internal audit department of Flextix Corporation, a watch manufacturer, hired an electronic data processing (EDP) auditor. The auditor recently completed a review of the administrative accounting systems and the system-development methodology used to implement the systems. He noted that no post-implementation audit had been performed. He discussed his concern with the system-development director and the corporate controller. The director argued that the post-implementation audit was a waste of time because he and the controller maintained close contact with all user problems. The director also said it was the internal audit department's job to perform all auditing work in order to have an objective opinion on the status of a new system. The auditor argued that it was system development's responsibility to perform the audit. Are post-implementation audits needed? If so, who should perform them?

5. Many of the Cobb Company's data-processing systems were developed in the early to mid-1970s, before there was widespread acceptance of the structured design and structured programming approaches. Although the systems are working properly and they meet management's information needs, an increasing percentage of system development's time is spent in maintaining existing programs. Currently, about 65 percent of the effort in system development is concentrated on maintenance of these existing systems. In addition, in the past two years the internal audit department has hired two EDP auditors, who specialize in auditing computer information systems. In performing their duties, they must often review the code in these programs. They have found, however, that it is almost impossible to follow the logic of the code. Therefore, they have abandoned direct review of program code as an audit technique. Do you think that Cobb has a problem? If so, what is the nature and cause of the problem? What do you recommend to correct it?

6. Smith's is a regional department store chain located in the Middle Atlantic states. Smith's extends credit to all of its creditworthy customers and has a large number of outstanding accounts receivable. About 60 percent of Smith's sales are on credit. The company has had an on-line accounts receivable system for the past eight years. Recently, this accounts receivable system has been redesigned and recoded to operate as a data base management system. In the design process, most of the input screens and output screens, and much of the program logic, were modified to better meet user and customer needs. The new system has been thoroughly tested and is now ready for conversion. The manager of systems development advocates using a direct conversion approach. Under a direct approach the new system would be implemented at all stores and the old system would be abandoned at the same time. But, others in the organization prefer a pilot approach, whereby two or three stores would be converted initially. The manager of systems development feels that direct conversion is the most appropriate for the following reasons: (1) the new system has been thoroughly tested, (2) employees can be trained in the use of the new system before conversion, and (3) employees are familiar with the use of an on-line accounts receivable system. Would you support either a direct or a pilot conversion, or some other method? Support your position.

7. Servo-Motor, Inc., a manufacturer of special and standardized electric motors, started a project to provide their managers with better, more reliable information. It was decided that the best alternative would be to develop a new computer system. John Lucas was chosen as the project manager for the whole systems life cycle. Since development was being rushed by top management, Mr. Lucas decided to neglect producing complete procedural manuals, and rely on his own memory to maintain and run the system. Is documentation an important part of the development life cycle, and if so should Mr. Lucas develop better documentation for its new system?

Application Development by End Users ▌ Chapter 8

CHAPTER OUTLINE

Introduction

Problems with Conventional Application Development
Increasing Labor Cost
Long Time Span Required
Slow Implementation of Changes
Work Overload
Prespecified versus User-Driven Computing

Methods for User Development of Application Software
Personal-Computer Tools
Query Languages and Report Generators
Graphics Generators
Decision-Support/Financial-Modeling Tools
Application Generators

Blending User Development with Conventional Development
Types of Application Development
Data-Base Administration
End-User Development and Computer-Aided Software Engineering (CASE)
Some Cautions about Application Development by End Users

Information Centers

Changing Roles of System Analysts and Programmers

Summing Up

Key Terms

Review Questions

Discussion Questions and Cases

■ INTRODUCTION

**APPLICATION DEVELOP-
MENT BY END
USERS**
This approach to application
development is often called
end-user computing or
application development
without programming.

END USERS
Persons who ultimately use
application software.

**FOURTH-GENERATION
LANGUAGE**
User-friendly computer
software that enables end users
to create application software in
one-tenth the time required by
typical third-generation
languages such as BASIC,
FORTRAN, and COBOL.
Examples of fourth-generation
languages are Lotus 1-2-3,
dBase III, and Focus.

Many information-system experts believe that a large percentage of business applications can be developed by users. *Application development by end users* means that the *end users* acquire and/or develop software without the assistance of programmers, and quite often without system analysts. This approach is often called application development without programming.

There are essentially three ways that end users can create or obtain application software without programming. First, users can be given powerful but easy-to-use computer tools to create their own application software without assistance from system analysts or programmers. These tools are often called *fourth-generation languages.* An example is an electronic spreadsheet. Second, consultants or system analysts can work directly with end users to generate application software through the use of fourth-generation languages that are too technical for end users to employ without assistance. Third, preprogrammed application software packages can be purchased from outside vendors.

We will examine some of the problems associated with the conventional application-development approach. Next we will discuss a variety of methods end users can employ to develop application software, and then cover the blending of user development with conventional development. Finally, the impact of user-developed software on the conventional information-system organization will be examined. We will also discuss information centers and the changing role of system analysts and programmers.

Keep in mind that application development by end users does not make obsolete the basic steps used in the system-development life cycle we studied in Chapters 6 and 7. As we stated at the end of Chapter 6, application development by end users only changes the degree to which these steps are performed and how they are performed, not whether they are performed.

■ PROBLEMS WITH CONVENTIONAL APPLICATION DEVELOPMENT

Conventional application-system development is the process studied in the last two chapters. Figure 8–1 illustrates the conventional system-development life cycle using the structured approach. It has several shortcomings as discussed below.

Increasing Labor Cost

The conventional development cycle is a labor-intensive, time-consuming process. The labor costs associated with system analysis and programming continue to increase, while the price of computer hardware continues to decline (see Figure 8–2). In the late 1970s the cost of hardware became lower

Figure 8–1
Structured Development Life Cycle

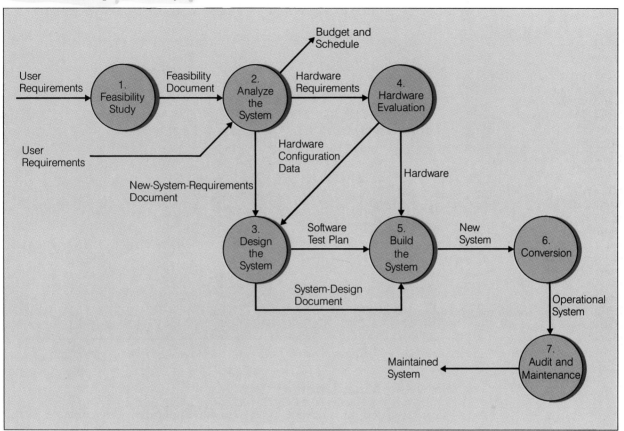

than labor cost for information-system organizations. This relationship between labor and hardware costs makes it economical to substitute hardware for labor.

With application development by end users, software is developed directly by end users through the use of computers and fourth-generation languages. This eliminates part of the labor cost of programming, and to some extent, system analysis. Obviously, it increases hardware costs because computers have to be used to execute fourth-generation languages. Also, these languages usually do not produce program code that executes as efficiently as program code written by programmers. However, this is of little concern because of the dramatic decline in hardware costs.

Long Time Span Required

A major disadvantage of the conventional approach is the long time span (months and sometimes years) required for the development of application software. Because of the dynamic nature of most businesses, the needs for the software (which were originally defined in the feasibility stage) may have changed substantially by the time the system is operational. Therefore, the system is sometimes obsolete by the time it is implemented.

Figure 8–2
Software Costs versus Hardware Costs

As fourth-generation languages become more widely used, software costs should begin to decline.

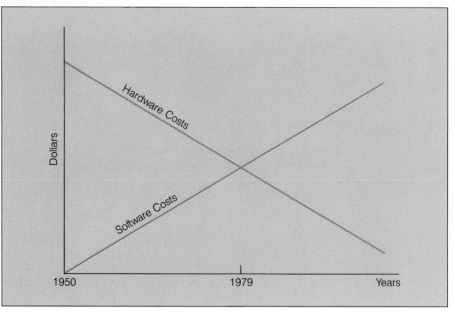

Slow Implementation of Changes

JAMES MARTIN
James Martin is a well-known author and lecturer who specializes in data-base management systems and fourth-generation languages. He is recognized as one of the premier authorities in these areas.

Closely related to the long time span for application development is the typically slow implementation of changes to the system. *James Martin* has stated that the mere act of implementing a system changes the requirements for that system. In other words, after a system is implemented it will affect the user organization in unforeseen ways. Martin maintains that it is impossible to foresee all the effects of a new system on an organization's information needs. There will be requests for changes to the system immediately, as it is implemented, since the user really cannot experience the new system until it is implemented. If systems are going to be successful, we must be able to implement changes rapidly. This is often difficult to do with the conventional development cycle.

Work Overload

Maintenance of application software is a major concern. In fact, most mature information-system organizations find that 50 to 75 percent of their programming effort is in the maintenance of existing systems as opposed to the programming of new systems. If this trend continues, we may find firms spending almost all their programming effort on maintaining existing systems!

Due to the declining price of hardware, many new users have purchased computers. If we depend on programmers to write the software for these computers, there will not be enough programmers to go around. In fact, for

Figure 8–3
Prespecified versus User-Driven Computing

Prespecified Computing

- Formal requirement specifications are created.
- A development cycle [such as that in Fig. 8–1] is employed.
- Programs are formally documented.
- The application development time is many months or years.
- Maintenance is formal, slow, and expensive.

Examples: Compiler writing, airline reservations, air-traffic control, and missile-guidance software development.

User-Driven Computing

- Users do not know in detail what they want until they use a version of it, and then they modify it quickly and often frequently. Consequently, formal requirement specification linked to slow application programming is doomed to failure.
- Users may create their own applications, but more often with an analyst who does this in cooperation with them. A separate programming department is not used.
- Applications are created with a fourth-generation language more quickly than the time to write specifications.
- The application development time is days or at most weeks.
- Maintenance is continuous. Incremental changes are made constantly to the applications by the users or the analyst who assists them.
- The system is self-documenting, or interactive documentation is created when the application is created.
- A centrally administered data-base facility is often employed. Data administration is generally needed to prevent chaos of incompatible data spreading.

Examples: Administrative procedures, shop-floor control, information systems, decision support, and paperwork-avoidance systems.

James Martin, *Application Development Without Programmers,* © 1982, p. 55. Reprinted by permission of Prentice-Hall Inc., Englewood Cliffs, NJ.

years there has been a shortage of application programmers. If new computer users are to get even minimal use of their hardware, we must find new ways of creating application software.

Prespecified versus User-Driven Computing

Martin has classified computing into two categories: prespecified and user-driven. In **prespecified computing,** processing requirements can be determined ahead of time. Therefore, formal requirement specifications can be created, and the conventional development cycle can be used. In contrast, in **user-driven computing** users do not know in detail what they want until they use a version of it. The users are in charge, they often develop their own systems, and they may modify the systems frequently and quickly. User-driven computing is the same as end-user computing. Figure 8–3 summarizes the differences between prespecified and user-driven computing.

Today it is not clear what percentage of business computing should be prespecified and what percentage should be user-driven. However, as users gain experience developing their own applications, user-driven techniques are certain to become the predominant approach. Martin states: "The requirements for management information systems cannot be specified beforehand and almost every attempt to do so has failed. The requirements change as soon as an executive starts to use his terminal. The point is *not* that conventional application development should be abandoned, but rather *it only works for certain types of systems*."[1]

METHODS FOR USER DEVELOPMENT OF APPLICATION SOFTWARE

Application development by end users became practical in the late 1970s and early 1980s owing to the availability of very powerful software. There are many of these fourth-generation tools. To be called fourth generation, a language should:

1. Enable users to develop software in one-tenth the time required by third-generation languages such as BASIC, COBOL, and FORTRAN.
2. Be user-friendly, user-seductive, and easy to learn and remember.
3. Be appropriate for use by both end users and information-system professionals.

This software can be classified into the six categories illustrated in Figure 8–4.

Personal-Computer Tools

There are a wide variety of **personal-computer tools** for end users. Electronic spreadsheets (Lotus 1-2-3 and Supercalc), data-base management systems (dBase III), and *integrated tools* (Enable, Framework, and Symphony) all may be easily applied by users. The ideal first step for those who are new to computers is to learn how to use one of these tools.

Query Languages and Report Generators

Query languages are usually associated with data-base management systems. They allow a user to search a data base or file, using simple or complex selection criteria. The results of the search can be displayed in detail or in summary format. For example, the query might state "List all customer accounts that are thirty to sixty days overdue and have a balance in excess of a thousand dollars." This type of software is widely available today. Many of the packages also allow update of the data base as well as data retrieval.

　　Report generators are similar to query languages except that they can perform more complex data-processing tasks and produce reports in almost any format. Generally, query languages are designed to be used without assistance from MIS professionals, whereas report generators sometimes do require help from system analysts or other professionals. One popular report generator, RPG, is discussed in Module B.

Graphics Generators

Graphic output is becoming increasingly important to today's business management. **Graphics generators** allow users to retrieve data from files or

INTEGRATED TOOL
A PC package that typically includes the functions of electronic spreadsheet, word processing, data-base management, and communications.

---

[1]James Martin, *Application Development without Programmers* (Englewood Cliffs, NJ: Prentice-Hall, 1982), 52.

Figure 8–4
Categories and Examples of Development Tools

Generally the easier-to-use tools run on personal computers. But some of the mainframe application generators such as Focus and Nomad 2 are also very user-friendly.

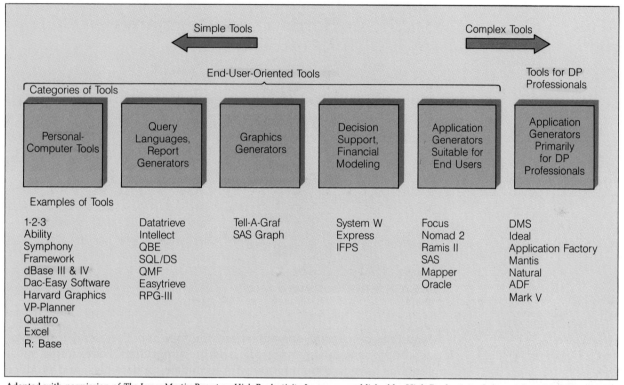

Adapted with permission of *The James Martin Report on High-Productivity Languages*, published by High-Productivity Software, Inc., Marblehead, MA.

data bases and display these data graphically. Users can specify the data they wish to graph and the basic format of the graph, such as pie, line, or bar. Figure 8–5 illustrates a graph made by a generator.

Decision-Support/Financial-Modeling Tools

The easiest to use **decision-support/financial-modeling tools** are electronic spreadsheets such as Lotus 1-2-3. More capable decision-support tools are available for large computers. Examples are System W, Express, and Integrated Financial Planning System (IFPS). These tools allow the construction of complex business models.

Application Generators

Application generators can create an entire information-system application including input, input *validation*, file update, processing, and *report generation*. The user usually specifies what needs to be done, and the application generator decides how to do it. In other words, the application generator generates program code based on the user's requirements.

VALIDATION
To check input for errors.

REPORT GENERATION
To produce information output.

Figure 8–5
A Graph Produced by a Graphics Generator

Graphics generators have substantially decreased the costs of producing professional-quality graphics.

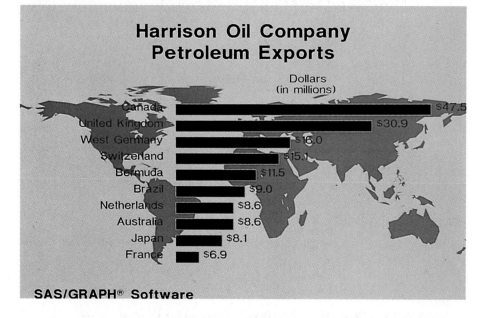

Many data-processing operations are routine, and they tend to be performed in the same manner regardless of the application. For example, most applications have to communicate with terminals, update files, and produce reports. These types of operations are preprogrammed in **generalized modules** in the application generator. When these operations are required, the application generator retrieves the preprogrammed modules and modifies them slightly for the particular application's needs.

It is unlikely that everything an application requires can be generated by an application generator. Each application is likely to have unique requirements. Therefore, most application generators contain **user exits**. User exits allow a user or programmer to insert program code that takes care of these unique requirements of the application. User exit routines can be programmed in a variety of languages, such as BASIC and COBOL.

Most application generators are interactive. Sitting at a terminal, a user and/or a system analyst respond to questions from the application generator. Their responses define the application inputs, files, processes, and reports. Based on these responses, the application generator generates code to execute the application. In a matter of hours, a *prototype* of the application may be up and running. This allows the user to experiment with the new application and make modifications if necessary. As you will notice in Figure 8–4, some application generators are suitable primarily for data-processing professionals.

PROTOTYPE
An experimental version of a user-developed application.

Table 8–1 lists some of the tools just discussed. The packages are classified as being suitable for end users or requiring professional help. A package is suitable for end users if a typical end user can, in a two-day course, learn how it works and can still use the package after several weeks of not working with it. The package should be easy to learn so the user can gain confidence in his

Table 8–1 ■ Leading Fourth-Generation Language Products

Notice that some of the application generators run on the IBM personal computer. This allows them to employ the same language on both mainframes and PCs.

Category/Product	Vendor	Environment	Suitable for	
			End User	Analyst
Personal computer tools				
dBase IV	Ashton-Tate	IBM Personal Computer, Various	√	√
Framework	Ashton-Tate	IBM Personal Computer, Various	√	√
Symphony	Lotus Development	IBM Personal Computer, Various	√	√
1-2-3	Lotus Development	IBM Personal Computer, Various	√	√
Query languages and report generators				
Datatrieve	DEC	DEC	√	√
Easytrieve	Pansophic Systems	IBM, Siemons	√	√
Intellect	Artificial Intelligence	IBM, Honeywell	√	√
RPG-III	IBM	System 38	√	√
QBE	IBM	IBM	√	√
QMF	IBM	IBM	√	√
SQL/DS	IBM	IBM	√	√
Graphics				
Business Graphics	Business Professional Software	IBM Personal Computer, Various	√	√
Tell-A-Graf	Issco	IBM, DEC	√	√
Decision support and financial modeling				
Express	Management Decision Systems	IBM, Prime	√	√
System W	Comshare, Inc.	IBM, IBM Personal Computer	√	√
Application generators suitable for end users				
Focus	Information Builders	IBM, IBM Personal Computer, DEC	√	√
Nomad 2	D & B Computing	IBM, IBM Personal Computer	√	√
Ramis II	Mathematica	IBM, IBM Personal Computer	√	√
SAS	SAS Institute	IBM, IBM Personal Computer, DEC, DG	√	√

Table 8–1 ■ (continued)

Category/Product	Vendor	Environment	Suitable for	
			End User	Analyst
Application generators for DP professionals				
DMS	IBM	IBM		√
Application Factory	Cortex Corp.	DEC	★	√
Ideal	Applied Data Research	IBM	★	√
Mantis	Cincom Systems	IBM	★	√
Mark V	Informatics General	IBM	★	√
Natural	Software AG	IBM, DEC	★	√

*Subset may be suitable for end users. Adapted with permission of *The James Martin Report on High-Productivity Languages,* published by Technology Insight, Inc., Marblehead, MA.

or her ability to use the package quickly. The user will learn more sophisticated applications as more experience is gained.

Figure 8–6 shows how Nomad 2, an application generator, generates the report in Figure 8–7. Note that only a minimum amount of information must be included in the commands to produce a report. Nomad 2 can easily produce much more complex reports than the one shown in Figure 8–7. Individuals experienced in writing programs in COBOL, BASIC, or FORTRAN are pleasantly surprised at how simple it is to produce meaningful reports with a language such as Nomad 2.

BLENDING USER DEVELOPMENT WITH ■ CONVENTIONAL DEVELOPMENT

Types of Application Development

When a firm attempts application development by end users, three types of development usually evolves:

1. The traditional development cycle is used, as illustrated in Figure 8–1. This is often used for those applications whose requirements can be prespecified and are likely to remain stable over a reasonable period of time.

2. A fourth-generation language is used as a prototyping tool. The system analyst and the user quickly generate a **skeleton application program** which serves as a model for the application. The end user can interact and experiment with this prototype and thereby refine the system's requirements. After the final requirements have been defined, the application can be programmed in a conventional fashion. Often parts of the prototype code can be used directly in the conventional programming process.

3. A fourth-generation language is used to develop the entire application. No programmers are used with this approach. The prototype itself becomes the application software.

The second approach is more likely to be successful in applications that process very high volumes of data because of hardware efficiency considerations. The basic model of the application can be developed by using an application generator, but the final application program is written in a

Figure 8–6
A Nomad 2 Report Request

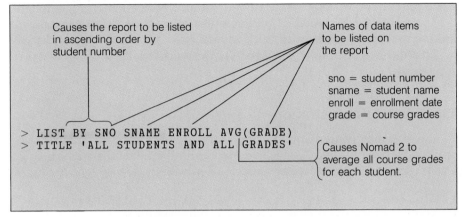

> LIST BY SNO SNAME ENROLL AVG(GRADE)
> TITLE 'ALL STUDENTS AND ALL GRADES'

Causes the report to be listed in ascending order by student number

Names of data items to be listed on the report

sno = student number
sname = student name
enroll = enrollment date
grade = course grades

Causes Nomad 2 to average all course grades for each student.

traditional programming language to produce code that is more efficient in terms of processing time and storage space. However, there are many business data-processing applications where the processing volume is not very high, and the number of times the program is run is very low. For example, some programs are of a one-time nature. Such applications are likely to use the third type of application development. The third type of application development is also more likely to be used whenever the application must be operational in a very short period of time and when the requirements are likely to change frequently.

We should also point out that the efficiency at which a particular program runs, that is, hardware efficiency, is becoming less and less important because of the declining cost of hardware. Therefore, the hardware efficiency reason for using application-development approaches 1 and 2 is declining in significance. Some would even argue that for most business data-processing applications, hardware efficiency is not a significant consideration. By the mid-1990s most application development will be done using the third approach.

Figure 8–7
The Report Produced by the Nomad 2 Report Request in Figure 8–6.

The sequence of this report could be changed by simply saying "by sname" instead of "by sno" in Figure 8–6.

```
PAGE 1
                ALL STUDENTS AND ALL GRADES

 STUDENT      STUDENT                ENROLLMENT      AVG
 NUMBER       NAME                      DATE        GRADE
 -------      -----------------      ----------     -----
      76      PAUL BRAXTON           SEP 78          2.0
      92      ANITA MACDONALD        SEP 78          3.5
     167      BRAD WHITLOCK          SEP 79          2.3
     198      ANN DISCALA            SEP 79          3.1
     436      JOSEPH PANE            SEP 78          3.1
     466      MARTHA LEVIN           SEP 79          3.3
     468      GARY ZANDER            SEP 78         no grade
```

Table 8–2 illustrates the effects of these three types of application development on the various steps of the application-development cycle. Note that when application development is done without professional programmers, the cycle is radically modified and compressed in time. The development process becomes a quick, informal, and interactive process. The user directly or with the aid of a system analyst creates and modifies his or her own applications.

Data-Base Administration

By now you may be thinking that application development by end users will result in isolated users creating their own redundant data files, which could result in chaos. How can we have users from various departments going off

Table 8.2 ■ Effects of Types of Application Development on the Application Development Cycle

	TYPE 1 Conventional Application Development	TYPE 2 Application Generator Used as a Prototyping Aid Followed by Programming	TYPE 3 Application Development Without Professional Programmers
Requirements Analysis	A time-consuming formal operation, often delayed by long application backlogs.	The user's imagination is stimulated. He may work at a screen with an analyst to develop requirements.	The user's imagination is stimulated. He may develop his own requirements, or work with an analyst.
System Specification Document	Lengthy document. Boring. Often inadequate.	Produced by prototyping aid. Precise and tested.	Disappears.
User Sign-off	User is often not sure what he is signing off on. He cannot perceive all subtleties.	User sees the results and may modify them many times before signing off.	No formal sign-off. Adjustment and modification is an ongoing process.
Coding and Testing	Slow. Expensive. Often delayed because of backlog.	The prototype is converted to more efficient code. Relatively quick and error-free.	Quick. Inexpensive. Disappears to a large extent
Documentation	Tedious. Time consuming.	May be partly automated. Interactive training and HELP response may be created online.	Largely automatic. Interactive training and HELP responses are created online.
Maintenance	Slow. Expensive. Often late.	Often slow. Often expensive. Often late.	A continuing process with user and analyst making adjustments. Most of these adjustments can be made very quickly—in hours rather than months.

James Martin, *Application Development Without Programmers*, © 1982, pp. 66–67. Reprinted by permission of Prentice-Hall, Inc., Englewood Cliffs, NJ.

and creating their own files containing redundant and uncoordinated data which cannot be accessed by other legitimate users? For example, data in a payroll system are often used by both the payroll and personnel departments.

The solution to this potential problem is effective **data-base administration.** Data bases are essential to the effective use of application development by users; thus the role of the *data-base administrator* becomes very important. He or she must assure that the data contained in the data base are sufficient to meet the needs of various users and that one or more users cannot modify the data in such a way as to destroy their usefulness to other people. Does this mean that each user is constrained in the ways that the data can be used because of the needs of other people in the firm? Certainly not. A user can extract portions of the data base and set these data up in his or her own files. The data can then be modified and massaged in any way the user sees fit, without harming the data in the data base.

DATA-BASE ADMINISTRATOR
The person responsible for coordinating the data base, including provisions for data security and prevention of data redundancy.

End-User Development and Computer-Aided Software Engineering (CASE)

Many of the application generator tools used by programmers and analysts to assist users through rapid prototyping are the same as (or very similar to) the application generators used in computer-aided software engineering (CASE). The underlying concept of using computers to assist in the creation of software is the foundation of both CASE and application development by end users. CASE tools are changing the methods that analysts and programmers use to create software, and fourth-generation languages are allowing end users to develop software. These two methods of creating software are tending to merge, with end users creating the relatively simple software and programmers and analysts creating the larger, more complex systems. However, programmers and analysts work directly with users and create rapid prototypes of these complex systems so that users can provide immediate feedback on their reactions to the prototypes.

Some Cautions about Application Development by End Users

As with most new approaches to solving problems, application development by end users is not without its potential pitfalls. Users are often not aware of or do not follow important software development standards, such as adequate documentation, built-in controls and edits, and proper testing. For example, let's assume that Jennifer West developed a complex real-estate-investment spreadsheet application for her firm. She did not document the application because she knew in detail how it worked, since she developed it. Furthermore, she was the only one to use the spreadsheet. The spreadsheet required the input of twenty-three pieces of data, and she did not build in any edits to check whether each data item was within a reasonable range. Jennifer had no problem using the spreadsheet. However, a year after completing the spreadsheet she left the firm, and her replacement, Emily, had to spend many hours figuring out how to use the spreadsheet. Also, the spreadsheet was designed to use a loan amortization calculation of only fifteen or thirty years. When Emily entered a loan term of twenty-five years, the spreadsheet appeared to work properly, but in reality the information it produced was erroneous. The firm was led to invest in a large real-estate venture in which they lost a substantial sum of money.

Another potential drawback of application development by end users is that it may not make sense for a highly paid professional or manager to spend a great deal of time developing software that a lesser-paid programmer or analyst could perhaps develop more economically. In essence, the professional or managerial user must decide whether to develop the software or delegate the software development to a computer professional, even though he or she will have to spend a great deal of time explaining the software requirements to the developer. Obviously, the answer to this question depends on the facts of each software development project. The decision is even more difficult if you, as a professional or managerial user, like to work with computers. In effect, you may ignore your job as accountant, manager, or whatever as you spend a great deal of time developing software.

Firms that have successfully applied application development by end users are aware of these problems. They establish standards for end-user software development and they manage software development by end users with the goal of preventing these pitfalls.

■ INFORMATION CENTERS

If application development by end users is to succeed, it must be coordinated and managed. The purpose of an **information center** is to manage the support for application development by users. Its primary objective is to encourage and accelerate the use of new software tools. The reasons for managing application development by users are:

1. To encourage the rapid adoption of application development by end users.
2. To assist users in their development efforts.
3. To prevent redundancy in application creation.
4. To ensure that data used in various applications are coordinated and not redundant.
5. To ensure that data are not created and stored in isolated, personal files.
6. To ensure that the systems created are controlled and auditable.

Figure 8–8 shows the typical organization of an information-system department that has an information center. **Technical Specialists** are experts on the various software tools and can assist in training end users to utilize the tools. In a smaller organization, the information center usually relies on technical specialists from the software vendor. For example, if a firm were using Focus and a technical problem occurred, the company would contact a specialist at Information Builders, the Focus vendor. Since application development by users is often done on PCs, there are **personal-computer consultants** at the information center. The **user consultants** work directly with users in creating applications. The user consultants also work closely with the data-base administrator. This is necessary to ensure that data used in both convention-

Figure 8–8
Organization of an Information-System Department That Has an Information Center
Information centers began to be implemented in the early 1980s.

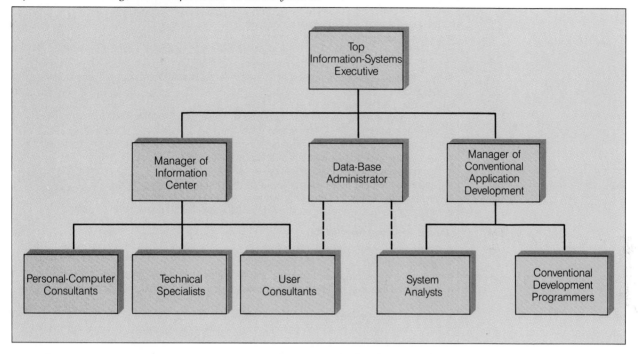

ally developed and user-generated applications are coordinated and not redundant. Figure 8–9 lists the functions typically performed by an information center.

CHANGING ROLES OF SYSTEM ANALYSTS
AND PROGRAMMERS

The advent of software that enables application development by end users causes the roles of system analysts and programmers to change. If fourth-generation software is to be used effectively, system analysts must recognize that there are many ways to create a new application and thus, move away from an over reliance on the conventional systems-development life cycle. In the requirements-analysis or feasibility-study phase, the system analyst must realize that there are many tools, any one of which may be appropriate for solving the user's problem. The tools for obtaining new applications are:

1. The conventional system-development life cycle.
2. The purchase of an application software package.
3. End users generating their own applications without outside help.
4. End users working with system analysts or information-center consult-ants, to generate the application.

Figure 8–9
Functions of an Information Center

By the Consultants:
- Training the users to employ the tools and create applications
- User encouragement, education, and selling
- Generation of applications (without programmers) in conjunction with users
- Generation and modification of prototypes
- Specification of changes to prototypes that may be needed to make them into working systems
- Consulting on user problems
- Determining whether a proposed application is suitable for Information Center development, and selecting the software and methods
- Demonstrations of Information Center capabilities to users, including senior management
- General communication with senior management
- Communication with traditional DP development
- Linking to the data administrator(s) in defining and representing data
- Maintaining a catalog of available applications and data bases
- Coordination to prevent duplicate or redundant application development

By the Technical Specialists:
- System set-up and support
- Dealing with technical and software problems
- Selection of languages and software and the versions of those which are used
- Assistance in choosing techniques or software for a given application (the job of the Techniques Analyst)
- Communication with vendors
- Monitoring system usage and planning future resources
- Charge-back to users
- Tuning or reorganizing an application for better machine performance
- Auditing system usage and application quality

James Martin, *Application Development Without Programmers,* © 1982, p. 306. Reprinted by permission of Prentice-Hall Inc., Englewood Cliffs, NJ.

5. System analysts and end users generating a prototype, experimenting with the prototype, and then coding the application in a conventional manner.

Many system analysts trained in conventional applications development find it difficult to change their roles. They continue to see themselves as the developers of systems, rather than serving as consultants to help end users develop their own systems. Perhaps the best way for a system analyst to encourage the use of these new software tools is to:

1. Search constantly for more effective and efficient ways of creating applications.
2. Avoid the use of programmers whenever possible.
3. Take on a consultant role and encourage users to employ the software themselves, rather than doing it for them.

Those of you who have planned a career in programming may be disturbed by the material in this chapter. It would be easy to imply that the demand for programmers will decrease drastically and perhaps even disappear as application development by end users continues to increase, which it will most certainly do. However, there will still be a large demand for programmers, for the following reasons:

1. The explosion in the use of computers has created a very large demand for application software developed both through conventional programming and by end users.

2. A significant proportion of all applications will continue to be of a prespecified nature, and therefore they will be well suited to the conventional development cycle.

3. System software such as operating systems and data-base management systems, as well as application software created by vendors, are likely to continue to be developed using conventional programming because of efficiency considerations. There is a large demand for programmers in this area. In fact, the most highly skilled programmers work for software vendors.

Summing Up

■ The conventional process of developing applications has several disadvantages:

    1. The high cost of programming expertise makes it very expensive.

    2. The time span for program development is usually very long.

    3. Program maintenance absorbs much programmer time, to the detriment of new-system development.

■ Computing can be classified into two categories:

    1. Prespecified.

    2. User-driven.

■ User-driven systems can be created through the use of five techniques:

    1. Personal-computer tools.

    2. Query languages/report generators.

    3. Graphics generators.

    4. Decision-support/financial-modeling tools.

    5. Application generators.

■ When application development by end users is employed, three types of application development usually evolves:

    1. Conventional application development cycle.

    2. Prototyping with a fourth-generation language and subsequent coding with a conventional language.

    3. Total system development with a fourth-generation language.

■ Data-base administration is very important when users develop their own applications. It has to ensure that data redundancy is minimized and that shared data resources are properly used by all.

■ The application development efforts of users can be coordinated by an information center. This center assists users in developing their own applications.

■ Many of the tools used in application development by end users are the same as those used in computer-aided software engineering.

■ If application development by end users is not well managed, software may be redundant, poorly documented, and not properly tested.

■ With more and more users creating their own applications, the roles of system analysts and programmers are changing.

■ Key Terms

application development by end users	generalized modules
end user	user exits
prespecified computing	prototype
user-driven computing	skeleton application program
personal-computer tools	data-base administration
query languages	information center
report generators	technical specialists
graphics generators	personal-computer consultants
decision-support/financial-modeling tools	user consultants
application generators	

■ Review Questions

1. What is application development by end users?
2. Which is more important for a MIS organization—labor costs or equipment costs?
3. How does the time span of conventional application development affect a system's utility?
4. Discuss the work overload on programmers and its implications.
5. Distinguish between prespecified and user-driven computing.
6. What is a query language?
7. Describe the basic purpose of a report-generator package.
8. Why are graphics languages becoming important for business people?
9. Explain the concept of an application generator.
10. What is the difference between a third-generation language and a fourth-generation language?
11. How does a report generator differ from an application generator?
12. Briefly describe three basic types of application development.
13. Discuss the role of the data-base administrator in a user-driven information-system environment.
14. Why is it important to have an information center to manage application development by end users?
15. Discuss the changing roles of programmers and system analysts.
16. What are some of the drawbacks of application development by end users?

■ Discussion Questions and Cases

1. Many large computer installations prescribe a standard language, such as COBOL or PL/I, for all programs to be executed on their equipment. Using a standard language would result in consistent documentation, but it could lead to certain problems. Based on the material discussed in this chapter, what problems would arise in this kind of environment?
2. Discuss whether each of the following applications is suitable for end user development. If so, which of the five methods of end user development would you use for each application? Explain the reasons for your choices.

    a. Sales forecast by territory
    b. Manufacturing process control
    c. Customer billing and accounts receivable
    d. Mailing list
    e. Course registration at a university
    f. Portfolio management

3. Frank Shields, the system development manager of the Carmel Corporation, has been inundated with requests to develop applications. In reviewing the file of unfulfilled requests, Frank began to wonder how many more requests have not been made known to him. Frank has been reading about this invisible, or shadow backlog of requests, and he does not know what to do. As much as Frank would like to maintain control over system development, he knows that one day he will have to let end users begin developing applications. What are some alternatives that Frank should consider in allowing end users to create their own computer application systems?

4. About two years ago, the JDF Corporation established an information center. Since then, the company has strongly supported application development by end users. Many end users are actively engaged in developing their own applications, both for personal computers and for the mainframe. Recently the internal audit department performed an audit of JDF's application-development by end user approach. The auditors found numerous instances of the same data being stored several times, both on the mainframe and on personal computers. In addition, they found that essentially the same application software had been created several times. For example, both the home-appliances division and the home-electronics division had created marketing-analysis systems using a mainframe program generator. Although the two systems are not identical, they are very similar. Based on their findings, the auditors have recommended that the corporation reassess its commitment to application development by end users. Do you agree with the auditor's recommendation? What recommendations do you have for the JDF Corporation?

5. Thomas Wesley is vice president of computer applications for a major U.S. corporation. He came to the company when it installed its first computer system twenty years ago. Mr. Wesley has never been convinced that application development by end users is a reliable way to produce computer applications. He would prefer that all computer applications be produced by programmers in his department. What advantages does application development by end users have that might change Mr. Wesley's mind? What arguments would Mr. Wesley use to refute those advantages?

PART THREE   ■ APPLICATION CASE

Corporate Programmers Lead the Way with CASE

By Janet Mason

Conditions were critical at Ramada Inc. in Phoenix, Ariz. "We're a small DP shop and we found that, more and more, we were addicted to buying mainframe software applications," said programmer/analyst Alexander Ingram. Accompanying this addiction was expensive software support and maintenance.

It's the classic story of a mainframe software backlog, and it rings particularly true in such information-intensive concerns as the financial industry and the U.S. government. The widening gap between technically advanced hardware and beleaguered software has left institutions with a dearth of new applications. Compounding this are mounting maintenance costs on some software applications that were developed more than a decade ago.

Along with a small, but rapidly growing, number of companies, Ramada is solving this problem by using personal computer- and mainframe-based computer-aided software engineering (CASE) tools.

CASE allows for more efficient development of software by automating routine analysis and programming tasks. Because it uses graphics, rather than the narrative style of traditional analysis, to demonstrate the data-flow diagram, users can more easily relate to CASE.

The basic concept of CASE is simple: It is software that assists in the development of software. Its finer details are more complex, however. There are two types of CASE. Front-end CASE aids in aligning the software strategy with business goals by analyzing the application. It also documents and designs the system with specifications residing in a dictionary or encyclopedia.

Back-end CASE takes the specifications and generates code to produce applications.

Both products run on a variety of hardware from PC to mainframe. Such vendors as Texas Instruments Inc. produce front- and back-end CASE tools. But many others, such as Index Technology Corp., produce one or the other, requiring interfaces to communicate with the other end.

While mainframes offer more memory and power, PCs present other advantages. "By using PCs we keep our development costs down because we don't have to tie up the larger VAX and IBM systems," pointed out Wayne Balmer, a senior systems analyst in the Information Engineering Association Division of E.I. du Pont de Nemours & Co.

"This keeps the software and hardware costs down considerably," added Mr. Balmer, whose Wilmington, Del., division is using CASE products to develop software for in- and out-of-house use.

Because CASE technology requires major changes in systems development and a substantial financial investment, many companies have hesitated to use it.

"It's really a cultural change from the emphasis of traditional systems design on writing code to doing analysis . . . and truly understanding the business problem," commented John Voss, systems development manager at Huntingdon National Bank, in Columbus Ohio.

At first glance, the investment figures are far less than enticing. "The software alone can cost anywhere between $5,000 and $20,000 per workstation, depending on the CASE tool used and the size of the application," noted Darvis Cormier, director of advanced system development for Touche Ross U.S.A.

Added to this is the training costs, which were placed at $5,000 to $10,000 per analyst for companies "aggressively" using CASE.

Mr. Cormier noted that this is "insignificant," compared to the money being spent in large shops for software development and maintenance.

"A lot of our clients are interested in CASE," he said, "But a smaller subset are starting to use it. In the next couple of years, I expect to see a dramatic increase."

Mr. Cormier is also a line partner in the management consultant practice of the firm's Dallas office, which offers CASE services.

"In an eight-year period of developing and maintaining in-house software with CASE, we estimate that it will cost $60,000 for each application," explained Ramada's Mr. Ingram, as "opposed to buying and maintaining commercial software for the same time period, which will cost us $180,000 for each application."

Mr. Ingram began his venture in CASE using Transform, a mainframe-based code generator from Transform Logic Corp., in Scottsdale, Ariz. After using Transform to generate hotel data bases and online ser-

PART THREE ▉ APPLICATION CASE

vice applications, he found the applications to be "more sophisticated than if they had been coded by hand."

"Transform generated 95 percent of the code on our IBM 4381, and we did the rest," said Mr. Ingram. "By using the tool, we were able to provide help screens for every field, every screen and transaction. These are niceties when coding by hand we would add if we had some slack time, which, of course, we never had."

Even with the benefits of using Transform, the staff was still doing manual analysis and design. So Ramada started using Excelerator/IS, from Index Technology Corp. of Cambridge, Mass., on its IBM PC XTs and ATs.

The analysis tool provided much the same benefits to the analysts that computer-aided design offers to engineers.

"The first draft of the data-flow diagram on Excelerator takes as long as doing it manually, which is about one day," explained Mr. Ingram. "But on subsequent drafts, after we show it to the end-user and refine it, we save an inordinate amount of time. [Manually] redrawing the diagram usually takes another day, but with Excelerator, I can change it in 10 minutes—and that's using a dot-matrix and not a laser printer."

Ramada designed its first system using CASE in about five months. Without CASE, it would have taken twice the time and a third more resources, Mr. Ingram noted.

Using the CASE tools required the staff to focus more on analysis than programming. With traditional systems design, stated Mr. Ingram, "You spend 25 percent of your time on upfront analysis and 75 percent coding the program. With the CASE tools we spend about 65 percent of our time on analysis and design and the rest on programming."

Consequently, everyone involved in the application development had an opportunity to sit down and talk to the users. "Everyone has the opportunity to learn more about how the business functions," continued Mr. Ingram. "We have had to start talking more like real people and less like computer people."

The CASE analysis forced the DP staff to standardize its practices. "We're all pretty much free spirits here and use different techniques for flow charting, program specifications, and so on," Mr. Ingram said.

"Using Excelerator forced us to develop consistent standards, and we are finding that we're becoming much more productive," he added.

The lack of standards presents a major snafu for many other CASE users. Dupont's Mr. Balmer said the major problem facing CASE is the large number of systems with different infrastructures. He added that incompatibility is particularly a problem when using the tools on different hardware platforms.

Still a Young CASE

Because CASE is relatively new, all of the bugs have not yet been ironed out of the products. "The major drawback of CASE is its immaturity," said Huntingdon National Bank's Mr. Voss, who has been using Texas Instrument's Information Engineering Facility to design customer information applications for the bank.

He added that he ran into a number of technical problems with the TI product that the vendor rapidly addressed. But since Mr. Voss is using a product that includes both front- and back-end CASE tools on a PC and mainframe, compatibility between products has not been a problem.

CASE users agree, however, that the technology's benefits far outweigh the drawbacks. "Looking at where software development is today, we believe that CASE is the future of software development. You can be with the leaders or the followers," said Mr. Voss.

Many users find that system documentation, which is stored in the dictionary, is high on the list of CASE's advantages.

"With online documentation we know exactly what we are working with," he continued. "It enables us to have more accurate system development."

Other users, including John Belbute with McDonnell Douglas Corp., find the emphasis on analysis a major benefit. The front-end analysis tool, even without using a code-generator, offers improved productivity and higher-quality systems.

"As an industry, we write great code," observed Mr. Belbute, a senior scientist with the McLean, Va., company that produces custom software for the Department of Defense. The major errors and maintenance problems stem from analysis and design, he maintained.

"The earlier errors are introduced into the system," he added," the more costly they are to repair."

Mr. Belbute works in the systems consulting division and uses Atlanta-based KnowledgeWare's Information-Engineering Workbench/Analysis Workstation to "make higher-quality software."

PART THREE ■ APPLICATION CASE

CASE keeps track of the details that are often over-looked in the traditional analysis process. "The KnowledgeWare tool shows a real-time representation of what is in the encyclopedia," he continued. "Consequently, when I change a data element in one place, it changes the same elements in all the other places as well."

While Mr. Belbute has already seen the tool improve the quality of systems development, he expects that major productivity improvements will be forthcoming.

A major advantage of CASE, stated Mr. Belbute, is that "everybody involved gets immediate feedback, including the end-users, systems analyst, and the IS [information system] manager.

"I've had users come in and sit down with me in the course of a morning, and go back to their office with data-flow diagrams," he noted. "This way, when the boss says, 'What did you do this morning?' they have a tangible product to show him."

While lauding the benefits of CASE, Mr. Belbute warns that it can't substitute for skills of a good analyst—only enhance them. The question that remains in the minds of many programmers is: Will they be replaced by code generators?

The answer from most CASE users is that the tool will elevate the programmer's status from code writer to analyst.

"Now instead of taking two weeks to write syntax, which CASE can generate in 45 minutes, they can spend their time on something much more exciting," said Sally Emery, director of corporate data resource management with UNUM, an insurance company in Portland, Maine.

Ramada's Mr. Ingram agrees. "We won't have too many people just sitting around writing code. People will have more interesting jobs if they want them."

Reprinted from *PC Week*, September 12, 1988 p. 51. Copyright ©: 1988 Ziff-Davis Publishing Company.

DISCUSSION QUESTIONS

1. What are the advantages of CASE?
2. Why are graphic techniques of system development superior to the traditional narrative techniques?
3. If CASE tools can be developed that automatically generate program code, do you think that CASE tools can be developed that generate data-flow diagrams, structured-English module documentation, and data dictionaries from existing program code? What advantages and impacts would such CASE systems have?

PART FOUR ■ Computer Resources

The Central Processing Unit and Storage Devices ■ Chapter 9

CHAPTER OUTLINE

Introduction

The Central Processing Unit
Primary Storage
Arithmetic-Logic Unit
Control Unit

Micros, Minis, Mainframes, and Supercomputers
Microcomputers
Minicomputers
Mainframe Computers
Supercomputers

Parallel Processing

Secondary Storage
Primary versus Secondary Storage
Magnetic Tape
Hard Disks
Floppy Disks
Laser-Optical Disks
Other Forms of Secondary Storage
Cache Memory

Summing Up

Key Terms

Review Questions

Discussion Questions and Cases

■ INTRODUCTION

The usefulness of a computer system for business purposes is largely determined by the characteristics of the **central processing unit (CPU)** and the storage devices. The CPU is the centerpiece of a computer system; strictly speaking, it is the computer (see Figure 9–1). Of course software and input/output devices are also important, but it is the traits of the CPU and storage devices, such as primary-storage size, that determine whether certain business applications are feasible on a given computer system. Therefore, understanding these basic characteristics is important to business users of computers.

In this chapter, we will cover the primary components of a CPU, explore the differences between mainframe, mini, and microcomputers, and examine

Figure 9–1
A Computer System

This chapter concentrates on the central processing unit and secondary storage. Chapter 10 covers data entry and data response.

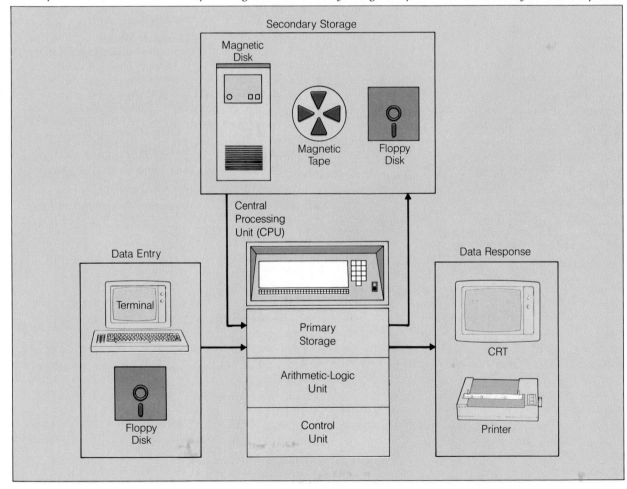

parallel processing. We will discuss primary and secondary storage, including the current media used in these two types of storage and the technology likely to be used in future computer systems.

■ THE CENTRAL PROCESSING UNIT

As illustrated in Figure 9–1, the central processing unit contains primary storage, the arithmetic-logic unit, and the control unit. We will discuss each of these below.

Primary Storage

Primary storage has three functions:

1. It stores operating-system programs which assist in managing the operation of the computer.
2. It stores the program being executed.
3. It stores data being processed by the CPU.

The bulk of data used by a computer application is stored in *secondary-storage* devices, but data must be stored in primary storage whenever the CPU is using them in processing. Therefore, data are continually being moved into and out of primary storage during the execution of a program (see Figure 9–2). For example, a complete customer record—that is, all the data associated with a particular customer—would most likely be stored in primary storage while the CPU was processing that customer's record.

Compared with secondary storage, primary storage allows faster access. Fast-access primary storage is necessary because the other components of the CPU, the control unit and the arithmetic-logic unit, operate at electronic speeds. If the CPU had to depend on mechanical movement to retrieve specific pieces of data, as is the case with disk- or magnetic-tape storage, the primary-storage access speed would become a major bottleneck for the CPU. This would decrease drastically the amount of work that could be performed by the CPU in a given amount of time. Ideally, the CPU should have a lot of very-fast-access primary storage; however, fast-access memory is more expensive than slower-access memory.

Early computer systems had modest amounts of primary storage. For example, a CPU with 64,000 bytes (characters) of primary storage was a large computer in the 1950s and 1960s. Many computers had 16,000 or less bytes of primary storage. Today, large computer systems may contain 5 to 500 megabytes of primary storage. Even personal computers have 128 kilobytes to 16 megabytes of primary storage.

The primary memory used in today's computers is made of very large scale integrated (VLSI) semiconductor chips. **Semiconductor chips** contain electronic circuits that can be reproduced photographically in a miniaturized form on silicon chips. These chips are often referred to as large-scale integrated (LSI) circuits or, in the case of advanced semiconductor technology, VLSI circuits. The development of semiconductor chips has revolutionized the

PRIMARY STORAGE
The storage within a central processing unit which holds the program being executed, the data the program is using, and all or part of the operating system. Primary storage is often also called memory, internal storage, main memory, and RAM (random-access memory).

SECONDARY STORAGE
A storage device that is not primary storage. In today's computers it is usually a magnetic or optical disk.

Figure 9–2
The Movement of Data Between Primary and Secondary Storage

Some programs, such as electronic spreadsheets, move a complete file into primary storage rather than part of it at a time. Others, such as data-base management systems, move only a few records from a file into primary storage at a time.

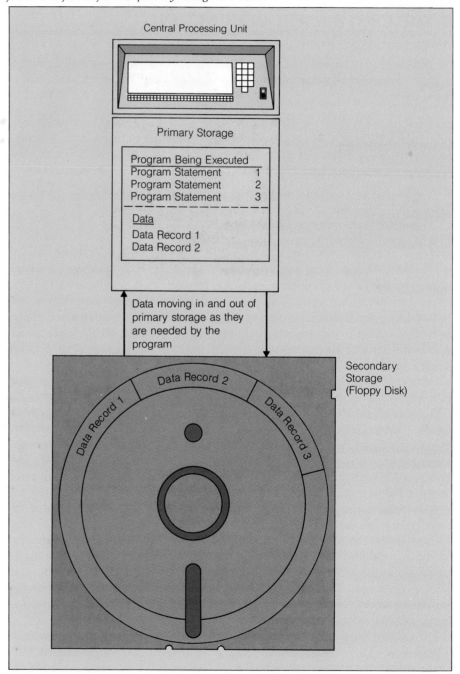

computer industry as well as other industries. For example, the calculator you can now buy at the grocery store for seven dollars would have cost more than a thousand dollars in the late 1960s.

The control unit and arithmetic/logic unit of a central processor can be placed on a single semiconductor chip. The processors on a chip are called **microprocessors** and are the basis for the microcomputer industry (see Figure 9–3). In fact, a CPU with much more computing power than the *ENIAC* computer of the 1940s can be placed on a chip approximately a quarter-inch square, whereas the ENIAC required a large room. Figure 9–3 shows a chip greatly magnified; the actual size is about a quarter-inch square. Figure 9–4 and 9–5 illustrate two of the tasks performed in manufacturing semiconductor chips.

It should be noted that microprocessors contain only the control unit and the arithmetic/logic unit. Primary storage is contained on separate (semiconductor) memory chips that plug into the system board.

There are two advantages of using the semiconductor chip in computer hardware. First, it can be reproduced in great quantities by automated means and is therefore inexpensive. A microprocessor (CPU) on a chip may cost less than ten dollars per copy. Second, the miniaturization of circuits has greatly enhanced the speed of the computer. The speed at which a CPU operates is limited by two factors—the speed at which electrical currents flow (about one-half the speed of light) and the distance over which they must flow.

ENIAC
The first electronic digital computer.

Figure 9–3
A VLSI Microprocessor

This is a 32-bit microprocessor, meaning that when it performs operations on data it moves 32 bits at a time (the equivalent of four characters).

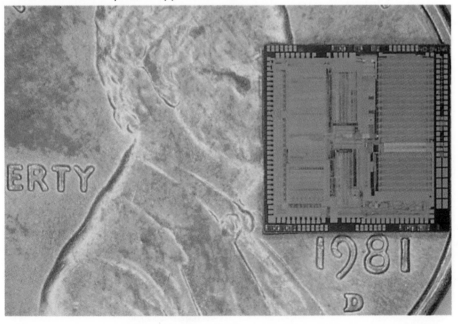

Figure 9–4
Seventy Thousand Parts per Quarter Inch

Tamara Bish inspects a reticle at NCR Corporation's microelectronics facility in Colorado Springs, Colorado. Comparable to a photographic negative, this reticle and others similar to it are used to pack more than 70,000 active microelectronic elements onto the NCR/32, a ¼-inch-square microcomputer chip. The reticle is inserted into a "wafer stepper" as part of the process of creating more than 100 microchips on a 5-inch silicon wafer.

Figure 9–5
Mirror, Mirror

Technician Rosa Burch reflects on four silicon wafers she is loading into a "plasma etcher" at NCR Corporation's microelectronics facility in Colorado Springs, Colorado. More than a hundred computer microprocessor chips can be etched on each wafer. Snow White's nemesis probably would have received a much more complex response had she been talking to this device rather than to a standard wall mirror.

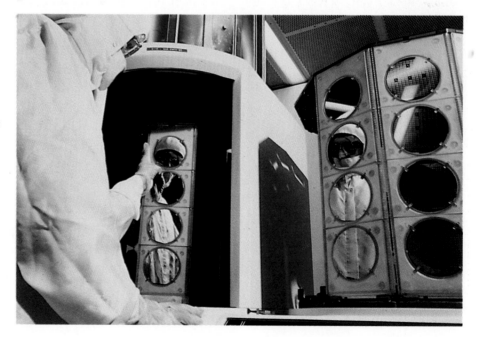

Computer designers have been able, through miniaturization, to greatly decrease this distance and thus greatly increase the speed of CPUs. Improvements in semiconductor technology are the primary driving force behind improvements in computer hardware. It appears that semiconductor technology has not yet reached its theoretical limits. Therefore, we can expect substantial additional improvements in hardware performance.

Semiconductors used in primary storage represent a *bit* of data by means of an individual circuit that either conducts or does not conduct electricity. From this fact arises the primary disadvantage of using semiconductors for primary storage. When the electrical supply to a CPU using semiconductor storage is interrupted, none of the circuits conducts electricity. Therefore, the CPU loses the data contained in primary storage, including any programs located there. Semiconductor storage is **volatile,** that is, the storage loses its data representation when electrical power is interrupted. This can be overcome with an uninterruptible power source (provided by back-up batteries and generators). The volatility of semiconductor storage is a relatively minor disadvantage compared with the advantages of this type of storage.

BIT
Either a 0 or 1. Synonymous with binary digit.

Sixty-four K-bit, 256K-bit, and 1-megabit chips are widely used as primary memory for computers. In addition, 4-megabit chips have been announced and will be used in future microcomputers. Table 9–1 illustrates the storage capacities of these chips.

There are two basic types of semiconductor memory: **random-access memory (RAM)** and **read-only memory (ROM).** The term RAM comes from the fact that access to a particular area of the memory can be performed on a *random* basis. RAM and the term *primary storage* as we have been using it are synonymous. This kind of memory stores the user's program while it is being executed and the data while they are being processed by the CPU. The CPU can perform read or write operations at any memory position of random-access memory at any point in time. RAM is volatile memory.

RANDOM
Having no specific order or pattern. In the case of RAM, random access means that the computer can access any memory position directly and in any order, and the time necessary to access data is independent of the data's location in memory.

Read-only memory can be read from but not written to. ROM comes from the manufacturer with programs already stored in it, so the computer user cannot modify it. Because the storage is permanent, ROM is nonvolatile memory. ROM is used to store programs that are frequently used by many computer applications. For example, some personal computers store a BASIC

Table 9–1 ■ Storage Capacities of Semiconductor Memory Chips

CHIP SIZE	CAPACITY IN BITS	CAPACITY IN BYTES (CHARACTERS)	CAPACITY IN DOUBLE-SPACED TYPED PAGES
64K-bit chip	65,536	8,192 or 8K bytes	5
256K-bit chip	262,144	82,768 or 32K bytes	19
1-megabit chip	1,048,576	131,072 or 128K bytes	75
4-megabit chip	4,194,304	524,288 or 512K bytes	300

Many personal computers contain 1 megabit memory chips. Each chip holds 128K bytes. To add 1 megabyte of memory to such a PC, you must buy nine memory chips; eight to hold the 1 megabyte of data, and one to do parity checking.

INTERPRETER
A program that translates a high-level language like BASIC into machine language.

PC-DOS
Personal Computer-Disk Operating System. This is the operating system used on most personal computers.

interpreter in ROM. They also store part of the *PC-DOS* operating system, the basic input/output system (BIOS), in ROM.

This technique of placing software or programs in hardware (the ROM semiconductor chip) is often termed **microcoding** (also called **microprogramming** or **firmware**).

The current trend is to replace more of the electronic logic circuitry with firmware. Microcoded programs in a computer can be changed simply by removing the ROM and replacing it with another ROM. Thus, computers can be tailored to meet the needs of specific users.

Arithmetic-Logic Unit

The **arithmetic-logic unit** performs arithmetic operations such as multiplication, division, subtraction, and addition. It also performs logic operations such as comparing the relative magnitude of two pieces of information. Arithmetic-logic operations are performed serially (that is, one at a time), based on instructions from the control unit.

Control Unit

The **control unit** decodes program instructions and directs other parts of the CPU to perform the tasks specified. The program instructions are in machine language. They consist of an **operation code** to be performed, such as add, subtract, move, or compare, and the **operands,** which are the entities to which the operation is applied, such as data and input/output units.

Two cycles are performed for each program instruction—the instruction cycle and the execution cycle. The process of executing an individual program instruction begins with the control unit moving the instruction from primary memory into the control unit for decoding. The operation code and the operands are examined and decoded. This process of decoding the instruction is called the **instruction cycle.** The **execution cycle** begins when the control unit causes the appropriate unit to perform the operation called for in the instruction. This unit may be the arithmetic-logic unit or an input/output unit. Input/output to or from primary storage in the CPU is handled by **channels,** which are, in effect, small specialized computers. Thus the main CPU does not have to perform the relatively mundane, standardized, and time-consuming task of handling input/output operations.

■ MICROS, MINIS, MAINFRAMES, AND SUPERCOMPUTERS

Microcomputers

The smallest and least expensive computer system is called a micro or **microcomputer** (see Figure 9–6). Since it is often used by one person, the term *personal computer* has become popular. Microcomputer systems typically have between 256K and 16 megabytes of primary storage, with 640K being

Figure 9–6
Microcomputer System

These computers are the IBM Personal System 2 Model 50. They are currently the most popular model of the PS/2 line. Many corporations are using them as personal workstations in computer networks.

most common. They can handle peripheral devices such as terminals, relatively slow-speed printers, cassette tapes, floppy disks, and Winchester hard disks. Because of their low cost, microcomputer systems are used by even the smallest of businesses.

Minicomputers

Minis or **minicomputers** are medium-sized systems that typically have from 512K to several megabytes of primary storage (see Figure 9–7). Their processing power is more than micros but less than mainframes. Minicomputers were first developed for use in process-control, scientific, and engineering applications. They were used, for example, to monitor automated manufacturing processes such as steel rolling and to adjust the equipment automatically in order to keep the output within specified tolerances. However, it was soon discovered that these computers had tremendous potential in data processing, especially for smaller companies.

Minicomputer systems can be equipped with most of the input/output devices and secondary-storage devices that the large mainframe systems can handle, such as terminals and hard disks. They are also used in **distributed data-processing** systems. Instead of a company having one large mainframe computer, it can distribute its data processing with a minicomputer at each of its remote locations, and connect them to each other through telecommunication links.

Figure 9–7
A Minicomputer System

This Unisys U 5000/35 minicomputer is compatible with a wide variety of operating systems and will communicate with other manufacturers' computers.

Mainframe Computers

Mainframes are large systems having 5 to 500 megabytes of primary storage and the input/output units associated with a large computer system (see Figure 9–8). They can support several hundred online terminals. For online secondary storage they use high-capacity magnetic-disk drives capable of storing up to 7.5 *gigabytes* of data in each disk-drive unit. Each computer can access several of these 7.5-gigabyte disk-drive units. Mainframe computers typically use high-capacity magnetic tape for *offline* storage of data. Most medium-sized to large companies have one or more mainframe computers, which perform the bulk of their information processing. Applications that run on mainframes tend to be large and complex, and the data and information must be shared by many users throughout the organization.

GIGABYTE
One billion bytes.

OFFLINE
Data or a device that is not under direct control of the computer. Usually a person must place an offline reel of tape on a tape drive before the computer can access data stored on it.

Figure 9–8
Mainframe Computer

The IBM 3090, shown here, is one of IBM's largest mainframes. It is widely used by large businesses.

Minis overlap mainframes, and micros overlap minis. As minis become more powerful, they tend to perform with equal efficiency the jobs that were done by mainframes. The boundary lines of the three types of computer systems are constantly changing.

Supercomputers

In terms of processing power, **supercomputers** are even larger than mainframes (see Figure 9–9). They are rarely used for business information systems. Their primary use is in scientific applications, especially where large simulation models are needed. In **simulation,** mathematical models of real-world physical systems are coded into software that is executed on a computer. The execution of the computer software then models the real-world system. For example, the National Oceanic and Atmospheric Administration uses supercomputers to model the world's weather system; such models improve weather predictions. Simulation models are often large and complex. For these models to execute in a reasonable length of time a supercomputer is necessary. This fact points to the primary difference between a supercomputer and a mainframe—most supercomputers have a processing speed that is four to ten times faster than mainframe computers.

Figure 9–9
A Supercomputer

This computer is capable of performing one billion combined arithmetic/logic operations per second! Its central processing unit is cooled with a liquid refrigerant to increase its speed.

■ PARALLEL PROCESSING

Almost all CPUs in today's computers execute programs and process data in a serial fashion; that is, they process one piece of data at a time. With the advent of inexpensive microprocessors on a chip, computer designers have produced CPUs that contain several of these microprocessors (some contain as many as 2,000). These computers are designed so that all the microprocessors work simultaneously on the same application. Computers that use multiple processors to execute a single application are known as **parallel processors.** Applications are divided into tasks that can be processed simultaneously by the various processors. This method greatly reduces the amount of time necessary to complete a given application. However, the difficulty in finding methods to divide applications into tasks that can be processed simultaneously is holding back the use of parallel processors. Current computers and programs are designed to process applications sequentially.

Although parallel processing was developed for scientific and military applications, it is now being used in business. For example, consider an application where the same process must be performed on a large number of records, such as calculating net pay for each employee on a company's payroll. If parallel processing were used, many payroll records could be processed simultaneously, instead of one at a time, as would be the case in a single processing system. Obviously, the processing time would be greatly reduced by parallel processing.

An elementary form of parallel processing has been in use by personal computers since the early 1980s. The IBM PC standard computers can contain a math co-processor chip that takes over the mathematical computations from the computer's main processor and thus, greatly speeds up math computations. Also, the IBM PS/2 can accommodate, in addition to the math co-processor, another microprocessor that operates parallel to the computer's main processor. This additional microprocessor gives the PS/2 more power so that it can readily perform specialized applications, such as computer-assisted engineering design.

Parallel processing is a quickly growing field in the computer industry; it is expanding at a rate of 35 percent a year. As parallel processing develops, it will no doubt become more important in the business world.

■ SECONDARY STORAGE

Primary versus Secondary Storage

Earlier in this chapter, we covered primary storage and its characteristics. As illustrated in Figure 9–1, primary storage is part of the CPU, and it must allow very fast access in order to increase the speed at which the CPU can operate. **Secondary storage,** on the other hand, is physically separate from the CPU. Why are there two types of storage? Why isn't the CPU designed with large amounts of primary storage so that all of the data can be randomly accessible at electronic speeds, with no mechanical movement? The answer is cost.

Figure 9–10
Data Stored on a Magnetic Tape

A character is recorded across the tape. The parity bit is used for checking purposes. Zone bits are needed only for encoding alphabetic and special characters, since only the four lower numeric bits are necessary to encode numeric data. In fact, when all the data to be stored are numeric, two numeric characters can be stored in one eight-bit byte. One of them is stored in the four zone bits. This type of storage is known as packed decimal.

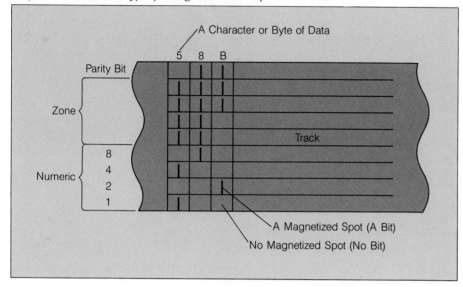

Primary storage is more expensive than secondary storage. Furthermore, the most widely used primary storage, semiconductor chips, is volatile. Secondary storage must be nonvolatile; that is, it must be able to retain the data stored in it even when the electrical current is off. All widely used secondary-storage media require mechanical movement for accessing data. Therefore, secondary storage is relatively slow, but in contrast to primary storage, it has the capability of storing large amounts of data at lower costs. Is it likely that computer systems in the future will use only one type of storage? Probably not, since the technologically most advanced, fastest, and therefore most expensive storage will be used in the CPU. Secondary storage will continue to use less expensive media.

Magnetic Tape

Magnetic tape has long been an important medium for secondary storage. Today, it is used almost exclusively for backup purposes. For mainframes it is supplied on reels up to 2,400 feet long; the tape is usually one-half-inch wide and, except for being larger, is similar in appearance to that used with tape recorders. Figure 9–10 illustrates data encoded on magnetic tape. Nine-track magnetic tape is by far the most common, although seven-, eight-, and ten-track tapes are available. They use different coding schemes for each character. Figure 9–11 illustrates a typical magnetic-tape drive.

Magnetic-tape cartridges with a storage capacity of 10 to 300 million characters are now being widely used to ***back up*** data stored on microcom-

BACK UP
To make an extra copy of current data and/or programs for use in case the original copy is partially or totally destroyed.

Figure 9–11
Magnetic-Tape Drives Used with Mainframes

Figure 9–11(a) shows in the background the tape drives that were used from the 1960s until the late 1980s. In the late 1980s these tape drives began to be replaced by those in the foreground of Figure 9–11(a). Figure 9–11(b) shows the two types of tape reels used by these drives. The larger reel is the older type. The new small reels will hold as much data as the larger reels.

(a)

(b)

puter hard disks (see Figure 9–12). As with all storage media, hard disks are subject to failure. Periodic copying of the data onto tape cartridges insures against loss of data and programs stored on hard disks.

The advantages of magnetic tape are as follows:

1. The cost of tape is low compared with other forms of secondary storage.
2. Computer systems can use several tape drives simultaneously.
3. The rate at which data may be transferred to and from tape is very high for sequentially organized files.
4. As a storage medium, magnetic tape is very compact and portable.
5. Magnetic tape is ideal as backup storage of data.
6. Magnetic-tape devices have several self-checking features; therefore, the recording and reading of data on magnetic tape are highly reliable.
7. Record lengths on magnetic tape can be very large, as long as they are within the limits of the individual computer system.
8. We can use magnetic tape over and over for storage of different data simply by writing the new data over the old. We can also correct mistakes by writing over the old data.

Disadvantages of magnetic tape include the following:

1. Magnetic tape is a sequential storage medium. Therefore, if a user wants to find an individual record stored on magnetic tape, the tape must be read up to the location of the desired record. This is very time consuming.
2. Damage to magnetic tape can result in the complete loss of data stored on the section of tape that is near the damage: therefore, critical data should be stored on a backup tape or another storage medium.
3. Magnetic tape is sensitive to dust, humidity, and temperature changes; consequently, the environment in which it is stored must be controlled.

Figure 9–12
A Cartridge Drive and Tape

Cartridge tapes are widely used to back up data stored on fixed hard disks in personal computers. Copying data onto tape is much faster than copying data onto floppy disks. Data is copied onto tape at the rate of five megabytes per minute. One cartridge tape can store from 125 to 500 megabytes of data.

Hard Disks

Magnetic disks are the most popular form of secondary storage. There are two basic types of disks: hard and floppy. Hard disks are widely used with all sizes of computers. They range in capacity from the 20-megabyte disk drives used with microcomputers to very high capacity disk drives such as IBM's 3380 Model K, which can store 7.5 gigabytes of data.

Hard disks are aluminum or magnesium rigid platters with an iron-oxide (rust) coating. Data are stored as magnetic patterns in the coating. Figure 9–13 illustrates one type of hard disk used with mainframes. It has eleven individual platters, each with two surfaces, top and bottom. Since this is a *removable disk* pack, data are not stored on the top surface of the top platter or the bottom surface of the bottom platter because of potential for damage to those surfaces. Therefore, there are twenty surfaces in the disk pack on which data can be stored. Within each surface, data are stored on *concentric tracks.* The same amount of data is stored on the outside tracks as on the center tracks, even though the circumferences of these tracks differ substantially. This is so because the time it takes for the disk to complete one revolution is the same for any track on the disk.

If the disk in Figure 9–13 has two hundred tracks on each surface, then the access arms can move horizontally and position themselves in two hundred different track positions. When an access arm is positioned over one of these

REMOVABLE DISK
A hard disk pack that can be removed from the disk drive.

CONCENTRIC TRACKS
Circular tracks that have a common center.

Figure 9–13
A Hard Disk

The access mechanism can position itself to access data from each of the two hundred cylinders. A cylinder is a set of all tracks with the same distance from the axis about which the disk pack rotates. In this example, there are twenty tracks in each cylinder.

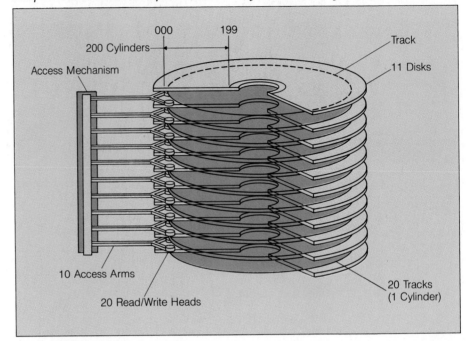

tracks, data can be read or written onto one track on each recording surface without the access arm moving. The twenty tracks located at one position of the read/write access arms make up a **cylinder.** When data are stored sequentially on a disk, they are stored by cylinder; that is, all the tracks in one cylinder are filled before any tracks in the adjacent cylinder are filled. The cylinder approach improves read and write access speeds to the disk. The speed of access to data on a disk is a function of the rotational speed of the disk, the speed with which the access arms move, and the relative position of the desired record to the read/write head once the correct track is located. Using the cylinder approach minimizes or eliminates the need for moving the access arms. Fixed and removable disk drives used with mainframes are illustrated in Figure 9–14 and 9–15.

Microcomputers use a type of hard disk known as a **Winchester disk** (see Figure 9–16). A Winchester disk unit contains a small (usually 5¼-inch) hard disk with multiple platters, and it typically stores twenty to three-hundred megabytes of data. It can be in the form of removable cartridge or *fixed disk.* A removable cartridge usually stores ten to twenty megabytes; whereas a fixed disk can store several hundred megabytes.

FIXED DISK
A hard disk pack that is permanently mounted in a disk drive and, therefore, cannot be removed.

Floppy Disks

Floppy disks (often called cassette disks, diskettes, or minidiskettes) are flat 3½ or 5¼-inch disks of polyester film with an iron-oxide magnetic coating. As

Figure 9–14
A Disk Drive with Fixed Disk

Fixed disks can hold more data than the same size removable disks. They are sealed within the unit and are much more stable than removable disk packs.

Figure 9–15
A Removable Disk Pack

Removable disk packs allow one disk drive to access many disks. However, they are being used less, owing to the labor required in mounting and dismounting them.

Figure 9–16
Inside a Winchester-Disk Drive

Note the access arms in the center. Since the disk pack is not removable, data are stored on the top of the top platter and on the bottom of the bottom platter, as well as all other platter surfaces in between.

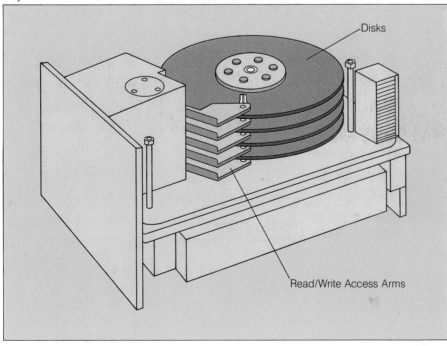

shown in Figure 9–17, the disk is covered with a protective jacket, and reading/writing from or to the disk is performed through the head access slot. A floppy disk has a capacity of 360K to 1.44 megabytes. Figure 9–18 has floppy-disk terminology, and Figure 9–19 shows some causes for data loss on floppy disks.

Floppy disks were developed by IBM in the early 1970s for use as secondary storage on minicomputers. However, they have become a widely used medium for secondary storage on microcomputers. Also, they are an important medium for *batch* data input to mainframe computers.

BATCH
An accumulation of data to be processed.

Users of PCs are switching from 5¼-inch disks to 3½-inch disks. The primary advantage of the 3½-inch disk is its higher storage capacity, even though it is smaller. The 3½-inch disk owes this storage advantage to its rigid protective cover. This cover protects the storage medium and thus, data can be stored more concisely and at a higher density. In addition, the rigid structure allows faster rotation of the disk.

The primary advantages of floppy disks are their relatively low cost, large capacity, and small size. The equivalent of 400 double-spaced typewritten pages can be stored on a 100K floppy disk.

The advantages of magnetic disks (both hard and floppy) include the following:

1. The magnetic disk is a **direct-access storage** medium; therefore, the user can retrieve individual records without searching through the entire file.

2. Although disks are more expensive than magnetic tape, their cost has steadily declined over the years.

Figure 9–17
5¼-Inch and 3½-Inch Floppy Disks

The 5¼-inch diskette is often called a minidiskette because the first floppy disk produced was an 8-inch diskette. It was introduced in the 1970s for use with minicomputers. The 3½-inch disk was first used in the Apple Macintosh and was later used by IBM on the PS/2 series.

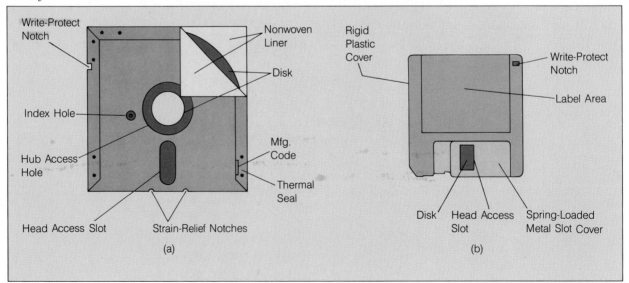

(a)   (b)

Figure 9–18
Floppy Disk Terminology

Disk or Diskette?

Definitions

- A disk is the circular-shaped media, inside the jacket on which the magnetic data are stored.
- A diskette is a combination of the disk and its flexible jacket.

Flexible-Disk Construction Features

Index Hole	Physical hole in diskette which, when detected, notifies drive that beginning of track is under read-write head.
Hub Access Hole	Hole in center of jacket into which drive hub of transport fits.
Hub Reinforcement or Hub Ring	Ring added to hub hole area. Provides increased strength and support for diskettes during clamping.
Jacket	Protective vinyl covering that encloses disk but allows access to disk by head and drive hub. This jacket is flexible on 5¼-inch disk and rigid on 3½-inch diskette.
Dust Cover	A protective paper or plastic cover for diskettes.
Liner	Soft, nonwoven synthetic material bonded to inner side of jacket. Primary purpose is to wipe surface of disk as it rotates in jacket.
Strain-Relief Notch	Notches cut into jacket near head access slot to reduce creasing when jacket is flexed.
Write-Protect Notch	Notch in jacket which prevents inadvertent recording on an 8-inch diskette and allows recording on a 5¼-inch and 3½-inch diskettes.
Write Enable/Protect Tab	Metalized, adhesive label which, when used to cover write-protect notch, prevents recording on a 5¼-inch diskette or allows recording on an 8-inch diskette.
Head Access Slot	Slotted area of jacket which allows drive-recording head physical access to media. All recording and data retrieval occur in this area.
Envelope	Outer protective covering that fits around diskette assembly to prevent damage and contamination during handling.

General Recording Terms

Bit	Smallest unit of information stored magnetically; usually it is the abbreviation for binary digit.
Byte	Eight bits equal one byte; usually equal to one alphanumeric character.

Media Terms

Oxide	Needle-shaped particles of iron oxide (rust). Used in manufacture of magnetic media.

Diskette Recording Terms

Sector	Division of magnetic surface of disk into separate, but contiguous, pie-shaped information zones by either magnetic or physical coding of disk.
Soft Sector	Sectors defined magnetically via software.
Hard Sector	Sectors defined physically by punching holes around inner or outer disk diameter.
Initialization/Formatting	Magnetically coded pattern recorded on disk to identify each track and sector.
Single Sided	Diskette made for use on disk drives with one recording head. Only one side of diskette is certified 100% error-free.
Dual Sided	Diskette made for use on disk drives with two recording heads. Both sides of diskette are certified 100% error-free.
Single Density	Machine-controlled method of recording data on diskette.
Double Density	Machine-controlled method of recording twice the amount on diskette as is possible with single-density method.
High Density	Machine-controlled method of recording twice or more the amount on diskette as is possible with double-density method.
Downward Compatibility	Using high-density or double-density diskette in double-density or single-density application.

Figure 9–19
Some Causes of Data Loss on Floppy Disks

As you can see, some very small particles look huge in comparison to the distance between the surface of a diskette and the read/write head. If these particles become lodged between the head and the surface of the diskette, the surface may be scratched, resulting in data loss. So be sure to keep the dust covers on your diskettes.

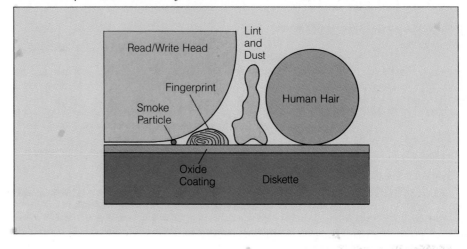

3. For online systems where direct access is required, disks are currently the only practical means of file storage.

4. Users can easily update records by writing new information over the area where old information was stored.

5. With removable disk packs or cartridges, a single disk drive can access a large number of disk packs. This method is especially economical with batch-processing applications which do not require frequent switching between disk packs. Because the same disk drive can be used to access more than one disk pack, the cost of the disk drive can be spread out over a larger volume of stored data.

6. Interrelated files stored on magnetic disk allow a single transaction to be processed against all of these files simultaneously. In addition, data can be retrieved from interrelated files simultaneously. This capability makes relational data-base systems possible, as we will see in Chapter 13.

The disadvantages of magnetic disks are as follows:

1. Compared with magnetic tape, hard disks are expensive.

2. Updating a master file stored on disk often destroys the old information. Therefore, disks may not provide an automatic *audit trail* and backup the way magnetic tape does. Subsequent to updating a master file stored on magnetic tape, there exist the old master file, the new master file, and the transaction file, on three separate reels of tape. When a disk is used, equivalent backup and audit trail require that each old master-file record be copied to another storage area prior to update.

3. For periodic batch-type systems where there is no need for between-run data retrieval from the files, magnetic tape serves just as well as disks for file-storage purposes—at substantially less cost.

AUDIT TRAIL
The capability of reconstructing processing steps and tracing information back to its origins.

Laser-Optical Disks

A type of secondary storage that is becoming increasingly popular is **laser-optical disks** (see Figure 9–20). These disks have the same technology as the digital compact disk (CD) players used with stereo systems. Originally, data could be written on them only one time; however, we now have erasable versions. The primary advantage of laser disks is large storage capacity at low cost; some of them cost less than ten dollars and hold 200 to 1,000 megabytes (one gigabyte) of data. Five hundred megabytes is the equivalent of 300,000 double-spaced typewritten pages, or the entire *Encyclopedia Brittanica* several times over! For mainframes, jukebox-like devices are being designed that will store and automatically retrieve large numbers of laser-optical disks. These devices will store hundreds of gigabytes of data or text. Optical disk drives for microcomputers cost 500 dollars or less.

The write-once optical disks are known by the acronym WORM, (write once, read many). They are often used for backup of hard disks. Once they are full, they can be discarded since they are inexpensive. WORM disks also are often used for storage of text and data that are infrequently updated, such as dictionaries and encyclopedias.

The primary disadvantage of these disks is their slow access time compared with hard disks. Accessing data on laser disks is approximately ten times slower than on hard magnetic disks.

Figure 9–20
Laser-Optical Disks

These optical storage disks can hold as much data as can be stored on fifty or more reels of magnetic tape.

Laser disks are used for storing large volumes of data that are not accessed or changed often. They are likely to replace magnetic tape for backup purposes. Laser disks can also provide microcomputer users with large data banks such as historical stock-market prices. One of the most promising uses for these disks is in libraries—card catalogs, microfilm holdings, and Library of Congress collections are being put on laser disks.

Other Forms of Secondary Storage

Another type of direct-access storage is the **mass-storage** device. These devices (such as the IBM 3850) can store very large amounts of data and access these data without human intervention (see Figure 9–21). The 3850 mass-storage subsystem can store up to 472 billion bytes of data. This is approximately the amount of data that can be stored on 47,200 reels of magnetic tape! Data in this system are stored on small, fist-sized cartridges which in turn are stored in honeycomb-like cells. Mechanical-cartridge access arms can remove the cartridges from the cells and place them on a read/write unit. The data are stored within the cartridge on a 3×770 inch strip of magnetic tape. Because of the relatively large amount of physical movement involved (even though it is machine movement), mass-storage data systems provide much slower access to data than a magnetic disk unit.

As technology continues to advance, new forms of storage are being developed. In the late 1970s, bubble storage was expected to make magnetic-disk storage obsolete. In a **bubble storage** system, data are stored through the polarization of microscopic bubbles that exist in certain crystalline substances. Bubble storage has potentially faster access time and vastly greater miniaturization than disk storage. One computer manufacturer ran advertisements claiming it was developing a bubble-storage device with the capacity of storing all the data in the New York Public Library in an area the size of an average closet. Bubble storage appears to be an almost ideal form of secondary storage. However, it has not yet been widely used because its production cost has failed to decline, while significant advances have been made in both magnetic and laser disk storage technology. It is, however, used today as internal storage for portable microcomputers and for military applications. Bubble storage has the advantage of being nonvolatile (the data are retained when the electricity is turned off).

Cache Memory

In this chapter, we learned that primary storage is fast-access memory. Its storage capacity is limited because it is relatively expensive. On the other hand, secondary storage is nonvolatile, has a large storage capacity, and is relatively inexpensive. Secondary-storage access time is always slower than primary storage. Often, a computer's CPU must wait idle while data are being read from or written to the relatively slow secondary storage. Cache memory helps in solving this problem of an idle CPU. **Cache memory** is semiconductor memory (RAM) that stores data temporarily while they are in transit, (in either direction) between primary and secondary memory. Thus, cache memory serves as a buffer between the access speeds of primary and secondary memory. The CPU deals only with the fast-access cache memory

Figure 9–21
Mass-Storage Device

This device is used when very large amounts of data must be stored. For example, the Internal Revenue Service uses these devices to store income-tax data.

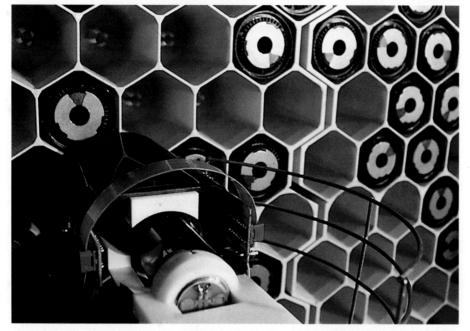

and can continue processing while data are in transit to and from cache memory and the slower secondary storage. Most computers today use cache memory to speed up processing.

Certainly, new forms of primary and secondary storage will be developed. However, magnetic disks and semiconductors will probably continue to be the major storage types of the 1990s and perhaps even longer, simply because improvements in these two technologies continue to significantly reduce their cost.

■ Summing Up

■ The central processing unit of a computer is its single most important component.
■ The primary-storage unit stores the program being executed and the data records being processed.
■ Primary storage must be a fast-access device in order for the CPU to be able to function at electronic speeds.
■ Random-access memory (RAM) allows the CPU to read any particular data or program statement on a random basis.
■ Read-only memory (ROM) can be read from but not written to. It is used to store programs that are frequently used by many computer applications and that do not need to be modified.

■ The arithmetic-logic unit performs arithmetic operations and logic comparisons on data.

■ The control unit interprets program instructions and arranges for their execution. Typically it calls on other units to execute the instructions.

■ Computers are classified into four groups: microcomputers, minicomputers, mainframes, and supercomputers.

■ Parallel processors use multiple processors to simultaneously execute multiple tasks in a single computer application.

■ Secondary storage is an essential part of a computer system. It stores the bulk of data and programs not in use. Secondary-storage devices usually use some mechanical movement to access data, thereby making it a relatively slow process.

■ Magnetic reel tape and cartridge tape are widely used secondary-storage media.

■ Magnetic tapes have the advantages of being inexpensive, compact, fast, accurate, portable, and reusable. However, it is necessary to handle them carefully and protect them from dirt and humidity.

■ Magnetic disk is the most popular form of secondary storage. Its major advantage is its random-access capability. Any piece of information on the disk can be accessed quickly with very little mechanical movement.

■ The cost of disk storage is steadily declining. It is a very useful direct-access medium for online systems. Its major disadvantage is that it does not provide an automatic audit trail or backup facility.

■ Laser-optical disks with large storage capacities (one gigabyte per disk) are becoming a very important form of secondary storage. They are used for storing large volumes of data that are not accessed or updated often.

■ Magnetic bubble storage and laser-optical disk storage will eventually increase in use. However, magnetic disk and semiconductor devices are expected to retain their importance for a long time.

■ Cache memory acts as a buffer between the fast access speed of primary memory and the slow access speed of secondary storage.

■ Key Terms

central processing unit (CPU)	operands
primary storage	instruction cycle
semiconductor chips	execution cycle
microprocessors	channels
volatile	microcomputers
random-access memory (RAM)	minicomputers
read-only memory (ROM)	distributed data processing
microcoding or microprogramming or firmware	mainframes
	gigabytes
arithmetic-logic unit	supercomputers
control unit	simulation
operation code	

parallel processors	Winchester disks
secondary storage	floppy disks
magnetic tape	direct-access storage
back up	audit trail
magnetic disks	laser-optical disk
hard disks	mass storage
tracks	bubble storage
cylinder	cache memory

1. What is the most important piece of equipment in a computer system?

Review Questions

2. List the three components of a central processing unit.

3. What are the major functions of the primary storage unit?

4. Why does primary storage have to be faster than secondary storage?

5. Describe the advantages of semiconductor memory.

6. Why is nonvolatile memory more desirable than volatile memory?

7. Describe random-access memory, and explain its advantages.

8. Why is the arithmetic-logic unit crucial to a computer's operation?

9. Describe the two cycles performed by the control unit.

10. How can you differentiate between mainframes, minis, and micros?

11. How does parallel processing increase the amount of work that a CPU can perform?

12. Why is a computer's memory divided into primary and secondary storage?

13. List four advantages of using magnetic tape for secondary storage.

14. Describe the concept of a cylinder in connection with magnetic disks.

15. What is the advantage of a direct-access storage device?

16. What is cache memory, and how does it increase the amount of work that a CPU can perform?

1. Small businesses are rapidly adopting microcomputer systems to automate their record-keeping functions. Some data-processing experts believe these small computer systems are not a wise choice in the long run because businesses will soon outgrow them or have trouble using them because they lack computer expertise. It may be better to rent computing power from an outside agency, or buy a minicomputer. What criteria should the business person use in deciding whether to buy a microcomputer, buy a minicomputer, or rent computer time?

Discussion Questions and Cases

2. A large primary-storage unit enables the computer to retrieve and store data quickly, and thus operate at a high speed. However, primary storage is more expensive than secondary storage. What factors need to be considered when deciding on the amount of primary storage to purchase? Give one example of a business application that would require a large primary storage, and one that would require a small primary storage.

3. Magnetic tape is a suitable storage medium for data that must be processed sequentially (for example, printing all the addresses on a mailing list). On the other hand, magnetic disk is more efficient for applications requiring random access (for example, finding the quantity available for a specific inventory item). How would you go about deciding whether to use a sequential- or direct-access device for a particular application?

4. Mary Delafore is a freshman in an introductory information-system class. She is an aspiring accounting major and hopes to become an auditor with a large accounting firm. The first topics in the course are the internal design of the computer and the differences in various sizes of computers including supercomputers, mainframes, minicomputers, and microcomputers. She feels this study of hardware is a waste of time because it does not have anything to do with accounting and auditing. Can you think of any situations in which Mary will need to know about computer hardware and processing in her career as an auditor?

5. Lowes Incorporated is a medium-sized regional department store. The company has a medium-sized IBM mainframe at its central headquarters. Accounts receivable is run on this mainframe, and terminals have been placed in the various stores so that inquiries can be made concerning customer accounts. Some store managers think accounts receivable should be kept locally at each store. They argue that a microcomputer such as the IBM PS/2 Model 70 could be used to keep up with the accounts receivable at each store. People in the central data-processing department argue that the volume of customers is too great for micros to handle accounts receivable. The managers counter this with the argument that two or more micros can be networked together to provide the necessary capacity, and that the micros in the various stores can be networked together. Which direction do you think Lowes should go? Should the firm maintain accounts receivable on the mainframe, as it is doing now, or should it convert the system to microcomputers?

6. Hunter Martin is the proprietor of a small but rapidly growing business. He is still using a manual record-keeping system, which is becoming large and very complex. Mr. Martin has decided that a personal computer with the adequate software would help him run his business better. How should Mr. Martin go about choosing the right personal computer for his business? What features offered by the personal computer might interest him?

7. Anthony Wilson has just been given a proposal to add laser-optical disk storage systems to the company's computer systems to replace three magnetic-tape systems that are currently used for backup purposes. Mr. Wilson does not involve himself in the use of computers, and he is not very familiar with computer technology. He does know that laser-optical disk storage is a new technology likely to be used widely in the future. How would you explain laser-optical disks to Mr. Wilson? What effect would this system have on the secondary-storage capabilities of the company? Would the benefits gained outweigh the costs of laser-optical disk storage? Where would you advise Mr. Wilson to go to get additional information on which to base his decision?

Data Entry and Information Response

Chapter 10

CHAPTER OUTLINE

Introduction

Data Entry
  Offline versus Online Data Entry
  Key-to-Diskette Data Entry
  Key-to-Disk Data Entry
  Interactive Data Entry
  Source-Data Automation

Information Response
  Visual Display Terminals
  Printers
  Computer-Output Microfiche
  Laser-Optical Disks
  Graphics
  Other Output Media

Summing Up

Key Terms

Review Questions

Discussion Questions and Cases

■ INTRODUCTION

Communication between computers and people has been an area of great innovation. As we saw in Chapter 2, exotic devices (such as a mouse) are used to communicate with a computer. But the human/computer interface is still a very important problem in the application of computers. Ideally, we should be able to communicate with computers in many different ways. Most people would like to use a spoken language, such as English. Computers can talk to us, and some can understand spoken English. The various ways to communicate with computers are discussed in this chapter.

Data-entry and **information-response** devices provide a link between the central processing unit (CPU) and the people who use it. Data-entry devices are used to provide input to the CPU. Information-response devices provide output from the CPU. Advances are continually being made in the human/computer interface, making it easier and more natural for us to communicate with the computer. The term *peripheral device* often refers to any hardware device that is not the CPU. Thus, data-entry, storage, and output devices are also called **peripheral devices.** As we examine data-entry devices, note that often the same media (such as magnetic disks) are used for data entry and secondary storage.

A distinction is usually made between the media and devices used for data entry, storage, and output. The **medium** (such as a magnetic disk) is the material on which the data are recorded, whereas the **device** (such as a disk drive) is the complete unit that reads or writes on the medium. Similarly, a printer is an output device, and paper is an output medium.

Many types of data-entry and information-response devices are available. This chapter will cover the most common ones and those expected to be in widespread use in the near future.

■ DATA ENTRY

Offline versus Online Data Entry

In offline data entry, data are entered through devices that are not connected (they are not online) to the CPU or to the disk master files that are to be updated. Thus, after being keyed in, data are transmitted to the processing CPU either electronically or by someone taking the storage medium (floppy disk or magnetic tape) to the processing CPU for input. Key-to-diskette and key-to-disk data entry (discussed below) are both offline data-entry methods.

With online data entry, the input device is connected electronically to the processing CPU, and the data are usually processed immediately after being entered. Interactive data entry is a type of online data entry, whereas source-data automation can be offline or online. Both interactive data entry and source-data automation will be discussed in this chapter.

Key-to-Diskette Data Entry

Key-to-diskette data entry is a form of offline data entry where data are keyed in through a keyboard and then stored on a floppy disk. Devices were designed to be used exclusively for this type of data entry in the early 1970s. However, with inexpensive microcomputers now available, almost all key-to-diskette data entry is performed using general purpose microcomputers. The primary advantages of key-to-diskette data entry are the same as those for key-to-disk, which will be covered in the next section. However, key-to-diskette data entry does have the additional advantage that the equipment required is very inexpensive and well suited for small operations.

Key-to-Disk Data Entry offline

Many medium- and large-sized companies use **key-to-disk** data input, as shown in Figure 10–1. With this approach, a minicomputer (or sometimes a network of microcomputers) performs the data-entry function. This minicomputer supports a number of terminals that are online to it. Also online to the minicomputer is a hard-disk unit that stores the data that have been keyed into the system. The typical procedure for using a key-to-disk input system is to key the data initially from the *source document* onto the disk from a keyboard. As the data are keyed in, the minicomputer can execute programs to screen the data for errors. Errors, such as alphabetic data in numeric fields, can be detected without reference to the files to which the input data pertain.

SOURCE DOCUMENT
The form containing information that is being keyed into a computer system.

Figure 10–1
Key-to-Disk Data Entry

This type of system is generally used by large companies that have large volumes of data to input from source documents.

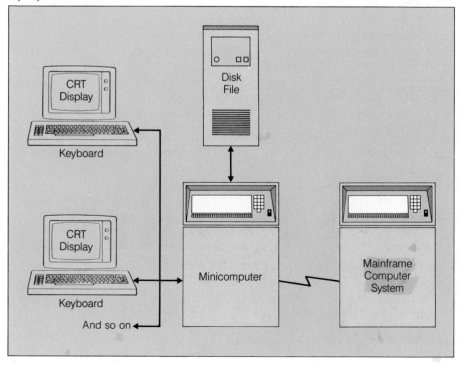

Once the data have been stored on the disk, **key verification** can be performed through a program executed by the minicomputer. Essentially, the data are keyed in a second time, and the key-verification program compares the data on the storage disk with the data that are keyed in the second time. After the data have been verified, the minicomputer produces *control totals* for balancing purposes. When the balancing phase has been completed and any necessary corrections to the data have been made, the data are transferred to the mainframe CPU for processing. This transmission is usually performed through electronic communication lines between the minicomputer and the mainframe CPU; however, it can be done by other means, such as magnetic tape.

We should emphasize that key-to-diskette systems (as discussed in the previous section) can operate like hard-disk systems if the input device is a microcomputer and can therefore execute input programs. The primary difference between the two systems is that the key-to-diskette system is for smaller-scale operations. Data-entry stations for key-to-hard-disk systems are shown in Figure 10–2.

The advantages of a key-to-disk input system are as follows:

1. A large percentage of the editing and control-total balancing can be performed at the time of data entry. Keying errors are often detected as they occur; therefore, the operator has a much better chance of correcting them.
2. Key verification is easily performed on a key-to-disk system where a mini or microcomputer is dedicated to the data-entry system.
3. The minicomputer can execute various programs that provide instructions, prompts, or *input masks* to assist the operator in entering data.

CONTROL TOTAL
A sum, resulting from the addition of a specified field from each record in a group of records; it is used for checking machine, program, human, and data reliability.

INPUT MASK
A form displayed on a monitor to guide the keying of input.

Figure 10–2
Data-Entry Stations

A minicomputer can service large numbers of data-entry stations.

4. The minicomputer can compile and report various statistics concerning the data-input operation, including operator-productivity statistics and error rates. These statistics can be very valuable in helping a company determine which operators need additional instruction.

5. A key-to-disk system relieves the mainframe of much input processing and allows the mainframe to do the jobs for which it is best suited.

The primary disadvantages of key-to-disk data entry are as follows:

1. The initial cost of a separate computer system dedicated to data input may be prohibitive to small firms. However, the cost of computer hardware continues to decline.

2. A separate computer data-entry system may not be necessary when a company's computer system has excess capacity and *multiprogramming* capability. In this case, the data can be entered directly to the mainframe system and processed immediately, or stored in batches for later processing in a batch system.

Interactive Data Entry

With **interactive data entry,** data are input directly to the production CPU through a data-entry terminal (see Figure 10–3), for either immediate processing against the master file or storage in batches on magnetic disks for later processing. A **production CPU** is the CPU that processes the application to which the input data pertain. If the system is a batch-processing application, this type of data input is very similar to key-to-disk, except that the production CPU handles the tasks that the minicomputer would handle. For

MULTIPROGRAMMING
The capability of a computer CPU to execute two or more programs concurrently and, therefore, serve two or more users at the same time. Synonymous with *multi-tasking.*

Figure 10–3
Interactive Data Entry

Interactive data entry is necessary for systems that maintain real-time files. Some companies may use interactive data entry also for batch systems when they have excess capacity on the mainframe computer.

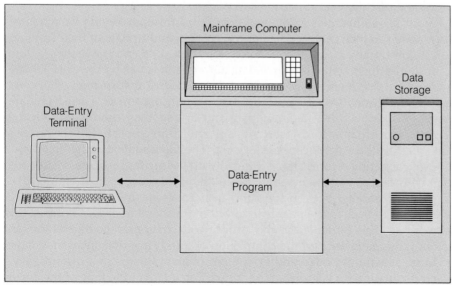

a real-time application, interactive data entry is the only practical type of input since the master file must be updated when an event occurs in order for it to reflect the current status of an activity.

Interactive input has all the advantages of a key-to-disk system, since the production computer can perform the same functions as a minicomputer. Other advantages are as follows:

1. Additional **data editing,** which is not possible with a minicomputer data-entry system, can be performed if the master files to which the transaction data pertain are online. Many edit checks depend on data stored in the master file. For example, if all valid employees have a master-file record, the input of weekly time data for an employee can be checked against the master file so the user can see whether the social-security number being input exists on the master file.
2. If excess capacity exists, the data-entry function can use production-CPU time that otherwise would not be used.

Disadvantages of interactive input are as follows:

1. The production CPU may not have enough excess capacity to perform the data-entry operation without increasing turn-around time on other jobs.
2. Unless master files are online and can be used for editing input data, a mini- or micro-computer can perform data-entry operations for batch-type systems more efficiently than a mainframe CPU.
3. The production CPU may be located far from where data are being entered, requiring the use of expensive communication lines.

Source-Data Automation

Source-data automation is the capture of data, in computer-readable form, at the location and time of an event. Often the capture of data is a by-product of some other operation. A good example is the capture of data by a computer-connected cash register upon the sale of merchandise.

Figure 10–4 illustrates traditional data entry through keying from source documents. As you can see, data-entry, editing, and update of the computer files involve many steps. Errors always occur in data entry, whether keying from source documents or source-data automation is used. However, keying from source documents has disadvantages in terms of correcting errors. As shown in Figure 10–4, if step 5 uncovers significant errors, corrections are keyed and key verified (as in steps 2 and 3) and then combined with the original data-entry records, and steps 4 and 5 are repeated. This process continues until no significant errors exist. The file update can then be done.

Also, correcting errors is more difficult with keying from source documents than with source-data automation. Since the process depicted in Figure 10–4 is usually separated both in time and distance from the original event, we often must go back to the people involved in the event in order to correct the data input. For example, if the event were customer payments on an account, the payment and the completion of the source document may have occurred several days ago and in another office, perhaps in a distant state. The individuals who completed the source document at the time of the event

Figure 10–4
Keying from Source Documents

When batch data are keyed, they are usually keyed to a disk, then key verified. The steps are the same in key-to-disk and key-to-diskette data entry.

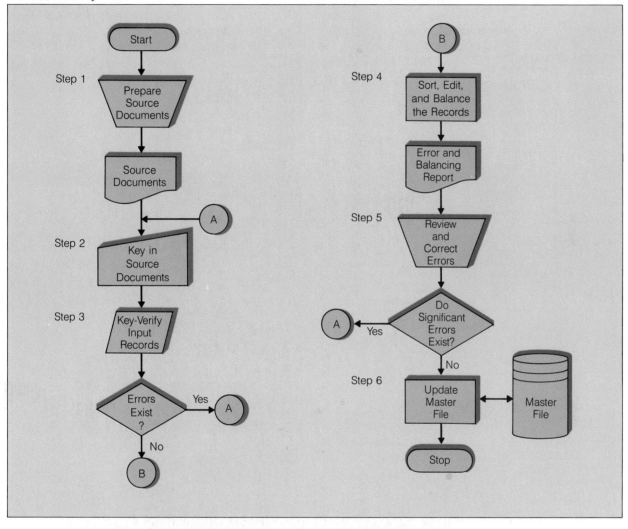

have the information needed to correct errors. It is preferable to detect and correct errors at the place and time of the event, since the particulars are at hand.

Figure 10–5 depicts source-data automation. When data are entered through a terminal located at the site of the event, the data can be immediately edited by the computer, and errors can be sent back to the terminal screen for correction. Source-data automation that allows immediate data entry and error correction has very significant advantages. However, not all source-data automation involves immediate error correction. For example, the **optical scan (opscan)** process depicted in Figure 10–5 is often a batch-processing operation performed separately, both in time and distance, from

Figure 10–5
Source-Data Automation

If possible, the input of data to a system should be done through source-data automation. Its advantages of reducing errors in data and reducing the human labor in data input are very significant.

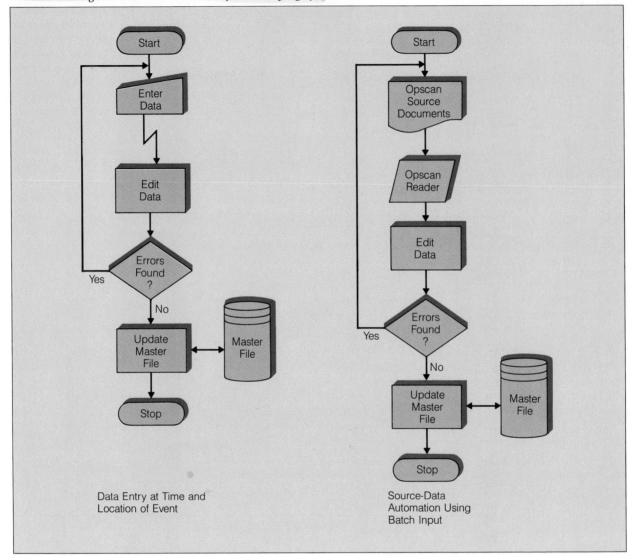

Data Entry at Time and Location of Event

Source-Data Automation Using Batch Input

the event. Therefore, it has many of the same disadvantages as keying from source documents.

Regardless of the type of source-data automation, it reduces the number of times the data have to be transcribed from one medium to another, and therefore significantly reduces chances for error. Furthermore, all source-data automation reduces the amount of human labor needed for data entry.

Source-data automation is often called distributed data entry. Essentially, what we are doing is changing from a centralized data-entry function to a situation in which data entry is distributed to the locations where significant

Figure 10–6
Point-of-Sale Data Entry

Have you ever examined your grocery receipt to see whether the computer made a mistake? It is extremely rare to find such errors because of the error-checking capabilities built into POS equipment. However, you may discover that the price stored in the computer is different from that marked on the shelf.

business events occur. In this way, we can capture data about those events directly and immediately with on-the-spot error correction.

POS Data Entry Source-data automation has given rise to **point-of-sale (POS)** equipment. In a typical POS configuration, as shown in Figure 10–6, cash registers are online to a minicomputer, that is in turn online to disk storage files containing such data as product descriptions, selling prices, and collected sales statistics. A **universal product code (UPC)** appears on each item sold (see Figure 10–7). It is read by the cash register with either a reader embedded in the checkout counter or a light-wand reader (see Figure 10–8). The UPC is transmitted to the minicomputer, which retrieves a description and selling price for the item and transmits them back to the cash register. Simultaneously, sales statistics are collected and used to update cash receipts and inventory master files. For small businesses, UPC readers can be attached directly to microcomputers, and the same functions can be performed as with larger minicomputers.

POS equipment is used most extensively by the grocery industry, although it can be applied to any merchandising operation. There are also other applications for POS equipment. For example, some libraries place UPC stickers on books and library cards. When books are checked out, the patron's identification number on the card and the code of each book are read by a light wand. Similarly, when books are returned, their code is also read with a light wand. Master files maintained by minicomputers contain book codes and the corresponding Library of Congress identification, titles, authors, and other information. Other files contain patron identification numbers, names, addresses, and information on checked out books.

Magnetic-Ink Character Recognition Magnetic-ink character recognition **(MICR)** was developed by the banking industry for use on checks. MICR

Figure 10–7
Universal Product Code (UPC)

Some railroad companies use a larger bar code (similar to this) on the side of railroad cars. Reading stations identify the cars as they pass by. In this way the railroad company can keep track of the progress of its rail shipments.

Figure 10–8
Light-Wand Reader Being Used in the Counting of Inventory
The UPC identification code is read from the tag. Then the inventory is counted and the count is keyed into the reader.

equipment reads data according to the shape of each individual character printed with magnetic ink. Preprinted checks contain the bank's identification number and the depositor's checking account number in MICR code at the bottom of the check, as shown in Figure 10–9. When a check is processed, the amount is printed in MICR code in the lower right corner. MICR codes are used for sorting and routing checks to banks and for updating the depositor's account. The use of MICR is limited mostly to the processing of checks and credit-card transactions.

Optical-Character Recognition and Optical-Mark Recognition   Optical- character recognition (OCR) devices read printed characters optically. Figure 10–10

Figure 10–9
MICR Coded Check

Banks process huge numbers of checks. Without the automated processing made possible by MICR, banking would be considerably more expensive for customers.

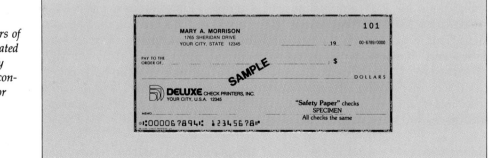

illustrates an OCR document. OCR devices can read almost all *fonts,* although their error rate increases with certain fonts. This equipment is very useful in word-processing applications. Essentially, it provides automated input of text that has been previously typed in a wide variety of fonts, including standard typewriter fonts.

Optical-mark recognition (OMR) equipment can detect marks on a specially prepared form. Figure 10–11 illustrates an OMR form. OMR is widely used in academic testing and is sometimes used on *turn-around documents* where the recipient marks data to be read subsequently by OMR equipment.

Other Input Media and Devices Voice-recognition systems have some limited applications. In **voice recognition,** a computer recognizes the patterns of an individual's (or several individuals') speech. Essentially, a person speaks into a microphone that converts the speech into analog electrical signals. These signals are recognized by the computer and converted into the digital signals of a digital computer system to represent individual word

FONT
A particular shape of printed or typed characters.

TURN-AROUND DOCUMENT
Any document originally prepared by a computer as output that is designed for subsequent input use

Figure 10–10
OCR Document and Input Device

OCR can be used to read identification tags on merchandise. It is also often used on bills that are turn-around documents, where a portion of the bill is sent back by the customer with payment and OCR equipment reads the bill.

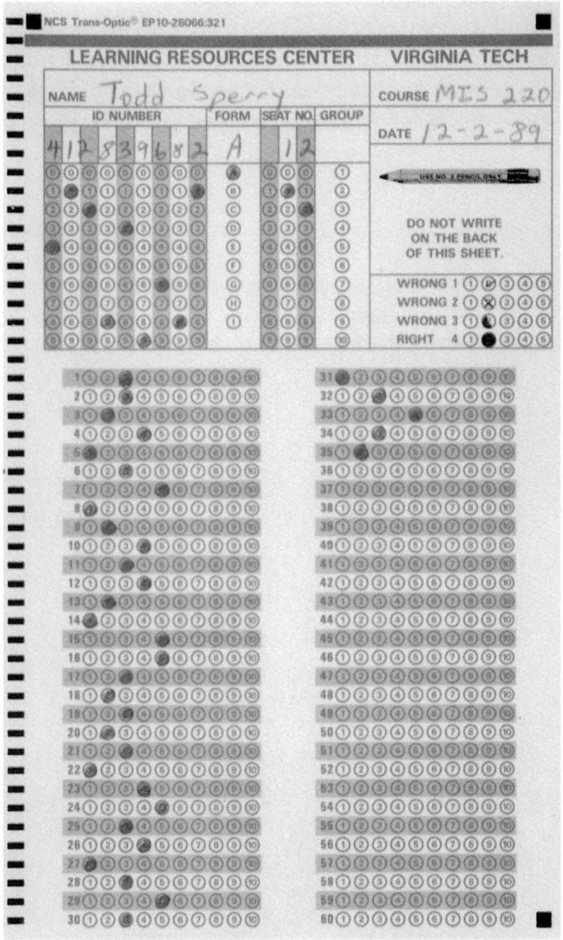

Figure 10–11
Optical-Mark Recognition Form

OMR is most often used in academic testing. Many universities also use it for student registration.

patterns. Several companies are working on a widely applicable voice-recognition system that could recognize normal human speech. This system is expected to be available in the mid-to-late 1990s. The potential market for such a system is enormous in word processing. Textual material could be dictated to a voice-recognition system, and the computer could produce typed copy directly. There are voice-recognition systems with very high accuracy (98 percent) over a very limited vocabulary. These are usually employed in a "hands busy" environment, such as when production-line workers are busy with their hands and therefore cannot enter data through a keyboard.

Telephone touch-tone devices, as illustrated in Figure 10–12 can be used to enter data directly over telephone lines into computer systems. Many variations of these devices exist.

Other data-entry devices becoming increasingly popular are **portable terminals** and portable (lap-top) personal computers (see Figure 10–13). These terminals have secondary-storage capability such as bubble storage (or floppy disk, in the case of portable PCs) so that data can be entered when the terminal is offline from the computer, and can be stored and subsequently transmitted at high speed to the central computer. One application for these portable computers has been designed for traveling salespeople. In a customer's office the salesperson can connect the terminal over a regular telephone line (perhaps using a toll-free number) to the company's computer. The salesperson can inquire about the availability of goods that the customer wishes to order and can immediately enter the

Figure 10–12
Telephone Touch-Tone Device

Any telephone can be used as a low-volume data-input device. If the computer has voice-output capabilities, the phone can also be used as an output device.

Figure 10–13
Portable Personal Computer

Portable PCs can be used in many applications to capture data for later processing by other computers.

customer's order into the computer. This can reduce the delivery time of the goods by several days.

■ INFORMATION RESPONSE

Visual Display Terminals

The most widely used output device is the **visual** (or video) **display terminal (VDT).** This terminal consists of a monitor with a cathode ray tube (CRT) and an attached keyboard (see Figure 10–14). Visual display terminals are also often called CRTs. The CRT is very similar to the picture tube in a television. VDTs have several advantages: they are inexpensive (less than five hundred dollars) and they produce output without making noise as most printers do. But perhaps their most important advantage is the speed with which they produce output. This speed is determined largely by the speed of the communication line between the VDT and the computer. Typical speeds range from 240 to 1,920 characters per second. The primary disadvantage of VDTs is that data must be read from a screen; many people prefer reading data from printed copy. Some people develop eyestrain from reading data on CRTs. Manufacturers are taking these complaints into consideration and are improving the readability of CRT screens.

Figure 10–14
Visual Display Terminal

Most VDTs can display only 80 characters across the screen, although high resolution graphics can display much more data both horizontally and vertically on the screen.

Many companies are replacing VDTs with personal computers. The personal computer can act as a terminal connected to a host minicomputer or mainframe. For a few hundred dollars more than what a VDT costs, a firm can have the equivalent of both a VDT and a personal computer in one device called a **personal workstation.** It can act as a display terminal as well as a data-entry terminal, it can upload and download information from the host computer, and it can act as a stand-alone personal computer. This is the approach most companies are taking.

A disadvantage of the CRT display is its bulkiness. The tubes are long, therefore causing the monitor to have a substantial depth. In some applications, such as lap-top portable computers, it is advantageous to have a very thin display (less than an inch).

An increasingly important type of VDT is the **flat-panel display.** There are several types of flat-panel displays, the most common being **liquid crystal diode (LCD) display.** LCD technology is the same as that used in digital watch displays. LCD displays available in the mid-1980s were difficult to read. However, substantial improvements have been made in LCD technology. Today's LCD displays use back lighting that makes them bright and very easy to read.

Printers

Printers produce printed copy of information output. Printed copy is often called **hard copy.** A wide variety of printers are available; they may be categorized as character, line, and page printers.

Character printers print one character at a time, similar to typewriters. The technology used for producing the print is usually either a **daisy wheel** or **dot matrix** (see Figures 10–15 and 10–16). Dot-matrix printers usually give lower-quality output. Therefore, when high-quality output is needed, such as in word processing, daisy-wheel or laser printers are often used. However,

Figure 10–16
Character Set for a Dot-Matrix Printer

As you can see, each character is made up of small dots. The near letter quality dot-matrix printers print at high speeds (up to 200 characters per second), producing draft-quality copy similar to what is shown here. When switched to the near-letter-quality mode, the printer produces about 70 characters per second by restriking the characters in each line. The dot pins are slightly offset when the character is struck again, so spaces between the dots of the first strike are filled in, and the copy looks better.

```
A B C D E F G H I J K L M N O P Q R S T U V W X Y Z
a b c d e f g h i j k l m n o p q r s t u v w x y z        Draft Quality
0 1 2 3 4 5 6 7 8 9 ` - = \ [ ] ; ' , . / ~ ! @ # $
% ^ & * ( ) _ + { } : " < > ?
```

```
A B C D E F G H I J K L M N O P Q R S T U V W X Y Z
a b c d e f g h i j k l m n o p q r s t u v w x y z        Near-Letter
0 1 2 3 4 5 6 7 8 9 ` - = \ [ ] ; ' , . / ~ ! @ # $        Quality
% ^ & * ( ) _ + { } : " < > ?
```

Figure 10–15
Daisy Wheel

You can see why this is called a daisy wheel. Characters are contained at the tip of daisylike spokes of the wheel. Daisy-wheel printers produce letter-quality copy.

Figure 10–17
A Line Printer

These printers are used with mainframes that have high-volume printed output. High-volume laser printers are making this type of impact line printer obsolete.

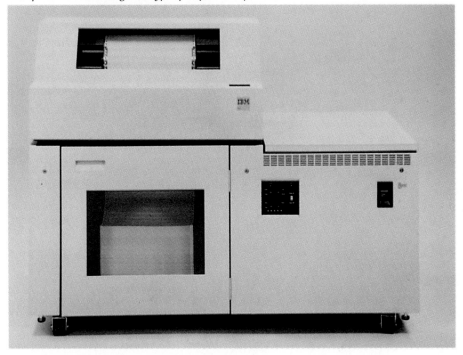

the newer 24-pin dot-matrix printers produce print that rivals the quality of print from daisy-wheel printers.

Line printers print a complete line in one operation (see Figure 10–17). Their speeds are as high as 2,000 lines per minute, and they are generally used for high-volume printed output. Line printers use print drums, print bands, or print chains to do the printing (see Figure 10–18).

Page printers print a complete page at a time. An example is a **laser printer,** which is a nonimpact printer. Thus far, we have described **impact printers,** which print characters and lines by having the type font strike the paper through an inked ribbon. **Nonimpact printers** do not use physical impact to transfer characters to paper. Examples are laser, ink-jet, and electrothermal printers.

Some page printers (such as ink-jet and laser) can produce very high quality, letter-perfect printing. For example, laser printers are capable of producing a wide range of type fonts and print quality equal to the best typewriters. Laser printers are also very fast, producing output at speeds of up to 21,000 lines per minute. Laser printers for personal computers cost about $1,200 to $2,500 and produce output at 250 to 450 lines per minute. Laser printer technology is very similar to that of copying machines. Ink-jet printers spray ink onto paper and produce print quality better than dot-matrix and not quite as good as laser printers. For PCs, they cost about $500, making them a good alternative to dot-matrix printers. Electrothermal printer output is of a lower quality, as it depends on dot-matrix technology to produce an image.

Figure 10–18
Chain, Band, and Drum Printer Mechanisms

These printing mechanisms operate in various high-speed impact printers.

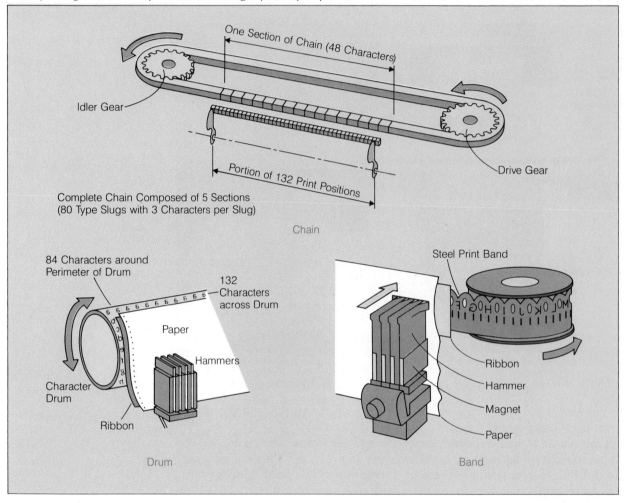

Other advantages of nonimpact printers over impact printers are that they are usually much faster and require less physical movement for printing; therefore, they are more reliable and quieter. A very significant advantage of laser, dot-matrix, and ink-jet printers is the ability to produce graphic output interspersed with text on the same page. Some printers can also produce color output, which is especially important for graphics applications.

Over the long run, nonimpact technologies such as laser and ink jet will, to a great extent, replace impact printers. Copying machines that print output from computers can be scattered throughout various offices and be connected to a central computer or a network so that high-quality output can be directed to local offices. Such a configuration could be an important part of an electronic mail system. If a high-quality hard copy of mail is needed, it can simply be routed to the office copier/nonimpact printer for printing. Table 10–1 provides a comparison of the speed and quality characteristics of various printing devices.

Table 10–1 ■ Comparative Characteristics of Printing Devices

Device	Category	Speed	Quality of Printout
High-Speed Line Printer	Impact Line Printer	High	Low/Medium
Dot-Matrix Printer	Impact Character Printer	Low/Medium	Low/Medium/High
Daisy-Wheel Printer	Impact Character Printer	Low	High
Laser Printer	Nonimpact Page Printer	Medium/High	Very High
Ink-Jet Printer	Nonimpact Character Printer	Medium	Very High

Most ink-jet printers can print in color. They can even print color onto transparencies used in overhead presentations.

Computer-Output Microfiche

Computer-output microfiche (COM) is used by many companies that need large amounts of computer-based data printed in a human-readable form. Figure 10–19 illustrates a COM card. This 4 × 6 inch card can hold up to 270 page images of data with 99 lines per page. Some COM machines read a reel of magnetic tape that holds the data to be produced. Others are connected directly to the CPU. Both types use a laser beam to image the data onto microfiche film. COM equipment can produce output at speeds of 10,000 to 20,000 characters per second and up to 10,000 pages per hour. The advantages of COM are the compact size of its output and the speed with which output can be produced. However, COM equipment is expensive, and microfiche is not directly readable by humans, although microfiche readers are inexpensive and easy to operate.

Laser-Optical Disks

Laser-optical disks have become important output media (see Figure 10–20). Their primary advantage is that they can store very large amounts of data—up to one billion bytes. In fact, predictions are that laser-optical disks will make

**Figure 10–20
Laser-Optical Disk**

Because of their large capacity (up to one billion bytes) and low cost (less than ten dollars each), these disks will have a revolutionary impact on computer output and secondary storage. Books and perhaps complete libraries can be stored on laser disks. Applications have just begun to be discovered.

**Figure 10–19
Computer-Output Microfiche**

Laser disks may replace the use of computer-output microfiche in the future. Laser-disks are less expensive to produce and can hold much more data.

computer-output microfiche obsolete. Their primary disadvantage is that a computer is necessary for users to view the output stored on them.

Graphics

The ability to display computer-based data directly in graphic form is an important business tool. Generally, the significance of data can be grasped much more easily by studying bar charts and line graphs than by examining the numerical data directly. Two types of graphics-output equipment are available: the **plotter,** which draws graphs directly on paper (see Figure 10–21); and the **graphics terminal.** Plotters and graphics terminals can produce both black-and-white and color output. Depending on the computer that supports the terminals and the communication lines available, graphics terminals can almost instantaneously display a complete graph on their screens. Therefore, management can quickly examine sales trends, profit trends, and other information. The newer personal computers, such as the PS/2 and the Macintosh, have very good graphic capabilities, for typical business uses. Thus, they are likely to decrease the need for specially designed graphics terminals.

Other Output Media

Many input and secondary-storage media, such as magnetic tape and disk, serve as output media as well. **Audio-response output** devices are also being used. For example, some railroads use audio-response devices for customer inquiries. Through a touch-tone telephone, customers can access the railroad's computer system, key in a shipment code, and receive an audio response indicating where their shipment is and when it is likely to arrive at their door.

Figure 10–21
A Plotter

Plotters usually have several color pens that draw the graph. These plotters are likely to be replaced by laser printers since laser printers now have the capability of producing color output.

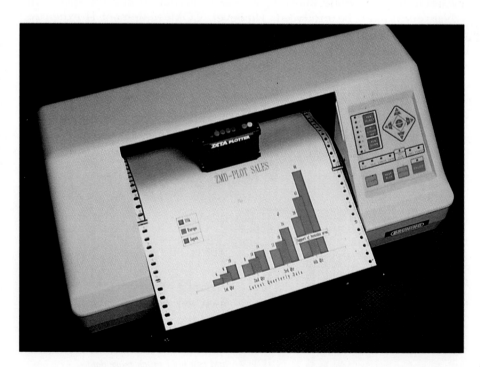

■ Data-entry and information-response devices provide a link between the central processing unit and the people who use it.

■ In a key-to-diskette data-entry system, data are transferred from the keyboard to a floppy disk. Floppy disks are low-cost, reusable storage devices.

■ A key-to-disk data-entry system allows some editing and verification of data upon entry. A mini or microcomputer is used to perform the editing and verification functions. It may also provide other data-input assistance, such as instructions, prompts, control totals, and error rates.

■ Interactive data entry allows the input of data directly to the production CPU. This kind of data entry is essential for real-time systems where the master file must be updated immediately. Since data are entered directly to the master file, it is possible to execute a large variety of edit checks, including comparisons with existing data.

■ Source-data automation permits the capture of data as a by-product of a business event. Some source-data-automation techniques are point-of-sale data entry, magnetic-ink character recognition, optical-character recognition, optical-mark recognition, voice recognition, and portable terminals.

■ Visual display terminals are the most widely used method of displaying output for reading by humans.

■ Printers are output devices that provide information response in the form of hard copy. Printers may be categorized as line, character, or page printers, or as impact versus nonimpact printers.

■ A line printer prints a complete line at a time, whereas a character printer prints a character at a time, just like a typewriter. A page printer prints a page at a time.

■ The type font of an impact printer actually strikes the paper to create character images. Nonimpact printers use techniques such as laser beams and ink jets to transfer information to paper.

■ Computer output microfiche can store large amounts of computer-generated data in human-readable form. Although it requires some expensive output devices, computer output microfiche can be produced at a high speed and requires very little storage space.

■ Plotters and graphics terminals are popular information-response devices. They help summarize business data by presenting them in an easy-to-understand pictorial format.

■ Key Terms

data entry	control totals
information response	input masks
peripheral devices	interactive data entry
medium	production CPU
device	data editing
key-to-diskette	source-data automation
key-to-disk	optical scan (opscan)
source document	point-of-sale (POS)
key verification	universal product code (UPC)

magnetic-ink character recognition (MICR)	daisy wheel
optical-character recognition (OCR)	dot matrix
	line printers
font	page printers
optical-mark recognition (OMR)	laser printer
turn-around document	impact printers
voice recognition	nonimpact printers
portable terminals	computer-output microfiche (COM)
visual display terminal (VDT)	laser-optical disks
personal workstation	plotter
flat-panel display	graphics terminal
liquid crystal diode (LCD) display	audio-response output
hard copy	
character printers	

◼ Review Questions

1. What is the primary function of data-entry and information-response devices?

2. Distinguish between data-storage and data-entry devices.

3. What is the difference between a data-input medium and a data-input device?

4. What are the major advantages of key-to-diskette data entry?

5. What are the major functions of the computer in a key-to-disk data entry configuration?

6. Explain the advantages of interactive data entry.

7. What is source-data automation?

8. What is the advantage of entering data at the time and place the actual business event occurs?

9. What do the initials UPC stand for?

10. Why are personal computers replacing visual display terminals?

11. What are the three ways to categorize printers?

12. List the advantages and disadvantages of computer-output microfiche.

13. What is the advantage of using graphics information response in business data processing?

14. What types of printers are most widely used with personal computers?

15. What are the major advantages of laser printers?

◼ Discussion Questions and Cases

1. Data-entry costs can be a significant portion of a business firm's total data-processing costs. If you had to choose between an online interactive and an offline key-to-disk data-entry system, what decision criteria would you use?

2. Interactive real-time data entry provides for up-to-date data files and powerful data-editing facilities. Unfortunately, processing costs for real-time data entry tend to be high. Batched data entry (such as key-to-disk) is much cheaper, but it involves a time lag between data entry and master-file updating. Which kind of data entry should a bank use for its deposits and withdrawals? Justify your answer by comparing the pros and cons of the suggested system.

3. While futurist writers predict paperless, computerized offices in the future, high-speed printers continue to print tons of paper every hour. If businesses want to control the quantity of paper they use, what are some suitable alternatives to printed output? Is it possible to continue using paper, but in a more economical and efficient manner? How?

4. The Smith Company is a manufacturer of envelopes and paper products. When employees need to purchase supplies or equipment, they fill out a form and send it to the purchasing department for processing. Several managers complain that the paper handling slows down the purchasing process by as much as two to three days. They recommend that a purchase request be initiated through online computer terminals. Under this proposal, the purchasing department would retrieve the purchase requisition on its own computer terminal, verify the information, and assign the purchase to a vendor.

Some people at Smith, including the internal auditors, argue that with paper forms, an individual authorized to make the purchase writes his or her signature on the purchase requisition. Thus the purchasing department has assurance that each purchase is authorized. They further argue that this vital control would be lost if an online terminal were used, since the purchasing department could not be assured that the individual inputting the purchase requisition was actually authorized to do so. Those advocating online terminals say that the person entering the purchase requisition would first have to enter a password that only he or she knows. The other group argues that passwords are easily misplaced and are often discovered by those who are not authorized to make a purchase. They argue that a signature is unique to an individual and cannot be easily copied by someone else. Which side of this argument would you support? State your reasons.

5. Lincoln Incorporated is developing a new budget-control system. This system will produce information on a weekly and monthly basis and will keep the managers informed of their spending in relation to their budget. Preliminary plans are to produce output only on personal computer workstations. Many managers already have workstations in their offices. When the new system is implemented, each manager will have a workstation and therefore will be able to call up budget information at any time.

John Decker is manager of manufacturing operations at Lincoln. John likes to play the role of a good old country boy, but in fact he is a very sharp and astute manager and very valuable to the company. In a recent meeting, system development presented the preliminary design of the system to the company's managers. When the plan to produce output only on workstations was discussed, John made this comment: "It seems that today, the only thing anyone ever mentions as far as computer output is concerned is workstations." He held up a piece of paper, and in his drawl said: "One of these days somebody is going to discover paper and say, 'Isn't this the best thing that has come down the pike? I can read it, I can write on it, I can put it in my briefcase, I can even take it to the bathroom with me.' " After the laughter died down, several managers joined John in insisting that output be available in traditional paper form. System development countered with the following arguments: many companies have almost been choked to death by paper; the trend is toward a paperless business environment through the use of sophisticated computer technology; and the sooner the company gets used to this environment the more competitive it will be. Which side of the argument would you support? Why?

6. Stephen Harris and Jim Howard were discussing their company's current high demand for high-quality documents. The company has been experiencing increased costs owing to the fact they have to go outside for such documents. Their discussion led to a possible need for laser printers, better word-processing software, and even desktop-publishing software. They were not terribly concerned about the cost of the software packages, which are reasonably priced. They were more concerned with the expense of buying laser printers when there are already a number of dot-matrix printers in the company. With the demand for high-quality documents so great, would a laser printer be worth the cost? Does the laser printer significantly increase the capability of producing high-quality documents?

7. Jonathan Symthe is the president of a large company, and he has decided to upgrade the company's computer system. Jennifer Jones, his MIS vice president, has given him a report on the alternatives available. The first choice is to update the current mainframe system and add terminals to additional offices that need them. The next alternative is to update the system by providing microcomputers to all users and then linking them to the mainframe, giving each employee that uses the computer system a personal workstation. What advantages would the second alternative have over the first in the long run, if any? What disadvantages would it have?

System Software

![■] Chapter 11

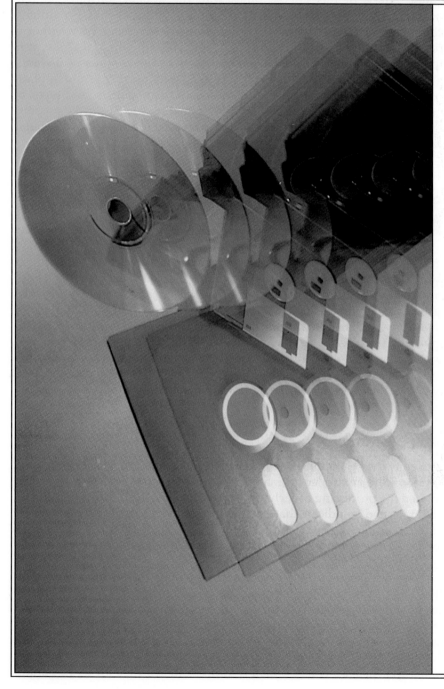

CHAPTER OUTLINE

Introduction

System Software versus Application Software
System Software
Application Software

Types of System Software
System Control Software
System Support Software
System Development Software

Types of Operating Systems
Batch Systems
Interactive Systems

Multitasking
Advantages of Multitasking
Disadvantages of Multitasking

Virtual Storage
Advantages of Virtual Storage
Disadvantages of Virtual Storage

Timesharing

Multiprocessing

Summing Up

Key Terms

Review Questions

Discussion Questions and Cases

Appendix: OS/2 versus DOS

■ INTRODUCTION

In most organizations, the computer is a very valuable resource. Among the resources a computer has are processing time, storage space, printers, and terminals. The management of these resources is performed largely by a type of system software called an operating system. When users interact with the computer, much of this interaction is with the system software. System software directly affects the ease with which users interact with a computer. Furthermore, system software is a significant determinant of whether a particular computer's resources are used optimally. For these reasons, it is important that computer users have a basic knowledge of system software.

In this chapter, we will distinguish between system software and application software, then we will explore the functions, components, and types of operating systems. Finally, we will see how operating systems make possible multitasking, virtual storage, timesharing, and multiprocessing computer systems.

■ SYSTEM SOFTWARE VERSUS APPLICATION SOFTWARE

There are two broad categories of software: system software and application software. **System software** is a set of programs that manages the resources of a computer system (processing time, storage space, and so on) so that they are used in an optimal fashion. This set of programs provides routine services (such as copying data from one file to another) and assists in the development of application programs. System software consists of general programs that help the computer efficiently execute application programs. **Application software,** on the other hand, performs specific tasks for the computer user. Figure 11–1 illustrates system and application software.

System Software

System software began to be used extensively in the early 1960s. Prior to this, computers were controlled primarily by human operators. These operators monitored the processing of each job. Typically, when a job ended, a bell rang or a light flashed to indicate that another job should be input to the computer and started by the operator. If a job ended while the operator was having a coffee break, the computer might have been idle for five or ten minutes or longer. In addition, the operator had to activate each peripheral device when that device was needed by the computer. This type of human intervention wasted large amounts of computer time and human resources. *Operating systems* were developed to automate these functions. These programs are stored partially in primary storage and partially in direct-access secondary storage so the computer can access them immediately when they are needed. With operating systems, a *job queue* can be read onto a disk. The operating system starts each job when system resources are available for its execution.

OPERATING SYSTEM
A set of integrated programs that controls the execution of computer programs and manages the storage and processing resources of a computer system.

JOB QUEUE
A line of programs awaiting their turn for execution.

Figure 11–1
Types of System and Application Software

Application software performs tasks for the computer user. System software assists in the control, support, and development of application software.

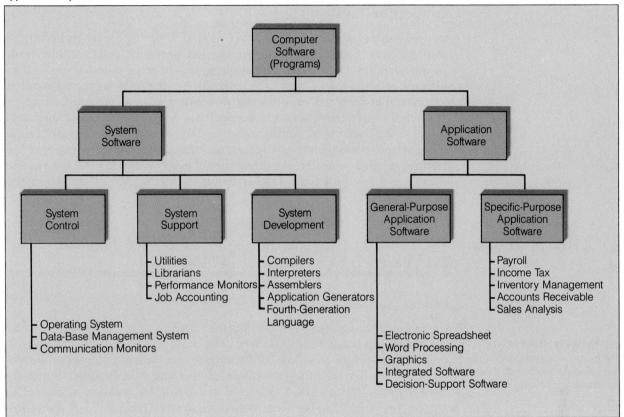

Since human intervention is eliminated, computer idle time is significantly reduced.

There are three types of system software:

1. System control programs control the execution of programs, manage the storage and processing resources of the computer, and perform other management and monitoring functions. The most important of these programs is the operating system. Other examples are data-base management systems and communication monitors.

2. System support programs provide routine service functions to other computer programs and computer users. Examples are utilities, librarians, performance monitors, and job accounting.

3. System development programs assist in the creation of application programs. Examples are language translators such as a BASIC interpreter, and application generators such as IBM's Application Development Facility.

System programs are developed and sold by both computer companies and specialized software firms. **System programmers** write system software. Most large firms have their own staff of system programmers who are capable of modifying an operating system to meet the unique requirements of the firm.

Application Software

An **application program** is a program written for or by a user to perform a particular job. **General-purpose application software,** such as electronic spreadsheet, has a wide variety of applications. **Specific-purpose application software,** such as payroll and sales analysis, is used only for the application for which it is designed. **Application programmers** write these programs.

Generally, computer users interact with application software as shown in Figure 11–2. The system software controls the execution of the application software and provides other support functions, such as data storage. For example, when you use an electronic spreadsheet on an IBM PC, the storage of the worksheet files on disk is handled by PC-DOS, the computer's operating system.

■ TYPES OF SYSTEM SOFTWARE

System Control Software

INITIAL PROGRAM LOAD
The initialization procedure that causes an operating system to commence operation.

BOOTSTRAP
When referring to personal computers, people often use this term instead of initial program load.

A very important part of system control software is the operating system, which performs many functions. Two of its more critical tasks are starting the computer (*initial program load* or *bootstrap*) and initiating the processing of each job. To understand these functions, let's examine the Personal Computer Disk-Operating System (PC-DOS) used in the IBM PC and compatibles. The components of PC-DOS are illustrated in Figure 11–3. Figure 11–4 shows the steps that PC-DOS goes through in bootstrapping the computer and loading an application program written in BASIC.

Operating systems on minis and mainframes also perform **job scheduling** functions by examining the priority of each job awaiting execution. Jobs with

Figure 11–2
The Interaction Between Users, Application Software, System Software, and Computer Hardware

Application and system software act as interfaces between users and computer hardware. If this software did not exist, very few people would be using computer hardware. As application and system software become more capable, people find computers easier to use.

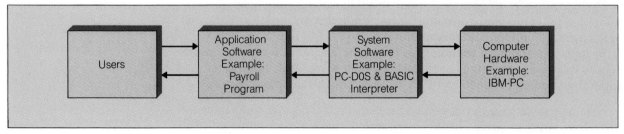

Figure 11–3
Personal Computer Disk-Operating System (PC-DOS) on the IBM PC

ROM-BIOS provides very fundamental services needed by the computer, such as a self-test of memory, starting up (booting) the computer, and input/output services between the central processing unit and peripheral devices such as printers and disks. It is stored permanently in ROM. The diskette boot record is a very short and simple program stored at the beginning of the DOS diskette. Its purpose is to begin the process of loading the operating system when the PC is first turned on. Nonresident means that it is not stored in RAM while the PC is operating. Both IBMBIO.COM and IBMDOS.COM are extensions of ROM-BIOS. They provide additional input/output interfaces with peripheral devices. They are stored on the DOS diskette, but they are hidden files. A hidden file is not displayed when a DIR (directory) of the diskette is produced. They are resident in RAM while the PC is operating. The primary job of COMMAND.COM is to process and interpret the commands that are typed in. It also contains the programs that execute several DOS commands. These programs are resident in RAM. The final part of DOS, the external commands, are not resident in RAM; these are moved from the DOS diskette to RAM whenever they are needed.

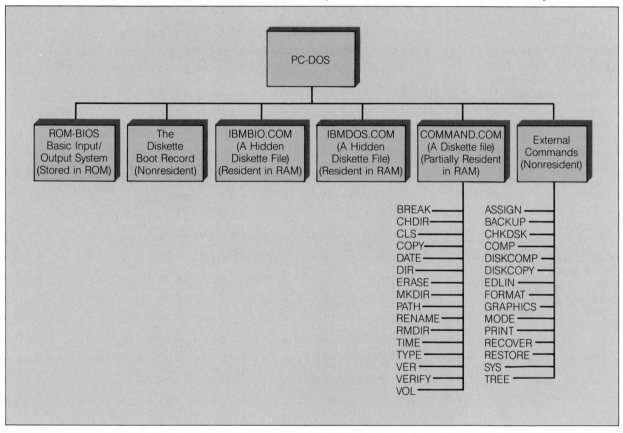

higher priorities are executed first. **Access security** is also an important function of the operating system. This function is carried out through various password schemes that identify valid users and determine which data files they may access.

Figure 11–5 illustrates the storage of a mini or mainframe operating system. The **system residence device** (a hard disk) stores the complete operating system. As portions of the operating system are needed for execution, they can be readily loaded into primary storage.

There are generally four types of operating-system programs: the **initial program loader (IPL),** the **supervisor,** the **job-control program,** and the

Figure 11–4
Loading an Application Program on a Personal Computer

Functions of the operating system are illustrated by the successive events required to load an application program. (1) Switching the computer on actuates a bootstrap program that loads the operating system into primary memory. The operating system transfers a file directory from disk memory to primary memory; in the file directory is listed the address, or position, of every program and data file recorded on the disk. In response to the next instruction, (2), the operating system finds the BASIC interpreter on the disk and, after making certain there is enough space for it, loads it into primary memory; the user is notified that the interpreter is ready. (Some personal computers perform step 2 automatically as part of the switching-on sequence.) The operating system is called on to load the application program itself. (3) Now, with the interpreter again in control, the application program can be run. Output will be a new data file in primary memory, which can be transferred to disk storage.

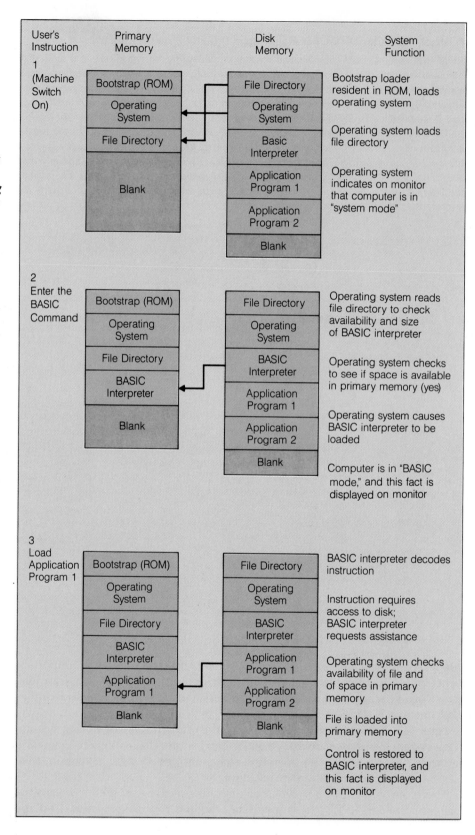

Figure 11–5
Storage of a Mini or Mainframe Operating System

A core-image library means that the programs stored on the disks can be moved directly into primary storage without modification. This improves the speed with which parts of the operating system can be moved into the supervisor transient area as needed.

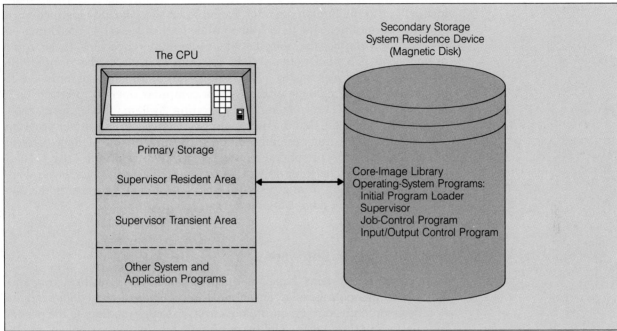

input/output (I/O) control program. In mainframe computers, the bootstrap program is known as the initial program loader. Its purpose is to start up operations. It performs this function by reading the resident portion of the supervisor from secondary storage and loading it into primary storage. Since the operating system is constantly supervising and monitoring the computer, a frequently used portion of the operating system, called the **resident supervisor,** is stored in primary storage while the computer is operating. Other parts of the supervisor are used less frequently. They are stored only temporarily in the supervisor transient area of primary storage when they are in use (refer to Figure 11–5).

Once the resident portion of the supervisor is loaded into primary storage, control is passed to the supervisor, and computer operation begins. The supervisor programs (often called **monitor** or **executive programs**) are the principal managers in an operating system. They organize and control the flow of work by initiating and controlling the execution of other computer programs.

As operating-system software replaced human operators in the control of mainframe computers, new languages were developed to enable users and programmers to communicate with the operating system. A **job-control language (JCL)** requires that the user include several job-control statements along with a program. The statements identify the job and its steps, and specify the system resources to be used (for example, expected run time, input/output device to be used, and memory space required). Job-control language also describes the data sets or files to be used in the various job steps. Job-control language is used primarily with large, multiuser computer systems, not with personal computers. The information provided through JCL can be furnished to a personal computer interactively by the user through the keyboard.

The supervisor and job-control programs acting together issue many instructions to the human operator. Examples of these include instructions to mount or dismount a tape or to load or unload a disk pack. If special forms are needed for printing the output, the programmer specifies these forms through the JCL statements. When the job is ready to be printed, the computer sends a message to the operator to mount the special forms on the printer. A large percentage of the work a computer operator performs is in response to instructions from the operating system. These instructions originate from the JCL that the programmer includes with his or her program.

Input/output control programs manage the movement of data between primary storage and peripheral devices such as disk and tape drives. These programs can also check for errors. For example, if an error is detected while a program is reading from a disk, the I/O control program rereads the data several times in an attempt to obtain error-free data.

System Support Software

Most computer systems have support software, called **utility programs,** which perform routine tasks. These programs sort data, copy data from one storage medium to another, output data from a storage medium to the printer, and perform other tasks. Utility programs are usually supplied by the computer manufacturer as part of the operating system. They may be called by any application program and used by that program.

Another common type of support software is a librarian. The primary function of the **librarian** is to maintain a catalog of the locations and usage of all program and data files. Librarians often execute password controls.

Performance monitors such as IBM's system management facilities (SMF) are a part of most system software. **Performance monitors** collect and record selected activities that occur within a computer system. For example, they collect data about CPU idle time, which operations are using the system (and how long they use it and what hardware they employ), whether each job is successfully executed, and the amount of primary storage each job employs. This information can be used in charging various departments for using the computer facility. Most firms feel that charging users for computer services is an important part of the control over computer resources.

Monitors also collect information about files used in performing a job. This provides an excellent audit trail concerning data and file usage. It is possible to determine, for example, which files were used when a particular program was run. It also identifies the user and the date and time of the access.

System Development Software

System development programs assist a programmer or user in developing and using an application program. Examples of these programs are language translators, linkage editors, and application generators.

A **language translator** is a computer program that converts a program written in a procedural language, such as BASIC, into machine language that can be directly executed by the computer (see Figure 11–6). Many different language translators exist—in fact, there is one for each programming language. They are categorized as compilers, interpreters, or assemblers. Programming languages and language translators are discussed in more detail in Module B.

Often in writing a program, a programmer calls prewritten subroutines (or subprograms), which are stored on the system residence device, to perform a specific standard function. For example, if a program requires the calculation of a square root, the programmer does not write a special program. He or she simply calls a square-root subroutine to be used in the program. The function of the **linkage editor** is to gather all these called subroutines and place them into the application program. The output from the linkage editor is called a load module. (The term *module* is often used synonymously with *program*.) A **load module** is a program that is suitable for loading directly into primary storage for execution.

Figure 11–6
Language Translation

Computers can execute only machine-language programs. Programs written in any other language must be translated into a machine-language load module, which is suitable for loading directly into primary storage.

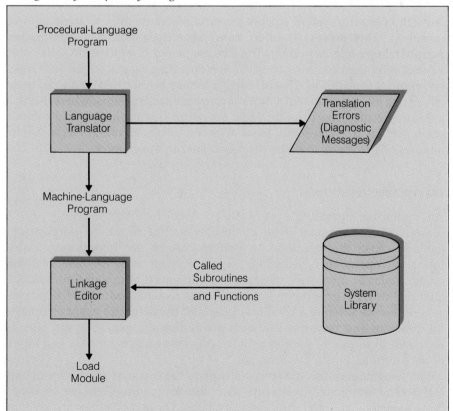

Application generators and **fourth-generation languages** are programming productivity tools that partially automate the programming process. For example, one type of application generator, the report generator, allows a programmer or user to simply describe the contents of a report rather than write the report in a procedural language such as COBOL. Some report generators (or query languages) even allow report requests to be made in conversational English. For example, a query language called Intellect will process the following query:

```
REPORT THE BASE SALARY, COMMISSIONS AND YEARS OF SER-
VICE BROKEN DOWN BY STATE AND CITY FOR SALES CLERKS
IN NEW JERSEY AND VIRGINIA.
```

Fourth-generation languages, such as FOCUS and ORACLE, are often employed by end users as well as programmers. These languages require many fewer statements to accomplish a task than typical third-generation languages such as BASIC and COBOL.

■ TYPES OF OPERATING SYSTEMS

There are basically two types of operating systems: batch and interactive.

Batch Systems

A **batch operating system** accepts jobs and places them in a queue to await execution. This process is often called **spooling** (short for **simultaneous peripheral operations on line**). The jobs are placed in a queue on a disk unit. As execution time becomes available, the operating system selects jobs based on priorities from this job queue. Batch jobs may be executed on a serial basis, where one job is executed at a time; or on a multitasking basis, where multiple jobs are executed concurrently. Most operating systems in personal computers work on a batch-serial basis without using spooling. Serial versus multitasking execution will be discussed later in the chapter.

Interactive Systems

An **interactive operating system** allows users to interact directly with a computer from a terminal. In effect, the user can interrupt a low-priority batch job and cause the computer to perform his or her high-priority work. Interactive operating systems must be multitasking systems. Also, real-time systems must be interactive since real-time files must be updated immediately after real-world events occur. An **interrupt** is required, which is the suspension of the execution of a computer program, caused by an event external to the program and performed in such a way that the execution can later be resumed. Examples of such external events are requests for data and inputs of data from an interactive terminal.

The remainder of this chapter will explore batch versus interactive operating systems and their relationships to multitasking, virtual storage, timesharing, interactive, and multiprocessing systems. These capabilities are predominant in mainframe operating systems today. Personal computer operating systems are moving toward many of these capabilities, such as multitasking and virtual storage.

■ MULTITASKING

Multitasking (sometimes called multiprogramming) is the capability of a CPU to execute two or more programs concurrently. In fact, multitasking operating systems for personal computers are called concurrent-processing operating systems. Multitasking capability is accomplished through the operating system. Essentially, two or more programs are stored concurrently in primary storage, and the CPU moves from one program to another, partially executing each program in turn. Early computer systems and many personal computers execute programs on a batch-serial basis; that is, each program is executed in the order in which it is read into the system, and only one program is executed at a time.

Advantages of Multitasking

Increased Throughput   There are several disadvantages of the batch-serial approach. First, throughput is not maximized. **Throughput** is a measure of the total amount of processing that a computer system can complete in a fixed period of time. The disadvantage is due to the relative speeds of computer system components. The CPU operates without mechanical movement, depending only on the flow of electronic pulses, which travel at about half the speed of light. Therefore, the CPU is very fast compared with the speed of input/output devices, which depend on mechanical movements or humans to operate them. Figure 11–7 depicts the elapsed time necessary to execute one job under batch-serial and three jobs under multitasking. Total throughput is significantly increased in multitasking, because the CPU is not waiting for input/output for the program it is executing. The CPU simply rotates to another program and begins executing.

Shorter Response Time   A second disadvantage of the batch-serial approach is its longer turnaround and response time. **Turnaround time** refers to the elapsed time between submission of a batch job and the availability of the output. **Response time** refers to the elapsed time between submission of a command to an online system and the completion of that command as evidenced by a message on the display screen. Turnaround on small jobs usually takes longer in a batch-serial environment than in a multitasking environment. Refer to Figure 11–7, and assume that jobs 1 and 2 are long, requiring ½ and ¾ hours of CPU time, respectively. Under the batch-serial approach, the turnaround time for job 3 would be 2¼ hours, plus execution time of about 1 minute. Under multitasking, the turnaround time for job 3 would be 3 to 4 minutes. Essentially, job 3 executes completely in a short elapsed time by utilizing the CPU, which otherwise would be waiting for I/O for jobs 1 and 2. Therefore, turnaround time for short jobs can be greatly

Figure 11–7
Elapsed Time under Batch-Serial and Multitasking System

In this illustration, three jobs are executed in four minutes under multitasking whereas only one job is executed in four minutes with a batch-serial operating system. The reason for the difference is that the multitasking operating system allows the CPU to execute other jobs while it is waiting for input/output to occur.

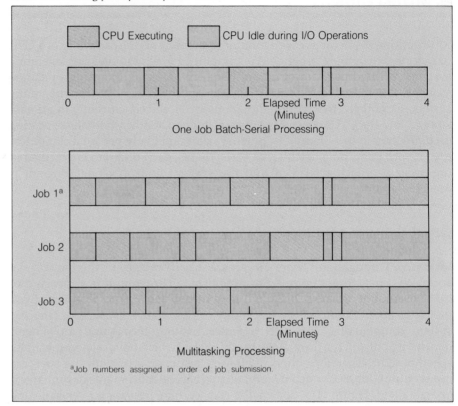

improved under multitasking. The turnaround time for long jobs is usually lengthened, since the CPU is devoting part of its time to short jobs. This is not a disadvantage, however, because long batch jobs usually have a lower priority. Multitasking systems usually have priority schemes whereby any job, including a long one, can be executed under a higher priority, if necessary.

Ability to Assign Priorities to Jobs Most multitasking systems have schemes for setting priorities for rotating programs. They specify when the CPU will rotate to another program, and which program it will rotate to. The user, through JCL or other specifications, can influence a job's priority.

Multitasking with priority schemes improves **system availability;** that is, it increases the speed with which the system can respond to high-priority, unanticipated requests of its resources. System availability under batch-serial mode can be very poor when long jobs are executing. With multitasking, high-priority jobs can be executed almost immediately.

Online, real-time, and timesharing systems would not be practical without multitasking. The response time at the terminals would be intolerably long if all instructions from the terminals and the batch jobs were executed on a batch-serial basis. Instructions from terminals must have high priority.

Improved Primary-Storage Allocation   In early multitasking systems, the programs being executed all had to reside in primary storage until their execution was complete. A constraining factor on the throughput of a multitasking system is the number of jobs that can reside in primary storage at one time. If only two large programs can fit in main memory, the CPU may be idle a large percentage of the time while waiting for I/O. The greater the number of programs that primary storage can hold, the greater the probability that the CPU will be able to execute at least one program while waiting for I/O for other programs. This line of reasoning led to the approach of writing out to secondary storage the programs that were waiting for I/O. In the vacated primary storage space, a program that was ready and waiting for execution was written in. This approach cleared main storage of all programs waiting for I/O. Therefore, in principle, all the programs residing in primary storage were either running or awaiting execution. This technique led to the concept of virtual storage, which will be discussed later in the chapter.

Disadvantages of Multitasking

Multitasking does have disadvantages, but they are minor. First, multitasking is implemented through an operating system, which is a program requiring space in primary storage since it must be executed by the CPU. The operating system overhead costs (its primary-storage requirements and CPU execution time requirements) are greater with multitasking than with batch-serial.

Another disadvantage of multitasking systems is the potential for **interprogram interference,** either intentional or accidental. While executing, a program can theoretically write to any area of primary storage. Under multitasking, other areas of primary storage contain other programs or their data. While two programs are concurrently executing, one of them could accidentally or intentionally modify the other. So that this is prevented, operating systems assign each program its own unique password while it is executing. In order to write to or read from, let's say, program A's assigned area of primary storage, the writing or reading program must present the proper password. This password is known only to program A. Therefore, only program A has access to its area of primary storage.

■ VIRTUAL STORAGE

Virtual storage is primary storage that does not actually exist. It gives the programmer the illusion of a primary storage that is, for all practical purposes, unlimited. The computer system itself maintains this illusion through a combination of hardware and software techniques.

Before a program can be executed, each of its instructions must be resident in the real primary storage, but not all instructions of a program have to be resident at the same time. Essentially, virtual storage involves storing in primary storage only the instructions that are currently executing, and storing the remainder on less expensive secondary storage, such as disks. Figure 11–8 illustrates virtual storage.

A virtual-storage system divides every program into pages, each of which has a size of, let's say, 4K. The operating system rolls pages of programs into primary memory as they are needed for execution. Under virtual storage, only the page of the program that is currently executing must be stored in primary storage. All other program pages can be stored on a peripheral disk unit until each is required for execution. The operating system also maintains tables that tell the CPU where each page of a program is located in primary storage. Figure 11–9 illustrates **paging.**

Advantages of Virtual Storage

Virtual storage has two major advantages. First, the CPU is utilized more fully. Pages of many different programs can reside in main storage simultaneously, since only one page of each program is resident in primary storage at any time. Thus primary storage can contain pages of many different programs before encountering size constraints.

The second advantage of virtual storage is that programmers no longer need to worry about primary-storage size constraints when writing programs. When the complete program has to reside in primary storage, as is the case with most PC operating systems, the program's primary-storage requirements cannot exceed the primary storage remaining after the operating system's requirements have been met. Under virtual storage, there is no practical limit on a program's primary-storage requirements.

Figure 11–8
Overview of Virtual Storage

Virtual storage allows the computer to execute a program even though only part of the program is in primary storage. The parts of a program are called pages, and they are swapped in and out of primary storage as they are needed for execution.

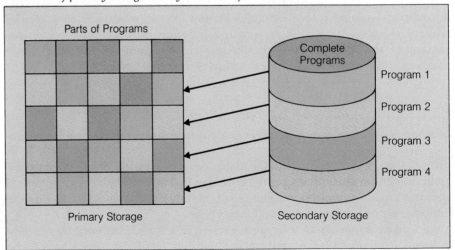

Figure 11–9
Paging in a Virtual-Storage System

Notice that to store all three illustrated programs would require 48K. However, because of the virtual-storage capability, the CPU can execute all these programs concurrently even though there is only 16K of primary storage available. For execution of a program to occur, only one page of the program must be in primary storage.

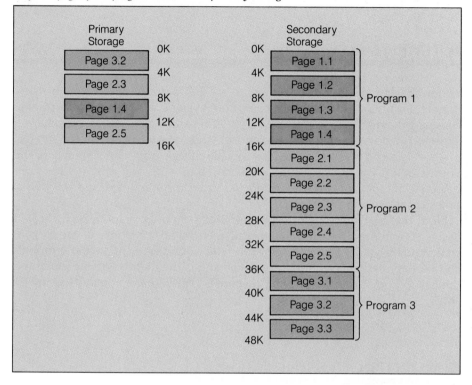

As mentioned before, PC operating systems are moving toward virtual-storage capabilities. This allows them to execute larger programs. For example, the size of most electronic spreadsheets is constrained by primary-memory size. Virtual-storage capabilities accommodate much larger spreadsheets.

Current developments in virtual storage are tending toward a single-level storage concept. Single-level storage treats all storage, primary and secondary, as a single unit or level. Therefore, the real difference between primary and secondary storage is *transparent* to the programmer.

Disadvantages of Virtual Storage

As one might expect, there are disadvantages to virtual storage. Overhead costs increase. CPU time is required to page (read/write) all those pages in and out of main storage. Additional primary storage is needed to store the tables that keep track of the pages, and to hold a virtual-storage operating system.

TRANSPARENT
An element of a computer system that a user or programmer can ignore when using the system.

Another potential problem is **thrashing,** which occurs when one or more pages of a program have to be paged in and paged out of primary storage frequently during program execution. Thrashing could reach a point where the CPU is spending too much time on paging in and out compared with executing the program.

■ TIMESHARING

A **timesharing** system allows access to a CPU and data files through many remote terminals. The central computer system is often owned by the company whose employees use it, but there are also public timesharing systems (owned by a timesharing vendor) where the users pay for the service. The cost is based on a fixed rate plus a usage charge. The services (such as The Source and Dow Jones News Retrieval) that you can access with your personal computer to retrieve data or order products execute on public timesharing systems.

From the user's viewpoint, the computer system appears to be dedicated exclusively to the user's terminal because of the fast response of the CPU to commands from the terminal. In reality, the CPU is servicing many terminals and perhaps several batch jobs. Multitasking is the method of implementing timeshared operations, since fast response to terminal commands is necessary.

■ MULTIPROCESSING

As explained earlier, a multitasking system executes two or more programs concurrently on a single CPU. In contrast, under **multiprocessing,** a single program is processed by two or more CPUs. The most typical type of multiprocessing occurs in systems that support both a batch mode and many remote terminals (see Figure 11–10). When a system has only a few remote terminals to support, the main CPU can handle all the terminal interrupts and trivial jobs, such as editing. However, the processing requirements of a large number of remote terminals can overload the main CPU. In this case, terminal interrupts and trivial jobs can be handled by a mini-computer, which, in the configuration shown in Figure 11–10, is called a **front-end processor.** The main CPU processes batch jobs and executes interactive programs that the front-end processor cannot handle.

Personal computers often use multiprocessing. For example, many PCs use a math co-processor that handles mathematical processing at speeds up to 80 times faster than the PC's microprocessor.

Multiprocessing systems substantially increase the throughput capabilities of a system with an overloaded CPU. Another advantage of multiprocessing is the backup CPU capability provided by two or more CPUs, which are, in some cases, identical.

Figure 11–10
A Multiprocessing System

Multiprocessing is widely used with large computers. Some mainframe systems may have several communication processors attached to them.

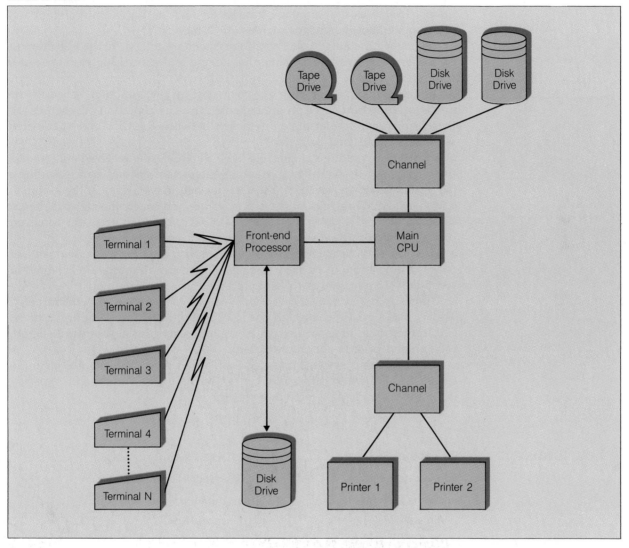

■ System software is a set of programs that manages the resources of a computer system, provides routine services such as copying data from one file to another, and assists in the development of application programs.

■ Application programs are written to perform specific jobs for computer users.

■ System control programs control the execution of programs, manage the storage and processing resources of the computer, and perform other management and monitoring functions. The most important of these programs is the operating system. Other examples are data-base management systems and communication monitors.

▪ Summing Up

■ System support programs provide routine service functions to other computer programs and users. Examples are utilities, librarians, performance monitors, and job accounting.

■ System development programs assist in the creation of application programs. Examples are language translators such as BASIC interpreters and fourth-generation languages such as FOCUS.

■ The major functions of an operating system are to control the execution of computer programs and manage the storage and processing resources of a computer system.

■ The programs in an operating system start up the computer, schedule the execution of various user programs, supervise the allocation of resources to these programs, and facilitate interaction between the CPU and I/O devices such as terminals and printers.

■ Batch-type operating systems line up jobs in the order received and process them when time is available. In contrast, interactive systems start executing a job as soon as it is received, so the user does not have to wait at the terminal.

■ The major advantages of multitasking are improved throughput, better turnaround, and shorter response time. These advantages are achieved primarily through the use of job rotation and priority schemes.

■ The concept of virtual memory refers to storing only the active segments or pages of a program in primary storage. The rest of the program is stored in secondary storage, and parts of it are called in when required.

■ A timesharing system allows many people to use the CPU concurrently. This is made possible through the use of multitasking operating systems. CPU processing time is distributed among users by a sophisticated job-rotation and priority-allocation system.

■ Multiprocessing systems allow the same job to be run on two or more CPUs. This improves system throughput by letting the various CPUs specialize in those functions which they perform best.

■ Key Terms

system software	access security
application software	system residence device
operating systems	initial program loader (IPL)
job queue	supervisor
system control programs	job-control program
system support programs	input/output (I/O) control program
system development programs	resident supervisor
system programmers	monitor *or* executive programs
application program	job-control language (JCL)
general-purpose application software	utility programs
specific-purpose application software	librarian
application programmers	performance monitors
initial program load *or* bootstrap	language translator
job scheduling	linkage editor

load module

application generators

fourth-generation languages

batch operating system

spooling (simultaneous peripheral operations on line)

interactive operating system

interrupt

multitasking

throughput

turnaround time

response time

system availability

interprogram interference

virtual storage

paging

thrashing

timesharing

multiprocessing

front-end processor

1. What is system software? How is it different from application software?
2. Describe the major functions of an operating system.
3. What are the functions of the three types of system software?
4. What is a JCL? What functions does it perform for an application program?
5. For what kind of job would you use a utility program?
6. Briefly describe the two types of operating systems.
7. Why is an interrupt-handling capacity necessary for an interactive operating system?
8. What are the disadvantages of the batch-serial approach to computer job execution?
9. How does multitasking overcome the disadvantages of the batch-serial approach to computer job execution?
10. Explain the concept of job rotation in a multitasking system.
11. What is paging?
12. What are the advantages of virtual storage?
13. How are timesharing, interactive computing, and multitasking related?
14. Give an example of a multiprocessing system.

■ Review
■ Questions

1. Assigning processing priorities to users can often be a difficult task. Operating-level personnel may desire a higher priority because they need a short turnaround time to keep production moving. Middle managers might feel that precious executive time is wasted in waiting for computer output because the operating-level people overload the CPU with long, routine jobs. How would you approach the problem of assigning user priorities in a large business firm? Is it feasible to allow the same person to use different priorities, depending on the importance of the job? How would you control the abuse of such a system?
2. Electronic Games, a small manufacturer of simple electronic games, has decided to purchase a computer system. One vendor recommends a system with multitasking capability. Karl Spear, the owner of Electronic Games, does not understand what multitasking means. Briefly explain multitasking to

■ Discussion
■ Questions
and Cases

him. Discuss what factors he should consider before deciding whether to buy the system.

3. The Getrichquick Company is overhauling its information and computer systems. The president is considering installing a real-time system to obtain quick answers to company problems (he feels the present batch system is outdated). He is even thinking about having a video display terminal in his office.

Getrichquick sells construction materials and supplies to commercial contractors. The construction materials are usually heavy steel and equipment, usually ordered so far in advance that only nominal inventories are maintained on them. Small orders and orders for supplies are creating problems. An extensive inventory is maintained for supplies, but many out-of-stock conditions (stockouts) occur because of unpredictable demand and supply problems. Sales personnel have long advocated a better computer system to help ordering and shipping problems and to reduce stockouts. Describe how you would advise the president about a real-time system. If a real-time system is not recommended, what type of system would you recommend? If a real-time system is recommended, what information should be handled on a real-time basis? What misconceptions does the president have? How would you advise him about these misconceptions?

4. The First Federal Savings and Loan Association is a small local firm. Its recordkeeping is done through timesharing with a computer service bureau. The association is satisfied with the timesharing service. However, several software firms have recently presented the firm with a complete package (including software and personal computers) that could perform the association's information processing needs locally. The software companies claim that their systems are flexible and can produce a wide variety of information for management needs. They also maintain that processing customer records locally would improve the confidentiality of the association's records. They argue that there have been instances of customer data being divulged to unauthorized persons at service bureaus. Do you think the savings and loan association should continue using the timesharing service, or install its own system?

5. Tieko, Incorporated, is trying to decide which of two personal computers to choose as the company's standard. The computer selected will be used throughout the company. One of the machines has a multitasking operating system, which allows the personal computer to execute two or more programs concurrently. The other computer does not have a multitasking operating system, but otherwise it is somewhat superior to the first machine. Those in the organization who favor the machine without the multitasking operating system argue that a personal computer can have only one user at a time, therefore there is no need for a multitasking operating system. How would you respond to this position?

6. In a recent staff meeting of the Tate Corporation, the idea of multitasking came up in the report concerning personal computer systems. Amy Wilkes, a new staff member, pointed out that employees must wait a considerable amount of time for reports because of the increasing use of their PCs. Jim Porter, executive vice president of Tate, stated that a multitasking system had been suggested before but was never looked into because of software and hardware costs. He added that the last time the issue came up was about two years ago, before Tate's employees used their computers so extensively. Since Tate's employees are using their computers more and more, would a multitasking operating system improve their efficiency? What advantages and disadvantages would it provide the company?

7. William Baxter, chairman of the board at Baxtercorp, just came into the central computer center to see what's going on. He has never shown any interest in the computer center before; he has simply let it run itself. Your boss is at lunch, meaning you have to show Mr. Baxter the operation. As you give him a tour, he asks you about virtual storage. He wants to know how it works and what you think its advantages are. Knowing your answer could make or break your future with Baxtercorp, how would you answer Mr. Baxter's inquiries about virtual storage?

Appendix ■ OS/2 versus DOS

■ INTRODUCTION

Many of you will be making a decision as to whether to purchase the OS/2 or the DOS operating system. This appendix briefly discusses their differences. Much has been said about the new operating system, OS/2, since IBM marketed it. In technological terms, OS/2 is the next generation of operating systems beyond DOS. However, many businesses and individual users are questioning how OS/2 can improve their productivity and efficiency. Some of the important questions in this ongoing debate are:

■ Is the added capability and power of OS/2 necessary for all users?
■ Will OS/2 have the same support and longevity that DOS has had?
■ Is the expense of switching to a new operating system justified?
■ When will application software that uses the power of OS/2 be available?

■ A LOOK AT DOS

The DOS (disk operating system) was designed for the Intel 8086 or 8088 processors found in the IBM PC, XT, PS/2 Models 25 and 30, and compatible computers. DOS is the most widely used operating system in the world. Currently, most people use DOS 3.3, 3.4, or 4.0. These versions have the following characteristics.

DOS 3.3

1. It is a single-user operating system.
2. It can run only one application at a time.
3. It has a 640-kilobyte memory limitation for RAM and a 32-megabyte limitation for hard disk drives.

DOS 3.4

1. This version provides the ability to address more than 640 kilobytes of RAM.
2. It provides a window and menu system that includes pull-down menus and help screens.
3. It has improved file-handling capability, which makes it easier and faster for users to add, delete, and organize files.

DOS 4.0

This version overcomes many of the DOS shortcomings. DOS 4.0 features menus, windows, and mouse capabilities:

1. It is menu-driven, and therefore easier to learn.

2. The user interface of the operating system is similar to that of the OS/2 Presentation Manager, but it does not require a high-resolution graphics monitor. This user interface follows IBM's Systems Application Architecture (SAA) design, meaning it has pull-down menus (called by typing the <F10> key) and optional mouse support.

3. The shell's heart is a file manager, which displays the disk directory in a tree-structure and in a file-by-file list.

4. It works in a number of graphic modes. For older monochrome monitors, the product works in text mode but still provides many easy-to-use features. On newer, higher-resolution displays, the product makes use of icons.

5. Some DOS functions still require the old-style command line user interface.

6. Another feature of DOS 4.0 is the breaking of the 32-megabyte limitation on the size of single volumes on a hard disk drive. It can create disk partitions of up to 1,024 megabytes instead of 32 megabytes. The Expanded Memory Specification (EMS) 4.0, which is built into the system, allows for files of up to 32 megabytes of RAM and is an ideal alternative to OS/2 for users who simply require more space for large spreadsheets and data bases.

7. It costs only slightly more than DOS 3.3 (about $150).

DOS is still alive, as other updated versions are expected in the future.

■ OS/2 DESCRIPTION

OS/2, released by IBM and Microsoft is the latest operating system for personal computers. OS/2 runs on IBM PS/2 Models 50, 55, 60, 70, and 80; IBM PC ATs; IBM PC XT Model 286, and clones. It requires a 80286, 80386, or 80486 microprocessor, a hard disk, and 1.5 megabytes of memory (2 megabytes to run both OS/2 and DOS applications). OS/2 is available in both a standard and an extended edition.

Standard Edition

Presentation Manager   OS/2's Presentation Manager provides a graphics/-icon user interface as an integral part of the operating system. Users start and track graphics-based applications by selecting icons with a mouse, rather than by using commands as in early versions of DOS. This icon user interface is very similar to the interface used on a Macintosh.

Multitasking   OS/2 has the capability of running multiple applications simultaneously within the same or different programs. Application programs (known as processes) can be grouped together to form sessions. Twelve sessions can be run simultaneously. These applications are said to be running in the foreground or in the background as they are being executed. Tasks that have control of the screen and keyboard are processing in the foreground; all other tasks are processing in the background. Foreground tasks have higher processing priority than background tasks.

Enhanced Memory   One of the biggest advantages of OS/2 is its breaking of the 640-kilobyte RAM barrier. OS/2 can use up to 16 megabytes of RAM. Actually, 16 megabyte is only a physical memory limit. Virtual storage capabilities can extend the memory capability to a virtual gigabyte (one billion bytes). The 32-megabyte hard-disk limitation still exists because of DOS compatibility but will be removed in a later version of the operating system.

DOS Emulation   OS/2 has downward compatibility with most DOS applications. Thus, it can run most applications that run under DOS.

Data Exchange   In OS/2, data can be exchanged between two applications in a number of ways.

Application Protection   OS/2 provides an environment where applications are protected from one another. OS/2 does much more than DOS in the way of resource management. OS/2 isolates processes, so if one process stops working, it does not cause further damage to any processes still running.

Extended Edition (EE)

Additional Memory Requirements   OS/2 EE requires 3 to 4 megabytes of physical memory, and the installed system takes up almost 20 megabytes of hard disk storage.

Data-base Manager   The data-base manager consists of a structured query language (SQL)-based relational data base, called Data Services, and a query language for the data base called Query Manager. The data-base manager is very compatible with the DB2 data base, which runs on IBM mainframes and minicomputers.

Networking   The Communication/LAN Manager of the Extended Edition uses OS/2 to allow any application written to run under OS/2 to access data and services across a network. In an OS/2 network, it is possible for all PC users to work concurrently on a single copy of a file. An OS/2 workstation can interact simultaneously with several other systems. A user can check parts inventory on a mainframe data base, check a customer data base on another OS/2 system on a local network, and stock prices through Dow Jones News Retrieval.

Disadvantages of OS/2

OS/2 has several disadvantages, although many of them exist because OS/2 is still a new operating system. Time and enhancements will lead to improvements in the system.

Parallel Operating Systems   The introduction of OS/2 has allowed for two parallel operating systems. There is much confusion among users whether to use DOS, OS/2, or both. In fact, DOS 4.0 has many features that OS/2 has. DOS 3.4 and 4.0 both overcome the former RAM memory limitation.

High Cost   The $325 standard version of OS/2 is about three times the cost of DOS, and this price does not include application programs. To run OS/2 and the Presentation Manager, the computer must have an Intel 80286, 80386, or 80486 processor, an IBM Enhanced Graphics Adapter or Video Graphics Array, 3 megabytes of RAM, a hard disk, and a mouse. Add this to the $325 cost of the operating system, application software upgrades, and user retraining and it could reach several thousand dollars per PC.

Large Memory Requirements   There is no certainty about minimum memory requirements for OS/2. Microsoft says that OS/2 requires 3 megabytes of RAM, whereas IBM says the system needs 3 to 4 megabytes.

High Training Costs   Industry experts expect costs of initial training to be high—perhaps 2 to 3 times that required for DOS.

DOS Compatibility Problems   OS/2 can be difficult because it is a hybrid. Although it moves beyond the 640 K memory limit of DOS and allows multitasking, it must remain compatible with DOS.

Hardware Compatibility Problems   Because OS/2 is very hardware-dependent, codes previously located in device drivers are now incorporated into OS/2, which handles all interaction with the system hardware. As a result, many peripherals that work with DOS may not work with OS/2. This incompatibility among different hardware configurations may raise problems for users who have not purchased all their equipment from one vendor.

Problems with Executing DOS Applications   OS/2 allows users to run only one DOS application program at a time and in a smaller RAM partition than is possible with DOS. DOS mode works fine for most applications but is not always compatible. DOS may occasionally need to be externally booted up to run troublesome programs. Existing DOS programs cannot be multitasked and are not protected. Thus, a DOS application that runs astray could wipe out the entire system. Also, DOS programs cannot use physical memory beyond 640 K and their execution time is greater under OS/2 than under DOS.

Lack of Applications   Technology without applications is meaningless. Although application software has been promised, not much has materialized. However, this is likely to change in the near future.

Only Promises   When fully developed, OS/2 will include a graphics interface, communications, multi-user capabilities, and a data-base manager that allows for a free exchange of data among mainframes, minis, and PCs. However, some of these capabilities may only be promises.

Advantages of OS/2

Memory Expansion   One of the biggest advantages of OS/2 is the shattering of the 640 K barrier. Expanded memory allows complex and large programs to run easily on OS/2 and allows developers to create highly sophisticated data-base systems. Under OS/2, PC data bases gain the power to emulate many characteristics of mainframe data-base systems, including enormous speed increases over DOS systems, improved multi-user capabilities and sophisticated file-recovery features.

Multitasking   The multitasking environment allows different programs to run concurrently. OS/2 juggles tasks to maximize the system's response to the user's foreground task. Thus, the advantage of OS/2 is its ability to bring a background task forward and suddenly focus most of the computer's processing power on it.

Graphics Interface   The Macintosh-like, icon-based, graphics interface is a superior way for humans to interface with a computer. IBM plans to use this interface for all its computers, from PS/2s to mainframes. Thus, users will feel comfortable using any size of computer.

Better Applications   Multitasking, the graphics interface, and memory expansion enable software developers to create much more sophisticated applications than under DOS. Because of the 640-kilobyte limit, DOS severely constrains programmers. 640 K is very little space in which to store DOS, the application programs, and data.

Increased Throughput   Multitasking features and the expanded memory greatly increase the amount of work that a single computer can perform in a given amount of time.

Disk Caching   This is another important productivity addition. The memory set aside for DOS compatibility can also be used for disk caching. Disk caching acts as a buffer between the fast microprocessor and the relatively slow hard disk. It accomplishes this by storing the most recently used data and programs in RAM. Thus, often these data and programs can be accessed from fast RAM instead of the slower hard disk.

Terminate and Stay Resident (TSR)   TSRs are DOS utilities (for example, calculators, notepads, outliners, and keyboard macros) that come with existing applications. TSRs provide a version of multitasking, sometimes with disastrous results when various programs trying to operate inside the 640 K memory limit crash into each other and bring the system down with them. OS/2, however, provides a class of programs known as device monitors that simplify, standardize, and enhance multitasking.

Connectivity   The OS/2 Extended Edition's built-in networking provides the capability of networking not only PCs, but also mainframes and minicomputers. Thus, connectivity between all types of computers is enhanced.

■ TRENDS

About fifty application software companies have started work on "protected mode" programs to run under OS/2. A survey by Forrester Research,

Incorporated, of Cambridge, Massachusetts, estimates that it will be 1990 before OS/2 outsells PC-DOS. Forrester's Professional Automation Report estimates that 235,000 copies of OS/2 will be sold in 1988, compared to 3.3 million copies of DOS. By the middle of 1989, OS/2 will begin a steep climb, until it surpasses DOS in 1990, selling 3.7 million copies versus 1.5 million for DOS.

According to another survey, DOS will retain its lead until 1990, when OS/2 will begin to gain steam as more applications become available for the system.

■ CONCLUSION

As of 1989, there is no clear-cut answer to the question of which operating system to use. It is up to users to decide which operating system they want for now. But based on the trends and on the efficiency of some of the OS/2 features, we may predict that OS/2 will dominate the future. But, many users will stay with DOS for the next few years. There is no question about the benefits of OS/2 or its overshadowing of DOS. The primary question is how quickly worthwhile applications will be developed for it.

Data Storage and Processing

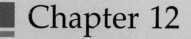 Chapter 12

CHAPTER OUTLINE

Introduction

Data Representation
True Binary Representation
EBCDIC Representation
ASCII Representation
Hexadecimal Representation
Parity Bits

Record-Access Methods
Primary and Secondary Keys
Sequential Access
Random Access

File Organization
Terminology Used with Files
Sequential File Organization
Direct File Organization
Indexed File Organization
Selecting a File Organization

Information-Processing Modes
Batch Processing
Immediate Processing
Batch-Sequential
Batch-Direct
Immediate-Direct

Online Direct-Access Systems

Real-Time Systems

Summing Up

Key Terms

Review Questions

Discussion Questions and Cases

■ INTRODUCTION

In Chapter 1, we briefly covered data storage and processing. Here we will discuss these concepts in more detail. Recall the components of the data hierarchy, listed in descending order of complexity:

1. Data base
2. File
3. Record
4. Field or item
5. Byte
6. Bit

By now you should feel fairly comfortable with these terms. (If you don't, go back and review data storage in Chapter 1.) In this chapter, we will first look at how bits are used to represent data. We will also explore file organization. And finally, information-processing modes and their relationships to online direct-access and real-time systems will be examined.

■ DATA REPRESENTATION

True Binary Representation

As you will recall from Chapter 1, all data in digital computers are represented by a **bit** being either on or off. Bit is short for binary digit. Since bits can store only two states, on or off, they are binary in nature. To store a large number of different alphabetic, numeric, and special characters, computers combine several bits into one byte. A **byte** is a combination of bits that represent one character of data. We will examine several ways that bits are combined to represent data.

True binary representation uses the **binary number system.** To illustrate this system, we need to first look at the **decimal number system** with which we are all familiar. The decimal number system uses the number ten as a base.

Each place within a decimal number has a certain value. Refer to Figure 12–1. At the bottom of the figure is a table that indicates the **place value** of each place within a decimal number. Starting with the right-most digit in the number, we see that the first place has a value of 1 (10^0), the second a value of 10 (10^1), the third a value of 100 (10^2), and so on.

Any number in any number system can be converted to a decimal number by multiplying each digit in the number by its respective place value. To illustrate, let's convert the decimal number 14,635 (shown at the top of Figure 12–1) to a decimal number. (Of course, the conversion of a decimal number to a decimal number produces the original number.) First, we multiply the digit 5 by its place value of 10^0 (or 1). Then, we multiply 3×10^1, and so on. When we add up all of these products, we find that the total is 14,635—the original number.

Let's now look at the binary number system, a system with the number two as a base. Recall that the typical storage media for computers—semiconductor

RAM and magnetic disk—store data by either conducting/not conducting electricity or by the positive/negative polarity of a magnetic spot. Only two possible states are represented. Thus, a binary number system, which has a base of two, is ideal for representing numbers in a computer system. At the bottom of Figure 12–2, we see the place values of a binary number system. The first place from the right has a value of 1 (2^0), the second place a value of 2 (2^1), the third place a value of 4 (2^2), et cetera. Note that these place values exactly double each time, since we're raising two to a power to derive the place values.

Figure 12–1
Conversion of a Decimal Number to a Decimal Number

The decimal number system is based on 10. Therefore, each place in the number system has a value that is a power of 10.

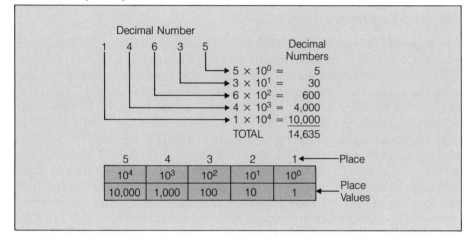

Figure 12–2
Conversion of a Binary Number to a Decimal Number

The binary number system is based on 2. Therefore, each place in the binary number system has a value that is a power of 2.

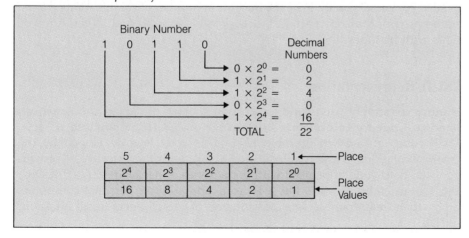

We convert a binary number to a decimal number in exactly the same way we converted the decimal number. We multiply the digit in each place by its respective place value, as illustrated at the top of Figure 12–2 (0×2^0 is equal to 0, 1×2^1 is equal to 2, et cetera). Adding up these products we get 22, so the binary number 10110 is equivalent to the decimal number 22.

True binary representation is used only to store numeric data. The primary advantage of true binary representation is that it requires fewer bits than other coding schemes do to store a given number. For example, the number 3985 can be stored in twelve bits if true binary representation is used. With twelve bits we can store any number from 0 through 4095, since in twelve bits there are 4096 (2^{12}) possible combinations of binary digits. If we use another binary coding scheme, EBCDIC—which we mentioned in Chapter 1 and will discuss next—the computer needs a minimum of sixteen bits to represent the number 3985.

EBCDIC Representation

The **Extended Binary Coded Decimal Interchange Code** or **EBCDIC** (pronounced *ib-si-dick*) is used on mainframe computers and is an IBM-developed binary code that represents each numeric, alphabetic, or special character with eight bits per byte (character). For example, the decimal digit 9 is represented by the code 11111001. Table 12–1 lists the EBCDIC codes for uppercase alphabetic characters and the numeric characters 0 through 9.

As shown in Figure 12–3, the eight bits in EBCDIC are divided into four numeric bits and four zone bits. You will notice in Table 12–1 that only the four right-most bits, the numeric bits, are necessary to code the numeric digits 0 through 9, since the four zone bits are always turned on and do not vary. The zone bits are used to code uppercase and lowercase alphabetic characters as well as special characters, such as commas and question marks. EBCDIC can code up to 256 different characters ($2^8 = 256$). This ability to code a wide range of characters is one of the primary advantages of EBCDIC.

Another advantage of EBCDIC is that we can represent two numeric digits within the eight bits of the EBCDIC code. If the data are all numeric, the computer divides the eight-bit code into two four-bit codes; in other words, the zone bits are used just like numeric bits. This form of data representation is called **packed decimal.** Since the maximum number of combinations we can represent with four bits is 16 (2^4), it is possible to represent all ten numeric digits with just four bits.

ASCII Representation

Another commonly used code for encoding bytes of data is the **American Standard Code for Information Interchange** or **ASCII** (pronounced *As'-key*). ASCII codes are shown in Table 12–1. This code was developed by the American National Standards Institute (ANSI), with the objective of providing a standard code to be used with many types of hardware. Like EBCDIC, ASCII is an eight-bit code, but it is used primarily on personal computers rather than mainframes. The advantages of ASCII include all those of EBCDIC.

Table 12–1 ■ EBCDIC and ASCII Coding Schemes

With 8 positions in a byte, EBCDIC and ASCII can encode up to 256 alphabetic characters, numbers, special characters, and symbols. This table shows only a portion of the characters that can be coded in EBCDIC and ASCII.

CHARACTER	EBCDIC BIT PATTERN	ASCII BIT PATTERN
A	1100 0001	0100 0001
B	1100 0010	0100 0010
C	1100 0011	0100 0011
D	1100 0100	0100 0100
E	1100 0101	0100 0101
F	1100 0110	0100 0110
G	1100 0111	0100 0111
H	1100 1000	0100 1000
I	1100 1001	0100 1001
J	1101 0001	0100 1010
K	1101 0010	0100 1011
L	1101 0011	0100 1100
M	1101 0100	0100 1101
N	1101 0101	0100 1110
O	1101 0110	0100 1111
P	1101 0111	0101 0000
Q	1101 1000	0101 0001
R	1101 1001	0101 0010
S	1101 0010	0101 0011
T	1110 0011	0101 0100
U	1110 0100	0101 0101
V	1110 0101	1010 0110
W	1110 0110	0101 0111
X	1110 0111	0101 1000
Y	1110 1000	0101 1001
Z	1110 1001	0101 1010
0	1111 0000	0011 0000
1	1111 0001	0011 0001
2	1111 0010	0011 0010
3	1111 0011	0011 0011
4	1111 0100	0011 0100
5	1111 0101	0011 0101
6	1111 0110	0011 0110
7	1111 0111	0011 0111
8	1111 1000	0011 1000
9	1111 1001	0011 1001

Figure 12–3
EBCDIC Place Values

Since EBCDIC is encoded in a binary number system, its place values are also powers of 2.

Place Values in EBCDIC							
Zone Bits				Numeric Bits			
8	4	2	1	8	4	2	1

Hexadecimal Representation

Often, programmers must examine the content of a storage location within the computer in order to debug a program. The internal storage is in binary form. To print out (or dump) the contents of memory in binary form would be of little use since the programmer would see only a string of ones and zeros on the printout. Conversion to decimal equivalents would be laborious and time consuming. Thus, some computer systems perform *memory dumps* in hexadecimal representation.

MEMORY DUMP
To print the contents of primary storage.

Hexadecimal has a base of 16; that is, there are 16 symbols in hexadecimal: 0 through 9 and A through F. Table 12–2 illustrates binary, hexadecimal, and decimal equivalent values. When hexadecimal is used, the contents of each four bits are converted to the corresponding hexadecimal symbol and printed out on the memory dump. For example, if the four bits are 1110, the hexadecimal symbol E would be printed out. Sixteen symbols are used since the maximum number of bit combinations of four bits is 16 (2^4).

The decimal equivalent of a hexadecimal number can be determined by multiplying each digit by its appropriate power of the base 16 and summing the products, just like we did in converting decimal and binary numbers to the decimal system. The primary advantages of a hexadecimal system are that conversion from hexadecimal to decimal is much easier than from binary to decimal, and hexadecimal generates a much smaller volume of printout than binary.

Parity Bits

The encoding of data using EBCDIC or any other coding scheme includes an extra (or check) bit. This **parity bit** detects errors. For example, with an even parity machine, the computer expects the number of bits turned on in a byte to always be even (in an odd parity machine, the number of bits turned on should always be odd). Refer to Table 12–3, which illustrates parity bits. Notice that when the number of on bits in the regular eight bits of the code is even, the parity bit is off; whereas if the number of on bits in the regular eight bits is odd, the parity bit is turned on to make the total number of on bits even. Bits can be erroneously changed from on to off (or off to on) when data are moved from one storage location or medium to another. If such an erroneous bit change occurs, the number of bits on are not even, thus signaling an error. Various environmental factors (such as dust) can cause these errors to happen. It is very important for computer hardware to contain automatic parity checking to detect errors in bit patterns.

Table 12–2 ■ Binary, Hexadecimal, and Decimal Equivalents

Notice that you can add up the place values of the binary system for the bits that are on, and the sum will be equal to the number in the decimal system.

BINARY SYSTEM (PLACE VALUES)				HEXADECIMAL SYSTEM	DECIMAL SYSTEM
8	4	2	1		
0	0	0	0	0	0
0	0	0	1	1	1
0	0	1	0	2	2
0	0	1	1	3	3
0	1	0	0	4	4
0	1	0	1	5	5
0	1	1	0	6	6
0	1	1	1	7	7
1	0	0	0	8	8
1	0	0	1	9	9
1	0	1	0	A	10
1	0	1	1	B	11
1	1	0	0	C	12
1	1	0	1	D	13
1	1	1	0	E	14
1	1	1	1	F	15

Table 12–3 ■ EBCDIC with Even Parity

Each row of bits represents a byte. Count the number of on bits in each row, and see whether it adds up to an even number.

DECIMAL EQUIVALENT	P*	8	4	2	1	8	4	2	1	←PLACE VALUES
0	0	1	1	1	1	0	0	0	0	EBCDIC
1	1	1	1	1	1	0	0	0	1	Code with
2	1	1	1	1	1	0	0	1	0	Parity Bit
3	0	1	1	1	1	0	0	1	1	
4	1	1	1	1	1	0	1	0	0	

*Parity Bit

■ RECORD-ACCESS METHODS

Primary and Secondary Keys

As discussed in Chapter 1, the storage of data in an information system can be considered a data hierarchy. Data bases contain files, files contain records, records contain fields, fields contain bytes (or characters), and bytes are represented by bits. A major concern of business information systems is the way we access individual records within files.

Records contain data on subjects. For example, a subject in a student registration system would be an individual student; in a payroll system, an individual employee. For this information to be of use we must be able to access it. To access an individual record, we must be able to uniquely identify it. We do this through a **primary key,** which is a field that uniquely identifies the record and thus separates it from all other records in the file. A student record is illustrated in Figure 12–4. The primary key of the record is the social security number, since an individual's social security number is different from all other social security numbers in the file. Normally, users or programs access individual records by supplying the primary key. Primary keys are also used when we change data within a record or delete a record. In performing these operations, we must uniquely identify the record on which the delete or change is being made.

Records may also be accessed through **secondary keys.** Any field within a record can be a secondary key. Secondary keys do not have to be unique. For example, in a student-records file, as illustrated in Figure 12–4, there would be many freshmen. We might make class a secondary key, since we may often need to retrieve all the records of freshmen. Since secondary keys allow us to retrieve information based on any field within the record, they are very valuable.

Sequential Access

In **sequential access,** we process every record in the file. Starting at the front of the file, we process the records in a record-by-record order. Sequential access is efficient only in terms of time, when the file-activity ratio is high. The file-activity ratio is a percentage of file records used in a given processing run. For example, most payroll systems would use sequential access when

Figure 12–4
Primary and Secondary Keys

Since the primary key must be unique, there can be only one record with a social security number of 410–39–3864. Since name, class, and grade-point average are used only as secondary keys, there could be multiple Robert E. Smiths, multiple freshmen, and multiple 3.70 grade-point averages.

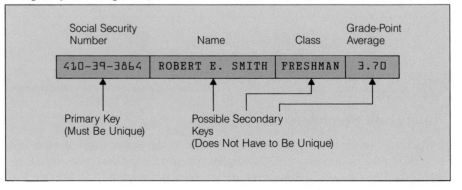

producing paychecks since most, if not all, employees of a company receive a paycheck in each payroll period. A very large percentage of the payroll file records would be used during such a run. In much of the routine, high-volume business information processing, there is a high file-activity ratio; thus, sequential access is an efficient approach.

Random Access

Often, we need to retrieve only one record from a file. Thus, the percentage of records we use in the file is extremely low. The need for these individual records usually occurs *randomly*. For example, when a grocery clerk uses a uniform-product-code scanner, the grocery items are passed over the scanner in a random order. The computer must be able to immediately retrieve individual records from the pricing file in order to price each item. It obviously could not access these price records sequentially, since there would be thousands of individual records—one for each item in the grocery store. File organization methods must be used that will allow quick, direct access to these randomly occurring requests for pricing data. Keep in mind there may be fifteen to twenty checkout machines going simultaneously, all serviced by the same computer. Just as there is a need to process records sequentially, there is also a very large need in business information systems today to access individual records randomly. Many applications, like airline reservations, must have **random access** because information needs to be processed immediately.

RANDOM
Something that occurs in no particular order.

■ FILE ORGANIZATION

Terminology Used with Files

There are a few terms we should define before discussing **file organization.** First, the term *address* identifies the location in which the record is stored. Note the difference between address and primary key. Primary key uniquely identifies a record, whereas address identifies where it is stored on the storage medium, which is usually magnetic disk. For example, your name identifies you but it does not identify where you live—your address does. There are two types of addresses: physical and relative (see Figure 12–5). A **physical address** deals with the physical characteristics of the storage medium. For example, on magnetic disk the physical address is composed of a **cylinder,** a **track,** and a **sector** (see Figure 12–6). To find an individual record on a magnetic disk, a computer ultimately must know its physical address. Some file organizations, such as index-sequential access, produce physical addresses for records. However, the most common file organizations today use **relative addressing** (refer again to Figure 12–5). In relative addressing an individual record's address depends on its relative position in the file. If it is the third record in the file, then it has a relative address of 3. Thus, what we are doing is assigning an address based on the record's relative position from the beginning of the file. As mentioned earlier, a relative address must

Figure 12–5
Relative and Physical Addresses

A physical address is equivalent to your street address. A relative address is equivalent to your saying, "I live in the fourth house on the left from the street intersection."

		Physical Address			
Relative Address		Cylinder	Track	Sector	
1	Data Record	9	3	1	Data Record
2	Data Record	9	3	1	Data Record
3	Data Record	9	3	2	Data Record
4	Data Record	9	3	2	Data Record
5	Data Record	9	3	2	Data Record

ultimately be converted to a physical address in order for us to find a record. The methods by which this is done are not important here.

Individual data records may contain the relative address of other data records. They are used to link together similar records. A file containing pointers of this type is called a **linked list.** In Figure 12–7 the records that contain the same class are linked. As you can see, all the freshmen records are linked together. The first freshman record has a pointer to the relative address of the second freshman record, and it has a pointer to the third freshman record which is in relative address 5, and so on.

A **directory** is a list of file names contained on a particular storage medium such as a magnetic disk pack. Figure 12–8 illustrates a PC file directory. It lists all the files stored on one floppy disk.

Figure 12–9 is an overview of the file organizations covered in this section. There are three basic types: sequential, direct, and *indexed*. We will discuss fully indexed files as well as a class of indexes called tree indexes. The balanced tree (B-Tree) index is becoming a very popular method for indexing files.

INDEX
A list used to indicate the address of records stored in a file. It is similar to a book index.

Sequential File Organization

With **sequential file organization,** records are stored either in the order they are entered into the file or in ascending order by primary key. For example, in a sequential student-records file, the records would be in ascending order by the students' social security numbers. For an individual record to be found, a sequential search, beginning at the first record in the file, must be performed. Each record must be examined until the required one is located. There is no index to the file.

Such a search can be time consuming when the file is large. Therefore, sequential organization is impractical for an application that requires imme-

Figure 12–6
Cylinder, Track, and Sector Addresses

The set of all tracks with the same distance from the center of the disk form a cylinder. The number of cylinders on a disk pack is equal to the number of tracks across a disk surface. The number of tracks within a cylinder is equal to the number of disk surfaces on which data are stored.

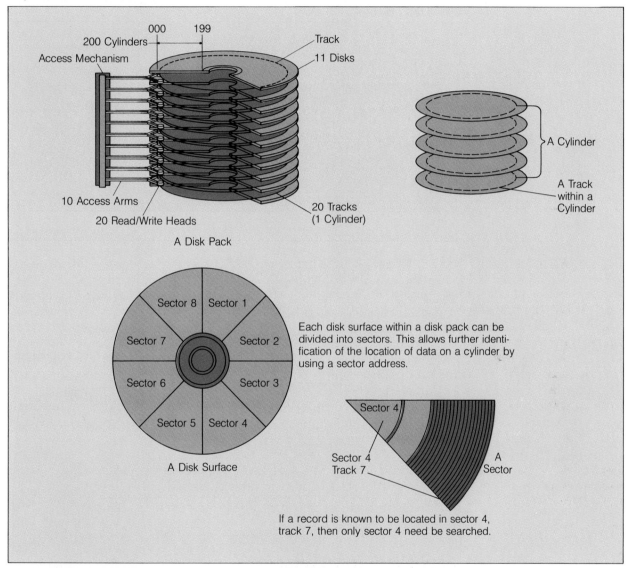

diate access to individual records. On the other hand, sequential organization is good for a payroll system that produces paychecks every week, since almost every record in the file must be accessed.

Certain storage media, like magnetic tape, allow only sequential file organization. In order for a record on a reel of magnetic tape to be located, the tape must be read sequentially, beginning with the first record. It is physically impossible for a tape drive to locate individual records directly because of the

Figure 12–7
A Linked List

After reading the first freshman record we can directly read each additional freshman record without reading nonfreshman records. Record 1 points to record 4, record 4 points to record 5, record 5 points to record 7, and record 7 indicates (with a zero in the pointer field) the end of that linked list.

Relative Address		Class	Pointer (to a Relative Address)
1	Other Data	Freshman	4
2	Other Data	Sophomore	3
3	Other Data	Sophomore	6
4	Other Data	Freshman	5
5	Other Data	Freshman	7
6	Other Data	Sophomore	8
7	Other Data	Freshman	0
8	Other Data	Sophomore	0
9	Other Data	Junior	0

Figure 12–8
A Personal-Computer File Directory

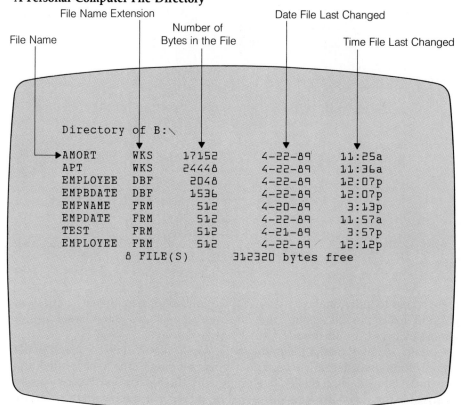

File Name Extension

Number of Bytes in the File

Date File Last Changed

File Name

Time File Last Changed

```
Directory of B:\

AMORT     WKS    17152    4-22-89    11:25a
APT       WKS    24448    4-22-89    11:36a
EMPLOYEE  DBF     2048    4-22-89    12:07p
EMPBDATE  DBF     1536    4-22-89    12:07p
EMPNAME   FRM      512    4-20-89     3:13p
EMPDATE   FRM      512    4-22-89    11:57a
TEST      FRM      512    4-21-89     3:57p
EMPLOYEE  FRM      512    4-22-89    12:12p
          8 FILE(S)       312320 bytes free
```

Figure 12-9
Overview of File Organizations

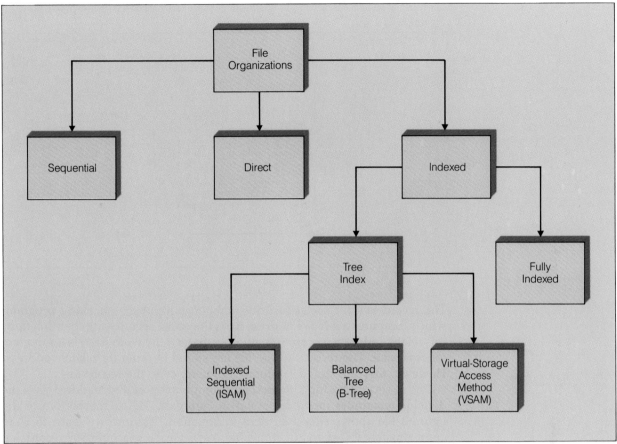

amount of winding and rewinding that must be performed. However, a direct-access storage device (DASD), such as a disk, allows sequential, direct, and indexed file organization.

Direct File Organization

A **direct file organization** allows immediate, direct access to individual records in a file. The organization scheme must allow retrieval of the individual record with little, if any, searching among the records on file. A direct file organization is usually used when there is a high volume of random requests for individual records and there is relatively little need to print out the complete file in sequential order by record key. An example of such an application is a grocery-store checkout. Grocery items are processed at several checkout lanes in a random order. The price file has to be accessed very quickly so the checkout process is not slowed.

The essence of direct addressing is being able to quickly produce a relative address from a record's primary key. Figure 12-10 shows how this is done.

Figure 12–10
Overview of Direct Addressing

One method by which a hashing program can derive a relative address is illustrated in Figure 12–11.

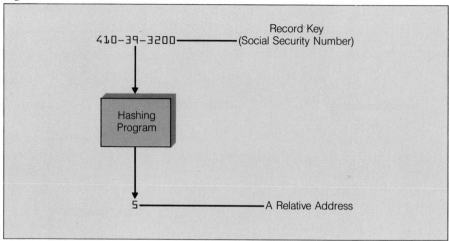

The record key for social security number is input to a hashing program, which computes a relative address from the social security number. In effect, this relative address is a random number. In fact, the word **hash** is a synonym for *randomize*. The records in the file are stored in order by relative address. However, they are stored randomly in reference to the record key.

One of several hashing methods for computation of direct addresses is the **division/remainder method,** shown in Figure 12–11. At the bottom of the figure a file shows stored student information. Assume we want to store approximately 950 students in this file. We set aside space for 999 records on a magnetic disk. There are 999 record-storage locations, each with a relative address that shows the record's position within the file. The division/remainder method divides the record key, in this case the social security number, by a number very near the number of storage locations set aside in the file. In our example, we will divide by the number 999. The remainder of this division process is added to the number 1, and the result is used as the relative address. The remainder will always be between 0 and 998. When 1 is added to the remainder, a social security number is very quickly converted into a random number between 1 and 999, which we use as a record's relative address. After placing the record in its relative-address location, we can retrieve it by simply supplying the social security number (which is the primary key); our hashing program will quickly compute the relative address.

The primary advantage of direct file organization is that we can access an individual record in a very small fraction of a second, even if the file has millions of records. Imagine how long it would take to find an individual record in a sequential file if the file contained ten million records.

A disadvantage of direct file organization is that space must be set aside on the disk for all the records we expect to store. In our example we set aside space for 999 records. When we don't have this number of records, we have empty space on the disk that cannot be used for other purposes.

Figure 12–11
Computation of Direct Addresses by the Division/Remainder Method

Try dividing some of the social security numbers in the file by 999 to see whether your result matches the relative address shown. Divide your own social security number by 999 to see at what address your record would be placed.

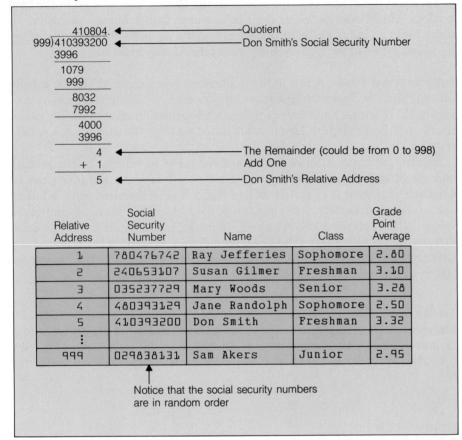

Relative Address	Social Security Number	Name	Class	Grade Point Average
1	780476742	Ray Jefferies	Sophomore	2.80
2	240653107	Susan Gilmer	Freshman	3.10
3	035237729	Mary Woods	Senior	3.28
4	480393129	Jane Randolph	Sophomore	2.50
5	410393200	Don Smith	Freshman	3.32
⋮				
999	029838131	Sam Akers	Junior	2.95

Notice that the social security numbers are in random order

Another disadvantage of the direct file organization is that the records are stored in a random order. As you can see in Figure 12–11, the records are not in sequential order by social security number. What if we had a need to produce a report of these records in sequential order by social security number? If the need for this report was only occasional and the file wasn't too large, we could simply sort a copy of the file in order by social security number. We could also maintain a linked list similar to the one shown in Figure 12–7, except in this case we would be linking the records in order by social security number. Each pointer would point to the relative address of the next social security number, in ascending sequence. However, it takes computer time to maintain linked lists, since they must be changed when records are added or deleted. Also, space must be set aside in the record to store the pointer. Generally, when records in a file must be produced in some sequence on a frequent basis and accessed directly, an indexed file organization is used.

Indexed File Organization

An **indexed file organization** has another file associated with it, which is used to indicate the address of the records stored in the primary file. The file that stores these addresses is called an index file, and it is similar to a card catalog in a library. When you look for a book in the library, you first go to the card catalog, which is an index to the books stored in the library. Similarly, an index file is an index to the records stored in the primary file. We will discuss two basic types of index files: fully indexed and tree indexed.

Fully Indexed Files   A full index is illustrated in Figure 12–12. In a **fully indexed file,** the index includes an entry for each record in the primary file. Figure 12–12 shows a full index on the social-security-number primary key of the file we used in Figure 12–11. A full index may be constructed on any field within a file.

As files get large, a lot of time could be spent searching for the relative address of an individual record in the index. However, a full index can be searched rapidly if it is stored in RAM and if it is searched with a binary search. A **binary search** splits the index file in half and then determines in which half the desired key is stored. That half is then split in half again to determine in which quarter the key is stored, and so on until the required key is found. A binary search is considerably more efficient than a sequential search of the index file.

Tree Indexed Files

Indexed Sequential File Organization   The **indexed sequential file organization,** or indexed sequential-access method (ISAM, pronounced *i-sam*), is a cross between sequential and indexed file organizations. The records within the file

Figure 12–12
A Full Index

In a full index, the relative address of each record in a file is stored. Although this may seem to be the best way to derive relative addresses, the process is time consuming because the full index itself must be both maintained and searched.

Primary Key	
Social Security Number	Relative Address
029838131	999
035237729	3
240653107	2
410393200	5
480393129	4
780476742	1
⋮	
998396732	128

are stored sequentially, but random access to individual records is possible through an index. Thus, records may be accessed either sequentially or randomly.

Figure 12–13 illustrates a cylinder and track index for an ISAM file. Notice that this index has a treelike structure. (Actually, it resembles an upside-down tree.) For a record to be found, the cylinder index is searched to locate the cylinder address, and then the track index for the cylinder is searched to locate the track address of the record. Using Figure 12–13 to illustrate, let's say the required record has a primary-key value of 225. The cylinder address is 2, since 225 is greater than 84 but less than 250. Then we search the track index for cylinder 2 and find that 225 is greater than 175 and equal to 225; therefore, the track address is 4. With the cylinder address and the track address known, the disk control unit can then search through the records on track 4 within cylinder 2 to retrieve the record. As you may have noticed, the ISAM technique provides a physical address (cylinder and track) rather than a relative address.

The ISAM approach is useful when records must be retrieved randomly and processed in sequential order by the primary key. An example is checking accounts: customers randomly access their accounts through automated teller

Figure 12–13
ISAM Cylinder and Track Index
Notice the treelike structure of an ISAM index.

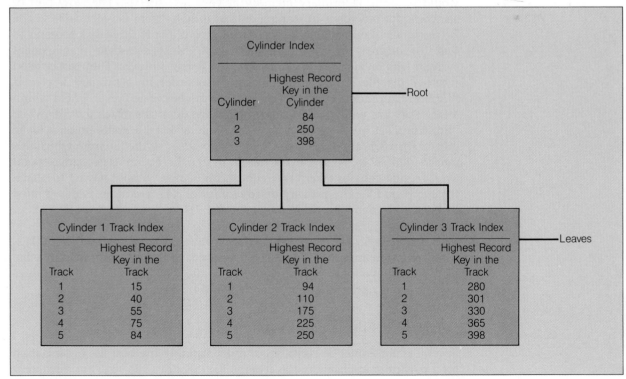

machines, and the bank processes checks on a batch basis once a day. The check-processing run would have a high file-activity ratio, and thus would access the file sequentially.

B-Tree Index   A widely used indexing technique is the **B-Tree index** (balanced tree index). Such an index is illustrated in Figure 12–14. This index is called a balanced tree index because all the leaves are on the same level of the tree. The B-Tree index in Figure 12–14b is an index to the primary file shown in Figure 12–14a. A search of the B-Tree index begins at the root. Let's assume we need to know the address of a record whose primary key is 72. We look at 54 in the root and decide that 72 is greater than 54, and then branch to the right. If the primary key we were looking for was less than 54, we would branch to the left. We then examine the primary keys in the next lowest level index. Since 72 is greater than 63 but less than 85, we go to the primary keys that branch between 63 and 85. At this point we are at the leaves that contain the relative address of each record. We find that 72 is in relative address 6. With three accesses (at the root, at the intermediate level, and at the leaves), we have found one address out of eleven records.

B-Tree indexes are very efficient in search time. This is true because we can put a large number of primary keys in each of the nodes. For example, what if we put a hundred primary keys in each of the nodes in Figure 12–14? We would have a hundred primary keys in the root node, ten thousand primary keys in the intermediate nodes, and one million primary keys in the leaf nodes. With such a B-Tree index, we could find the address of one in one million records with just three disk accesses! Of course, we would have to do some searching within the hundred primary keys in each root node, but this would be done in primary memory at very fast speeds. The slow part of searching for records is in reading data or indexes from magnetic disks. The B-Tree index of one million records would require only three disk accesses to find the address of an individual record. Most data-base management systems (run on all types of computers) use B-Tree indexes. They can be used whether the file is physically in sequential order by a primary key or is physically in random order. B-Tree indexes can be created on any field within a file. They are very good at servicing ad hoc queries such as the following: "Provide a list of all students who are seniors, have a grade-point average greater than 3.2, and have taken a Spanish course." If the file from which this information is to be retrieved has a B-Tree index on class, grade-point average, and courses taken, the request can be met without having to search the complete file. The primary disadvantage of a B-Tree index is that it must be kept up-to-date.

Virtual Storage Access Method   The **virtual storage access method (VSAM)** is used on IBM mainframes. It uses a B-Tree index to retrieve records from a file. VSAM is independent of hardware (hence the word *virtual*); that is, it does not store and retrieve data by cylinders and tracks.

Selecting a File Organization

Several factors must be considered in determining the best file organization for a particular application: file activity, file volatility, file size, and file query

Figure 12–14
A B-Tree Index

Most indexes used with personal computers are B-Tree.

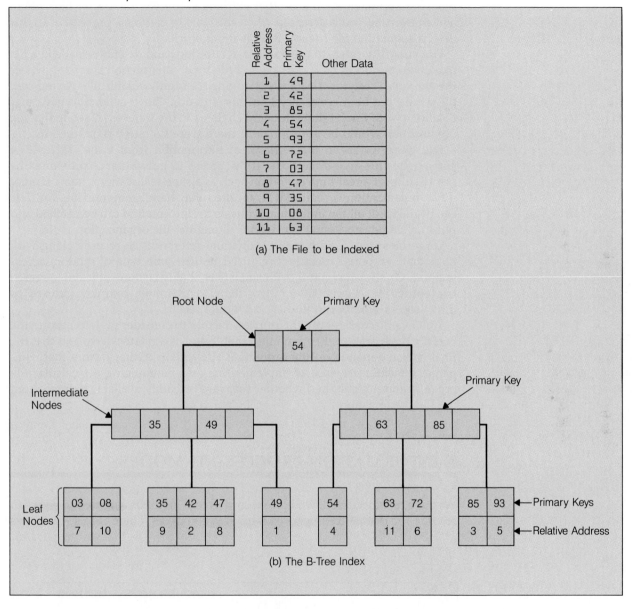

(a) The File to be Indexed

(b) The B-Tree Index

requirements. We defined **file activity** earlier as the percentage of file records used or accessed in a given processing run. At one extreme (with a low file activity) is an airline-reservation application, where each transaction is processed immediately and only one file record is accessed. If the file is rarely processed sequentially, the direct-access method would be used. In-between is the bank-checking application, where the records must be accessed both randomly and sequentially. This file is best organized using one of the indexing approaches. At the other extreme is the payroll master file, where almost every record is accessed when the weekly payroll is processed. In this case, a sequential file organization is more efficient.

File volatility refers to the number of additions and deletions made in a file in a given period of time. The payroll file for a construction company where the employee roster is constantly changing is a highly volatile file. An indexed file would not be a good choice in this situation, since many additions and deletions would necessitate frequent changes in the indexes. A sequential file organization would be appropriate if there were no query requirements.

File query refers to the retrieval of information from a file. Table 12–4 summarizes file-access methods. If the access to individual records must be fast to support a real-time operation such as airline reservations, some kind of direct organization is required. If, on the other hand, requirements for data can be delayed, all the individual requests for information can be batched and put in a single processing run with a sequential file organization.

Large files that require many individual references to records along with immediate response must be organized under some type of random-access method. On the other hand, with small files, it may be more efficient to search the entire file sequentially rather than to maintain complex indexes or direct-access schemes to find an individual record.

We have discussed only the primary factors to consider in determining the best file organization. Keep in mind that "best" is a relative term and that the final choice depends on the individual application. Other factors that companies consider are ease of implementing and maintaining a particular file organization, its cost, and whether software is readily available to implement the file organization.

■ INFORMATION-PROCESSING MODES

We have just discussed two basic record-access methods: sequential access to records and direct access to records on a random basis. There are also two ways

Table 12–4 ■ Summary of File-Access Methods

A direct file organization allows sequential record access if the records are linked together in sequential order with a linked list.

	RECORD-ACCESS METHOD	
FILE ORGANIZATION	**Sequential**	**Random**
Sequential	Yes	No
Direct	Usually No	Yes
Indexed Sequential	Yes	Yes
Balanced Tree	Yes	Yes
Virtual Storage	Yes	Yes
Fully Indexed	Yes	Yes

to process data—batch and immediate. We will first discuss batch and immediate processing. Then we will examine how the two types of record-access methods combine with the two ways to process data to form three information-processing modes: batch-sequential, batch-direct, and immediate-direct. Immediate-sequential is impractical, since records cannot be retrieved randomly from sequential files that are not indexed.

Batch Processing

Under **batch processing,** changes and queries to the file are stored for a period of time, and then a processing run is made periodically to update the file and to obtain the information required by the queries and scheduled reports. The batch runs may be made on a scheduled basis (such as daily, weekly, or monthly) or on an as-required basis.

Figure 12–15 illustrates batch processing with a sequential file stored on magnetic tape. As shown in the figure, a new master file on a separate volume of tape is produced whenever the file-storage medium is magnetic tape. If the storage medium is direct access, then the updating is in-place updating, and the new master-file records reside physically in the same area of the direct-access storage device (DASD) as the old records. In-place updating,

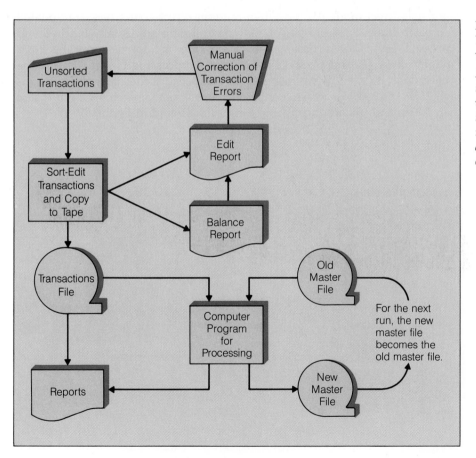

Figure 12–15
Batch-Sequential Processing with Tape Files

If the files were stored on disks, the only difference is that there would be no old and new master files, since each record in the master file would be updated and then written back to its original location on the disk.

sometimes referred to as destructive updating, simply writes the new data over the physical area that the old data occupied on the DASD.

Immediate Processing

Under **immediate processing,** transactions are processed to update the file immediately or shortly after a real-world event occurs. Usually, these real-world events occur in a random order. Immediate processing is illustrated in Figure 12–16.

Batch-Sequential

The **batch-sequential mode** was illustrated in Figure 12–15. With this type of processing, changes and queries to the file are batched and processed periodically on a sequential-access basis. In a practical sense, the only way to process a sequential-access file is on a batch basis since there is no random direct access to individual records. Earlier data-processing applications were always batch-sequential, but the mode is declining in popularity because of the decreasing costs of direct-access storage devices.

Batch-Direct

The **batch-direct mode** is used when random direct-access files are updated on a batch basis. For example, weekly payroll data are usually batched and processed on a batch basis even if the file is stored according to a random-access file organization. Batch-direct processing is sometimes done even though it is inefficient in a payroll run because the file-activity ratio is high. The batch-direct mode is most efficient when the activity ratio is less than 50 percent. Batch-direct processing is illustrated in Figure 12–17.

Figure 12–16
Immediate Processing

Immediate processing is likely to be the predominant method of processing business transactions in the future.

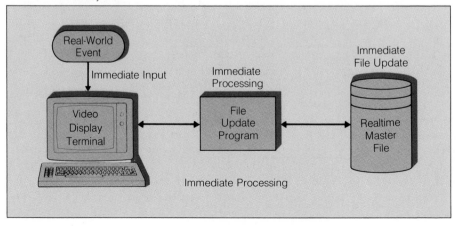

Figure 12–17
Batch-Direct Processing

Contrast this illustration with Figure 12–15. Here, the files are stored on a direct-access storage device, allowing random updating.

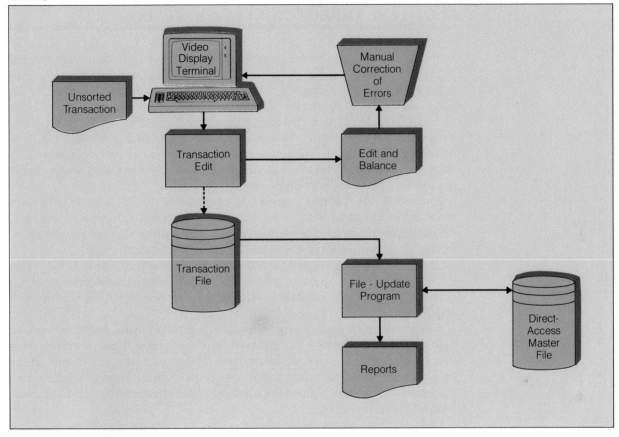

Immediate-Direct

Immediate processing of random direct-access files is the approach that information processing is moving toward. The **immediate-direct mode** is essential for real-time files, which are required in many information systems. For example, an airline-reservations system could not function without real-time files. Other examples of information systems that require real-time files are finished-goods inventory files where order entry is computerized, and student-record files for course-registration systems.

Many other applications use immediate-direct processing because if transactions are captured near the point of the event, errors can usually be corrected with relative ease. A properly designed, immediate-direct processing system can potentially control input much better than a batch-processing system. All of the edit checks performed on batch input can also be performed on immediate input. In addition, under an immediate-direct system, errors are communicated immediately to the data-entry operator, who is thus better able to correct them. Also, the computer can provide the operator with instructions and aids through the terminal. Figure 12–18 illustrates immediate-direct processing.

■ ONLINE DIRECT-ACCESS SYSTEMS

In the term *online direct-access systems*, **online** refers to any computer system, peripheral device, or file, that the CPU can control without direct human intervention. A reel of magnetic tape in the library cannot be processed by the CPU without human intervention and therefore is not online. In contrast, a disk pack mounted on a disk drive that is accessible to the CPU is online. Peripheral devices or files not in direct communication with the CPU are **offline. Direct access** refers to a file organization where records can be retrieved by the CPU without much searching. Direct and indexed file organizations allow direct access.

An **online direct-access system** has several terminals (or workstations) in direct communication with the CPU, which in turn can retrieve data from one or more files directly for immediate processing without human intervention. Figure 12–19 shows a typical online direct-access system.

Online terminals without online direct-access capability would be impractical. The turnaround time and processing costs would be intolerable if an operator had to mount each file requested and the record search were performed sequentially.

Random direct-access files are usually associated with online terminals. One of the primary reasons for random direct-access files is to allow for immediate processing of inquiries and updates to the file from online terminals scattered throughout the user organization. Therefore, the terms *online* and *direct-access* are usually used together when referring to a complete computer system.

Online direct-access systems serve three primary functions—inquiry, update, and programming. Inquiry terminals retrieve information from files

Figure 12–18
Immediate-Direct Processing

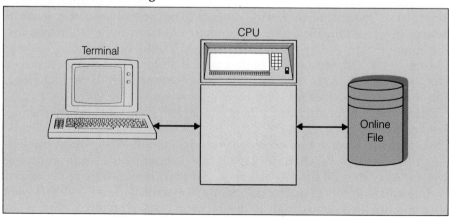

Figure 12–19
A Typical Online Direct-Access System

The terminals (or workstations) at the left may access the communication processor through a direct line, through a local area network, or through regular telephone dial-up lines. A communication processor handles all communications with the terminals, thereby relieving the main CPU of this task.

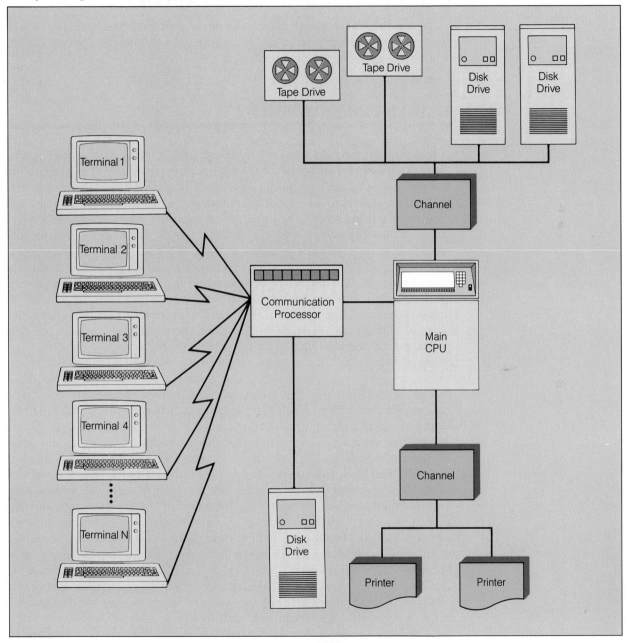

in response to inquiries. Update terminals access files, modify data, and provide information in response to inquiries. Programmers use online direct-access systems widely when they write or change program code. Copies of production or new programs are stored in a programmer area on an online disk pack, and coding is done through a CRT terminal on the programmer's desk.

Online direct-access systems are not necessarily real-time systems, though the two terms are often used interchangeably. The distinction between them will be discussed in the next section.

■ REAL-TIME SYSTEMS

A **real-time information system** can immediately capture data about ongoing events or processes and provide the information necessary to manage them. Examples of real-time systems are manufacturing-process control and airline-reservation systems. An essential component of a real-time system is real-time master files, which are updated immediately after a real-world event occurs. Consequently, at any point in time, the data in real-time master files should accurately reflect the status of the real-world properties they represent. For example, when a customer reserves a seat on an airline flight, the agent keys in the customer's reservation, and the inventory of available seats on that flight is immediately updated to reflect one less seat. Obviously, an immediate processing system is necessary to respond to customer inquiries about available seats. A batch system would be inadequate because the data on the master file would not be up-to-date.

Many colleges and universities use real-time systems to register students for classes. The students request classes through a computer terminal. They can be notified immediately about whether their schedules are confirmed because the inventory of unfilled seats in each class is on a real-time file. Figure 12–20 illustrates a real-time system.

Real-time systems are most useful at the transaction-processing and operational decision levels—for example, in order-processing systems that depend on real-time inventory master files. Management decisions at the tactical and strategic levels generally do not require real-time information. Information that is a day, a week, or even a month old, such as profit and loss statements, can be just as valuable as real-time data for tactical or strategic decision making. However, as the cost of storage and processing declines, more real-time systems are being implemented for transaction processing. More of the data used in tactical and strategic decisions are becoming available on a real-time basis. For example, tactical sales-analysis data can be retrieved from real-time point-of-sale systems, even though in some cases it is not necessary for such data to be real-time.

Certain transaction-processing applications do not require real-time updating. For example, updating the payroll master file on a real-time basis for hours worked by each employee is unnecessary. If payroll checks are produced weekly, the information can be updated every week via the batch-processing method.

Figure 12–20
A Real-Time System

In a real-time system, the terminals as well as files must be online to the CPU.

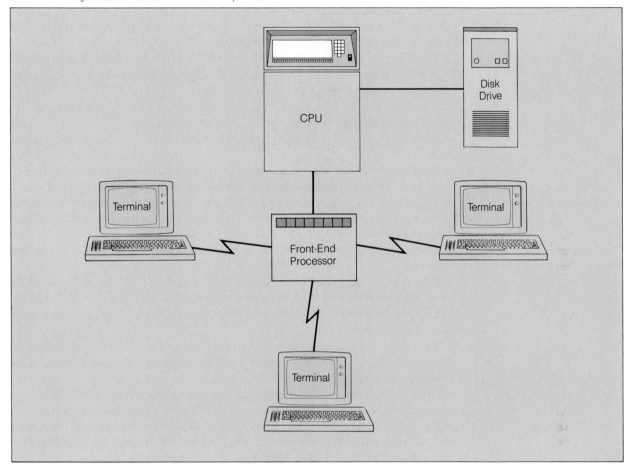

The computer configuration to support a real-time system must allow online direct access to data. The files must be structured to allow random access, since fast response to inquiries is required, and update transactions are processed as they occur, rather than on a delayed, batch basis. Thus, real-time systems are online, direct-access systems. However, an online, direct-access system does not have to have real-time files. For example, a payroll system may allow online, direct access to answer queries, but the files may be updated in a batch basis at the end of each pay period.

Real-time systems have the primary advantage of providing timely information. Certain computer applications can function only on a real-time basis. Others are most cost-effective using a batch mode. The primary disadvantages of real-time systems are that hardware and communication costs are greater, and the operating system and application software necessary to support them are more complex.

■ Summing Up

■ Data are internally represented in the computer in the form of binary digits. Any number can be converted to binary representation by expressing it in terms of the powers of two.

■ The Extended Binary Coded Decimal Interchange Code (EBCDIC) represents a character or a digit as a combination of eight bits, called a byte. This code is used extensively on IBM hardware.

■ The eight-bit American Standard Code for Information Interchange (ASCII) is another popular coding scheme used by many hardware manufacturers. ASCII is widely used on personal computers.

■ If it is necessary to examine the contents of the computer's memory, the hexadecimal system may be used. Since this system represents numbers in powers of 16, it is much more compact and readable than binary representation.

■ Usually, a byte of data has an extra bit, called a parity bit. The computer sets the value of the parity bit such that the total number of on bits in every byte is either always even or always odd. If a byte has an odd number of on bits in an even parity computer, it means the data have been damaged and must be corrected.

■ There are two types of access to records stored in files: sequential and random.

■ Data records stored in a sequential file are ordered by the order in which they were entered or by record key. Sequential files are usually used for batch-type processes where most of the records have to be accessed every time the program is run.

■ Direct file organization allows rapid access to any individual record by converting its primary key directly to an address. This is usually done through the division/remainder approach.

■ Indexed files are associated with another file called an index, which is used to locate individual records in the indexed file on a random-access basis.

■ The indexed sequential-access method (ISAM) uses an index to determine the cylinder and track location of a record, and then that track is searched sequentially for the desired record.

■ B-Tree indexes are widely used because they allow fast access to very large files and they can be used on any field in the file.

■ To select the best file organization for an application, it is necessary to consider many factors, including file volatility, file activity, file size, and file query requirements.

■ In a batch-processing system, queries and updates to the system are accumulated for some time and then are executed all in one run. On the other hand, with immediate processing, transactions are individually entered into the files soon after the real-world event occurs.

■ Three modes of information processing are used: batch-sequential, batch-direct, and immediate-direct. Most applications are now being designed for the immediate-direct mode.

■ An online direct-access system consists of several terminals (or workstations) connected to a CPU, which in turn is connected to several random-access files.

■ A real-time information system is a special kind of online direct-access system. It captures data immediately after an event occurs, processes it right away, and returns information that is used to manage ongoing events.

bit

byte

binary number system

decimal number system

place value

EBCDIC (Extended Binary
Coded Decimal Interchange Code)

packed decimal

ASCII (American Standard
Code for Information Interchange)

memory dump

hexadecimal

parity bit

primary key

secondary key

sequential access

random access

file organization

physical address

cylinder

track

sector

relative address

linked list

directory

sequential file organization

direct file organization

hash

division/remainder method

indexed file organization

fully indexed file

binary search

indexed sequential file organization
(ISAM)

B-Tree index

virtual storage access method (VSAM)

file activity

file volatility

file query

batch processing

immediate processing

batch-sequential mode

batch-direct mode

immediate-direct mode

online

offline

direct access

online direct-access system

real-time information system

■ Key Terms

■ Review Questions

1. Explain the relationship among the elements in the data hierarchy.

2. What is the difference between a binary number and a decimal number?

3. Why is it necessary to use a coding scheme such as EBCDIC or ASCII-8 to store data instead of using pure binary representation?

4. Describe the advantages of a hexadecimal system.

5. How is a parity bit used to ensure data accuracy?

6. What are the three basic types of file organization?

7. Briefly explain how the direct addressing technique of data retrieval is performed.

8. Explain the differences among the three types of indexed file organization.

9. List the criteria used in selecting a file organization method.

10. Explain the difference between batch processing and immediate processing.

11. Is it possible to process direct-access files in a batch mode?

12. List the benefits of the immediate-direct approach to data processing.

13. What makes a system online?

14. Why is direct-access storage necessary for an online system?

15. What makes an online direct-access system a real-time system?

▪ Discussion
▪ Questions
and Cases

1. What type of file organization would be best suited for each of the following files?

  a. A payroll master file from which paychecks are issued biweekly.

  b. An accounts-receivable master file in a large retail department store.

  c. A batch transaction file for a material inventory system in which the master file has an ISAM organization.

  d. The master file for a work-in-process job order system used by management for operational control of production.

  e. An online class-registration master file used by a university for student registration from online terminals.

2. Sequential file organization is conceptually simple and requires a minimum of storage space. Direct file organization, on the other hand, requires complex access methods and extra storage space for indexes. Discuss some business reasons for the increasing popularity of direct-access systems despite their higher costs. What technological developments have aided in this process?

3. Managers at a large bank with branches in several cities within a state are re-evaluating the bank's demand deposit accounting (DDA) system. They feel there are three basic approaches to DDA:

  a. A centralized batch DDA system updated for changes on a daily basis. Microfiche (COM) would be produced every business day and would contain the beginning balance, the day's transactions, and the ending balance for each depositor. By 8:00 A.M. every day, a courier service would deliver to each branch the COM containing the above information for all its depositors. The daily cutoff for the DDA system would be 2:00 P.M. Therefore, the COM would reflect any transactions that had cleared by 2:00 P.M. the previous day. This COM would be used for depositors' inquiries concerning their accounts.

  b. A centralized batch DDA system similar to the system in alternative *a* (above), but with no COM produced. Instead, CRT terminals (connected online through leased lines with the central CPU) would be used by each branch for processing depositors' inquiries about their accounts.

  c. A real-time DDA system in which both transactions and inquiries are processed immediately by branch CRT terminals through leased communication lines.

What are the advantages and disadvantages of the three alternatives? How would the necessity of using dial-up lines affect your choosing alternative *c*?

4. Basic Hardware is a medium-sized chain of hardware stores located primarily in the southeastern states. The company is considering some type of point-of-sale capture of sales data through cash registers for input to sales analysis and inventory reordering systems. The choices are a true real-time system and a batch system that is updated daily. With a real-time system, each cash register would be online to the central computer through regular telephone lines during business hours. Under the batch system, each cash register would have the capability of storing one day's worth of sales data. At the end of the day, the data would be transmitted to the central computer.

Although the real-time option has the advantage of providing real-time information, it also is more expensive, primarily because it would tie up long-distance telephone lines during business hours. With the batch approach, a line would be in use for approximately fifteen minutes at the end of each day. Do you think real-time information in this situation would justify the additional communication costs?

5. The Lowery Engineering Consulting Company employs about seventy-five engineers who work with clients in product design for farm equipment. Leroy Jones, a computer consultant, was recently hired to design a computerized timekeeping system that allows the firm to keep track of consultant hours charged to various projects. The new system requires that each engineer complete a weekly time sheet indicating the number of hours charged to specific projects. The time sheets would be batched and would update the system on weekends. Leroy envisions three computer files: an employee master file, a project file, and a file of hours charged to projects per employee. Leroy still needs to determine the best file organization. Can you help him?

6. Bower Lumber Company is a small, regional chain of stores specializing in building supplies. Robert Bower, owner of the chain, purchased and implemented an online computer system a number of months ago. The computer system maintains the inventory for each store and automatically orders inventory when necessary. The inventory files are also linked with the cash registers, so that inventory is instantly updated when a sale is made. The system also maintains a customer list and a list of overdue bills. Mr. Bower is not yet convinced the system has improved his business. Do you think the online computer system was needed to make Bower Lumber Company run better? If so, what could you tell Mr. Bower which would convince him an online system was necessary? What suggestions could be made to better utilize the system?

Data-Base Management Systems

■ Chapter 13

CHAPTER OUTLINE

Introduction

The Traditional Approach to Information Processing
Data Redundancy
Lack of Data Integration
Program/Data Dependence
Lack of Flexibility

The Data-Base Approach to Information Processing
Logical versus Physical Views of Data Storage
The Users
The Data-Base Management System
The Data-Base Administrator
The Data-Base

Logical Data-Base Structures
Tree Structures
Network Structures
Relational Structures

Advantages and Disadvantages of the Data-Base Approach
Advantages
Disadvantages

Summing Up

Key Terms

Review Questions

Discussion Questions and Cases

■ INTRODUCTION

Perhaps the most important challenge facing information-system developers is to provide users with timely and versatile access to data stored in computer files. In a dynamic business environment, there are many unanticipated needs for information. Often the data to satisfy these information needs are contained in computer files but cannot be accessed and output in a suitable format on a timely basis. Data-base management systems have the potential to meet this challenge. In this chapter we will first contrast the traditional and the data-base approach to information processing. Then we will look at some of the logical ways users view data stored in a data base. And finally, we will explore the advantages and disadvantages of data-base management systems.

■ THE TRADITIONAL APPROACH TO INFORMATION PROCESSING

The traditional approach to information processing is file-oriented. Prior to the advent of the data-base management system (DBMS), each application maintained its own master file and generally had its own set of transaction files. Figure 13–1 illustrates this traditional approach. Files are custom-designed for each application, and generally there is little sharing of data among the various applications. Programs are dependent on the files and vice versa; that is, when the physical format of the file is changed, the program also has to be changed. The traditional approach is file-oriented because the primary purpose of many applications is to maintain on the master file the data required to produce management information. Therefore, the master file is the centerpiece of each application. Although the traditional, file-oriented approach to information processing is still widely used, it does have some very important disadvantages. Among them are the following.

Data Redundancy

Often, identical data are stored in two or more files. Notice that in Figure 13–2 each employee's social security number, name, and department are stored in both the payroll and personnel files. Obviously, such **data redundancy** increases data editing, maintenance, and storage costs. In addition, data stored on two master files (which in theory should be identical) are often different for good reason; but such differences inevitably create confusion.

Lack of Data Integration

Data on different master files may be related, as in the case of payroll and personnel master files (refer again to Figure 13–2). For example, management may want a report displaying employee name, department, pay rate, and occupation. However, the traditional approach does not have the mecha-

Figure 13–1
Traditional Approach to Information Processing
Notice that each application has its own master file.

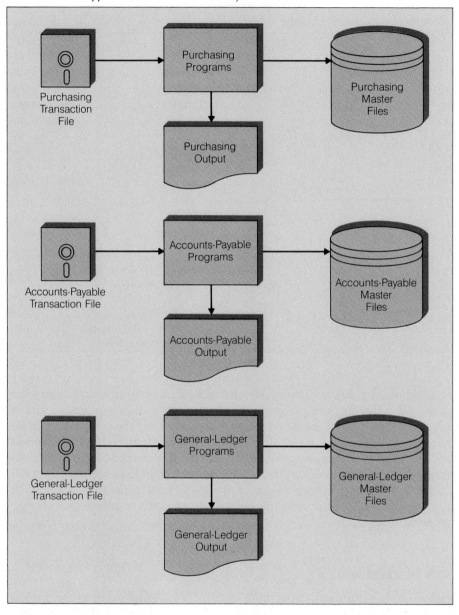

nisms for associating these data in a logical way to make them useful for management's needs.

Program/Data Dependence

Under the traditional, file-oriented approach, programs are tied to master files and vice versa. Changes in the physical format of the master file, such as

Figure 13–2
Data Redundancy and Lack of Integration among Files

A payroll file stores data concerning employees' wages and salaries. A personnel file contains data about employees' work and education histories as well as occupational skills. Many large firms have separate payroll and personnel departments. A data-base management system would allow the two departments to share data.

Payroll File

Social Security Number	Employee Name	Pay Rate	Year-to-Date Earnings	Department
385686293	Joseph Hawkins	$14.50	4005.50	380
390328453	Samuel Smith	$15.25	5100.60	390
410686392	Theodore Thatcher	$ 6.50	2495.60	312
425786495	Robert Benson	$28.80	8135.50	312
510933492	Thomas Benson	$14.50	4005.50	095
511945893	Jane Benson	$32.50	9617.55	100

Personnel File

Social Security Number	Employee Name	Department	Date Hired	Occupation
385686293	Joe Hawkins	380	03 JAN 83	Manager
390328453	Sam Smith	390	05 SEP 65	Salesperson
410686392	Ted Thatcher	312	15 JUN 81	Clerk
425786495	Bob Benson	312	20 JUL 64	Vice-President
510933492	Tom Benson	095	31 DEC 68	Accountant
511945893	Jane Benson	100	20 JUL 64	President

the addition of a data field, require changes in all programs that access the master file. Consequently, for each of the application programs that a programmer writes or maintains, he or she must be concerned with data management. There is no centralized execution of the data-management function; data management is scattered among all the application programs. Think of the thousands of computer programs that had to be altered when the U.S. Postal Service changed from a five-digit to a nine-digit zipcode. A centralized DBMS could have minimized the number of places this change had to be made.

Lack of Flexibility

The information-retrieval capabilities of most traditional systems are limited to predetermined requests for data. Therefore, the system produces information in the form of scheduled reports and queries which it has been programmed to handle. If management needs unanticipated data, the information can perhaps be provided if it is in the files of the system. Extensive programming is often involved. Thus, by the time the programming is completed, the information may no longer be required or useful. This problem has long plagued information systems. Management knows that a particular piece of information can be produced on a one-time basis, but the expense and time involved are generally prohibitive. Ideally, information processing should be able to mix related data elements from several files and produce information with a fast turnaround to service unanticipated requests for information.

THE DATA-BASE APPROACH TO
■ INFORMATION PROCESSING

A **data-base management system (DBMS)** is a set of programs that serves as an interface between application programs and a set of coordinated and integrated *physical files* called a data base. A DBMS provides the capabilities for creating, maintaining, and changing a data base. A **data base** is a collection of data. The physical files of a data base are analogous to the master files of application programs. However, with DBMS the data among the physical files are related with various **pointers** and keys, which not only reduce data redundancy but also enable the unanticipated retrieval of related information. Figure 13–3 illustrates the DBMS approach.

PHYSICAL FILE
The actual storage of data on storage media.

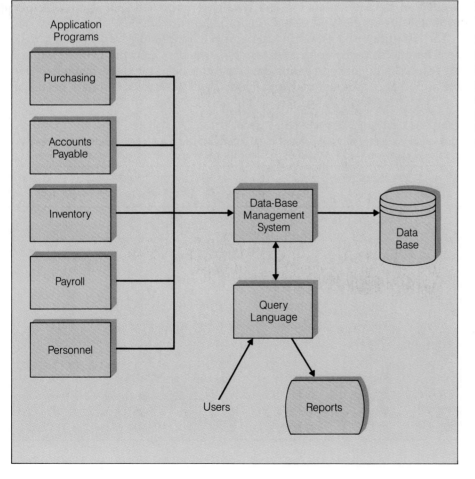

Figure 13–3
The DBMS Approach

The data-base management system stores, updates, and retrieves data for all application programs. Data can be readily shared among these programs to prevent data redundancy. Easy-to-use query languages allow users to produce ad-hoc reports.

Logical versus Physical Views of Data Storage

With most traditional data-storage techniques, the programmer needs to be aware of the physical layout of data records on storage devices and thus needs to understand the technical characteristics of many kinds of hardware. The problem gets even more complex in a multi-user environment where one programmer may have to use data files designed by another programmer. Often, a lot of time is wasted just trying to figure out what a particular data field is supposed to represent.

A DBMS overcomes this problem by providing two views of data: physical and logical. The **physical view** of data is similar to traditional file systems. It deals with the actual location of bits and bytes on memory devices. Some MIS personnel need this information in order to make efficient use of storage and processing resources. However, knowledge of all these details would serve no useful purpose for the application programmer who is interested only in using the information, no matter how it is stored.

The **logical view** represents data in a format that is meaningful to the user and the application programmer. The emphasis here is on interrelating data fields and records such that they represent the underlying business reality. For instance, a marketing executive's logical view of sales data may resemble Table 13–1. In this format, the data can easily be used to generate reports needed in decision making. The data-base approach allows the user to maintain this kind of conceptual (logical) view of data.

The data might be physically disaggregated and stored on magnetic disk according to some complex addressing mechanism, but the DBMS assumes the responsibility of aggregating the data into a neat, logical format whenever the application program needs it. Thus, application programmers need not

Table 13–1 ■ Logical View of Sales Data

This is only one logical view of sales data. Manufacturing managers might be interested in sales data by product, instead of data on salespersons and regions, as shown here.

SALESPERSON			YEAR-TO-DATE SALES		
I.D. #	Name	Region	Product A	Product B	Product C
223	Smith	S.W.	6,395	4,328	5,875
227	O'Neill	S.W.	4,326	898	1,587
241	Maxwell	S.W.	12,331	8,976	7,215
256	Ware	East	8,232	6,554	7,321
257	Charles	East	2,111	4,573	5,321
258	Scholar	Midwest	5,221	6,632	6,331
276	Williams	Midwest	11,213	10,709	9,318
283	Mufti	Midwest	2,124	5,335	6,326
285	Cadd	Midwest	7,224	5,019	2,020
300	Harris	N.E.	3,423	3,302	8,824
307	Bentley	N.E.	8,635	5,661	3,624
310	Curtis	N.E.	10,728	7,187	8,721
322	May	N.E.	7,853	5,354	6,332

worry about tracks and cylinders; instead, they can concentrate on the business aspects of the problem to be solved.

Figure 13–4 shows how the DBMS insulates the user from physical-storage details. The user or application programmer can refer to data items by using meaningful (logical) names, such as EMPLOYEE-NAME and SALARY. He or she no longer has to worry about specifying physical storage information, such as the number of bytes in a field.

The data-base environment has four components: the users, the DBMS software, the data base, and the data-base administrator. Figure 13–5 illustrates the interaction of these components.

The Users

Users consist of both the traditional users (such as management) and application programmers, who are not usually considered to be users. Users interact with the DBMS indirectly via application programs or directly via a simple *query language.* The user's interactions with the DBMS also include

QUERY LANGUAGE
A high-level and easy-to-use
computer language used to
retrieve specific information
from a data base.

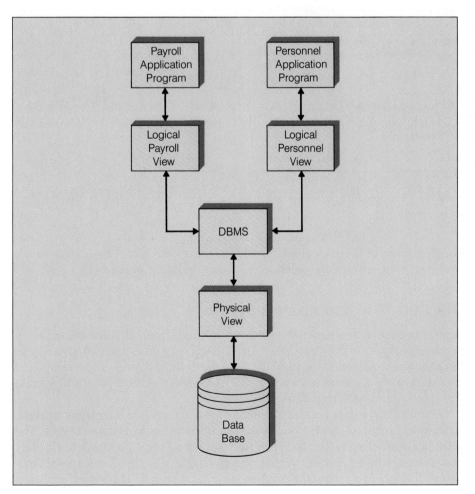

Figure 13–4
Logical versus Physical
Views of Data

The ability to establish different logical views of the same data while insulating the user from concerns about how the data are physically stored has been a major contribution to the user-friendliness of information systems.

Figure 13–5
Interaction among DBMS Components

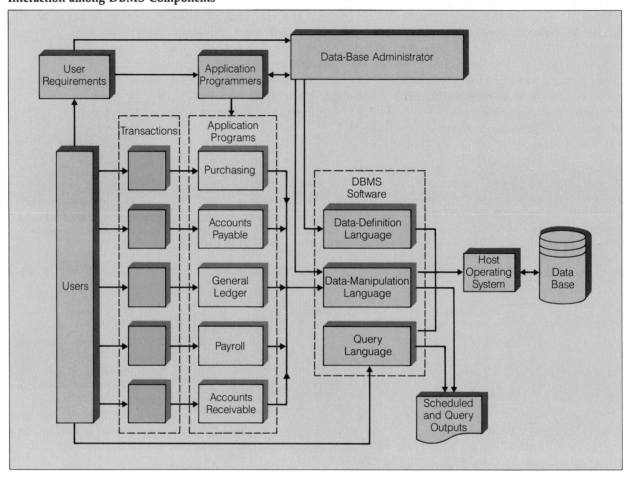

the definition of the logical relationships in the data base (the logical view), and the input, alteration, deletion, and manipulation of data.

The Data-Base Management System

The data-base management system is software that enables the user to communicate with the data base. The DBMS interprets user commands so that the computer system can perform the task required. For example, it might translate a command such as GET CUSTNO, AMOUNT, INVNO into "retrieve record 458 from disk 09."

Conceptually, a data-base management system uses two languages—a **data-definition language (DDL)** and a **data-manipulation language (DML).** The DDL is essentially the link between the logical and physical views of the data base. As discussed earlier, logical refers to the way the user views data; physical refers to the way the data are physically stored. The logical structure of a data base is sometimes called a **schema.** A **subschema** is the way a particular application views the data from the data base. There may be many users and application programs utilizing the same data base, therefore many different subschemas can exist. Each user or application program uses a set of DDL statements to construct a subschema that includes only the data elements of interest. Figure 13–6 shows statements from a data-definition language.

The DDL is used to define the physical characteristics of each record: the fields within the record, and each field's logical name, data type, and length. The logical name (such as SNAME for the student name field) is used by both application programs and users to refer to a field for the purpose of retrieving or updating the data in it. The DDL is also used to specify relationships among the records. The primary functions of the DDL are to:

1. Describe the schema and subschemas.
2. Describe the fields in each record and the record's logical name.
3. Describe the data type and name of each field.
4. Indicate the keys of the record.
5. Provide for data security restrictions.
6. Provide for logical and physical data independence.
7. Provide means of associating related data.

Figure 13–6
Statements from a Data-Definition Language

Notice that this DDL is describing the physical characteristics of the data, such as the data type and length of each field.

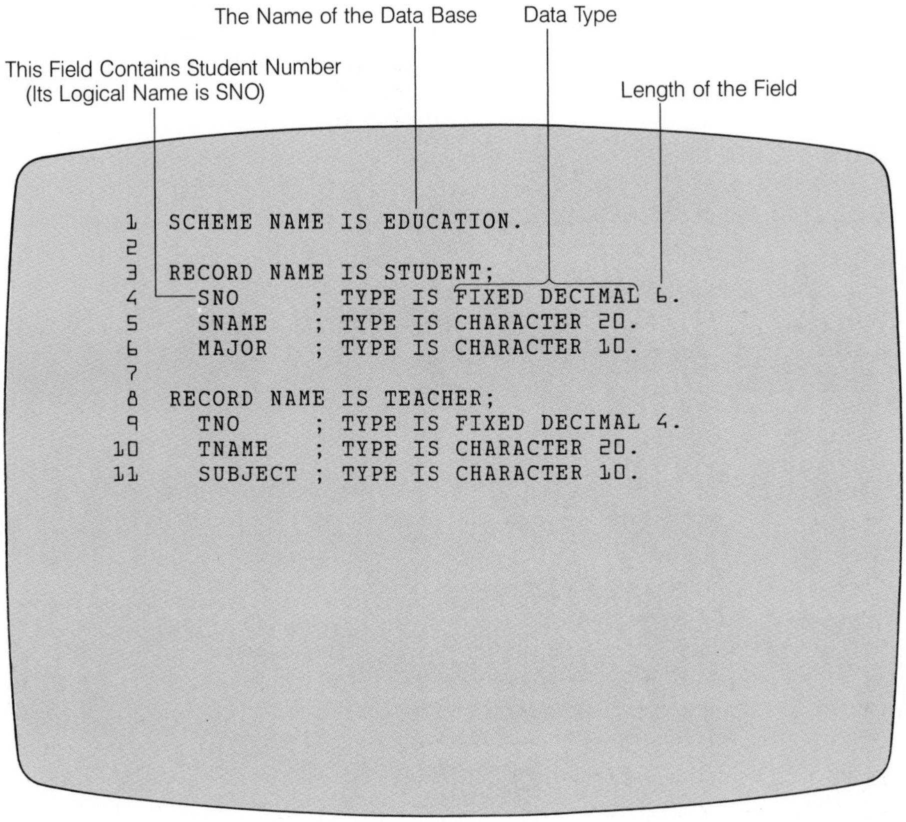

The Name of the Data Base   Data Type

This Field Contains Student Number
(Its Logical Name is SNO)

Length of the Field

```
 1   SCHEME NAME IS EDUCATION.
 2
 3   RECORD NAME IS STUDENT;
 4     SNO     ; TYPE IS FIXED DECIMAL 6.
 5     SNAME   ; TYPE IS CHARACTER 20.
 6     MAJOR   ; TYPE IS CHARACTER 10.
 7
 8   RECORD NAME IS TEACHER;
 9     TNO     ; TYPE IS FIXED DECIMAL 4.
10     TNAME   ; TYPE IS CHARACTER 20.
11     SUBJECT ; TYPE IS CHARACTER 10.
```

Table 13–2 ■ Data-Manipulation-Language Verbs

The verbs in this table are combined with operands to manipulate data. For example, a command might be DELETE CUSTNO 5.

VERBS	OPERANDS
Delete	Record Key, Field Name, Record Name, or File Name
Sort	Field Name
Insert	Record Key, Field Name, Record Name, or File Name
Display	Record Key, Field Name, Record Name, or File Name
Add	Field Name

OPERAND
An entity to which an operation is applied; that which is operated upon.

The data-manipulation language (DML) provides the techniques for processing the data base such as retrieval, sorting, display, and deletion of data or records. The DML should include a variety of manipulation verbs and operands for each verb. Table 13–2 contains some of these verbs and corresponding *operands*. Figure 13–7 shows statements from three data-manipulation languages.

Most data-manipulation languages interface with high-level programming languages such as COBOL and PL/I. These languages enable a programmer to perform unique data processing that the DBMS's data-manipulation language cannot perform.

A key feature of a DML is that it uses logical names (such as CUSTNO for customer number) instead of physical storage locations when referring to data. This capability is possible since the data-definition language provides the linkage between the logical view of data and their physical storage. The functions of a DML are to:

Figure 13–7
Statements from Three Data-Manipulation Languages

The verbs in data-manipulation languages differ widely. For example, the verbs (such as find, move, and select) used in these three languages all differ from the verbs shown in Table 13–2.

```
1. Data-Base Task Group (DBTG) DML defined for COBOL

   PERFORM UNTIL FLAG = 'RED'
       FIND NEXT OVERDUE WITHIN ACCOUNTS
       IF EOF NOT = 'YES'
           IF OVERDUE = 'YES'
               MOVE 'RED' TO FLAG
           END-IF
       END-IF
   END-PERFORM

2. Information Management System (IMS) DML (DL/1)

       GU ACCOUNTS (OVERDUE = 'YES'
   VA GN ACCOUNTS (OVERDUE = 'RED'
       go to VA

3. Structured Query Language (SQL)

   SELECT ACCTNO FROM ACCOUNTS
       WHERE OVERDUE = 'YES'
```

1. Provide the techniques for data manipulation such as deletion, replacement, retrieval, sorting, or insertion of data or records.

2. Enable the user and application programs to process data by using logically meaningful data names rather than physical storage locations.

3. Provide interfaces with programming languages. A DML should support several high-level languages such as COBOL, PL/I, and FORTRAN.

4. Allow the user and application programs to be independent of physical data storage and data-base maintenance.

5. Provide for the use of logical relationships among data items.

The Data-Base Administrator

The **data-base administrator (DBA)** and staff perform the following functions:

1. Maintains a data dictionary. The data dictionary defines the meaning of each data item stored in the data base and describes interrelations between data items. Since the data base is shared by many users, it is necessary to have clear and commonly agreed upon meanings for the stored items. A portion of a data dictionary is shown in Figure 13–8. The trend in DBMS is to combine the functions of the data-definition language and data dictionary into an **active data dictionary.** It is called "active" because the DBMS continuously refers to it for all the physical data definitions (field lengths, data types, and so on) that a DDL would provide.

2. Determines and maintains the physical structure of the data base.

3. Provides for updating and changing the data base, including the deletion of inactive records.

4. Creates and maintains edit controls regarding changes and additions to the data base.

5. Develops retrieval methods to meet the needs of the users.

6. Implements security and disaster-recovery procedures.

7. Maintains configuration control of the data base. **Configuration control** means that changes requested by one user must be approved by the other users of the data base. One person cannot indiscriminately change the data base to the detriment of other users.

8. Assigns user access codes in order to prevent unauthorized use of data.

The data-base administrator is extremely important, working very closely with users in order to create, maintain, and safeguard the data base. In effect, the DBA is the liaison between the data base and its users and therefore, must be familiar with their information requirements. The administrator must also be technically competent in the areas of DBMS, data storage, and processing. Data-base administration is becoming an attractive career option for individuals with programming, systems, and business backgrounds. Figure 13–9 indicates the position of the DBA in a business organization.

The Data Base

The data base is the physical collection of data. The data must be stored on direct-access devices, such as magnetic disks. However, well-managed instal-

Figure 13–8
A Data Dictionary

This portion of a data-dictionary entry describes data about an account in a general-ledger accounting system.

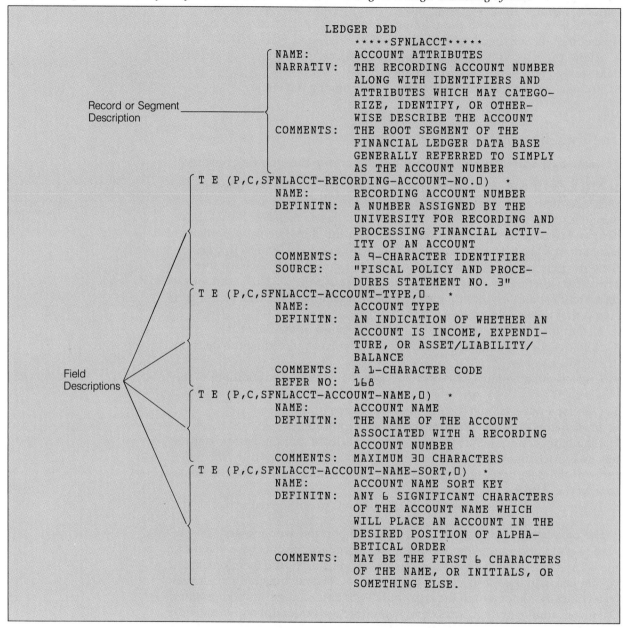

```
                              LEDGER DED
                              *****SFNLACCT*****
                    NAME:      ACCOUNT ATTRIBUTES
                    NARRATIV:  THE RECORDING ACCOUNT NUMBER
                               ALONG WITH IDENTIFIERS AND
                               ATTRIBUTES WHICH MAY CATEGO-
                               RIZE, IDENTIFY, OR OTHER-
                               WISE DESCRIBE THE ACCOUNT
                    COMMENTS:  THE ROOT SEGMENT OF THE
                               FINANCIAL LEDGER DATA BASE
                               GENERALLY REFERRED TO SIMPLY
                               AS THE ACCOUNT NUMBER
          T E (P,C,SFNLACCT-RECORDING-ACCOUNT-NO.0)  *
                    NAME:      RECORDING ACCOUNT NUMBER
                    DEFINITN:  A NUMBER ASSIGNED BY THE
                               UNIVERSITY FOR RECORDING AND
                               PROCESSING FINANCIAL ACTIV-
                               ITY OF AN ACCOUNT
                    COMMENTS:  A 9-CHARACTER IDENTIFIER
                    SOURCE:    "FISCAL POLICY AND PROCE-
                               DURES STATEMENT NO. 3"
          T E (P,C,SFNLACCT-ACCOUNT-TYPE,0   *
                    NAME:      ACCOUNT TYPE
                    DEFINITN:  AN INDICATION OF WHETHER AN
                               ACCOUNT IS INCOME, EXPENDI-
                               TURE, OR ASSET/LIABILITY/
                               BALANCE
                    COMMENTS:  A 1-CHARACTER CODE
                    REFER NO:  168
          T E (P,C,SFNLACCT-ACCOUNT-NAME,0)  *
                    NAME:      ACCOUNT NAME
                    DEFINITN:  THE NAME OF THE ACCOUNT
                               ASSOCIATED WITH A RECORDING
                               ACCOUNT NUMBER
                    COMMENTS:  MAXIMUM 30 CHARACTERS
          T E (P,C,SFNLACCT-ACCOUNT-NAME-SORT,0)  *
                    NAME:      ACCOUNT NAME SORT KEY
                    DEFINITN:  ANY 6 SIGNIFICANT CHARACTERS
                               OF THE ACCOUNT NAME WHICH
                               WILL PLACE AN ACCOUNT IN THE
                               DESIRED POSITION OF ALPHA-
                               BETICAL ORDER
                    COMMENTS:  MAY BE THE FIRST 6 CHARACTERS
                               OF THE NAME, OR INITIALS, OR
                               SOMETHING ELSE.
```

Record or Segment Description

Field Descriptions

lations create backup copies of the data base on offline storage media such as magnetic tape. These security measures are extremely important in a data-base environment, since many departments and application programs may be dependent on a single, centralized data base.

Data-base management systems are designed with a view toward optimizing the use of physical storage and CPU processing time. The logical view

Figure 13–9
The Data-Base Administrator

Some companies have three people involved in the data-base administrator's job: a data strategist, a data-base administrator, and a data-base designer. The data strategist helps the end-user management define its logical data needs. The data-base designer handles the physical aspects of data storage.

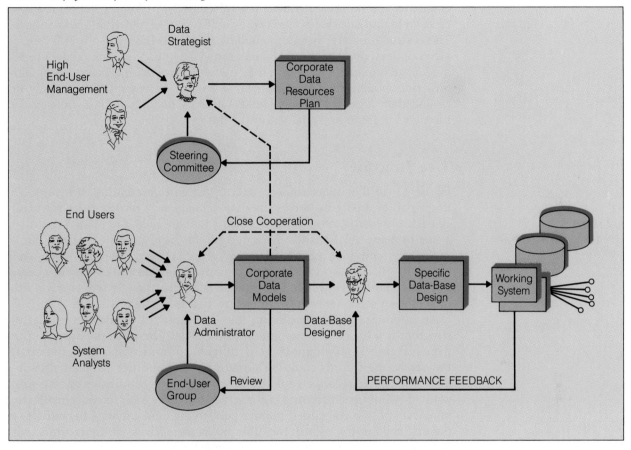

may contain redundant data items in order to make them more understandable to users. But the physical implementation of the DBMS attempts to make the physical storage nonredundant. This not only saves space, but also precludes the possibility of different values existing for the same data item at one time. The DBMS also uses other techniques to optimize resource utilization. Data records that are seldom used could be placed on inexpensive, slow-memory devices, whereas frequently used data could be put on faster, more expensive media.

■ LOGICAL DATA-BASE STRUCTURES

Two key features of a DBMS are the ability to reduce data redundancy and the ability to associate related data elements such as related fields and records.

These functions are accomplished through the use of keys, embedded pointers, and linked lists. An **embedded pointer** is a field within a record containing the physical or relative address of a related record in another part of the data base. The record referred to may also contain an embedded pointer that points to a third record, and so on. The series of records tied together by embedded pointers is a **linked list** (discussed in Chapter 12). Three basic types of logical structures are used by a DBMS: tree, network, and relational. These structures are, in effect, models on which the user can build logical views of data. Some real-world data-base management systems allow users to model and implement data on a tree, network, or relational basis; others allow only one model, such as relational. A tree or network DBMS usually ties related data together through linked lists. A relational DBMS relates data through information contained in the data.

Tree Structures

SEGMENT
Often used as synonym for *record* **in a DBMS.**

Figure 13–10 illustrates student data in a tree (hierarchical) structure. The lower part of the figure shows the data fields in each record. A **tree structure** consists of records (often called *segments*) that are linked to related records in a one-to-many relationship. Each record can have only one parent but an unlimited number of children. The top record is called the root. As shown in Figure 13–10, each student can attend many semesters and take many courses in each semester. However, each course is tied to a single semester, and the data in each semester record are in turn tied to a single student.

An important point concerning tree (and network) structures is that the structure is a logical representation of the data. The physical storage of the data in Figure 13–10 might be quite different from that shown in the figure. Physically, the records could be stored one after another (sequentially) on a disk. The related records would be linked together by addresses or embedded pointers within each record. With a tree structure, each record must have a minimum of two embedded pointer fields. One field contains the address of the first child of the record; the other holds the address of the record's twin. In Figure 13–10, for example, the fall-semester record contains the address of course CIS 1010 (the first child) as well as the address of the spring semester (the twin of the fall semester). Tree structures can represent many types of data and are widely used in data-base management systems. For example, IBM's Information Management System (IMS), a mainframe DBMS, uses tree structures for modeling data.

Network Structures

NODE
In data-base structures, the point at which subordinate records or segments originate.

A **network structure** allows a many-to-many relationship among the *nodes* in the structure. Figure 13–11 illustrates a network structure between courses and students. Each student can enroll in several classes; each class has many students.

The physical storage as well as data linkage in a network structure involve embedded pointers in each record, as in a tree structure. There are several schemes for using pointers with network structures. One is similar to the

Figure 13–10
A Tree Structure

In this data structure, each student can attend many semesters and take many courses in each semester.

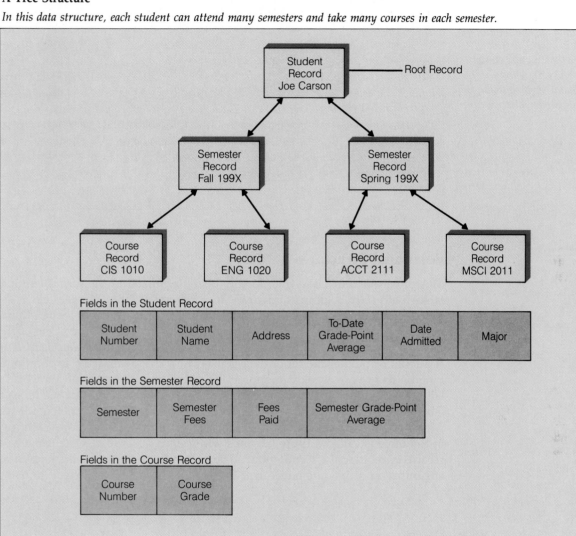

scheme used with tree structures, where each course record (for example, course 1) contains the address of the first student in the course, and then the first student record, in turn, contains the address of the second student in the course, and so on, thereby forming a linked list.

Data represented by a network structure can also be represented by a tree structure through the introduction of redundancy, as illustrated in Figure 13–12. As can be seen, the tree structure requires that the student information be stored two or more times, depending on the number of classes in which a student is enrolled. Tree structures are inefficient if there is substantial redundancy. The avoidance of redundancy is an advantage of network structures when many-to-many relationships exist in the data.

Figure 13–11
A Network Data Structure

Notice that with a network data structure, the course records are stored only once. Contrast this with the tree structure shown in Figure 13–10, where the course record must be stored for each student who takes a particular course.

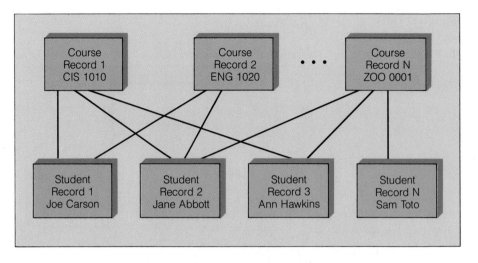

Relational Structures

Most business data have traditionally been organized in the form of simple tables with only columns and rows. In a relational DBMS, these tables are called relations (see Table 13–3). This data structure is known as the **relational model,** since it is based on the mathematical theory of relations. One of the greatest advantages of the relational model is its conceptual simplicity. The relational or tabular model of data is used in a large variety of applications, ranging from your weekly shopping list to the annual report of the world's largest corporation. Most people are familiar with the relational model as a table. But the relational model does use some unfamiliar terminology. What we have come to know as a file is called either a **table** or relation. Each row in the table is called a **tuple** (rhymes with *couple*). A tuple is the same as a record in regular file terminology. The columns of the table are known as **attributes,** and they are equivalent to fields within records. Instead of using

Figure 13–12
Tree Representation of the Network Data Shown in Figure 13–11

Some data-base management systems do not allow data to be stored in a network structure. As shown here, however, if the DBMS does allow a tree structure, network data can be stored by introducing redundancy.

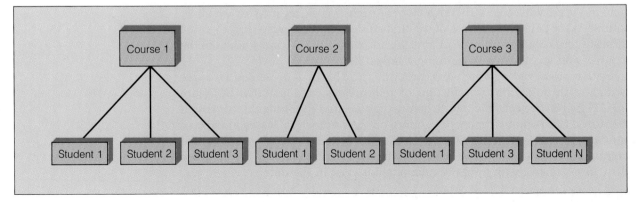

Table 13–3 ▪ Terminology of a Relational DBMS

The correct (formal) terms for a relational DBMS are relation, tuples, and attributes. However, the terms shown in parentheses are often used.

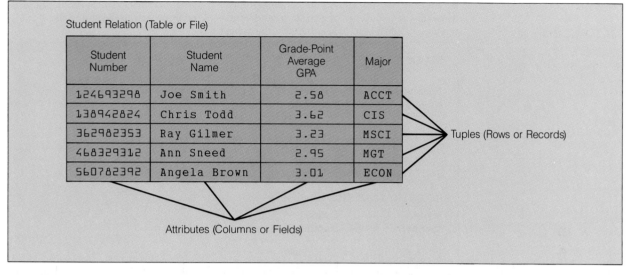

the formal relational terminology, we will use the more familiar terms (files, records, and fields), as do most real-world relational data-base systems.

Table 13–4 shows how a college registrar may perceive data in a relational DBMS. A relational DBMS allows a conceptually simple view of data but also provides a set of powerful data-manipulation capabilities. For example, if the registrar wanted a report listing student number, student name, course number, and grade of all students enrolled in CIS 1010, the report could easily be derived from the files shown in Table 13–4. But how would the information needed for the report be related? It's in two different files, and there are no linked lists or pointers! This leads to the second major advantage of a relational DBMS: the relationships among data are carried in the data themselves. As long as two or more files contain the same field, a relational DBMS can relate the files. In Table 13–4, both the student file and the registration file contain student number, therefore the relational DBMS can relate (technically, the word is *join*) the two files. In addition, both the registration file and the course file contain the course number. Thus we can join together all three of these files, producing any imaginable combination of information. The join is an extremely powerful and important capability.

Now, let's see how we would produce the registrar's report. Using a simple DML statement such as the one shown in Figure 13–13a, we get the report shown in Figure 13–13b. With a traditional, file-oriented system it would have been necessary to write a complex computer program to perform this kind of data manipulation. A tree- or network-structured data base would have allowed this manipulation, but only if it had been anticipated at design time and the necessary pointers had been embedded in the records. Since the relational approach does not have either of these restrictions, it is a very effective tool for quickly generating unanticipated reports for management.

Table 13–4 ■ Student Data-Base Relations

Notice that these tables are subject-oriented. The student file contains information about students, the registration file contains information about student registration for particular courses, and the course file contains information about courses. The subjects of these three files are students, registration, and courses. One approach to designing files for a relational DBMS is to concentrate on the subjects.

STUDENT FILE

Student Number	Student Name	Grade-Point Average GPA	Major
124693298	Joe Smith	2.58	ACCT
138942824	Chris Todd	3.62	CIS
362982353	Ray Gilmer	3.23	MSCI
468329312	Ann Sneed	2.95	MGT
560782392	Angela Brown	3.01	ECON

REGISTRATION FILE

Student Number	Course Number	Grade
124693298	CIS 1010	B
124693298	ACCT 2111	B
138942824	CIS 1010	A
362982353	MSCI 3840	A
468329312	CIS 1010	C
468329312	MGT 3010	A
560782392	ECON 2111	C

COURSE FILE

Course Number	Course Title	Instructor
ACCT 2111	PRINCIPLES OF ACCOUNTING	PATON
CIS 1010	INFORMATION SYSTEMS	HICKS
ECON 2111	PRINCIPLES OF ECONOMICS	SAMUELSON
MGT 3010	MANAGEMENT PRINCIPLES	TAYLOR
MSCI 3840	APPLIED SIMULATION	FORRESTOR

Relational data bases are being implemented at a rapid pace, and they will be the dominant data base of the future.

Structured Query Language   The establishment of a **structured query language (SQL)** for relational database management systems would be an advantage for end users. If all relational DBMSs contained this standard language, end users, after learning the language, could manipulate and retrieve data from any DBMS without having to learn a new retrieval language. It appears that SQL will become the defacto standard query language. SQL was originally developed by IBM and it is now implemented in many DBMSs, including dBASE IV, Oracle, and DB2 — the database manager in the extended edition of IBM's new personal computer operating system, OS/2. DB2 also is IBM's relational DBMS for mainframe systems.

The data manipulation language shown in Figure 13–13a is SQL. As you can see from this figure, the structure of SQL is easy to understand. The general structure of an SQL command is

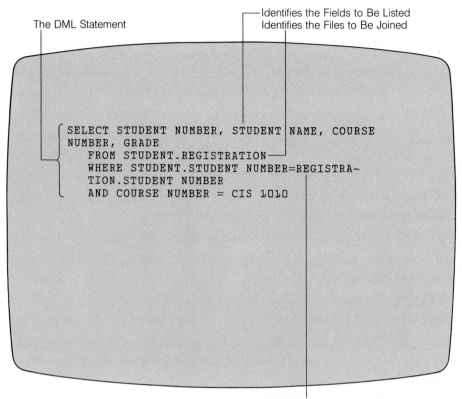

The DML Statement

Identifies the Fields to Be Listed
Identifies the Files to Be Joined

```
SELECT STUDENT NUMBER, STUDENT NAME, COURSE
NUMBER, GRADE
    FROM STUDENT.REGISTRATION
    WHERE STUDENT.STUDENT NUMBER=REGISTRA-
    TION.STUDENT NUMBER
    AND COURSE NUMBER = CIS 1010
```

Identifies the Fields to Match in the Join

(a)

Figure 13–13
A Relational Data-Base Query

If the registrar wants the report in an ascending order by grade, a line reading ORDER BY GRADE is added to the DML statement.

```
The Report                                        DATE 02 MAY 8X
STUDENT NUMBER       STUDENT NAME     COURSE NUMBER       GRADE

   124693298         JOE SMITH        CIS 1010              B
   138942824         CHRIS TODD       CIS 1010              A
   468329312         ANN SNEED        CIS 1010              C
```

(b)

SELECT A_1, A_2, ... A_n (A_1, A_2, ...A_n represent columns in a relational file or table)

FROM R (R represents a relational file or the name of a two-dimensional table)

WHERE condition 1 AND condition 2 .... AND condition n

The SELECT clause specifies the columns or fields to be displayed, the FROM clause identifies the file from which the data is to be extracted, and the WHERE clause allows the user to specify what conditions the records in the file must meet before they will be displayed.

The restrictions on the conditions that may follow the WHERE statement are very flexible. These conditions can be applied to any of the fields (columns) in the relation specified in the FROM clause. The conditions can be simple arithmetic comparisons (such as equal to, not equal to, less than, not less than, greater than, and not greater than), connectives (such as AND, OR, and NOT), set operations (such as UNION and INTERSECT), and set membership conditions (such as X not in S, where S is a set). An example of a connective in the WHERE clause is:

    SELECT suppliername, suppliercode, supplieraddress
    FROM suppliers
    WHERE item = 'shoes' or item = 'shirts'

Other examples of WHERE statements are:

    WHERE lastname = 'Richards'

    WHERE balance < 1000

    WHERE balance > (100 + SALARY/12)

The SELECT clause allows you to manipulate data stored in the columns without changing it. An example is:

    SELECT lastname, ss#, salary/12

    FROM ....

where the annual salary of the employee is stored in the column SALARY and can be divided by 12 to give a monthly salary without affecting the original value.

SQL queries can also retrieve information from two relations, using the syntax as shown below:

    SELECT customername, address, balance
    FROM customerfile, account
    WHERE customercode > 150 AND amount > 10000

In this example, values are obtained from two relations (or tables), customerfile and account. The information on customername and address is pulled from customerfile, whereas account provides information on the customer's balance. Also, the first condition is being checked in relation customerfile and the second condition in the relation account.

SQL statements can also contain ORDER BY clauses that specify the order in which the output is to be sorted. For example:

    ORDER BY customername

will sort the output of the example above in order by customer name.

SQL also allows you to perform nonquery operations such as update, deletion, and creation of records. The SQL language includes facilities for security authorization, data-base administration, data-base recovery, and operations control. Thus, SQL can be implemented as a full relational DBMS. However, most end users will only use it as a query language.

Finally, SQL does have some limitations. It is a command-driven query language. It does not have a full-screen menu or graphics type user interface. Neither does it have a report generator. In spite of its limitations, it appears that SQL will become a widely used query language for end users.

■ ADVANTAGES AND DISADVANTAGES OF THE DATA-BASE APPROACH

Advantages

Elimination of Data Redundancy Under a DBMS, data that are normally stored at two or more places are stored in one location. This reduces both storage costs and the confusion that may occur when data are stored at two or more locations.

Ability to Associate Related Data The ability to associate related data not only allows data redundancy to be reduced but also provides the ability to process unanticipated requests for data. This capability is best met by a relational DBMS.

Program/Data Independence With a DBMS, programs can be changed without data storage being changed, and data storage can be changed without programs being changed. The DBMS serves as an interface between programs and data so that the programs are concerned only with the logical symbolic names of the data, not physical storage. This advantage frees the programmer from the detailed and complex task of keeping up with the physical structure of the data.

Improvement of the Interface between the User and the System A DBMS provides simple query languages through which the user, or the user assisted by an application programmer, can quickly retrieve information to fill unanticipated needs for information. In addition, these languages enable users to write their own programs to retrieve information on an ad-hoc basis.

Increased Security and Integration of Data The data-base administrator's primary function is to provide for the integration, physical storage, and security of the data. Thus, data contained in a data base are likely to be more secure and better integrated than data in traditional files. Under the traditional approach, several individuals handle this job.

Considering these advantages of a DBMS, you can see how important a DBMS is to management. The ability to associate related data in processing unanticipated requests for data and the improvement of the interface between user and system are indispensable tools in a MIS. As you learned in Chapter 4, a DBMS is also central to many decision-support systems.

Disadvantages

The disadvantages of data-base management systems are relatively few and in the long-run are outweighed by the advantages. One disadvantage is that DBMS software is complex; the concepts used are often new to users. Therefore, a DBMS requires sophisticated data-processing personnel and sometimes a re-education of users. The current trend is to produce data-base management systems that are easier for users to understand. In fact, many PC-based DBMSs are very easy to learn and used for simple tasks.

Another disadvantage is that DBMS software creates additional overhead costs because it requires computer time to execute, disk space for storage, and so on. However, as we discussed in Chapter 11, this is a disadvantage of all system software. It is not likely to be a major problem in the future as the cost of computer hardware declines.

■ Summing Up

■ Traditional information processing is file-oriented, where each application has its own separate data storage. This approach has several disadvantages:

1. Redundant data may be stored.
2. It is difficult to integrate data from various sources.
3. Data storage is tied up with specific application programs.
4. It is difficult to respond to unanticipated information requests.

■ The data-base approach integrates the data into one large storage structure that may be used by many users and application programs.
■ The physical view of data defines the layout of data records on actual physical devices such as disk packs.
■ The logical view represents the data in a way that is meaningful to users and application programmers.
■ The data base may be accessed by users either directly or through an application program.
■ A data-base management system is a complex program that manages a firm's data resources. It uses a data-definition language to link the logical view with actual physical storage.
■ A data-manipulation language allows the user to input, access, modify, and retrieve data in a data base. It is often used in conjunction with a regular programming language to process data in ways the DBMS by itself cannot.
■ The data-base administrator (DBA) is a key person in a data-base environment.
■ The DBA is responsible for:

1. Maintaining a data dictionary.
2. Ensuring physical security of the data.
3. Controlling changes in the logical and physical structures of the data base.

■ The data base is usually stored on direct-access devices. The DBMS tries to arrange data storage in a way that minimizes storage and processing costs.
■ A nonrelational DBMS uses embedded pointers and linked lists to reduce data redundancy and to establish logical relationships among data elements.
■ A tree structure is a logical data model that arranges data according to some natural hierarchy on a one-to-many basis.
■ A network structure allows logical relationships among entities on a many-to-many basis.
■ A relational structure organizes data in the form of two-dimensional tables. The data in these tables may be manipulated in many ways. Because of its conceptual simplicity and ability to relate data, this data model is rapidly becoming more popular.
■ SQL has become a defacto standard relational data base query language.
■ The data-base system has these major advantages:

1. It eliminates data redundancy.
2. It integrates related data.
3. It provides data independence.
4. It provides an interface between users and data through query languages.

■ The disadvantages of a DBMS are that it can be complex and can require substantial computer resources to execute.

■ **Key Terms**

data redundancy	data-base administrator (DBA)
data integration	active data dictionary
program/ data dependence	configuration control
data-base management system (DBMS)	embedded pointer
data base	linked list
pointers	tree structure
physical view	network structure
logical view	nodes
users	relational model
query language	table
data-definition language (DDL)	tuple
data-manipulation language (DML)	attributes
schema	SQL (structured query language)
subschema	

■ **Review Questions**

1. What is the relationship between a traditional file and an application program?

2. Explain the concept of data redundancy.

3. Why is program/data dependence undesirable?

4. Distinguish between a data file and a data base.

5. What is the difference between a logical and a physical view of data? Which view is most relevant to the application programmer?

6. What are the four components of a data-base environment?

7. How does a data-base management system use its data-definition language? Its data-manipulation language?

8. Describe the major tasks performed by a data-base administrator.

9. What is the difference between a data base and a data-base management system?

10. What kind of logical relationship may be expressed with a tree structure?

11. Describe the major characteristics of a network structure.

12. What is the conceptual advantage of using a relational structure? What other advantages does the relational model offer?

13. Why are indexes used by a DBMS?

14. How does a DBMS improve data independence?

Discussion Questions and Cases

1. Clemento Corporation has a large information-processing facility that uses separate tape and disk files for separate applications such as production, sales, distribution, and payroll. You have been appointed to the newly created post of data-base administrator. It is your job to design a data base for the corporation. You are also expected to convince the line and staff managers that it is to their advantage to switch from files to a data base. Outline the plan of action you will use to achieve these goals.

2. Many data-base users prefer one logical model over others. Proponents of the tree structure present a number of strong arguments in favor of that model: (a) The tree structure is an excellent way to represent many hierarchical relationships that exist in the business world; (b) Hierarchical data structures are efficient from the point of view of optimizing storage space and data-access time; and (c) IBM's Information Management System, one of the most widely used DBMSs, is based on the tree concept.

Enthusiasts of the recently developed relational model hold that the relational model (a) seems more natural to business users since they have used it for centuries; (b) provides much easier data manipulation since pointers and chains are not needed; and (c) is reasonably efficient because with decreasing hardware costs, machine efficiency is not as important a consideration as it once was.

Evaluate the merits and demerits of each model. Which model would you select for your firm?

3. If you are designing an inventory data base for a grocery store, for which attributes would you provide indexes? Remember, an index is a tool for quick retrieval of data. It is useful to set up indexes only for attributes frequently used as a basis for retrieving records.

4. During the last five years, Bohlin Incorporated has been converting its existing applications to IBM's Information Management System (IMS). IMS is a hierarchical, tree structured DBMS. The company has also developed most of its new applications on the IMS. The initial expectation was that the IMS data-base management system software would assist in producing highly integrated application systems. This would allow managers to easily associate related data within the data-base management system. However, this expectation has not been fulfilled. Personnel manager Chuck Bloss is very disappointed that the system does not integrate the personnel and payroll systems. When he retrieves data from the personnel system and attempts to retrieve related data from the payroll system, he finds no link between the two systems. In numerous other cases, integration of the systems is lacking on the DBMS. How do you think this situation occurred? Are all data-base management systems designed to produce integrated systems that can associate related data? Would the same problem exist if Bohlin had used a relational DBMS?

5. The Lord Delaware High School recently purchased IBM personal computers for both students and teachers. Cheryl Haymes, a math teacher, is in charge of acquiring software. She has been trying to decide whether to buy a data-base management system, but she is confused by many of the software ads for data-base packages. Cheryl knows that relational data-base structures are the latest in technology, and many software vendors claim that their packages are true relational data bases for a personal computer. What uses would a high school have for a PC data-base management system? What capabilities of a relational DBMS should Cheryl look for in choosing a package?

6. You have just been hired by Navigator Technologies, which has a very large information-processing center. In changing jobs, you received a big promotion as Navigator Technologies' new data-base administrator. Since the last administrator has already retired, there is no one to explain the data-base system to you. How important is it that you understand the data-base management system of the company, and how would you learn about it? What do you expect your responsibilities to be as the data-base administrator of a large multinational company?

7. Over the last several years, Herald Aircraft Corporation has invested a large amount of money in a traditional information-processing system. This system was developed before DBMS software was available and is considered one of the best in the aircraft industry. Herald Aircraft has hired an outside consulting firm to determine what improvements could be made to the system. The consultants' only suggestion is a DBMS. The Board of Directors is reluctant to dump the old system and invest a large amount of money in a DBMS. What advantages of a DBMS could the consultants include in their report to convince the Board of Directors to make the change?

Distributed Data Processing and Office Automation

■ Chapter 14

CHAPTER OUTLINE

Introduction

Data Communication
Types of Data Communication
The Data Transmission Process
Communication Hardware
Network Systems

Distributed Data Processing
The Need for Decentralized
*   Processing*
Hardware Distribution
Software Distribution
Data Decentralization

Office Automation
Word Processing
Desktop Publishing
Electronic Mail
Voice Mail
Computer and Video Conferencing
Electronic Calendaring
Facsimile Transmission
Image Storage and Retrieval
Forms Processing
Integrated Word Processing/Data
*   Processing*
Office Decentralization and
*   Productivity*
Human Factors

Summing Up

Key Terms

Review Questions

Discussion Questions and Cases

■ INTRODUCTION

In the early days of electronic data processing (EDP), the computer was a highly centralized company resource. High equipment costs and difficult-to-operate software systems prevented the spread of EDP resources to user departments. During the last decade, however, this situation has changed dramatically. The cost of hardware has decreased sharply, and software is becoming easier to use. As a result, many people can now use the computer without the help of EDP specialists. By carefully dispersing computer resources throughout the organization, a business can significantly reduce paperwork costs and improve turnaround time on applications. The management of dispersed EDP facilities is generally known as **distributed data processing (DDP)**. In this chapter we will discuss the major concerns in designing and operating a DDP system.

The entry of computer equipment into user departments has far-reaching effects on office procedures. While managers are delighted to see the productivity of their offices grow rapidly, they have to ensure that office personnel willingly adopt the new procedures. Nothing could be more disastrous for a distributed data-processing system than a hostile attitude among users. In the last section of this chapter we will discuss the automation of some major office procedures and look at issues arising from the human–machine interface.

Distributed data-processing facilities depend heavily on the communication of data between computers. Designing a communication system is a complex engineering task, generally beyond the competence of a business manager. Nevertheless, it is important for managers to understand the fundamentals of data communication. This can help them recognize communication problems and formulate policies regarding the efficient use of alternative communication methods. We will start this chapter with a discussion of the basic concepts of data communication.

■ DATA COMMUNICATION

The communication of data from one point to another is a crucial business function. Methods of **data communication** vary from the use of existing telephone lines to satellite transmission. In a DDP environment, the communication function can become very complex as a result of growth and integration of previously independent systems. Every DDP system has a unique communication system to link its devices together. This typically evolves as a response to the company's growth and the information-processing strategy employed by management.

Types of Data Communication

There are three basic configurations in data communication: computer/peripheral device, computer-to-computer, and communication through a data switch.

Computer/Peripheral-Device Communication   This involves the transfer of data between a CPU and a peripheral device, such as a terminal or a storage medium. The storage or terminal device is under the complete control of the CPU. It is customary to call this kind of setup a **master-slave relationship.** The master (the CPU) determines when and how data are to be transferred to and from the slave (the peripheral device).

As illustrated in Figure 14–1, it is possible to place a number of terminals on a single line from the computer. The computer addresses each terminal in turn for input or output (I/O). Such terminals are considered intelligent, since they know when the computer is talking to them. There are also dumb terminals, which must be connected to the computer through separate lines. A dumb terminal does not know when it is being addressed; it assumes that any signal coming down the line is meant for it. Figure 14–2 shows a number of dumb terminals linked to a CPU.

Computer-to-Computer Communication   Often it is necessary to transfer data from one computer to another. For instance, some grocery-store chains

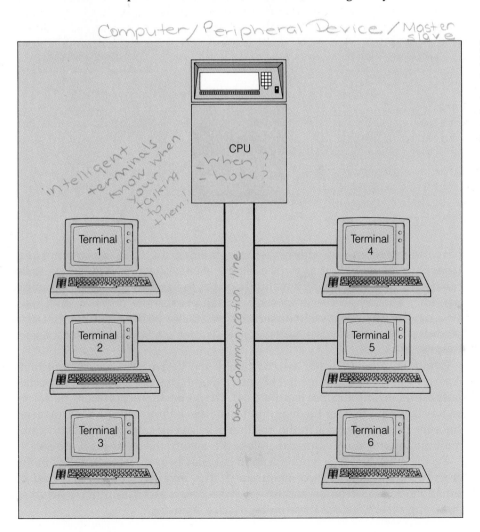

Figure 14–1
Intelligent Terminals Connected to a CPU

An intelligent terminal contains a microprocessor that allows it to detect which signals are meant for it.

Figure 14–2
Dumb Terminals Connected to a CPU

Under this configuration, the CPU addresses each terminal separately on a different communication line.

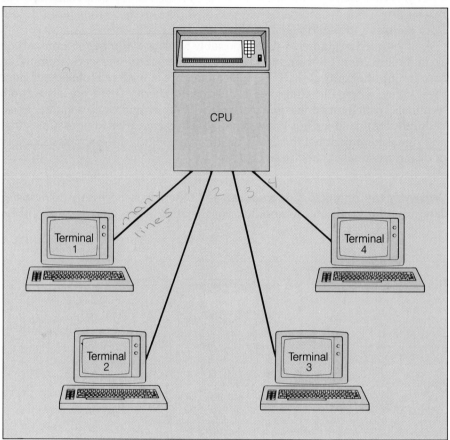

have linked their computers to the computers of their major suppliers through communication lines (see Figure 14–3). When an item needs to be reordered, the computer automatically places the order over the communication line. The supplier's computer can then process the order immediately. This procedure not only eliminates the possibility of human error, but also permits better inventory management by speeding up the reordering process.

Communication between two computers may be a master-slave connection. An example is the relationship between a mainframe computer and a special-purpose minicomputer (see Figure 14–4). The minicomputer typically performs an auxiliary function for the mainframe, such as editing input data. However, since the minicomputer is in the position of a slave, it cannot initiate any communication with the mainframe unless the mainframe allows it to do so.

On the other hand, a communication link may be between equals. As in the grocery-store example, two mainframe CPUs may interact. In this kind of situation, each computer has to have the consent of the other machine's operating system before it can initiate a data transfer.

Communication through a Data Switch A **data switch** is a device similar to a telephone exchange. A number of CPUs and peripheral devices are linked to it, and it can connect any two of them together on demand. This kind of arrangement has advantages: a user can access many computers from the

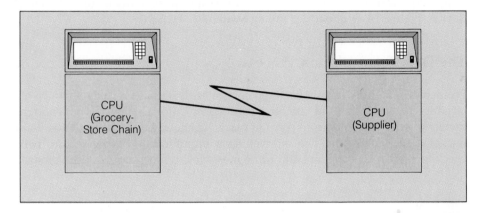

Figure 14–3
CPU-to-CPU
Communication
This type of data communication is increasing with the widespread use of personal computers.

Figure 14–4
Mainframe-Minicomputer Link
The master-slave relationship depicted here indicates that the minicomputer is subservient to the mainframe. The mainframe controls all communication between the two computers.

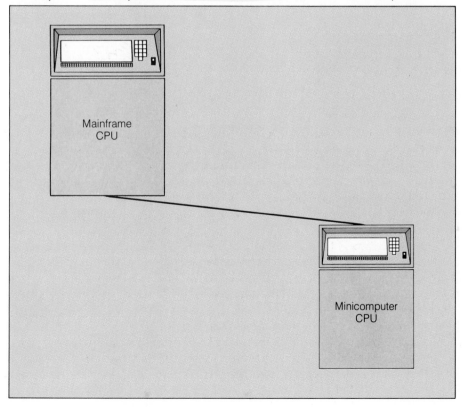

same terminal or workstation, and a CPU can exchange data with any one of
the other CPUs on the *network*.

A data switch can be used not only to link communication lines, but also to
provide various translation services. As we will see in the next section,
hardware devices differ in the way they organize the flow of data. The data
switch, which is actually a minicomputer, can change the format of data in
transit so that it conforms with the hardware requirements of the receiving
device. Figure 14–5 illustrates a data switch.

The Data Transmission Process

Protocols   The flow of data between computer devices is basically a stream of
bits, represented by "on" or "off" line conditions. Unfortunately, it is not enough
merely to send raw data from place to place; it is necessary to package the data
into blocks or messages. The intervening communication hardware can then
check for transmission errors and route messages to their correct destinations.

Figure 14–5
A Data Switch

*Data switches are used quite often in companies that have multiple CPUs. The data switch
allows a terminal or workstation to communicate with any of the CPUs.*

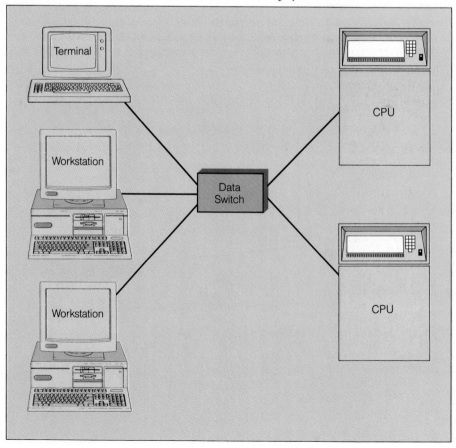

A **communication protocol** is a set of rules governing information flow in a communication system. These rules define the **block format,** or **message envelope,** which packages each message to be transmitted. This envelope usually contains control characters to mark the message's beginning and end, as well as an address, so that data can be directed to particular workstations. It might also contain characters used for error detection. Figure 14–6 shows a typical message envelope. A workstation that conforms to an error-checking protocol operates error-free, since it automatically retransmits any data that does not arrive correctly. Communication protocols enable workstations to be bunched together on a single line, because these workstations can be selectively addressed or **polled** by the CPU. The computer polls the workstations by addressing each one in turn. If a workstation does not respond, the computer goes to the next one.

Unfortunately, there are many incompatible and competing communication protocols. Two of the most common protocols are the RS232C standard, which is often used for communication between microcomputers, and IBM's BISYNC protocol, which is used with mainframes.

Transmission Mode   Data are usually sent along a single line, defining successive intervals of time as consecutive bits in a byte. The coding scheme used to represent a byte (a character of data) is typically the seven-bit American Standard Code for Information Interchange (ASCII). We discussed ASCII in Chapter 12.

Two possible conditions, "on" and "off" (representing binary digits one and zero, respectively), are imposed on the line by the transmitter. The receiver monitors this train of signals and reconstructs the incoming byte. This can be done in two ways.

The simpler method, typically used in microcomputers, is **asynchronous transmission** (see Figure 14–7). In this type of transmission, the condition always goes "off" for one interval before a byte is sent and always reverts to "on" for at least one interval after the byte has been sent. This allows the receiver to synchronize with the transmitter at the beginning of each byte and

Figure 14–6
A Message Envelope

This protocol is IBM's widely used BISYNC (Binary Synchronous Communication Protocol).

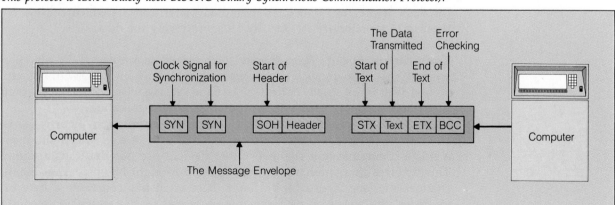

Figure 14–7
Asynchronous and Synchronous Bit Streams Transmitting the Name TOM

With asynchronous transmission, a start bit is transmitted before each byte. With synchronous transmission, a clock signal synchronizes the sender and receiver so that several bytes can be transmitted without a start bit being sent prior to each byte.

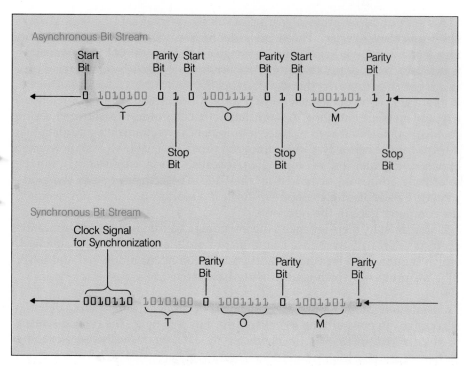

start reading at the correct time. The two extra bits per byte increase the number of transmitted bits from eight to ten, but the real information content of the package, including the necessary parity bit, is only eight bits. Since 20 percent of the data transmitted is merely control information, this method is considered inefficient in terms of line usage. It is, however, easy to implement.

A more economical method, used by complex, high-speed terminals, is **synchronous transmission** (refer to Figure 14–7). With this method, the receiver's clock is not synchronized with the sender's for each individual byte. It is synchronized at the beginning of the transmission session and can run continuously. Therefore, it is not necessary to send signals at the beginning and end of each byte. However, if there are gaps in the data stream, they must be filled with "idle" bytes to maintain synchronization. At the beginning of the data stream there is a predetermined pattern of bits which causes the receiver to synchronize its clock and start receiving the data.

Transmission Speed   Data transmission speed is measured in **bits per second (bps)**. Sometimes the term *baud* is used interchangeably with bits per second. This is not strictly correct, since baud rate is a telegraphic concept that is not necessarily applicable to computer data communication.

Some devices employ a technique called **serial transmission**. Figure 14–7 is an example. A byte is transmitted one bit at a time, in a serial fashion, over a single communication channel. Other devices use **parallel transmission**. This involves the simultaneous transmission of eight bits across an eight-channel line (see Figure 14–8). Since these eight bits constitute a byte or character, the speed of such systems is quoted in characters per second.

Figure 14–8
Parallel Transmission

Since there are eight channels in this parallel transmission, a complete byte of eight bits can be transmitted in the time it takes one bit to be transmitted with serial transmission.

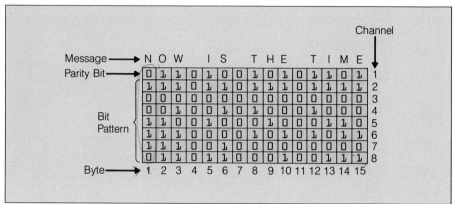

Parallel transmission is faster than serial. Most microcomputers communicate with their printers in parallel mode. Communication between microcomputers, over regular telephone lines, is done in serial mode since these lines can transmit only one bit at a time over the single channel that is available.

Transmission Direction   Data transmission can also be characterized by the direction that a communication channel allows. There are three combinations of transmission directions, as shown in Figure 14–9. A **half-duplex channel** can send and receive data, but only in one direction at a time. With a **full-duplex channel**, data can be sent and received at the same time. Full-duplex channels are usually used in computer-to-computer communication. A **simplex channel** allows data to be transmitted only in one direction. This channel is rarely used, since usually data must flow in both directions between a terminal and a CPU or between two CPUs.

Communication Hardware

Modems   Many different media are used to convey data. Satellite communication is being used more and more for long-distance transmission. Short- and medium-distance communication is done primarily through traditional telephone lines that were meant to carry voice messages. These lines operate only in analog waveform. Before transmission, the digital data signals must be converted into analog form (see Figure 14–10). This conversion process is called **modulation**. At the receiving end, the sound signals are converted back to digital form through a **demodulation** process. A device called a **modem** (short for modulator-demodulator) is used for this purpose. PC modems transmit 300 to 2,400 bits of data per second and use an asynchronous mode. Figure 14–11 shows a typical modem.

Data communication is moving away from analog transmission with modems. Many of the networks discussed later in this chapter use digital

Figure 14–9
Simplex, Half-Duplex, and Full-Duplex Channels

Data communication over regular telephone lines is normally done in half duplex. When large-volume transmissions are required between CPUs, a full-duplex channel is usually established.

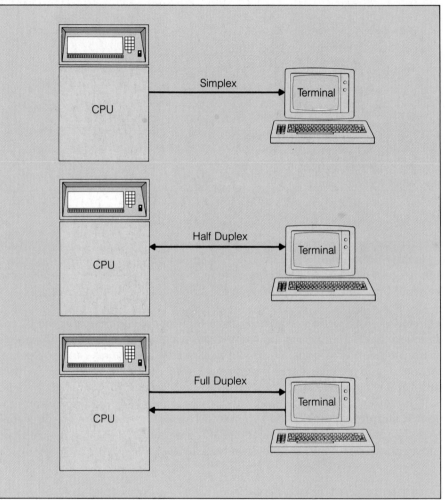

transmission. Furthermore, most voice messages will likely be transmitted and stored by digital means in the future. Companies are installing digital telephone systems that transmit and store voice, images, and data in a digital fashion. In effect, the telephone system becomes a computer network over which you can talk. In the not-too-distant future, even the public phone system will be a digital computer network.

Multiplexors   While information is being keyed into a *buffer* at a terminal or is being processed by the CPU, the communication line remains idle. If a number of terminals are installed at one location, idle time can be reduced by having the terminals share the line. A sophisticated modem known as a

BUFFER
A storage device used to compensate for a difference in rate of data flow, or time of occurrence of events, when transferring data from one device to another.

Figure 14–10
Conversion of Digital Signals to and from Analog Form

Modems are designed to send and receive data over analog telephone lines. Thus, the same modem can perform both modulation and demodulation depending on the direction in which the data are flowing.

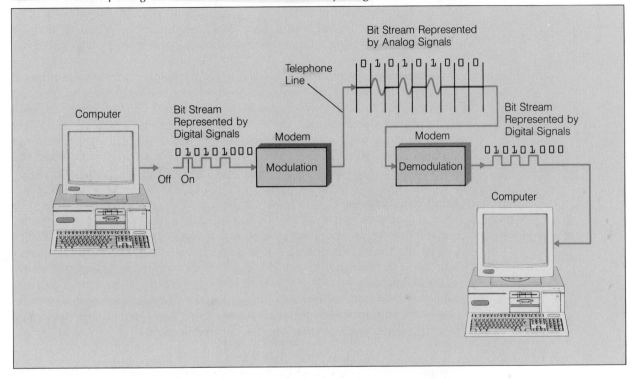

Figure 14–11
Modems and Communication Software

When using a modem with a personal computer, you must have communication software. This software executes on the PC and performs such tasks as dialing the other computer and handling the data communication itself.

multiplexor is used. Frequency division multiplexors divide the telephone line into different frequency bands, each of which is allocated to a separate terminal. Time-division multiplexors divide the transmission into small time slices. Each terminal is allowed one time slice in turn (see Figure 14–12). A statistical multiplexor is similar to a time-division multiplexor but is a more intelligent device that allocates more transmission time to terminals that are sending and receiving a larger volume of data (see Figure 14–13).

Data-Switching Networks   One of the most complex hardware configurations is a **data-switching network**. As discussed earlier, this kind of setup allows communication among many terminals and CPUs. Using statistical multiplexors, the network converts many low-speed data streams into a few high-speed streams. These are then transmitted in digital form over long-distance lines. Some of these networks transmit data at over 50 million bits per second.

Front-End Processors   With most hardware, a CPU has to communicate with several terminals at the same time. Routine tasks such as polling, synchronization, and error checking can absorb a large proportion of the CPU's processing time. This often leads to degraded performance on more important jobs. In order not to waste this precious mainframe CPU time, many systems have a small computer that is dedicated solely to the communication function. Known as a **front-end processor,** this computer manages all routine communication with peripheral devices. Figure 14–14 depicts a network that uses front-end processors to manage communication.

Network Systems

The rapid growth of the data communication industry has given birth to literally hundreds of types of networks. Many of these systems are designed

Figure 14–12
Multiplexing

The multiplexors here are dividing a communication line among several computer terminals. There is also a voice/data multiplexor, which, by dividing a home phone line, allows you to talk on your phone while your PC is using the line for data communication.

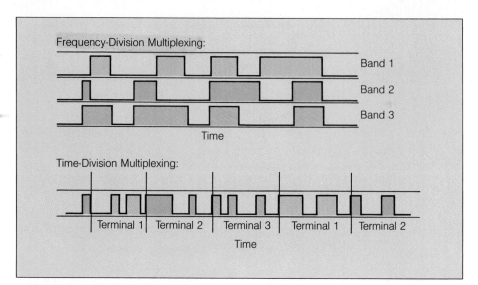

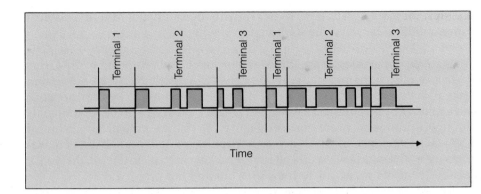

Figure 14–13
Statistical Multiplexing

Terminal 1 is using the communication line less than terminal 2, therefore the multiplexor allocates more time to terminal 2.

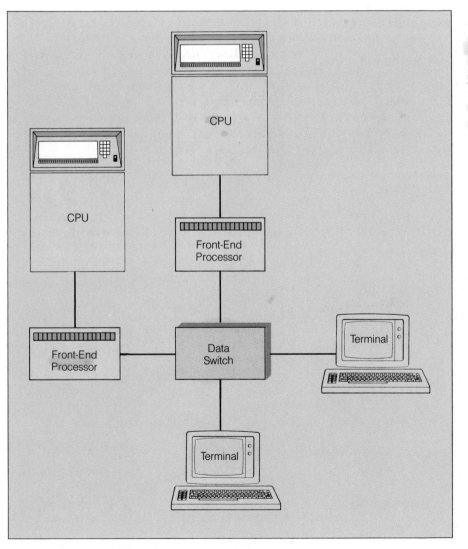

Figure 14–14
Front-End Processors in a Communication Network

The front-end processor performs the routine tasks associated with communication, thereby freeing the CPU to do more important work.

to work primarily with one vendor's products. Others try to establish communication between different vendors' equipment.

System Network Architecture (SNA)   Developed and promoted by IBM, this system fulfills all the communication needs for a distributed data-processing system built with IBM equipment. The basic structure of **system network architecture (SNA)** consists of a large CPU that controls a number of terminals through a front-end processor (see Figure 14–15). An enhanced version of SNA allows several CPUs to access a population of terminals or personal computers through a network of front-end processors. If one of the CPUs breaks down, its work can be transferred to another processor.

Advanced Information System/Net 1   A project of the large telecommunications company AT&T, this system is still in the development stage. When it is fully operational, the **advanced information system/net 1 (AIS)** is expected to provide comprehensive data-switching facilities. Like a telephone exchange,

Figure 14–15
Basic Structure of SNA

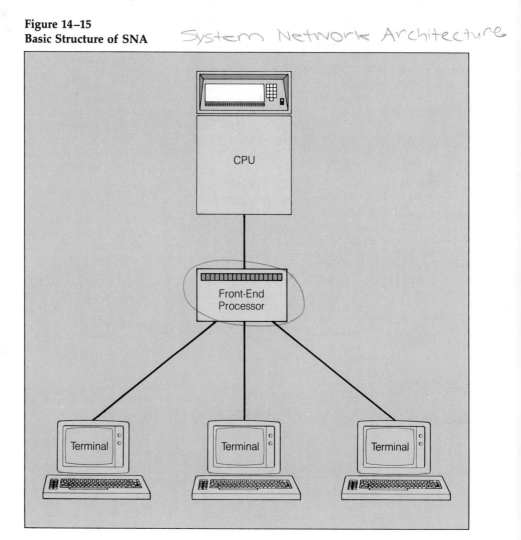

this network can put through "calls" between terminals and computers connected to it. Each terminal or CPU is referred to as a node. Unlike the hierarchical structure of SNA, AIS treats all nodes as equals. It is expected that the AIS will ultimately be able to link up with most computer hardware and thereby provide a truly public wide-area data-switching network. Many large firms have established their own wide-area private networks.

Local Area Networks   An even more widespread phenomenon is the establishment of the **local area network (LAN)**. Firms are installing these networks to provide for local communication needs. For example, an individual plant might have its own LAN. LANs are often PBX (Private Board Exchange) based so that they handle both voice and data communications. They transmit information between all sizes of computers in a digital format on a single-channel cable system at very high speeds—56 thousand to 50 million bits per second.

Local area networks are also being widely used to network personal computers. These networks usually consist of three components: a networking expansion board to be installed in an expansion slot on a PC, the necessary cable for connections between computers, and software to control the network. The cost is typically about $1,000 for every PC connected. These networks not only allow data communication between PCs, but they also allow PCs to share expensive peripherals such as high-capacity disk drives and laser printers.

■ DISTRIBUTED DATA PROCESSING

Spreading the data-processing function throughout an organization entails more than merely dispersing physical equipment and providing for data communication. It requires creative programming and system design, so that maximum benefits can be derived from the distributed data-processing system. The following section considers some of the major reasons for adopting DDP and the types of problems to be expected when implementing it. This will be followed by a discussion of how to distribute hardware, software, and data resources. Remember, computers that are distributed can be either mainframe, mini, or micro. Also, the concepts presented apply to DDP networks regardless of whether they are mainframe-, mini-, or PC-based or a combination of the three.

The Need for Decentralized Processing

DDP offers several advantages over centralized processing. First, it is often cheaper to use a micro or minicomputer instead of a mainframe to perform certain tasks. Using smaller computers may also reduce data communication costs, because more processing is done at branch locations. Second, system reliability may be improved, because if one CPU crashes, its workload can be distributed to others. Third, and probably most important, DDP allows the end users to interact directly with the computer. Although this creates some control problems, it has a favorable effect on employee productivity.

DDP also offers many advantages to the system designer. Since system components may be added as demand grows, DDP is extremely modular. This is in contrast to a traditional system where a large computer has to be installed in anticipation of future workload additions, even though current needs do not justify it. Moreover, the system designer can tailor the DDP system to the firm's organizational structure. A centralized firm may want the central computer to closely supervise branch-office computers. A decentralized firm might require only a loose connection between home-office and branch-office processors.

Distributed data processing also has a number of disadvantages.

1. Communication costs can easily run over the budget, unless line usage is carefully controlled.
2. Incompatible hardware existing at various locations may be difficult to link together.
3. Software written at different locations may be incompatible.
4. Locally developed systems may not be able to aggregate data to meet central management's need for information.

Some of the most difficult problems arise in selling the DDP system to employees. Data-processing managers often resent their loss of control. User employees sometimes resist working directly with a computer. Some opposition to change is expected; however, a distributed data-processing system requires widespread acceptance and support from users. The list of DDP systems that have failed because of user indifference is long.

Hardware Distribution

To be considered a DDP setup, a system should have more than one CPU. The CPUs are arranged in one of many configurations. Here we explore some of the more common ones. Keep in mind that the CPUs connected by the network can be of any size, although they usually are mainframes, minis, and micros.

Star Configuration   Under a **star configuration,** remote computers are connected radially to a central processor, as depicted in Figure 14–16. The remote computers perform I/O operations as well as data processing. For example, minicomputers at the branch offices of a bank may process deposits and withdrawals and then transmit summary data to the head office.

Ring Configuration   A **ring configuration,** another popular setup, joins a number of CPUs in a circular pattern. As can be seen in Figure 14–17, each computer can communicate with its neighbors. Actually, a CPU can communicate with any other CPU on the ring, it merely has to ask the intervening computers to send the message along to its destination. Ring configurations are being used widely in personal-computer networks.

Hybrid Configuration   A **hybrid configuration** is a ring-structured network where every node is the center of a star network. Such an arrangement is often used in a data-switching environment. The nodes on the ring (see Figure 14–18) perform only data-communication functions. The actual processing is done by the computers that are on the tips of the stars.

Figure 14–16
A Star Configuration

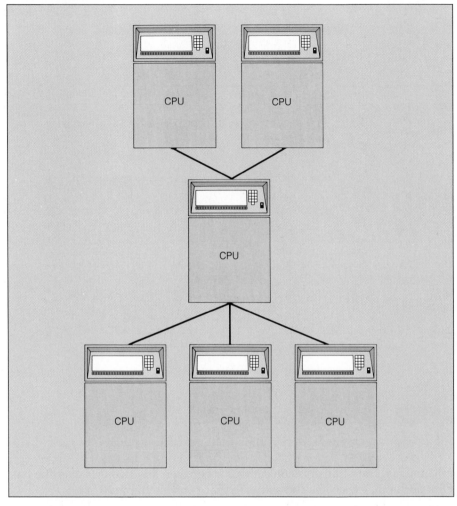

Broadcast Configuration A **broadcast configuration** is an extension of the ring configuration. All computers can directly communicate with each other (see Figure 14–19). Although communication between CPUs is faster, the hardware and communication costs may be much higher.

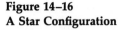**Tree Configuration** As Figure 14–20 shows, a **tree configuration** links a number of computers in a hierarchy. This arrangement might be suitable for a large, centralized firm. A central mainframe would control the operations of several computers in regional offices. Each regional-office computer would, in turn, be responsible for supervising a number of minicomputers at branch locations. And these minicomputers might in turn be networked to personal computers.

Bus Configuration A network often used with personal computers is a **bus configuration** (see Figure 14–21). Each PC is connected to a single cable,

Figure 14–17
A Ring Configuration

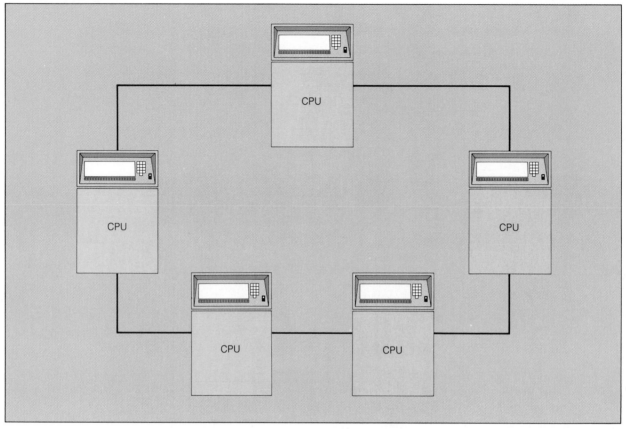

called a bus. Data transmission can occur between any two PCs over the bus. One of the PCs executes the software that controls the network.

Software Distribution

A distributed system provides communication among several CPUs. However, these CPUs do not usually spend most of their time communicating with each other. In most cases, a CPU uses the bulk of its time to process locally and only a small fraction of it to communicate with other computers.

Many application programs executed by a computer are specific to that location. For example, the various divisions in a large firm may run their own specialized applications on their computers (see Figure 14–22). This makes it possible to decentralize the tasks of application development and maintenance. Each functional area (manufacturing or marketing, for example) develops its own application software and assumes the responsibility of maintaining it.

In effect, this situation requires that application development know-how be dispersed throughout the organization, a notion perhaps unappealing to system development managers who feel it would undermine their authority.

Figure 14–18
A Hybrid Configuration

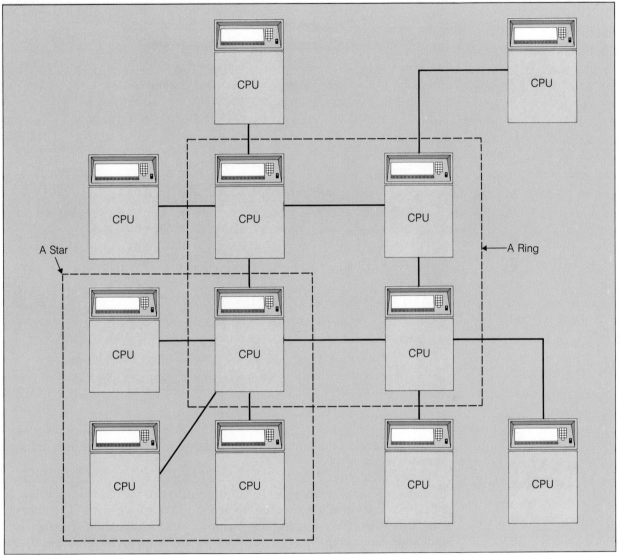

But with the demand for application software increasing rapidly, it is necessary to decentralize application development. User departments should be able to create their own application programs, either by training non-data-processing staff or by setting up their own specialized application-development departments.

Although some application programming may be distributed, some of it has to be done centrally. For instance, a large holding company may allow its subsidiaries to develop their own manufacturing and marketing software but may want to develop most financial software at headquarters. In general, most application software used in a communication network must be developed centrally. Moreover, the central information systems department should

Figure 14–19
A Broadcast Configuration

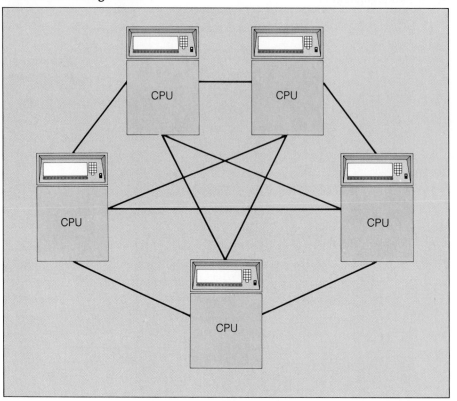

ensure that uniform documentation standards and security controls are used by local departments.

A major concern in DDP systems is the system software. The complexity of the hardware configuration places a great burden on the operating system. In a DDP environment, a computer has access to the storage and I/O devices of other computers. Its operating system must have the capability of recognizing and addressing these foreign devices in addition to its own peripheral equipment.

As we will discuss in the following section, a DDP system might involve the maintenance of a **distributed data base**. In this case, the DBMS must be capable of accessing storage devices on various machines. Again, this involves interaction among the operating systems of various computers. Centralized programming is required in this situation.

Data Decentralization

When data processing is distributed, the problem of data storage tends to get very complex. A decision has to be made as to where the data should be stored. Some of these data are shared among various nodes, and these **shared data** must be made accessible to them all. However, a lot of data are used only

Figure 14–20
A Tree Configuration

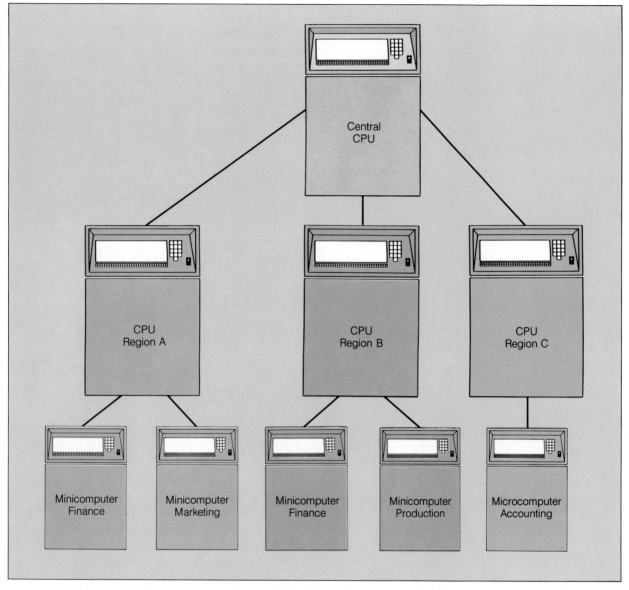

locally and thus are referred to as **local data**. It would serve no useful purpose to make these data available to the whole network.

Whether data are stored in files or in a data base, it is necessary to keep track of what is stored, and where. The data-base administrator must maintain an up-to-date data dictionary for all shared data.

DDP is often used for real-time applications, such as inventory control, hotel reservations, and law enforcement. Since real-time applications are best supported by a data-base management system, it is not surprising that distributed data bases have become a major concern in the DDP field. Each

Figure 14–21
A Bus Configuration

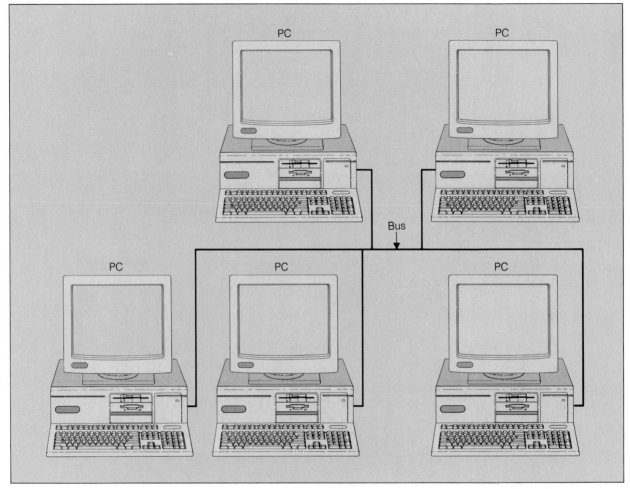

DDP system develops its own unique distributed data base depending on its hardware configuration and user demands. The local data present no special problems. The DBMS can access this data since it is stored locally (see Figure 14–23). However, there are two approaches to maintaining shared data: partitioning and replication.

Partitioning   With **partitioning,** a particular kind of record is stored at the location that uses it the most (see Figure 14–24). When another node requests that record, the DBMS consults the data dictionary to determine the record's location, and retrieves it from there. For instance, a bank may store a customer's account balance at the branch where the customer usually does business. On rare occasions the customer might execute a transaction at another branch. At such times, the DBMS would have to retrieve the data via communication lines. Since most data retrievals are done locally, communication costs are minimized.

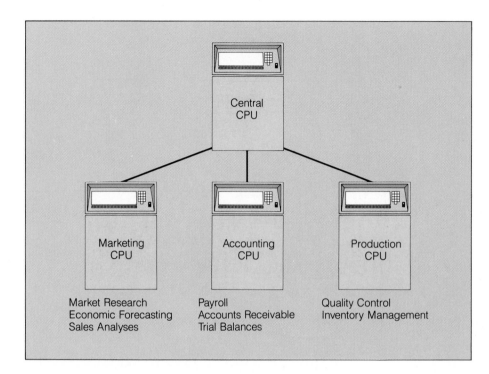

Figure 14–22
Applications Specific to
Each Division within a Firm

Replication With **replication,** duplicate copies of the data base are stored at all locations that have a need for the data. Changes to the data base are periodically copied to all these locations. This approach is useful with small data bases, where it is cheaper to store multiple copies of the data than to use communication lines to retrieve individual records from distant locations. A

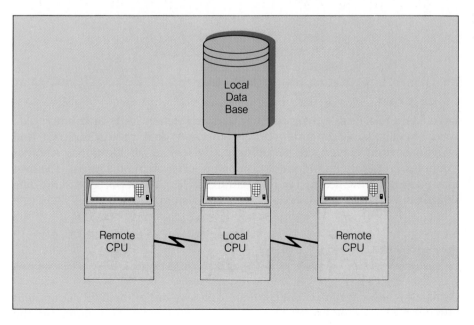

Figure 14–23
A Local Data Base

Figure 14–24
A Partitioned Data Base

Any of the CPUs in this net-
work can access any of the three
data bases. However, data are
stored at the CPU that uses
them most often.

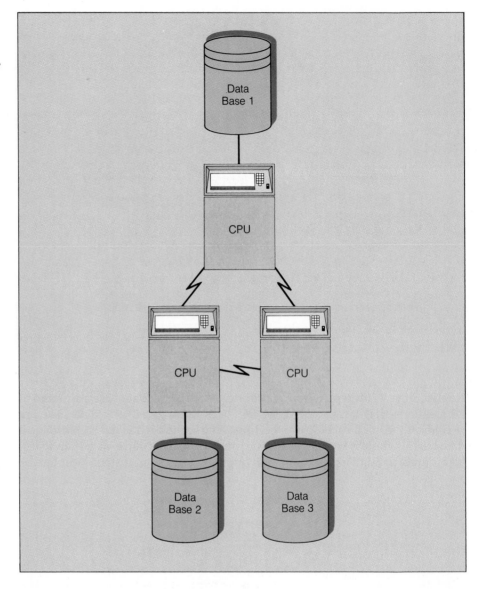

large East Coast textile manufacturer uses replication in its distributed data base. The data base, containing orders, customer data, production data, and warehouse information, is periodically updated at all locations. Another example of replication is a local decision-support system on a micro. The user may periodically replicate from the central data base those portions of the data which supports his or her decision-support system.

■ OFFICE AUTOMATION

As data-processing equipment continues to move out of the EDP department and into users' offices, office workers depend more and more on the computer to do their daily jobs. Some of the most significant effects of this distribution of computer processing have been in the area of **office automation.** The remainder of this chapter describes the changes that are occurring in today's computerized office and how they affect office personnel.

Word Processing

Just as computers can process numerical data, they can also process words. Textual material such as letters, reports, and books can be stored on the same storage media as numerical data. A **dedicated word-processing system** is essentially a small computer with one or more VDT input stations, a high-quality printer, and disk storage that is used solely for word processing (see Figure 14–25). Word processors basically are small computer systems that cost from $5,000 to $25,000.

From a hardware standpoint, one of the most important parts of a typical word-processing system is the high-quality printer. These printers are usually based on ink jet or laser technology. The workstation is a standard video

Figure 14–25
A Typical Word-Processing Configuration
One or more workstations can be connected to a word-processing CPU.

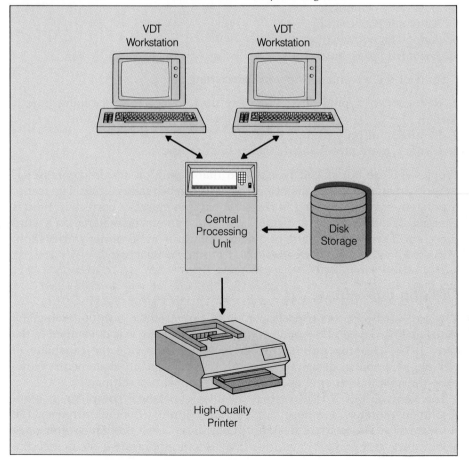

display terminal that enables the operator to see the words being processed. The CPUs in word processors are relatively low-powered microprocessors. The processing of words requires comparatively little processing capacity. Storage may be either floppy or hard disk. Some word-processing systems have only one workstation, others have many—sometimes a hundred or more.

Much word processing is being done on personal computers as well. Inexpensive software, such as Word and WordPerfect, make the PC a very efficient word processor. WordPerfect is covered in Appendix C.

The advantages of word processing are based on the fact that the system can store textual data on a disk, and retrieve, modify, and print these data on command. A report, for example, can be typed through a workstation, stored on disk, and printed. Corrections to the report can be made directly through the workstation. Words, sentences, paragraphs, and even whole pages can be inserted, deleted, and moved before a final copy of the report is printed. Among the capabilities of word processing are the following:

1. Detection and correction of spelling errors.
2. Automatic changing of margin width. This is done without retyping the material. The operator simply tells the system the new margins, and the CPU automatically sets them.
3. Deletion, insertion, or modification of any text material.
4. Automatic centering.
5. Automatic underlining.
6. Automatic hyphenation of words.
7. Automatic page numbering.

Some of the advantages of word processing are:

1. Reduction of typing time (some say up to 50 percent of typing time is saved).
2. Reduction of proofreading time.
3. Cleaner, more professional-looking final copies.

People who are not skilled typists find that typing on a word processor is easier than on a typewriter, since corrections can be made readily. The fear of making an error and having to correct it with an eraser or correction fluid is eliminated. If the material is dictated, the typist enters the material on a word processor. Then the originator of the text calls it up on his or her workstation, reviews it, makes final corrections, and prints the final copy.

Desktop Publishing

Because word-processing packages could not produce output having the same quality of typeset documents, desktop publishing was developed in the early 1980s. **Desktop publishing (DTP) systems** provide the capability of writing, assembling, designing, and printing high-quality documents. However, the quality is not yet as good as professional typesetting.

The hardware of a DTP system includes a personal computer, a high-resolution monitor, a mouse, and a laser printer. General-purpose DTP software is at the heart of desktop publishing. These programs offer page layout, text, and graphics features. Images and graphics are easily incorporated into DTP documents. Figure 14–26 shows a document produced by a DTP system.

The advantages of DTP include lower cost, reduced lead time for producing final output, and easier and faster modifications. Also, many companies are using DTP to improve the attractiveness of their internal communications, which in the past were printed by regular word-processing systems.

Desktop publishing does have some disadvantages. First, the programs are complex, and it takes a while to learn to use them. Perhaps the biggest disadvantage is that designing high-quality documents is an art. Simply buying a desktop publishing package and learning how to use it will not give the user the ability to design attractive and professional printed documents. Unless a company produces a large volume of high-quality documents, it may be better off contracting with someone outside to do the desktop publishing.

There are many printing firms that offer desktop publishing at a reasonable price.

Electronic Mail

Many companies with networked information-processing systems are expanding them into an **electronic mail** network (see Figure 14–27). Since the

Figure 14–26
A Document Produced by a Desktop Publishing System

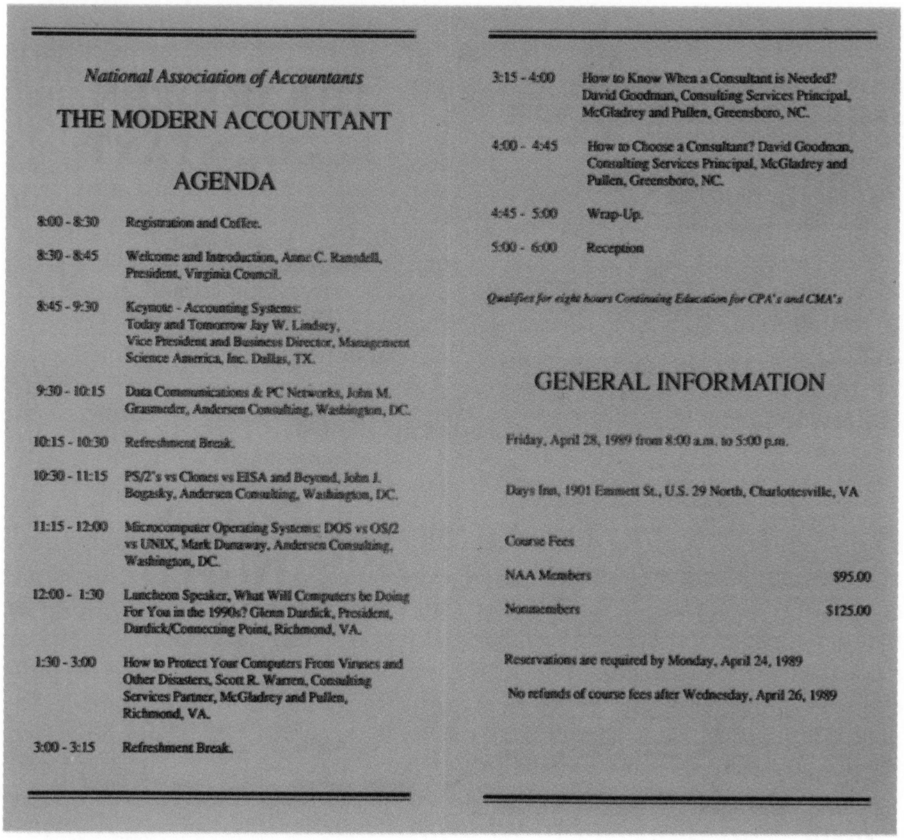

National Association of Accountants

THE MODERN ACCOUNTANT

AGENDA

8:00 - 8:30	Registration and Coffee.
8:30 - 8:45	Welcome and Introduction, Anne C. Ransdell, President, Virginia Council.
8:45 - 9:30	Keynote - Accounting Systems: Today and Tomorrow Jay W. Lindsey, Vice President and Business Director, Management Science America, Inc. Dallas, TX.
9:30 - 10:15	Data Communications & PC Networks, John M. Grasmeder, Andersen Consulting, Washington, DC.
10:15 - 10:30	Refreshment Break.
10:30 - 11:15	PS/2's vs Clones vs EISA and Beyond, John J. Bogasky, Andersen Consulting, Washington, DC.
11:15 - 12:00	Microcomputer Operating Systems: DOS vs OS/2 vs UNIX, Mark Dunaway, Andersen Consulting, Washington, DC.
12:00 - 1:30	Luncheon Speaker, What Will Computers be Doing For You in the 1990s? Glenn Dardick, President, Dardick/Connecting Point, Richmond, VA.
1:30 - 3:00	How to Protect Your Computers From Viruses and Other Disasters, Scott R. Warren, Consulting Services Partner, McGladrey and Pullen, Richmond, VA.
3:00 - 3:15	Refreshment Break.
3:15 - 4:00	How to Know When a Consultant is Needed? David Goodman, Consulting Services Principal, McGladrey and Pullen, Greensboro, NC.
4:00 - 4:45	How to Choose a Consultant? David Goodman, Consulting Services Principal, McGladrey and Pullen, Greensboro, NC.
4:45 - 5:00	Wrap-Up.
5:00 - 6:00	Reception

Qualifies for eight hours Continuing Education for CPA's and CMA's

GENERAL INFORMATION

Friday, April 28, 1989 from 8:00 a.m. to 5:00 p.m.

Days Inn, 1901 Emmett St., U.S. 29 North, Charlottesville, VA

Course Fees

NAA Members	$95.00
Nonmembers	$125.00

Reservations are required by Monday, April 24, 1989

No refunds of course fees after Wednesday, April 26, 1989

Figure 14–27
Electronic Mail

Electronic mail is becoming widespread within large firms. It is used much less between firms.

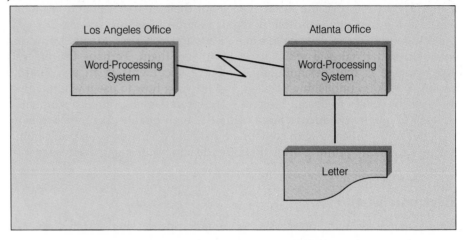

textual material is stored in electronic form in the word-processing system, it can be easily transmitted over long distances through regular commercial channels such as microwave and telephone lines. Some companies, such as Amoco Oil and Citicorp, have extensive electronic-mail capabilities.

When an executive receives electronic mail on his or her local workstation, the message can be read from the screen. Also, a printed copy is readily available if needed. These systems have several advantages:

1. The time between creation of information and its receipt by interested parties is minimized.
2. By relying on typed messages rather than voice communications, managers do not have to waste time dialing the phone, only to hear a busy signal.
3. Messages and documents do not need to be physically copied in order to be routed to many people on a distribution list.
4. Electronic mail may be filed by the recipient or dispatched to an "electronic wastebasket." The wastebasket retains messages for a period of time before destroying them.

Voice Mail

DIGITIZE
To convert voice, images, or other items to digital signals so they can be processed and stored by a digital computer.

Since the human voice can be *digitized*, stored, and transmitted by computers, many firms have installed voice-mail capabilities. **Voice mail** has the same advantages as electronic mail. A voice message may be stored or routed to many people on a distribution list. However, voice mail has one major advantage over electronic mail. Voice mail is easier to use because typing skills are not necessary and it is faster to talk than it is to type a message. Voice mail is often installed as a part of digital switches, which are computer-based telephone networks where voice, image, text, and data are transmitted and stored by the digital network. This digital network is, in effect, a computer network.

These systems provide other capabilities, such as camping on a person's phone. Camping on is useful when you are trying to reach someone by phone, but the line is busy. With camping on, the telephone digital switch rings both the caller and receiver's phone simultaneously once the receiver's phone becomes free.

Computer and Video Conferencing

Computer conferencing is a type of electronic mail. A number of individuals can exchange information, data, and comments interactively over a computer network, thus removing the necessity for long-distance travel to a conference. These conferences may occur over a specified short period of time, or they may last for days or even weeks.

Another form of long-distance conferencing is **video conferencing,** where two-way TV systems are set up among all sites of the conference. Thus, individuals can interact both verbally and visually with the other participants. Many firms have their own video-conferencing facilities. Others rent them from hotels and telephone companies.

Electronic Calendaring

Office automation systems also provide **electronic calendaring** capabilities. The appointment calendars of employees and resources, such as conference rooms, are kept on the computer so that they can be accessed by people throughout the organization. Through workstations, personnel can reserve conference rooms and schedule employees to attend meetings.

Facsimile Transmission

Facsimile transmission (usually called **fax**) has been in existence since the 1960s. In the late 1970s and 1980s it became more popular as the capabilities of fax machines increased and their costs decreased. These machines, costing as little as $500, scan a document bit by bit and transmit a complete image of the document (including photos, graphics and text) to remote locations over standard telephone networks. At the receiving end, the facsimile machine creates an exact copy of the document transmitted. Typical transmission rates are one page per minute, but these are increasing. Facsimile machines are as easy to operate as a copying machine and enable the transmission of documents anywhere in the world that has telephone lines and a receiving fax machine. Personal computers can also transmit text and images directly to a receiving fax machine.

Fax machines have been a factor in increasing the number of people who work at home. With a fax machine, a personal computer, and a copier, many people can perform their office work at home.

Image Storage and Retrieval

One of the most difficult problems in an office is storage of paper documents. Paper files can get very voluminous, and the time necessary to retrieve and refile documents can be substantial. Copies of paper documents are often called images. Companies have long used microfiche and microfilm images to reduce the volume of paper storage. However, retrieving and reading microfiche and microfilm can be slow and expensive. Microfiche systems are being combined with computer retrieval of microfiche images to decrease the time and expense of image retrieval and refiling.

In addition, systems are now available that will scan documents and convert them to digital code (digitize them) so that their images can be stored on regular computer disks rather than on microfiche. These documents can be quickly retrieved and displayed on high-resolution graphics terminals. This digital image storage and retrieval of documents is certainly the direction of the future in this area. Eventually, very few paper documents will be stored.

Forms Processing

Companies have traditionally used forms for a great deal of their internal transmission of data from one person to another. Thus, employees feel very comfortable filling out forms. In recent years, **forms-processing** software has become available that automates filling out forms as well as the transmission and storage processes. Forms that look very much like paper forms can be created on computer workstations, and employees can fill them out.

Forms-processing systems can be front ends to data-base management systems, where the input data are captured and processed by data-base management systems in a traditional way. Or, the forms can be transmitted and stored as if they were paper forms.

Forms-processing systems are an example of a concept known as direct manipulation of objects of interest. Under this concept, computers allow personnel to directly manipulate objects in a fashion similar to the way they did these tasks prior to computers. Thus, forms-processing systems allow personnel to directly manipulate forms or directly use forms on the computer. Human/computer interfaces are moving toward this concept of direct manipulation of objects of interest.

Integrated Word Processing/Data Processing

Very often, businesses need to combine the output of their data-processing system with textual material to create a final document. If data processing and word processing are performed on separate systems, it is necessary to retype some of the information in order to obtain the final printout. **Integrated word processing/data processing (WP/DP)** systems can save this extra labor by processing the data and then using the results as input to a word-processing operation.

Customer Mailing Lists   Data from accounting or marketing records can be combined with text to create high-quality correspondence material. For instance, a hospital computer can search patient records to find people who have not had a checkup in over a year. After checking the current appointments file, the system can automatically produce letters to remind patients to come in for their annual visit. This capability on a personal computer is often

Figure 14–28
A Personalized Letter Produced by Integrated Word Processing/Data Processing

The word-processing capabilities of integrated personal-computer packages such as Ability and Symphony can integrate data into a report or letter from a spreadsheet, a data base, or a graph.

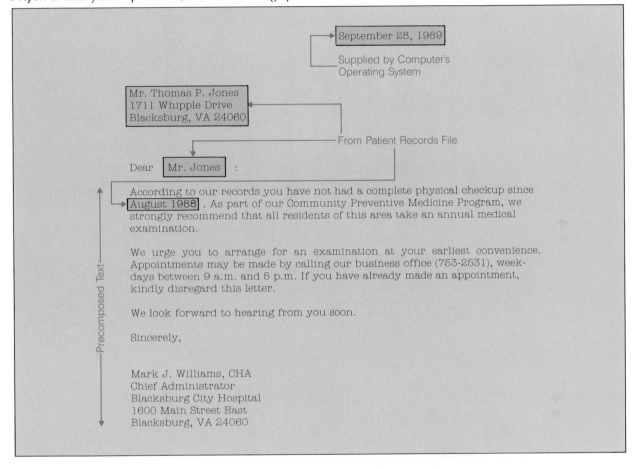

called **mail merge**. Figure 14–28 shows how the system would print a high-quality letter by merging data files with precomposed text.

Report Generation Managers frequently prepare reports that include both data and descriptive text. For example, a report from a regional sales manager may include detailed sales data as well as a subjective evaluation of the future market. Figure 14–29 illustrates how an integrated WP/DP system would produce a tabular report combined with the manager's remarks. In addition, systems are now available that can insert graphics output on a report along with the data and text.

Integrated Personal-Computer Software The equivalent of integrated mainframe WP/DP on a personal computer is the software that combines spreadsheet, word processing, graphics, data-base management, and communication. Examples are Ability, Symphony, Framework, Enable, and Jazz software packages.

Figure 14–29
Sales Report Including Both Data and Text

This capability is very useful to most businesses. Executives like to have data reports analyzed and explained through text comments, as shown here.

Green Forest Products, Inc.
Quarterly Sales Summary ($'000)
Southwest Region
2nd Quarter 1989

Product	% Change	April	% Change	May	% Change	June
White Paper	+1.4%	162	+ 0.62%	163	− 7.89%	150
Hardboard	+0.85%	85	+ 2.35%	87	+ 5.75%	92
Plywood	+1.43%	123	+ 4.88%	129	+ 6.20%	137
Wallpaper	+3.15%	55	−23.64%	42	+21.43%	51

Comments

1) White paper sales dropped in June, mainly owing to school and office vacations.
2) Hardboard and plywood sales were up sharply because of a seasonal rise in construction activity.
3) Wallpaper sales fell drastically during May. The major reason was the low introductory prices of a new competitor, Frisco Paper Company. However, we were able to regain our market share in June, because of aggressive marketing and an increase in Frisco's prices.

Office Decentralization and Productivity

A major incentive for office automation is improved productivity. Information-processing technology serves the cause of productivity in two ways. First, computers perform many of the routine tasks that people used to perform manually. This not only speeds up the work, but also reduces errors in the results. Second, information-processing equipment lets people produce output in greater quantities and of better quality.

Using distributed data processing, many firms are now decentralizing their office operations. Marketing professionals use portable terminals to enter data from remote places. Executives save on travel time by employing "teleconferencing." Technical experts improve their productivity by staying home and working through personal computers and fax machines. This not only saves people much commuting time, but also helps them avoid the distractions of the office. In short, office automation reduces the need for direct person-to-person contact and accelerates the throughput of work.

Unfortunately, this increased productivity is not an unmixed blessing. Many workers do not like to work in isolation. The opportunity to socialize in the work environment is of significant value to them. To take it away would have a negative impact on their morale. The business itself may suffer if employees do not interact on a personal basis. Many new ideas and strategies

377

develop during informal communication between employees. Excessive de-centralization of the office would be detrimental to such brainstorming.

Human Factors

Just as the "scientific management" techniques of the early twentieth century caused concern among factory workers, "office automation" is a disturbing phenomenon for many office personnel today. Since the technology is still evolving, there is great uncertainty about its ultimate impact on office life.

Many white-collar workers fear losing their jobs to a machine. These fears are not justified. Although computers do automate many manual functions, they also tend to create new jobs that are more interesting and challenging. What is really needed is a retraining of existing personnel to take over the newly created jobs. Most data-processing installations arrange seminars and hands-on training courses for user department personnel. Many private firms and software vendors provide similar services on a commercial basis.

People often prefer reading printed text rather than text displayed on computer screens. Also, electronic mail suffers from lax pickup—that is, people often do not read their electronic mail promptly.

As more experience is being gained with office machines, the design of computer equipment is being more closely tailored to human needs and comfort. Design engineers are making keyboards and video display screens to fit the human physique better. These improvements favorably affect the work environment of clerical personnel, who have to use computer terminals for long periods of time.

Some executives are reluctant to use computer terminals because they don't like to type. Light pens, mice, and touch-sensitive screens can help them overcome this "terminal phobia." Letter-quality printing and graphic output are other means of winning over skeptical top managers.

One major obstacle to users' acceptance of a system is poorly designed software. Sometimes, a program is written without much regard for whether users can easily interact with it. A good system designer must always keep in mind the technical competence and knowledge level of the end user. Although actual system design depends on the unique requirements of the business, the following guidelines should be considered in order to make the software "user-friendly" or ideally, "user-seductive."

1. Screen messages should be clear and concise, so that a nonprogrammer can understand them. Unnecessary abbreviations must be avoided.
2. Whenever possible, provide complete error messages online instead of listing error numbers. The user probably has more important things to do than to search through heavy manuals to find out what error number "X953-E22$G" stands for.
3. Provide online help facilities. If a user does not know what to do at any point in the program, the system should display the available options.
4. Use menu-driven systems that allow the user to choose among several options as a way of providing instructions to a computer. A menu-driven system is easier to use than a system that requires users to type in commands.
5. Design input and output formats to coincide with the user's conceptual view of documents.

6. Supply easy-to-use but comprehensive user manuals. These should be written in plain language, not programmer jargon. For instance, a record may simply be called a line or a row, and an attribute, a column. The purpose is to aid the user in operating the system, not to write a formal technical document. A friendly, easy-to-use system is much more likely to be accepted by office personnel than an exacting and intolerant program that does not allow any human error.

Summing Up

■ In recent years, there has been a tendency to disperse data-processing facilities throughout the user organization. As a result, office procedures and work habits are rapidly changing.

■ A distributed data-processing (DDP) system is crucially dependent on the data communication system used to connect various devices.

■ Three basic configurations are used in a data communication network:

1. Computer/peripheral-device communication.
2. Computer-to-computer communication.
3. Communication through a data switch.

■ The flow of information is governed by a set of rules known as the communication protocol. The protocol also determines whether transmission will be asynchronous or synchronous.

■ Depending on the characteristics of the communication channel, data may be transmitted either a bit at a time or a character at a time. The mode of the terminal and the type of communication channel determine whether data flow in only one direction or in both.

■ A large number of devices facilitate data communication, using either telephone lines or special digital cables. The most important devices are modems, multiplexors, statistical multiplexors, and front-end processors.

■ Two of the most important data communication systems are IBM's SNA and AT&T's AIS/Net 1.

■ Distributed data processing (DDP) offers several advantages, including more efficient CPU time utilization, sometimes lower data communication costs, and direct interaction between users and the computer. Further, the system designer is better able to tailor the system to a company's need.

■ The disadvantages of DDP include sometimes higher communication costs and equipment incompatibility problems. The most difficult part of implementing a DDP system is obtaining the active support of user personnel.

■ There are many ways of arranging computers in a distributed system. The most important configurations are star, ring, hybrid, broadcast, tree, and bus.

■ In a DDP system, software development and maintenance are often distributed among user departments. It is, however, necessary to centralize system software and those application programs which are shared among nodes.

■ In a distributed data-base environment, some of the data are shared among the nodes, whereas some are used only locally. Local data are stored at the appropriate node. Shared data are stored at the node that uses them most or are replicated and stored at all locations.

■ Office automation can enhance office productivity in many ways.

1. Word processing greatly improves the ability of typists and professionals to produce typed materials.

2. Electronic and voice mail enable personnel to communicate quickly and effectively through written and vocal messages.

3. Computer and video conferencing allow dispersed personnel to hold meetings without the costs of traveling.

4. Electronic calendaring employs computers in scheduling physical facilities and personnel for various commitments.

5. Facsimile transmission (fax) has become a widely accepted method for instantaneous transmission of documents over long distances.

6. Image storage and retrieval systems employ computers to store documents in microfiche or digital form.

7. Forms-processing systems provide for the filling out of forms by keying data onto a form displayed on a computer screen and for the transmission and storage of these forms by computers.

■ Word processing can be combined with the company's data-processing facilities. This leads to the efficient generation of high-quality output for mailing lists, management reports, and so on.

■ Distributing the data-processing function allows the decentralization of office facilities in some cases. This may improve productivity because users reduce their travel time and avoid the distractions of a large office.

■ The reactions of personnel to office automation critically affect the success of a DDP system. The automation of the office can raise questions about job security and the quality of the work environment.

■ The design of friendly software systems is an important element in selling DDP to user departments. Programs must be written with the user's convenience in mind.

■ Key Terms

distributed data processing (DDP)

data communication

master-slave relationship

data switch

communication protocol

block format or message envelope

polled

asynchronous transmission

synchronous transmission

data transmission speed

bits per second (bps)

serial transmission

parallel transmission

half-duplex channel

full-duplex channel

simplex channel

modulation

demodulation

modem

multiplexor

data-switching network

front-end processor

system network architecture (SNA)

advanced information system/net 1 (AIS)

local area network (LAN)

star configuration

ring configuration

hybrid configuration

broadcast configuration

tree configuration

bus configuration

distributed data base

shared data

local data

partitioning

replication

office automation

dedicated word-processing system

desktop publishing (DTP)

electronic mail

voice mail

computer conferencing

video conferencing

electronic calendaring

facsimile transmission (fax)

image storage and retrieval

forms processing

integrated word processing/data processing (WP/DP)

mail merge

■ Review
■ Questions

1. Explain the three basic types of data communication.
2. Why are communication protocols necessary?
3. What is the difference between asynchronous and synchronous data transmission?
4. How is data transmission speed measured?
5. What is the function of a modem in data communication?
6. What is a multiplexor?
7. Explain the advantage of using a front-end processor.
8. What is a local area network?
9. List the advantages of decentralized processing.
10. How does the star network configuration differ from the tree configuration?
11. Explain the concept of software distribution.
12. Explain the terms shared data, local data, partitioning, and replication.
13. What is electronic filing?
14. How can a DBMS be used to manage large volumes of textual data?
15. What are the major capabilities of the various technologies of office automation systems?
16. How does DDP improve office productivity?
17. Why are human factors considered in the design of a computer system?
18. List some techniques that can be used to make software user-friendly.

■ Discussion
■ Questions
and Cases

1. Spreadout Incorporated has decided to connect its computers in twelve states with a data communication network. Elmer Ware, the president, is not sure how a communication network functions. Explain to him the important functions of a communication system and how they relate to Spreadout's data-processing operations.
2. Describe the job of a data-base administrator in a DDP environment. Would the DBA maintain one data dictionary for the whole system or a separate dictionary for each location? How would he or she convince user departments to make their data available to departments at distant locations? If software development is highly decentralized, does that pose special problems for data-base design? Explain.

3. What kind of personnel grievances can be expected when automating an office? What can an office manager do if data-entry operators complain of excessive eyestrain from looking at video displays. How does he or she pacify disgruntled executives complaining about slow response time during peak hours?

4. Dublin Furniture is a medium-sized furniture manufacturing operation in Virginia, with five plants scattered over five counties in the southwest part of the state. The company has one central computer, an IBM mainframe. Each plant has access to the central computer through a variety of online terminals. For the last few months, manufacturing managers at the various plants have been building a case for distributed data processing. They argue that manufacturing resources planning (MRP) systems are becoming essential to effective manufacturing management. Their plan calls for a minicomputer to be purchased for each plant. Each plant would run its own MRP system. In addition, they argue, other applications could be distributed from the central computer to these minicomputers. For example, each plant could maintain its own personnel system. If you were chief executive officer of Dublin Furniture, would you approve the distributed-data-processing proposal?

5. Managers at the Real-Time Orange Juice Company are concerned about the growing amount of paperwork inundating the corporate headquarters. A computer is being considered as a way of eliminating some paperwork. One manager suggested using the value-added concept of transaction processing for the purchasing department. A manager in a department would complete a purchase requisition on a computer terminal and would authorize it with a password and a user identification number. The requisition would be sent electronically to purchasing for approval. Each purchasing agent would have an electronic "in basket," or computer file, in which requisitions would be stored until approved. The purchasing agent would "add value" to each item in the computer file by attaching his or her identification number to the item. This "electronic signature" would serve as the approval to purchase the item. The document would then be sent through the proper channels until the items had been ordered and the invoice paid. The computerized document would be stored on a magnetic-tape history file. What would be some considerations in implementing this type of paperless purchasing system?

6. Allied Innovators, Incorporated has a computer problem concerning the communication of information among its worldwide operations. Each division takes care of its own processing needs with its own minicomputer or mainframe. Computer communications among the divisions, the divisions and their remote locations, and the divisions and corporate headquarters are handled overnight, using standard long-distance lines. Allied Innovators' problem is twofold. First, certain divisions have begun to receive defense contracts, making security an important issue. Second, the communication between divisions has increased significantly; and overnight communication is causing problems when information is needed quickly. What suggestions would you make to Allied Innovators to improve its communications and security?

Fast-Food Distributor Counts on LANs for Swift Service

By Craig Zarley

The menu for fast-food delivery is about to change at Martin-Brower Company, the nation's largest distributor of fast foods.

With McDonald's, Long John Silver's, Arby's, and Red Lobster restaurant chains among its clients, the company operates 31 regional distribution centers throughout the United States and Canada, and owns more than 500 semitrailer trucks that deliver food and paper products to more than 6,600 fast-food restaurants.

Based in Des Plaines, ILL., Martin-Brower is a technical leader in the trucking industry with its use of automated routing systems and on-board computers that monitor the mechanical performance of each truck. Now it is on the verge of installing local area networks (LANs) at each of its distribution centers. The LANs will be used to merge vehicular data with the transportation-routing data base to further improve operational efficiency.

"The key to our business is on-time service," said Mark Cartwright, Martin-Brower's manager of transportation services. "A restaurant manager typically schedules more employees to coincide with our deliveries to help unload the truck. If we say that we'll be there at 10 a.m. and don't show up until 1 p.m., he's paying people to stand around."

For this reason, Martin-Brower promises delivery within 15 minutes of the scheduled time. To help meet stringent schedules, the company has, since 1984, been using an automated routing system called Trucks, from STSC Inc., in Rockville, Md.

Trucks previously ran on the company mainframe, but just over a year ago it was switched to an IBM PS/2 Model 80 to take advantage of enhanced graphics capabilities with the latest version of the software. Instead of viewing a column of statistics, dispatchers can now see an on-screen video map of each delivery route.

A Trucks system is used at each of the 31 distribution centers. The data bases at each site include street and highway maps of all possible road segments used by Martin-Brower trucks in that territory, as well as the location of each restaurant served by the distribution center.

Based on factors such as time commitments, available trucks, speed limits, distances, and what is being delivered, Trucks runs algorithms to plot the most efficient delivery route. While once it used to take two people 40 to 60 hours to develop between 50 and 75 routes using paper maps and calculators, Trucks can now build 100 routes in 20 minutes, according to Mr. Cartwright.

"We've been able to reduce our mileage by 10 to 15 percent while increasing our load factor on each truck by 10 percent with Trucks," he said.

Although Trucks does help improve operational efficiency, Martin-Brower has had no way to monitor how well drivers are actually meeting their delivery deadlines. To remedy the problem, the company is in the process of using a LAN to compare and analyze data from vehicular monitoring computers on its trucks with the information from the Trucks routing system.

Each Martin-Brower truck is equipped with a CADEC 300 Vehicle Information System from CADEC Systems Inc. of Londonerry, N.H. The system monitors engine performance factors such as speed, rpm, and mileage. The system also features an internal clock which times how long it takes to drive each road segment, as well as how long the driver spends at each stop. The driver activates the clock by entering a numerical code on the system's keyboard for each route and for each restaurant. The data are recorded on a cassette tape, and at the end of each day are fed into an IBM AT at each distribution center for processing.

The company has been using the CADEC system for three years, but until now the data have been used primarily to monitor driver performance and to increase fuel efficiency. "The data tell us on a daily basis if the driver has been speeding or if he has been running the rpm up too high before shifting into the next gear," explained Don Campbell, senior systems analyst at Martin-Brower. By analyzing speed and rpm, the company can improve driver safety and increase fuel economy by monitoring and adjusting driving habits.

The company now intends to further tighten its delivery schedule by combining the actual delivery information from this CADEC system with the theoretical data from Trucks. Martin-Brower's McDonald's Division has already installed a Novell LAN running PC/

PART FOUR

APPLICATION CASE

Focus data-base management system from Information Builders Inc., of New York, at its Atlanta distribution center. Trucks and CADEC software both include routines that allow users to format output files so they can be loaded into PC/Focus.

From this new combined data, the company has designed a special focus report, called the Transportation Information System (TIS). This report compares the distances and times that Trucks predicts will be needed to complete a delivery route with the actual figures gleaned from the CADEC system. "We want to take the actual driving and unloading times and put them back into Trucks so that we can fine-tune that system and make it a more accurate transportation-planning tool," said Mr. Cartwright.

In the initial tests at its Atlanta facility, Martin-Brower has found that mileages and times on the Trucks system have been as much as 90-percent accurate. But approaching 100-percent accuracy is still a corporate priority. "It's extremely advantageous to us in the budgeting process to be able to predict our operating expenses for the coming year," said Mr. Campbell. "With TIS, we'll be able to adjust road speeds in the Trucks system to meet actual driving conditions and thus achieve greater accuracy with our routing system."

The PS/2 used for Trucks and the AT running the CADEC system will be the initial nodes on the networks, along with one each for the transportation and distribution manager at each distribution center. Mr. Cartwright expects that the number of network nodes on each LAN will eventually grow to about 10 to accommodate general business applications at the distribution center. A PS/2 Model 80 will be the file server for the LANs.

"We chose the Model 80 as a file server because we needed the disk-storage capacity," explained Mr. Campbell. "And because we already have a Model 80 at each site, we'll have a backup to run Trucks in a stand-alone mode if the file server ever goes down."

Timetable Wrinkle

Mr. Campbell said that the LANs should be installed in all distribution centers within a year. Current plans call for sending TIS data from the LANs to a minicomputer at each center. The LAN-minicomputer link has not yet been determined because Martin-Brower is reassessing its choice of IBM System/36s and System/38s,

in light of recent announcements of their successor, the AS/400. The company has already installed 14 System/36s at regional sites but wants to evaluate the AS/400 before proceeding further.

Once minicomputer hardware is chosen, TIS data will be sent to the minicomputer and shipped quarterly via Systems Network Architecture (SNA) leased lines to the corporate IBM 3081 and 3083 mainframes.

Mr. Cartwright said that connecting the distribution LANs to corporate headquarters will be vital in maintaining the Trucks automated routing system. As new restaurants are added to the distribution network, typically at a rate of 10 to 20 per week, road segments necessary to service the new stops must be added to the data base. A Trucks maintenance staff at corporate headquarters adds new roads to the system by tracing digitizers over paper maps and entering geographic coordinates for each new restaurant.

Currently, updates to the Truck data base are shipped to the centers on disks or magnetic tapes via overnight mail. "Our goal is to get the changes out to the distribution centers within one hour," said Mr. Cartwright. "Once the LANs are in place, we will send the changes via modem and Carbon Copy [communications software from Meridian Technology Inc., in Irvine, Calif.]."

"With the LANs linked to corporate headquarters, we can maintain the transportation systems from Des Plaines, instead of hiring maintenance experts at each site," said Mr. Cartwright.

With the ability to track all deliveries, Martin-Brower is betting it can make the fast-food business even faster.

Reprinted from *PC Week*, August 22, 1988 p. 33. Copyright ©: 1988 Ziff-Davis Publishing Company.

DISCUSSION QUESTIONS

1. Does Martin-Brower's Trucks system give it a competitive advantage? If so, what are the competitive advantages?

2. Assume you are a competitor of Martin-Brower. What would you do to overcome Martin-Brower's competitive advantage?

3. Are there other types of business that such a system could be applied to? If so, what are they, and how would you apply the system?

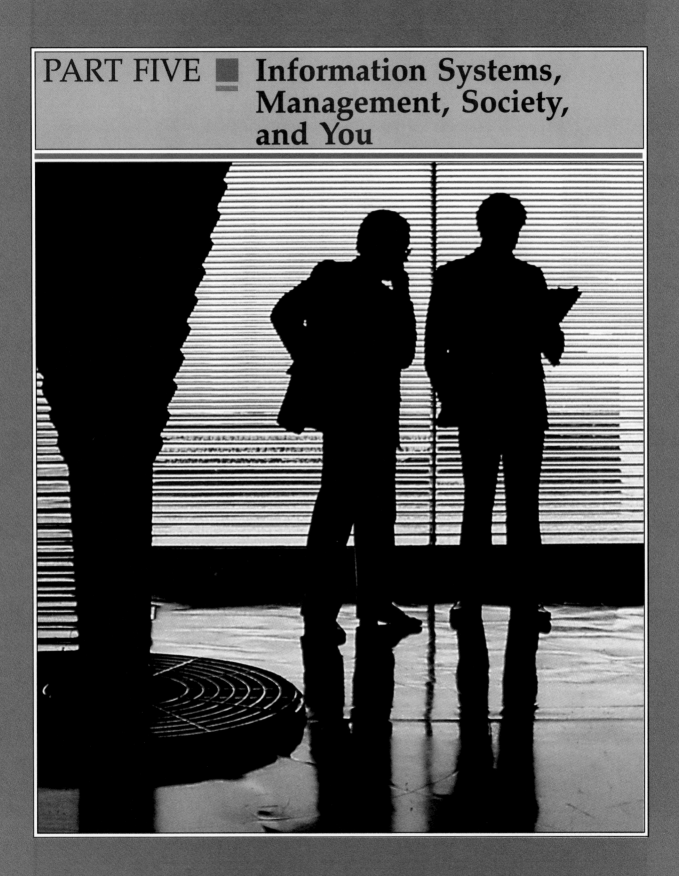

PART FIVE ▪ Information Systems, Management, Society, and You

Managing the Information-System Resource

Chapter 15

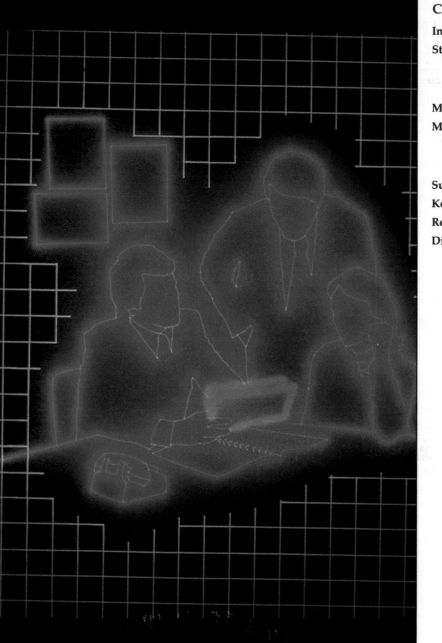

CHAPTER OUTLINE

Introduction

Structure of a MIS Function
*The Organizational Location
of MIS*
The Internal Structure of MIS

Managing System Development

Managing System Operations
System Maintenance
Data-Processing Operations
Physical Security

Summing Up

Key Terms

Review Questions

Discussion Questions and Cases

■ INTRODUCTION

Management of information systems has seen significant changes in recent years. In the 1960s and 1970s, information-system managers gradually increased their power and influence within most organizations. Typically, they moved from managerial positions within a department, such as accounting, to full-fledged vice presidents of information systems. These managers were looked upon as experts in information processing and, in effect, they held the keys to the computer resource. In recent years, however, the role of the information-system manager has been changing. With users directly purchasing hardware and either purchasing or creating software, many people see the role of the information-system manager changing to that of a consultant, advisor, and coordinator. Of course, we will continue to have centralized computer facilities, especially for large batch runs and large data bases that support many users concurrently. The challenge of administering centralized data bases and communication networks with distributed computing means that information-system managers will continue to play a crucial role in the management of business organizations.

In this chapter, we will discuss the structure of the management information system (MIS) function, and then we will look at managing system development, system maintenance, and data-processing operations. Finally, we will cover physical security of computer operations.

■ STRUCTURE OF A MIS FUNCTION

The Organizational Location of MIS

Typically the MIS function is located in one of two areas in an organization. The chief MIS executive may be reporting to the vice president and controller, as shown in Figure 15–1, or he or she may be vice president of management information systems and be reporting directly to the president, as depicted in Figure 15–2. There are advantages and disadvantages of both cases.

The **controller,** being the chief accounting officer in a corporation, is looked upon as the primary provider of financial management information. In addition, functions in the controller's area such as payroll, accounts payable, and accounts receivable were often the first computerized applications. Therefore, the MIS function often originated and matured within the controller's organization. The primary disadvantage of the chief MIS executive reporting to the controller is that the computer resource may be dominated and used primarily to solve problems within the controller's area, and therefore other functions may be neglected. Marketing, engineering, and production applications of the computer are of equal or more importance than many of the applications in the accounting area. The primary advantage of the chief MIS executive reporting to the controller is that accounting is an information-oriented discipline, and accountants are well trained in the area of control. Accountants may produce a computer system that is much more controlled and auditable.

Figure 15–1
Chief MIS Executive Reporting to the VP/Controller

This organizational location for the chief MIS executive often occurs in smaller and medium-sized companies or in firms that are just beginning to install computer information systems.

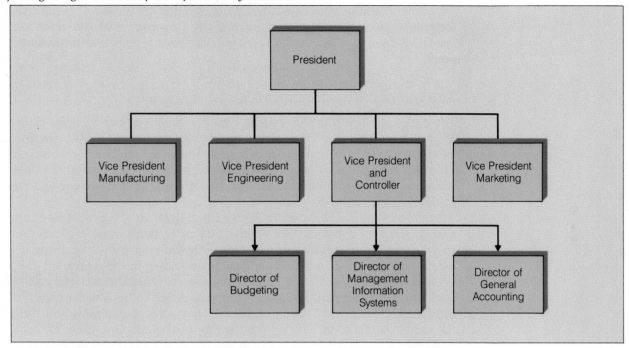

Figure 15–2
Chief MIS Executive Reporting to the President

In large firms where a MIS has been developed to its full potential, the MIS vice president usually reports to the president.

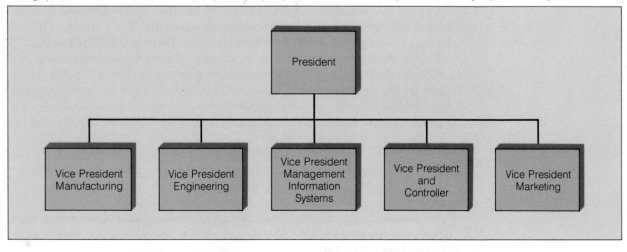

Most of the larger, more mature MIS organizations are separate and have a chief MIS executive who is a vice president and reports directly to the president, as illustrated in Figure 15–2. This location for the MIS function helps to ensure that each of the areas receive unbiased attention from the MIS department. Today, with computers penetrating many areas and being used for competitive advantage, it is particularly important that the chief MIS executive be a member of the unbiased vice-presidential level of management.

The Internal Structure of MIS

The organization of the MIS function itself varies from firm to firm. Figure 15–4 on pages 392 and 393 depicts a typical MIS organization in a large firm. In smaller firms, many of these functions would be consolidated or would not exist. For example, in a small firm all software may be purchased, so there would be no need for the systems and programming department and the system software function.

At the manager level shown in Figure 15–4, there are six distinct functions that should be carried out within the MIS or through outside sources. A specific MIS organization chart may look quite different. However, the major functions concerning an MIS organization are shown in the figure.

The **information center** is responsible for coordinating and supporting application development by users. The staff consists of technical experts on software such as Lotus 1–2–3 and Focus. They act as consultants and assist the user in application development without programming. Since the personal computer is an important tool in this effort, the coordination of personal computing is often carried out by the information center. As discussed in Chapter 2, the personal computer has brought several challenges, including PC management. The responsibilities of the coordination group are listed in Figure 15–3.

The **system software department** installs and maintains system software such as operating systems and data-base management systems. The staff are technical and very highly skilled programmers who rarely deal directly with users.

Application software is developed by (or selected and purchased with the help of) the **systems and programming department.** The personnel in this department interact heavily with users as they develop user applications.

The **technical support staff** is in charge of maintaining hardware and establishing data-processing standards. **Standards** are very much like procedures for the data-processing function. They include such things as program, data, and application naming conventions; procedures for maintaining the integrity of communication systems; and standards that govern the content of user procedure manuals.

The **data-processing operations department** manages the day-to-day operations of the computer hardware. It also monitors the processing of computer jobs and assists where human intervention, such as mounting tapes, is required.

A relatively new function in most larger MIS organizations is **data-base administration (DBA).** The DBA department is responsible for coordinating the data base, which includes providing for data security.

Figure 15–3
Responsibilities of the Personal-Computer Coordination Group

Personal-computer coordination groups originated in the early 1980s. Information processing by PCs and application development by users represent up to 75 percent of the total information processing of firms.

- Standardizing hardware purchases
- Standardizing software purchases
- Providing PC access to mainframe data bases
- Preventing the redundant development of software
- Preventing the redundant creation and storage of data
- Assuring that data stored on personal computers are secure
- Providing personal-computer training
- Organizing and supporting personal-computer user groups
- Maintaining the firm's in-house "personal computer store" where users can try out a wide variety of PC hardware and software

The MIS steering committee is an important part of the MIS function. A **steering committee** is made up of high-level managers from each department within the business, including marketing, accounting, MIS, manufacturing, and so on. Its purpose is to guide the overall direction of the MIS. For example, the steering committee decides the priorities for implementing specific application systems. Much of the high-level planning for the MIS is either performed or approved by the steering committee. Ideally, the steering committee provides the broad perspectives and guidance necessary to assure that the MIS supports the objectives of the business as a whole.

■ MANAGING SYSTEM DEVELOPMENT

Perhaps the most important aspect of managing the system development effort is the **system development methodology** used. In previous chapters we discussed the structured approach to system development, system prototyping, and application development by users. It is important that a structured methodology, combined with system prototyping and application development by users, be used to develop new systems.

Another aspect of managing system development is the process by which development efforts are actually controlled. Most system development organizations use a **project management approach,** meaning that each application development of significant size is assigned to a project development team. This team is usually headed by a senior system analyst or sometimes a user department manager who has system development experience. Sufficient resources in the form of programmers, system analysts, hardware, and software, are assigned to the team to complete the project.

Each project is assigned its own financial budget and time schedule. The financial budget performance is tracked by periodic reports that compare actual expenditures to budgets. Schedule performance is managed and controlled through one of several tools, such as the **program evaluation and review technique (*PERT*), critical path management (*CPM*),** and the *Gantt chart.* There are several good project-manager software packages available for personal computers, such as the Harvard Total Project Manager and the

PERT and CPM
These two scheduling methods use graphic networks to depict the activities and time that are necessary to complete a project. The minimum amount of time in which a project can be completed is computed by these methods. They also highlight those activities whose completion are most critical to the on-time completion of the project.

GANTT CHART
A graph where output activities are plotted as bars on a time scale. This chart was developed by Henry L. Gantt in 1917. Gantt charts indicate who is assigned responsibility for completing certain tasks, the estimated or planned dates on which tasks are to be started and completed, and the actual dates on which particular tasks have been started and completed.

Figure 15–4
Large MIS Organization

As computer information systems have become more important to organizations, the MIS organization itself has grown in size and influence. The area that is growing most rapidly is the information center, with its personal-computer coordination and support of application development by users.

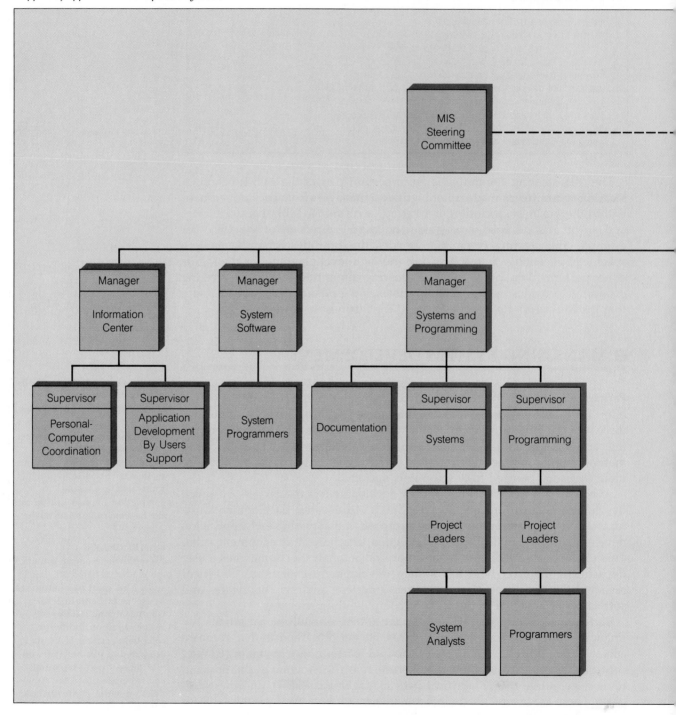

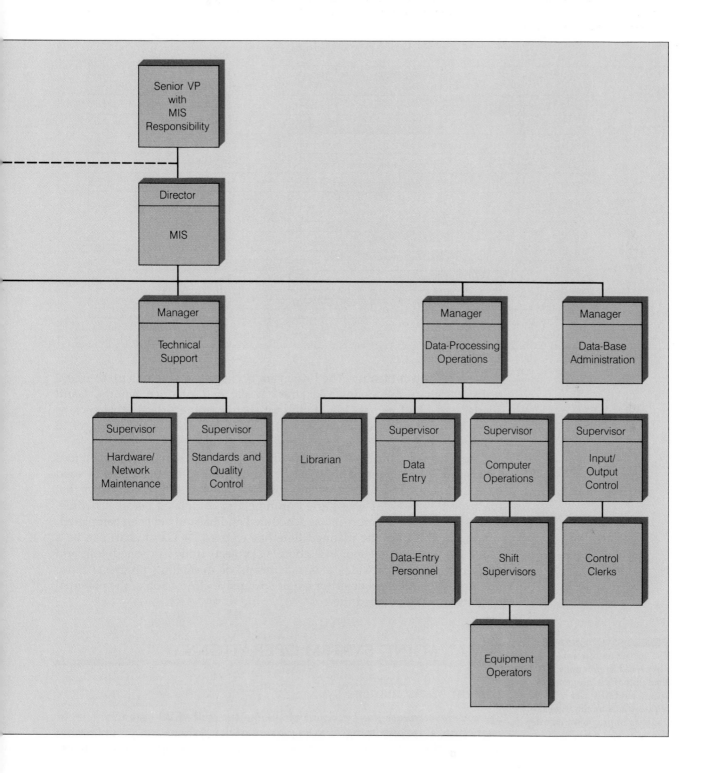

Figure 15–5
Gantt Chart

Gantt charts are easily understood tools that allow managers to visualize the schedule for a project. Inexpensive PC plotters produce these charts quickly.

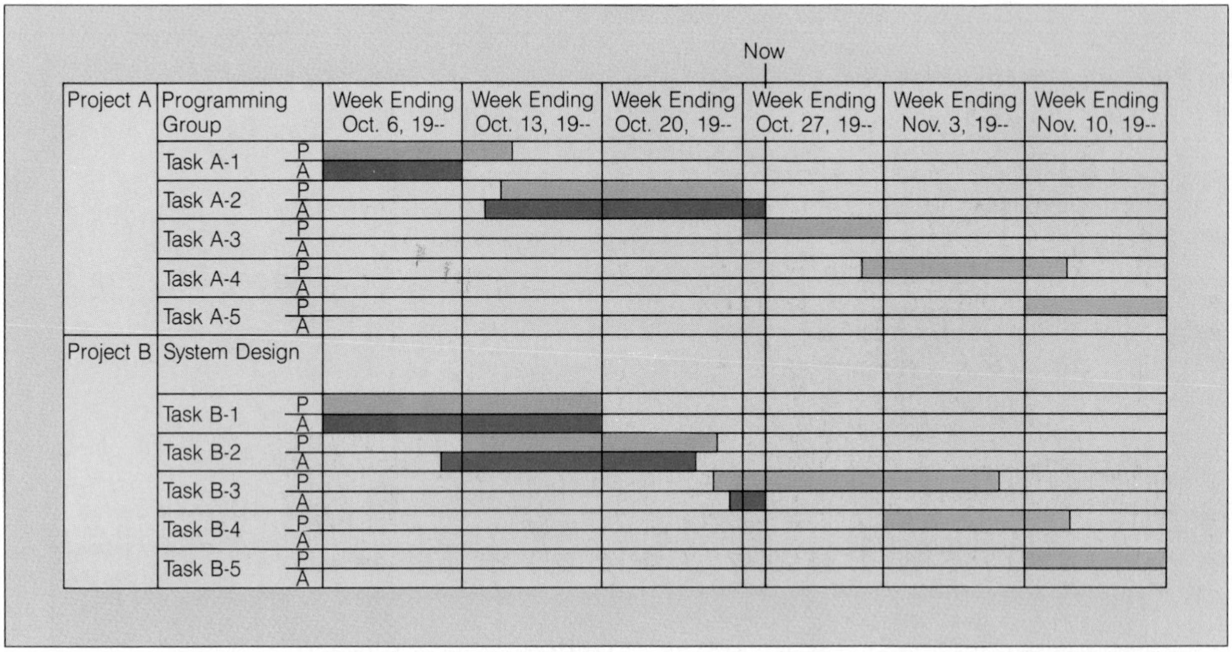

Primavera Project Planner. The Primavera package can schedule up to 10,000 tasks; assign resources to tasks; track costs; and produce reports, Gantt charts, and PERT charts. It is important that computer-based tools such as these be used in project management. They allow the project manager to quickly see the impact of schedule and resource changes.

Gantt charts are the most conceptually simple of the scheduling techniques (see Figure 15–5). Planned times for the various tasks are represented by solid bars; the actual times are shown by cross-hatched bars. The chart shows that for project A, task A-1 was started on time and completed before schedule. Task A-2 was started before it was scheduled and has not yet been completed, although more than the planned time has elapsed. A Gantt chart can be a valuable measurement tool in a complex project. It aids in scheduling and coordinating, and provides a visual means of evaluating progress. Since preparing a Gantt chart does not require extensive effort or data, the potential benefits generally exceed the cost.

SYSTEM MAINTENANCE
The correction of errors discovered in programs and the changing of the programs to satisfy modified user requirements or conditions. Changes in programs are often also necessary when new hardware is introduced.

■ MANAGING SYSTEM OPERATIONS

System Maintenance

System maintenance has become a challenge for many MIS organizations. In many cases it is consuming 70 to 80 percent of the systems and programming resources. Such situations leave little resources for developing new systems.

Methods for decreasing the cost of system maintenance are of paramount concern to MIS managers.

As with managing system development, the adoption of a structured methodology will greatly enhance the ability to manage system maintenance. Efficient and effective system maintenance requires that personnel understand the program to be modified. Structured methodologies produce programs that are easier to understand. Programming personnel must be able to make the change by changing the program statements in a confined and isolated area of the program. If a change requires modification in many different areas of the program or system, system maintenance becomes an almost impossible task. As we learned in previous chapters, structured methodologies produce programs that are modular. Each of these modules is as independent and self-contained as practical. Therefore, changes are likely to affect only a restricted area of one module.

An **active data dictionary** simplifies system maintenance by restricting both the number and location of program changes. This dictionary allows data to be defined in one location, and this definition is used by all programs that process those data. The programs use the data simply by referring to data names like ZIP CODE for an address zip code. The information's physical format, such as its type (character or numeric) and length, must be known to each program that uses it. So instead of the physical-format definition of the same data item being buried in many different programs, it is stored in one place, the active data dictionary. The term *active* is used since each program "actively" uses the data dictionary for definitions.

To understand how an active data dictionary aids in system maintenance, consider the U.S. Postal System change from a five-digit to a nine-digit zip code. Many firms have literally hundreds of programs that use zip codes. To search through all these programs, locate where the format of zip code is defined, and make the change from five to nine digits would be a monumental task. With an active data dictionary, only one change in the dictionary is needed. Usually, none of the programs that use the data dictionary has to be manually changed. Each of them may have to be recompiled, but this is an automated process.

Requests for changes in programs originate with the users. A formalized **change authorization form** should be used. On this form the user identifies the program and/or system to be changed and outlines the changes desired. An important part of this form is the authorization signatures, which must be obtained prior to changing the programs. These signatures typically include user management, the systems and programming manager, and sometimes the data-processing steering committee. Figure 15-6 shows a change authorization form.

Program changes must be well managed and controlled. After the changes have been made, the system must be thoroughly tested prior to implementation. The same set of tests used when the system was developed should be run before the changed system is implemented.

Data-Processing Operations

Managing data-processing operations is much like managing any production shop within an organization. Management must be concerned with maintain-

Figure 15–6
Change Authorization Form

The authorization and documentation of changes made to systems are crucial to well-maintained systems. Without such documentation, fraudulent changes could easily occur or the system could be changed to the point where no one really knows what the system does.

REQUEST FOR SYSTEM MODIFICATION

User Name:

Department:

Telephone No.:

System Name:

Module(s) to be changed (if known):

Please describe the change(s) desired and explain the reasons thereof:

Signature	Approved	Rejected	Comments
Requestor			
Dept. Manager	☐	☐	
MIS Liaison Officer	☐	☐	
Manager, Systems and Programming	☐	☐	

ing sufficient capacity to process the computer jobs. Users of the resource should be charged for the resources they use. Personnel must be hired, managed, and sometimes dismissed, and the machines must be maintained in operable condition.

Processing capacity may be limited by any number of factors, including primary-storage size, secondary-storage size, CPU power, number of terminals, and so on. Any of these can become the **bottleneck** that limits the capacity of the computer system. Data-processing management must monitor these resources and determine whether one is likely to become a bottleneck in the future. Additional resources can be obtained if the potential bottleneck is identified promptly. *Software monitors* such as IBM's systems management facility (SMF) are very valuable in determining the levels of use of various system resources. For example, we could determine the percentage of time various terminals are being used and the time of day they are being used. We could also determine whether the CPU is running close to its maximum capacity at any given point during the day. Trends of system resource utilization enable us to project when various resources will be used at their capacity, and therefore when expansion should be planned.

Hardware monitors are sometimes used to detect bottlenecks and determine utilization levels for various devices. Figure 15–7 shows the output of a hardware monitor used to control resource usage.

One of the best ways to ensure that the computer is used efficiently is to charge people for their use of various computer resources, including CPU time, disk space, tapes, and printing. Under a **user-billing system,** the data-processing operations department is set up as a service center for the rest of the firm. Its services are available to anyone in the firm who is willing to pay for them. Rates should be similar to outside rates, such as what a service bureau would charge.

BOTTLENECK
The component of a computer system that limits the amount of work it can perform.

SOFTWARE MONITOR
A program that monitors the usage and performance of various computer system devices.

HARDWARE MONITOR
A device that monitors usage and performance of various computer system devices.

Physical Security

In many computer systems today, the MIS resource is a crucial asset. Even a temporary loss of this resource through fire, sabotage, or other disaster can be very costly. You may learn the importance of contingency planning with backup of files firsthand someday. After you have worked for several days on an electronic spreadsheet, program, or word-processing file, you may accidentally lose or erase it. One such experience usually teaches the importance of planning for disasters. Imagine the cost to a large business of failure to plan for disasters. Imagine if it lost all its files in a fire and no backups had been made!

File backup is a technique for recovering from a disaster after it occurs. In this chapter we examine physical security that helps prevent disasters from occurring. We will cover controls for five areas: entry, sabotage and virus, fire, natural and environmental disaster, and power.

Entry Control A well-designed **entry control** system will control entry to the computer facility. Only operations personnel are allowed to enter the computer facility itself. Manually delivered programs and data are passed through a window of the computer room. Of course, most programs and data today are transmitted electronically to and from the computer. Entry control is usually done through a locked door to the computer room. The doors are opened through various means, such as plastic cards with magnetic strips (similar to credit cards) or a combination of a plastic card and a memorized entry code.

Figure 15–7
Sample Hardware-Monitoring Report

This graph displays eight variables being monitored. Each variable has a value of 0 to 100 percent. The length of the asterisks away from the center of the graph illustrates the magnitude of each variable. For example, the CPU is active 78.5 percent of the time, whereas the CPU only is busy 10.5 percent of the time. Notice that the "CPU active" and "CPU wait" add up to 100 percent. The "CPU only busy" and the "CPU plus any device busy" add up to the 78.5 percent time that the CPU is active. When the CPU is active, it is either executing the operating system (which is called the supervisor) or it is executing a particular application program called a problem. Therefore, the total of the supervisor state and the problem state is 78.5 percent, the same as the "CPU active" percent.

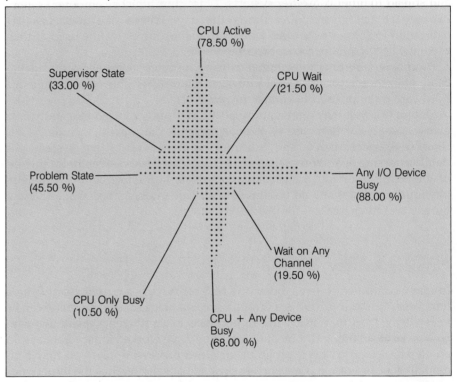

Plastic cards and keys can be lost or misplaced, though. Providing 100 percent positive identification has been difficult. There has been a wide variety of techniques and machines tested to provide positive identification of personnel entering computer facilities. One machine examines the pattern of the person's fingerprints. You cannot misplace your fingerprints! But it has been found that a photocopy of a person's fingerprints will trick the machine into unlocking the door. Another technique works in a similar way, except you have to kiss the machine! Lip prints uniquely identify a person. But aside from its obvious drawbacks, a photocopy of one's lip prints would also mislead this machine. Another device shines light into a person's eyes and makes an identification based on the patterns within his or her eyeballs! Although the technique is harmless, employees probably would not accept it. Eventually we will have machines that are highly reliable in identifying a particular person.

Sabotage and Virus Control **Sabotage control** of the hardware, programs, and data is achieved to a large extent through passwords and by physical-entry controls of the computer facility itself. Firms that have specifically designed a secure computer facility usually construct the computer room to bomb-proof specifications. It is interesting to note that when computers were first used in the 1950s and 1960s, it was common for a firm to show off its computer facilities by having large glass windows surrounding its computer center. A saboteur could have easily tossed a bomb through these windows.

Computer viruses, a new form of computer sabotage, came about in the late 1980s. These viruses are computer programs designed to replicate themselves and spread to other computer systems. Once they infect a computer system, their actions can range from the relatively harmless, like displaying the message "Gotcha" on workstation screens, to the very destructive, like erasing all the computer system's disk files.

Viruses can spread from computer to computer through network connections or through shared storage media among computers. Some of the most notorious virus attacks have spread quickly (in a few hours) all over the country through national computer networks. Such attacks have consumed many hours of computer and human time in efforts to purge computer systems of the virus.

Writing a computer virus program is an easy task for a skilled programmer, especially for a system programmer. Although writing and intentionally spreading a virus program is reprehensible and illegal, we can expect to have computer viruses around for the foreseeable future.

The analogy with biological viruses is most appropriate. Even the protections against computer viruses are called vaccines. These vaccines are programs that monitor a computer system to detect and purge a system of a virus before it does damage. There are vaccines available for all types of computers. But unfortunately, as with biological virus vaccines, computer virus vaccines do not protect a system against all viruses, particularly new ones. Thus, backup of critical computer files is a very important protection against virus attacks.

Fire Control The most likely physical threat to a computer facility is fire. The best **fire control** is to store backup copies of data and programs at another location and to arrange for emergency use of alternative computer hardware. In addition, many computer centers use a fire-suppression gas known as halon. The halon is released by fire and smoke detection systems and is effective in extinguishing fires. The primary disadvantage of halon is its cost. If the gas is accidentally released, a firm may have to pay several thousand dollars to replace it. Less expensive gases exist but are impractical because they are poisonous. Halon is nonpoisonous.

Natural and Environmental Disaster Control Firms need to consider **disaster controls** when choosing the site for a computer room. Natural and environmental hazards include floods, hurricanes, and bursting pipes. Water can destroy the sensitive electronic equipment of a computer. Fire-control water sprinklers on floors above the computer room are an environmental hazard that is sometimes overlooked. Water leaking down through pipe holes and other crevices onto computer equipment, tapes, and disks can be very damaging. For this reason, the floor above the computer room should be thoroughly sealed to prevent water leakage.

Power Control   Large computer systems should have uninterruptible and controlled power supplies. Plugging such computer systems directly into electrical lines is not a good idea. If the power goes off, even momentarily, the data and programs stored in semiconductor primary storage are lost because semiconductor storage is volatile. Furthermore, power spikes (increases in the current voltage) can heavily damage a computer system. Such power spikes are often caused by electrical thunderstorms. Some computer centers guard against this type of power spike by shutting down computer operations during such storms. Often, however, this is not a viable alternative.

Many organizations use power-supply systems as their **power control.** These systems consist of batteries and backup generators. The batteries are continuously being charged by the incoming electrical service, and the computer draws its power from the batteries. Thereby the computer is insulated from the electrical service lines, and power spikes are prevented. If there is a power outage, the batteries will be sufficient for a short duration. Longer-lasting power outages are covered by the backup generator.

As organizations become more dependent on computer systems, managing information-system resources becomes more critical. Many of you will, in varying degrees, be involved in this management. In the next two chapters we will see how computers impact society and you.

■ Summing Up

■ In recent years, the role of the information-system manager has changed as users have become more actively involved in data processing.
■ The MIS function may be located within the controller's organization, where the controller is considered to be the primary provider of information. On the other hand, many organizations treat information systems as a separate function headed by a vice president who reports directly to the president.
■ It is important that a structured methodology be used for system development. Usually, system development is carried out using the project management approach for project control.
■ With a structured methodology, program maintenance becomes a much easier task. All changes must be authorized and properly documented in order to prevent confusion and chaos.
■ Active data dictionaries substantially reduce the number of program changes that must be made when the data format changes.
■ Operations should be constantly monitored in order to detect bottlenecks and inefficiencies. Users should be billed to ensure efficient use of resources.
■ Physical security of the EDP system is a major responsibility of system management. Procedures should be implemented for both the prevention of disasters and the recovery from disasters such as fires, floods, and viruses.

■ Key Terms

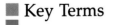

controller	system software department
information center	systems and programming department

technical support staff

standards

data-processing operations department

data-base administration (DBA)

steering committee

system development methodology

project management approach

program evaluation and review technique (PERT)

critical path management (CPM)

Gantt chart

system maintenance

active data dictionary

change authorization form

bottleneck

software monitors

hardware monitors

user-billing system

entry control

sabotage control

computer viruses

fire control

disaster control

power control

1. What developments are causing a change in the role of the information systems manager?

2. What are two possible locations for an MIS department within a firm? How do they differ?

3. Identify the major functions within an MIS organization.

4. Explain the project management approach. List some tools that may be used to control a project.

5. What are the primary factors of concern to managers of system maintenance?

6. Why is it important to have formal change authorization procedures?

7. List several factors that could limit processing capacity.

8. What is user billing? What are its advantages?

9. Briefly describe the idea of entry controls.

10. What controls can be used to limit the threat of fire?

11. List some major natural disasters that may threaten a computer installation.

12. What is a computer virus? How does it spread, and what damage can it do?

13. How can you prevent damage caused by irregularities in the power supply?

1. As president of Hi-Tek, Incorporated, you must decide whether the director of the MIS department should report to the controller or to you. Which alternative do you choose? Why? If you think neither arrangement is suitable, what do you suggest instead?

2. Assume you are redesigning the EDP facilities of a company located on the eleventh floor of a downtown office building. What physical security features must be built into the new design? Give reasons to justify the cost of these security features.

3. The Cancun Corporation recently acquired a fourth-generation software package that allows end users to quickly write their own programs to produce ad hoc management reports from the corporation's data base. The package is so successful that people in user departments are implementing their own systems without the aid of the system development department. The manager of system development worries that users do not know the importance of specifying new systems according to an established development methodology. She also thinks that information stored in the various systems might be redundant. Should application development by users be controlled? If so, in what way?

4. Jim Brown, a cost accountant for the Southern Pines paper-processing plant, made extensive use of a popular spreadsheet program. He created several programs for analyzing overhead accounts, and everyone in the cost-accounting department used them. The firm's policy was for the cost-accounting manager to review the logic of all spreadsheet programs before they were used for everyday reporting.

A vice president of the company asked Jim to make a change in a spreadsheet program format. Jim made the change without approval from the cost-accounting manager, and in the process he accidentally changed a cost-calculation formula as well. The vice president used the erroneous information in a bid, and the company lost the bid because the cost estimate was too high. The following week, the cost-accounting manager noticed the faulty spreadsheet calculation. Both Jim and the vice president were fired. What controls could possibly have prevented this situation?

5. Thomas Incorporated has a large, centralized computer operations facility. The computers operate seven days a week, twenty-four hours a day. Ray Harper is considered by operations management to be its most valuable computer operator. He is highly experienced and very loyal to the company. Whenever a problem arises, he can be counted on to diligently work toward its solution. In fact, Ray is so dedicated that in the last five years he has not taken a vacation. From the standpoint of the company, do you see any problem with the fact that Ray has declined a vacation in the last five years?

Information Systems and Society

■ Chapter 16

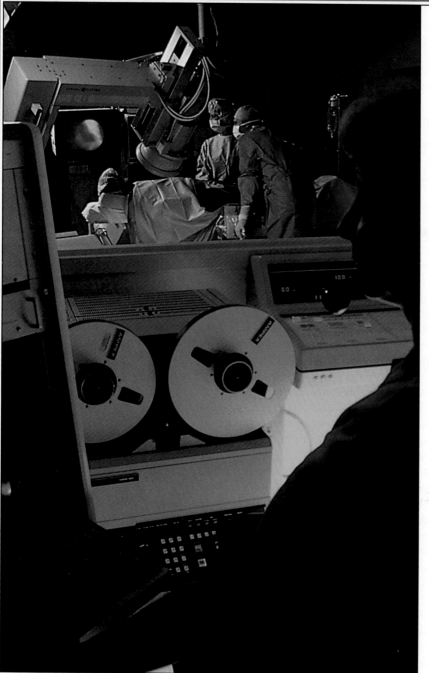

CHAPTER OUTLINE

Introduction

The Potential Impact of Computer Information Systems
The Information Revolution
Working at Home
Control Problems

Displacement of Human Beings
Automation
Artificial Intelligence

Computers and Individual Privacy
Potential Problems
Privacy Legislation

Personal Computers

International Data Transfers

Computer Crime Cases
Equity Funding
Pacific Bell
Wells Fargo

Summing Up

Key Terms

Review Questions

Discussion Questions and Cases

■ INTRODUCTION

Our assumption throughout this text has been that the application of computers will enhance both our work and personal lives. Most people agree with this assessment, although some say these enhancements have been slow in coming and the computer has not yet produced the revolution it promised. We will first examine the potential impact of computer information systems; we will then explore automation and artificial intelligence. Next, we will consider privacy questions associated with computerized information and the very significant effects that personal computers are having on our lives. Finally, we will explore the problems of international data transfers and computer crime.

THE POTENTIAL IMPACT OF ■ COMPUTER INFORMATION SYSTEMS

The Information Revolution

Information is wealth. Although some say the computer has caused information to be wealth, information has always been wealth. For example, if you have information about where a major highway is to be built before others know the location, purchasing land in that area is almost certain to increase your wealth. The computer is simply a new source of significant amounts of information. Those who can afford to buy a computer and have the skills to use it will be better able to acquire information than those who cannot use the technology. Will the computer revolution produce two new classes in our society—the information-rich and the information-poor?

There are proposals to produce electronic newspapers. You would simply connect your personal computer through regular telephone lines to the newspaper's large computer. Through key words, you would be able to retrieve any news item—current or up to several years old. You could even select only those articles of interest. In effect, you would be making your own newspaper! For example, you could enter the name of your favorite sports team and retrieve all articles about the team. But in reading newspapers we acquire a broad spectrum of information. Would the ability to select our reading material tend to make our knowledge base more narrow?

Already there are **information services,** such as *The Source* and *Dow Jones News Retrieval*, which allow you to obtain a wide variety of information. Information services allow you to retrieve stock-market quotes, order airline tickets, and order merchandise. With such a service, you could save money (and thereby increase your wealth) by having the computer search for the least expensive airline fare when you plan to travel.

Some people suggest that we establish an information-assistance program, similar to current food-assistance programs for the disadvantaged in our society. They argue that without such a program, the poor will become further disadvantaged because they can't access the information that personal and business computers provide. Whether we should have an information-assistance program, of course, is a political decision. In any case, this concern illustrates the degree of impact that some feel the computer revolution may have on society.

If we reach the point where we do a significant amount of our shopping through electronic means, work at home on a personal computer connected to an office computer, and receive most of our entertainment as well as our educational instruction through cable TV, some very significant questions arise. Can we all retreat into our electronic cottages and still function as a society? Possibly not. Many would argue that a democratic society requires frequent **face-to-face contact** among its citizens. Further, an electronic society provides very great threats to privacy, as we will discuss later in the chapter. These threats decrease our personal freedom and increase the ability of others to manipulate and monitor our personal lives. The potential is there, as we will see.

Working at Home

Would you really want to work for a company where you did all of your work at home through electronic means? Off the top of your head, you might answer with an enthusiastic "yes." No doubt there would be many advantages to such an arrangement. You could live almost anywhere you wanted and spend more time with your family. But working where you have direct contact with people also has advantages. The social interaction and exchange of ideas among co-workers is a significant contributor to the mental well-being of most individuals. In fact, surveys show that the most common way to meet a marriage partner is at work.

In any case, you may in the near future have a chance to decide whether to work at home or at a traditional workplace. If a significant number of people decide to work at home, there will be noticeable impacts on society. However, it is a good guess that most individuals will quickly become bored with working at home and will prefer at least a portion of their work to be in a workplace.

Control Problems

To illustrate another potential problem of computers and the emerging communication technology, let's consider the **electronic shopping** systems such as QUBE. The **QUBE system** has been tested in Columbus, Ohio. It is essentially a combination of a cable TV system and computer technology that allows TV viewers to respond electronically to such things as surveys and merchandise sales. Some people say this system could produce instant responses to surveys, allow shopping by electronic mail, and even allow instant electronic democracy where voters could respond to an issue through their QUBE terminal systems. Such proposals are questionable, however. For example, how do we know who is pushing those buttons? Is it an adult or a three-year-old child?

Picture our presidential candidates stating their positions in a TV debate. After the debate is over, we push our buttons and elect the president! This, of course, is absurd. The control problems would be horrendous. Consider the case of a straight-as-an-arrow married couple who subscribed to the QUBE system. They began receiving sexually explicit materials through the mail. To their amazement, they found that their four-year-old child had actually ordered the materials by pushing the appropriate button while watching a cable TV program. Since the parents were the cable TV subscriber, the materials were shipped in their name, and they, of course, ended up on the mailing lists of places dealing with such materials. What if your five-year-old turned on your personal computer and started transferring your bank-account funds? Certainly, many of these example problems have solutions, but as yet the problems still exist.

■ DISPLACEMENT OF HUMAN BEINGS

In the 1950s, many people were concerned that computers were going to displace large numbers of people, especially clerical workers. They worried that as clerical functions became automated, there would be no need for people with clerical skills. This did not occur to the extent predicted. In general, more jobs were created than were lost, although the new jobs often called for different skills, such as programming and system analysis.

Automation

In general, managements use computers to generate more or better quality information. They do not use them to generate the same information as before and thereby reduce the labor force. However, this is beginning to change. Computers are being used to control robots that are quickly replacing human workers on assembly lines in industry (see Figure 16–1). In some factories, the whole production line is automated on certain shifts; the only human beings are security guards. The robots can even repair themselves when they break down. For example, when a drill bit breaks, the machine simply replaces it from a bin of replacement bits. These factories do require maintenance personnel during the same shifts.

Office automation is likely to reduce the need for typists, clerks, and other office personnel. Prior to personal computers, computers were primarily used for high-volume tasks. Many of the day-to-day tasks were still done manually. Personal computers are rapidly changing this situation.

If computers do displace significant numbers of workers, will society support the retraining of these workers? Will there be enough alternative jobs? It seems there will. There is always something to be done, regardless of how many tasks are performed by computers and machines. And usually the new jobs are more interesting. The computer often does the dull and routine jobs such as assembly-line and clerical work. The bottom line, though, is that anytime we can replace a human being with a machine at a cheaper cost, society as a whole benefits because the standard of living rises.

Artificial Intelligence

Artificial intelligence is a computer application where the computer makes decisions or judgments that appear to require human intuition, reasoning,

Figure 16–1
A Robot

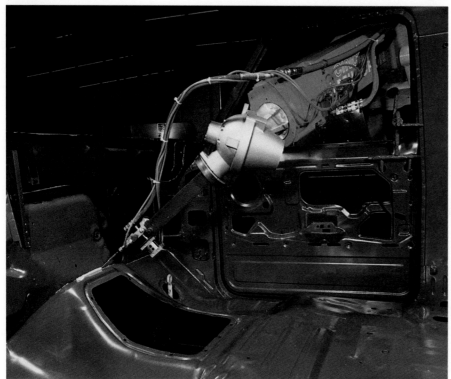

and intelligence. One type of artificial intelligence being rapidly adopted is the expert system. **Expert systems** attempt to provide the same judgmental advice that human experts such as doctors provide. In the areas where they have been successful, these systems can equal and often surpass the best judgments made by humans. For example, they have been applied to the diagnosis of illnesses. Given the symptoms of the patient, the expert system may ask more questions, request additional laboratory tests, and eventually arrive at a diagnosis that is as good as or better than that of the best doctors in limited areas of medicine. One approach to developing these expert systems is to model the thought processes of a physician making a diagnosis. This not only results in an artificial intelligence system, but also provides very interesting insights into how humans reason and make judgments.

Will these systems ever replace experts such as doctors, lawyers, engineers, accountants, and information-system consultants? Certainly some of these expert systems may make better judgments than the least competent people in these areas, but most professionals will use the systems as tools. A medical diagnosis expert system could assist doctors greatly in narrowing down a possible diagnosis.

Will the professionals accept these systems, which may seem to diminish the experts' importance to society? I think they will. Most true professionals are always looking for ways to improve their productivity and the quality of service they provide to their clients.

One danger is that people may think expert systems are infallible since they are computer-based. Nothing can be further from the truth. These systems are models of the human judgment process; thus many human imperfections are found in expert systems. Professionals, such as doctors, must continue to know enough about their field to recognize when the computer-based expert system is providing unreasonable answers or diagnoses.

■ COMPUTERS AND INDIVIDUAL PRIVACY

Potential Problems

If I were asked by a totalitarian regime how to provide almost total surveillance over the country's population, I would suggest establishing a pervasive **electronic funds transfer system (EFTS)** and eliminating paper, coin, and check money as much as possible. I would also recommend installing two-way cable TV systems with centrally located computers as part of the cable system, and perhaps a computer in each home. You may be wondering what this has to do with surveillance. In fact, it appears to be the direction we are headed in our society. Think for a minute—what actions can you perform in our society, or in any modern society, without spending money? You cannot travel, you cannot buy food, and you cannot rent a motel room. You can do very little without spending money. If every time you spent money, you gave the merchant, the airline, or the gas station a plastic card, your transaction could be recorded through a communication system to a central data base. Your funds would be electronically transferred from your account to the merchant's account. The computer could easily record the time of the transaction, the day, your location, and other surveillance information. In fact, we could keep a record of all of your movements and all your purchases, and through the cable TV system we could learn what programs you are watching on TV. You can see that we could very easily obtain a great deal of information about almost all your actions and know approximately where you are at any point in time.

You may think that such a situation could never occur in this country. Certainly the technology is here for this system, and we are moving rapidly toward these capabilities as electronic funds transfer, two-way cable systems, home electronic shopping, and other systems are implemented.

Consider one actual case. In Columbus, Ohio, where the QUBE system was installed, a local theater owner was taken to court over an allegedly pornographic movie shown at his theater. Currently, the test that the Supreme Court applies as to whether a movie is pornographic is whether or not it goes beyond the moral values and standards of the community where it is being shown. By coincidence, the same movie had recently been shown on the local QUBE system. So the theater owner's defense lawyer summoned the records from QUBE to determine who in the community watched the allegedly pornographic movie on the cable network. This was a brilliant move by the lawyer. If a significant number of people watched the movie, including supposedly outstanding citizens, then the movie did not go beyond the community's moral values. But do you want judges, lawyers, and jurors reviewing the records of what you have watched on cable TV? Is this an invasion of your privacy? Fortunately, the judge in this case kept all names confidential. The case against the theater owner was dismissed.

Privacy Legislation

From the examples just given, you can see some of the problems related to privacy. Through two-way cable systems, computers could constantly monitor our financial transactions and the entertainment and goods we purchase. In addition, government agencies and private businesses maintain large data bases with information that concerns private individuals. Substantial legislation has been passed that addresses the privacy issues of these data bases.

In the nongovernmental area, the major legislation was the **Fair Credit Reporting Act** of 1970. Many lending agencies and credit bureaus maintain records concerning your credit worthiness and your financial transactions. The act helps you ensure this information is correct. First, you have a right to access the data stored about you, and second, you have a right to challenge the data in order to correct any inaccuracies. You should know, however, that institutions still have the right to maintain information about you—it just has to be correct, and they must allow you access to it.

Perhaps the greatest effect of privacy legislation has been on the operations of the federal government. There are four acts in this area. The first, the **Freedom of Information Act** of 1970, allows individuals to access any information about them that is stored in a federal government data base or file.

The **Educational Privacy Act** applies to educational institutions that are funded by the federal government. This applies to almost all educational institutions because almost all receive at least some federal funds. The act states that a student's educational records may be accessed by both the student and his or her parents, and that information can be collected only by authorized individuals and distributed only to authorized individuals and agencies. The rights provided for under this act may be waived by the student.

The **Privacy Act of 1974** applies only to federal government agencies and provides that:

1. Information collected for one purpose cannot be used for other purposes unless the individual gives consent.
2. There must be no secret collections of data.
3. Individuals must have a right to access and correct erroneous data.

Agencies collecting information are responsible for assuring its accuracy and protecting against its misuse.

The **Right to Financial Privacy Act** of 1978 addresses a threat to privacy that exists within financial institutions. Currently, every check and credit-card transaction you make is recorded on microfilm by your bank and stored for five years. Prior to the Right to Financial Privacy Act, governmental investigative bodies such as the IRS and FBI could access these microfilm records and examine them without your knowledge. As we have seen, a great deal of information can be collected from these financial transaction records. The act provides that if an investigative body wishes to access your personal financial data stored at a financial institution, you must be notified. This notification provides you with an opportunity to challenge the access in court.

The federal privacy legislation does not apply to most state institutions, with the exception of state educational systems. So, most states have passed their own privacy legislation. The provisions of the state laws are usually similar to the provisions of the federal Privacy Act of 1974.

■ PERSONAL COMPUTERS

We have explored personal computers in other sections of this book. However, it would be useful here to examine some of the impacts they are likely to have on society. Earlier in this chapter we indicated that access to personal-computer technology may differentiate between those who can use information to produce wealth and those who cannot.

One of the most significant questions is, will we lose many of our current mental skills as the computer performs tasks for us? For example, most of the math that engineers learn in college and use in their day-to-day work and certainly all basic mathematical functions can be performed by the computer. Children in elementary and secondary schools are using the computer to complete their math homework. Will this dependence on the computer cause us to lose our math skills?

Perhaps a more significant question is, does it make any difference if we lose a skill that we can purchase for a few hundred dollars or less? Certainly as we have advanced over the centuries, we have lost many skills that were absolutely necessary to our survival in earlier times. Today, there are very few people, if any, who have the necessary skills to survive through hunting and food gathering in a stone-age fashion, without the use of modern firearms. This question of losing mental skills is an important controversy—some say it won't make any difference; others are very concerned about it.

On a more positive note, there is no question that personal computers are going to make our lives more productive and take away some of the more boring tasks we have to perform. These electronic tools are going to become much more **user-friendly.** In fact, many people already find them very easy to use.

■ INTERNATIONAL DATA TRANSFERS

Most countries now restrict the movement of secret, classified data outside of their country. But what about nonclassified data? Multinational firms have offices and factories in many countries. On their large computer networks, data can very quickly move all the way around the world. Some countries, particularly European ones, have been concerned about data flowing out of their nations. This concern has brought about legislation that restricts the international flow of data from some countries.

On what basis can a country justify such legislation? Remember, earlier in the chapter we argued that information is wealth. Many countries currently restrict the transfer of wealth or funds outside their borders. There are, of course, several examples of valuable information such as engineering design data, or financial and economic data. Customer lists can be very valuable from a marketing standpoint, or a country may simply want to protect its citizens from unsolicited mailorder campaigns that originate outside its borders.

In 1992, the European Common Market countries are scheduled to remove all trade barriers between their member countries. A part of this integration of their economies is the provision for free flow of economic data among the Common Market countries. However, the Common Market countries will also develop standards for the electronic transmission of economic transaction data by firms that are selling goods and services to firms in the Common Market. These standards have the potential of making data transmission more efficient among Common Market firms. However, the standards could also make it more difficult for firms outside the Common Market to do business with Common Market firms, since they may have to comply with a new set of electronic transmission standards. Thus, electronic data transmission controls and standards have the potential to be used as barriers to trade.

Restrictions on **international data transfers** are a threat to the free movement of goods and ideas among countries. They would also hamper a multinational corporation's ability to function smoothly. Most international economists agree that such consequences would diminish international economic growth, particularly the growth of a country that severely restricts international data transfers.

■ COMPUTER CRIME CASES

Another very important area of the computer's impact on society is **computer crime.** Several sensational computer crimes have been uncovered. Most experts, however, maintain that the computer crime discovered thus far is only the tip of the iceberg; most of it remains hidden. A computer system that is not well controlled provides almost unlimited opportunities for a person wanting to steal funds or goods and conceal the theft. The amount of money taken in an average armed robbery is very small compared with the amounts taken through computer theft. Often, those who perpetuate a computer crime are not prosecuted when they are caught. Managers sometimes feel that the organization would be embarrassed if the public learned of the crime. Perhaps the public would lose confidence in the firm's ability to function effectively. Let's look at three cases.

Equity Funding

The management of Equity Funding Life Insurance Company used the computer to perpetrate a major fraud against investors and creditors. The company generated bogus insurance policies with a total face value of over two billion dollars. These policies were then sold to reinsurers. Computer programs were rigged so that the auditors could not easily access the files of the nonexistent customers. The fraud was finally exposed when a former employee disclosed it, and the stockholders lost enormous amounts of money.

Pacific Bell

In this case, a teenager retrieved passwords, user manuals, and other confidential documents from the trashcans outside the phone company's office. He then proceeded to steal equipment from supply centers. Using his knowledge of the company's computer system and a remote terminal, he altered accounting records to show the thefts as a bona fide use of equipment. The fraud was not discovered until an accomplice turned himself in.

Wells Fargo

Two employees of the Wells Fargo Bank collaborated with an account-holder to make fraudulent deposits to his account. Using the computerized inter-branch settlement system, the bank employees would make an offsetting entry to another branch's account, showing that the funds deposited were to come from another branch. This entry would be extended every ten days so that no actual payment was demanded from the other branch. The criminals withdrew $21.3 million before the fraud was discovered, which occurred when they made an improper entry.

Summing Up

■ Information is wealth, and computers assist us in obtaining this wealth. Those who do not possess knowledge about the computer might end up being poor because they lack the information necessary to compete with others.

■ Working at home with a remote terminal might seem like an interesting option. It could, however, lead to boredom and social isolation.

■ Although automation does take away jobs temporarily, in the long run it creates more jobs. Moreover, it helps raise society's standard of living.

■ Artificial intelligence aids experts in making better-informed decisions in areas such as medicine and engineering. These systems, however, do not replace human intelligence; rather, they complement it with the computer's immense memory and fast speed.

■ The computer can potentially be used to monitor most of our actions, thus robbing us of privacy. Recognizing this threat to our basic freedom, Congress has enacted several laws to protect the privacy of citizens.

■ The advent of personal computers could cause us to lose some of our basic skills. On the other hand, personal computers could make our lives more interesting by performing many of our routine chores for us.

■ Some countries are concerned about transborder flows of data and have imposed restrictions on them. This could hamper world economic growth by restricting the free movement of information among countries.

■ Computer crime is a growing threat to society. The average take in a computer fraud is many times greater than in a traditional robbery.

Key Terms

information services	Freedom of Information Act
face-to-face contact	Educational Privacy Act
electronic shopping	Privacy Act of 1974
QUBE system	Right to Financial Privacy Act
artificial intelligence	user-friendly
expert systems	international data transfers
electronic funds transfer system (EFTS)	computer crime
Fair Credit Reporting Act	

Review Questions

1. Explain the phrase "information is wealth."
2. What are the advantages of working at home? What are the disadvantages?
3. Discuss some control problems that may be encountered when using data communication technology?
4. In the long run, how does automation create more jobs than it eliminates?
5. Is it possible for an artificial intelligence system to replace a human mind? If not, what functions can such a system perform?
6. Describe how computer technology could be used to monitor a person's actions.
7. How does computer technology constitute a threat to individual privacy?
8. What rights do you have under the Fair Credit Reporting Act of 1970?
9. List the major provisions of the Privacy Act of 1974.
10. What is the likely effect of personal computers on our basic mathematical skills?
11. What are the arguments for and against allowing free transfer of data across borders?
12. Why are victims of computer fraud often reluctant to report the crime?
13. How could Pacific Bell have prevented the computer fraud perpetrated against it?

Discussion Questions and Cases

1. "Computerization will ultimately lead us to the point where we will push buttons for everything. There will be no room for creativity or original thought." Discuss this statement.
2. Expert systems are based on models of human thought processes. In what ways is such a system superior to traditional computer programs? Can you think of any applications of artificial intelligence other than those discussed in this chapter?
3. Very little legislation or case law on the subject of computer crime exists. Discuss some of the problems a court would face when trying a case of computer fraud. Why is it difficult to use precedents from traditional criminal law?
4. The Fairfax Company is developing a computer-based accounting system, which will result in the loss of ten clerical positions in the accounting

department. Over all, though, the company will not experience a reduction in personnel owing to the new system. New positions will be created both in systems development and in accounting. However, these new positions will require different and higher-level skills than the clerical personnel have. Retraining for the new positions is feasible for three of the employees. The other seven are long-time employees of the company, and most will reach retirement age in approximately ten years. Management has decided that retraining these employees is not feasible. Even if it were possible, these employees probably would not want to go through the retraining. If you were the manager making the decision about the future of these seven employees, what would you do?

5. Carolyn Short is a programmer for the Appalachian Tire Company. The main language used in Appalachian's computer information system is CO-BOL. To help reduce the application backlog, the computer center management recently purchased personal computers for some user departments. It also started thinking about buying application-productivity tools for prototyping and for managing system development. Management has assured Carolyn that COBOL will still be the main language, and that she will have plenty of work to do. Carolyn is worried, though, that her current skills in COBOL may not be needed in the future if COBOL is eventually replaced by a high-level language that nonprogrammers can easily use. Is Carolyn justified in her worries that she could be replaced?

6. Midland Bank, a medium-sized bank in a Virginia city, has recently discovered that an employee used the computer to embezzle $75,000 from the bank. The bank's management has decided to handle the case in the following manner. It will confront the employee with the evidence it has concerning embezzlement. If the employee returns a substantial portion of the $75,000, the management will dismiss the employee without calling in law enforcement officers, and the case will be closed as far as the bank is concerned. The management will handle the dismissal as a normal resignation and give the employee favorable recommendations for any new job he might pursue. The bank's primary rationale for this approach is that it cannot afford the adverse publicity that would ensue if the embezzlement were reported in the newspaper. Questions over the security of deposits might cause the bank to lose customers. Evaluate the bank's approach.

Information Systems and You

Chapter 17

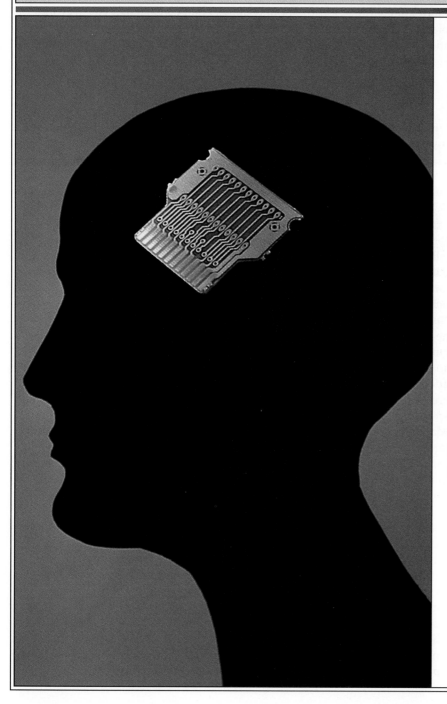

CHAPTER OUTLINE

Introduction

The Effect of Computers on Professional Careers

Information-System Careers
Programmer
System Analyst
EDP Auditor
Data-Processing Operations
Data-Base Administrator
Knowledge Engineer
Information-System Consultant
Information-System Manager

Professional Associations
AFIPS
DPMA
ACM
ASM
SIM
EDP Auditors Foundation

Professional Certification Programs
The CDP and CCP
CISA

Information-System Education

Summing Up

Key Terms

Review Questions

Discussion Questions and Cases

415

■ INTRODUCTION

Most of us realize that computer information systems have had and will continue to have a significant impact on our lives. Many experts agree that computers will be even more pervasive and useful in the future. In this chapter we examine the effect of computers on professional careers, and explore the various information-system careers available. We also look at professional organizations and certification programs associated with information systems. Finally, we discuss two suggested models for information-system education.

THE EFFECT OF COMPUTERS ON ■ PROFESSIONAL CAREERS

Very few careers, if any, are unaffected by computers. Business professionals rely heavily on computers for their record keeping and information needs. Certainly, those who know how to use computer technology effectively are at a competitive advantage. As we discussed in the previous chapter, artificial intelligence or expert systems affect the most prestigious careers, such as medicine, law, and accounting. These and other careers are based on information or expert knowledge. Computer systems may be able to provide much of this expert knowledge more effectively and at a lower cost.

Business professionals find that computers relieve them of many boring, time-consuming, and repetitive details of their jobs and allow them to pursue the more exciting and challenging aspects of their careers. By using computers, you will probably be much more productive in your career than your predecessors. But regardless of how sophisticated computer systems become, there will always be areas of knowledge and action that require human discretion.

Many experts say we are entering the **information age** because of computer information systems. A greater percentage of the workforce are employed as **information workers.** Large amounts of information are almost instantly available to decision makers, who must understand not only the information technology but also the decision models, such as economic-order quantity and linear programming, on which computer information systems rely. A decision maker must be able to decide whether the information supplied by the computer or the action that the computer recommends is reasonable. As business professionals, we cannot simply turn the decision making over to the computer without understanding what is going on.

In summary, the computer provides us with a great deal of information, but we must understand the underlying processes. Otherwise, the actual intelligence behind these systems, the human mind, loses control. We must continue to exercise creative thinking and control. If professionals want to maintain their competitive advantage, they should view the computer as simply a very important tool that must be used effectively.

■ INFORMATION-SYSTEM CAREERS

The largest impact of the computer revolution will be on information-system careers. The bureau of labor statistics predicted that the number of jobs for all information-system professionals will increase substantially from 1986 to the year 2000. The increases in specific fields are as follows:

■ System analysts—an increase of 76 percent.
■ Programmers—an increase of 70 percent.
■ Computer operators—an increase of 48 percent.

The number of information-system specialists recruited is expected to be greater than any other business profession.

The primary reason for this increase is the declining cost of hardware and therefore, the increase in the number of computers. Once businesses and other organizations acquire computers, they want them to perform specific jobs. This takes software, which in turn usually requires programmers and system analysts. Someone must also operate the computer and service it.

This forecasted large increase in jobs in the information-system area does not mean these jobs are recession-proof. In the 1982 recession, the job market dried up for entry-level programmers without experience, as there was an oversupply of them. At the same time, the market was still very good for programmers who had three to four years of experience.

Figure 17–1 illustrates the relationships among the main careers in information systems. Let's look at some of these positions.

Programmer

As we discussed in previous chapters, there are two types of **programmers:** application programmers and system programmers. System programmers write and maintain system software such as operating systems, compilers, utilities, and data-base management systems. These individuals usually have a degree in computer science. They often work for computer manufacturers and software development firms. Most large computer systems require a few system programmers, whereas most medium-sized and smaller ones do not employ a full-time system programmer.

Most jobs in programming are for application programmers. These people write computer programs that perform jobs specified by the user, such as inventory control, accounts receivable, accounts payable, airline reservations, marketing analysis, and personnel information systems.

It is possible to obtain a job as an application programmer without a four-year college degree. Individuals who obtain their programming education in technical schools and community colleges quite often become application programmers. Many of them, however, have college degrees in computer science, information systems, mathematics, or a host of other areas. Most employers prefer that application programmers not only have training in the computer area, but also have education or experience in their application area. For example, it is helpful to a programmer writing application programs in the accounting area to have accounting expertise; or in the

Figure 17–1
The Information-System Department

College graduates entering the information system field usually start in the information center or the system department. Both types of consultants within the information center are currently high-visiblity positions with a lot of exposure to different user applications.

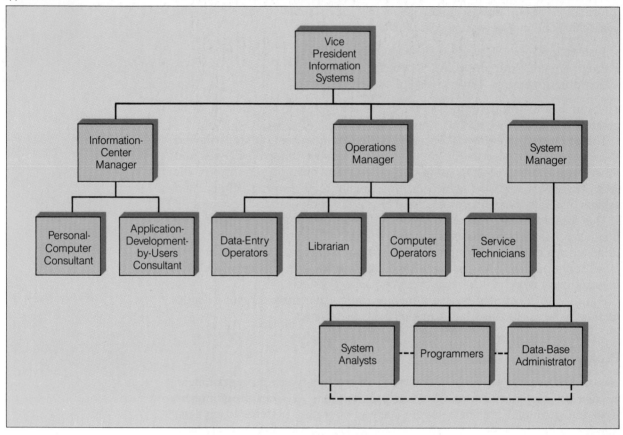

marketing area, to have marketing expertise. Therefore, many employers are seeking application programmers who have a broad, business-oriented degree with a major in information systems, and who have taken all the other general business courses, including accounting, finance, economics, business law, marketing, management, and quantitative methods.

Although the demand for programmers is projected to remain large, there is certainly the possibility that new programming tools, such as application generators, will decrease the demand for programmers. In addition, application development by users without programmers is likely to become much more prevalent in the future.

System Analyst

A system analyst may be compared to an architect. The **system analyst** analyzes and designs application systems. In carrying out their responsibility, the analyst is heavily involved with the system-development life cycle from analysis through implementation. Often, the analyst is looked upon as an intermediary between the users and programmers. Most analysts do not perform programming, and they do not have to be highly skilled programmers. However, the analyst should be familiar with several business-oriented languages. Some firms have positions known as **programmer/analysts.** In this case, the system analyst performs both programming and analysis functions and therefore must be competent in programming as well.

It is more important that system analysts have competence in the application area in which they are working than in programming. The analyst must deal directly with users and must understand their applications in order to design a new system. For these reasons, an analyst sometimes has a formal education in an area such as marketing, economics, accounting, or management. But the best combination is to have an education in one of these application areas plus an information-system education. In fact, system analysts are often employed by the user organization rather than the information-system function. They analyze and design new systems and then turn the specifications over to the information-system organization for programming.

Whereas programmers often work with machines and program code, system analysts work directly with people (user personnel and programmers) most of the time. A good system analyst must have highly developed communication skills. Listening, persuasion, teaching, and consulting skills help ensure success for a system analyst.

The job outlook for system analysts is indeed bright. They can initially pursue a career in system analysis, and then decide whether to remain in the information-system organization or move into management in the application area in which they are trained, such as finance, accounting, or marketing. They are usually actively recruited by user organizations because of their computer expertise. Even if users develop many of their own applications in the future, they will need individuals with the expertise of system analysts to guide them in the use of new software such as application generators and data-base management systems.

EDP Auditor

A subspecialty of the auditing field is EDP auditing. An **EDP auditor** has computer expertise and thus can assist traditional auditors both in the review of computer controls and in the production of audit information through the use of computers. Currently, there is a high demand for EDP auditors. Some people think that in the long run traditional auditors will acquire the necessary computer expertise and EDP auditors will no longer be needed. This probably will not happen. It is very difficult for one individual, an auditor, to maintain a high level of expertise in computer technology, auditing, and accounting at the same time. Furthermore, computer technology will continue to advance. In the foreseeable future, there will continue to be a need for specialist EDP auditors who keep abreast of the latest computer technology and the methods for controlling application systems based on that technology.

Data-Processing Operations

Data-entry operators, librarians, and computer operators work in the field of data-processing operations. A **data-entry operator** keys data from source documents into computer-readable form, usually disk storage. Job openings in this area are expected to decline in the future. This is owing primarily to source-data automation where terminals, cash registers, and other devices capture data at the point of an event or transaction. Data-entry operators generally have only a high-school diploma. There is no need for advanced education at the college level. The primary skill required is good typing.

A **librarian** is responsible for storage of program and data files. These files are stored on tape or disk. The job entails keeping records of the use and storage of these files and operating equipment that tests the storage media (such as tape and disk) to assure that data are stored without error. A high-school diploma is sufficient for this job.

Computer operators run the computer equipment. Most have only a high-school diploma. However, the operator must be able to operate various types of equipment, such as printers, card readers, tape drives, disk drives, plotters, CPUs, and data switches. This requires some technical training. In addition, the operator must be able to convey to programmers and sometimes system analysts and users the nature of problems that occur in the execution of computer jobs.

Data-Base Administrator

A **data-base administrator (DBA)** is responsible for the design and control of a company's data base. This is a management position. In medium-sized and larger firms there are several individuals in the DBA's department. Data-base administrators must have a high level of technical data-base expertise. They also must be able to communicate effectively with various user groups, since their primary responsibility is meeting the often conflicting needs of users. The major duties of the DBA are: designing data bases; developing data dictionaries; designing and implementing procedures that ensure the accuracy, completeness, and timeliness of data stored in the data base; mediating and resolving conflicts among users' needs for data; and advising programmers, analysts, and users about the efficient use of the data base.

Knowledge Engineer

A **knowledge engineer** is a computer professional who builds expert systems. The major task in building any expert system is the construction of the knowledge base. This knowledge base consists primarily of if-then rules. Knowledge engineers work closely with human experts to elicit their knowledge, and they codify this knowledge into the expert system's knowledge base. The knowledge engineer may use programming languages, such as LISP or PROLOG, to build a complete expert system, including the knowledge base and the inference engine. Or alternatively, they may use an expert system shell. An expert system shell already contains the inference engine; thus only the knowledge base must be created.

Ideally, knowledge engineers should have some expertise in the area in which they are applying expert systems. However, some do not. Certainly, after building a successful expert system, the knowledge engineer will know a great deal about the area of application. As expert systems become more widely used, the number of knowledge engineers required will increase dramatically.

Information-System Consultant

An **information-system consultant** is very much like a system analyst. This individual may be employed within an organization's information department or by outside management consulting firms or CPA firms. The consultant's role ranges from helping a user develop an application to performing a complete analysis, design, and implementation of a system.

A consultant employed in a firm's information center may hold a specialized position as a personal-computer consultant or an information-center consultant. Personal-computer consultants coordinate usage and assist users in applying personal computers. Information-center consultants may also assist PC users, but generally their efforts are directed toward helping users retrieve and manipulate data stored on mainframe data bases. As personal-computer hardware and software become more powerful, the jobs of these two consultants are likely to merge. They both are currently aimed at assisting the user in developing applications without programming.

Consultants who work for outside consulting firms are more likely to be involved in the complete development of a system. Often, a firm employs them as an alternative to developing a system in-house.

Many information-system consultants, particularly those employed by outside consulting firms, hold advanced degrees, such as a master's in business, information systems, or accountancy. To be a successful consultant requires a special set of skills and experience, including maturity, the ability to communicate effectively, a high level of technical knowledge of computer systems and applications, and the ability to recognize problems and come up with solutions quickly without getting bogged down in details.

Information-System Manager

In all the information-system careers discussed, there are management positions. Usually a person starts out in one of the careers and then moves up to a management position in that area. In addition to needing technical expertise, **information-system managers** need the management skills that are universal to all management positions. These include the ability to communicate both orally and in written form; ability to plan, organize, and implement; and human-relations skills, which are so necessary in the supervisory function of management. Almost all information-system managers have a college education.

■ PROFESSIONAL ASSOCIATIONS

There are several professional associations in the field of computer information systems. Most have as their primary purpose the continuing education of computer professionals and the exchange of ideas. Some also offer professional certification programs. Many of these associations welcome student members. In fact, some, such as the Association for Computing Machinery, have local student chapters on many campuses.

AFIPS

The **American Federation of Information Processing Societies (AFIPS),** 1815 North Lynn Street, Arlington, Virginia 22209, (703) 558–3600, is a federation of information-processing societies. Among the societies represented by AFIPS are the Data Processing Management Association (DPMA), the Association for Computing Machinery (ACM), the Institute of Electrical and Electronic Engineers (IEEE), the American Statistical Association (ASA), and the American Institute of Certified Public Accountants (AICPA). The primary activities of AFIPS are to sponsor the yearly national computer conference and exposition, and to represent its constituent professional societies in a similar international group called **International Federation of Information Processing Societies (IFIPS).**

DPMA

The **Data Processing Management Association (DPMA),** 505 Busse Highway, Park Ridge, Illinois 60068, (312) 825–8124, was founded as the National Machine Accountants Association. Its name was changed to DPMA in 1962. The association holds monthly meetings at its local chapters, holds an annual data-processing conference, sponsors an annual information-system education conference, publishes a monthly journal called *Data Management*, and sponsors various educational programs. This is a business-oriented data-processing association. Its membership is made up largely of practicing business data-processing professionals. However, there are also more than four hundred student chapters of DPMA.

ACM

The **Association for Computing Machinery (ACM),** 11 West 42nd Street, New York, NY 10036, (212) 869–7440, has as its primary objective the advancement of the science and art of information processing. It is the largest technical, scientific, and educational computing organization. Many of its members are computer-science faculty members at universities. The ACM has many **special-interest groups (SIGs).** For example, ACM members who have a special interest in small computers are members of SIGSMALL. Other special-interest groups are Data Base, Computer Science Education, Programming Languages, and Business Data Processing. Active ACM chapters are located on many college campuses and in most cities.

ASM

The **Association for Systems Management (ASM),** 24587 Bagley Road, Cleveland, Ohio 44138, (216) 243–6900, was founded in 1947 and is a national organization. The ASM publishes a monthly journal called *The Journal of Systems Management* and has local chapters in most cities. It holds an annual conference, and its membership is made up largely of system analysts and information-system managers.

SIM

The **Society for Information Management (SIM),** 111 East Wacker Drive, Suite 600, Chicago, Illinois 60601, (312) 644–6610, was founded in 1968. Its members include information-system managers, business system analysts, and educators. The SIM holds an annual conference and also co-sponsors the annual International Conference on Information Systems. The latter has in recent years become an important event, where papers and ideas are exchanged among business information-system educators.

EDP Auditors Foundation

The **EDP Auditors Foundation,** 455 Kehoe Boulevard, Suite 106, Carol Stream, Illinois 60188, (312) 653–0950, is a professional association of auditors who specialize in EDP auditing. It has local chapters in all major cities and holds an annual conference. In addition, it publishes a journal called *The EDP Auditor.* One of the more important activities of this foundation is sponsorship of the Certified Information Systems Auditor (CISA) exam. This will be discussed in the next section.

■ PROFESSIONAL CERTIFICATION PROGRAMS

There are several professional certification programs in the information-system area. Students who plan careers in information systems should take the exams relating to their career interests. Even though the requirements for certification include professional experience, one may sit for the exams prior to completing the experience requirements. The best time to sit for these exams is during the senior year or shortly after graduation, since the tests are based on material learned in an undergraduate program.

The CDP and CCP

The **Certificate in Data Processing (CDP)** examination and the **Certificate in Computer Programming (CCP)** examination are administered by the **Institute for Certification of Computer Professionals (ICCP),** 2200 East Devon Avenue, Suite 268, Des Plaines, IL 60018, (312) 299–4227. This organization is nonprofit and was established in 1973 with the purpose of testing and certifying computer professionals. As with AFIPS, the ICCP is made up of several constituent societies. The CDP examination originated with DPMA but was turned over to the ICCP in 1974. Candidates for the CDP exam must have at least three years of professional experience in information systems. The exam consists of five sections: computer hardware, computer programming and software, principles of management, methods and application, and system analysis and design. The CCP is also a five-part exam and is designed to test the knowledge and skills required of a senior-level programmer.

CISA

The **Certified Information Systems Auditor (CISA)** exam is administered by the EDP Auditors Foundation, 455 Kehoe Blvd., Suite 106, Carol Stream, Illinois 60188, (312) 653–0950. This is a multiple-choice exam that covers the following general areas:

- Application-system controls.
- Data integrity.
- System-development life cycle.
- Application development.
- System maintenance.
- Operational-procedures controls.
- Security procedures.
- System software.
- Resource acquisition.
- Resource management.
- Information-system audit management.

In addition to passing the exam, the applicant must have a minimum of five years of practical experience in EDP auditing in order to become certified.

■ INFORMATION-SYSTEM EDUCATION

Two professional organizations have been active in designing **model curriculums** for information-system education. Both the ACM and the DPMA published model curriculums in the early 1980s. Outlines of these curricu-

Figure 17–2
DPMA Model Curriculum for Computer Information Systems

This curriculum is oriented toward undergraduate information-system programs in business colleges.

List of Courses
CORE COURSES

CIS/86-1	Introduction to Computer Information Systems
CIS/86-2	Microcomputer Applications in Business
CIS/86-3	Introduction to Business Application Programming
CIS/86-4	Intermediate Business Application Programming
CIS/86-5	Systems Development Methodologies: A Survey
CIS/86-6	Data Files and Data Bases
CIS/86-7	Information Center Functions
CIS/86-8	Systems Development Project

ELECTIVE COURSES

CIS/86-9	Advanced Office Systems
CIS/86-10	Computer Graphics in Business
CIS/86-11	Decision Support and Expert Systems
CIS/86-12	Artificial Intelligence in Decision Making
CIS/86-13	Advanced Business Applications Programming
CIS/86-14	Computer Control and Audit
CIS/86-15	Distributed Intelligence and Communication Systems
CIS/86-16	Programming Languages: Procedural, Nonprocedural, and Fourth Generation
CIS/86-17	Computer Hardware, System Software, and Architecture
CIS/86-18	Information Resource Planning and Management
CIS/86-19	Systems Development Project with Information Center Techniques
CIS/86-20	CIS Communication, Reporting, and Documentation Techniques

BUSINESS SUPPORT COURSES

BUS-1	Financial Accounting Practices
BUS-2	Managerial Accounting Practices
BUS-3	Quantitative Methods in Business
BUS-4	Principles of Management
BUS-5	Principles of Marketing
BUS-6	Principles of Finance
BUS-7	Organizational Behavior
BUS-8	Production and Operations Management
BUS-9	Business Policy

From *The DPMA Model Curriculum for Undergraduate Computer Information Systems*, copyright 1985, Data Processing Management Association Education Foundation. All rights reserved. Reprint permission granted.

lums are shown in Figure 17–2 and 17–3. As you can see, the course titles of these two curriculums differ substantially. The primary difference between the two is that the ACM curriculum has a more theoretical and conceptual basis, whereas the DPMA model curriculum is more practical and applied in nature. Another difference is that the DPMA model curriculum emphasizes that information-system education should be housed within business colleges.

It is rare that an information-system curriculum at a specific university or college exactly matches either of these two curriculums. Model curriculums are designed to be just that—models that are modified to fit the particular needs of a particular university or college. You do not have to follow these model curriculums exactly to receive a good information-system education.

Figure 17–3
ACM Model Curriculum for Information Systems
The ACM model curriculum has been implemented at both the undergraduate and graduate levels.

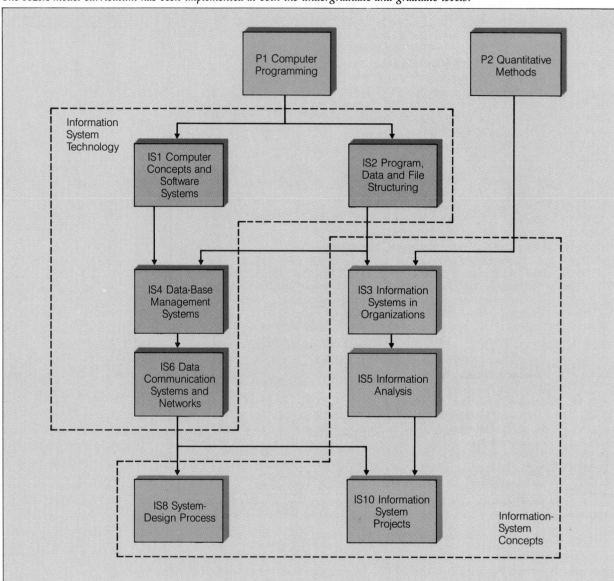

◼ Summing Up

◼ Most business professionals now have to rely on computer-generated information to perform effectively in their jobs. However, in order to make informed and responsible decisions, they must also understand the processes used by the computer in generating the information.

◼ The bureau of labor statistics has predicted a large increase in information-system jobs by the year 2000. Careers in information systems may be categorized as follows:

Programmer.
System analyst.
EDP auditor.
Data-processing operations.
Data-base administrator.
Knowledge engineer.
Information-system consultant.
Information-system manager.

■ There are many professional associations for information-system personnel. Some of the more prominent are:

American Federation of Information Processing Societies (AFIPS).
Data Processing Management Association (DPMA).
Association for Computing Machinery (ACM).
Association of Systems Management (ASM).
Society for Information Management (SIM).
EDP Auditors Foundation.

■ Several professional certifications exist in the information-system area. The Certificate in Data Processing (CDP), Certificate in Computer Programming (CCP), and Certified Information Systems Auditor (CISA) are widely recognized qualifications for EDP personnel.

■ Key Terms

information age

information workers

programmers

system analyst

programmer/analysts

EDP auditor

data-entry operator

librarian

computer operators

data-base administrator (DBA)

knowledge engineer

information-system consultant

information-system managers

American Federation of Information Processing Societies (AFIPS)

International Federation of Information Processing Societies (IFIPS)

Data-Processing Management Association (DPMA)

Association for Computing Machinery (ACM)

special-interest groups (SIGs)

Association of Systems Management (ASM)

Society for Information Management (SIM)

EDP Auditors Foundation

Certificate in Data Processing (CDP)

Certificate in Computer Programming (CCP)

Institute for Certification of Computer Professionals (ICCP)

Certified Information Systems Auditor (CISA)

model curriculums

■ Review Questions

1. Why is it important to understand the decision models used by computers?

2. What is the primary cause of the increase in demand for information system specialists?

3. Distinguish between an application programmer and a system programmer.

4. What kind of educational background is needed for a career as an application programmer?

5. Why would the use of application generators decrease the demand for programmers?

6. What is the difference between a programmer and a system analyst?

7. Describe the functions of an EDP auditor.

8. Why is a librarian necessary in the data-processing department?

9. Distinguish between a data-base administrator and a data-processing manager.

10. What skills are needed for a career as an information-system consultant?

11. Briefly describe each of the professional associations discussed in this chapter.

12. What is the purpose of the CDP examination?

13. What do the initials CISA represent?

14. What are the primary differences between the model curriculums suggested by the ACM and the DPMA?

Discussion Questions and Cases

1. Some experts argue that tools such as application generators and easy-to-use computer languages will greatly reduce the need for programmers in coming years. Does this mean that programming jobs will be the next victims of automation? If so, will it be possible to retrain computer programmers to do some other kind of productive work?

2. If you decide to build a career in the information systems area, which professional associations would you like to join? How would they contribute to your professional development?

3. Professions such as medicine, law, and accounting have strict state licensing requirements for practitioners. Why is there no such requirement in the information systems profession? Is such a requirement likely to be imposed in the future?

4. Susan has tentatively decided that she would like to pursue a career in computer information systems. She feels that computers are going to become increasingly important in the future. Being practical, she agrees with the advice that it is easier to ride a horse in the direction it is traveling than to make it go in a different direction. But she has a nagging doubt. You see, Susan is really a "people person." She likes dealing with people, and she is afraid that computer careers are technology- and machine-oriented. Are there careers for people-oriented individuals, like Susan, in computer information systems?

5. The Abbett Company is considering a policy requiring that all of its computer professionals, including EDP auditors, have an appropriate professional certification. Individuals within the system development department could hold either the Certificate in Computer Programming or the Certificate in Data Processing. EDP auditors would need to be Certified Information Systems Auditors. Abbett management believes that this policy would build a spirit of professionalism among computer personnel. Managers feel this is now lacking and to some extent accounts for the high staff turnover the company has seen in these areas. Do you think this is a good policy?

6. Campbell Manufacturing Company is a large, diversified manufacturer of industrial and consumer products. Campbell is considering encouraging employees in user departments to transfer to the MIS department for a minimum period of two years, and encouraging employees in the MIS department to transfer to user-type jobs in marketing, finance, personnel, and so on, also for a minimum of two years. Campbell's management feels that this cross-training will be very useful in the future, especially as users begin to develop applications themselves. Do you think this is a good policy? Would you be willing to make such a transfer if you were an employee?

7. A personnel officer of the Computer Consulting Company was interviewing a prospective employee and looking at his resume. She noticed that the interviewee held a bachelor's degree in accounting and a master's degree in information systems. He also was a CPA and had held five jobs working with computers over the last eight years. The personnel officer stated to the interviewee, "Your resume looks impressive with your education and certifications. You have also worked with some major companies and have had many duties that indicate you perform well. But I have one question: Why do you change jobs so often, if I may ask?" The prospective employee replied that he was always looking for a challenge, since new computer technology is always being developed. He commented, "Your firm seems to be on the leading edge of this technology in the system development field." The personnel officer was not quite satisfied with the answer; she wondered whether she should hire someone who had switched jobs every one or two years. Should she hire this person?

PART FIVE   ■ APPLICATION CASE

Microcomputer Managers Need Well-Rounded Backgrounds

By Meghan O'Leary

"I created it myself . . . out of a need," said Mike Connery about his position as micro manager at Government Electronics Systems Division (GESD), of Syracuse, N.Y.

Sixteen months ago, Mr. Connery was part of a test-engineering group that had implemented its own successful PC-business system. GESD was integrating PCs with its mainframe system and needed someone to provide training and support.

With one PC success under its belt, plus years of engineering and manufacturing experience, Mr. Connery's group seemed the logical choice for GESD.

The rise of Mr. Connery gives one example of a corporation that draws on the business and technical experience of its users (and, often, its data-processing staff) to meet the broadly based requirements of a PC manager's job.

In bringing computing power to the masses, the microcomputer has added some new dimensions to computer-management needs. The need for development and systems planning grew, but a centralized MIS department had little hope of closely monitoring such applications development and corporatewide PC data processing.

The nature of microcomputing called for a different style of computer management. Although mainframe computing remained the domain of highly technical personnel, microcomputer management required a more personalized program, geared toward the needs and applications of each department or user. It often thrived under technically able managers and clerical workers.

While much of their technical competence was acquired on the job, such ad hoc PC coordinators often had non-technical experience that better enabled them to cope with the problems and needs particular to their users.

Micro managers of all levels of experience agree that a well-rounded background has its advantages, but they disagree on the ideal proportions of technical-to-non-technical experience, as well as on the identity of the pivotal PC-management quality.

"I brought street smarts [to my job]," Mr. Connery said, referring to his experience as an user. Based on the assertion that the company's MIS department was out of touch with users' needs, "questioning the status quo was the biggest thing I wanted to bring along."

In his eight years at GESD, Mr. Connery worked in departments all over the company, with an eye toward "understanding the full concept of the business." He admitted that engineering and technical experience play critical roles in his job, but that knowledge of administrative policies and corporate philosophy were equally important. He is currently working toward an MBA to improve his grasp of business and management procedures.

Other micro managers share Mr. Connery's enthusiasm for micro management from non-technical vantage points. Dee Lalliss, senior systems analyst and PC coordinator for Eaton-Kenway Corp.'s engineering support division in Salt Lake City, suggested that a background too strictly geared toward technical training could mean trouble.

"You can't have a micro manager who doesn't understand the system," said Mr. Lalliss. "You lose your audience if you can't service it. Your control of the information now goes to someone else and your credibility goes down the tube."

Despite such warnings, there are advocates of unadulterated technical experience. "A person with applications-development experience in systems is pretty well-rounded," said Bill McClatchie, manager of information services and quality assurance for General Electric's Plastic Business Group in Pittsfield, Mass. Mr. McClatchie, whose background is mostly technical, added that users at GE tend to be technically sophisticated and thus less reliant on his group for support and applications development.

Cynthia Carter of Intermec Corp., in Lynnwood, Mass., agreed that technical proficiency is the skill around which others should revolve. Though she admitted that one of the highlights of her position as office-systems support manager at the Barcode Systems Manufacturing Co., a subsidiary of Intermec, is its personnel aspect, she stressed that she would have

PART FIVE

▇ APPLICATION CASE

been unable to meet the demands of the position without technical training.

Ms. Carter, who first learned about data processing through courses at a local college, said that such programs offer a promising pool of potential micro-manager candidates. Surprisingly, her hopes for that student pool hinge as much on its data-processing experience as on the fact that many of the students with whom she is familiar have four-year, liberal-arts backgrounds as well.

However, as Phil Karp, assistant secretary of General RE Services Corp., of Stamford, Conn., pointed out, what is true in classroom theory is often not true in practice. "I went through a master's degree program [in computer science] without ever opening a file," he said. Mr. Karp, who oversees the reinsurance concern's Client Based Systems group, said that six months on the job taught him more about managing a computer system than his entire doctoral program.

Other PC coordinators agree that on-the-job experience far outweighs classroom training in utility and professional value because it teaches how to couple theory to actual system design in an applications environment. "You have to understand what the user wants, what the user does," said Mr. Lalliss. "I have a negative feeling for the way universities turn out systems analysts. They run them through accounting or management and they say, 'I'm a systems manager.' They don't understand the relationship between the design and the machine."

Even micro managers who have completed MBA programs agree that professional business and management experience are the keys to managing a PC system to meet business needs. Indeed, good technical management and farsighted planning are considered critical to the success of a corporatewide PC system.

Mr. Lalliss stressed the importance of documentation and an organized approach to systems development. A micro manager who rises from the technical staff may be promoted because of technical ability, but a lack of organizational skills can hinder his ability to manage a system, he warned.

Still, micro managers agree, technical management can be learned. It's harder, they said, to learn to manage people and to provide creative solutions to the problems of users.

"There are a lot of people doing things they've never done before," said Mr. Connery. "A micro manager needs an appreciation of the struggles of the user in the learning process. While experience as user can help to cultivate a sympathetic approach, a professional background in education is a plus for those without user experience."

Mr. Karp believes that his teaching background enables him to break down complex technical concepts to simple elements that even a raw beginner can grasp. Very technically oriented people generally make poor trainers because they take a certain level of technical knowledge for granted.

"User computing is the goal," said Mr. Connery. "We're out here to support this professional staff." The background and hands-on experience a micro manager takes to his position are, simply and ultimately, the tools he needs to do his or her job.

Reprinted from *PC Week*, May 19, 1987 p. 51. Copyright ©: 1987 Ziff-Davis Publishing Company.

DISCUSSION QUESTIONS

1. Is it harder to learn to manage people than to learn the technical aspects of computer information systems?
2. What are the relative advantages of "university learning" versus "on-the-job learning"? Are there ways that universities can provide some of the learning that comes from on-the-job experience? Should universities attempt to provide a type of on-the-job learning?
3. Assume you plan a career in computer information systems. Which educational background would best prepare you for such a career—computer science, management information systems, liberal arts, accounting, management, or some other major?

Module A ▪ History of the Computer Industry

MODULE OUTLINE

Introduction

Early Developments in Data Processing
The Abacus
Mechanical Calculators
Jacquard's Loom
Babbage's Engines and Ada, Countess of
  Lovelace

Punched-Card Equipment
Metcalfe's Cards
Hollerith's Punched Cards
Powers's Punched Cards
Mark I Electromechanical Computer

The First Electronic Computers
The ENIAC
The Binary Number System
The EDVAC and EDSAC

First-Generation Computers: 1951–1958
UNIVAC-I
First-Generation Software

Second-Generation Computers: 1959–1964
Hardware Advances
Software Advances

Third-Generation Computers: 1965–1971
Hardware Advances
Software Advances

**Fourth-Generation Computers:
1971–Present**
Hardware Advances
Software Advances

History of Personal Computers
PC Hardware
PC Software

Future Computers

Summing Up

Key Terms

Review Questions

Discussion Questions and Cases

▪ INTRODUCTION

The computer industry is unique in many ways. How many products or services have steadily declined in price while their quality and performance have dramatically increased? Very few! The computing power you can buy today for one thousand dollars in the form of a personal computer would have cost more than one million dollars in the early 1960s. The history of the computer industry is short but interesting. It is a classic case of human innovation!

Advances in computer hardware and software are generally classified into generations. The first generation started in 1951 and the current (fourth) one in 1971. This module will cover the significant developments of each computer generation. We will also speculate about the characteristics of future computer systems. But first, we will discuss the early developments in data processing and see how they eventually led to punched-card equipment and the first electronic computers.

▪ EARLY DEVELOPMENTS IN DATA PROCESSING

The Abacus

Movable beads on a wire frame constituted the first known calculating device, called an **abacus** (see Figure A–1). The abacus was used by the ancient Greeks and Romans, although most of the significant contributions to its design were made by the Chinese. The Chinese abacus is called *suan pan*, which means counting board. Beads are stored at one side of the frame, and calculations are performed at the other side by moving beads against that side of the frame. The significant conceptual contribution of the abacus is the use of position to represent value, as shown in Figure A–1.

Mechanical Calculators

The **mechanical calculators** used until about 1970 resembled a calculating machine invented in 1642 by **Blaise Pascal,** a French mathematician and philosopher. Pascal developed a gear-driven machine capable of addition, subtraction, and multiplication. Manipulations were performed by rotating wheels, and a mechanism made possible an automatic carry. The automatic carry was the significant contribution from Pascal's machine.

In 1671, the German mathematician and philosopher **Gottfried von Leibnitz** improved Pascal's design and built a machine that multiplied, divided, and determined square roots (see Figure A–2). This calculator consisted of a

Figure A–1
The Abacus

Although the abacus is an ancient calculating instrument, it is still used in many parts of the Far East. (I once saw one used by an elderly Japanese man in a small restaurant in Hawaii. Using an abacus, he calculated all the meal checks faster than most people could with an electronic calculator.)

Figure A–2
Gottfried von Leibnitz's Calculator
Mechanical calculators that are descendants of Leibnitz's machine were used in the 1960s.

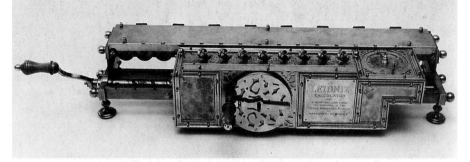

cylindrical drum with nine teeth along its surface. The teeth varied in length, and when the drum rotated, some of them engaged a sliding gear on the axle. This gear principle was employed in many mechanical calculators until they were replaced by electronic calculators in the 1960s.

Jacquard's Loom

In 1801 a Frechman named **Joseph Jacquard** perfected a **loom** that was controlled by holes in cardboard **punched cards** (see Figure A–3). The design for woven fabric was represented by a series of holes punched in the card. In the loom's control mechanism, mechanical fingers were activated by the presence or absence of a hole in the card. The movement of the fingers determined what threads were to appear in the fabric. By sequencing the cards, the loom could produce a large number of patterns and designs. When the cards for a particular pattern were repeated, the pattern would be repeated automatically. As we will see, punched cards were later used extensively in processing data. Also, Jacquard's punched cards were, in effect, a program for the loom. They stored the various fabric designs. There is a similarity between Jacquard's cards and stored programs in a computer.

Babbage's Engines and Ada, Countess of Lovelace

In 1812 **Charles Babbage,** an English mathematician and inventor, found that certain principles from Jacquard's loom could be used in numerical computation. He saw that if computing steps could be stored in advance of computation, it would be possible for a machine to process data unaided. Babbage thus developed the concept of the **stored program** for data processing—the capability that differentiates computers from calculators. He is generally recognized as the first person to propose the concept of the computer.

Babbage called his first machine a **difference engine** and designed it to calculate logarithm tables (see Figure A–4). A series of levers was to enter the data, and a device similar to a typewriter was to print the output. Unfortu-

Figure A–3
Jacquard's Loom

Notice the punched cards at the top of the diagram near the letter C. They were strung together and rotated to produce the fabric pattern.

nately, the metallurgy technology of that time was not sufficiently advanced to allow a practical difference engine to be built.

Babbage did not give up easily. He went on to design an **analytical engine**. It was designed to add, subtract, multiply, and divide through the use of a stored program. The program was to be entered on a series of punched cards similar to those used on the Jacquard loom.

The four major components of the analytical engine were input and output devices, an arithmetic unit to perform the calculations, and a memory to store the intermediate calculations. Modern computers are organized in a similar manner. Despite the advanced design features of this engine, Babbage never succeeded in building this machine either. However, in 1871, after Babbage's death, his son built a working model of the analytical engine. Perhaps if someone had carried on Babbage's research we would have had computers sooner.

A significant contributor to Babbage's research was **Augusta Ada Byron,** Countess of Lovelace. Babbage met her when he was working on his analytical engine. She was the daughter of Lord Byron, the famous English poet. Ada Bryon was an accomplished mathematician, and she recorded and analyzed

Figure A–4
Babbage's Difference Engine

The idea for a difference engine that would compute mathematical tables such as logarithms was first conceived by Babbage in 1812. After twenty years of labor, he had to stop because of financial difficulties, and the machine was never completed.

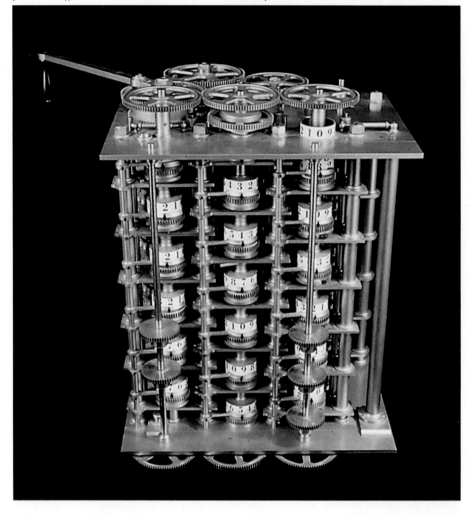

many of Babbage's ideas. Because of her work in developing (programming) the mathematical tables for the analytical engine, she is recognized as the first programmer. The programming language, Ada, is named after her.

■ PUNCHED-CARD EQUIPMENT

Metcalfe's Cards

The next significant historical development took place in the 1870s at the Frankford Arsenal in Philadelphia. When Lieutenant **Henry Metcalfe** started to reorganize the arsenal's cost-accounting system, he found he could not produce the information that management needed because records were kept in leather-bound ledgers by department. Retrieving information from these ledgers and sorting it in the order required for reports was a laborious and often impractical task. Extrapolating from the practice of librarians who index books on cards, Metcalfe transferred some of the arsenal's accounting records from ledgers to cards. Then the decks of cards could be manually sorted, summarized, and manipulated to better meet the information needs of management. This system required a sophisticated **coding scheme,** a well-defined **unit record,** and a system design that specified the flow of data.

Today, computer information systems electronically perform many of the functions of Metcalfe's system. The concept of a record and the use of codes in storing information were developed by Metcalfe.

Hollerith's Punched Cards

At about the same time as Metcalfe was developing his coding scheme, the federal government began to encounter problems in data processing. It took seven years to compile the statistics from the 1880 census, and it became apparent that it would be time to begin a new census before the analysis of the previous one was completed. In 1880 **Herman Hollerith,** a statistician employed by the United States Census Bureau, began experimenting with punched cards for use in data processing. Although punched cards were used in process control, as with Jacquard's loom, they had not been successfully employed in data processing (Metcalfe's cards were not punched). Hollerith designed a device called the **tabulating machine,** which used machine-readable punched cards (see Figure A–5). Initially, Hollerith's cards had round holes and forty-five columns. His machine reduced tabulating time on the 1890 census to one-eighth the time required by the old methods. Hollerith founded the Tabulating Machine Company in 1896 to manufacture and sell his new inventions. In 1911 the company merged with the International Time Recording Company, the Dayton Scale Company, and the Bundy Manufacturing Corporation to form the Computing-Tabulating-Recording Company (CTR). CTR was renamed the International Business Machines Corporation (IBM) in 1924.

Powers's Punched Cards

James Powers, an engineer who worked for the Census Bureau, produced several refinements of Hollerith's machine and patented a punched-card machine in 1908. Powers developed the concept of **simultaneous punching.** The operator depressed keys to cause punching, but holes were not actually punched until all keys for the card had been depressed and the release key was depressed. Thus, corrections could be made prior to punching. Powers also developed a sorting machine and tabulators that were used in the 1910 census. He formed the Powers Accounting Machine Company, which in 1926 merged with Remington Rand Corporation. Later, Remington Rand Corporation merged with Sperry Gyroscope Company to form Sperry Rand Corporation, which produced UNIVAC computers.

Figure A–5
Hollerith's Tabulating Machine

This machine, which helped in the 1890 census, was a forerunner of the IBM Corporation. From the early 1900s to about 1950, the mainstay of IBM's business was tabulating equipment.

Punched-card data processing was widely used until the early 1960s when electronic computers began to replace punched-card equipment in significant numbers. Several types of electromechanical devices were used to process punched cards, including **key-punches, key-verifiers, sorters, reproducers, collators,** and tabulating machines. Two of these devices, the key-punch and key-verifier, were also used with electronic computer systems, since cards were an important type of input to these systems. However, card input has been largely replaced by CRT terminal or floppy-disk input. Very few companies today use cards in the data-processing function.

Until the beginning of World War II, only two companies in the United States were involved in the punched-card data-processing business. IBM Corporation produced machinery that used the **eighty-column Hollerith card** and Remington Rand Corporation produced machinery that employed the **ninety-column Powers card.** The war created great demands for high-speed calculating equipment. Developments in long-range artillery, aircraft, and the atomic bomb required machines that could calculate at speeds never before dreamed possible.

Mark I Electromechanical Computer

In 1937 **Howard Aiken** of Harvard University started to build a machine that integrated punched-card and calculating technology. Aiken received help from graduate students and IBM engineers, and in 1944 the **Mark I** digital computer was completed (see Figure A–6). This machine had an automatic sequence-controlled calculator that was operated entirely by mechanical switches and electromagnetic relays. It was an **electromechanical computer,** not an electronic one. Ironically, Babbage's analytical engine was displayed at Harvard University; however, Aiken had almost completed Mark I before he became aware of Babbage's work. Mark I was the first machine to successfully perform a long series of arithmetic and logical operations. Several Mark I machines were built for the United States Navy, and they made a significant contribution to the war effort.

Commodore **Grace Murray Hopper** programmed the MARK I while at Harvard. Hopper became an important contributor to computer languages, especially COBOL, as we will discuss later in this chapter.

■ THE FIRST ELECTRONIC COMPUTERS

The ENIAC

In 1939, at the Moore School of Electrical Engineering at the University of Pennsylvania, **John W. Mauchly** and **J. Presper Eckert, Jr.** led a team that developed the first electronic digital computer, called the ENIAC (see Figure A–7). The **ENIAC (Electronic Numerical Integrator and Calculator),** completed in 1946, used **vacuum tubes** in place of electromagnetic relays. The substitution increased the calculation speed by a thousand times. This

Figure A–6
The Mark I Automatic Calculator

This machine used electromagnetic relays for switches. When the machine was running, the clicking of all the relays produced a very loud noise.

Figure A–7
The ENIAC

Since the ENIAC was based on electronic parts (vacuum tubes), it could perform a multiplication in three-thousandths of a second. The Mark I, based on mechanical electromagnetic relays, took about three seconds to perform a multiplication. Thus, the ENIAC was a thousand times faster.

machine was built for the United States Army and was designed to calculate the mathematical tables for artillery trajectories.

The ENIAC was an enormous computer by today's standards. It weighed 30 tons and covered 1,500 square feet of floor space. The ENIAC used 150,000 watts of electricity, equal to about 200 horsepower. The ENIAC could solve in half a minute a problem usually requiring twenty hours with a desk calculator.

The original ENIAC design was partially controlled by a combination of switches and a telephone-switchboard-like arrangement of "patch cords." Several hours of manual disconnecting and replugging these patch cords into new locations were necessary to change a program. The ENIAC was a stored-program computer in the sense that once the machine was wired properly for a given task, the program was in effect stored. However, changing to a different task required "rewiring" for the new program. It is interesting to note that the electromechanical punched-card equipment of the 1940s also had the switchboard-like patch-cord technology, which enabled the machines to perform different tasks. Therefore, it was natural for Mauchly and Eckert to use this approach in their computer. A computer that stores programs electronically, the same way data are stored, has significant advantages over the ENIAC.

The Binary Number System

In 1945 **John von Neumann,** a Princeton mathematician, suggested that both data and programs be stored internally, in high-speed memory, using the **binary number system.** This number system uses the digits zero and one rather than the ten digits in the decimal system. On and off, magnetized and not magnetized, are states that generally describe the condition of electronic components. The use of the binary system greatly facilitated the design of electronic computers because zero and one are used to represent the condition of electronic components. Von Neumann demonstrated how the instructions could be coded using the binary system. These concepts form the basis of today's electronic computer.

The EDVAC and EDSAC

In 1946 Mauchly, Eckert, and their colleagues began to construct a computer based on the concepts suggested by von Neumann, the **EDVAC (Electronic Discrete Variable Automatic Computer).** However, Eckert and Mauchly left the Moore School over patent disagreements in 1946. This seriously impeded progress on the EDVAC. It was completed in 1952 and was used by the United States Army. Meanwhile, **Maurice Wilker** of Cambridge University in England attended a course taught by Eckert and Mauchly entitled "The Theory and Techniques for Design of Electronic Digital Computers." He returned home and began work on the **EDSAC (Electronic Delay Storage Automatic Computer).** The EDSAC was completed in 1949, about two years before EDVAC was finished. Therefore, the EDSAC is credited as the first **stored-program electronic digital computer.**

In 1946 Mauchly and Eckert formed their own company, which was acquired by Remington Rand in 1951. From this point on in the early 1950s, the development of computers has been classified in terms of **generations.** Major technological developments caused each new generation to supersede the last. These developments have increased capabilities and reduced costs.

■ FIRST-GENERATION COMPUTERS: 1951–1958

UNIVAC-I

In 1951 Remington Rand produced the first commercially available computer, **UNIVAC-I (Universal Automatic Computer);** see Figure A–8. The UNIVAC-I was first used by the U.S. Census Bureau in 1951. This machine was retired in 1963 after 73,500 hours of operation. It was the first commercial computer to use a compiler to translate program language into machine language. General Electric acquired one of these machines in 1954 and installed it in the GE Appliance Park in Louisville, Kentucky. This event marked the first business data-processing application of a computer.

Figure A–8
UNIVAC-I

Although this machine marked the first use of a computer for business data processing, many UNIVACs were also used for scientific applications.

First-generation computers used vacuum tubes for switching and controlling functions. **Magnetic drums** were used for primary storage, and punched cards or punched paper tape were used for secondary storage. The tubes generated a great deal of heat, which meant that large air-conditioning units were needed to control the environmental temperature of the machine. First-generation machines were very large and required continuous maintenance because of the large number of vacuum tubes they contained (see Figure A–9).

First-Generation Software

The biggest advance in software was the use of **symbolic languages** for programming. All computers execute only **machine-language** programs, which are in the binary form of ones and zeros. Programming in machine language is very time consuming and difficult. A symbolic language expresses operation codes (op codes) of instructions and data addresses in symbols understood by users, rather than in machine language. For example, a programmer could write the word "add" for an operation code instead of the binary numbers which the machine understands for the addition operation code. A **translator** program translates the symbolic language into the binary machine language that the computer executes. Symbolic-language programming increased programmer productivity by a large factor. First-

Figure A–9
Vacuum Tubes, Transistors, and Chips

The vacuum tubes are on the left, the transistors are on the right, and the small items on the bottom are chips. By 1990 more than four million transistors were being packed on a quarter-inch-square chip.

generation computers were applied primarily to relatively simple business functions, such as processing payroll.

■ SECOND-GENERATION COMPUTERS: 1959–1964

Hardware Advances

In 1948 a small **semiconductor** device called a **transistor** was developed by Bell Laboratories. Unlike the vacuum tube, the transistor does not depend on a heat filament. It is much smaller, much more reliable, and when employed as a switching device, much faster than the vacuum tube. Besides making possible the pocket radio, the transistor made possible the second generation of computers.

Second-generation computers were considerably smaller. The need for air conditioning was reduced, and a significant increase in speed was realized. Speeds were measured in microseconds (millionths of a second), and maintenance costs were significantly lower because new and better components were used in the computer. The most widely used business-oriented second-generation computer was the IBM 1401; the IBM 7090–7094 series were the most widely used scientific computers.

A new type of primary storage, **magnetic core,** was developed. This donut-shaped iron core could be magnetized either positively or negatively by sending electrical currents through the wires that run through the center of each core. Thus, it is a binary storage device, capable of representing zero or one.

Magnetic tape was used extensively for secondary storage of data. Magnetic tape provided much faster input and output of data compared to punched cards. In fact, most large, second-generation computers were configured to accept only input or output on magnetic tape. Cards were transferred to magnetic tape, and reports were printed from magnetic tapes by separate, smaller computers. This approach allowed the larger computers to operate at greater speeds; they did not have to wait on the relatively slow input of data from cards or output to printers. Processing was performed under the batch mode, with sequentially ordered files.

Later in this period, magnetic disks were developed for secondary storage (see Figure A–10). Magnetic disks allowed for random file organization whereby a particular record could be retrieved immediately.

Software Advances

Operating systems—software that controls execution of programs and manages computer resources—were developed for use in second-generation computers. These systems were primitive batch serial systems that allowed execution of only one program at a time.

Figure A–10
Magnetic Disks

Magnetic disks were an extremely useful innovation for data storage. They made data randomly accessible, enabling computer systems to respond fast to information queries. They first appeared in the 1960s.

A major evolution in programming languages occurred during the second generation: the development of **high-level procedural languages,** such as **COBOL (Common Business-Oriented Language)** and **FORTRAN (Formula Translator).** COBOL was developed by the **Committee on Data Systems Languages (CODASYL)** of which Hopper was a prominent member. CODASYL has been a major force in the continuing evolution of the COBOL language. COBOL and FORTRAN are much more like English than machine and symbolic languages are. Procedural languages facilitate the programming of certain procedures. With FORTRAN the procedures are scientific; with COBOL they are business-oriented. Updated versions of both languages are still widely used today.

■ THIRD-GENERATION COMPUTERS: 1965–1971

Hardware Advances

In the 1960s, the development of **integrated circuits** brought about the third generation of computers. Integrated circuits contain transistors that are deposited photochemically on a silicon chip (see Figure A–11). The primary contributions of integrated-circuit technology were miniaturization and decreased costs. Miniaturization also increased speed, because the distance that electronic pulses had to travel decreased. The nanosecond (one billionth of a second) became the new standard for measuring access and process time. This generation of computers began with IBM's System/360 computers.

The first minicomputer was developed in the mid-1960s by the Digital Equipment Corporation (DEC). Minicomputers, which are smaller versions of the large mainframe computers, were originally developed for process control and military applications. However, as with earlier computers, business applications quickly developed. Today, minicomputers are very powerful, containing many more capabilities and features than the largest computers of the 1960s.

Online, real-time systems first became popular with third-generation computers. These systems were possible because of advances in disk-storage technology, enabling large amounts of data to be stored with immediate random retrieval.

**Figure A–11
A Silicon Chip**

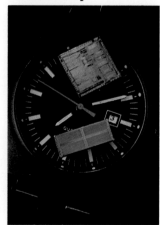

Software Advances

Online, real-time systems are only possible with multiprogramming operating systems, which were developed for third-generation computers. **Multiprogramming operating systems** allow the concurrent execution of two or more programs. For example, while the computer is executing a batch payroll program, a salesperson can query the inventory system through a terminal to determine the quantity on hand of a particular item in the warehouse. This was a major advance in operating-system software. One computer can simultaneously handle high-priority online, real-time queries and time-consuming batch processing. Through a **remote terminal** over regular telephone lines or leased lines, users can access data from almost any location. In addition, these remote terminals can be used to initiate the execution of programs from remote locations and print out the results at the remote location. Many users can interact with the computer at the same time. This approach is called **timesharing.** Multiprogramming operating systems make timesharing possible.

This generation of computers was the first to handle business and scientific applications equally well. IBM developed **PL/I,** a general-purpose language designed to replace FORTRAN and COBOL. However, PL/I never replaced these languages, primarily because they had already become firmly established. Making the change to PL/I would have required tremendous retraining and reprogramming costs.

Along with vastly improved operating systems, the other major development in the software area during the third generation was the beginning of the software industry. Software firms write general-purpose application and system software and sell or lease it to computer users. Examples of software that can be purchased are payroll, accounts-receivable, and general-ledger applications.

FOURTH-GENERATION COMPUTERS: 1971–PRESENT

Hardware Advances

The major technological development that distinguishes fourth-generation computers is the use of **large-scale integrated (LSI)circuits** for both logic and memory circuits. The primary computer to use this technology is the IBM 370 series, introduced in 1971. The more recent fourth-generation computers are employing **very-large-scale integrated (VLSI) circuits.** With this technology, it is possible to place a complete CPU on one very small semiconductor chip. These circuits increase the speed of computers and drastically reduce the production cost. In fact, a major feature of the fourth generation is the decreased cost and increased performance of computer hardware. The processing power that could have been purchased for approximately one million dollars in the 1960s can be purchased now in the form of a personal computer for less than one thousand dollars.

In the fourth generation, LSI and VLSI circuits have replaced magnetic core as the dominant form of primary storage. Significant advances have also been made in the storage capacity, access speed, and cost of disk storage. It is common for manufacturers to offer new disk storage with double the capacity at no increase in cost or at a reduced cost.

Video display terminals have become very widespread as processing moves from a batch mode to online. In the late 1970s **graphics terminals,** which can display charts and graphs in color, provided a new and exciting way of presenting information to management.

The dramatic decrease in the cost of computers has led to **distributed data processing (DDP).** DDP is the installation of micro- or mini-computers at a company's remote locations. Local data processing is handled by a computer at the remote location.

The widespread use of video display terminals and DDP has made **data communication** more important. This has led to new competitors (IBM and companies such as MCI) for American Telephone and Telegraph Company (AT&T) in the data-communication business. In the early 1980s AT&T divested its local operating companies so that its Long Lines Division could better compete in the data-communication market and enter the computer field.

The fourth-generation development most likely to directly affect people is the microcomputer or **personal computer (PC).** As mentioned earlier, the ability to place a complete CPU on a single chip dramatically reduces the cost of computer hardware. For less than $1,000, an individual can purchase a personal computer that can assist in many household and personal-business tasks, such as recipe filing, list keeping, checkbook balancing, and personal budgeting. In addition, this machine can entertain with computer games and provide security with fire and burglar alarm systems. These small computers are suitable for most elementary and secondary schools and are appearing in increasing numbers in their classrooms. More sophisticated personal computers with hard disk drives and better-quality printing currently cost $1,500 to $5,000.

Software Advances

There have also been significant advances in computer software during the fourth generation. Data-base management systems, which assist in storing and retrieving large amounts of data, were introduced. The primary development in operating systems was the addition of **virtual-storage operating systems.** These systems allow secondary storage to be used as if it were primary storage, hence the term *virtual storage* (the secondary storage is virtually primary storage).

Another trend in software was the development of **user-friendly systems,** especially electronic spreadsheets and word-processing packages. The idea was to develop software that would make computers easier to use. Some of this software, fourth-generation languages, allows users to develop applications without the assistance of programmers and system analysts. The trend toward user-friendly systems results partly from the increasing demands for computer software and the corresponding increase in costs to develop it. Characteristics of the computer generations are shown in Table A–1.

■ HISTORY OF PERSONAL COMPUTERS

PC Hardware

The personal computer has become so important that we should examine its relatively short history. The first personal computer, the **Altair 8800,** appeared in 1975. A company called MITS sold it as a kit for $397. The Altair was bought

Table A–1 ■ Characteristics of Computer Generations

First Generation: 1951–1958

Drum primary storage

Punched-card and paper-tape secondary storage

Vacuum-tube circuits

Continuous maintenance required

Applications: payroll and other simple applications in large companies

Batch processing

Machine and symbolic language programming

Different computers for scientific and business applications

Second Generation: 1959–1964

Magnetic-core primary storage

Tape secondary storage

Transistor circuits

Greater reliability and speed

High-level procedural languages: FORTRAN and COBOL

Applications: payroll, inventory, and accounts receivable in large and medium-sized companies

Batch processing

Third Generation: 1965–1971

Magnetic-disk secondary storage

Online real-time processing

Multiprogramming operating systems

Integrated circuits

Increased miniaturization, speed, and reliability

Multipurpose computers capable of performing both scientific and business tasks

Development of minicomputers

Applications: order processing, airline-reservation systems, and real-time inventory control

Fourth Generation: 1971–Present

Large-scale and very-large scale integrated circuits

Semiconductor primary storage

Dramatic decrease in hardware cost

Increasing costs of software

Development of the micro/personal computer

Development of electronic spreadsheet

Point-of-origin data capture and entry

Widespread use of video display terminals

Data-base management systems

Application development by users

User-friendly software

Virtual-storage operating systems

Distributed data processing

Increased use of data communication and computer networks

Graphics terminals

Applications: corporate modeling, decision-support systems, electronic funds transfer, electronic spreadsheet, word processing, and small business applications

Table A–1 ■ **Continued**

Future Computers
Organic chips
Decreasing costs of software
Decreasing costs of hardware
Integrated data, voice, images, and video
The merging of high-definition TV and computers
Super and ultra personal computers
Increased miniaturization
Vast improvements in the price-performance ratio
Applications: artificial intelligence, robots, expert systems, large-scale corporate modeling, weather-system modeling, star-wars systems, and personal robots

by electronic hobbyists, who found it difficult to assemble. Even if a person was successful in assemblying the Altair, there was virtually nothing that could be done with it! The Altair 8800 had no keyboard or monitor. Both programs and data had to be painstakingly entered in binary form via 16 switches that could be turned on or off. Output was displayed, also in binary form, by 36 light-emitting diodes. Since there were no application programs available for the Altair, a user had to write them in binary machine language.

The Altair was a great machine for those who input, think, and see in binary form, but I know of no human who does. Yet thousands of Altair 8800s were sold. It was an instant success. Why? Prior to the Altair, only large corporations and organizations could afford this wondrous machine called a computer. At the time, the only IBM computer that came close to being a personal computer was the 5100, which sold for $19,000. Few individuals bought it. But many people could afford an Altair. I suspect that many Altair owners saw their computer as a status symbol.

Let's think like entrepreneurs. If thousands of people will pay $397 for a box of electronic parts that are difficult to assemble into a computer that does nothing useful, there must be an incredible market for personal computers! Several entrepreneurs jumped at this opportunity. From 1975 through 1978, IMSAI sold a machine similar to the Altair. Both MITS and IMSAI were fertile breeding grounds for personal-computer entrepreneurs. Bill Millard, who started Computerland, was associated with IMSAI. Both Bill Gates, a founder of Microsoft Corporation, and David Bunnell, a founder of *PC Magazine* and *PC World*, were employees of MITS. But most important, this opportunity spurred the second generation of personal computers. The most prominent were introduced in 1977: the **Apple II** and Radio Shack's **TRS–80**. These computers had features that the Altair lacked, such as monitors, keyboards, and more primary memory. They were very successful. In its first month, the TRS–80 sold three times the number projected for the entire year of 1977.

Even more remarkable was the success of the Apple II. Apple Computer was started in a garage in 1977, and in less than seven years was one of the largest five hundred corporations. The company was started by Steve Wozniak, a young electronics engineer from Hewlett-Packard, and Steve Jobs who, in his early twenties, was new to the entrepreneurship game. They both were avid members of the Homebrew Computer Club, a group of Altair 8800 enthusiasts. Wozniak sold his Hewlett-Packard calculators and Jobs sold his

Volkswagen bus to raise money to start Apple. As they grew, they had the good sense to hire professional business managers and a first-rate advertising agency. Today, Apple Computer, with its MacIntosh, is in perhaps a life or death struggle with IBM for the business PC market. And both Wozniak and Jobs have left Apple. Jobs has started a new computer company, NEXT Inc. Wozniak is promoting rock concerts.

IBM was a latecomer to the PC market when it introduced the **IBM PC** in September 1981. Prior to the PC, IBM had built computers around its own *proprietary* technology. This protected the market for its computers. Competitors had difficulty building similar computers without violating patent or copyright laws. However, IBM adapted to the open nature of the personal-computer market by encouraging others to build both hardware and software that would operate with the IBM PC. IBM even chose an outside vendor, Microsoft Corporation, for the **disk operating system (DOS).** The IBM PC is literally an assembly of many components from several companies.

Since its operating system and most of its hardware components are not proprietary to IBM, many other companies have produced IBM PC compatible machines, the most successful being Compaq. The IBM PC quickly gave legitimacy to the personal computer in the business world and became a standard for the industry.

In 1987, IBM introduced a new generation of personal computers, the **Personal System 2 (PS/2).** In contrast to, the original IBM PC, the PS/2 family contains patented proprietary chips. IBM's apparent strategy was to establish a new PC standard that it owns the rights to, and in this way squeeze out the clone manufacturers. However, nine clone manufacturers joined ranks and created a new PC design called the **extended industry standard architecture (EISA).** Currently the outcome of this competition is not clear. The EISA machines could become a success, or the clone manufacturers could clone the PS/2 and pay IBM royalties. Two PS/2 clones have already appeared.

In 1989, Steve Jobs introduced the **NEXT computer,** which is designed primarily for higher education uses. However, many observers expect this computer to be used for business purposes as well.

PC Software

In PC software, the most significant application software development was **VisiCalc** (Visible Calculator), introduced in 1979. VisiCalc automated the very widespread business chore of calculating spreadsheets. It was indeed revolutionary! VisiCalc gave almost every business a reason to own one or more personal computers. Two Harvard MBA students originated the VisiCalc idea.

One of VisiCalc's former employees, Mitch Kapor, along with a single programmer, produced Lotus 1–2–3. An improved electronic spreadsheet, **Lotus 1–2–3** was designed for the IBM PC. Suddenly, it became the standard spreadsheet and produced another fast-growth company, Lotus Development Corporation.

Other software has contributed to the usefulness of personal computers, particularly word processing. The first word-processing program for PCs was **Electric Pencil,** developed by Michael Shrayer. It was developed for the Altair but was subsequently rewritten to run on many PCs. Currently, the most widely used word-processing software is **WordPerfect.** Today, a wide range of software such as data-base managers, project managers, communication software, and desktop publishing software are contributing to the widespread use of PCs. We will see much more application software in the future.

A part of IBM's 1987 introduction of its PS/2 computers was the OS/2 operating system. This system provides multitasking capabilities and has a graphics user interface called Presentation Manager. Presentation Manager is icon-based and is similar to the popular Macintosh interface. IBM's plan is to provide the same user interface for all its computer systems, including minis and mainframes. OS/2 also contains capabilities that will enable closer network connections between personal systems, minis, and mainframes. OS/2 is likely to be the standard operating system for business purposes in the 1990s.

■ FUTURE COMPUTERS

By the end of 1982 there were more computers on earth than there were people—more than five billion computers were in use, from microchips to mainframes. They are literally everywhere: in automobiles, appliances, business information systems, and military hardware. With electronic technology advancing rapidly, the use of computers is expected to grow even faster in coming years. We will explore some areas of potential growth based on current trends.

One computer prediction is a sure bet. Computers will increase in performance and decrease in size and cost. As shown in Figure A–12, these trends began with the first generation of computers. Software costs have continued to increase, because software grows in complexity and its development is labor-intensive. However, new approaches to developing software, such as the structured system development life cycle, prototyping, and application development by end users, are beginning to lower the costs of producing software. In addition, the costs of software packages are expected to decline.

Some people wonder why we need faster computers. The fact is, many problems cannot be adequately solved at the speed at which today's computers operate. For example, the future ability of computers to recognize human speech, spoken at normal speed, is largely dependent on the use of faster computers. Also, an extremely important application of computer technology is modeling and simulation. Diverse users such as business strategic forecasters, government economists, design engineers, and geologists *simulate* real-world events on computers to aid in better decision making. Faster turnaround on these applications could lead to significant savings owing to more timely decisions.

Even with existing hardware technology, there are many fields in which electronic information processing has not yet been applied to full advantage. In coming years, industry is expected to increase the use of **computer-aided design and computer-aided manufacturing (CAD/CAM)** techniques. This will

SIMULATE
To build a model or imitation of something that exists in the real world, such as a business, a weather system, or an aircraft. Simulations built with computers are mathematical models.

Figure A–12
Computer Hardware and Software Trends

Computer hardware has become so inexpensive that it is a relatively minor part of the information-processing costs of today's organizations.

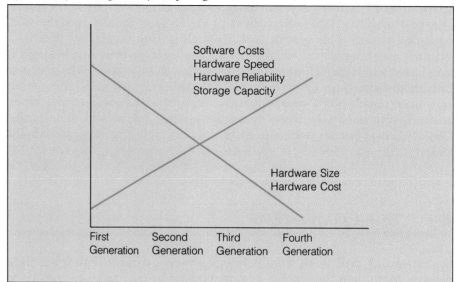

require, among other things, refinement of graphics techniques, improvement of production-control software, and developments in robot technology.

The revolutionary increase in computer hardware performance is just beginning. New and faster microprocessors for personal computers appear about every three years. These new microprocessors effectively quadruple computing power at nearly the same cost as the previous microprocessor. Currently, the most widely used microprocessors are the Intel 80286 and the Intel 80386. The Intel 80486 has been released and should appear in PCs by late 1989. The 80486 chip has 1.2 million transistors compared with about 275,000 for the 80386, and it offers up to four times the processing power of the 80386. The 80586 chip, with speeds three to four times that of the 80486 should be released in the early 1990s. It is expected by 1995 that PCs will be executing 100 million instructions per second (MIPS), far faster than any mainframe runs today. Also, substantial strides have been made in improving the access speed of RAM memory. RAM used in the machines of the early 1990s will be about four times as fast as that used in the late 1980s.

The biggest change that we will see in computer systems in the 1990s is **integrated services digital networks (ISDN).** ISDN will greatly enhance the ability of computers of all sizes to communicate with one another. Computers and their networks will be able to store, process, and communicate data, voice, and images in an integrated fashion. As our telephone systems become digital, they in effect become computer networks. After your voice is digitized, it is communicated and stored by a computer in a fashion very similar to the way music is stored on a cassette disk. In fact, musical cassette disks and computer laser disks use the same technology. Vast quantities of information, in the form of data, text, voice, music, and still and moving images, will be stored on laser disks. Let's say you need to write a paper on the French Revolution. Instead of walking to the library, you could connect your personal workstation to the library's computer and review extensive material on the French Revolution, including a video reenactment of the storming of the Bastille. In fact, you could stop the video at any point and interview the participants, almost as if you were actually there in 1789. The interactive random access nature of laser disks allows this capability. Of course, your questions would have to be anticipated by the video producers. To help illustrate your research presentation to your class, you may want to download portions of the video to your portable workstation and replay them on the large flat-screen monitor in your classroom.

Closely related to the above capabilities is the emergence of high-definition TV (HDTV). HDTV promises to provide TV pictures with the resolution and quality of 35-millimeter photographs. Digital computer technology will be used for HDTV. Thus, TV and computer technology will merge. The HDTV monitors will become our high-resolution (definition) computer monitors. In the 1990s we will see music, TV, telephone, and communications technology all becoming digital and thus merging with computer technology. In fact, much of this revolution is already well under way.

The opportunities this revolution offers are vast. Innovative firms will find many applications for this technology. For example, instead of flipping through a mail-order catalog to order clothes, you may find yourself viewing a high-resolution video of a coat you are considering purchasing. You could zoom in on the fabric to see the detail. After entering your measurements, your order would be transmitted to the factory where a computer-controlled machine would cut the fabric to an exact fit. After sewing and pressing, the coat would be shipped to you. You may think this senario is futuristic, but the technology to do it is now available. Our abilities to communicate and to design and manufacture specialized products will be transformed in the 1990s.

We will have much more information at our computer keyboard fingertips— so much information that a huge market will exist for software that can scan this information and extract only the portion that interests us at the moment. Such software will require artificial-intelligence capabilities.

Another area in which advances are being made is parallel computing. In parallel computing, multiple processors work simultaneously on a single application. The problem in designing practical parallel computing is a software problem. Multiple microprocessors can be easily tied together to create parallel hardware. However, the operating system or the application software must be able to break an application apart so that each part can be processed simultaneously on separate processors. Current computers are designed to process applications sequentially, thus our application software is designed to be executed sequentially. But some business applications could be processed in a parallel way. For example, imagine a parallel computer with a thousand microprocessors that is used only for data-base processing. Up to one thousand terminals tied to this computer could simultaneously access and update the data-base, with each processor working on only one person's problem. Parallel computers promise to substantially increase computer speed and perhaps lower hardware costs. Microprocessors are inexpensive.

Behind some of these advances in computer technology are researchers in both Japan and the United States who have embarked on the ambitious **fifth-generation project** to produce major advances in hardware and software. In Japan this effort is subsidized by the Japanese government. The United States effort is being led by the Microelectronics Computer Corporation, a consortium of several U.S. computer companies. IBM has not joined this consortium and is pursuing fifth-generation research independently. The goal of the fifth-generation projects is to produce radically different computer systems whose primary characteristic is **artificial intelligence.**

Other researchers believe it will soon be possible to use the chemistry of living cells to produce computers. These organic computers may operate at speeds well above today's supercomputers and could store much more data. The researchers feel that these computers would have significant advantages over silicon-based chips—they would not generate heat and could be much smaller. An organic chip may be able to store one billion times as much data as a similar-sized silicon chip. The direction of this research seems to confirm the fact that the human brain is the most remarkable of all computers. This fact is not likely to change in your lifetime.

Even with current technology, the office of the future should be a more efficient and productive place. As office workers, from the receptionist to the president of the firm, learn more about the computer, it will become a much larger part of their daily routine.

Like any other technology, computer information systems are expected to give rise to some undersirable phenomena. When billions of dollars' worth of assets are controlled and processed by computers, the risk of fraud is extremely high. Businesses have a strong interest in ensuring that only authorized transactions are executed by their information systems. This should lead to the development of sophisticated computer security and computer audit techniques. The growth of distributed data processing and data-communication usage will further enhance the importance of such control mechanisms.

ERGONOMICS
The science of designing computer hardware and software in a way that makes them easier for people to use

Office managers and *ergonomists* are voicing their concern over the harmful effects of computer usage in the office, such as eyestrain, exposure to radiation, and general fatigue for users operating a video display terminal for long hours. As a result, design improvements are expected in both hardware and software products. Strong competition in the information-systems market will force vendors to make their products more suitable for human use, rather than requiring that people adapt themselves to the computer.

■ Summing Up

■ The abacus, invented by the Chinese and used by the ancient Greeks and Romans, is the first known calculating device.

■ Mechanical calculators were used from 1642 to about 1970. French mathematician Blaise Pascal is credited with inventing these machines. Later Gottfried von Leibnitz improved Pascal's design for a calculator.

■ In the early nineteenth century, Joseph Jacquard used punched cards to control textile-mill operations.

■ Charles Babbage proposed the construction of an analytical engine using punched cards. This machine, like today's computers, would have had input and output devices, a CPU, and memory space.

■ Ada Byron, Countess of Lovelace, is recognized as the first programmer for her work in developing (programming) mathematical tables for Babbage's analytical engine.

■ In the 1870s, Henry Metcalfe developed the unit-record concept. By storing cost-accounting information on cards, he was able to manipulate it much more easily than was possible with traditional leather-bound ledgers.

■ Starting with the 1880 U.S. Census, punched-card equipment was increasingly used for data processing by government and industry. Herman Hollerith and James Powers developed this equipment. The need for computing equipment during World War II greatly stimulated the beginning of the computer industry.

■ In 1944, Howard Aiken of Harvard University built the first electromechanical computer, the Mark I.

■ Commodore Grace Murray Hopper programmed the Mark I and was a major contributor to the COBOL language.

■ The first electronic computer capable of running stored programs was completed at the University of Pennsylvania in 1946 by John Mauchly and Presper Eckert. This was soon followed by computers using the binary number system for internal storage.

■ First-generation computers (1951–1958) used vacuum tubes for switching and controlling functions A major breakthrough of this generation was the use of translators to convert symbolic-language programs into machine-language instructions.

■ The second-generation machines (1959–1964) offered a number of improvements over the first generation. The vacuum tubes were replaced by transistors, which reduced size and increased speed. Faster memory devices such as magnetic cores, tapes, and disks were extensively used. The major software developments in this period were the use of operating systems to control program execution and the creation of high-level procedural languages such as COBOL and FORTRAN.

■ Third-generation computers (1965–1971) were even smaller and faster, thanks to the development of integrated circuit technology. Online, real-time applications could be run on multiprogramming operating systems. Through the use of remote terminals, these systems allowed a much larger number of users to access the computer from their own locations.

■ Fourth-generation computers (1971–present) employed very sophisticated technology to improve processing speed and reduce production costs. The application of semiconductor technology has greatly reduced the cost of memory space. Lower costs have led to the widespread use of computers in applications ranging from simple household budgeting to extremely complex distributed data-base systems.

■ The first personal computer, the Altair 8800, was produced by MITS. It was in kit form and had very limited capabilities.

■ The TRS–80 and Apple II were second-generation personal computers that were purchased by many individuals.

■ The IBM PC was introduced in September 1981. It legitimized the personal computer in the business market and established itself as the standard.

■ VisiCalc, the first electronic spreadsheet, was a major factor in making personal computers useful to the business professional.

■ In the future, computers are expected to be much faster and smaller. Personal computers will have today's super-computer capabilities. They will be able to solve many problems that today's computers cannot cope with owing to speed and memory limitations. Video, sound, data, images, and text will be processed, stored, and communicated by integrated service digital computer networks. Sophisticated systems will be developed to automate work in the factory as well as in the office. At the same time, it will be necessary to improve control over computerized systems so that unauthorized operations cannot be performed.

■ Key Terms

abacus

mechanical calculators

Blaise Pascal

Gottfried von Leibnitz

Joseph Jacquard

Jacquard's loom

punched cards

Charles Babbage

stored program

difference engine

analytical engine

Augusta Ada Byron

Henry Metcalfe

coding scheme

unit record

Herman Hollerith

tabulating machine

James Powers

simultaneous punching

key-punches

key-verifiers

sorters

reproducers

collators

eighty-column Hollerith card

ninety-column Powers card

Howard Aiken

Mark I

electromechanical computer

Grace Murray Hopper

John W. Mauchly

J. Presper Eckert, Jr.

ENIAC (Electronic Numerical Integrator and Calculator)

vacuum tubes

John von Neumann

binary number system

EDVAC (Electronic Discrete Variable Automatic Computer)

Maurice Wilker

EDSAC (Electronic Delay Storage Automatic Computer)

stored-program electronic digital computer

generations

UNIVAC-I (Universal Automatic Computer)

magnetic drums

symbolic languages

machine language

translator

semiconductor

transistor

magnetic core

magnetic tape

operating system

high-level procedural languages

COBOL (Common Business-Oriented Language)

FORTRAN (Formula Translator)

Committee on Data Systems Languages (CODASYL)

integrated circuits

online, real-time systems

multiprogramming operating systems

remote terminal

timesharing

PL/I

large-scale integrated (LSI) circuits

very-large-scale integrated (VLSI) circuits

video display terminals

graphics terminals

distributed data processing (DDP)

data communication

personal computer

virtual-storage operating systems

user-friendly systems

Altair 8800

Apple II

TRS–80

IBM PC

disk operating system (DOS)

Personal System 2 (PS/2)

extended industry standard architecture (EISA)

NEXT computer

VisiCalc

Lotus 1–2–3

Electric Pencil

WordPerfect

computer-aided design and computer-aided manufacturing (CAD/CAM)

integrated services digital networks (ISDN)

fifth-generation project

artificial intelligence

ergonomists

Review Questions

1. How is Jacquard's loom related to computers?
2. Who was Charles Babbage, and what did he contribute to computer development?
3. Trace the developments in punched-card technology.
4. Who developed the first electronic computers?
5. What were the characteristics of the first electronic computers?
6. Distinguish between the characteristics of each generation of computer hardware.
7. Distinguish between the characteristics of each generation of computer software.
8. Describe the first personal computer.
9. Who is Steve Jobs? What is the nature of his involvement with computers?
10. Why did the IBM PC become an industry standard?
11. What are the various PC standards that now compete in the marketplace?
12. What were the first widely used electronic-spreadsheet and word-processing software for PCs?
13. What are the Intel 8086, 80286, 80386, and 80486 chips?
14. What are the integrated digital networks?
15. What is the relationship between high-definition TV, cassette sound disks, digital telephones, and computers?

458

■ Discussion
■ Questions
and Cases

1. Are future computer systems likely to have the powers of the human mind, such as reasoning ability, creativity, and learning?

2. The early days of personal computer hardware and software (in the late 1970s and the 1980s) were typified by many small start-up companies, some of which were phenomenally successful. Are these types of companies likely to be successful in the future in the PC industry, or has their time gone by?

3. Is software lagging behind hardware, or is hardware lagging behind software in applying personal computers to business problems?

4. Identify new business opportunities that may accompany the merging of communications, high-definition TV, sound, video, text, data, and computer technology.

5. Susan Wright is a freshman at a large state university. She is taking a course entitled Introduction to Computer Information Systems primarily because it is required for her major. Susan has stated several times that "with the rapid advances expected in computer hardware and software, computers will become as easy to use as a telephone. I didn't have to take a course in how to use the telephone and study how a telephone works. The computer is just a tool, like a telephone. Why should I spend my time studying something that in a few years will be very simple to use? I'll even be able to converse with the computer in English!" Do you agree or disagree with Susan? Why?

6. Many experts now anticipate that computers will be used for very practical artificial intelligence systems within the next ten years. These computers will be able to reason, see, converse in English, make expert judgments, and perhaps even learn. If this occurs, the world may change dramatically. The major characteristic that distinguishes humans is our ability to reason. Are we on the brink of creating a machine that has greater reasoning powers than 95 percent of the human population? Will we need as many human experts, such as doctors, lawyers, and system snalysts? Will expert computer systems produce a profound increase in the quality of human existence? Let's assume the experts' predictions come true. What impacts, both positive and negative, will artificial intelligence have on the career you plan to pursue?

Module B ▪ Programming Languages

MODULE OUTLINE

Introduction

Types of Programmming Languages
Machine Language
Symbolic Languages
Procedural Languages
Fourth-Generation Languages

Language Selection

Summing Up

Key Terms

Review Questions

Discussion Questions and Cases

▪ INTRODUCTION

Software for large, complex, and/or unique applications is usually written by an application programmer to fulfill a particular user or application requirement. The development of application software should be performed using structured methodology, as discussed in Chapters 6 and 7. Before any coding (programming) is done, the application must be analyzed and a structured physical design developed, which is in effect the programmer's blueprint for coding the application. From this structured design specification, a suitable language is used to code the program(s). A **program** is a set of instructions executed by the computer. The instructions cause the computer to perform a desired task. The selection of a language depends primarily on the nature of the problem or application, as well as the programmer's choice, the standard language used by the company, and the hardware capabilities.

This module will introduce you to the most widely used programming languages. In addition, factors influencing the selection of a language will be discussed.

▪ TYPES OF PROGRAMMING LANGUAGES

Machine Language

The evolution of software is characterized by various stages or generations, beginning with the tedious machine language, and evolving to the present-day **high-level languages. Machine language,** as the name implies, is a machine-oriented language. Programmers using such a language must be extremely familiar with the design, operation, and peripherals of a particular computer. This creates a **semantic gap** between the application and the programming language. In other words, a programmer cannot write a machine-language program directly from the structured design specifications

459

developed for the application, and expect any similarities between the program and the specifications. In fact, the machine code would be unintelligible to most users. For example, a program that computes tax, written in machine code, is in no way similar to the English description of the computation.

A machine-language program is a set of instructions that have a one-to-one correspondence to every operation that must be performed. It is the only language that a computer can understand. All programs written in other languages must be compiled or translated into machine language for execution. A machine-language program is also known as *object code.* Object code is machine-readable and requires no translation process before execution. This feature allows for extremely fast processing time and efficient use of primary storage.

Programming in machine language is very tedious because the programmer is concerned not only with problem definition but also with the clerical tasks such as manually assigning primary-storage locations in which to store the data and program. The programmer must keep track of each memory location used throughout the program. This task makes writing and debugging a machine-language program extremely difficult. The probability of a programmer inadvertently writing data or instructions into primary-storage locations that contain other data or instructions, and thereby destroying them, is very high. Changes in instructions are extremely difficult to make because the programmer must reassign all references to storage locations manually, making the program inflexible. Because of the difficulties of programming in machine language, it is not used today. Instead, symbolic or high-level procedural languages are used.

Symbolic Languages

As the evolution of software continued, **symbolic languages** were developed. The IBM **assembly language,** which uses **mnemonics** or symbols for each machine-language instruction, is an example. Assembly language allows the programmer to specify constants and storage locations symbolically. This feature takes some of the tediousness out of programming in machine language, and gives the responsibility to a program called an assembler. Like machine language, an assembly language is designed for a specific machine. Therefore, the program makes efficient use of the time and resources of the CPU. In general, there is still a one-to-one correspondence between instructions and actual computer operations. Each symbol corresponds to one machine operation and is descriptive of that particular operation. The *assembler* translates the assembly-language program into machine code and then references and assigns all addresses and storage locations. An assembly, or higher-level language program, is known as *source code.* It is written by an application programmer and must be translated or compiled into object code (machine-language code) before it is executed.

Since machine-language code and assembly languages are difficult to comprehend, a simple example will be used to illustrate the nature and complexity of programming in these languages. Figure B–1 illustrates a simple program that adds two variables, X and Y, and then places the result in a third variable, *SUM.* In **pseudocode,** the program would be expressed as follows:

OBJECT CODE
A machine-language program that has been produced from a higher-level language through the compilation process. It is called object code since its production is the *objective* of compilation or translation.

ASSEMBLER
A computer program that translates an assembly-language program into machine language.

SOURCE CODE
A program written in a higher-level language than machine language. It is called source code because it is the starting point or *source* in the compilation process to produce object code.

Figure B–1
A Program Coded in Machine and Assembly Language

These two programs are merely adding X + Y and placing the result in SUM. What an incredible amount of detail to perform such a simple operation! It is no wonder higher-level languages for computers were developed.

Machine Code				Assembly Language		Explanation
MEMORY LOCATION	OBJECT CODE	ADDR1	ADDR2	STMT	SOURCE STATEMENT	
000000				1	ADD CSECT	;IDENTIFIES BEGINNING\NAME OF PGM
000000			00000	2	USING *,15	;IDENTIFIES R15 AS BASE REGISTER
000000	5820 F010	00010		3	L 2,X	;LOAD "1" INTO R2
000004	5A20 F014	00014		4	A 2,Y	;ADD '2' TO CONTENTS OF R2
000008	5020 F018	00018		5	ST 2,SUM	;STORE CONTENTS OF R2 IN SUM
00000C	07FE			6	BR 14	;RETURN CONTROL TO CALLER PGM
00000E	0000					
000010	00000001			7	X DC F'1'	;RESERVE MEMORY LOCATION FOR X, INIT TO '1'
000014	00000002			8	Y DC F'2'	;RESERVE MEMORY LOCATION FOR Y, INIT TO '2'
000018				9	SUM DS F	;RESERVE MEMORY LOCATION FOR SUM
				10	END	

```
program ADD;
   declare X        real initial (1),
           Y        real initial (2),
           SUM      real;
   SUM = X + Y;
end ADD;
```

To illustrate the complexity of machine code, we will look at only the LOAD instruction in Figure B–1. The LOAD instruction is broken down as follows:

58 2 0 F 010

where   58   is the hexadecimal representation for the
              LOAD operation code
         2   is the hexadecimal representation for
              "register 2"
         0   is the hexadecimal representation for the
              index register (not used in this example)
         F   is the hexadecimal representation for the
              base register
         010 is the hexadecimal representation for the
              relative location of contents to be loaded

REGISTER
A storage location in the CPU used to store and manipulate data.

This example shows the clerical detail involved in coding the program. The programmer must determine which storage areas (or *registers*) will be used in the program. In statement 2 of the assembly-language program, register 15 is designated as the **base register** from which all storage locations associated with the program are determined. The base register contains the relative address of the next instruction, which is the LOAD instruction (statement 3) at relative location 000000. Statements 3 through 5 use register 2 for temporary storage during the addition process. Statement 3 is the instruction that loads register 2 with the contents of the memory location (000010), designated X. Statement 4 adds to register 2 the contents of the memory location (000014), designated Y. Statement 5 stores the contents of register 2, the sum of X and Y, in the memory location (000018), designated SUM.

Today, application programmers seldom write in assembly language, though some use it to write programs that are executed many times (such as arithmetic functions and specialized input/output programs). Assembler is also used to provide access to operating-system resources that may be unavailable in high-level languages, such as graphics and physical input and output. Because assembly language is efficient in terms of processing time and primary-storage utilization, it is generally used by system programmers who write operating-system programs. For these programs, execution time is a primary consideration.

Procedural Languages

The third stage of software evolution brought about the development of procedure-oriented high-level languages, such as FORTRAN, COBOL, and PL/I. A **procedure-oriented language** is a language in which the programmer gives step-by-step instructions to the computer. A **compiler** generates the necessary machine-language instructions for the computer. These languages help bridge the semantic gap between problem definition and the language.

With these machine-independent languages, the programmer needs to know very little about the machine on which the program is executed. Programming is now simpler because there is a buffer, the compiler, which handles all cross-referencing and storage allocation. The high-level-language program must go through three processes before it is ready to be executed:

1. Translation (compilation): The translator (compiler) program translates the source code into object code (machine-language code).

2. Linking: The linkage editor combines with the program any *called* instructions or *library routines*.

3. Loading: The loader program *loads* the object code and its appended library functions/instructions into main memory for execution

Figure B–2 illustrates these processes. They are performed for most high-level programming languages.

Our discussion will include six procedure-oriented languages: FORTRAN, COBOL, PL/I, BASIC, PASCAL, and ADA. We will illustrate selected languages with an example that calculates and prints a payroll report called the Payroll Register. A description of the program is as follows:

CALL
The action of bringing a computer program, a routine, or subroutine into effect; for example, to summon a library routine for use in a program.

LIBRARY ROUTINES
Standard programs that are often used as part of another program, such as a program that sorts data in ascending sequence. Library routines are stored on disk, and the linkage editor combines them with any program that calls them so that the program does not have to rewrite them each time they are used.

LOAD
To bring a program into primary storage for execution.

Figure B–2
Translating Source Code into Executable Object Code

The object code is machine code, as illustrated in Figure B–1. The translator or compiler is a program that converts the source code of a high-level language (such as COBOL) into the machine-language object code.

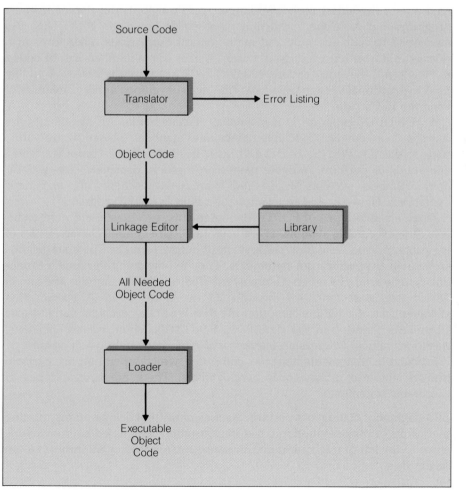

1. Print the *header* for the payroll register.

2. For each employee, read in a record containing the job code which identifies the type of job the employee holds, the employee's social security number, the number of hours worked, and the current hourly wage.

a. If the job code is equal to 1111, then the employee works part-time and no deductions are taken except for federal and state income taxes.

b. If the job code is equal to 1120, then the employee works full time and all deductions are taken except for credit-union dues.

c. If the job code is equal to 1122, then the employee works full time and all deductions are taken.

3. Calculate the payroll for each employee with a valid job code, or print an error message.

4. Finally, when the end of the input file is reached, print the total for the Payroll Register.

This program is designed to process any number of employees and print the total net earnings. A sample of the output, the Payroll Register, is illustrated in Figure B–3.

FORTRAN   FORTRAN (FORmula TRANslator), created in 1954, is considered one of the oldest high-level languages. Prior to its development, most programming was done in machine or assembly language. FORTRAN was developed to code scientific and mathematical expressions. Therefore, *algorithms* dealing with processing of numbers or *arrays* of numbers can be coded in FORTRAN. Several versions of FORTRAN have been released. A widely used instructional version called **WATFIV** was developed at the University of Waterloo in Canada.

A FORTRAN program is a sequence of **statements.** All statements are composed of keywords, variable names, and symbols. **Keywords** are verbs, such as READ, WRITE, STOP, DO, and IF, that tell the computer which operations to perform. Variable names are used to designate storage locations. Symbols such as +, –, and * are used primarily for arithmetic operations. Figure B–4 is an example of a FORTRAN 77 program.

There are two types of FORTRAN statements: executable and nonexecutable. **Nonexecutable statements** are used to declare various characteristics of the program, such as data types and input/output formats. These statements are known as **specification statements.** They tell the computer how information is to be arranged when it is transferred between the computer and an I/O device (see statements 47 through 53 in Figure B–4). A specification statement can also tell the computer the **data type** of a particular variable (see statements 1 and 2 in the figure). In FORTRAN, a *real variable* can have fractional values, whereas an *integer variable* can have only whole values.

Executable statements tell the computer which operation to perform through the use of keywords and symbols. There are several types of executable statements.

1. Assignment statements perform a series of arithmetic operations, placing the results of the operation into a storage location designated by the variable name to the left of the equal sign. Examples are statements 60 through 67 in Figure B–4.

Figure B–3
Payroll Register

The term register is often used for computer reports, especially those which are accounting oriented.

Job Code	Employee Number	Hours Worked	Hourly Wage	Gross Pay	Social Security Tax	Federal Income Tax	State Income Tax	Credit Union	Retirement	Net Pay
1111	400941648	33.00	4.51	148.83	0.00	1.04	1.19	0.00	0.00	146.60
1122	22499460	40.00	5.10	204.00	13.67	23.05	6.12	10.20	10.20	140.76
1120	90022792	44.00	4.51	207.46	13.90	23.44	6.22	0.00	10.37	153.52
1122	22485493	45.00	7.25	344.38	23.07	38.91	10.33	17.22	17.22	237.62
1111	900120001	25.00	3.25	81.25	0.00	0.57	0.65	0.00	0.00	80.03

Total Earnings: 758.53

Figure B–4
Payroll Program Written in FORTRAN

Indenting nested statements within a program improves its readability. For example, statements 18, 22, and 40 are all part of a single IF-THEN-ELSE statement. Notice we have indented the nested IF-THEN-ELSE statements within the first level. For example, the second level is represented by lines 23, 37, and 39, which make up another IF-THEN-ELSE statement.

```
 1          REAL EXTRA,OTIME,TOTAL,FCRATE,FTRATE,STRATE,CURATE,RTRATE,
          1    HOURS,RATE,GROSS,FICA,FIT,SIT,RETIRE,CUNION,NET,WHRS
 2          INTEGER EMPNO,JOBCODE
 3          COMMON  WHRS,OTIME,FCRATE,FTRATE,STRATE,RTRATE,CURATE,TOTAL,
          1         HOURS,RATE,GROSS,FICA,FIT,SIT,RETIRE,CUNION,NET
 4          COMMON JOBCODE,EMPNO
 5          DATA TOTAL/0.0/
 6          WRITE (6,300)
 7          WRITE (6,500)
 8          WRITE (6,400)
 9    10 CONTINUE
10          READ (5,200,END=100) JOBCODE,EMPNO,HOURS,RATE
11          OTIME=0.0
12          WHRS=HOURS
13          FCRATE=0.0
14          FTRATE=0.0
15          STRATE=0.0
16          RTRATE=0.0
17          CURATE=0.0
18          IF (JOBCODE.EQ.1111)THEN
19             FTRATE=0.007
20             STRATE=0.008
21             CALL CALC
22          ELSE
23             IF ((JOBCODE.EQ.1120).OR.(JOBCODE.EQ.1122))THEN
24                FCRATE=0.067
25                FTRATE=0.113
26                STRATE=0.03
27                RTRATE=0.05
28                IF (JOBCODE.EQ.1122)THEN
29                   CURATE=0.05
30                END IF
31                IF (HOURS.GT.40.0) THEN
32                   EXTRA=HOURS-40.0
33                   OTIME=EXTRA*RATE*1.5
34                   WHRS=40.0
35                END IF
36                CALL CALC
37             ELSE
38                WRITE (6,900)
39             END IF
40          END IF
41          GO TO 10
42    100 CONTINUE
43          WRITE (6,500)
44          WRITE (6,700) TOTAL
45          WRITE (6,800)
46          STOP
47    200 FORMAT (I4,I9,F5.2,F4.2)
48    300 FORMAT ('1',50X,'Payroll Register')
49    400 FORMAT (' ',56X,'Social',5X,'Federal',5X,'State'/
          1      ' ',4X,'Job',5X,'Employee',5X,'Hours',4X,'Hourly',5X,
          2      'Gross',5X,'Security',5X,'Income',4X,'Income',4X,'Credit',
          3      20X,'Net'/
          4      ' ',2X,'Code',7X,'Number',5X,'Worked',5X,'Wage',7X,'Pay',
          5      8X,'Tax',9X,'Tax',8X,'Tax',6X,'Union',4X,'Retirement',
          6      6X,'Pay'/)
50    500 FORMAT (' ',1X)
```

Figure B–4 (continued)

```
51        700 FORMAT (' ',95X,'Total Earnings: ',F8.2)
52        800 FORMAT ('1',1X)
53        900 FORMAT (' ',2X,'Invalid Job Code.')

54            END
55            SUBROUTINE CALC
56            REAL EXTRA,OTIME,TOTAL,FCRATE,FTRATE,STRATE,CURATE,RTRATE,
          1        HOURS,RATE,GROSS,FICA,FIT,SIT,RETIRE,CUNION,NET,WHRS
57            INTEGER EMPNO,JOBCODE
58            COMMON WHRS,OTIME,FCRATE,FTRATE,STRATE,RTRATE,CURATE,TOTAL,
          1        HOURS,RATE,GROSS,FICA,FIT,SIT,RETIRE,CUNION,NET
59            COMMON JOBCODE,EMPNO
60            GROSS=(WHRS*RATE)+OTIME
61            FICA=GROSS*FCRATE
62            FIT=GROSS*FTRATE
63            SIT=GROSS*STRATE
64            RETIRE=GROSS*RTRATE
65            CUNION=GROSS*CURATE
66            NET=GROSS-(FICA+FIT+SIT+SIT+RETIRE+CUNION)
67            TOTAL=TOTAL+NET
68             WRITE (6,600) JOBCODE,EMPNO,HOURS,RATE,GROSS,FICA,FIT,SIT,
          1                  CUNION,RETIRE,NET
69        600 FORMAT (' ',2X,I4,5X,I9,4X,F6.2,4X,F6.2,4X,F7.2,5X,F6.2,6X,F6.2,
          1        4X,F6.2,4X,F6.2,6X,F6.2,6X,F7.2)
70            RETURN
71            END
```

2. Control statements control the order of execution within the program. Figure B–4 illustrates the use of the IF-THEN-ELSE statement. Statement 18 determines whether the job code of the present time card is equal to 1111. If it is, 0.7 percent for federal withholding and 0.8 percent for state withholding are deducted. If the job code does not equal 1111, then statements 23 through 39 are performed. The END IF, at line 40, signals the end of the IF-THEN-ELSE statement.

3. Input/output statements instruct the computer from which input device or to what output device data are to be transferred. In Figure B–4, statement 10 reads in the input values, using statement 47 to describe how the input data is to be arranged. Statement 44 transfers data to an output device, the printer, using statement 51 to describe the layout of the data.

FORTRAN has a large amount of experience behind its design, implementation, and standardization. It has a vast library of mathematical, statistical, and engineering subroutines. Although FORTRAN was primarily designed for scientific applications and efficient mathematical manipulations, the language has been used for business data-processing and file-handling applications. However, before the advent of FORTRAN 77, which allows for **structured programming** techniques, logical problems were difficult to express in FORTRAN. The FORTRAN 77 version has made writing and debugging programs easier and faster. FORTRAN processes large volumes of mathematical calculations efficiently and has good input/output facilities. However, FORTRAN can be expensive in terms of primary-memory allocation for variables and constants. Another disadvantage of FORTRAN is that it is "non-English-like" and requires extensive internal *documentation*.

DOCUMENTATION
English statements that describe the steps in a program.

FORTRAN has been implemented on personal computers. However, the standardization level of microcomputer FORTRAN varies, ranging from various additional nonstandard features to a lack of very basic features. The most common version used with microcomputers is FORTRAN IV.

COBOL   COBOL (Common Business-Oriented Language) is one of the leading and most widely used business-oriented programming languages today and is considered to be the industry standard. COBOL was first conceived in 1959 by a group of users, programmers, and manufacturers from the government and business sectors, referred to as the CODASYL Committee (Conference On DAta SYstems Languages). The goal of this committee was to design and implement an English-like common business language. By December 1959, the initial specifications for COBOL had been drafted with the basic objectives of being highly machine-independent and *self-documenting*.

The first version of COBOL was published in 1960, known as COBOL–60. The second verison, COBOL–61, was released in 1961 and included many changes in the procedure division. An extended version of COBOL–61 became available in 1963, which included sorting and report-writing routines. In September 1962, the American National Standards Institute (ANSI) formed a committee to standardize COBOL. Grace Hopper was a member of this committee (see Module A). Several versions of COBOL were developed since 1962, and the committee chose COBOL–68 as the standard. The standardization process was very strict, thereby solving the *portability* problem of having too many dialects of the language. COBOL is now a truly common language. The CODASYL committee meets every year to update the language.

COBOL is English-like, making the language easy to read and code. COBOL can be loosely compared to an English composition which consists of headings, sections, paragraphs, and sentences. A program written in COBOL is shown in Figure B–5.

A COBOL program has four major parts, called **divisions.** Each division and its function is listed in the order it must appear within a program:

1. The *identification division* identifies the name and various documentary entries of the program.
2. The *environment division* identifies the input/output hardware needed to support the program.
3. The *data division* identifies the storage-record layout for input, output, and the intermediate results (working-storage).
4. The *procedure division* contains the instructions that tell the computer what operations to perform. This division is most like programs written in other languages.

All divisions except the identification division are further divided into **sections.** The procedure division has a structure different from the other divisions. It consists only of **sentences**, which are combinations of **statements.** For example, statement 64 in Figure B–5,

```
MOVE 0.067 TO WS-FRATE.
```

is an imperative sentence, which tells the computer to assign the value 0.067 to the variable, WS–FCRATE. Statements 54 through 56,

```
IF I-JOBCODE IS EQUAL 1122
```

SELF-DOCUMENTING
A characteristic of a computer language whose statements are easy enough to understand so that English descriptions of the program steps are not necessary.

PORTABILITY
The ability to move a computer program from one type of computer to another.

Figure B–5
Payroll Program Written in COBOL

Notice how long this program is compared with the payroll-register programs of other languages. No wonder COBOL is considered wordy! This wordiness supposedly improves COBOL's readability. Examine the procedure division starting at statement 33, and determine whether you think COBOL is more understandable than the other languages discussed in this module.

```
         IDENTIFICATION DIVISION.
         PROGRAM-ID.
            PAYROLL.

         ENVIRONMENT DIVISION.
         CONFIGURATION SECTION.
         SPECIAL-NAMES.
            C01 IS TOP-OF-PAGE.
         INPUT-OUTPUT SECTION.
         FILE-CONTROL.
            SELECT CARD-IN-FILE ASSIGN TO UT-S-SYSIN.
            SELECT LINE-OUT-FILE ASSIGN TO UT-S-SYSOUT.

         DATA DIVISION.
         FILE SECTION.
         FD  CARD-IN-FILE
            LABEL RECORDS ARE OMITTED.
         01  CARD-IN-RECORD.
            05  I-JOBCODE          PICTURE X(4).
            05  I-EMPNO            PICTURE X(9).
            05  I-HOURS            PICTURE 999V99.
            05  I-RATE             PICTURE 99V99.
            05  FILLER             PICTURE X(58).
         FD  LINE-OUT-FILE
            LABEL RECORDS ARE OMITTED.
         01  LINE-OUT-RECORD        PICTURE X(133).
         WORKING-STORAGE SECTION.
1        77  WS-EXTRA              PICTURE 999V99.
         77  WS-OTIME              PICTURE 999V99.
         77  WS-TOTAL              PICTURE 999V99 VALUE ZEROES.
         77  WS-FCRATE             PICTURE 9V999.
         77  WS-FTRATE             PICTURE 9V999.
         77  WS-STRATE             PICTURE 9V999.
         77  WS-RTRATE             PICTURE 9V999.
         77  WS-CURATE             PICTURE 9V999.
         77  WS-WHRS               PICTURE 999V99.
         77  WS-GROSS              PICTURE 9999V99.
         77  WS-FICA               PICTURE 999V99.
         77  WS-FIT                PICTURE 999V99.
         77  WS-SIT                PICTURE 999V99.
         77  WS-CUNION             PICTURE 999V99.
         77  WS-RETIRE             PICTURE 999V99.
         77  WS-NET                PICTURE 9999V99.
2        01  OUT-OF-CARDS-FLAG     PICTURE X VALUE 'N'.
             88  OUT-OF-CARDS                 VALUE 'Y'.
3        01  FLAG                  PICTURE X VALUE 'N'.
         01  WS-DETAIL-LINE.
4            05  FILLER            PICTURE XXX VALUE SPACES.
             05  JOBCODE           PICTURE X(4).
5            05  FILLER            PICTURE X(5) VALUE SPACES.
             05  EMPNO             PICTURE X(9).
6            05  FILLER            PICTURE X(4) VALUE SPACES.
             05  HOURS             PICTURE ZZ9V99.
7            05  FILLER            PICTURE X(4) VALUE SPACES.
             05  RATE              PICTURE ZZ9V99.
8            05  FILLER            PICTURE X(4) VALUE SPACES.
             05  GROSS             PICTURE ZZZ9V99.
```

Figure B–5 (continued)

```
 9            05  FILLER             PICTURE X(5) VALUE SPACES.
              05  FICA               PICTURE ZZ9V99.
10            05  FILLER             PICTURE X(6) VALUE SPACES.
              05  FIT                PICTURE ZZ9V99.
11            05  FILLER             PICTURE X(4) VALUE  SPACES.
              05  SIT                PICTURE ZZ9V99.
12            05  FILLER             PICTURE X(4) VALUE SPACES.
              05  CUNION             PICTURE ZZ9V99.
13            05  FILLER             PICTURE X(6) VALUE SPACES.
              05  RETIRE             PICTURE ZZ9V99.
14            05  FILLER             PICTURE X(6) VALUE SPACES.
              05  NET                PICTURE ZZZ9V99.
15            05  FILLER             PICTURE X(14) VALUE SPACES.
          01  WS-HEADER-LINE.
16            05  FILLER             PICTURE X(51) VALUE SPACES.
              05  FILLER             PICTURE X(16)
17                VALUE 'Payroll Register'.
18            05  FILLER             PICTURE X(66) VALUE SPACES.
          01  WS-COL-LINE-1.
19            05 FILLER              PICTURE X(57) VALUE SPACES.
              05 FILLER              PICTURE X(28)
20                VALUE 'Social     Federal       State'.
21            05 FILLER              PICTURE X(58) VALUE SPACES.
          01  WS-COL-LINE-2.
22            05 FILLER              PICTURE XX VALUE SPACES.
              05 FILLER              PICTURE X(118)
23                VALUE 'Job       Employee     Hours    Hourly    Gross
     -            '  Security    Income     Income    Credit
     -            '               Net'.
24            05 FILLER              PICTURE X(16) VALUE SPACES.
          01  WS-COL-LINE-3.
25            05 FILLER              PICTURE XXX VALUE SPACES.
              05 FILLER              PICTURE X(117)
26                VALUE 'CODE       Number    Worked     Wage     Pay
     -            '     Tax         Tax        Tax     Union  Reti
     -            'rement     Pay'.
     -            'rement       Pay'.
27            05  FILLER             PICTURE X(16) VALUE SPACES.
          01  WS-FOOTER-LINE.
28            05  FILLER             PICTURE X(96) VALUE SPACES.
              05  FILLER             PICTURE X(16)
29                VALUE "Total Earnings:  '.
              05  TOTAL-EARNINGS     PICTURE ZZZZ9.99
30            05  FILLER             PICTURE X(14) VALUE SPACES.
31        01  EMPTY-LINE             PICTURE X(133) VALUE SPACES.
          01  ERROR-MSG              PICTURE X(21)
32            VALUE 'Invalid job code'.

33        PROCEDURE DIVISION.
          MAIN-LINE-ROUTINE.
34            OPEN INPUT CARD-IN-FILE
                   OUTPUT LINE-OUT-FILE.
35            PERFORM HEADER-PARAGRAPH.
36            READ CARD-IN-FILE
37                AT END MOVE 'Y' TO OUT-OF-CARDS-FLAG.
38            PERFORM PROCESS-PAYROLL
                   UNTIL OUT-OF-CARDS.
39            PERFORM FOOTER-PARAGRAPH.
40            CLOSE CARD-IN-FILE
                     LINE-OUT-FILE
          MAIN-LINE-ROUTINE-EXIT.
41            STOP RUN.
```

Figure B–5   (continued)

```
          HEADER-PARAGRAPH.
42            WRITE LINE-OUT-RECORD FROM WS-HEADER-LINE
                 AFTER ADVANCING TOP-OF-PAGE.
43            WRITE LINE-OUT-RECORD FROM WS-COL-LINE-1
                 AFTER ADVANCING 2 LINES.
44            WRITE LINE-OUT-RECORD FROM WS-COL-LINE-2
                 AFTER ADVANCING 1 LINES.
45            WRITE LINE-OUT-RECORD FROM WS-COL-LINE-3
                 AFTER ADVANCING 1 LINES.
46            WRITE LINE-OUT-RECORD FROM EMPTY-LINE
                 AFTER ADVANCING 1 LINES.
          PROCESS-PAYROLL.
47            MOVE 'Y' TO FLAG.
48            MOVE ZEROS TO WS-OTIME, WS-FCRATE, WS-FTRATE, WS-STRATE,
                          WS-RTRATE, WS-CURATE
49            MOVE I-HOURS TO WS-WHRS.
50            IF I-JOBCODE IS EQUAL 1111
                 THEN
51                   PERFORM JOBCODE-1111-PARA
                 ELSE
52               IF I-JOBCODE IS EQUAL 1120
                     THEN
53                       PERFORM JOBCODE-1120-PARA
                     ELSE
54                   IF I-JOBCODE IS EQUAL 1122
                         THEN
55                           PERFORM JOBCODE-1120-PARA
56                           PERFORM JOBCODE-1122-PARA.
57            PERFORM COMPUTE-PAYROLL-PARAGRAPH.
58            PERFORM WRITE-LINE-PARAGRAPH.
59            READ CARD-IN-FILE
60               AT END MOVE 'Y' TO OUT-OF-CARDS-FLAG.

          JOBCODE-1111-PARA.
61                MOVE 0.007 TO WS-FTRATE.
62                MOVE 0.008 TO WS-STRATE.
63                MOVE 'N' TO FLAG.

          JOBCODE-1120-PARA.
64            MOVE 0.067 TO WS-FCRATE.
65            MOVE 0.113 TO WS-FTRATE.
66            MOVE 0.03  TO WS-STRATE.
67            MOVE 0.05  TO WS-RTRATE.
68            IF I-HOURS  IS  GREATER THAN 40.0
                 THEN
69                   SUBTRACT 40.0 FROM I-HOURS GIVING WS-EXTRA
70                   COMPUTE WS-OTIME ROUNDED =
                             WS-EXTRA * I-RATE * 1.5
71                MOVE 40.0 TO WS-WHRS.
72            MOVE 'N' TO FLAG

          JOBCODE-1122-PARA.
73            MOVE 0.05 TO WS-CURATE.
74            MOVE 'N' TO FLAG.

          COMPUTE-PAYROLL-PARAGRAPH.
75            COMPUTE WS-GROSS ROUNDED = (WS-WHRS * I-RATE) +WS-OTIME.
76            MULTIPLY WS-GROSS BY WS-FCRATE GIVING WS-FICA ROUNDED.
77            MULTIPLY WS-GROSS BY WS-FTRATE GIVING WS-FIT  ROUNDED.
78            MULTIPLY WS-GROSS BY WS-STRATE GIVING WS-SIT  ROUNDED.
79            MULTIPLY WS-GROSS BY WS-RTRATE GIVING WS-RETIRE ROUNDED.
80            MULTIPLY WS-GROSS BY WS-CURATE GIVING WS-CUNION ROUNDED.
```

Figure B–5   (continued)

```
81              COMPUTE WS-NET = WS-GROSS -
                      (WS-FICA + WS-FIT + WS-SIT + WS-RETIRE + WS-CUNION)
82              ADD WS-NET TO WS-TOTAL.
                WRITE-LINE-PARAGRAPH
83                  IF FLAG = 'N'
                    THEN
84                      MOVE I-JOBCODE TO JOBCODE
85                      MOVE I-EMPNO TO EMPNO
86                      MOVE I-HOURS TO HOURS
87                      MOVE I-RATE TO RATE
88                      MOVE WS-GROSS TO GROSS
89                      MOVE WS-FICA TO FICA
90                      MOVE WS-FIT TO FIT
91                      MOVE WS-SIT TO SIT
92                      MOVE WS-CUNION TO CUNION
93                      MOVE WS-RETIRE TO RETIRE
94                      MOVE WS-NET TO NET
95                      WRITE LINE-OUT-RECORD FROM WS-DETAIL-LINE
                            AFTER ADVANCING 1 LINES
                    ELSE
96                      WRITE LINE-OUT-RECORD FROM ERROR-MSG
                            AFTER ADVANCING 1 LINES.

                FOOTER-PARAGRAPH.
97                  MOVE WS-TOTAL TO TOTAL-EARNINGS.
98                  WRITE LINE-OUT-RECORD FROM WS-FOOTER-LINE
                        AFTER ADVANCING 2 LINES.
99                  WRITE LINE-OUT-RECORD FROM EMPTY-LINE
                        AFTER ADVANCING TOP-OF-PAGE.
```

```
        THEN
            PERFORM JOBCODE-1120-PARA
            PERFORM JOBCODE-1122-PARA.
```

are statements that form a conditional sentence where

```
PERFORM JOBCODE-1120-PARA.
```

is a statement beginning with the verb PERFORM. A statement is a combination of **words,** symbols, and phrases beginning with a COBOL verb. COBOL words are of three types:

1. Reserved words have special meaning to the compiler. The COBOL verbs COMPUTE, ADD, and SUBTRACT are examples.

2. User-defined words are created by the programmer. Examples (in Figure B–5) are CARD-IN-FILE, LINE-OUT-FILE, and MAIN-LINE-ROUTINE.

3. System names are supplied by the hardware manufacturer to allow certain elements in the program to correspond with various hardware devices. Examples are UT-S-SYSIN specifying the card reader, and UT-S = SYSOUT specifying the line printer in the input-output section of the environment division in Figure B–5.

COBOL is a very standardized language and therefore can be used by different kinds of computers fairly easily. The advantage of COBOL is that it was conceived especially for data processing. It can manipulate many types of data files, and it is much more readable and self-documenting than most languages. However, efficiency in terms of coding and actual execution is sacrificed because of its wordiness. Also, because of the nature of the syntax of COBOL, **semantic errors** can occur that are very difficult to detect. For report generation, COBOL can be an extremely useful tool because of its report-writer facility. COBOL has limited facilities for mathematical notation but excellent capabilities for character and file processing. COBOL compilers are available for personal computers.

PL/I PL/I (Programming Language/I) is a comprehensive language with a wide variety of applications. PL/I can be used for scientific, business data processing, text processing, and system applications. The language was developed in the 1960s when programmers were divided into three distinct groups: scientific, business/commercial, and special-purpose.

IBM, along with SHARE and GUIDE (a scientific user group and a commercial user group, respectively), developed PL/I with the following objectives in mind:

1. Machine independence.
2. Access to the machine's operating system.
3. Structured and modular programs.
4. Easy-to-learn language.
5. Readable and easy-to-write code.
6. A bridging of the gap between commercial and scientific high-level languages.

In 1964 the specifications for the language were presented to GUIDE and SHARE. The specifications incorporated features from FORTRAN, COBOL, and ALGOL (expressive algebraic language). Although PL/I met the objectives, it is not as widely used as FORTRAN and COBOL. The language was standardized by ANSI in 1976 after further development.

A PL/I program consists of statements separated by semicolons (see Figure B–6). Being a **block-structured language,** PL/I programs are headed by labeled statements and terminated by an END statement. The header statement in Figure B–6 is statement 1:

```
payroll:PROCEDURE OPTIONS (MAIN);
```

where "payroll" is the program name. Another major block resides within the program, and it must also be headed by a labeled statement (statement 42). This block of statements is called an **internal subroutine.**

The most widely used statements are discussed next by statement type.

Data Definition Data elements are introduced into a PL/I program through the use of the DECLARE statement. This statement specifies the data element, its data type, and its precision level. For example,

```
DECLARE total FIXED DECIMAL (6,2)  INITIAL (0)
```

tells the PL/I compiler that the variable "total" has a type of fixed decimal (for business applications) and a *precision* as follows:

```
XXXXVXX
```

PRECISION
The number of digits that a number is allowed to have.

where the "X"s are numeric digits and "V" is an implied decimal point. The initial value of zero is also placed in the variable at compilation time.

Figure B-6
Payroll Program Written in PL/I

PL/I is a structured programming language. Statement 12, the DO-WHILE, is a structured loop that ends with statement 40. Statements 12 through 40 are executed over and over until an end-of-file (eof) is encountered in the input file.

```
 1      payroll:PROCEDURE OPTIONS (MAIN);
 2          DECLARE empno                           FIXED DECIMAL (9),
                    (fcrate,ftrate,strate,curate,
                    rtrate)                         FIXED DECIMAL (4,3),
                    (extra,otime,hours,whrs,fica,
                    fit,sit,cunion,retire)          FIXED DECIMAL (5,2),
                    rate                            FIXED DECIMAL (4,2),
                    (gross,net)                     FIXED DECIMAL (6,2),
                    total                           FIXED DECIMAL (6,2)
                                                        INITIAL (0),
                    jobcode                         FIXED DECIMAL (4);
 3          DECLARE(eof,no)                         BIT(1) INITIAL ('0'B),
                    yes                             BIT(1) INITIAL ('1'B);
 4          DECLARE sysin                           FILE STREAM INPUT,
                    sysprint                        FILE STREAM OUTPUT;
 5          ON ENDFILE (sysin) eof = yes;
 6          PUT PAGE EDIT ('Payroll Register')(X(50),A);
 7          PUT SKIP(2) EDIT ('Social      Federal      State')(X(56),A);
 8          PUT SKIP EDIT ('Job','Employee','Hours','Hourly','Gross',
                    'Security','Income','Income','Credit','Net')
                        (X(1),A,X(5),A,X(5),A,X(4),A,X(5),A,X(5),A,X(5),A,
                        X(4),A,X(4),A,X(20),A);
 9          PUT SKIP EDIT ('Code','Number','Worked','Wage','Pay','Tax','Tax',
                    'Tax','Union','Retirement','Pay')
                        (X(2),A,X(7),A,X(5),A,X(5),A,X(7),A,X(8),A,X(9),A,
                        X(8),A,X(6),A,X(4),A,X(6),A);
10          PUT SKIP;
11          GET SKIP EDIT (jobcode,empno,hours,rate)(f(4),f(9),f(5,2),f(4,2));
12          DO WHILE (eof = no);
13              otime = 0.0;
14              whrs = hours;
15              fcrate = 0.0;
16              ftrate = 0.0;
17              strate = 0.0;
18              rtrate = 0.0;
19              curate = 0.0;
20              IF jobcode = 1111
                    THEN DO;
21                      ftrate = 0.007;
22                      strate = 0.008;
23                      CALL calc_payroll;
24                      END;
25                  ELSE
                IF jobcode = 1120 | jobcode = 1122
                    THEN DO;
26                      fcrate=0.067;
27                      ftrate=0.113;
28                      strate=0.03;
29                      rtrate=0.05;
30                      IF jobcode=1122
                            THEN curate=0.05;
31                      IF hours > 40.0
                            THEN DO;
32                          extra = hours - 40.0;
33                          otime = extra * rate * 1.5;
34                          whrs = 40.0;
35                          END;
36                      CALL calc_payroll;
37                      END;
```

Figure B–6 (continued)

```
38              ELSE
                  PUT SKIP EDIT ('Invalid Job Code.')(X(3),A);
39              GET SKIP EDIT (jobcode,empno,hours,rate)
                              (f(4),f(9),f(5,2),f(4,2));
40      END;
41      PUT SKIP(2) EDIT ('Total Earnings: ',TOTAL)(X(96),A,F(7,2));
42  calc_payroll:PROCEDURE;
43      gross = (whrs * rate) + otime;
44      fica = gross * fcrate;
45      fit = gross * ftrate;
46      sit = gross * strate;
47      retire = gross * rtrate;
48      cunion = gross * curate;
49      net = gross - (fica + fit + sit + retire + cunion);
50      total = total + net;
51      PUT SKIP EDIT (jobcode,empno,hours,rate,gross,fica,fit,sit,cunion,
                       retire,net)(X(2),F(4),X(5),F(9),X(4),F(6,2),X(4),
                       F(6,2),X(4),F(7,2),X(5),F(6,2),X(6),F(6,2),X(4),
                       F(6,2),X(4),F(6,2),X(6),F(6,2),X(6),F(7,2));
52  RETURN;
53  END;

54  END;
```

Control Statements   Statements that control the flow of execution through the program in Figure B–6 are as follows:

1. The IF-THEN-ELSE statement.
2. The DO-WHILE statement.

The IF-THEN-ELSE was introduced in the FORTRAN section. Statement 12 is the beginning of a DO-WHILE which will perform the statements up to statement 40, the END statement, until the end of the input file is reached. In other words, the DO-WHILE is a repetitive loop in which statements are executed while the condition in statement 12 is being met.

Input/Output Statements   Examples of input/output statements in Figure B–6 are the GET EDIT and the PUT EDIT statements. Statement 11 is an **edit-directed** input statement, which means the programmer must tell the computer how the data are arranged when they are read into the program. Statements 6 through 10 are edit-directed output statements. Again, the programmer specifies the layout of the data to be printed.

Assignment Statements   The assignment statement is in the following form:

   variable = expression;

where the expression specifies that a particular computation takes place, and the results of the computation are assigned to the variable to the left of the equal sign.

For the novice programmer, PL/I is easy to learn because of its *default* features. If the programmer is vague in specifying any features within the program, the compiler assumes (defaults to) the most frequently used

DEFAULT
An alternative value, attribute, or option that is assumed when none has been specified.

specifications. Also, PL/I is well-suited for the experienced programmer because the language is designed so that the programmer can better utilize the resources of the computer.

PL/I has substantial character-handling facilities and is well-suited for business data processing. Like COBOL, PL/I has very good file-handling characteristics, but PL/I is not limited to particular types of applications as COBOL is. PL/I is a powerful language; however, efficiency in terms of compilation time, execution, and storage is sacrificed for this power.

PL/I is not generally available on microprocessors owing to the size of the compiler, although variations (PL/M and MPL) are available.

BASIC   BASIC (Basic All-Purpose Symbolic Instruction Code) is a programming language that has been implemented on virtually every type of computer—from the smallest micro to the largest mainframe. BASIC was conceived in 1963 and implemented in 1964 at Dartmouth College. The language was designed as an easy-to-learn, easy-to-use, interactive language, with no particular application area targeted. BASIC was created because of the trend away from batch processing toward *interactive* systems.

There are many versions of BASIC that have the essence of the Dartmouth version in their design. An effort to standardize BASIC began in 1970, and an ANSI standard was established in 1978. Although a standard does exist, the term BASIC refers to a classification of the language, not to the particular, standard version.

As previously stated, BASIC is an easy language to use, once the following core statements have been learned. These statements are used in almost every version of BASIC implemented. Refer to Figure B–7.

Data-Definition Statements   The data-definition statement DIM is used to define arrays, and DEF is used to define functions in the program.

Control Statements   Control of the flow of execution is performed by the GO-TO, IF-THEN, FOR-NEXT, and GOSUB-RETURN statements. The GO TO statement causes an unconditional branching to a designated statement. The IF-THEN statement (see statement 230 in Figure B–7) causes a conditional two-way branching. The FOR-NEXT construct allows for repetitive looping. The statements are executed at least once before the condition is tested. In other words, there is no pretest of the condition. The GOSUB used in conjunction with a RETURN, allows modularity through the use of subroutines. The statements between the referenced statement in the GO-SUB, and the RETURN are executed, and the flow of execution returns to the statement following the GOSUB.

Input/Output Statements   Input of data is performed either by the INPUT statement for interactive mode, or the READ statement (see statement 220) for batch mode. The READ statement reads in the data contained in the DATA statements (see statements 640 through 681). Output is performed by the PRINT statement, which sends output back to the terminal.

Assignment/Arithmetic Statements   Assignment and arithmetic statements are similar to those in FORTRAN, except these statements are prefixed with the key word LET (see statement 460). The syntax is as follows:

INTERACTIVE
An application in which each entry calls forth a response from a system or program, as in an inquiry system or an airline-reservation system. An interactive system may also be conversational, implying a continuous dialogue between the user and the system.

Figure B–7
Payroll Program Written in BASIC

Notice this is the shortest program in the module. Because of this conciseness and the lack of structured programming statements, BASIC programs can be difficult to read. Readability can be improved by liberal use of REM statements in the program (for example, statements 340 and 380).

```
100     PRINT TAB(51),'Payroll Register'
101     PRINT ' '
110     PRINT TAB(57),'Social',TAB(68),'Federal',TAB(80),'State'
120     PRINT ' '
130     PRINT TAB(2),'Job',TAB(13),'Employee',TAB(26),'Hours',TAB(35),
140     PRINT 'Hourly',TAB(46),'Gross',TAB(56),'Security',TAB(69),'Income',
150     PRINT TAB(79),'Income',TAB(89),'Credit',TAB(115),'Net'
160     PRINT TAB(3),'Code',TAB(14),'Number',TAB(25),'Worked',TAB(36),
170     PRINT 'Wage',TAB(47),'Pay',TAB(58),'Tax',TAB(70),'Tax',TAB(81),
180     PRINT 'Tax',TAB(90),'Union',TAB(99),'Retirement',TAB(115),'Pay'
190     PRINT ' '
200     LET T =   0.0
210     REM......read in job code,empno, hours, and hourly rate
220     READ O1,E1,H,R3
230     IF O1 = 0.0 THEN 580
240        LET W = H
250        LET O2 = 0.0
260        LET F1 = 0.0
270        LET F2 = 0.0
280        LET S1 = 0.0
290        LET R1 = 0.0
300        IF O1 = 1111 THEN 340
310        IF O1 = 1120 THEN 400
320        IF O1 = 1122 THEN 380
330        GO TO 610
340     REM....for job code 1111
350        LET F2 = 0.007
360        LET S1 = 0.008
370        GO TO 450
380     REM....for job code 1122
390        C1 = 0.05
400     REM....for job code 1120 and 1122
410        F1 = 0.067
420        F2 = 0.113
430        S1 = 0.03
440        R1 = 0.05
450     REM....calculate payroll and print line
460        LET G = (W * R3) + O2
470        LET F3 = G * F1
480        LET F4 = G * F2
490        LET S2 = G * S1
500        LET C2 = G * C1
510        LET R2 = G * R1
520        LET N = G - (F3 + F4 + S2 + C2 + R2)
530        LET T = T + N
540        PRINT TAB(3),O1,TAB(12),E1,TAB(25),H,TAB(35),R3,TAB(45),G,
550        PRINT TAB(57),F3,TAB(69),F4,TAB(79),S2,TAB(89),R2,TAB(101),C2,
560        PRINT TAB(113),N
570     GO TO 210
580     REM....write total net earnings
590     PRINT TAB(96),'Total Earnings: ',TAB(117),T
600     GO TO 690
610     REM ....write error message
620     PRINT TAB(3),'Invalid job code.'
630     REM ....data cards
640     DATA 1111, 400941648, 33.00, 4.51,
650     DATA 1122, 224949460, 40.00, 5.10,
660     DATA 1120, 900221792, 44.00, 4.51,
```

Figure B–7 (continued)

```
670     DATA 1122, 224885493, 45.00, 7.25,
680     DATA 1111, 900120001, 25.00, 3.25,
681     DATA 0, 0, 0, 0
690     END
```

LET variable = expression

Comment Statements   Figure B–7 also includes REMARK statements (abbreviated REM). A REM statement is used when the programmer internally documents the program.

BASIC is used, with much innovation, on most microcomputers. Even though BASIC is standardized, many versions are available. Consequently, the **portability** of the language (the transferability of programs from one machine to another) is low. In other words, one version of BASIC may not be compatible with a compiler or interpreter of another version. BASIC is very popular with users of small computers even though it is an unstructured language and has very limited screen-handling facilities. A major reason for this popularity is that the language is easy to learn and is applicable to many areas, from a simple arithmetic program to a complicated file-handling system. However, the availability of these capabilities depends on the BASIC version being used.

PASCAL   The programming language **PASCAL** (named after Blaise Pascal, a French mathematician) was developed as an educational tool to encourage the writing of well-structured, readable programs. It is adaptable to business and scientific applications and is considered a simple, yet versatile language. PASCAL was first implemented in 1970 in Zurich, Switzerland. The PASCAL design is very similar to ALGOL-60 (as is PL/I). PASCAL was intended to be a low-cost, student-oriented language. By low cost, we are speaking in terms of storage and processing time.

PASCAL, like PL/I, is a block-structured language (see Figure B–8). It consists of groups of statements enclosed within a BEGIN statement (statement 24) and an END statement (statement 76). Header statements are needed for a major block of code. In Figure B–8, the statement:

```
PROGRAM payroll (INPUT,OUTPUT);
```

is needed for the main program. As in PL/I, the internal procedure (located at the beginning of the PASCAL program) must also have a header statement (statement 9). Note that the procedure is also enclosed with BEGIN and END statements.

PASCAL is similar to PL/I in statement structure; however, there are minor differences in the use of the BEGIN and END statements, and PASCAL uses semicolons as statement separators instead of as statement terminators.

Data-Definition Statements   Data within a PASCAL program may be introduced through the use of the VAR statement (statements 2 through 7). The

Figure B–8
Payroll Program Written in PASCAL

PASCAL is also a structured programming language. Notice the WHILE-NOT statement (no. 37) and the IF-THEN-ELSE
starting with statement 47.

```
  1 |       PROGRAM payroll (INPUT,OUTPUT);
  2 |          VAR
  3 |             empno,jobcode : INTEGER;
  4 |             fcrate,ftrate,strate,curate,rtrate : REAL;
  5 |             extra,otime,hours,whrs,rate : REAL;
  6 |             fica,fit,sit,cunion,retire : REAL;
  7 |             gross,net,total : REAL;
  8 |
  9 |       PROCEDURE calculate_payroll;
 10 |          BEGIN
 11 |             gross := (whrs * rate) + otime;
 12 |             fica := gross * fcrate;
 13 |             fit := gross * ftrate;
 14 |             sit := gross * strate;
 15 |             retire := gross * rtrate;
 16 |             cunion := gross * curate;
 17 |             net := gross - (fica + fit + sit + retire + cunion);
 18 |             total := total + net;
 19 |             WRITELN (jobcode:6,empno:14,hours:10:2,rate:10:2,gross:11:2,
 20 |                      fica:11:2,fit:11:2,sit:11:2,cunion:10:2,retire:12:2,
 21 |                      net:13:2)
 22 |          END;
 23 |
 24 |          BEGIN
 25 |             total :=0.0;
 26 |             PAGE;
 27 |             WRITELN ('Payroll Register':66);
 28 |             WRITELN (' ');
 29 |             WRITELN ('Social       Federal       State':84);
 30 |             WRITELN ('Job' :7,'Employee':13,'Hours':10,'Hourly':10,
 31 |                      'Gross':10,'Security':13,'Income':11,'Income':10,
 32 |                      'Credit':10,'Net':23);
 33 |             WRITELN ('Code':6,'Number':13,'Worked':11,'Wage':9,'Pay':10,
 34 |                      'Tax':11,'Tax':12,'Tax':11,'Union':11,'Retirement':14,
 35 |                      'Pay':9);
 36 |             WRITELN (' ');
 37 |             WHILE NOT EOF DO
 38 |                BEGIN
 39 |                   READLN (jobcode,empno,hours,rate);
 40 |                   otime := 0.0;
 41 |                   whrs := hours
 42 |                   fcrate := 0.0;
 43 |                   ftrate := 0.0;
 44 |                   strate := 0.0;
 45 |                   rtrate := 0.0;
 46 |                   curate := 0.0;
 47 |                   IF jobcode = 1111
 48 |                   THEN BEGIN
 49 |                      ftrate := 0.007;
 50 |                      strate := 0.008;
 51 |                      calculate_payroll
 52 |                          END
 53 |                   ELSE
 54 |                 IF (jobcode = 1120) OR (jobcode = 1122)
 55 |                   THEN BEGIN
 56 |                      fcrate := 0.067;
 57 |                      ftrate := 0.113;
 58 |                      strate := 0.03;
 59 |                      rtrate := 0.05;
```

Figure B–8   (continued)

```
60 |                        IF jobcode = 1122
61 |                           THEN curate := 0.05;
62 |                        IF hours > 40.0
63 |                           THEN BEGIN
64 |                               extra := hours - 40.0;
65 |                               otime := extra * rate * 1.5;
66 |                               whrs := 40.0
67 |                                  END;
68 |                        calculate_payroll
69 |                           END
70 |                ELSE WRITELN ('Invalid Job Code.':24);
71 |            END;
72 |        WRITELN (' ');
73 |        WRITELN ('Total Earnings: ':110.total:9:2);
74 |        PAGE;
75 |        WRITELN (' ')
76 |    END.
```

programmer can specify the **data type** of the variables as REAL, INTEGER, CHARACTER, or BOOLEAN. The language has strong data-structuring capabilities provided by the compiler, making less work for the programmer. In other words, the programmer does not include precision levels for the variables when declaring them, as is done in PL/I.

Control Statements   Statements that control the flow of execution in a PASCAL program are as follows:

1. The IF-THEN-ELSE statement.
2. The WHILE-DO statement.
3. The REPEAT-UNTIL statement.
4. The CASE statement.

The IF-THEN-ELSE and WHILE-DO were illustrated in previous sections. The REPEAT-UNTIL is similar to the WHILE-DO in that it is a repetitive loop. However, the statements within the loop are executed before the condition is checked. Therefore, the statements are always executed at least once. The CASE statement is similar to a series of IF-THEN-ELSE statements. A certain path through the program is taken, depending on which multiple condition is true.

Input/Output Statements   Input into a PASCAL program is done by utilizing READ or READLN statements. The READ statement reads until a blank character appears in the input file, whereas the READLN reads the input until the end of the line or card image. Data types are checked by the system, so the programmer need not specify the format of the input file as with PL/I.

Output is performed through the use of WRITE or WRITELN statements. The WRITE statement writes the data out to the output device, one data element at a time, without moving to the next output line. Therefore, the next output statement places the data on the same line immediately following the previous data element. The WRITELN writes the data out to the output device, then moves to a new line. Thus when the next output statement is encountered, the data will be written on the next line.

Assignment/Arithmetic Statements   The syntax of the assignment statement in PASCAL is as follows:

variable   : =   expression;

The assignment statement is essentially the same as that used in PL/I, except the assignment operator is ": =" as illustrated in Figure B–8, statements 11 through 18.

PASCAL is an excellent language for a microcomputer because its compiler is of a manageable size, and it is cost-efficient in terms of memory allocation. Other factors are the language's simplicity, versatility, fast execution time, and character-manipulation capabilities. PASCAL is fairly standardized (de facto). The language is also extremely compact in that there are few reserved words to learn. A disadvantage of PASCAL is its poor character-handling facilities. The language only processes one character at a time, requiring the use of arrays which can be very cumbersome.

ADA   From 1975 to 1979, progressively comprehensive specifications were developed by the U.S. Department of Defense (DOD) for a new programming language. As a result of this effort, in 1979, **ADA** was designed (named for Augusta Ada Byron, the first programmer; see Module A). ADA, based on PASCAL, was created for the DOD as a portable, well-structured language to be used primarily in a multiprocessor environment for scientific and system programming. The language was developed because the DOD needed a common language to meet its programming needs. Thus ADA is versatile enough to be used in a wide variety of applications.

ADA is a block-structured language that provides for a strict form of modular programming. All major blocks of code are headed by declarative statements and are set off by BEGIN-END statements. Subroutines are located at the beginning of the program, as shown in Figure B–9. Modularity is enhanced through the use of modules that can be written and compiled separately from the main procedure. **Modules** are collections of variables, constants, statements, subroutines, or other modules. Modules are of two types:

1. Packages—logical collections of entities (declarations, statements, procedures, et cetera) that cover a certain logical aspect of the application.
2. Tasks—independent collections of statements that are executed in the order required by the system, without any dependency or order among the tasks. These tasks facilitate the multiprocessor environment.

ADA is similar to PASCAL in syntax, but there are minor variations. The language uses **terminating keywords** (END IF, END LOOP, END CASE) in place of BEGIN-END statements, and semicolons are used as statement terminators as in PL/I, not as statement separators as in PASCAL.

Data-Definition Statements   In ADA, data types are declared in the data-definition statements. This feature was inherited from PASCAL. The declaration statements for variables are in the form:

Figure B–9
Payroll Program Written in ADA

Notice the similarity of this ADA program to the PASCAL program shown in Figure B—8.

```
 1 |         WITH TEXT_IO; USING TEXT_IO;
 2 |         PROCEDURE payroll IS
 3 |            PRAGMA MAIN;
 4 |               empno Jobcode : INTEGER;
 5 |               fcrate,ftrate,strate,curate,rtrate : FIXED;
 6 |               extra,otime,hours,whrs,rate : FIXED;
 7 |               fica,fit,sit,cunion,retire : FIXED;
 8 |               gross,net,total : FIXED;
 9 |
10 |         PROCEDURE calculate_payroll IS
11 |            BEGIN
12 |               gross :=(whrs * rate) + otime;
13 |               fica := gross * fcrate;
14 |               fit := gross * ftrate;
15 |               sit := gross * strate;
16 |               retire := gross * rtrate;
17 |               cunion := gross * curate;
18 |               net := gross - (fica + fit + sit + retire + cunion);
19 |               total := total + net;
20 |               PUT (jobcode,6);
21 |               PUT (empno,14);
22 |               PUT (hours,10,2);
23 |               PUT (rate,10,2);
24 |               PUT (gross,11,2);
25 |               PUT (fica,11,2);
26 |               PUT (fit,11,2);
27 |               PUT (sit,11,2);
28 |               PUT (cunion,10,2);
29 |               PUT (retire,12,2);
30 |               PUT (net,13,2);
31 |               PUT (NEWLINE);
32 |            END;
33 |
34 |            BEGIN
35 |               total := 0.0;
36 |               PUT ('Payroll Register',66);
37 |               PUT (NEWLINE);
38 |               PUT ('  ');
39 |               PUT (NEWLINE);
40 |               PUT ('Social      Federal      State',84);
41 |               PUT (NEWLINE);
42 |               PUT ('Job      Employee      Hours      Hourly',40);
43 |               PUT ('      Gross      Security      Income      Income',44);
44 |               PUT ('      Credit                Net',33);
45 |               PUT (NEWLINE);
46 |               PUT (' Code      Number      Worked      Wage' ,39);
47 |               PUT ('      Pay      Tax      Tax      Tax',43);
48 |               PUT ('      Union  Retirement      Pay',34);
49 |               PUT (NEWLINE);
50 |               PUT ('  ');
51 |               PUT (NEWLINE);
52 |               WHILE NOT END_OF_FILE LOOP
53 |                    GETLN (jobcode,empno,hours,rate);
54 |                    otime := 0.0;
55 |                    whrs := hours;
56 |                    fcrate :=0.0;
57 |                    ftrate :=0.0;
58 |                    strate := 0.0;
59 |                    rtrate := 0.0;
60 |                    curate := 0.0;
```

Figure B–9 (continued)

```
61 |                        IF jobcode = 1111 THEN
62 |                            ftrate := 0.007;
63 |                            strate := 0.008;
64 |                            calculate_payroll;
65 |                        ELSIF jobcode = 1120 OR jobcode = 1122 THEN
66 |                            fcrate := 0.067;
67 |                            ftrate := 0.113;
68 |                            strate := 0.03;
69 |                            rtrate := 0.05;
70 |                            IF jobcode = 1122 THEN
71 |                                Curate := 0.05;
72 |                            END_IF;
73 |                            IF hours > 40.0 THEN
74 |                                extra := hours - 40.0;
75 |                                otime := extra * rate * 1.5;
76 |                                whrs := 40.0;
77 |                            END_IF;
78 |                            calculate_payroll;
79 |                        ELSE
80 |                            PUT_LINE ('Invalid Job Code.',24);
81 |                        END_IF;
82 |                    END_LOOP;
83 |              PUT ('  ');
84 |              PUT (NEWLINE);
85 |              PUT ('Total Earnings: ',110);
86 |              PUT (total,9,2);
87 |              PUT (NEWLINE);
88 |              PUT ('  ');
89 |              PUT (NEWLINE);
90 |          END payroll;
```

variable : data type;

Examples in Figure B–9 are statements 4 through 8.

Control Statements Statements that control the flow of execution in an ADA program are as follows:

1. The IF-THEN-ELSIF-ELSE statement.
2. The LOOP statement.
3. The WHILE-LOOP statement.
4. The FOR-LOOP statement.
5. The CASE-OF statement.

The IF-THEN-ELSE statement (statements 61 through 81) is similar to other languages; however, a new keyword ELSIF is used. The ELSIF allows for nested conditional statements. The LOOP is an infinite repetitive loop terminated only by the EXIT statement, which flags an exception. This loop would be used in a program that constantly monitors an apparatus or device. The WHILE-LOOP statement (statement 52) performs a pretest before executing the repetition, and the FOR-LOOP statement is an iterative repetition that is controlled by counting. The CASE-OF statement is similar to the CASE statement used in PASCAL.

Input/Output Statements ADA provides a package for input/output facilities. Subroutine calls are used for input/output functions. All text output in Figure B–9 is performed by the procedure PUT (statements 20 through 31), which is similar to the WRITE in PASCAL. This procedure uses parameters specifying variable types and the layout of these variables. Input of data is performed by the procedure GET, which is equivalent to the READ in PASCAL. In Figure B–9, input is performed by the GETLIN procedure (statement 53), which is equivalent to the READLN in PASCAL.

Assignment/Arithmetic Statements The syntax of the assignment statement in ADA is as follows:

```
<<label>> variable := expression;
```

where the statement *label,* enclosed in double-angle brackets, is optional.

ADA is a versatile and up-to-date language incorporating new technology and experiences of other languages. Therefore, it is an efficient, modular language that is very flexible. However, ADA is a complex language to learn and use, a disadvantage that may outweigh the advantages.

Fourth-Generation Languages

A **fourth-generation language (4GL)** is a flexible development tool that enables users and programmers to develop applications by describing to the computer what they want rather than by writing a procedural program. A procedural program specifies the detail steps that a program must execute. Because 4GLs do not specify the detail steps, they are often called **nonprocedural languages.** Examples of fourth-generation languages include electronic spreadsheets, query languages, and application generators.

Many fourth-generation languages are available, and they execute on all sizes of computers. Fourth-generation languages are one of the primary reasons that application development by users is possible. This section examines three 4GLs: FOCUS, dBASE, and RPG.

FOCUS FOCUS was developed in the mid-1970s by Information Builders. Initially, it could be used only on IBM mainframes. However, today it can execute on a wide variety of mainframes, minis, and personal computers, and it is the most widely used 4GL of its type. FOCUS is best classified as an application development tool that is suitable for both programmers and end users.

FOCUS has data storage, data maintenance, and data analysis capabilities. In data storage, it has a complete data-base facility that stores data in a hierarchical, a relational, or a combination of hierarchical and relational forms. A master file description is used in FOCUS to establish a data base. Figure B–10 illustrates a master file description of an employee file. This file is hierarchical, with segments on two levels, as illustrated in Figure B–11. FOCUS also has an interactive facility called FILETALK, which creates a master file description for the user. This facility interactively asks the user for the information required in a master file description and simultaneously creates the description at the bottom of the display screen. FOCUS also accesses data stored in a wide variety of non-FOCUS data bases and files, such

Figure B-10
FOCUS Master File Description of an Employee File

```
                    FILE=EMPLOYEE,SUFFIX=FOC

                    SEGNAME=EMPINFO,SEGTYPE=S1
                        FIELDNAME=EMP_ID        ,ALIAS=EID,FORMAT=A9      ,$
Employee                FIELDNAME=LAST NAME     ,ALIAS=LN ,FORMAT=A15     ,$
Information             FIELDNAME=FIRST NAME    ,ALIAS=FN ,FORMAT=A10     ,$
                        FIELDNAME=DEPARTMENT    ,ALIAS=DPT,FORMAT=A10     ,$

                    SEGNAME=PAYINFO,PARENT=EMPINFO,SEGTYPE=SH1
Pay                     FIELDNAME=DAT_INC       ,ALIAS=DI ,FORMAT=I6YMD   ,$
Information             FIELDNAME=PCT_INCREASE,ALIAS=PI ,FORMAT=F6.2,     ,$
                        FIELDNAME=SALARY        ,ALIAS=SAL,FORMAT=D12.2M  ,$
                        FIELDNAME=JOBCODE       ,ALIAS=JC ,FORMAT=A8      ,$

                    SEGNAME=ADDRESS,PARENT=EMPINFO,SEGTYPE=S1
                        FIELDNAME=ADDRESS_TYPE,ALIAS=AT ,FORMAT=A4      ,$
Address                 FIELDNAME=ADDRESS_LN  ,ALIAS=A  ,FORMAT=A20     ,$
Information             FIELDNAME=ADDRESS_LN  ,ALIAS=A  ,FORMAT=A20     ,$
                        FIELDNAME=ADDRESS_LN  ,ALIAS=A  ,FORMAT=A20     ,$

                    SEGNAME=UNION,PARENT=EMPINFO,SEGTYPE=U
Union                   FIELDNAME=UNION_ID      ,ALIAS=UI ,FORMAT=A6      ,$
Information             FIELDNAME=DATE_ENTERED,ALIAS=DE ,FORMAT=I6YMD   ,$
                        FIELDNAME=UNION_LOCAL ,ALIAS=UL ,FORMAT=A6      ,$
```

as IBM's Information Management System (IMS) data-base management system.

In the data maintenance area, FOCUS has complete transaction processing facilities. Input data may be validated and logged before files are updated. Transaction data may originate from disk, tape, or online terminals. FIDEL (FOCUS Interactive Data Entry Language) enables the user to easily develop formatted screens for online data entry and display.

Figure B–11
Hierarchical Structure of the Employee File in Figure B–10.

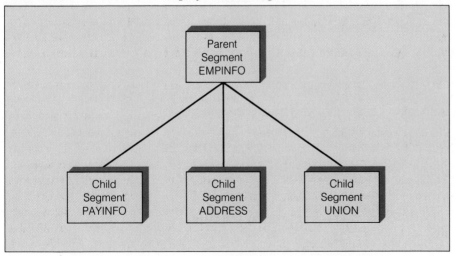

The data analysis and reporting facilities of FOCUS allow reports, queries, monochrome and color graphics, statistical analysis, and financial modeling. FOCUS also has its own electronic spreadsheet, called FOCCALC.

Reports are produced in FOCUS through the TABLE command. Figure B–12 illustrates a FOCUS procedure that produces the same payroll register as the procedural programs described earlier. First, notice how short this procedure is compared to the procedural programs. FOCUS automatically handles many of the details that COBOL and other languages require a programmer to specify at great length. In the first part of the procedure, the programmer used the DEFINE FILE PAYFILE ADD command to create temporary files to hold the appropriate rates for taxes, retirement, and union dues. These rates vary, depending on the employee's job code. FOCUS allows the IF-THEN-ELSE selection logic for the rates to be coded directly in the arithmetic assignment statements, as illustrated.

The command TABLE FILE PAYFILE produces the payroll register. First, the user prints the report heading. Then, the user tells FOCUS which data fields to print in each column of the report. Notice that most of the fields are computed in the PRINT command with the COMPUTE verb. The column headings for EMPNO, HOURS, and RATE are picked up from headings entered in the master file description. Column headings for the computed fields are entered in the COMPUTE statement with the AS phrase. Finally, the user tells FOCUS to sum the net field and to print it as a total at the bottom of the column.

Figure B–12
Payroll Program Written in FOCUS

Notice how concise this program is compared with the third-generation programs. They all produce the same payroll register.

```
DEFINE FILE PAYFILE ADD
  FCRATE/D4.3 = IF JOBCODE EQ 1120 OR 1122 THEN.067
               ELSE 0.0;
  FTRATE/D4.3 = IF JOBCODE EQ 1111 THEN .007
               ELSE IF JOBCODE EQ 1120 OR 1122 THEN .113
               ELSE 0.0;
  STRATE/D4.3 = IF JOBCODE EQ 1111 THEN .008
               ELSE IF JOBCODE EQ 1120 OR 1122 THEN .03
               ELSE 0.0;
  RTRATE/D4.3 = IF JOBCODE EQ 1120 OR 1122 THEN .05
               ELSE 0.0;
  CURATE/D4.3 = IF JOBCODE EQ 1122 THEN .05
               ELSE 0.0;
TABLE FILE PAYFILE
  HEADING CENTER
   "PAYROLL REGISTER"
  PRINT JOBCODE AND EMPNO AND HOURS AND RATE AND COMPUTE
    GROSS AS 'Gross,Pay' =
      IF HOURS LE 40.0 THEN WHRS * RATE
      ELSE (40.0*RATE)+((HOURS-40.0)*RATE*1.5);
    FICA AS 'Social,Security,Tax' = GROSS*FCRATE;
    FIT AS 'Federal,Income,Tax' = GROSS*FTRATE;
    SIT AS 'State,Income,Tax' = GROSS*STRATE;
    CUNION AS 'Credit,Union' = GROSS*CURATE;
    RETIRE AS 'Retirement' = GROSS*RTRATE;
    NET AS "Net,Pay" = GROSS-(FICA+FIT+SIT+RETIRE+CUNION);
  SUM NET AND COLUMN-TOTAL
END
```

FOCUS has an interactive reporting facility called TABLETALK, which works with reports as FILETALK does with master file descriptions. TABLETALK interactively queries the user for the specifications necessary to produce a report while simultaneously creating the TABLE FILE procedure at the bottom of the screen.

Fourth-generation languages such as FOCUS will be used widely in the future. They have many advantages. Applications can be developed up to ten times faster with 4GLs than with third-generation languages. In addition, 4GLs allow end users to develop many of their own applications.

Unfortunately, FOCUS and other fourth-generation languages do have disadvantages. Generally, they do not perform well in a high-volume, online, transaction-processing application in which a large number of terminals update files simultaneously. With such a system, they produce terminal response times that are much too slow. For example, a motor vehicles system using a 4GL language was built for the state of New Jersey. The system was supposed to handle 1,000 terminals. But, with only 220 terminals online, it bogged down and frequently produced response times of one to two minutes. The transaction-processing parts of the system had to be rewritten in COBOL to solve the response time problem. It should be noted, however, that the high-volume transaction-processing capabilities of 4GLs are gradually being improved. Also, as computers become more powerful, they will execute the 4GLs faster.

dBASE   dBASE II, dBASE III, and most recently dBASE IV are versions of **dBASE,** a relational data-base management system marketed by Ashton-Tate for use with personal computers. Although many people only use dBASE's interactive query language, the package also comes with the ability to create program files that access and manipulate data-base files (see Figure B-13). These program files are made up of the commands available in the interactive query language and of certain program control commands (for example, DO WHILE, IF-ELSE) that can be used only within a program or command file.

Users of dBASE create command files for a number of reasons. They may routinely issue a set of commands to input or extract certain information from a data base. It takes less time to link these commands together in a command file than to type them in each time they are used. Longer, more complicated programs are written by many dBASE users to create a user interface of menus, screens, and reports that guide users through a set of tasks.

dBASE is used almost exclusively for business applications. It is considered by most to be a fourth-generation programming language. It has a number of advantages over other languages. First, since dBASE is part of a data-base management system, easy-to-use but very powerful file management commands are available to the user. Consider the payroll application used as an example throughout this module. A dBASE program that accesses that same payroll file and prints the employee number and the hours worked for all employees who worked more than forty hours could be written in one line:

```
LIST EMPNO, HOURS FOR HOURS>40 TO PRINT
```

A program to accomplish this in a third-generation language would require a number of lines set into and around a loop that sequentially accesses the file.

Figure B–13
Payroll Program Written in dBASE

Although dBASE is a fourth-generation language, programs written in dBASE do have procedural characteristics. Notice how similar the steps within the DO WHILE loop in this program are to those in third-generation programs.

```
PROCEDURE MAIN
SET MARGIN TO 5
SET TALK OFF
SET PRINT ON
? "                                                    SOCIAL        FEDERAL
  STATE"
? " JOB         EMPLOYEE     HOURS HOURLY    GROSS   SECURITY      INCOME
INCOME CREDIT                 NET"
? "CODE          NUMBER      WORKED WAGE      PAY     TAX          TAX
  TAX  UNION    RETIREMENT  PAY"
?
SET PRINT OFF
USE PAYFILE
DO WHILE .NOT. EOF()
   STORE 0 TO FTRATE
   STORE 0 TO STRATE
   STORE 0 TO FCRATE
   STORE 0 TO RTRATE
   STORE 0 TO CURATE
   IF JOBCODE=1111
      STORE 0.007 TO FTRATE
      STORE 0.008 TO STRATE
      DO CALC
    ELSE
      IF JOBCODE=1120 .OR. JOBCODE=1122
        STORE 0.067 TO FCRATE
        STORE 0.113 TO FTRATE
        STORE 0.03 TO STRATE
        STORE 0.05 TO RTRATE
        IF JOBCODE=1122
           STORE 0.05 TO CURATE
        ENDIF
        DO CALC
      ELSE
        DO ERROR
      ENDIF
   ENDIF
   SKIP
ENDDO
SUM NET TO RAMNETPAY
SET MARGIN TO 62
SET PRINT ON
?
? "TOTAL NET EARNINGS ARE:",RAMNETPAY
?
SET PRINT OFF
SET MARGIN TO 0
CLOSE DATABASES
RETURN

PROCEDURE CALC
STORE 0 TO OTIME
IF HOURS>40
   STORE (HOURS-40)*RATE*1.5 TO OTIME
  REPLACE GROSS WITH (40*RATE)+OTIME
ELSE
  REPLACE GROSS WITH (HOURS*RATE)
ENDIF
```

Figure B–13 (continued)

```
REPLACE FICA WITH GROSS*FCRATE
REPLACE FIT WITH GROSS*FTRATE
REPLACE SIT WITH GROSS*STRATE
REPLACE RETIRE WITH GROSS*RTRATE
REPLACE CUNION WITH GROSS*CURATE
REPLACE NET WITH GROSS-(FICA+FIT+SIT+RETIRE+CUNION)
SET PRINT ON
? JOBCODE,EMPNO,HOURS,RATE,GROSS,FICA,FIT,SIT,CUNION,RETIRE,NET
SET PRINT OFF
RETURN

PROCEDURE ERROR
SET PRINT ON
? JOBCODE,EMPNO,HOURS,RATE,"**ERROR: INVALID JOB CODE**"
SET PRINT OFF
RETURN
```

The dBASE program states *what* it wants, not *how* to do it. Languages of this sort are called nonprocedural because they state only the result of a procedure and not the steps in the procedure itself.

dBASE also provides tools for screen, report, and even application generation. A screen generator is a tool by which a user can quickly design a screen on which data are input or read. The dBASE report generator is a fill-in-the-blanks tool by which a person can format a report generated from one or more files without ever writing a line of program code. In fact, the payroll program illustrated in this module could be very quickly and easily generated in this manner. An application or program generator uses screen and menu definitions, file structures, report forms from the report generator, and so on to generate actual program code for an application. The combination of ease of use and power that dBASE provides makes it an extremely popular PC programming language.

RPG RPG (Report Program Generator) is a nonprocedural language. The programmer or user describes the report desired, and the RPG system creates it. The basic objective of RPG is to simplify and facilitate the generation of reports from files.

RPG was introduced in 1964, and improved versions, RPG II and RPG III, followed. RPG is designed for only one application: to update and produce output from other files. RPG is a descriptive language. The input into the RPG system are specification forms on which the programmer describes the report to be generated.

A report is composed of three major parts: the header, detail lines, and footer. The programmer uses the specification forms to describe the input record layout and field definitions; indicators used in the program; intermediate calculations performed; and the formats of the header, detailed lines, and footer.

RPG is a very machine-dependent language, primarily supported by IBM. Other manufacturers have their own versions: therefore, there is no standard. RPG is very limited in scope and is generally used for report generation in data-processing applications. The language is not suited for complex problems requiring extensive programming logic. An advantage of RPG is that it can be implemented at small computer installations because it has minimal storage requirements.

■ LANGUAGE SELECTION

Here, we do not make comparisons among the languages just discussed. Rather, we explain the factors that influence language selection. Selecting a language for a particular programming application is an important and sometimes difficult task. The first consideration is: how relevant is the language to the application? Many languages are designed for a particular application and are second choices for other applications. For example, COBOL was designed for the business data-processing application and does not have the facilities to support complex numerical computations character-istic of scientific applications.

A second question is: can the language be efficiently implemented on the existing system? Efficiency is measured in terms of compilation time, execu-tion time, primary-storage requirements, and labor. For example, PASCAL and BASIC are good languages for personal computers because these lan-guages require very little primary storage for compilation and execution.

Organizational aspects must also be considered. Staff requirements should be determined, and the cost of training the staff should be weighed against the cost of acquiring new talent. The language can play a big role in determining the time and cost required for orientation. Also, the language should be versatile and flexible enough to meet the changing needs of the organization. The selector must consider all the objectives and try to make an optimal decision. No language satisfies all objectives, and the selector must allow for trade-offs among desired objectives.

The following is a brief outline of essential features determining a lan-guage's effectiveness:

1. Readability/overall writing features:
   Modularity
   Structural clarity
   Compactness
   Simplicity
2. Application-oriented features:
   Functional support
   Flexibility
   Versatility
3. Standardization and portability features
4. Software development features:
   Editing/debugging facilities
5. Efficiency features:
   Compilation
   Execution
   Primary-storage requirements
   Labor efficiency

These features should be viewed with varying degrees of importance, depending on how and in what environment the language will be used. For example, in an interactive system, execution time is critical. That is not necessarily the case in a batch-processing environment where jobs can be run overnight.

Desirable qualities of a language are ease of overall writing and readability. These can directly affect personnel costs associated with learning and acquiring proficiency of the language. Modularity and structural clarity are essential in enhancing readability and coding; it should be possible to break down the program into more visible logical units. These features also aid in the development and continual maintenance and modification of structured software throughout its life cycle. Examples of a modular language with structural clarity are PASCAL and PL/I.

Other features desirable for ease of overall writing are compactness and simplicity. Compactness refers to the ability to write a program with a minimum number of keywords and symbols. These features also aid in the maintenance of the language. Examples of a compact language are PASCAL and BASIC. COBOL is not a compact language, because in being English-like, it requires words, instead of symbols, when coding.

Once again, relevance of a language to a given application is very important. When selecting a language, evaluate the language's functional support facilities. Does the language support facilities that enhance its performance within a given application, thereby making less work for the programmer? For example, FORTRAN has several built-in functions for evaluating complex numerical equations; and dBASE supports a built-in report-writer, application generator, and data-base management system. Flexibility is essential in meeting the changing needs of the organization. Application software that can be quickly and accurately altered to specification is most important. Versatility is another feature that enhances a language's performance. PL/I is a versatile and flexible language because it is suitable for both business and scientific computing.

For most business information systems, an important consideration is the ability to run a program on different computers. This capability is known as portability, as discussed earlier. It is most important to be able to upgrade to new hardware without having to modify programs. The standardization of languages, which contributes greatly to portability, is a continuing challenge to the profession. The most prominent organization to produce standardization is the American National Standards Institute.

Software development aids should not be overlooked. The selector should evaluate the implementation's editing and debugging facilities—are the *compile-time* and *execution-time diagnostics* adequate? The WATFIV version of FORTRAN is an example of an implementation with superior debugging facilities (that is, descriptive diagnostics which aid in debugging).

Finally, efficiency of a programming language is measured by compilation time, execution time, and primary-storage requirements. Machine and assembly languages utilize these resources very efficiently at the expense of portability, flexibility, and programmer time. PL/I has a large compiler and therefore uses a lot of primary storage and takes a long time to compile, whereas PASCAL uses very little primary storage. The machine efficiency of programming languages is becoming less important as hardware costs decline. Much more important is the human labor required to use the language.

COMPILE-TIME DIAGNOSTICS
Error diagnostics that are produced when a program is compiled.

EXECUTION-TIME DIAGNOSTICS
Error diagnostics that are produced when a program is executed.

■ Summing Up

■ Software may be purchased or developed in-house. If it is developed in-house, a suitable programming language must be selected.

■ Machine language, which is written in binary representation, is the only language the computer understands. Programs written in other languages must be translated into machine language, with the help of a compiler or translator.

■ Assembly language is similar to machine language in that every machine operation must be individually described. But in assembly language, operations and variables are represented by mnemonics instead of by binary numbers. This makes assembly-language programs easier to read.

■ A high-level language (procedural or fourth-generation) is much easier for people to write and understand. The compiler automatically generates most of the routine machine instructions, making life easier for the programmer.

■ FORTRAN is one of the oldest high-level languages. Although it was originally designed for scientific applications, it is sometimes used in business data processing.

■ COBOL is an English-like language designed for business applications. A COBOL program contains paragraphs, sentences, and clauses. The major advantages of this language are high portability and self-documentation.

■ PL/I is a comprehensive language suitable for both business and scientific programming. It is a powerful language because both the novice and the experienced programmer can use it. Versatility in handling character data and strong file-management capabilities make PL/I a good candidate for business applications.

■ BASIC is an all-purpose language that is easy to learn. Although it is not well structured, it is extremely popular among PC users. Many vendors and users have developed their own versions of BASIC, thereby reducing its portability.

■ Like PL/I, PASCAL is a well-structured language suited to both business and scientific applications. It can be used on microcomputers because the compiler does not require an excessive amount of storage space.

■ One of the newest high-level languages, ADA, is intended to be portable, well-structured, and versatile. ADA was developed by the Department of Defense, primarily for use in a technical environment.

■ Fourth-generation languages, the latest generation, provide facilities that allow users to develop many of their own applications.

■ Focus is the most popular fourth-generation language. It runs on personal computers, minicomputers, and mainframes. It has many facilities that both programmers and users can employ to develop applications.

■ dBASE is a PC data-base management system. Since program (command) files can be created in dBASE, many business applications can be programmed in dBASE. It is the most widely used PC data-base management system.

■ RPG is a popular nonprocedural language, used widely on small computers. Its basic function is to generate date files and reports, although some limited data-manipulation features are available.

■ When evaluating a computer language, the selector should consider the following characteristics:

1. Readability/overall writing features
2. Application-oriented features

3. Standardization and portability
4. Software development aids
5. Efficiency

program	documentation
high-level languages	COBOL
machine language	divisions
semantic gap	sections
object code	sentences
symbolic languages	statements
assembly language	words
mnemonics	reserved words
assembler	user-defined words
source code	system names
pseudocode	semantic errors
register	PL/I
base register	block-structured language
procedure-oriented language	internal subroutine
compiler	edit-directed
translation	BASIC
linking	portability
loading	PASCAL
FORTRAN	data type
WATFIV	ADA
statements	modules
keywords	packages
nonexecutable statements	tasks
specification statements	terminating keywords
data type	fourth-generation language (4GL)
executable statements	nonprocedural languages
assignment statements	FOCUS
control statements	dBASE
input/output statements	RPG
structured programming	

1. What is machine language? How does it differ from assembly language?
2. In what ways do procedural languages aid the programming process?
3. Describe the three processes that a procedural language program must go through before it is executed.

4. What are the two basic types of FORTRAN statements?
5. Describe the three types of executable statements in FORTRAN.
6. What were the objectives in developing COBOL?
7. Discuss the functions of the four major divisions in a COBOL program.
8. List the objectives of developing PL/I.
9. Briefly explain the four kinds of statements in a PL/I program.
10. What was the motivation for creating BASIC?
11. Discuss the disadvantages of BASIC.
12. In what respects is PASCAL a better language than PL/I?
13. List the advantages and disadvantages of ADA.
14. What are the functions of the specification forms used by RPG?
15. Explain the difference between a procedural and a nonprocedural language.
16. What are some facilities of a fourth-generation language such as FOCUS?
17. What essential features would you consider when determining the effectiveness of a language?

Discussion Questions and Cases

1. Your firm, Hokies International, plans to install a new, computerized order-processing system. Fast-Code, a software firm, has offered to sell you its package FAST-SELL. It is a complete order-processing program written in dBASE. Fast-Code agrees to maintain it for three years. The chief programmer at Hokies International believes that she can write a more efficient program in COBOL. This would cost only two-thirds of what Fast-Code charges for its package. Which alternative would you choose, and why?

2. Some people believe that the existence of many programming languages is undesirable. Some disadvantages of multiple languages are as follows:

- It is difficult to transport programs among installations.
- Training programmers in more than one language is costly and redundant.
- It is difficult to integrate programs written in different languages.

In spite of these arguments, computer languages continue to proliferate. What are the possible reasons for this? Should the number of languages be controlled?

3. FOCUS is a useful language for writing quick, informal programs. On the other hand, COBOL is suitable for writing formal, well-documented programs. For each of the following applications, decide which of these two languages is preferable.

a. A one-time, strategic report for top management.
b. A program occasionally used by middle managers to compare actual sales with budgeted sales.
c. A statistical computation used by the factory engineer to schedule machine-maintenance checks.
d. An accounts receivable system that processes about eight hundred transactions daily.

4. Jill Johnson is creating a personnel tracking system for King William County. She was at the library using a personal computer to design some of the computer programs in BASIC when she saw her friend Susan Cox, a consultant for a CPA firm. Susan asked Jill why she was programming in

BASIC. Jill said that BASIC was the only language she knew and that it was an excellent choice for implementing the system. Susan replied that there were many relational data-base management system packages, such as dBASE, on the market, and that dBASE would be more efficient; it would reduce programming time because of its data-base capabilities. Jill was adamant about not changing the language because she had already done quite a bit of programming. Do you think that Jill should continue writing in BASIC, or should she try an alternative?

5. The Hercules Company recruits a large number of business graduates with majors in management, marketing, finance, management science, and accounting. Ramon Noegel is director of personnel. Several operational managers in the company have suggested that he require all new-hires to have taken at least one programming course in their college career. They argue that a person must understand programming in order to use computers effectively and to really understand what the computer is doing. Ramon maintains that programming is becoming an obsolete skill. He states that business personnel can certainly utilize the computer in many effective ways without knowing how to program. He cites the fact that there are many user-friendly packages available for personal computers, such as electronic worksheets, report generators, data-base management systems, and graphics, which can be used without programming. Do you think that learning at least one programming language is useful to a business student?

Module C ■ Computer System Evaluation and Acquisition

MODULE OUTLINE

Introduction

**Conducting an Evaluation of
a Computer System**
Development of a Request for Proposal
Proposal Evaluation
Evaluation of Purchased Software
Vendor Selection

Financing Options
Purchasing
Renting
Leasing

**Sources of Information-System
Equipment and Services**
Computer Manufacturers

Retail Computer Stores
Software Vendors
Service Bureaus
Timesharing Services
Computer Lessors
Facilities-Management Vendor
Peripheral-Hardware Manufacturers
Information-System Consultants

Summing Up

Key Terms

Review Questions

Discussion Questions and Cases

■ INTRODUCTION

Users have become increasingly involved with the evaluation and acquisition of computer hardware and software. Often managers serve on user committees responsible for selecting a computer system. Even when the information-systems function is not a routine responsibility of managers, they sometimes help select a computer system because of the computer's impact on their departments.

Many techniques discussed in this module are useful in evaluating and acquiring any size computer, from mainframe to personal computer. There are several check-lists that should be considered when purchasing computer hardware and software. When purchasing a PC, you may also want to use the checklist for microcomputing needs in Figure 2–22.

We first discuss how computer systems and software are evaluated. We then examine the methods for financing computer systems. Finally, we explore the various sources for information-system equipment and services.

■ CONDUCTING AN EVALUATION OF A COMPUTER SYSTEM

Approaches to acquiring computer hardware and software have changed over the years. In the past, the hardware and software available to users were much more limited. Purchasing a particular manufacturer's hardware usually locked the buyer into that company's software and utility programs since they were sold as a package. This practice was known as **bundling.** Hardware components of different manufacturers were usually incompatible. **Plug-compatible** hardware units (units produced by other manufacturers that directly replace hardware units produced by major manufacturers such as IBM) did not exist. Therefore, acquiring a computer tended to be very informal. Decisions were based on a review of the manufacturer's specifications, what competitors were doing, other computer users' recommendations, or the desire to buy from a favorite manufacturer. Today, sophisticated computer users employ a more structured approach. The range of systems and costs within the computer industry is simply too broad for an unstructured evaluation to be successful.

As illustrated in Figure C–1, the evaluation process has five primary steps:

1. System feasibility study.
2. System analysis.
3. Development of a request for proposal (RFP).

Figure C–1
Steps in Evaluation and Purchase of Computer Hardware and Software
Determining your hardware and software requirements through structured system analysis is an important step. Many firms have purchased inappropriate hardware and software because they did not first determine their requirements.

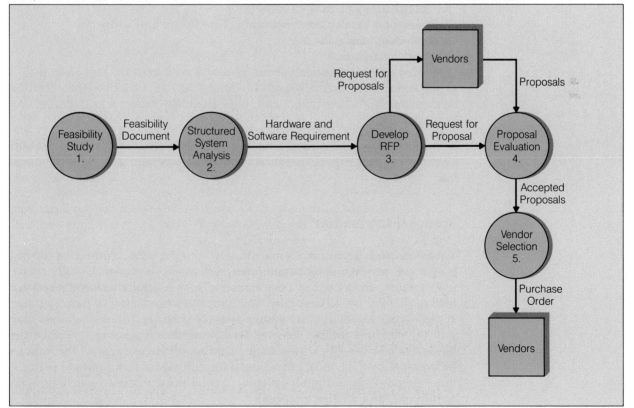

VENDOR
A supplier of computer
hardware and/or software.

4. Proposal evaluation.
5. *Vendor* selection.

Although we discuss the evaluation steps sequentially, the actual process can be highly iterative, and the steps can overlap. Steps 1 and 2 were discussed in Chapter 6, System Analysis; therefore, this module begins with step 3, which is the first task to be completed when purchasing hardware or software.

Development of a Request for Proposal

The **request for proposal (RFP) document** puts the requirements for equipment and software in a form that vendors can respond to. It serves as a communication tool between the potential buyer and vendor. Among the areas an RFP should cover are:

1. A description of present and proposed applications, including for each application: processing mode (batch or interactive), input/output volumes, data-flow diagrams, file descriptions (including size), data-base characteristics, and how often the application will be run.
2. Reliability requirements.
3. Backup requirements.
4. Vendor service requirements.
5. Outline of specific hardware or software features required, such as printer speed or disk capacity.
6. Criteria for evaluating proposals.
7. Plans for a vendor demonstration of hardware and software.
8. Implementation schedule.
9. Price constraints.
10. List of specific questions about hardware and software characteristics.
11. Procedures for clarifying and submitting the RFP, including the person to contact for RFP clarification and the scheduled date for submitting the proposal.

The RFP is sent to each prospective vendor, along with an invitation to bid. The buyer should expect a notification from each vendor as to whether it will bid.

Proposal Evaluation

Hardware and Software Demonstration In the first phase of proposal evaluation, vendors demonstrate their systems to the users. Usually only a few vendors are invited to demonstrate. They generally present the major features of their proposals orally. The complete system may be demonstrated at the buyer's location, if the system is easily portable. If not, the buyer may visit the vendor's facility. The vendors' presentations enable several of the buyer's employees to gain an understanding of the features of the various proposals. However, most buyers use more substantial techniques to evaluate these proposals than merely listening to oral presentations, watching demonstrations, and reading proposals.

Evaluation Techniques Performance evaluation of computer hardware and software is a major tool used in the selection of new equipment. For each proposal, the buyer would like to know the performance characteristics (execution time, throughput, idle time, response time, and so on) when executing current and planned applications. Obtaining such information is obviously impossible. Planned applications have not been developed, and current applications may not execute on the various equipment without program modification. However, there are techniques available to assist the buyer in obtaining approximate performance data. Performance evaluation techniques fall into two categories. Traditional techniques provide very gross measures of a system's performance. Current techniques provide the buyer with much more reliable and extensive measures of a system's performance.

Traditional Techniques The traditional techniques of performance evaluation compare performance characteristics such as number of bits processed in each operation by the CPU, primary and secondary memory access time, millions of instructions per second (MIPS) executed by the CPU, an average time for a mix of instructions, and for PCs, the clock speed of the microprocessor (typically stated in terms of megahertz, such as 16 megahertz). All are very gross measures of computer performance. They have limited usefulness— and then only when the various computers have similar internal organization. With these techniques, the effects of software on system performance are ignored.

Another traditional technique is the **kernel program,** which is a small sample program executed on each proposed computer. In some cases the kernel program is not actually executed, but the run time is derived on the basis of instruction execution time. This approach may be helpful in standard mathematical applications, but it is not very useful for business systems since software and input/output effects are ignored.

Current Techniques More reliable techniques are benchmark programs, workload models, simulation, and monitors. **Benchmark programs** are sample programs or test jobs that represent at least part of the buyer's primary computer workload. They include software considerations and can be current application programs or new programs that have been designed to represent planned processing needs. The buyer can design these programs to test any characteristic of the system. For example, the benchmark might test the average response time for inquiries from workstations when the system is also executing a *compute-bound* batch job.

The speeds of personal computers are often compared using benchmarks. In periodicals such as *PC Magazine*, writers compare PCs by using benchmarks such as the time necessary to do a dBASE sort, recalculate a Lotus 1-2-3 sort, or search a ten-page document for spelling errors. Such benchmarks can be very helpful to a user trying to decide on a PC to buy.

Figure C–2 illustrates benchmark tests that can be used to evaluate a data-base management system.

Workload models are computer programs that accurately represent the buyer's planned computer workload. The programs require the same demand for computer resources that the buyer's application programs will require. For example, if the buyer's total workload is expected to contain 15 percent high

COMPUTE-BOUND JOB
A computer run that requires large amounts of CPU time and relatively little input and output.

Time to Create the Structure of a File
Time to Enter a Sample of Standard Data
Time to Execute a Standard Task
Time to Perform a Sort
Time to Retrieve Records Randomly
Time to Create a Standard Report on the Screen
Time to Execute a Standard Report to the Screen

Figure C–2
Benchmark Tests for a Data-Base Management System

Tests such as these can produce valuable data for judging software and hardware.

CPU demand work, 10 percent compilation, 30 percent workstation input/output, and 45 percent data-base processing, the workload model programs should contain the same mix. Workload models differ from benchmark programs in that the latter usually do not accurately represent the buyer's complete planned workload.

Simulation techniques have been used extensively to evaluate complex alternative systems where it is not possible to analytically determine which system is preferable. For example, an airline could use a computer simulation to determine which aircraft would be the best buy, given its present fleet, its expected route, and its passenger demand. Simulation is equally applicable to the evaluation of computer systems.

A simulation program can work with almost any computer system. Input to this program includes descriptions of expected workloads, files, input/output volumes, and the vendor's equipment. The program simulates running the user's expected workload on the equipment. Simulating the equipment of different vendors is accomplished by changing the equipment-description input. Validity of the simulation greatly depends on how accurately the simulation models the equipment and the buyer's anticipated workload. Since a valid simulation can be difficult to achieve and even to recognize, it should be used by only the more sophisticated computer buyers.

Monitors are hardware or software devices that monitor the operation of a computer and provide operating statistics such as idle time of the CPU and average job-execution time. Software monitors are programs that periodically interrupt processing to collect statistics. They are part of the operating system and therefore have access to all operating-system data. Hardware monitors are devices attached to the hardware component being monitored. They collect data on whatever characteristic is being measured.

Monitors are used primarily in the evaluation and **fine tuning** of existing computer systems, rather than in the selection of new systems. Used as a fine-tuning tool, they can indicate where bottlenecks occur within the system. For example, the CPU may not be fully utilized while jobs are waiting in queue because input-output channels are operating at capacity.

We have discussed several traditional and current techniques for evaluating computer systems. For most firms, a combination of benchmarking and workload models is the best technique for evaluating performance. Often, vendors already have the results of several benchmark runs which the buyer can use. The extent to which benchmarking and workload models are used depends on the size of the computer being purchased. Personal computers are often purchased without the buyer using either technique. However, a wise PC buyer makes comparisons using published benchmark tests.

Other Evaluation Criteria

Equipment Criteria Many technical criteria should be considered in selecting computer equipment, including:

1. Primary-memory (RAM) size.
2. Storage-device characteristics.
   a. Disk drives (including *access time*, capacity, and whether it is removable or fixed).

ACCESS TIME
The speed with which a peripheral device moves data to and from the CPU.

b. Tape drives (including capacity, access time, and recording density).

3. *Bus* characteristics, such as size.

Software Criteria In software, the primary areas of concern are operating systems and application programs. Operating systems have a major impact on the efficiency of computer processing. Some features to evaluate are:

1. Multiprogramming capabilities.
2. Job management features.
3. Availability of utility programs.
4. CPU time and primary-storage-space overhead required by the operating system.
5. Quality of the operating system's documentation.
6. User-friendliness of the user interface.

The user should also determine whether the major compiler to be used is available and whether it is well supported by the vendor.

The availability, capabilities, and reliability of necessary application programs must be considered as well. Users may want to purchase application software and make minor modifications to adapt the programs to their particular needs. In such a case, the extent of the documentation and the ability of the programs to be modified are important considerations. The reliability and capabilities of application software usually can be best determined by consulting current users and referring to published reviews of the software. The evaluation of purchased software is covered in more detail later in this module.

General Criteria More general criteria to evaluate when selecting a computer system are vendor support, compatibility, and modularity. **Vendor support** is crucial to the success of a computer system in a variety of areas, including:

1. Personnel training.
2. Repair and maintenance.
3. Installation.
4. Preinstallation testing.
5. Hardware backup arrangements.

Vendor support is generally adequate among the larger, more established computer vendors. However, there are many new firms in the minicomputer and PC industry, and in some cases their support is minimal. In addition, even with larger computer vendors, repair and maintenance services may be slow and expensive when the user is located in rural or remote areas.

Compatibility can be divided into two parts: hardware and software compatibility. Users should know how compatible a potential vendor's hardware is with the hardware of other vendors. Compatibility enables a buyer to consider other vendors for certain components of the system. For example, since many companies sell remote terminals, the buyer could realize substantial savings by purchasing them from the smaller computer vendors. In addition, some computer manufacturers specialize in less expensive, plug-compatible units that can replace the major components (the CPU, for example) of the large vendors' systems. However, the use of mixed systems (plug-compatible units) can increase management problems, because it is

BUS
One or more conductors for transmitting signals between system units.

difficult to assign responsibility for hardware failures when there are two or more vendors' units.

The primary concern about software compatibility is whether the user's existing software can execute on the proposed system. In addition, the user should determine whether the new software is compatible with other computer systems, both from other vendors and from the proposed vendor. If the compatibility of proposed new software is limited, this can be a major restriction to a buyer who later wants to change systems. Vendors often offer families of computers (such as the IBM PS/2 and 3090 series). Transition from one member to another of these families is very easy since peripheral equipment and operating systems are compatible.

A final general criterion to evaluate is **modularity,** which is a computer system's ability to add capacity or components. Modularity allows for growth without changing systems. For example, additional main memory or disk units can be added when processing requirements dictate such expansion. This capability is crucial if the user's information-processing requirements are expected to increase.

Evaluation of Purchased Software

System software is almost always purchased from a vendor or supplied as a package along with the hardware. There is also a trend toward purchasing application software instead of developing it *in-house.* In this section we discuss the evaluation of purchased software. In-house development was covered in Chapters 6, 7, and 8.

Purchasing application software packages has several advantages:

1. Software development is basically labor-intensive and therefore is becoming increasingly expensive. Costs per user can be cut by spreading development and maintenance costs over many users.
2. Purchased software is often better documented.
3. Purchased packages are often very flexible. They can be adapted to fit specific user needs without modifying programs.
4. Applications can be implemented faster, since the long lead time involved in software development is eliminated.
5. The risk of large cost and time overruns of in-house development is reduced.

Among the disadvantages of purchased software are:

1. Purchased software is not likely to meet the needs of the user as closely as software developed in-house.
2. Certain uncontrollable risks are assumed when software is purchased. For example, the vendor may go out of business, or fail to maintain and update the software.
3. With purchased software, *the expertise* is outside the user company, whereas with software developed in-house, that expertise is also in-house.

There are many sources for application software. To find out what packages are on the market, the buyer should consult **software directories** such as those published by International Computer Programs, Auerbach, and Datapro.

The overall approach to evaluating software packages is very similar to that of evaluating hardware. The primary factors are:

1. Does the package meet the user's needs, or can it be modified at a reasonable cost?

2. What are the initial and yearly costs of the package?

3. Is the system easy to install, and is installation help available?

4. How efficient is the package? How much of each computer resource (run-time, primary storage, and secondary storage) does the package require?

5. Will additional hardware be required?

6. What are the operating-system requirements of the package?

7. How satisfied with the package are similar users?

8. Is the package well documented?

9. Can data be easily entered, manipulated, and corrected?

10. Are there easy-to-use query facilities for displaying the data contained in the system's files?

11. Are thorough backup facilities and procedures provided?

12. Are screens and menus easy to access and use?

13. What online help is available?

14. What level of computer expertise is required from the user?

15. Are there user groups for the software?

16. Does the vendor provide the user's employees with extensive training for using the package?

17. Is local support offered, and is a hotline available?

18. Is the vendor viable? What is the vendor's financial status? How long has the firm been in business?

19. Does the package appear to be viable over the long run? Can it accommodate changes in hardware and operating systems as well as changes in the user company's needs?

20. Are the performance claims of the vendor specifically guaranteed by the terms of the contract?

21. Does the vendor provide a free trial period? Is this period sufficiently long, given normal implementation time spans?

22. Does the package provide adequate data editing, audit trail, and other control features?

Vendor Selection

In most cases, more than one computer system or software package can meet a user's needs. A widely used method for ranking competing systems is to assign points based on the degree to which each system meets important criteria, and then total the points to obtain a ranking (see Table C–1). Of course, the difference among vendors on one or two factors can override the total score. For example, vendor support could be so poor that it precludes the purchase of an otherwise outstanding system. Communicating with the vendors about the point ranking system can be an effective tool for helping them respond more effectively to the RFP.

◼ FINANCING OPTIONS

There are three ways to pay for computer systems: a user can purchase, rent, or lease. Usually all three options are available from manufacturers or their

Table C–1 ■ A Point Ranking System

The maximum points are assigned, based on the relative importance the buyer feels each system characteristic should have. Usually, a team of two to four people independently rank each system being considered.

System Characteristics	Maximum Points	POINTS ASSIGNED System			
		A	B	C	D
Hardware					
Memory size	20	10	15	20	10
Bus characteristics	10	10	8	5	10
Disk capacity	20	20	5	15	10
Modularity	30	30	20	25	15
Compatibility	30	30	10	15	20
Software					
Operating System	30	20	15	25	30
Languages	20	15	10	15	20
Application programs	40	30	40	20	25
Compatibility	30	30	30	25	25
Vendor support	40	20	30	35	40
Cost	50	30	40	40	50
Benchmarking results	50	50	40	45	30
Total	370	295	263	285	285

THIRD PARTY
A company other than the user or the computer-system manufacturer.

representatives, and rental and lease arrangements can also be made through a *third party*. Many companies rent or lease computer hardware and software.

Purchasing

The primary advantage of purchasing equipment is the potential cost savings if the equipment is kept for its useful life, normally three to six years. Furthermore, the purchaser can depreciate the equipment for tax purposes if it is used for business. The rental or lease payment is also tax-deductible.

Although purchasing equipment generally results in lower overall costs, the buyer assumes the **risk of obsolescence** and does not have the **flexibility** of canceling the arrangement. Furthermore, purchasing requires capital that may be better utilized elsewhere.

Another consideration when purchasing computer equipment is maintenance. If the equipment is rented, the manufacturer usually provides maintenance services. If the equipment is purchased, the user has several maintenance alternatives:

1. Purchase a maintenance agreement that provides for all maintenance, parts, and labor.
2. Pay for maintenance on a per-call basis, as required.
3. Use the company's own employees for maintenance.

Renting

Under the rental option, the equipment is rented on a monthly basis directly from the manufacturer or a third party. Most agreements have a minimum rental period, such as ninety days. After the minimum period, the user can cancel the agreement with short notice—one to two months. Personal computers can be rented for as short a period as one day. This flexibility is perhaps the major advantage of renting. However, the value of this flexibility is often overestimated, since the user may have a large investment in training, preparation, and implementation.

Mainframe rental agreements generally provide for 176 hours of equipment use per month (8 hours per day $\times$ 22 average work days per month = 176 hours). Using the equipment for more than eight hours a day may require an additional rental payment, although at a reduced rate.

Renting is the most costly approach in terms of overall cash flow. However, the user does not need the large capital outlay required in purchasing equipment. In addition, the risk of obsolescence and the responsibility for maintenance are borne by the equipment owner. In some cases, renting equipment may lead to more contact with, and support from, the manufacturer.

Leasing

Leasing is a compromise between purchasing and renting. Typically, leasing costs less than renting but more than purchasing. Most risks of obsolescence can be transferred to the lessor through an option to purchase the equipment at the end of the lease. If, at the end of the lease, the equipment is obsolescent then the lessee can simply not purchase the equipment. If the equipment is still useful, the lessee can exercise the option to purchase. Leasing is not as flexible as renting because the lessee is locked in to the agreement until the lease expires—typically after five years. However, sometimes the lease can be terminated early through the payment of a termination charge.

Lessors are often third-party, independent leasing companies. The lease agreement may provide a maintenance contract and does not usually charge for operation beyond 176 hours per month. Leasing offers substantial cost savings over renting for the user who is willing to forego the additional flexibility that renting offers.

The ultimate choice of financing involves a trade-off among risks of obsolescence, flexibility, and costs. These trade-offs are illustrated in Figures C–3 and C–4. The flexibility variable has become less important because computer systems themselves are now designed to be much more flexible. They can be upgraded through additional primary storage, secondary storage, or attached processors.

SOURCES OF INFORMATION-SYSTEM ■ EQUIPMENT AND SERVICES

Information-system equipment and services are widely available. The computer industry is intensely competitive, and this has been a major factor in the rapid technological advancement of the industry. Suppliers are innovative, and they continually look for unfilled customer needs. This competitive

**Figure C–3
Costs versus
Risk-of-Obsolescence
Trade-offs of Financing
Alternatives**

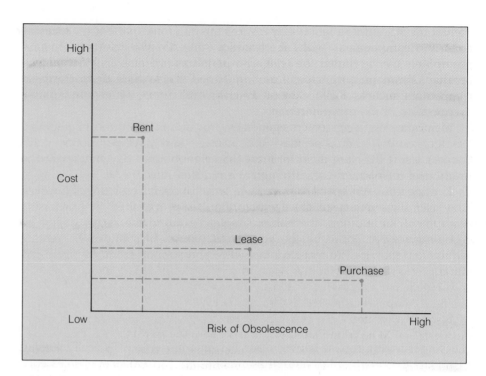

atmosphere can result in substantial cost savings for the buyer. In this section, we discuss the major equipment and service options available.

Computer Manufacturers

Many manufacturers produce complete lines of computer systems, including mainframes, minis, and personal computers. IBM dominates with more than

**Figure C–4
Costs versus Flexibility
Trade-offs of Financing
Alternatives**

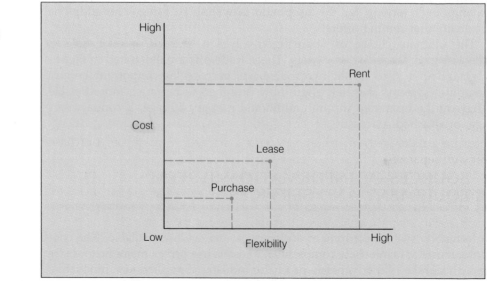

50 percent of the information-processing market. However, IBM was late to enter the competition. When it introduced its IBM 650 computer in the mid-1950s, Sperry Univac was already established. However, IBM quickly became dominant and successfully defended its market against strong competitors such as RCA, General Electric, and Xerox, all of which have dropped out of the computer business.

Producers of large computers now include Unisys, Amdahl, Cray Research, Hewlett-Packard (HP), National Cash Register (NCR), Digital Equipment Corporation (DEC), and Control Data Corporation (CDC). These manufacturers tend to specialize, often in areas that IBM historically has not covered well. Cray Research specializes in very large supercomputers that usually have scientific, military, or space applications. Control Data Corporation also tends to specialize in scientific computers but no longer makes supercomputers. Unisys deals in banking applications, although it does have small business computers. Hewlett-Packard and DEC tend to specialize in engineering and scientific applications, with their minicomputers, microcomputers, and interactive computer systems. The primary manufacturers of small business computers are IBM, NCR, and Unisys.

Personal computers are now used extensively in both large and small businesses. IBM has dominated this market with the IBM-PC and PS/2. There are, however, a host of other PC manufacturers, including Apple, Compaq, Radio Shack, Zenith, and many of the mainframe and minicomputer manufacturers. Medium-size and large companies usually purchase personal computers directly from the manufacturer. Small firms buy them from retail computer stores and local offices of computer manufacturers.

Many of these manufacturers also sell software for their computers.

Retail Computer Stores

We discussed sources of personal computers in Chapter 2. Recall that **retail computer stores,** including mail-order firms, have become a very large supplier of personal computer hardware and software. These stores began appearing in the late 1970s. They have been a significant factor in making PC hardware and software accessible to individuals and small businesses.

Software Vendors

In the early 1970s, court decisions required hardware manufacturers to sell their hardware without also requiring the customer to purchase the manufacturer's software. The outcome was a new market for companies that do not manufacture computers, but do produce software. Since hardware and software no longer came as one package, the user was free to purchase software separately.

The advent of personal computers has spawned a large number of software vendors. Buying from software vendors often has significant price and performance advantages. The complete range of software, including application programs, application generators, data-base management systems, utility programs, and operating systems, is available from these vendors. A software vendor often has specialized application programs, such as packages for project scheduling, that are not available from computer manufacturers.

Service Bureaus

Service bureaus are companies that provide computer processing services on an as-needed basis. They generally charge by the hour. These bureaus are a primary source of computer services for small businesses, and they routinely handle standard applications, such as payroll and accounts receivable. Either the service bureau or the customer provides the programs.

Using a service bureau can reduce costs and allow the user to test programs prior to installing a new computer. It also allows a company that owns its own computer to arrange backup services. Service bureaus also handle data entry and temporary processing overloads.

The main disadvantage of service bureaus is that companies may lose control over data. This could result in serious security problems. Related to the question of data security is the problem of data-file ownership. Users of service bureaus or timesharing services should be sure they retain all rights of file ownership, including access and use. Another potential problem with service bureaus is lengthy processing turnaround, since the user may not have control over the processing schedule.

Timesharing Services

Timesharing services provide the user with access to a computer through a remote terminal located at the users place of business. The CPU and secondary storage are located at the site of the timesharing service. Execution of user programs is initiated through commands issued at the terminal. Turnaround is very fast because programs are executed under a multitasking operating system that rotates among programs, allowing each program a CPU time slice. Thus, many independent users can gain access to a computer system at the same time. The characteristics of a typical timesharing system include the following:

1. Each user has access to the computer system through one or more terminals, typically a video display device with hardcopy print capability.
2. Data and instructions arrive at the CPU simultaneously from many users, and all users are serviced concurrently by giving each some small time slices of CPU time on a rotating basis.
3. Each user feels that he or she is the sole user of the system.
4. Each user's data files are stored by online, direct-access storage devices at the central computer site and are protected by password access systems. This allows the user immediate access to data.
5. Users can have their own application programs or use the public programs provided by the timesharing service.

Timesharing in commercial firms tends to be limited to jobs with small amounts of input and output, such as statistical programs and financial-planning models. However, timesharing is ideally suited for scientific jobs since they usually have a small amount of input/output and relatively more computation.

Computer Lessors

As mentioned earlier, a potential computer user can lease hardware rather than purchase it. Many companies specialize in leasing computers. Generally the user can lease a computer for substantially less than it costs to rent one. However, the lessee gives up flexibility, since leasing is a long-term commitment.

Facilities-Management Vendor

A **facilities-management vendor** specializes in managing, staffing, and operating computer information systems for users. This may include all aspects of the system, including computer operations, programming, and system analysis. Typically users own or lease the hardware installed at their sites. The user establishes the guidelines under which the facilities-management vendor operates the computer.

This approach is advantageous primarily to the company installing its first computer. A facilities-management vendor can offer its expertise and its experienced personnel to the new user. An established, smoothly operating installation has its own expertise. The primary disadvantage of facilities management is that outsiders manage an extremely important segment of a company's operations.

Peripheral-Hardware Manufacturers

Much of the peripheral hardware in a computer system can be acquired from vendors other than the CPU manufacturers. Components such as tape drives, disk drives, and printers are plug-compatible with hardware produced by computer manufacturers. In fact, some companies produce CPUs that can be used in IBMs or other big-name computers. Such equipment can be significantly less expensive. However, the user may encounter service and maintenance problems when dealing with more than one vendor. When equipment fails, it may be difficult to pinpoint which vendor's equipment is responsible.

Information-System Consultants

Certified Public Accountant (CPA) firms and management consulting firms both provide information-system consulting services. Consultants can be invaluable to new users and to experienced users who are making major changes in their systems. Equipment salespeople are not always accurate in their performance claims. **Information-system consultants** can help the user evaluate these claims and choose a satisfactory system. The services provided by a consultant range from help in selecting hardware and software to doing the complete system development life cycle for a large custom-built system. These services may include programming. Consulting is a rapidly growing industry.

■ Generally, users are heavily involved with the evaluation and acquisition of computer hardware and software. Management consulting firms and CPA firms aid in evaluating and installing computer information systems.

■ The primary topics in this module are system evaluation, finance options, and sources of information-systems equipment and services.

■ Summing Up

■ A system evaluation consists of the following steps: feasibility study, structured system analysis, development of a request for proposal, proposal evaluation, and vendor selection.

■ Three financing alternatives for computer acquisition are available: purchasing, renting, and leasing. The trade-offs among the three options primarily involve cost considerations, capital availability, risks of obsolescence, and flexibility.

■ The buyer or user of computer information systems has a wide choice of sources for equipment and services. Among them are:

1. Computer manufacturers.
2. Retail computer stores.
3. Software vendors.
4. Service bureaus.
5. Timesharing services.
6. Computer lessors.
7. Facilities-management vendors.
8. Peripheral-hardware manufacturers.
9. Information-system consultants.

■ Key Terms

bundling	compatibility
plug-compatible	modularity
request for proposal (RFP) document	software directories
kernel program	risk of obsolescence
benchmark programs	flexibility
compute-bound	retail computer stores
workload models	service bureaus
simulation techniques	timesharing services
monitors	facilities-management vendor
fine tuning	information-system consultants
vendor support	

■ Review Questions

1. What are the five primary phases of evaluating computer systems?
2. What areas should be covered in a request for proposal?
3. What are some current techniques a buyer can use to evaluate a computer system's performance?
4. Distinguish between a benchmark program and a workload model.
5. How can simulation be used to evaluate computer systems?
6. Describe and evaluate the usefulness of monitors.
7. What are the primary criteria that should be used to evaluate a computer system?
8. Discuss the importance of compatibility as a criterion for evaluating a computer system.
9. What finance options are available to the computer user?
10. What are the available sources of computer equipment and services?

11. Are monitors used more in the selection of new systems or in the evaluation of existing systems? Why?

12. What is modularity, and why is it an important consideration in selecting a computer system?

13. Identify four criteria for equipment that should be considered when selecting a vendor.

14. Identify six criteria for software that should be considered when selecting a computer system.

1. Janet Smith, owner and manager of a small business that produces delicate engineering instruments, has decided to acquire a computer system. She plans to use it for accounts receivable, accounts payable, payroll, and manufacturing control. Her company deals with few customers and suppliers. Most orders are large and designed to customer specifications. Janet is an engineer and has managed operations first-hand, usually relying on her own observations for control. Her management philosophy is that no reports are as beneficial as "seeing it for yourself." She has always been fascinated with gadgets and computer technology. Based on the information presented, should she acquire a computer system? Why or why not?

2. The Cascade Company has just reviewed five proposed computer configurations. Based on the review, the firm rated the five configurations on a scale of one to ten (ten being the most desirable rating). The results appear in the following table. Examine the table, and determine which configuration (A, B, C, D, or E) should be selected for the Cascade Company. Justify your choice. The weighting factor expresses the importance of each characteristic. Each configuration rating is multiplied by the weighting factor and the results are summed for each configuration to obtain an overall rating.

■ Discussion
■ Questions
   and Cases

Characteristic	Weighting Factor	CONFIGURATION RATING				
		A	B	C	D	E
Hardware						
Memory size	0.9	10	9	8	7	5
Bus characteristics	0.5	10	10	6	9	8
Disk capacity	0.8	9	8	10	7	9
Modularity	1.0	8	7	10	9	8
Capatibility	1.0	10	9	10	10	10
Software						
Operating system	0.9	6	10	8	7	10
Languages	0.6	10	10	9	10	10
Application programs	0.4	10	5	5	9	8
Compatibility	0.9	6	9	8	5	10
Vendor support	1.0	2	9	6	9	8
Cost	1.2	7	10	8	7	9
Benchmarking results	1.1	10	8	10	7	10

3. Curtis Company operates in a five-county industrial area. The company uses a manual system for all its record keeping except payroll, which is processed by a local service bureau. Other applications were not computerized because they could not be cost-justified. However, the company's sales have grown at an increasing rate over the past five years, so a computer-based system seems more practical. Consequently, Curtis recently hired a management consulting firm to conduct a feasibility study for converting its record-keeping system to a computer-based system. The consulting firm reported that a computer-based system would improve the company's record keeping and also provide material cost savings. Therefore, Curtis decided to develop a computer system, and they hired a person with experience in system development as manager of systems and data processing. The manager's responsibilities is to oversee the entire systems operation, with special emphasis on the development of the new system. Describe the major steps that will be undertaken to develop and implement Curtis Company's new computer-based system. (Adapted from CMA Examination, June 1976, Part 5, No. 4).

4. American Chemical is a large chemical company headquartered on the West Coast. About two years ago, American decided it needed a new computer-based accounts-payable system. After doing a feasibility study and developing a requirements document, the company decided to purchase an accounts-payable package from a large and reputable software house. Based on demonstrations of the system and on subsequent evaluations, American decided the package should be modified to fit American's specific needs. A contract was developed with the software house to make the necessary modifications. About eight months later, it became apparent that the software house was not going to succeed in making these modifications. By this time, American had invested several hundred thousand dollars in the package, but the software house could not get the package to execute after the modifications. In an attempt to salvage its investment, American hired another software development firm to try to straighten out the mess. This attempt was unsuccessful as well. Primarily because of this disastrous experience, the director of MIS for American Chemical instituted a policy which stated that before an outside software package can be purchased, the package must meet American's needs close enough so that no modification is required, or alternatively, American Chemical must be able to change its way of doing business to fit the way the package operates, without modification. Evaluate this policy.

5. Carolina Manufacturing is considering installing a manufacturing resources planning (MRP) system. Carolina has had extensive experience in the use of computers, having installed its first computer-based system in the late 1950s. In addition, Carolina has many manufacturing experts on its staff. However, no one in the company has experience with MRP systems. The director of manufacturing and the director of MIS currently disagree on how to gain the necessary MRP experience to implement this system. Angela Battle, the director of MIS, advocates hiring an outside consulting firm to guide the company in the implementation of the MRP system. Consulting rates in the area are $125 per hour, and it is expected that the total consulting fee would be approximately $100,000. Jim Johnson, the director of manufacturing, thinks Angela should hire someone with MRP experience to join the MIS staff. Such an individual could be hired for about $50,000 per year, which includes fringe benefits. Which approach do you think Carolina should take?

Glossary

Sources

The many differing definitions of information systems terms are often a barrier to our understanding of information systems. The American National Standards Institute (ANSI) has attempted to standardize the definitions of these terms through publication of the *American National Standards Dictionary for Information Processing.* Whenever possible, we use ANSI definitions. Definition sources are identified as follows:

1. ANSI definitions are preceded by an asterisk. An asterisk to the left of the term indicates that the entire entry is reproduced with permission from American National Standards Committee X3 Technical Report *American National Standards Dictionary for Information Processing Systems*, X3/TR-1-82 copyright 1982 by The Computer and Business Equipment Manufacturers Association (CBEMA). Copies of this publication can be purchased from CBEMA, 311 First Street N.W., Suite 500, Washington, D.C. 20001. When definitions from other sources are included in the entry, ANSI definitions are identified by an asterisk to the right of the term. The term "(ISO)" at the beginning of a definition indicates that the definition is from the *ISO Vocabulary-Information Systems* developed by the International Organization for Standardization.
2. Definitions from *Dictionary of Computing*, IBM Publication C-20-1699-07 (1987), are indicated by "(IBM)," which precedes the definition.

access: to read, write, or update information, usually on secondary storage such as a disk.

* access arm: A part of a magnetic disk storage unit that is used to hold one or more reading and writing heads. (ISO) In a magnetic disk unit, an arm on which magnetic heads are mounted.

access controls: The controls that limit access to program documentation, program and data files, and computer hardware.

* access time: (ISO) The time interval between the instant at which a call for data is initiated and the instant at which the delivery of data is completed.

accounts payable system: A computer system that helps provide control over payments to suppliers, issues checks to these suppliers, and provides information necessary for effective cash management.

accounts receivable system: A computer system used for billing customers, maintaining records of amounts due from customers, and generating reports on overdue amounts.

* accuracy: (1) (ISO) A quality held by that which is free of error. (2) (ISO) A qualitative assessment of freedom from error, with a high assessment corresponding to a small error.

acoustic coupler (IBM): A type of telecommunication equipment that permits use of a telephone handset as a connection to a telecommunication line for data transmission by means of sound transducers.

action construct: A construct in a program where a single action is performed.

ADA (IBM): A high-level programming language based on PASCAL that was developed by the U.S. Department of Defense.

* address: (1) (ISO) A character or group of characters that identifies a register, a particular part of storage, or some other data source or destination. (2) (ISO) To refer to a device or a data item by its address.

algorithm: Synonym for *program.*

alphabetic character (IBM): A letter or other symbol, excluding digits, used in a language.

* alphanumeric: Pertaining to a character set that contains letters, digits, and usually other characters, such as punctuation marks. Synonymous with *alphameric.*

American National Standards Institute (ANSI) (IBM): An organization consisting of producers, consumers, and general-interest groups, that establishes the procedures by which accredited organizations create and maintain voluntary industry standards in the United States.

* analog: Pertaining to data consisting of continuously variable physical quantities.

* analog computer: (ISO) A computer that processes analog data.

* analyst: (ISO) A person who defines problems and develops algorithms and procedures for solutions to the problems.

anticipation check: A control based on the fact that certain fields in an input record should always be nonblank or that an input record is expected for each master file record.

APL (IBM): A general-purpose programming language for diverse applications such as commercial data processing, system design, mathematical and scientific computation, data-base applications, and the teaching of mathematics and other subjects.

application: A specific use of a computer to perform a business task.

application controls: Controls applied directly to the individual computer application including: (1) input controls, (2) processing controls, and (3) output controls.

application development by users: The development of application programs by users, with only limited support from programmers and system analysts.

application generator: A software system that generates computer programs based on the user's needs. It consists of a large number of precoded modules that perform various functions. The user merely specifies the functions needed for his or her application, and the system invokes the appropriate modules and runs them.

application program (IBM): A program, written for or by a user, that applies to the user's work, such as a program that does inventory control or payroll.

application programmer: A programmer who writes and maintains application programs. Contrast with *system programmer.*

application software: Programs, written for or by a user, that have to do with a particular application of the computer. A payroll program is application software.

application systems: Computer programs written to perform specific business tasks.

archival storage: Storage, not under direct control of the computer, on which backup information and old records are kept.

arithmetic assignment: The assignment of the results of an arithmetic operation to a numeric variable.

* arithmetic and logic unit: (ISO) The part of a computer that performs arithmetic, logic, and related operations.

arithmetic operator: A symbol that represents the performance of an arithmetic operation, such as addition, subtraction, multiplication, or division.

arithmetic proof checks: A control that verifies the results of mathematical operations.

array: An arrangement of elements in one or more dimensions.

* artificial intelligence (AI): The capability of a device to perform functions that are normally associated with human intelligence, such as reasoning, learning, and self-improvement.

* ASCII (American Standard Code for Information Interchange): The standard code, using a coded character set consisting of 7-bit coded characters (8 bits including a parity check), that is used for information interchange among data processing systems, data communication systems, and associated equipment. The ASCII set consists of control characters and graphic characters.

* assemble: (ISO) To translate a program expressed in an assembly language into a computer language equivalent.

* assembler: (ISO) A computer program that is used to assemble. Synonymous with *assembly program.*

* assembly language: (ISO) A computer-oriented language whose instructions are symbolic and usually in one-to-one correspondence with computer instructions and that may provide other facilities such as the use of macroinstructions. Synonymous with *computer-dependent language.*

assignment: Placing a certain value in a variable.

assignment statement: A program statement that performs some computations and assigns the resulting value to a variable.

asynchronous transmission: A data transmission method in which each byte is transmitted separately.

attribute: A characteristic or property that an entity has.

audit trail: The capability to reconstruct processing steps and trace information back to its origins.

backup copy: A duplicate of data or programs used to restore the original if it is lost or destroyed.

backup file: A file that contains redundant copies of programs and data which are used to reconstruct current files in case current files are partially or totally destroyed.

backup procedure: A control procedure that provides additional evidence about the integrity of stored information.

base register: A register (in the CPU) that is used as a reference point to specify all other storage locations for the program.

BASIC (Beginner's All-Purpose Symbolic Instruction Code) (IBM): A high-level programming language with a small number of statements and a simple syntax that is designed to be easily learned and used and that is widely used for interactive applications on microcomputers.

batch (IBM): An accumulation of data to be processed.

batch-direct: The processing method where changes and inquiries to the file are batched and processed periodically under a direct-access file-organization method.

* batch processing: (1) The processing of data or the accomplishment of jobs accumulated in advance, in such a manner that the user cannot further influence processing while it is in progress. (2) The processing of data accumulated over a period of time. (3) Loosely, the execution of computer programs serially. (4) Pertaining to the technique of executing a set of computer programs such that each is completed before the next program of the set is started.

batch-sequential processing: The processing method where changes and inquiries to the file are batched and processed periodically under a sequential-file access method.

batch-serial execution: A method of data processing where each program is executed in the order in which it was read into the system; only one program is executed at a time.

batch total: The sum resulting from the addition of a specified numeric field from each record in a batch of records which is used for control and checking purposes. See *control total* and *hash total*.

* baud: A unit of signaling speed equal to the number of discrete conditions or signal events per second. Synonymous with *bits per second (bps)*.

benchmark program: A sample program that is representative of at least part of the buyer's primary computer workload and that is executed on various computer configurations to provide information useful in making a computer acquisition decision.

bidirectional printing: The ability of a printer to print onto the paper when the carriage is moving either to the right or to the left. This speeds up printing because it eliminates carriage returns during which no printing can take place.

binary: (1) A condition that has two possible values or states. (2) A number system whose base is two.

* binary digit (bit): (ISO) In binary notation, either of the characters 0 or 1. Synonym for *bit*.

binary representation: A number system that uses only the digits 0 and 1, rather than the ten digits in the decimal system. This system is used to represent electronic computer design since its two digits are used to present the two conditions (on-off) present in electronic components.

binary search: A method of searching for a value in an array which is in ascending or descending order. The array is split in two, and one half is searched for the value. The half is in turn split into two parts. This process continues until the required element is found.

* bit: (1) (ISO) In the pure binary numeration system, either of the digits 0 and 1. Synonymous with *binary digit*. (2) (ISO) Synonym for *binary element*.

bit mapped: A system in which each possible dot of a CRT display is controlled by a single bit of memory.

* block: (1) (ISO) A string of records, words, or characters that for technical or logical purposes are treated as a unity. (2) A collection of contiguous records that are recorded as a unit, and the units are separated by interblock gaps.

block format: The format of each individual message sent through a communication system. This includes control characters to mark the beginning and end of the message, and error-detection characters.

bootstrap: A program used to start (or "boot") the computer, usually by clearing the primary memory, setting up various devices, and loading the operating system from secondary storage or ROM.

bottleneck: A slowdown in one part of the system that can cause the whole system to operate below capacity.

boundary: The area that separates one system from another.

bpi (IBM): Bits per inch.

bps: Bits per second.

branching: The transfer of execution to nonsequential statements.

break: A key on most keyboards that is used to tell the computer that the current operation is to be aborted.

bubble sort: A method of sorting the elements of an array. Each element is compared with the next element, and if they are out of order, they are switched.

bubble storage: A nonvolatile memory device that stores data by polarizing microscopic bubbles in a crystalline substance.

buffer area: An area in primary memory where data are stored temporarily after being retrieved from secondary storage or before being placed in secondary storage. The data may be modified by a program while in the buffer.

* bug: A mistake or malfunction.

bundling: The selling of hardware and software together as a package.

* burst: (1) In data communication, a sequence of signals counted as one unit in accordance with some specific criterion or measure. (2) To separate continuous-form paper into discrete sheets.

bus: A communication link that connects the CPU to its peripheral devices.

byte: (1) * (ISO) A binary character string operated upon as a unit and usually shorter than a computer word.

cache (IBM): A high-speed buffer storage that contains frequently accessed instructions and data, it is used to reduce access time.

CAD: An acronym for computer-aided design or computer-assisted design. The term covers a wide range of systems that function as tools to expedite mechanical and electronic design.

calculate: To perform one or more arithmetic functions including addition, subtraction, multiplication, and division.

* calculator: (ISO) A device that is especially suitable for performing arithmetic operations, but that requires human intervention to alter its stored program, if any, and to initiate each operation or sequence of operations. A calculator performs some of the functions of a computer but does not usually operate without frequent human intervention.

call: To cause a module to begin execution.

CAM: An acronym for computer-aided manufacturing or computer-assisted manufacturing.

capacity: The amount of data that can be stored on a disk, most often expressed in kilobytes or megabytes (1,024 and 1,048,576 bytes, respectively). Because most disks use some area for storing format and location information, capacities are usually given as both unformatted and formatted.

* card punch: (ISO) An output unit that produces a record of data in the form of hole patterns in punched cards.

* card reader: (1) (ISO) An input unit that reads or senses the holes in a punched card, transforming the data from hole patterns to electrical signals. (2) An input device that senses hole patterns in a punched card and translates them into machine language. Synonymous with *punched card reader.*

card sorter: (ISO) A device that deposits punched cards in pockets selected according to the hole patterns in the cards.

cartridge: For tape, one of the ways that recording tape is packaged. Cartridges include two tape reels and a set of guide rollers inside a shell that looks like a fat audio cassette. For disks, cartridges are plastic shells that hold removable hard disks.

cassette: A package for magnetic tape similar in appearance to a standard audio cassette, but filled with tape optimized for digital recording.

cathode ray tube (CRT) (IBM): A vacuum tube in which a beam of electronics can be moved to draw lines or to form characters or symbols on its luminescent screen.

cell (IBM): In a spreadsheet, an area at the intersection of a column and a row that may contain a value computed according to a defined relationship with other cells; for example, a value representing a total of the cell values in a column or row or an average of those values. When a cell value is changed, the values in all affected cells are recalculated automatically.

* central processing unit (CPU): (ISO) That part of a computer that includes the circuits that control the interpretation and execution of instructions. Synonymous with *central processor.*

central processor (IBM): A processor that contains the sequencing and processing facilities for instruction exe-

cution, interruption action, timing functions, initial program loading, and other machine-related functions.

chained list (IBM): (ISO) A list in which the data elements may be dispersed but in which each data element contains information for locating the next. Synonymous with *linked list.*

chaining (IBM): A method of storing records in which each record belongs to a list or group of records and has a linking field for tracing the chain.

channel: (1) * A path along which signals may be sent; for example, an output channel. (2) (IBM) A device that connects the processing unit and main storage with the I/O control units. (3) The individual magnetic tracks along the length of the tape.

* character: (ISO) A member of a set of elements that is used for the organization, control, or representation of information: the elements may be letters, digits, punctuation marks, or other symbols.

character data: Data on which arithmetic calculations cannot be done.

* character printer: (ISO) A printer that prints a single character at a time. Synonymous with *serial printer.*

* character set: An ordered set of unique representations called characters; for example, the 26 letters of the English alphabet, boolean 0 and 1, the set of symbols in the Morse code, and the 128 ASCII characters.

character string assignment: The assignment of a literal value to a string variable.

* check bit: A binary check digit; for example, a parity bit.

checkpoint: (1) * A sequence of instructions in a program for recording the status of execution for restart purposes. (2) (IBM) A point at which information about the status of a job and the system can be recorded so that the job step can be later restarted.

chief programmer team: An organizational structure often used for programming projects. A small group (consisting of a chief programmer, assistant programmers, a librarian, and a back-up programmer) works independently on a programming task with very little supervision.

* chip: (1) A minute piece of semiconductive material used in the manufacture of electronic components. (2) An integrated circuit on a piece of semiconductive material.

circuit board: See *printed circuit board.*

classify: The identification of an item of data with a certain category. For instance, a sales transaction can be classified as cash or credit.

clock/calendar: A hardware and software feature that automatically sets the time and date when the computer is started or rebooted.

clustered system: A data entry system in which several keyboards are connected to one or two magnetic tape drives.

* COBOL (Common Business-Oriented Language): A programming language designed for business data processing.

CODASYL (IBM): Conference on Data Systems Languages.

code: (1) * (ISO) A set of rules that maps the elements of one set, the coded set, onto the elements of another set, the code element set. Synonymous with *coding scheme.* (2) * A set of items, such as abbreviations, that represent the members of another set. (3) (IBM) Loosely, one or more computer programs, or part of a computer program. (4) (ISO) To represent data or a computer program in a symbolic form that can be accepted by a processor. (5) (IBM) To write a routine.

code inspection: A review of program code by a review team. The programmer walks the reviewers through the code, and they check it for compliance with design specifications.

* coding scheme: (ISO) Synonym for *code (1).*

* collator: (ISO) A device that collates, merges, or matches sets of punched cards or other documents.

* column: A vertical arrangement of characters or other expressions. Contrast with *row.*

* command: (1) A control signal. (2) Loosely, a mathematical or logic operator. Synonym for *instruction.*

communication protocol: A set of rules governing the flow of data through a communication system.

communications processor: A device that converts data to a standard protocol before transmitting it over communication lines, and decodes received data for the computer's own use.

compare: To examine two pieces of data to determine whether they are equal or one is greater than the other.

compatible (IBM): Pertaining to computers on which the same programs can be run with appreciable alteration.

* compile: (1) (ISO) To translate a computer program expressed in a high-level language into a program expressed in an intermediate language, assembly language, or machine language. (2) To prepare a machine language program from a computer program written in another programming language by making use of the overall logic structure of the program, or by generating more than one computer instruction for each symbolic statement, or both, as well as performing the function of an assembler.

* compiler: (ISO) A computer program for compiling. Synonymous with *compiling program.*

compiler diagnostics: Errors detected in a computer program during its compilation.

compile-time diagnostics: Error diagnostics that are produced when a program is compiled.

compressed format: A data format that eliminates necessary blanks between data values.

compressed printing: By reducing the horizontal distance between dots in a dot-matrix printer, characters can be made to be printed narrower, although they remain the same height, so that there are more characters per inch and thus a compressed format.

* computer: A device that consists of one or more associated processing units and peripheral units that is controlled by internally stored programs and that can perform substantial computations including numerous arithmetic operations, or logic operations, without human intervention during a run. A computer may be a stand-alone unit or it may consist of several interconnected units.

computer-assisted instruction (CAI) (IBM): A data-processing application in which a computing system is used to assist in the instruction of students. The application usually involves a dialogue between the student and a computer program that informs the student of mistakes as they are made.

* computer crime: A crime committed through the use of software or data residing in a computer.

computer fraud: Illegal use of computer facilities to misappropriate corporate resources. This includes unauthorized changes to both software and hardware systems.

* computer graphics: That branch of science and technology concerned with methods and techniques for converting data to or from visual representation, using computers.

computer operator: An employee who monitors the performance of the CPU and storage devices. He or she performs most of the human functions necessary to keep the system running.

* computer output microfilm (COM): Microfilm that contains data recorded directly from computer-generated signals.

* computer program: (ISO) A sequence of instructions suitable for processing by a computer. Processing may include the use of an assembler, a compiler, an interpreter, or a translator to prepare the program for execution, as well as the execution of the program. The sequence of instructions may include statements and necessary declarations.

computer service technician: A trained technician who is responsible for the repair and maintenance of hardware devices.

concatenation: The process of joining together two or more literals to form a single literal.

concentric tracks: Circular tracks that have a common center.

* concurrent: (1) (ISO) Pertaining to processes that take place within a common interval of time during which they may have to alternately share common resources; for example, several programs are concurrent when they are executed by multiprogramming in a computer having a single instruction control unit. (2) Contrast with *consecutive, sequential,* and *simultaneous.*

connection: A link between two modules showing which module calls the other.

* consecutive: (1) (ISO) In a process, pertaining to two events that follow one another without the occurrence of any other event between them. Contrast with *concurrent, sequential, simultaneous.*

* console: The part of a computer that is used for communication between the operator or maintenance engineer and the computer.

constant: (IBM) (ISO) In programming languages, a language object that takes only one specific value.

consultant: An EDP information systems expert who assists users in developing and debugging their own applications.

control: The process of comparing actual results to planned results.

control data: Data the program uses solely for making processing decisions.

control group: A personnel group separated from computer operations which maintains input-output controls and reviews output prior to distribution to users.

* control program: (ISO) A computer program designed to schedule and to supervise the execution of programs of a computing system. See *operating system.*

control program for microcomputers (CP/M): A popular operating system for personal computers.

control statement: A statement that regulates the order of execution in a program; for example, an IF statement.

control total (IBM): A sum, resulting from the addition of a specified field from each record in a group of records, that is used for checking machine, program, and data reliability. Synonymous with *hash total.*

control unit: (1) A subsystem contained within the transformation process of every information system. A control component selects, interprets, and executes programmed instructions so that the system can function. In total, it controls the actions of a system. (2) That part of the central processing unit that decodes program instructions and directs the other components of the computer system to perform the task specified in the program instruction.

conversion (IBM): (1) The process of changing from one method of data processing to another. (2) The process of changing from one form of representation to another; for example, to change from decimal representation to binary representation.

copy protected: Means that disks or tapes have been recorded in a way that prevents the data on them from being copied, although they can be read and used.

* core storage: (ISO) A storage device that uses magnetic properties of certain materials in which the data medium consists of magnetic cores.

counter: A variable used to keep track of the number of times a loop has been executed. Its value is increased (or decreased) by one every time the loop is traversed.

couple: A data item that moves from one module to another.

CPU time (IBM): The amount of time devoted by the processing unit to the execution of instructions. Synonymous with *CPU busy time.*

* CRT display: See *cathode ray tube.*

cursor (IBM): (ISO) A movable, visible mark used to indicate the position at which the next operation will occur on a display surface.

cursor key: A key that, when pressed, causes the cursor to move in a designated direction. Arrows engraved on the keys indicate direction of cursor movement: up, down, right, left, or home (top left corner of screen).

* cycle: An interval of space or time in which one set of events or phenomena is completed.

cylinder: (1) (ISO) In a disk pack, the set of all tracks with the same nominal distance from the axis about which the disk rotates. (2) (IBM) The tracks of a disk storage device that can be accessed without positioning the access mechanism.

daisy wheel: A print element for several popular printers consisting of a plastic or metal disk with spokes radiating from the center portion (like the petals on a daisy flower). At the end of each spoke is a circular area with a typeface impression on it.

DASD (IBM): See direct-access storage device.

* data: (1) (ISO) A representation of facts, concepts, or instructions in a formalized manner suitable for communication, interpretation, or processing by humans or by automatic means. (2) Any representation such as characters or analog quantities to which meaning is, or might be, assigned.

* data base: A collection of interrelated data, often with controlled redundancy, organized according to a schema to serve one or more applications; the data are stored so that they can be used by different programs without concern for the data structure or organization. A common approach is used to add new data and to modify and retrieve existing data.

data-base administrator: The person responsible for coordinating the data base, including provisions for data security.

data-base machine: A computer dedicated entirely to the use of a data-base management system.

data-base management system (DBMS): A computer program that stores, retrieves, and updates data that are stored on one or more files.

data block: A set of data values processed as a whole.

data cartridge (IBM): A removable storage device that consists of a housing containing a belt-driven magnetic tape wound on a supply reel and, in some cartridges, a take-up reel.

* data communication: (1) (ISO) The transfer of information between functional units by means of data transmission according to a protocol. (2) The transmission and reception of data.

data definition: The process of creating a schema by identifying and describing data elements and their relationships that make up the data-base structure.

* data definition language (DDL): A language that is used to define the relationship between the logical and physical views of a data base.

data dictionary: A dictionary that defines the meaning of each data item stored in a data base, and describes interrelationships among them.

data editing: Synonymous with *editing*.

data entry: The process of entering data into a computer system in order to communicate with it.

data entry operator: An employee who keys data from source documents into computer-readable form such as disk or tape.

data-flow diagram: A graphic representation of the movement and transformation of data within an organization.

data independence: A lack of dependence between the physical structure of data storage and the structure of application programs.

data item: The smallest element of data stored or used by a program.

* data management: In an operating system, the programs that provide access to data, perform or monitor organization and storage of data, and control input/output devices.

data manipulation language (DML): A language used to define operations in a data base, such as retrieval, sorting, and updating of records.

data processing: The capture, storage, and processing of data to transform it into information that is useful for decision making.

data redundancy: Occurs when identical data are stored in two or more files.

data set (IBM): The major unit of data storage and retrieval, consisting of a collection of data in one of several prescribed arrangements and described by control information to which the system has access. Synonymous with *file*.

data structure diagram: A graphical representation of the logical relationships between various data files.

data switch: A device similar to a telephone exchange, which can establish a data communication link between any two devices connected to it.

* data transmission: (ISO) The conveying of data from one place for reception elsewhere by telecommunication means.

data type: The category that a data item belongs to, for example, numeric or alphabetic.

* debug: (ISO) To detect, diagnose, and eliminate errors in programs.

decimal number system: A number system whose base is ten; that is, it represents numbers in terms of the powers of ten (for example, units of tens, hundreds, and so on). This is the number system we normally use in our everyday lives.

decision-making: The process of selecting one course of action from two or more alternatives, based on the value(s) of one or more variable(s).

decision model: A set of rules used in making a choice between two or more alternatives.

* decision table: (1) (ISO) A table of all contingencies that are to be considered in the description of a problem, together with the actions to be taken for each set of contingencies. (2) A presentation in either matrix or tabular form of a set of conditions and their corresponding actions.

decision tree: A graphic representation of all contingencies to be considered, together with the actions that must be taken for each of them.

default format: A data format automatically assigned by the computer, if the programmer does not specify one.

* default option: An implicit option that is assumed when no option is explicitly stated.

demand listing: A report generated only when a user requests it. Typically used to fill irregular needs for information.

demodulation (IBM): (1) The process of retrieving intelligence (data) from a modulated carrier wave. (2) The reverse of modulation.

* **density:** See *recording density.*

desk checking (IBM): In system development, manual simulation of program execution to detect errors in function or syntax through step-by-step examination of a source program.

* **desktop publishing:** Computer-aided publishing that uses data-processing equipment small enough to fit on a desktop or table and suitable for an end user.

destructive process: A process that destroys the existing value of a variable it is operating on.

device (IBM): A mechanical, electrical, or electronic contrivance with a specific purpose.

device controller: A part of the CPU that manages communications between the CPU and peripheral devices.

diagnostics: A set of routines used to detect errors in a program or system malfunctions, or to carry out standard performance tests. Errors and failures are detected by comparing the results with known correct results.

dial-up terminal: (IBM) A terminal on a switched line.

* **digital computer:** (1) A computer that consists of one or more associated processing units and that is controlled by internally stored programs; it may be a stand-alone unit or it may consist of several interconnected units. (2) A computer in which discrete representation of data is used.

digitize: To convert voice or other patterns to digital signals so they can be processed and stored by a digital computer.

DIP switches: A collection of small switches on a Dual In-line Package (DIP), used to select options on circuit boards without having to modify the hardware.

direct access: (1) (ISO) The facility to obtain data from a storage device, or to enter data into a storage device in such a way that the process depends only on the location of those data and not on a reference to data previously accessed. (2) (IBM) Contrast with *sequential access.*

* **direct-access storage:** A storage device that provides direct access to data.

direct-access storage device (DASD) (IBM): A device in which the access time is effectively independent of the location of the data.

direct conversion: A method of converting to a new information system, such that the old system is discontinued one work day and the new system is started the next day.

direct file organization: A file organization that allows direct access to a record without sequentially examining a large number of other records.

directory (IBM): (1) (ISO) A table of identifiers and references to the corresponding items of data. (2) an index used by a control program to locate one or more

blocks of data that are stored in separate areas of a data set in direct-access storage.

disaster controls: Controls that minimize the risk of loss owing to natural disasters such as flooding and hurricanes.

* **disk:** A flat, circular plate with a magnetizable surface layer on which data can be stored by magnetic recording.

disk-controller card: A printed circuit board that interfaces disk storage drives to the CPU of a personal computer.

disk drive: A device that houses a disk or diskette while it is in use. It contains a motor and one or more magnetic heads to read and write data on the disk.

diskette: Synonymous with *floppy disk.*

display: (1) * (ISO) A visual presentation of data. (2) (IBM) (ISO) To present data visually.

distributed data base: A data base that resides on two or more computers simultaneously. The data base can be either partitioned between the two computers or replicated at both locations.

distributed data processing: The concept of distributing the load of data processing through the installation of minicomputers at a company's remote locations, so the local data-processing needs are handled by the remote location's own local computer.

* **document:** A medium and the information recorded on it that generally has permanence and that can be read by humans or machines.

documentation: The aids provided for the understanding of the structure and intended uses of an information system or its components, such as flowcharts, textual material, and user manuals. (2) A collection of documents on a given subject.

documentation standards: Specific procedures for system documentation, including flowcharting conventions, coding conventions, and documentation revision procedures.

DOS: disk operating system.

* **dot-matrix printer:** (ISO) A printer or a plotter that prints characters or line images that are represented by dots. Synonymous with *matrix printer.*

double-density diskette: A diskette that can hold twice as much data as a diskette having standard density.

double-sided diskette: A double-sided diskette provides two surfaces on which data may be written by the computer.

DO-WHILE construct: A construct in a program where an operation is performed repeatedly as long as a certain logical condition remains true.

downloading: The process by which information from within a data base, stored in a remote mainframe or minicomputer, is brought "down" to a personal computer for manipulation.

DP operations department: MIS personnel who are responsible for managing the day-to-day operations of data-processing facilities.

* drum printer: (ISO) An impact printer in which a full character set, placed on a rotating drum, is made available for each printing position.

* dump: (1)(ISO) Data that have been dumped. (2) (ISO) To write at a particular instant the contents of a storage onto another data medium for the purpose of safeguarding the data.

duplex: (IBM) Pertaining to communication in which data can be sent and received at the same time. Synonymous with *full duplex*.

* duplication check: A check based on the consistency of the results of two independent performances of the same task.

EBCDIC (IBM): Extended binary-coded decimal interchange code. A coded character set consisting of 8-bit coded characters.

* echo check: (ISO) A check to determine the correctness of the transmission of data in which the received data are returned to the source for comparison with the originally transmitted data.

* edit: (ISO) To prepare data for a later operation. Editing may include the rearrangement or the addition of data, the deletion of unwanted data, format control, code conversion, and the application of standard processes such as zero suppression.

edit directed I/O: Input or output of formatted data.

editor: A program through which text can be entered into the computer memory, displayed on the screen, and manipulated as the user chooses. An editor is an aid for writing a program. It is also the central component of a word processor.

EDP auditor: An auditor who specializes in auditing computer-based information systems.

* electronic data processing (EDP): (ISO) Data processing largely performed by electronic devices.

electronic disk: Software that permits extra primary memory to be used as if it were a disk drive by simulating disk drives within the system's RAM.

electronic funds transfer system: A computerized system that can transfer money from one point to another immediately, using data communication lines.

electronic mail: The transmittal of messages among computer users over a data communication network.

electronic shopping: Selecting merchandise and ordering it through a remote terminal installed in your home.

embedded pointer: A field within a record which contains the address of a related record.

emulation (IBM): (ISO) The imitation of all or part of one system by another, primarily by hardware, so that the imitating system accepts the same data, executes the same programs, and achieves the same results as the imitated computer system.

encoding: Storage of data in coded form. It cannot be accessed by a user who does not know the code.

encryption: To convert programs or data into a secret code or cipher.

end users: Persons who ultimately use application software.

entity: A subject on which data are kept in an information system.

entry controls: Controls over entry to areas where computer parts, such as CPUs and storage devices, are installed.

* erasable storage: (ISO) A storage device onto which different data can be written at the same storage location. Contrast with *read-only storage*.

ergonomics: The science of designing computer hardware and software to make them more easy and comfortable for humans to use.

error handling: Procedure for detecting errors in input data, and ensuring that they are corrected before the data are processed.

* error message: An indication that an error has been detected.

error recovery: The ability of a system to continue operating normally after the user has made an input error.

exception report: A report generated only if an activity or system gets out of control and requires human attention.

executable statement: A program statement that instructs the computer to perform a certain action.

execution: To run a computer program.

execution path: The specific set of program instructions used by the computer.

execution time (E-Time) (IBM): (1) Any instant at which a program is being executed. (2) The time during which an instruction in an instruction register is decoded and performed.

execution-time diagnostics: Error diagnostics that are produced when a program is executed.

* executive program: Synonym for *supervisory program*.

expansion board: A printed circuit board that accommodates extra components for the purpose of expanding the capabilities of a computer.

expansion slot: A slot for installing additional expansion boards that perform functions not provided by the computer's standard hardware.

expert systems: Systems that possess artificial intelligence.

expression: A variable, constant, function, or any combination of these elements separated by arithmetic or relational operators.

extract: (1) * (ISO) To select and remove from a set of items those items that meet some criteria; for example, to obtain certain specified digits from a computer word as controlled by an instruction or a mask. (2) (IBM) To remove specific items from a file.

facilities management vendor: A firm that specializes in managing, staffing, and operating computer installations for its customers.

feasibility study: The first step in the system development life cycle. At this step, the system analyst identifies the objectives of the present system and determines whether an attempt to develop a new system would be cost-effective.

fiber optics: A laser-based data communication technique that transmits data over glass fibers by means of light waves (photonic—light-based—mode of data transmission).

* field: (ISO) On a data medium or in storage, a specified area used for a particular class of data; for example, a group of character positions used to enter or display wage rates on a screen.

* file: (ISO) A set of related records treated as a unit; for example, in stock control, a file could consist of a set of invoices.

file activity ratio: The proportion of master file records that are actually used or accessed in a given processing run of the file or during a given period of time.

file area: The area on the disk available for storage of files containing data or programs.

file directory: The disk area allocated to hold a directory that names and indicates the area occupied by each file and the available space on the disk.

* file layout: (ISO) The arrangement and structure of data or words in a file, including the order and size of the components of the file.

file-maintenance inputs: All file changes that are not originated by transactions.

* file organization: The physical order of records in a file, as determined by the access method used to store and retrieve them.

file protected (IBM): Pertaining to a tape reel with the write-enable ring removed.

file-protection ring: A plastic ring that must be inserted into a reel of magnetic tape before it can be written on. (An alternative is a no-write ring, which prevents the file-protection ring from being inserted and therefore prevents files from being written on when it is inserted in a reel of tape.)

file-protect notch: The cut-out area in the upper right corner of a floppy disk; it is used to prevent accidental destruction of data.

file query: The retrieval of some specific information from a file.

file volatility ratio: The proportion of additions and deletions in a file during a given period of time.

fine tuning: Removing bottlenecks and reallocating work among system resources in order to obtain maximum output from the given resources.

fire controls: Controls that minimize the risk of losses from fire. These include both emergency procedures and preventive measures.

fixed disk: A disk that is permanently mounted in its disk drive, or the disk and drive combination.

fixed-length record (IBM): A record having the same length as all other records with which it is logically or physically associated. Contrast with *variable-length record.*

fixed-point constant: Synonymous with *integer constant.*

* flag: (1) Any of various types of indicators used for identification; for example, a word mark. (2) A character that signals the occurrence of some condition, such as the end of a word. (3) (ISO) Synonym for *sentinel.*

flat file: A file containing only fixed-length records of equal length.

floating parameter: A variable within the definition of a user-defined function. It has no meaning outside the function definition.

floppy disk: A data storage medium that is a 3½-, 5¼-, or 8-inch disk of polyester film covered with a magnetic coating.

* flowchart: (ISO) A graphical representation in which symbols are used to represent such things as operations, data, flow direction, and equipment for the definition, analysis, or solution of a problem. Synonymous with *flow diagram.*

* font: A family or assortment of characters of a given size and style: for example, 9-point Bodoni Modern.

format: To put the magnetic track and sector pattern on a disk, which is needed before the disk can store any information. Formatting completely erases any previously stored data.

* FORTRAN (Formula Translation): A programming language primarily used to express computer programs by arithmetic formulas.

fourth-generation language: A flexible application development tool, such as an electronic spreadsheet, query language, or application generator, that allows you to develop an application by describing to the computer what you want rather than programming it in a how-to, step-by-step fashion.

front-end processor: A computer configuration where the minor jobs or communication tasks are handled by a mini-CPU, allowing the main CPU to handle all batch jobs and programs the front-end processor cannot handle.

full duplex (IBM): Synonym for *duplex.*

function: A preprogrammed set of statements that can be called by a one-line reference, and that returns one single value to the calling program.

functional area: An organizational unit of a business corresponding to its major duty or activity, such as engineering or finance.

functional information system: A set of application systems that satisfies the information needs within a functional area of the business.

functional primitive: The lowest level of a data-flow diagram, where the actual processing of data is described.

functional reference: A call to a function at some point in the program. This is done simply by giving the function name and a value for its parameter(s).

Gantt chart: A graph where activities are plotted as bars on a time scale.

general controls: Overall managerial controls applied to all software, hardware, and personnel involved in the information system.

generalized module: A precoded module that performs some commonly used function. It can be used by many users for a variety of purposes.

generations (IBM): A means of referencing items with respect to time and ancestry such that an item without antecedents is designated as the first generation, and subsequent derivations are designated as the nth generation, where n-1 is the number of derivations from the original.

giga: (G)(IBM): Ten to the ninth power; 1,000,000,000 in decimal notation. When referring to storage capacity, two to the thirtieth power; 1,073,741,824 in decimal notation.

gigabyte: One billion bytes.

grandparent-parent-child backup: A file backup system in which the current version and the two previous versions of a file are always retained.

graphics (IBM): (1) The making of charts and pictures. (2) Pertaining to charts, tables, and their creation. (3) See *computer graphics.*

graphics language: A computer language that can be used to retrieve data from files or data bases and display them graphically.

* hacker: (1) A computerphile. (2) A computerphile who uses his or her knowledge and means to gain unauthorized access to protected data or software.

* half duplex: In data communication, pertaining to an alternating, one way at a time, independent transmission. Contrast with *duplex.*

half-inch tape: The big reels of tape used with mainframes and minicomputers.

hanging separator: A symbol used at the end of a PRINT statement which causes the next PRINT statement to continue writing on the same output line.

hard copy: (1) In computer graphics, a permanent copy of a display image that is portable and can be read directly by human beings; for example, a display image that is recorded on paper. (2) (IBM) A printed copy of machine output in a visually readable form; for example, printed reports, listings, documents, and summaries. Contrast with *soft copy.*

* hard disk: (ISO) A rigid magnetic disk.

hard error: An error in disk data that persists when the disk is reread.

* hardware: (ISO) Physical equipment as opposed to programs, procedures, rules, and associated documentation. Contrast with *software.*

hardware monitor: A machine device that monitors usage and performance of various computer-system devices.

hardware study: An analysis of hardware requirements for an information system. It normally leads to a tentative selection of equipment.

hardwired terminal: A terminal that is directly wired to the computer. See *dial-up terminal.*

* hash total: The result obtained by applying an algorithm to a set of data for checking purposes; for example, a summation obtained by treating data items as numbers.

* head: A device that reads, writes, or erases data on a storage medium; for example, a small electromagnet used to read, write, or erase data on a magnetic disk or magnetic tape.

header: (1) The top part of a report, including the column headings. (2) In a file, the first record that contains descriptive information concerning the file.

header label (IBM): A file or data set label that precedes the data records on a unit of recording media.

header value: A special value specified before a loop is executed. It tells the program how many times the loop is to be performed.

hexadecimal representation: A number system used to represent data internally in a computer and for memory dumps. The digits of a hexadecimal number represent powers of sixteen.

hierarchical network: A distributed system design where a superior/subordinate relationship exists among distributed computer installations.

high-level language (HLL) (IBM): A programming language that does not reflect the structure of any particular computer or operating system.

* Hollerith card: A punch card characterized by eighty columns and twelve rows of punch positions.

horizontal network: A distributed system design where each local installation is equal and has the capability of communicating with all other installations. Synonymous with *ring network*.

host computer (IBM): In a computer network, a computer that provides end users with services such as computation and data bases and that usually performs network control functions. (2) The primary or controlling computer in a multiple computer installation.

human factors: The positive and negative behavioral implications of introducing EDP systems into the workplace.

hybrid network: A ring-structured communication network where each node on the ring is also the center of a star network.

icon (IBM): A symbol on a display screen that a user can point to with a device such as a mouse in order to select a particular operation or software application.

IF-THEN-ELSE construct: A construct in a program where one of two possible courses of action is taken, depending on whether a certain logical condition is true or false.

immediate-direct processing: The immediate processing of transactions and inquiries with direct-access files.

immediate mode: A mode of processing under which transactions are processed to update the master file shortly after they occur.

* impact printer: (ISO) A printer in which printing is the result of mechanical impact.

implementation: A phase in the system development cycle when coding, testing, and manual-procedure development are done.

index: A list used to indicate the addresses of records stored in a file. An index is much like an index to a book.

index file: A file used to indicate the addresses of records stored on secondary storage devices.

index replication (IBM): In VSAM (virtual storage access method), the use of an entire track of direct access storage to contain as many copies of a single index record as possible; replication reduces rotational delay.

indexed sequential access method (ISAM): A file organization where records are stored sequentially, yet direct access can be made to individual records in the file through an index of the records' absolute address.

indexed sequential organization (IBM): A file organization in which records are arranged in logical sequence by key. Indexes to these keys permit direct access to individual records.

inference engine (IBM): In artificial intelligence, the components of an expert system, such as a cluster of connected processors and associated software, that apply principles of reasoning to draw conclusions from the information stored in a knowledge base.

infinite loop: A loop in a program that has no exit. The computer keeps performing the loop indefinitely unless some external action is taken to stop the program.

* information: (1) (ISO) The meaning that is currently assigned to data by means of the conventions applied to that data. (2) In a conceptual schema language, any kind of knowledge about things, facts, or concepts of a universe of discourse that is exchangeable among users.

information center: In an organization, a service department that assists users in developing their own computer applications.

information processing (IBM): The systematic performance of operations on information in conjunction with a computer system to obtain, manipulate, duplicate, exchange, or communicate its meaning; for example, file management, word processing, document interchange, facsimile, and videotext. See also *data processing*.

* information retrieval (IR): (ISO) Actions, methods, and procedures for recovering stored data to provide information on a given subject.

information-system consultant: An individual who assists users with various problems, ranging from simple troubleshooting to complete system design and implementation.

information-system manager: An MIS professional who is responsible for managing the entire EDP department or some part of it.

information-system master plan: An outline of the overall strategy for implementing an information system.

information workers: People who create, process, and use substantial amounts of information as a regular part of their jobs.

in-house development: When a firm produces its own application software.

initial program load (IPL) (IBM): The initialization procedure that causes an operating system to commence operation.

initialize: To assign an initial value to a variable before beginning a specific process. Counter variables are often initialized to zero before they start counting the number of loops executed.

ink-jet printer (IBM): A nonimpact printer that forms characters by projecting a jet of ink onto paper.

input controls: Controls ensuring that all inputs are authorized, accurate, and properly converted to machine-readable format.

* input data: (1) Data being received or to be received by a device or a computer program. Synonymous with *input*. (2) Data to be processed.

input mask: A form displayed on a terminal to guide the keying of input.

input/output control system (IOCS) (IBM): A group of routines provided by IBM for handling the transfer of data between main storage and auxiliary storage devices.

input/output statement. A program statement that causes the computer to either read input data or produce output.

* input unit: (ISO) A device into which data may be entered for use by a data-processing system.

inquiry (IBM): A request for information from storage; for example, a request for the number of available airline seats, or a search for information from a file.

* instruction: (ISO) In a programming language, an expression that specifies one operation and identifies its operands, if any.

integer constant: A constant number that does not contain a decimal point or a fractional part.

integrated circuit: A device containing transistors that have been deposited photochemically on a chip of silicon material. Because of this device, computer speed has greatly increased while computer size has greatly decreased.

integrated package: A personal-computer package that typically includes the functions of electronic spreadsheet, word processing, data-base management, and communications.

integrated word-processing equipment (IBM): Word-processing equipment that has its associated control unit contained within the body of the machine.

intelligent terminal: (1) (IBM) Synonym for *programmable terminal*. (2) A user terminal that has computation capability. (3) A terminal that can be programmed to perform user-determined functions.

interactive (IBM): Pertaining to a program or system that alternately accepts input and then responds. An interactive system is conversational; that is, a continuous dialogue exists between user and system. Contrast with *batch*.

interactive data entry: The process of entering data directly into the computer through a data-entry terminal.

* interface: (1) (ISO) A shared boundary between two functional units defined by functional characteristics, common physical interconnection characteristics, signal characteristics, and other characteristics, as appropriate. The concept involves the specification of the connection of two devices having different functions. (2) A point of communication between two or more processes, persons, or other physical entities.

* interleave: (ISO) To arrange parts of one sequence of things or events so that they alternate with parts of one or more other sequences of the same nature so that each sequence retains its identity.

internal storage: (1) (ISO) Storage that is accessible by a processor, without the use of input/output channels. (2) (IBM) Synonym for *processor storage*.

international data transfer: The movement of data across national boundaries through data-communication networks.

interpreter: A program that translates a high-level language, such as BASIC, into a machine language so it can be used in the computer. It is slower and less efficient than a compiler but easier for programmers to use.

* interrupt: (ISO) A suspension of a process, such as the execution of a computer program, caused by an event external to that process, and performed in such a way that the process can be resumed.

* inverted file: (1) A file whose sequence has been reversed. (2) In information retrieval, a cross-index file in which a keyword identifies a record; the items, numbers, or documents pertinent to that keyword are indicated.

* I/O: Input/output.

* ISO: The International Organization for Standardization.

*item: (ISO) An element of a set of data; for example, a file may consist of a number of items such as records which, in turn, may consist of other items. Synonym for *data item*.

job: (1) * (ISO) A unit of work defined by a user, and to be accomplished by a computer. This term is sometimes loosely used to refer to a representation of a job; the representation may include a set of computer programs, files, and control statements related to the operating system. (2) (IBM) A collection of related programs, identified by appropriate job-control statements.

* job-control language (JCL): A problem-oriented language designed to express job statements that are used to identify the job or to describe its requirements to an operating system.

job queue: A line of programs awaiting their turn for execution.

job schedules (IBM): The part of a control program that reads and interprets job definitions, schedules jobs for processing, indicates and terminates the processing of jobs and job steps, and records job output data.

kernel program: A small sample program executed on various computer configurations to provide information useful to a person or firm making a computer-acquisition decision.

key: (1) *(ISO) Within a set of data, one or more characters that contain information about the set, including its identification. (2) (IBM) To enter information from a keyboard.

keyboard (IBM): (1) An arrangement of typing and function keys laid out in a specified manner. (2) A group of numeric keys, alphabetic keys, or function keys used for entering information into a terminal and into the system.

key-to-disk data entry: The process of recording data on disk before inputting it to the computer.

key-to-diskette data entry: The process of recording data on a diskette before inputting it to the system.

key-to-tape data entry: The process of recording data on magnetic tape before inputting it to the computer.

keypunch: (ISO) A keyboard-actuated punch that punches holes in a data medium. Synonymous with *keyboard punch.*

key verifier: A machine verifying that data were keypunched correctly.

keyword: In a programming language, a special word that tells the computer which operation to perform.

kilobyte: 1,024 bytes of memory, which stores 1,024 characters of data or programs. Kilobyte is usually abbreviated as K. 256 K of memory holds 256 times 1,024 (or 262,144) characters of data. In contexts other than computers, the word *kilo* or the symbol K indicates 1,000. In terms of computers, K is a power of 2 (it is 2^{10} or 1,024) because of the binary nature of computer memory.

knowledge base (IBM): A data base that contains information about human experience in a particular application and data resulting from problems previously solved. See also *expert system.*

knowledge engineering (IBM): The branch of computer science that pertains to the design and development of expert systems.

label: (1) * (ISO) An identifier within or attached to a set of data elements. (2) * (ISO) In programming languages, an identifier that names a statement.

language: In relation to computers, any unified, related set of commands or instructions that the computer can accept. Low-level languages are difficult to use but closely resemble the fundamental operations of the computer. High-level languages resemble English.

language translator (IBM): A general term for any assembler, compiler, or other routine that accepts statements in one language and produces equivalent statements in another language.

laser printer: A high-quality, nonimpact printer that is capable of producing a wide variety of type fonts.

laser storage: A memory device that makes use of laser beams for storing data. These laser beams form microscopic patterns to represent characters on various surfaces.

leasing: A contract arrangement that binds a user to rent a system over a relatively long period of time. Leasing usually costs less than renting.

left justify: To line up characters such that the first nonblank character in each line is on the left margin.

letter quality: Printed output that appears to have been typed on a typewriter.

leveled data-flow diagram: A hierarchically partitioned data-flow diagram. Each level describes in more detail the data flows shown in the level above it. Increased partitioning at lower levels keeps the diagrams of manageable size.

librarian: An MIS employee responsible for the storage of program and data files. These files are usually stored on tape or disk.

* library: (1) A file or a set of related files; for example, a set of inventory-control files in stock control. (2) A repository for demountable recorded media, such as magnetic disk packs and magnetic tapes.

* library routine: A proven routine that is maintained in a program library.

light pen: An input device that allows the console operator to choose among alternatives. When a menu is presented on the screen, for instance, a number of choices are given, each with a box next to it. The operator positions the light pen to a box representing his or her choice and then presses the entry button on the pen. The pen contains a light sensor that returns a signal indicating to the computer which choice the operator has made.

limit/reasonableness checks: See *reasonableness checks.*

linear search: A sequential search of the elements of an array for the purpose of locating a particular value.

line feed: The action of advancing the paper in a printer or the cursor on a screen to the next line.

* line printer: (ISO) A printer that prints a line of characters as a unit. Synonymous with *line-at-a-time printer.* Contrast with *character printer, page printer.*

* linkage editor: A program for creating a load module from one or more object modules.

link-attached terminal (IBM): A terminal whose control unit is connected to a computer by a data link.

link edit (IBM): To create a loadable computer program by means of a linkage editor.

linking: Synonymous with *link editing.*

* list: (1) (ISO) An ordered set of items of data. (2) To print or otherwise display items of data that meet specified criteria. (3) (ISO) Synonym for *chained list*.

literal: Synonymous with *string constant*.

lithium battery: An easily removable battery, lasting twelve to eighteen months, that is usually used to power clock/calendars in personal computers.

load: (1) (ISO) To enter data or programs into storage or working registers. (2) (IBM) To bring a load module from auxiliary storage into main storage for execution.

load module: (ISO) A module that is the output of a linkage editor and is in a form suitable for loading into main storage for execution.

loading (IBM): Adding inductance (load coils) to a transmission line to minimize amplitude distortion.

local area network (LAN): (ISO) A data network, located on a user's premises, in which serial transmission is used for direct data communication among data stations. Communication within a local area network is not subject to external regulation; however, communication across the network boundary may be subject to some form of regulation.

local data: Data that are used by only one computer in a distributed data-processing environment.

logical model: A system model that emphasizes what is to be done, rather than who or what does it.

logical record: (1) * A record independent of its physical environment; portions of one logical record may be located in different physical records or several logical records, or parts of logical records may be located in one physical record. (2) (IBM) A record from the standpoint of its content, function, and use rather than its physical attributes; that is, a record defined in terms of the information it contains.

logical view: Representation of data in a data base in a format that is meaningful to the application programmer and end user.

logoff (IBM): The procedure by which a user ends a terminal session.

logon (IBM): The procedure by which a user begins a terminal session.

loop: A set of statements that are repeatedly performed during program execution. (Also used as a verb.)

loop variable: A variable used as a counter in a FOR-NEXT loop. It keeps track of the number of times the loop has executed.

machine cycle: The time required by the CPU to perform one machine operation.

* machine language: (1) An artificial language whose elements are machine instructions. (2) (ISO) Synonym for *computer language*.

machine operation: The smallest unit of processing done by a computer; for example, adding 0 to 1.

macro instruction: A set of program statements that can be invoked simply by issuing a one-line reference to the set.

mag tape: Magnetic tape.

magnetic core storage: See *core storage*.

* magnetic disk: (ISO) A flat, circular plate with a magnetizable surface layer on one or both sides of which data can be stored. Synonymous with *disk*.

* magnetic drum: (ISO) A circular cylinder with a magnetizable layer on which data can be stored.

magnetic-ink character recognition (MICR): *(ISO) The automatic recognition of characters printed with ink that contains particles of magnetic material. Contrast with *optical character recognition*.

* magnetic storage: (ISO) A storage device that utilizes the magnetic properties of certain materials.

magnetic tape: (ISO) A tape with a magnetizable surface layer on which data can be stored by magnetic recording.

* mainframe: A large computer, usually one to which other computers are connected in order to share its resources and computing power.

* maintainability: (ISO) The ease with which maintenance of a functional unit can be performed in accordance with prescribed requirements.

maintenance: Correcting errors discovered in programs, and updating the programs to satisfy changed requirements.

man-machine boundary: The line of demarcation between manual operations and computerized functions.

management controls: Control mechanisms that ensure proper management of EDP facilities in accordance with organizational objectives.

management information system (MIS): (1) *(ISO) Management performed with the aid of automatic data processing. (2) * An information system designed to aid in the performance of management functions. (3) A system for providing information for decision making; an automated system that uses a computer to process data.

* manual input: (1) Entering data into a device by hand. (2) The data entered manually.

mass storage: (ISO) Storage that has a very large capacity.

master file: (ISO) A file that is used as an authority in a given job and that is relatively permanent, even though its contents may change. Synonymous with *main file*.

matrix printer: (ISO) A printer that makes each character by using a pattern of dots. Synonymous with *dot printer*.

megabyte: 1,048,576 bytes of memory. A megabyte is often thought of as 1 million bytes, but more accurately it is 1,048,576 bytes, since it is 2^{20} bytes.

memory: (IBM) Synonymous with *primary storage*.

memory dump: To print the contents of primary storage.

memory module: Extra memory chips that can be added to personal-computer hardware in order to expand primary storage.

* menu: A displayed list of options from which a user selects actions to be performed.

* MICR: Magnetic-ink character recognition.

Microcoding (microprogramming): The technique of placing programs in hardware devices (like ROM). This is often used for system programs, such as operating systems.

microcomputer: The smallest of computer systems.

* microfiche: A sheet of microfilm capable of containing microimages in a grid pattern, usually containing a title that can be read without magnification.

microfilm: Microfilm whose medium is film (in the form of rolls) that contains microimages arranged sequentially.

microform: A medium that contains microimages; for example, microfiche and microfilm.

* microprocessor: (1) (ISO) A processor whose elements have been miniaturized into one or a few integrated circuits. (2) An integrated circuit that accepts coded instructions at one or more terminals, executes the instructions received, and delivers signals that describe its status. The instructions may be entered, integrated, or stored internally.

microprocessor chip: Contains the circuitry of the CPU—the portion of the computer that does the calculating and executes the program. This chip is mounted in one socket of the CPU board of a personal computer.

microsecond (IBM): One-millionth of a second.

millisecond (IBM): One-thousandth of a second.

minicomputer: A midsize computer generally used in midsize or smaller organizations by several users at the same time.

minimal BASIC: A basic set of commands recommended by the ANSI for inclusion in any version of the BASIC language.

* MIS: Management information system.

* mnemonic symbol: (ISO) A symbol to assist the human memory; for example, an abbreviation such as "mpy" for multiply.

modem (modulator-demodulator): A device that converts digital data from a computer to an analog signal that can be transmitted on a telecommunication line,

and converts the received analog signal to data for the computer.

* modularity: The extent to which a system is composed of modules.

modulation (IBM): The process by which a characteristic of a signal is varied according to a characteristic of another signal.

* module: (1) A discrete set of instructions, usually processed as a unit, by an assembler, a compiler, a linkage editor, or similar routine or subroutine. (2) A packaged functional hardware unit designed to be used with other components.

monitor: (1) (ISO) A functional unit that observes and records selected activities within a data-processing system for the purpose of analysis. (2) (IBM) Software or hardware that observes, supervises, controls, or verifies operations of a system. Synonym for *visual display unit*.

* monitor program: (ISO) A computer program that observes, regulates, controls, or verifies the operations of a data-processing system.

motherboard: A printed circuit board onto which other printed circuit boards connect.

mouse (IBM): (ISO) In computer graphics, a hand-held locator operated by moving it on a flat surface. A mouse generally contains a control ball or a pair of wheels.

MS-DOS (Microsoft disk operating system): An operating system used in personal computers, especially the IBM PC and its compatibles.

* multiplexing: (ISO) In data transmission, a function that permits two or more data sources to share a common transmission medium such that each data source has its own channel.

multiprocessing: (1) (ISO) A mode of operation for parallel processing by two or more processors of a multiprocessor. (2) Pertaining to the simultaneous execution of two or more computer programs or sequences of instructions by a computer.

multiprogramming: (1) *A mode of operation that provides for the interleaved execution of two or more computer programs by a single processor. (2) (IBM) Pertaining to concurrent execution of two or more computer programs by a computer.

* multitasking: (ISO) A mode of operation that provides for concurrent performance or interleaved execution of two or more tasks.

nanosecond (IBM): one-thousand-millionth of a second.

* nest: (1) (ISO) To incorporate one or more structures of one kind into another structure of the same kind; the structure may be a loop, a subroutine, or a set of statements. (2) (ISO) To place subroutines or data into other subroutines or data at a different hierarchical level so that the subroutines can be executed recursively and the data can be accessed recursively.

network (IBM): (1) An arrangement of nodes and connecting branches. Connections are made between data stations. (2) A configuration of data-processing devices and software connected for information interchange.

network data structure: A data structure that allows a many-to-many relationship among the nodes in the structure.

* node: (1) (ISO) In a network, the point at the end of a branch. (2) The representation of a state or an event by means of a point on a diagram. (3) In a tree structure, a point at which subordinate data items originate.

nonexecutable statement: A statement that does not cause the computer to perform any action. It merely informs the computer or a human reader about the format, characteristics, and nature of various data and processes.

nonimpact printer: (ISO) A printer in which printing is not the result of mechanical impacts; for example, thermal printers, electrostatic printers, photographic printers.

nonprocedural language (IBM): Synonyn for *nonprocedure-oriented language.*

nonprocedure-oriented language (IBM): A programming language that allows the user to express the solution to a problem in a form other than as an explicit algorithm. Synonymous with *nonprocedural language.*

nonprogrammable decision: A decision related to an ill-defined or unstructured problem.

nonrecurring costs: The initial costs of a computer system, which are not expected to arise in years subsequent to the initial installation.

nonvolatile storage: Primary or secondary storage that does not lose the data stored in it when the electrical power is interrupted.

numeric: (IBM) Pertaining to data or to physical quantities that consist of numerals. Synonymous with *numerical.*

numeric/alphabetic checks: A control assuring that input record fields which should contain only numeric characters do not contain alphabetic characters, and vice versa.

numeric data: Numbers on which arithmetic calculations will be performed.

numeric variable: A variable that can assume only numeric values.

nybble: Four bits.

object code: A machine-language program that has been produced from a higher-level language through the compilation process. It is called object code since its production is the objective of compilation or translation.

object module: (1) A portion of an object program suitable as input to a linkage editor. (2) A set of instructions in machine language produced by a compiler from a source program.

object program (IBM): (1) (ISO) A fully compiled or assembled program that is ready to be loaded into the computer. Contrast with *source program.*

office automation: The use of EDP systems to perform routine office chores and improve productivity.

offline: Data or devices that are not under direct control of the computer. Usually a person must place an offline reel of tape on a tape drive before the computer can access data stored on it.

* offline storage: Storage that is not under the control of a processing unit.

online: (1) (ISO) Pertaining to the operation of a functional unit when under the direct control of a computer. (2) Pertaining to a user's ability to interact with a computer.

online direct-access system: A computer system that has several terminals in direct communication with the CPU, which in turn is in direct communication with direct-access files.

online storage: (IBM) Storage under the control of the processing unit.

online system (IBM): A system where the input data enter the computer directly from the point of origin, or output data are transmitted to where they are used.

operand: (1) * (ISO) An entity to which an operation is performed. (2) (IBM) That which is operated upon. An operand is usually identified by the address part of an instruction.

* operating system: (ISO) Software that controls the execution of programs and provides services such as resource allocation, scheduling, input/output control, and data management. Usually, operating systems are predominantly software, but partial or complete hardware implementations are possible.

operation code (IBM): (1) The machine representation of the operation parts of the instruction of a computer. (2) A code used to represent the operations of a computer.

operational decision: A decision on how to carry out specific tasks effectively and efficiently.

operator: A symbol that indicates the performance of a mathematical operation such as division, multiplication, addition, or subtraction.

opscan: Synonymous with *optical scanner.*

* optical character recognition (OCR): Character recognition that uses optical means to identify graphic characters.

optical disk: A disk that records information and reads it back using light (laser beams).

optical reader (IBM): A device that reads hand-written or machine-printed symbols into a computing system.

optical scanner: (1) (ISO) A scanner that uses light for examining patterns. (2) A device that scans optically and usually generates an analog or digital signal.

order-processing system: A computer system that initiates shipping orders, keeps track of back orders, and produces various sales analysis reports.

origination: The creation of raw data as a result of a business event or transaction.

output: The information produced by a computer.

output controls: Controls that help assure the accuracy of computer results and proper distribution of output.

* output device: (ISO) synonym for *output unit*.

* output unit: (ISO) A device by which data can be conveyed out of a computer.

packed-decimal format (IBM): A format in which each byte in a field except the rightmost byte represents two numeric digits. The rightmost byte contains one digit and a sign. For example, the decimal value + 123 is represented as 0001 0010 0011 1111.

packaged software: A program designed for a specific application of broad, general usage, unadapted to any particular installation.

page: (ISO) In a virtual storage system, a fixed-length block that has a virtual address and is transferred as a unit between real storage and auxiliary storage.

page frame (IBM): (1) (ISO) In real storage, a storage location having the size of a page. (2) An area of main storage used to hold a page.

page printer (IBM): A device that prints one page as a unit; for example, a COM printer and a xerographic printer. Synonymous with *page-at-a-time printer*. Contrast with *character printer, line printer*.

paging: (1) (ISO) The transfer of pages between real storage and auxiliary storage. (2) * An allocation technique by which main storage is divided into page frames. A computer program need not be located in contiguous page frames in order to be executed. Synonymous with *page turning*.

paint: To draw directly on a video screen, as opposed to writing programs that create images.

palette: The overall selection of colors or shades available in a graphic display system.

parallel conversion: A method of converting to a new system whereby both the old and the new systems operate concurrently until management is satisfied that the new system will perform satisfactorily.

parallel port: A connection, through which data are transmitted eight bits at a time (or in parallel). Generally used with printers.

* parallel processing: The simultaneous execution of two or more processes in a single unit. Contrast with *serial processing*.

* parallel transmission: (ISO) The simultaneous transmission of the signal elements of a group representing a character or other data item. Contrast with *serial transmission*.

parameter: A constant value supplied to the program by the user. The execution of the program is in some way modified, based on the value of this parameter.

parameterized application package: Prewritten application programs that the user can modify to suit his or her own requirements. The modification is done simply by specifying values for certain parameters.

* parity bit: (ISO) A binary digit appended to a group of binary digits to make the sum of all the digits, including the appended binary digit, either odd or even, as predetermined.

* parity check: (ISO) A redundancy check by which a recalculated parity bit is compared with the predetermined parity bit.

partitioning: Decomposing a data-flow diagram into smaller, more detailed diagrams.

PASCAL: A block-structured, high-level computer language named after the pioneer computer scientist Blaise Pascal.

password (IBM): In computer security, a string of characters known to the computer system and a user, who must specify it to gain full or limited access to the system and the data stored in it.

* patch: (ISO) To make a temporary or expedient modification of a program in order to locate and correct an error.

payroll program: A computer program that prepares checks to pay employees and maintains payment information.

payroll register: A report that provides a recap of payment transactions for each employee and serves as an important part of the audit trail of the system.

payroll system: A computer system that assists in the preparation of salary checks, maintains payment records, and provides management reports related to payroll activities.

peripheral equipment: (IBM) A functional unit that provides services external to a processing unit.

personal computer: A computer small enough to be placed on a desktop and designed to be used by one person who possesses very little, if any, programming knowledge.

PERT-CPM: Scheduling methods using networks consisting of activities that consume resources and take time and events which mark the beginning and end of the activities. These methods allow the minimum amount of time in which a project can be completed and the critical path to be determined.

phased conversion: A method of converting to a new system whereby the old system is gradually phased out, and the new one is gradually phased in at the same time.

physical file: A collection of records that are physically located contiguous to one another. Contrast with *logical file*.

physical implementation: The way a system is actually performed in the real world. Manual systems and automated systems, such as computers, are different types of physical implementation.

physical record: A record whose characteristics depend on the manner or form in which it is stored, retrieved, or moved. A physical record can contain all or part of one or more logical record.

physical view: Representation of the data in a data base in terms of physical characteristics such as location, field length, and access method.

picosecond (IBM): One trillionth of a second; one thousandth of a nanosecond.

pie chart: A chart that shows the relative values of various quantities as arc-shaped sections of a circle.

pilot conversion: A method of converting to a new system where the new system is introduced in some selected departments. If it functions satisfactorily, it is extended to the whole organization.

pixel: The smallest dot that can be displayed on a screen. The word is derived from a contraction of *picture element*. All screen images, including both text and graphics, are made up of pixel combinations. The more pixels per screen, the finer the images that can be drawn.

planning: Part of the process of management decision making. Planning involves identifying the alternatives, selecting the criteria to be used in choosing an alternative, and selecting the plan of action to be implemented.

platter: The metal (or other rigid material) disk that is mounted inside a fixed-disk drive.

plotter: An output device, driven by the computer, that moves a pen across a sheet of paper to create a multiple-line pattern.

plug-compatible: A hardware unit produced by one manufacturer that can directly replace units produced by another manufacturer.

* pointer: (1) A data element that represents an address or location of a related stored record in a file. (2) An identifier that indicates the location of a data item.

point-of-sale (POS) data entry: Immediate entry of sales transactions into the computer through a cash register that is connected to the computer.

polarize: To cause a magnetic substance to contain a positive or negative charge.

polling: A process by which the CPU addresses various terminals in turn to check whether they have any input data for transmission to the CPU. A single line links all these terminals to the CPU.

port: An input/output (I/O) connection for interfacing peripherals and computers.

portability: (1) (IBM) The ability to transfer data from one system to another without being required to recreate or reenter data descriptions or to significantly modify the application being transported. (2) * The ability to run a program on more than one computer without modifying the program.

post-implementation audit: Usually consists of two steps: (1) an evaluation of a new system, using the objectives stated during the system-investigation phase, and (2) a review and evaluation of the system development cycle.

power controls: Controls that prevent the system from being damaged by voltage fluctuations and power breakdowns.

precision: The number of digits that a number is allowed to have.

prespecified computing: EDP applications for which processing requirements can be determined ahead of time and programmed in the conventional manner.

primary key: A field in a record whose value uniquely identifies the record. For instance, I.D. number may be a primary key for a file or data base pertaining to students at a university.

primary storage: The area in a central processing unit that stores the program while it is being executed, the data the program is using, and all or part of the operating system. Primary storage is often called memory, internal storage, core storage, or RAM (random access memory).

printed circuit board: A laminated plastic board, about 1/16-inch thick, onto which wiring is electroplated. This wiring connects components and sockets, which are fastened to the board. The sockets receive chips.

print spooler: Software that allows a memory area to hold output to be printed, enabling the user to simultaneously perform other tasks on the personal computer.

printer (IBM): A device that writes output data from a system onto paper or other media.

* procedure-oriented language: A problem-oriented language that facilitates the expression of a procedure as an explicit algorithm; examples include FORTRAN, AL-

GOL, COBOL, and PL/I. Synonymous with *procedural language*.

* **process:** (1) (ISO) To perform operations on data. (2) A course of events defined by its purpose or by its effect, achieved under given conditions. (3) To perform operations on data.

* **process control:** (ISO) Automatic control of a process in which a computer system is used to regulate the usually continuous operations or processes.

process description: A description of the data transformations that occur within the most detailed processes on a data-flow diagram.

processing controls: Controls that increase the integrity of processing.

processor storage (IBM): (1) The storage provided by one or more processing units. (2) In virtual storage systems, synonymous with *real storage*.

production: Refers to the jobs, programs, or files that are used in the daily tasks of an information system.

program: A set of instructions for the computer to follow:

program bug: An error in a computer program.

program code: The instructions used in a computer program.

program documentation: The documentation relating to individual programs.

* **program library:** (ISO) An organized collection of programs or parts of programs, and possibly other information pertaining to their processing. Synonym for *partitioned data set*.

program module: A small, identifiable unit of program statements that performs one program task.

program stubs: Dummy modules that are called by the parent module during the testing phase. This allows testing of the parent module before the lower-level modules are written.

programmable decision: A decision made within the guidelines of an established policy.

programmable read-only memory: A read-only memory into which data or programs can be written by an external programming device.

* **programmer:** A person who designs, writes, and tests computer programs.

programmer/analyst: An MIS professional who performs both programming and system-analysis functions.

* **programming:** (ISO) The designing, writing, and testing of computer programs.

* **programming language:** (ISO) An artificial language designed to generate or to express programs.

* **programming language one (PL/1):** A programming language designed for use in a wide range of commercial and scientific computer applications.

* **project management:** (ISO) The activities concerned with project planning and project control.

prompt: A symbol displayed on the screen to tell the user the operating system or program is ready to accept a new command or line of text.

proprietary: That which is exclusively owned by an individual or corporation, such as a patent.

protect: To safeguard data from unauthorized changes or destruction.

protocol: A set of codes that must be transmitted and received in the proper sequence to guarantee that the terminals or computers are hooked together and can "talk."

prototype: An experimental version of a computer application.

pseudocode: A description of program logic using English-language sentences, instead of computer-language statements.

* **punched card:** (1) (ISO) A card punched with hole patterns. (2) See *Hollerith card*.

QUBE system: A combination of cable TV and a computer system, which allows viewers to respond to a broadcast messages through a keyboard.

queries: Requests for information from a file.

query language: A high-level computer language used to retrieve specific information from a data base.

RAM: See *random access memory*.

RAM disk: See *electronic disk*.

random: Something that occurs in no particular order.

random access: An access technique in which logical records are obtained from or placed in a storage device in a nonsequential manner.

random-access memory: (RAM) Storage whose contents can be read and modified directly, without searching. RAM is usually used for primary storage.

random addressing: Synonymous with *direct addressing*.

randomizing (IBM): A technique by which the range of keys for an indirectly addressed file is reduced to smaller ranges of addresses by some method of computation until the desired address is found.

read-after-write: A mode of operation that has the computer read back each sector written to the disk, checking that the data read back are the same as recorded. This slows down disk operations, but increases reliability.

read-only memory (ROM): (IBM) Memory in which stored data cannot be modified by the user except under special conditions. (ISO) Synonym for *read-only storage*.

read-only storage (ROS): (ISO) A storage device whose contents cannot be modified, except by a particular user, or when operating under particular conditions; for example, a storage device in which writing is prevented by a lockout. Synonymous with *fixed storage*.

read/write head: (ISO) A magnetic head capable of reading and writing.

real constant: A constant that may contain a decimal point with or without a fractional part.

real storage: (ISO) The main storage in a virtual storage system. Physically, real storage and main storage are identical.

real-time information: Information about ongoing events that reflects the status of these events in a completely up-to-date manner.

real-time processing: (ISO) The manipulation of data that are required or generated by some process while the process is in operation; usually the results are used to influence the process, and perhaps related processes, while it is occurring.

real-time system: A computer system with the capability of immediately capturing data concerning ongoing events or processes and providing information necessary to manage these ongoing events.

reasonableness checks: Program controls that monitor the values of input data and make sure that they are within proper limits. For instance, a reasonableness check would trap a time card that showed 150 hours worked in one week.

* record: (ISO) (1) A group of related data elements treated as a unit. (2) A named and usually ordered collection of zero or more data items and data aggregates that represent the occurrence of a set of data values that describe the attributes of a particular entity.

* record layout: The arrangement and structure of data or words in a record, together with a definition of the order and size of the component elements of the record.

* recording density: The number of bits in a single linear track, measured per unit of length of the recording medium.

recurring costs: The costs expected to continually arise throughout the life of the computer installation.

redundancy check: A check that uses one or more extra binary digits or characters attached to data for the detection of errors.

register: (ISO) A storage device having a specified storage capacity such as a bit, byte, or computer word, and usually intended for a special purpose.

* relative address: An address calculated as a displacement from a base address.

relational data model: A logical view of a data base which treats all data as if they were stored in the form of tables.

relational operator: A symbol that represents the performance of a comparison operation between two quantities or values. *Is greater than* is a relational operator.

relevance: The usefulness of data in decision making.

reliability: A quality held by that which is dependable and can be trusted.

remote (IBM): Pertaining to a system, program, or device that is accessed through a telecommunication line.

remote job entry (RJE): (ISO) Submission of a job through an input unit that has access to a computer through a data link.

remote terminal (IBM): A synonym for *link-attached terminal*.

removable disk: A disk drive where the disk itself can be removed; in particular, a hard disk drive that has disks mounted in cartridges.

replication (IBM): See *index replication*.

report: Management information printed on a hard-copy medium such as paper.

report generation: To produce information output.

report generator: A high-level language that can be used to produce reports in almost any format.

report program generator (RPG) (IBM): A programming language specifically designed for writing application programs that meet common business data-processing requirements.

request for proposal: A document that specifies the requirements for equipment and software to be purchased.

reserved words: In a program, words that have a special meaning for the compiler. The user cannot use them for any other purpose.

resident: Pertaining to computer programs or data as long as they remain on a particular storage device.

resident supervisor: That part of the operating system which is used most often and is continuously stored in primary storage.

resolution: The fineness of detail that can be shown on a display screen. Resolution for computer displays is usually stated as the number of possible lines across the image, and the maximum number of possible dot positions in each line. The IBM PC has a maximum screen resolution of 640 dots across by 200 lines down.

resource (IBM): Facilities of a computing system or operating system required by a job or task, including main storage, input/output devices, the processing unit, data sets, and control or processing programs.

resource allocation: (ISO) The assignment of the facilities of a computer system for the accomplishment of jobs; for example, the assignment of main storage, input-output devices, or files.

resource management: Synonymous with *resource allocation*.

response time: (1) * (ISO) The elapsed time between the end of an inquiry or demand on a computer system and the beginning of the response; for example, the length of time between an indication of the end of an inquiry and the display of the first character of the response at a user terminal.

retrieve: To move data from secondary storage to the CPU so that they can be processed.

right justify: To line up characters such that the last nonblank character in each line is on the right margin.

rigid disk: A hard, flat, circular plate coated with magnetic material and used as a secondary storage device.

ring-network configuration: A communication network in which several CPUs are connected in a circular pattern. Each computer can communicate with either one of its neighbors in the circle.

risk analysis (IBM): In computer security, a determination of the possible threats to the security of a system and the undesirable events that can result.

* RJE: (ISO) See *remote job entry*.

ROM: See *read-only memory*.

rounding: The process of replacing a number with the closest possible number, after dropping some of its decimal digits.

* routine: (ISO) A program, called by another program, that may have general or frequent use.

* row: (1) A horizontal arrangement of characters or other expressions. (2) Contrast with *column*.

RPG: See *report program generator*.

RS-232C (serial) port: A personal computer I/O port through which data are transmitted and received serially, one bit at a time. It can be used in conjunction with modems, printers, and other serial devices.

* run: (ISO) (1) (ISO) A performance of one or more jobs. (2) (ISO) A performance of one or more programs.

sabotage controls: Controls that reduce the risk of sabotage in EDP operations.

* scan: To examine sequentially, part by part.

schema: The logical structure of a data base.

scheduled listing: A report produced at a regular interval, such as a week, a month, or a year.

scratch (IBM): To erase data on a disk or tape or delete their identification so that they can be used for another purpose.

scratch file (IBM): A temporary work file.

* search: (ISO) The examination of a set of items for one or more having a given property.

* secondary key: A key that is not a primary key, but for which an index is maintained; it can identify more than one record.

secondary storage: (1) * (ISO) A storage device that is not primary storage. (2) * Storage that supplements another storage. (3) (IBM) Data storage other than primary storage; for example, storage on magnetic tape or direct-access devices. Synonymous with *external storage, secondary storage*. (4) * Contrast with *primary storage*.

* section: (ISO) Deprecated term for segment.

* sector: (ISO) A predetermined angular part of a track or band on a magnetic drum or magnetic disk, that can be addressed.

seek: A movement of the disk read/write head in or out to a specified track.

segment: Often used as a synonym for *record* in a data-base management system.

segregation of functions: Dividing up the workload among employees such that the work of one becomes a check on the work of others.

self-documenting: A characteristic of a computer language whose statements are easy enough to understand, so that English descriptions of the program steps are not necessary.

semantic gap: A lack of correspondence between a problem definition and the computer code written to solve it.

semantic error: An error in the logic of the program, as opposed to a syntax error.

* semantics: (1) (ISO) The relationships of characters or groups of characters to their meanings, independent of the manner of their interpretation and use. (2) The relationships between symbols and their meanings.

semiconductor: A solid crystalline substance, such as silicon, that has a conductivity greater than good insulators but less than good conductors such as metal.

semiconductor storage: Storage that uses integrated electronic circuits on semiconductor material to represent bits of data. See *chip*.

* sentence: (1) (ISO) In text processing, a sequence of words that is terminated by an end punctuation mark. (2) In a conceptual schema language, a linguistic object that expresses a proposition.

sentinel (IBM): Synonym for *flag*.

sentinel value: Synonymous with *trailer value*.

sequence check: A control that verifies that input records are in ascending order by record-key field.

* sequential: (ISO) Pertaining to a process in which all events occur one after the other without any time lapse between them.

sequential access (IBM): (1) An access method in which records are read from, written to, or removed from a file, based on the logical order of the records in the file.

sequential construct: A construct in a program where two or more operations are performed in sequence.

sequential file organization: A file organization where records are usually in ascending order by record key.

* serial processing: Pertaining to the sequential or consecutive execution of two or more processes in a single device such as a channel or processing unit. Contrast with *parallel processing.*

* serial transmission: (ISO) The sequential transmission of the signal elements of a group representing a character or other entity of data. Contrast with *parallel transmission.*

service bureau: A company that provides batch computer processing service on an as-needed basis and charges for the service, based on an hourly rate.

shared data: Data that are used by two or more computers concurrently in a distributed data-processing system.

* sign bit: (ISO) A bit or a binary element that occupies a sign position and indicates the algebraic sign of the number represented by the numeral with which it is associated.

* simplex transmission: (ISO) Data transmission is one preassigned direction only.

simulate: To build a model or imitation of something that occurs in the real world, such as a business, weather system, or aircraft. Simulations built on computers are mathematical models.

* simulation: (ISO) The representation of selected characteristics of the behavior of one physical or abstract system by another system; for example, the representation of physical phenomena by means of operations performed by a data-processing system, or the representation of operations of a data-processing system by those of another data-processing system. Contrast with *emulation.*

simultaneous: Pertaining to the occurrence of two or more events at the same instant of time. (2) See also *concurrent, consecutive, sequential.*

skeleton application program: A simple program developed as a model for an actual application. It includes only the most essential capabilities needed in the actual application. Synonymous with *prototype.*

soft copy: An image on a video or other electronic screen, as opposed to hard copy on paper.

soft error: An error found when reading data (from the disk) that does not recur when those same data are reread.

soft-sectored: Disks that mark the beginning of each sector of data within a track by a magnetic pattern rather than by a physical hole in the disk.

* software: Programs, procedures, rules, and any associated documentation pertaining to the operation of a computer system. Contrast with *hardware.*

software directory: A reference book that lists a large number of software packages and describes their major characteristics.

software monitor: A software system that monitors the performance of various system devices.

* sort: (1) (ISO) To segregate items into groups according to specified criteria, without necessarily ordering the items within each group. (2) To arrange a set of items according to keys which are used as a basis for determining the sequence of the items; for example, to arrange the records of a personnel file into alphabetical sequence by using employee names as sort keys.

* sorter: (1) (ISO) A device that deposits punched cards into pockets selected according to the hole patterns in the cards. (2) A person, device, or computer routine that sorts.

* sort key: A key used as a basis for determining the sequence of items in a set.

sound synthesizer: An acoustic device which, when connected to a computer, can produce many different musical sounds.

source code: A program written in a higher level language than machine language. It is called source code because it is the starting point, or source, in the compilation process to produce object code.

source-data automation: The capture of data, in computer-readable form, at the place and time of an event.

source document: A form containing data that are being keyed into a computer system.

* source language: A language from which statements are translated.

* source program: (ISO) A computer program expressed in a source language. Contrast with *object program.*

specification form: A form used to specify computations, input file format, and report format in RPG.

specification statement: In a program, a passive statement that describes data characteristics to the computer but does not make it perform any action.

speed (IBM): In a document-copying machine, a measure of the light sensitivity of the coating of sensitized materials.

spindle: The center shaft of a disk.

spooling (simultaneous peripheral operation online): (ISO) The use of auxiliary storage as a buffer storage to reduce processing delays when transferring data between peripheral equipment and the processors of a computer.

spreadsheet: A program that allows the user to create a large, two-dimensional table on the computer screen, and to manipulate the data in the table in many ways.

stand-alone: Computer hardware or software that operates in an independent and separate manner.

standard: An acknowledged guideline or norm against which performance is measured.

star-network configuration: A communication network in which several microcomputers are connected to a central CPU.

* statement: (1) In a programming language, a language construct that represents a set of declarations or a step in a sequence of actions. (2) In computer programming, a symbol string or other arrangement of symbols.

statistical multiplexor: A multiplexing device that allocates transmission time to different terminals in proportion to their volume of data input/output.

storage: The process of retaining data, program instructions, and output in machine-readable form.

* store: (1) (ISO) To place data into a storage device. (2) (ISO) To retain data in a storage device.

stored program: A set of instructions, residing in the computer's memory, that can be executed without human intervention.

strategic decision-making: Involves making decisions at the upper or strategic level of the organization. These decisions affect the future of the organization and are made in an environment of uncertainty. Strategic decisions involve establishing goals, policies, and long-term resource allocations.

streaming tape: A tape-recording method used only to make backup copies of information from hard disks. Streaming tapes record data blocks close together, leaving too little room to be able to start and stop between blocks.

* string: (ISO) A sequence of elements of the same type, such as characters, considered as a whole.

string constant: A constant composed of alphabetic, numeric, and special characters, enclosed within double quotes.

string variable: A variable that can take on as a value any string of alphabetic, numeric, and special characters.

structure chart: A graphic representation of the hierarchical relationships between various modules.

structured: That which is highly organized.

structured analysis: A system-analysis methodology used in structured system development. A structured analysis moves from a study of the existing system to its logical model. Then the logical model of the new system is created and developed into a new physical system.

structured design: Development of the logic of program modules and their interfaces.

structured English: A tool for describing program logic in English-like terminology. It uses the vocabulary of English combined with the logical constructs of a programming language to make the logic understandable to humans.

structured programming: An approach to computer programming that restricts the flow of control to three basic constructs: sequence, loop, and conditional.

structured system development: A system-development methodology based on three major principles: partitioning into small modules, specification of interfaces between modules, and specification of processes within the modules.

* subroutine: (1)(ISO) A sequenced set of instructions or statements that can be used in one or more computer programs and at one or more points in a computer program. (2) A routine that can be part of another routine.

subschema: The logical view of that part of a data base which is of interest to a particular application.

subscript: A variable whose values uniquely identify individual elements of an array. Synonymous with *index*.

substrate: On a disk, the material beneath the magnetic coating. Hard disks are generally made of aluminum or magnesium alloys (or glass, for optical disks), whereas on floppy disks the substrate is usually Mylar.

subsystem: (1) (IBM) A secondary or subordinate system (or programming support) usually capable of operating independently of, or asynchronously with, a controlling system. (2) A part of the total system. All subsystems combine to comprise the system.

summary file: A file containing data extracted and summarized from other files.

supervisor (IBM): The part of a control program that coordinates the use of resources and maintains the flow of processing-unit operations. Synonym for *supervisory program*.

* supervisory program: (ISO) A computer program, usually part of an operating system, that controls the execution of other computer programs and regulates the flow of work in a data-processing system. Synonymous with *executive program, supervisor*.

surface: The top or bottom side of a disk platter.

* symbolic language: A programming language that expresses addresses and operation codes of instructions in symbols convenient to humans rather than in machine language.

synchronous transmission: A data-transmission method in which a long stream of bytes is transmitted without interruption. This method is economical for complex, high-speed equipment that processes large volumes of data.

* syntax: (1) The relationship among characters or groups of characters, independent of their meanings or the manner of their interpretation and use. (2) The structure of expressions in a language. (3) The rules governing the structure of a language.

* system: People, machines, and methods organized to accomplish a set of specific functions.

system analysis: (1) In system development, the systematic investigation of a real or planned system to determine the functions of the system and how they relate to each other and to other systems. (2) The evaluation of a set of alternatives in a system with a set of criteria.

system analyst: A person whose responsibility is to analyze, design, and develop information systems.

system commands: Operating-system commands issued by the user to facilitate the creating, editing, and execution of programs.

system-development life cycle: The phases a typical computer-based information system goes through in its development and use.

system-development controls: Control procedures to manage the system development, system documentation, and program-maintenance functions.

system documentation: Documentation that provides an overview of a system's features.

system flowchart: A flowchart providing an overall view of the inputs, processes, and outputs of a system.

system maintenance: Correcting errors discovered in programs and changing the programs to satisfy modified user requirements or conditions.

system network architecture (SNA): A data-communication system used to connect various IBM devices.

system and programming group: MIS personnel who develop or acquire application software systems.

system programmer (IBM): A programmer who plans, generates, maintains, extends, and controls the use of an operating system with the aim of improving the overall productivity of an installation.

system unit: The part of a personal computer that contains the central processing unit.

system software: A set of programs that controls the use of hardware and software resources. This software allocates system resources to application programs, based on the needs and the priorities of these programs.

table: (1) A two-dimensional data structure used as a logical model in relational data-base management systems. (2) * (ISO) An array of data, each item of which may be unambiguously identified by means of one or more arguments.

tactical decision-making: Involves making decisions at the middle or coordinating level of an organization. The decisions are made primarily to reach the current goals of the organization. A common decision on this level involves resource allocation.

* tape drive: (ISO) A mechanism for controlling the movement of magnetic tape, commonly used to move magnetic tape past a read or write head, or to allow automatic rewinding.

* task: (ISO) In a multiprogramming or multiprocessing environment, one or more sequences of instructions treated by a control program as a unit of work to be accomplished by a computer.

technical support staff: MIS personnel who are responsible for hardware maintenance and establishing data-processing standards.

telecommunications: Any communication between two computers, or devices with embedded computers, in various locations. This type of communication differs from networks in that it takes place over long distances and is usually carried out over phone lines, radio waves, or a satellite-transmission apparatus.

* temporary storage: In computer programming, storage locations reserved for intermediate results. Synonymous with *working storage.*

terminal: (1) * A point in a system or communication network at which data can either enter or leave. (2) (IBM) In data communication, a device, usually equipped with a keyboard and some kind of display, capable of sending and receiving information.

test data: Hypothetical data used to test a new program for errors. Test data should be comprehensive enough to cover all possible types of valid and invalid inputs so that program performance can be observed under all circumstances.

third-generation language: A programming language, such as FORTRAN, COBOL, PASCAL, or BASIC, which requires that the user instruct the computer in a procedural, step-by-step fashion.

third party: A company other than the user or the computer manufacturer.

thrashing (IBM): In virtual-storage systems, a condition in which the system can do little useful work because of excessive paging.

throughput: (ISO) A measure of the amount of work performed by a computer system over a given period of time; for example, number of jobs per day.

timeliness: The speed with which data are provided to the user for decision making.

timesharing: (1) (ISO) An operation technique of a computer system that provides for the interleaving in time of two or more processes in one processor. (2) (IBM) A method of using a computing system that allows a number of users to execute programs concurrently and to interact with the programs during execution. (3) (ISO) Synonym for *conversational mode*.

timesharing service: A service firm that rents out computer time to its customers. The customer typically accesses the CPU through a remote terminal located at its place of business.

topdown approach: A system-development approach that calls for the development of an integrated information system based on the objectives of the business.

topdown programming (IBM): The design and coding of computer programs, using a hierarchical structure in which related functions are performed at each level of the structure.

trace: (1) * A record of the execution of a computer program; it exhibits the sequence in which the instructions were executed. (2) (IBM) To record a series of events as they occur.

track: An invisible, magnetic, circle pattern written on a disk as a guide to where to store and read data.

track density: How closely the tracks are packed on a disk. The number is specified as tracks per inch (tpi), with most fixed disks in the hundreds or thousands.

tractor feed: A mechanism with a train of feed pins on each side that fit into the pinholes of continuous paper stock. Line-advance commands from the computer then cause the paper to advance.

trailer label: The last record in a file on magnetic tape; the record contains control information such as the total number of records in the file.

trailer value: A special data value that signals the end of a set of data. Synonymous with *sentinel value*.

transaction: A business event, such as a sale to a customer. In information systems, the term is often used to refer to any change made in a computer file.

transfer rate: For a disk or other peripheral device, the rate at which information is transferred from the device to memory, or vice versa.

* transform: (ISO) To change the form of data according to specified rules, without significantly changing the meaning of the data.

transform description: A description, at the lowest levels of a data-flow diagram, of how data are to be processed.

transistor (IBM): A small, solid-state semiconducting device that can perform nearly all the functions of an electronic tube, including amplification and rectification.

translation: Generation of object code from source code.

* translator: (ISO) A computer program that translates from one language into another language, and in particular from one programming language into another programming language. Synonymous with *translating program*.

tree data structure: A hierarchical data structure, characterized by a top node called a root, and nodes having a one-to-many relationship.

turn-around document: A document that is sent out to be read by people, and that is also read by the computer when it is returned. The punched card containing remittance advice that often comes with a utility bill is a turn-around document.

turnaround time: (1) (ISO) The elapsed time between submission of a job and the return of the complete output. (2) The elapsed time between submission of a batch job and the availability of output.

turnkey system: A complete system in which all hardware and software have been installed and debugged. In theory, all the user has to do is turn a key.

two-dimensional: Allowing only rows and columns.

unit record (IBM): (1) A card containing one complete record, a punched card. (2) Pertaining to card input/output or printer output.

universal product code (UPC): A bar-coded symbol printed on the package of a consumer product. This is detected by an optical reader and is used by the computer to identify and price the product.

update (IBM): To modify a master file with current information according to a specified procedure.

user (IBM): Anyone who requires the services of a computing system.

user affirmation: The process of asking the user whether he or she will enter more data. This process is used when executing programs that require interactive data entry.

user-driven computing: EDP applications for which users do not always know what information they will need, or when. In such systems, it is often necessary to modify the programs on short notice.

user-defined function: A function defined by a programmer, as opposed to a built-in fashion.

user-defined words: Words in a program that the programmer has defined as having specific meanings.

user exit (IBM): A point in an IBM-supplied program at which a user exit routine can be given control.

user-friendly systems: software systems that make it easy for noncomputer-oriented people to use computers.

utility program: (1) * (ISO) A computer program in general support of the processes of a computer; for example, a diagnostic program, a trace program, or a sort program. Synonymous with *service program*. (2) (IBM) A program designed to perform an everyday task such as copying data from one storage device to another.

vacuum tube: Glass-covered instruments that were used to regulate the flow of electrons through the circuits of early computer systems.

validation: (IBM) The checking of data for correctness, or compliance with applicable standards, rules, and conventions.

validity checks: A hardware control that monitors the bit structure of bytes to determine whether the combination of the on and off bits represents a valid structure within the character set of the computer.

* variable: A quantity that can assume any of a given set of values.

variable-length record (IBM): (1) A record having a length independent of the length of other records with which it is logically or physically associated. Contrast with *fixed-length record*. (2) Pertaining to a file in which the records are not uniform in length.

vendor support: Services provided by the seller of a hardware or software system. These typically include training, repair and maintenance, installation, testing, consulting, and backup arrangements.

verifiability: The ability to confirm the accuracy of data. Accuracy can be confirmed by comparing with other data of known accuracy or tracing back to the original source.

virtual drive: The use of a drive name (on the PC, a letter of the alphabet) to refer to part of a disk drive. Virtual drives are often for large-capacity hard disks.

virtual storage: (ISO) The storage space that can be regarded as addressable main storage by the user of a computer system in which virtual addresses are mapped into real addresses. The size of virtual storage is limited by the addressing scheme of the computing system and by the amount of auxiliary storage available, not by the actual number of main-storage locations.

virtual-storage access method (VSAM) (IBM): An access method for indexed or sequential processing of fixed and variable-length records on direct-access devices. The records in a VSAM data set or file can be organized in logical sequence by means of a key field (key sequence), in the physical sequence in which they are written on the data set or file (entry-sequence), or by means of relative-record number.

visual display terminal (IBM): Synonym for *visual display unit*.

visual display unit (VDU): A device with a TV-like display screen, usually equipped with a keyboard.

voice mail (IBM): The use of computers to alert recipients that recorded telephone messages are waiting. See also *electronic mail*.

voice-recognition system: A hardware or software device that interprets the patterns of an individual's speech, thereby enabling voice input to a computer.

VSE (virtual storage extended) (IBM): An operating system that is an extension of disk-operating system/virtual storage. A VSE system consists of: (a) licensed VSE/Advanced Functions Support, and (b) any IBM-supplied and user-written programs that are required to meet the data-processing needs of a user. VSE and the hardware it controls form a complete computing system.

volatile storage: (ISO) A storage device whose contents are lost when electrical power is off.

walkthrough: A step-by-step review of the documentation or other work produced by a system analyst or programmer.

Winchester disks: Hard disks that use a technology similar to an IBM model that had the Winchester name. These disks use the read/write heads that ride just above the magnetic surface, held up by the air dragged by the turning disk. When the disks stops turning, the heads land on the surface, which has a specially lubricated coating. Winchester disks must either be sealed or have a filtration system, since ordinary dust particles are large enough to be caught between the head and the disk.

window: (1) (ISO) In computer graphics, a predefined part of a virtual space. (2) A portion of a display surface in which display images pertaining to a particular application can be presented. Different applications can be displayed simultaneously in different windows.

word (IBM): (1) A character string considered as a unit for a given purpose. (2) A character string or a bit string considered as an entity.

word-processing system: A computer system that stores and processes text data. These systems typically include powerful editing and text-formatting capabilities.

word size: A measure of the amount of data the CPU can process simultaneously.

working storage: (ISO) Synonym for *temporary storage* and *working space*.

workload model: A set of one or more computer programs that are representative of the buyer's planned computer workload. These are typically executed on various computer configurations to provide information useful for acquisition decisions.

* write: (ISO) To make a permanent or transient recording of data in a storage device or on a data medium.

write-enable ring (IBM): A ring installed in a tape reel to permit writing on the tape. If tape is mounted without the ring in position, writing to the tape cannot occur and the tape is protected.

write-protect notch: A cut-out in one corner of a disk that is optically scanned to allow writing on a disk. If the notch is covered with tape, the drive cannot write on the diskette; thus the disk is write-protected.

write-read check: A control similar to a redundancy check. As data are written on magnetic tape or disk, they pass through a read head, which reads the data and compares them to the data that should have been written.

write-once: As applied to optical disks, technologies that allow the drive to store data on a disk and read them back, but not to erase them.

Index

Page numbers followed by an i refer to figures; page numbers followed by a t refer to tables.

Abacus, 433, 433i
Ability (software), 48, 98, 192, 375
Access arms, 226
Access security, 263
Access time, 500
Accounting software, 46–47, 46i
Account management, 131
Accounts payable, 127–28, 127i, 128i
Accounts receivable, 123–27
  management reports, 125i, 126i
  objectives of, 123–24
  structure chart of, 169i
Accuracy, 6, 86
Active data dictionary, 329, 395
ADA, 463, 481, 482–83i, 483–84
  assignment/arithmetic statements, 484
  control statements, 483
  data-definition statements, 481, 483
  input/output statements, 484
Address
  cell, 17
  physical, 295, 296i
Advanced Information System/Net 1, 358–59
Aiken, Howard, 438
Algorithm, 464
Altair, 447–48
American Airlines' Sabre system, 85
American Federation of Information Processing Societies (AFIPS), 422
American Hospital Supply, 85
American Institute of Certified Public Accountants (AICPA), 422
American National Standards Institute (ANSI), 290, 468, 491
American Standard Code for Information Interchange (ASCII), 11, 290, 291t, 351
American Statistical Association (ASA), 422
Analog signals, 353
  conversion of digital signals to and from, 355i
Analytical engine, 435
Apple Computer Company, 44–45, 448

Apple II, 448
Apple Macintosh; 33, 45, 65, 254
  business software for, 67–69
  finder, 66–67, 67i
  hardware for, 65
  HyperCard, 69–70
  interface, 66
  merging of standards, 70–71
Application, 88
Application development
  by end users, 187–88
  blending conventional development with, 195–200
  cautions about, 199–200
  changing roles of system analysts and programmers, 201–3
  definition of, 188
  information centers, 200–1
  methods for, 192–95, 193i
  problems with conventional, 188–92
  role of information systems department in, 72–74
  types of, 195–98, 198t
Application generators, 193–95, 268
Application packages, 21
Application program, loading, on a personal computer, 264i
Application programmers, 262
Application software, 260, 261i, 262, 262i
  definition of, 140
  methods of user development of, 192
Application systems, 89
Arithmetic-logic unit, 9, 218
Array, 464
Artificial intelligence, 406–8
Assembler, 460
Assembly language, 460, 461i
Association for Computing Machinery (ACM), 422
Association for Systems Management (ASM), 423
Asynchronous transmission, 351–52, 352i
AT&T, 447
Attribute, 11, 334
Audio output, 42
Audio-response output devices, 254
Audit, post-implementation, 181

Audit trail, 86–87, 230
Automation, 406, 407i
Automation decisions, impact of management information systems, on, 93
Avon, management information system at, 134–36

Babbage, Charles, 434–35
Back-ordered items, 122
Back up, 39, 223–24
Balanced-tree index, 304, 305i
Band printer mechanisms, 252i
Base register, 462
Basic All-Purpose Symbolic Instruction Code (BASIC), 99, 160, 188, 194, 195, 463, 476, 477–78i, 490
  assignment/arithmetic statements, 476–77
  comment statements, 477
  control statements, 476
  data-definition statements, 476
  input/output statements, 476
BASIC interpreter, 261
Batch, 228
Batch-direct mode, 308, 309i
Batch operating system, 268, 270i
Batch processing, 12–13, 14i, 15i, 307–8, 307i
Batch-sequential mode, 307i, 308
Benchmark programs, 499, 500i
Binary number system, 288–90, 441
  conversion of numbers into decimal numbers, 289i
Binary search, 302
Bit, 10, 217
Bit patterns, 11
Block format, 351
Block-structured language, 473
Bootstrap, 262
Bottleneck, 397
Broadcast configuration, 361, 364i
B-tree index, 304, 305i
Bubble storage, 248
Bubble storage system, 232
Buffer, 354
Bundling, 497

Bundy Manufacturing Corporation, 437
Bunnell, David, 448
Bus, 501
Bus configuration, 361, 366i
Business, impact of management
    information systems on, 92–93
Business cycle, 114–16, 115i
Business functions, and management
    information systems, 88–89
Byron, Augusta Ada, 435–36, 481
Byte, 11, 55

Cache memory, 232–33
Calculators, 433–34, 434i
Call, 170, 463
Careers
    effect of computers on, 416
    information-system, 417–21
Cartridge drive and tape, 225i
CASE. See Computer-aided software
    engineering
Cell, 17
Cell address, 17
Central process, in data-flow diagram,
    170
Central processing unit (CPU), 8–9, 9i,
    33, 212, 213
    arithmetic-logic unit, 218
    control unit, 218
    primary storage, 213, 215, 217–18
Certificate in Computer Programming
    (CCP), 424
Certificate in Data Processing (CDP)
    examination, 424
Certified Information Systems Auditor
    (CISA) exam, 424
Chain printer mechanisms, 252i
Change authorization form, 395, 396i
Channels, 218
Character data, 21
Character printers, 250
Chief-programmer teams, 179
Clerical workers, impact of
    management information systems
    on number of, 92–93
COBOL (Common Business-Oriented
    Language), 99, 160, 188, 194, 195,
    328, 329, 439, 445, 446, 463, 468,
    469–72i, 472–73, 490
    divisions in, 468
    reserved words in, 472
    sections in, 468
    semantic errors in, 473
    system names in, 472
    user-defined words in, 472
CODASYL (Committee on Data
    Systems Languages), 445, 468
Code inspection, 176
Coding, 176
Collators, 438
Columns, 17
COM (computer-output microfiche),
    253, 253i
Command, 51

Committee on Data Systems Languages
    (CODASYL), 445
Communication hardware, 353–54, 356
Communication program, 42
Communication protocol, 351
Compaq, 45, 450
Compatibility, 501–2
Competitive advantage, using
    information systems for, 85
Compile, 177
Compiler, 462
Compiler diagnostics, 177
Compile-time diagnostics, 491
Compute-bound batch job, 499
Computer(s)
    applications for, 15–24
    characteristics and capabilities of,
        5–6, 5i
    definition of, 4–5
    effect of, on career, 416
    electromechanical, 438–39, 439i
    electronic, 439–411, 440i
    first-generation, 441–42, 442i
    fourth generation, 446–47, 449t
    future of, 451–54, 452i
    and individual privacy, 408–10
    processing of data by, 12–15
    second-generation, 443–44, 449t
    storage of data by, 9–12
    stored programs for, 6–7
    third-generation, 445–46, 445i, 449t
Computer-aided design and computer-
    aided manufacturing (CAD/CAM)
    techniques, 451
Computer-aided design (CAD)
    software, 119
Computer-aided software engineering
    (CASE), 158, 173
    and end-user development, 199
    tools for, 158, 173
    use of, at Ramada, Inc., 206–8
Computer-based inventory systems, 117
Computer conferencing, 373
Computer crime, 411
    Equity Funding Life Insurance
        Company, 411–12
    Pacific Bell, 412
    Wells Fargo, 412
Computer information systems,
    potential impact of, 404–6
Computer-integrated manufacturing
    (CIM), 118–21, 120i
Computer lessors, 508–9
Computer manufacturers, 506
Computer operators, 420
Computer-output microfiche (COM),
    253, 253i
Computer/peripheral-device
    communication, 347, 347i, 348i
Computer reports, types of, 87–88
Computer system, 7–8, 7i, 8i, 212i
    central processing unit, 8–9, 9i
    evaluation of, 496–503, 497i
    financing options, 503–5
    input devices, 8
    output devices, 9

secondary storage, 9
    vendor selection, 503, 504t
Computer-to-computer communication,
    347–48
Computer viruses, 399
Computing-Tabulating-Recording
    Company (CTR), 437
Concentric tracks, 225
Conference on Data Systems Languages
    (CODASYL) Committee, 468
Configuration control, 329
Connection, 170
Control, 84
Controller, 388
Control totals, 240
Control unit, 9, 218
Conventional development, blending
    user development with, 195–200
Conversion, 180
Conversion activity, 114
Core-image library, 265i
Couple, 170
Critical path management (CPM), 393
CTR (Computing-Tabulating-Recording
    Company), 437
Cursor, 53
Customer mailing lists, 375–76
Cylinder, 226, 295, 297i

Daisy wheel printer, 250, 250i
Data, use of, in decision making, 87
Data base, 12, 78, 89, 102, 323, 329–31
Data-base administration, 198–99, 199,
    390
Data-base administrator, 199, 329, 331i,
    420
Data-base management, 47
Data-base management system (DBMS),
    12, 20–21, 192, 320, 326–29
    advantages of, 339
    disadvantages of, 339–40
    to information processing, 323–31,
        323i
    interaction among components of,
        326i
    management information systems
        and, 89–90
    query languages of, 88
    relationship between, and
        management information
        systems, 91i
    structures, 331–32
        network structures, 332–33, 334i
        relational structures, 334–38, 335i,
            336i, 337i
        tree structures, 332, 333i
Data communication, 42, 346, 447
    types of, 346–50
Data decentralization, 364–68, 367i
Data-definition language (DDL), 326,
    327
    statements from, 327i
Data dictionary, 149, 150–51, 329, 330i,
    366

Data editing, 242
Data entry
  interactive, 241–42, 241i
  key-to-disk data entry, 239–41, 239i
  key-to-diskette data entry, 238–39
  offline versus online data entry, 238
  source-data automation, 242–49, 243i
Data-entry devices, 238
Data-entry operator, 420
Data-entry stations, 240i
Data files, as component of management
  information system, 79
Data-flow diagram (DFD), 144, 149–50,
  169–70
  deriving structure charts from, 170
  symbols used in, 146i
Data hierarchy, 9–12, 11i
Data integration, 320–21, 339
Data-manipulation language (DML),
  326, 328–29
  statements from three, 328i
  verbs, 328t
Data processing, 395–97, 420
  definition of, 87
  early developments in, 433–36, 433i,
    434i, 435i, 436i
  orientation of, 78
  relationship between, and
    management information
    systems, 79i
Data Processing Management
  Association (DPMA), 422
Data-processing operations department,
  390
Datapro Reports on Microcomputer
  Software, 50
Data redundancy, 320, 322
  elimination of, 339
Data representation
  ASCII representation, 290, 291t
  EBCDIC representation, 290, 291t
  hexadecimal representation, 292, 293t
  parity bits, 292, 293t
  true binary representation, 288–90
Data storage, 9–12
  logical versus physical views of,
    324–25, 325i
  data representation, 288–93, 289i,
    291t, 292i, 293t
  file organization, 295–97, 296i, 297i,
    298i, 299–306, 299i, 300i, 301i,
    302i, 303i, 305i, 306i
  information-processing modes,
    306–10, 307i, 308i, 309i, 310i
  online direct-access systems, 310,
    311i, 312
  real-time systems, 312–13, 313i
  record-access methods, 293–95, 294i
Data switch, 350i
  communication through, 349–50
Data-switching networks, 356
Data transmission process
  communication hardware, 353–54,
    356
  data transmission speed, 352–53, 353i
  protocols, 350–51

  speed, 352–53, 353i
  transmission direction, 353
  transmission mode, 351–52, 352i
Dayton Scale Company, 437
dBase, 487, 488–89i, 489, 491
dBase III, 188, 192
dBase III Plus, 21
Decimal number system, 288
  conversion of binary number to, 289i
Decision(s)
  determination of, 80
  relationship between objectives, and
    information needs, 81i
  structured, 98
Decision making
  levels of, 81–83, 82i
    characteristics of, 82t
    characteristics of information
      required, 83t
    operational, 82t, 83t
    strategic, 82t, 83t
    tactical, 82t, 83t
Decision-support/financial-modeling
  tools, 193
Decision-support systems, 49
  building, 103, 104i
    design, 105
    evaluation, 105–6
    implementation, 105
    predesign, 103–5
  components of, 99i
  definition of, 91, 98–99
  functions of, 100–2
  hardware capabilities of, 101–2
  and management information
    systems, 90–91
  management need for, 102
  organization environment for
    successful, 102–3
  software for, 99–100
  tools for, 98, 99
    software, 99–100
Decision tables, 151, 153, 153i, 154
Decision-tree, 151, 154, 154i
Dedicated word-processing system, 369
De facto standards, 45
Default, 475
Demand reports, 88
Demodulation, 353
Dependent variable, 101
Design modules, 173
Desk check, 177
Desktop publishing, 370–71, 371i
Device, 238
Difference engine, 434–35
Digital Equipment Corporation (DEC),
  445
  development of XCON by, 106
Digital signals, conversion of, to and
  from analog form, 355i
Digital transmission, 353–54
Digitize, 372
Direct access, 310
Direct-access file, 12
Direct-access storage device (DASD),
  228, 307

Direct addressing, 300i
Direct file organization, 299–301
Direct manipulation of objects of
  interest, 374
Direct marketing, 131
Directory, 296, 298i
Disaster controls, 399–400
Disk caching, 284
Diskette. See Floppy disk
Disk operating system (DOS), 50, 51i,
  280, 448
  DOS 3.3, 280
  DOS 3.4, 280
  DOS 4.0, 280–81
Distributed data entry, 244–45
Distributed data processing (DDP), 376
  data decentralization, 364–68, 367i
  hardware distribution, 360–61, 361i,
    362i, 363i, 364i, 365i
  need for decentralized processing,
    359–60
  software distribution, 362–64
Distributed data processing (DDP), 346,
  446
Distributed data-processing systems,
  219
Division/remainder method of hashing,
  300, 301i
Divisions, of COBOL program, 468
DML (data-manipulation language),
  326, 328–29
Documentation
  in FORTRAN, 467
  in system development, 179
Dot-matrix printer, 39, 40i, 250–51
  character set for, 250i
Dow Jones News Retrieval, 59, 404
Download, 61
DPMA (Data Processing Management
  Association), 422, 424
Drum printer mechanisms, 252i

EBCDIC (Extended Binary Coded
  Decimal Interchange Code)
  representation of data, 290, 291t,
    292i
Eckert, J. Presper, Jr., 439, 440, 441
Edit-directed input statement, 475
EDP auditor, 419–20
EDP Auditors Foundation, 423
EDSAC (Electronic Delay Storage
  Automatic Computer), 441
Educational Privacy Act, 409
EDVAC (Electronic Discrete Variable
  Automatic Computer), 441
EFTS (electronic funds transfer system),
  408
EISA (Extended Industry Standard
  Architecture), 45, 450
Electric Pencil, 450–51
Electromechanical computer, 439
Electronic bulletin boards, 59
Electronic calendaring, 373
Electronic data processing (EDP), 346

Electronic Delay Storage Automatic Computer (EDSAC), 441
Electronic Discrete Variable Automatic Computer (EDVAC), 441
Electronic funds transfer system (EFTS), 408
Electronic mail, 371–72, 372i, 377
Electronic Numerical Integrator and Calculator (ENIAC), 439–41, 440i
Electronic shopping systems, 405
Electronic spreadsheets, 17–20, 17i, 18i, 19i, 20i, 21i, 47, 192
Electrothermal printer output, 251
Embedded pointer, 332
Enable, 192, 375
End users, 188. *See also* Users
   application development by, 72, 187–200
   blending with conventional development, 195–200
   and computer-aided software engineering (CASE), 199
ENIAC (Electronic Numerical Integrator and Calculator), 215, 439–41, 440i
Entity, 11
Entry control system, 397–98
Equity Funding Life Insurance Company, 411–12
Ergonomics, 454
Error reports, 88
Excel (software), 17, 47, 67–68
Excelerator, data-flow diagram produced by, 159i
Exception reports, 88
Executable statements, 464
Execute, 6
Execution cycle, 218
Execution paths, 6
Execution-time diagnostics, 491
Executive programs, 265
Expert systems, 100, 106, 407–8
   advantages of, 106–7
   components of, 107–8, 108i
   components of rule-based, 108i
   definition of, 106
   developing, 109
   picking right problem for, 107
Expert system shell, 109
Express (software), 193
Extended Binary Coded Decimal Interchange Code (EBCDIC)
   representation of data, 290, 291t, 292i
Extended Industry Standard Architecture (EISA), 45, 450
External files, 102

Face-to-face contact, 405
Facilities-management vendor, 509
Facsimile transmission, 373
Fair Credit Reporting Act (1970), 409
Feasibility study, 143–44
Feedback, and management control, 84

FIDEL (FOCUS Interactive Data Entry Language), 485
Field, 11
Fifth-generation project, 454
File, 12, 13i
File-access methods, 306t
File activity, 305
File backup, 397
File conversion, in system development, 180
Filemaker Plus, 68
File organization
   direct, 299–301
   indexed, 302, 302i
   selecting, 304–6
   terminology used with files, 295–96
File query, 306
FILETALK, 484, 487
Finance activity, 114
Financial functions, with decision-support system, 101
Financial management software, 47
Fine tuning, 500
Finished goods, 116
Fire control, 399
Firing of rules, 108
Firmware, 218
First-generation computers, 441–42, 442i
First-generation software, 442–43, 449t
Fixed disk, 226
Flat-panel display, 250
Flexibility, in hardware acquisitions, 504, 506i
Floppy disk, 9, 38–39, 226, 228, 228i, 230
   causes of data loss on, 230i
   terminology, 229i
Floppy-disk drive, 39i
Focus (software), 188, 268, 484–87, 485i, 486i
FOCUS Interactive Data Entry Language (FIDEL), 485
Font, 247
FORTRAN (Formula Translator), 99, 160, 188, 195, 329, 445, 446, 463, 464, 466–67i, 467–68, 491
   assignment statements, 464
   control statements, 467
   executable statements, 464
   input/output statements, 467
   keywords, 464
   nonexecutable statements, 464
FORTRAN IV, 468
FORTAN 77, 467
4th Dimension (software), 68
Fourth-generation computers, 446–47, 449t
Fourth-generation language, 160, 268, 484
   definition of, 160, 188
   products of, 195–96t
   as prototyping tool, 196
Frame-based expert system, 107
Framework, 48, 192, 375
Freedom of Information Act (1970), 409
Front-end processor, 274, 356, 357i

Full-duplex channel, 354i
Fully indexed files, 302, 302i
Functional area, 88–89
Functional information systems, 88–89
Functional primitives, 151

Gantt charts, 393, 394, 394i
Gates, Bill, 448
General business software, 46–48, 46i
Generalized modules, 194
General ledger, 130
General-purpose application software, 262
Gigabyte, 220
Goal seeking, with decision-support system, 101
Go-to-less programming, 170
Graphics, 254
   with decision-support system, 101
Graphics generators, 192–93, 194i
Graphics plotting, 42, 42i
Graphics terminals, 9, 254, 446
Graphics workstations, 119, 121i
GUIDE, 473

Hackers, 59
Half-duplex channel, 353, 354i
Hands-on exposure, 23–24
Hard copy, 250
Hard disks, 39i, 225–26, 226i,
Hardware
   costs of, 190i
   demonstration of, 498
   first-generation, 441–42, 442i, 443i, 449t
   fourth-generation, 446–47
   for personal computer, 33–36, 34i, 35i, 36, 36i, 37i, 38–39, 38i, 39i, 40i, 41, 41i, 42, 42i, 447–48, 450
   input/output devices, 36, 36i, 38–39, 38i, 39i, 40i, 41–42, 42i
   system unit, 33–36
   second-generation, 443–44, 449t
   the Apple Macintosh, 65
   third-generation, 445, 445i, 449t
Hardware industry, 42, 44–45
Hardware monitors, 397, 398i
Harvard Total Project Manager, 393
Header, 464
Hewlett-Packard, 448
Hexadecimal representation of data, 292, 293t
Hierarchical partitioning, 140–41
High-definition TV (HDTV), 453
High-level languages, 459
Historic information, in planning, 84
Hollerith, Herman, 437
Hollerith card ninety-column Powers card, 438
Hollerith's punched cards, 437, 438, 438i
Hopper, Grace Murray, 439, 468

Human beings, displacement of, 406–8
Human-resource information system, 131
Hybrid configuration for distributed data processing, 360, 363i
HyperCard, 69–70
HyperText, 69

IBM (International Business Machine Corporation), 437
  application development facility, 261
  systems management facility (SMF), 397
IBM PC, 33, 45, 448, 450
  buying, 53, 55
  merging of standards, 70–71
  software for, 450–51
IBM PS/2, 33, 45, 254
Icons, 53
IFPS (Integrated Financial Planning System), 47, 48i, 101
IF-THEN rules, 109
Illegal access, 59
Image storage and retrieval, 373–74
Immediate-direct mode, 309–310, 310i
Immediate processing, 13–15, 16i, 308, 308i
Impact printer, 251, 252i
Independent variable, 101
Index, 296
Indexed file organization, 302, 302i
Indexed sequential-access method (ISAM), 302–4, 303i
Inference engine, 107
Information
  in decision making, 83t, 87
  impact of management information systems on quality of, 93
  management uses of, 84
  qualitative characteristics of, 85–86
    accuracy, 86
    relevance, 86
    timeliness, 86
    verifiability, 86–87
Information center, 201i, 390
  functions of, 202i
Information needs
  determination of, 80
  relationship between objectives, decisions and, 81i
Information processing, 87
  applications for, 116i
  costs of, 93
  data-base approach to, 323–31, 323i
  modes, 306
    batch-direct, 308, 309i
    batch processing, 307–8, 307i
    batch-sequential, 307i, 308
    immediate-direct, 309–10, 310i
    immediate processing, 308, 308i
  traditional approach to, 320–23, 321i
Information response
  audio-response output devices, 254

computer-output microfiche (COM), 253, 253i
  graphics, 254
  laser-optical disks, 253–54, 253i
  printers, 250–53
  visual display terminals, 249–50, 249i
Information-response devices, 238
Information revolution, 404–5
Information services, 404
Information-system careers, 417
  data-base administrator (DBA), 420
  data-processing operations, 420
  EDP auditor, 419–20
  information-system consultant, 421
  knowledge engineer, 420–21
  programmer, 417–18
  system analyst, 418–19
Information-system consultant, 421, 509
Information-system department, 418i
  organization of, 201i
  role of, in applications development, 72–74
Information-system education, 424–25, 425i, 426i
Information-system equipment and services
  sources of, 505–9
Information-system manager, 421–22
Information-system reports, 89i
Information systems
  definition of, 4
  reasons for studying, 4
  using, for competitive advantage, 85
Information workers, 416
Infoworld, 55
In-house development of software, 502
Initial program load, 262
Initial program loader (IPL), 263
Ink-jet printer, 251
Ink jet technology, 252
Input, 8
Input devices, 8
Input masks, 240
Input/output (I/O) control program, 265
Institute for Certification of Computer Professionals (ICCP), 424
Institute of Electrical and Electronic Engineers (IEEE), 422
Instruction cycle, 218
Integer variable, 464
Integrated circuits, 445
Integrated Financial Planning System (IFPS), 47, 48i, 101, 193
Integrated personal-computer software, 375
Integrated services digital networks (ISDN), 452
Integrated software, 48–49, 91
Integrated tool, 192
  definition of, 192
Integrated Word Processing/Data Processing (WP/DP), 374–75, 375i, 376i
Intellect, 268

Interactive, 476
Interactive data entry, 241–42, 241i
Interactive operating system, 268–69
Interface, 141
Internal auditors, 181
Internal subroutine, 473
International data transfers, 410–11
International Federation of Information Processing Societies (IFIPS), 422
International Time Recording Company, 437
Interpreter, definition of, 218
Interprogram interference, 271
Interrupt, 268
Inventories, 116–17
Inventory carrying costs, 117
Inventory management reports, 119i
Inventory system, 116–17
IPL (initial program loader), 263
ISAM (indexed sequential-access method), 302–4, 303i
ISDN (integrated services digital networks), 452
Item, 11

Jacquard, Joseph, 434
Jacquard's loom, 434, 435i
Jazz (software), 375
Job-control language (JCL), 265–66
Job-control program, 263
Job queue, 260
Jobs, Steve, 45, 448, 450
Job scheduling, 262–63
Just-in-time inventory systems, 117

Kapor, Mitch, 450
Kernel program, 499
Keyboard, 8, 36, 36i
Key decisions, 103–4
Key-punches, 438
Key-to-disk data entry, 239–41, 239i
Key-to-diskette data entry, 238–39
Key verification, 240
Key-verifiers, 438
Keywords, 464
Kilobyte (K), 35
Knowledge base, 107
Knowledge engineer, 109, 420–21
Knowledge system, 99

Labor cost, in conventional development cycle, 188–89
Language. See Programming language
Language system, for decision-support system, 99
Language translator, 267, 267i
LAN (local-area network), 42, 359
Lap-top personal computers, 248
Large-scale integrated (LSI) circuits, 213, 446

Laser-optical disks, 231, 231i, 232, 253–54, 253i
Laser printer, 41, 251, 252
LCD (liquid crystal diode) display, 250
Lead tracking, 131
Leasing, of computer system, 505, 506i, 508–9
Letter-quality print, 39
Leveled data-flow diagrams, 145
Librarian
  in data-processing operation, 420
  support software, 266
Library routines, 463
Line department, 102–3
Line menu, 53
Line printer, 251, 251i
Linkage editor, 267
Linked list, 296, 298i, 332
Linking, 463
Liquid crystal diode (LCD) display, 250
LISP, 109, 421
Load, 463
Loading, 463
Load module, 267
Local-area network (LAN), 42, 44i, 359
Local data, 365
Local data base, 367i
Logical view of data, 324, 324t
Lotus 1-2-3, 17, 47, 68, 98, 99, 188, 192, 193, 450
  menu, 53

Machine cycle, 33
Machine language, 442, 459–60, 461i
Machine operations, 33
MacPaint, 69
Magnetic disks, 444
Magnetic drums, 442
Magnetic-ink character recognition (MICR), 245–46
Magnetic tape, 223–24, 297, 444
Magnetic tape cartridges, 39
Magnetic-tape drives, 224i
Mail merge, 376
Mainframe computer, 32, 220–21, 221i
  link with minicomputer, 349i
  magnetic-tape drives used with, 224i
Maintainability, of structured system, 157–58
Management
  need of, for decision-support systems, 102
  uses of information by, 84
Management by exception, 88
Management control, 84, 84i
Management information system (MIS), 77–78, 388
  at Avon, 134–36
  and business functions, 88–89
  and data-base management systems, 89–90
  and decision-support systems, 90–91
  definition of, 78

as federation of functional information systems, 90i
  impact of, on business, 92–93
  internal structure of, 390, 391–92i, 393
  managing system development, 393–94
  managing system operations, 394–400
  organizational location of, 388, 389i, 390
  parts of, 79–80, 80i
  relationship between data-base management systems and, 91i
  relationship between data processing and, 79i
Management-science models, with decision-support system, 101
Manual procedures, as component of management information system, 79
Manufacturing firms, 114
Mapping, 131
Marketing information system, 130–31
  account management, 131
  accounts payable, 127–28
  accounts receivable, 123–27
  computer-integrated manufacturing, 118–21
  direct marketing, 131
  human-resource information system, 131
  inventories, 116–17
  lead tracking, 131
  ledgers, 130
  mapping, 131
  marketing systems, 130–31
  order processing, 122–23
  payroll, 128–29
  sales forecasting, 131
  sales presentations, 131
  telemarketing, 131
Marketing management software, 47, 49i
Mark I electromechanical computer, 438–39, 439i
Martin, James, 190
Mass-storage device, 232, 233i
Master-slave relationship, 347, 348
Mauchly, John W., 439, 440, 441
MCI, 447
Medium, 238
Megabyte, 36
Memory dump, 292
Memory expansion board, 36, 36i
Memory modules, 34–35
Menu, 51, 52i, 53
Merchandise inventory system, 116, 117, 118i
Merchandising firms, 114
Message envelope, 351, 351i
Metcalfe, Henry, 436–37
Metcalfe's cards, 436–37
MICR (magnetic-ink character recognition), 245–46
Microcoding, 218
Microcomputer, 32, 218–19, 219i
Microcomputer chip, 216i

Microelectronics Computer Corporation, 454
Microprocessor, 33, 215
  speed of, 33
Microprogramming, 218
Microsoft Corporation, 448
Millard, Bill, 448
Million instructions per second (MIPS), 452
Minicomputer, 32, 219, 220i
MIPS (million instructions per second), 452
MIS steering committee, 393
Mnemonics, 460
Model, 100
  normative, 105
Model building, as function of decision-support system, 100
Model curriculums, 424
Modem, 42, 43i, 353–54, 355i
  conversion of data with, 43i
Modularity, 502
Modulation, 353
Module, 167, 170, 481. See also Subroutine
Monitor, 8, 9, 36, 38i, 265, 500
Mouse, 53
Multiplexing, 356i, 357i
Multiplexors, 354, 356
Multiprocessing, 274–76, 275i
Multiprogramming, 241
Multiprogramming operating systems, 445
Multitasking, 269–71, 270i
  advantages, 269–71
  disadvantages of, 271
  in OS/2, 281, 284

National Machine Accountants Association, 422
Natural and environmental disaster control, 399–400
Network, 350
Networking, in OS/2, 282
Network structures, for data-bases, 332–33, 334i
Network systems, 356–59
Next Computer, 45, 450
Nodes, 332
Nomad 2, 195
  report request, 197i
Nonexecutable statements, 464
Nonimpact printer, 251
Nonimpact technologies, 252
Nonprocedural language, 99, 100, 484
Nonprogrammable decisions, 83
Nonvolatile storage, 39
Normative model, 105
Numbering system
  binary, 288–90, 441
  in data-flow diagrams, 145
  decimal, 288
Numeric data, 21

Object code, 460
Objectives, relationship between decisions, information needs and, 80
Obsolescence, risk of, 504, 506i
Office automation, 368–69, 377
    computer conferencing, 373
    desktop publishing, 370–71, 371i
    electronic calendaring, 373
    electronic mail, 371–72, 372i
    facsimile transmission, 373
    forms processing, 374
    image storage and retrieval, 373–74
    integrated word processing/data processing (WP/DP), 374–75, 375i, 376i
    office decentralization and productivity, 376–78
    video conferencing, 373
    voice mail, 372–73
    word processing, 369–70, 369i
Office decentralization and productivity, 376–78
Offline, 220, 310
Offline data entry, versus online, 238
Omnis 3/Plus, 68
Online, 310
On-line applications, 14
Online data entry, versus offline, 238
Online direct-access systems, 310, 311i, 312
Operands, 218, 328
Operating system, 260, 444
    batch operating system, 268, 270i
    interactive operating system, 268–69
    multiprocessing, 274–76, 275i
    multitasking, 269–71, 270i
    storage on a mini or mainframe, 265i
    timesharing, 274
    virtual storage, 271–74, 272i
Operational decision making, 81–82, 82t
Operation code, 218
Optical-character recognition (OCR), 246–47, 246i, 247i
Optical scan (opscan) process, 243–44
ORACLE, 268
Order entry system, 122
Order processing, 122–23, 122i, 123i, 124i
Order-processing reports, 123, 124
OS/2, 281–94
    advantages of, 283–84
    application protection, 282
    data-base manager, 282
    data exchange, 282
    disadvantages of, 282–83
    DOS emulation, 282
    enhanced memory, 282
    memory requirements, 282
    multitasking, 281
    networking, 282
    presentation manager, 281
    trends in programs, 284–85
Out-of-stock situations, 117
Output, 8, 84
Output devices, 9

Pacific Bell, 412
Packaged design, 176
Pagemaker, 69
Page printer, 251
Paging, 272, 273i
Parallel computing, 453–54
Parallel processing, 222
Parallel transmission, 352–53, 353i
Parity bits, 293t
Partitioning, 366, 368i
PASCAL, 160, 463, 478, 479–80i, 480–81, 490, 491
    assignment/arithmetic statements, 481
    control statements, 480
    data definition statements, 480
    input/output statements, 480–81
Pascal, Blaise, 433, 478
Passwords, 59
Payroll, 128–29, 129i
Payroll system, subsystems within, 142i
PC-DOS, 218, 263i
PC Magazine, 55
PC Week, 55
PC Write, 59
Performance evaluation, 499–500
Performance monitors, 266
Peripheral device, 238
Peripheral-hardware manufacturers, 509
Personal computer, 9, 32, 34i
    buying hardware and software, 53, 55, 56–57i
        illegal access, 59
        software piracy, 58–59
    data communications, 42
    future directions of, 60–61
    hardware of, 33–36, 34i, 35i, 36, 36i, 37i, 38–39, 38i, 39i, 40i, 41, 41i, 42, 42i
    input/output devices, 36, 36i, 38–39, 38i, 39i, 40i, 41–42, 42i
    history of, 447–48
    impacts of, on society, 410
    in the home, 58
    lap-top, 248
    main circuit board of, 36i
    managing, 59–60, 60i
    multiprocessing, 274
    and self-service, 72–74
    software of, 46–51, 53
        general business software, 46–48, 46i
    types of, 33
    See also Microcomputers
Personal-computer consultants, 200
Personal-computer coordination group, responsibilities of, 393i
Personal Computer Disk-Operating System (PC-DOS), 218, 263i
Personal-computer mouse, 41, 41i
Personal-computer tools, 192
Personal Computing, 55
Personal System 2 (PS/2), 450
Personal workstation, 250
Personnel, as component of management information system, 79

PERT (program evaluation and review technique), 393
Physical address, 295, 296i
Physical implementation, 149
Physical security, 397–400
Physical view of data, 324
Place value, 288
PL/I (Programming Language/I), 328, 329, 446, 463, 473, 474–75i, 475–76, 491
    assignment statements, 475–76
    control statements, 475
    data definitions, 473
    input/output statements, 475
Plotter, 254, 254i
Plug-compatible hardware units, 45, 497
Pointers, 323
Point-of-sale (POS), 245, 245i
Portability, 468
Portable personal computer, 249i
Portable terminals, 248–49
Portfolio manager, 104
POS (point-of-sale), 245, 245i
Post-implementation audit, 181
PostScript, 68
Power control, 400
Powers, James, 437
    punched cards, 437–38
Powers Accounting Machine Company, 437
Power spikes, 400
Precision, 473
Predictive reports, 88
Presentation Manager, 451
Prespecified computing, versus user-driven computing, 191–92, 191i
Primary key, 294, 294i
Primary storage, 213, 215, 217–18
    allocation of, 271
    in CPU, 9
    movement of data between, and secondary storage, 214i
    versus secondary storage, 222–23
Primavera Project Planner, 394
Printers, 9, 250–53
    comparative characteristics of, 253t
    dot-matrix, 39, 40i
    letter-quality, 39, 41
Privacy
    and computers, 408–10
    legislation for, 409–10
Privacy Act (1974), 409
Problem-processing system, 99
Procedural languages, 99, 462–64, 467–68, 472–73, 476–78, 480–81, 483–87, 489–90
    with decision-support system, 100
Procedure development, 179
Process descriptions, 149–50, 151
Processing, 8
Process (or transform) descriptions, 151
Production CPU, 241
Professional associations, 422–23
Professional certification programs, 423–24

Program, 6, 459. *See also* Module
  stored, 6–7
Program bug, 178
Program code, 151
Program/data dependence, 321–22
Program/data independence, 339
Program evaluation and review
  technique (PERT), 393
Program flowchart symbols, 174i
Programmable decisions, 83
Programmer, 417–18
  changing roles of, 201–3
Programmer analysis, 167
Programming language, 160
  fourth-generation, 484
  high-level, 459
  machine language, 459–60, 461i
  procedural languages, 462–64,
    467–68, 472–73, 476–78, 480–81,
    483–87, 489–90
  selection of, 490–91
  symbolic languages, 460, 462
Program module, 23
Program stubs, 177
Project management approach, 393
PROLOG, 421
  use of, in expert system
    development, 109
Proposal, evaluation of, 498–502
Proprietary, 448
Protocols, 350–51
Prototype, 194
Pseudocode, 173, 460, 462
Public-domain software, 59
Public timesharing systems, 274
Punched-card equipment
  Hollerith's punched cards, 437, 438i
  Metcalfe's cards, 436–37
  Power's punched cards, 437–38
Punched cards, 434
Purchase order, 117
Purchase order notice, 117
Purchasing, 504

Quattro, 17, 47
QUBE system, 405–6, 408
Query language, 88, 192, 268, 325–26
  structured, 336–38, 337i

Radio Shack's TRS-80, 448
RAM (random-access memory), 34,
  217–18
Random, 217, 295
Random access, 295
Random-access memory (RAM), 34,
  217–18
Raw materials, 116
Read-only memory (ROM), 34, 217–18
Read/write head, 226
Ready-Set-Go, 69
Real-time applications, 14
Real-time information, 83

Real-time systems, 268, 312–13, 313i,
  445
Real variable, 464
Record, 11–12
Record-access methods, 293–94
  primary key, 294, 294i
  secondary keys, 294, 294i
Register, 462
Related data, ability to associate, 339
Relational structures, 334–38, 335i, 336i,
  337i
Relative address, 295, 296i
Relevance of information, 86
Reliability, 6
Remington Rand Corporation, 437
Remote terminal, 445–46
Removable disk pack, 225, 227i
Renting, of computer system, 504–5
Replication, 367
Report(s)
  accounts receivable management, 125,
    126
  definition of, 87
  inventory management, 119i
  order-processing, 123, 124
Report generation, 192, 193, 268, 375,
  376i
Report Program Generator (RPG),
  489–90
Reproducers, 438
Request for proposal, 498
Reserved words, 472
Resident supervisor, 265
Response time, 269
Retail computer stores, 507
Revenue activity, 114
Right to Financial Privacy Act (1978),
  409
Ring configuration, 360, 362i
Risk analysis, with decision-support
  system, 101
Robots, 120–21, 406, 407i
ROM (read-only memory), 34, 217–18
Rows, 17
RPG (Report Program Generator),
  489–90
Rule-based expert system, 107–8

Sabotage control, 399
Sales forecasting, 131
Sales presentations, 131
Satellite communication, 353
Scheduled reports, 87–88
Schema, 326
SDLC. *See* System-development life
  cycle
Secondary keys, 294, 294i
Secondary storage, 9, 213
  bubble storage system, 232
  floppy disks, 226, 228, 228i, 230
  hard disks, 225–26, 226i
  laser-optical disks, 231, 231i
  magnetic tape, 223–24
  mass-storage device, 232

  movement of data between primary
    storage and, 214i
  primary storage versus, 222–23
Second-generation computers, 443–44,
  449t
Sector, 295, 297i
Segments, 332
Self-documenting, 468
Self-service, and personal computers,
  72–74
Semantic errors, 473
Semantic gap, 459
Semiconductor, 10, 443
Semiconductor chips
  advantages of using, 215
  development of, 213, 215
  storage capacities of, 217t
Semiconductor memory, types of,
  217–18
Semiconductor storage, 10
Sequential access, 294–95
Sequential-access file, 12
Sequential file organization, 296–97, 298
Serial transmission, 352
Service bureaus, 508
Service firms, 114
SHARE, 473
Shared data, 364
Shareware, 59
Shipping orders, 122
Shrayer, Michael, 450–51
Simplex channel, 353, 354i
Simulate, 451
Simulation, 93, 221
Simulation models, 221
Simulation techniques, 500
Simultaneous peripheral operations on
  line (spooling), 268
Simultaneous punching, 437
Site preparation
  as aspects of conversion phase of
    system development, 180
Skeleton application program, 196
SMF (system management facilities),
  266
SNA (System Network Architecture),
  358, 358i
Society for Information Management
  (SIM), 423
Software
  for Apple Macintosh, 67–69
  costs of, 191i
  definition of, 140
  demonstration of, 498
  evaluation of, 501, 502–3
  first-generation, 442–43, 449t
  fourth-generation, 447
  general business, 46–48, 46i
  interacting with, 50–51, 53
  of personal computer, 46–51, 53,
    450–51
  piracy, 58–59
  second-generation, 444
  third-generation, 445–46
Software engineering, 158
Software monitors, 397

Software vendors, 507
Sorters, 438
Source, The, 59, 404
Source code, 460
Source-data automation, 242–49, 243i, 244i
Source document, 239
Spaghetti code, 170
Special-interest software, 50
Specification statements, 464
Specific-purpose application software, 262
Spending activity, 114
Sperry Gyroscope Company, 437
Sperry Rand Corporation, 437
Spooling (simultaneous peripheral operations on line), 268
Stand-alone, 49
Standards, 81–82, 390
  merging of, 70–71
Star configuration, 360, 361i
Statistical analysis, with decision-support system, 101
Steering committee, 393
Storage, 8
  semiconductor, 10
  volatile, 9
Stored program, 434
Strategic decision making, 81, 82t
Structure chart, 167–73, 168i
Structured decisions, 83, 98, 167i
Structured design, 166–67
  notational conventions used in, 171i
Structured development life cycle, 189i
Structured English, 151–52, 152i, 153i, 154
  conversion of, to pseudocode, 173
Structured program flowchart and pseudocode, 175i
Structured programming, 151, 467
Structured query language, 336–38, 337i
Structured system, 141
Structured system analysis, 144–57, 145i
Structured system development
  advantages of, 157–58
  life cycle of, 141–42
Structured walkthroughs, 176, 177
Suan pan, 433
Subroutine, 169, 170. *See also* Module
Subschema, 326–27
SuperCalc, 17, 99, 192
Supercomputers, 221, 221i
Supervisor, 263
Symbolic languages, 442, 460, 462
Symbols
  in data-flow diagrams, 146i
  in system-flowchart, 147i
Symphony, 48, 192, 375
Synchronous transmission, 352
Syntax, 151
System analysis, 22, 139–40
  definition of, 140
  feasibility study, 143–44
  structured system analysis, 144–57

System analysis and application development without programming, 159–60
System analyst, 81, 418–19
  changing roles of, 201–3
System availability, 270
System control software, 261, 262–66
System-development life cycle (SDLC), 22–23, 166i
  building system, 176–79
  chief-programmer teams, 179
  conversion, 180
  designing system, 166–76
  design modules, 173
  hardware evaluation, 142, 496–509
  packaging the design, 173–76
  post-implementation audit and maintenance, 181
  procedure development, 179
  structure chart, 167–73
  structured design, 166–67
  structured walkthroughs, 176
  subsystems within, 141–42, 143i
  top-down coding, 177
  top-down testing, 177–79, 178i
System development methodology, 393–94
System development software, 261, 266–68
System flowchart, 144
  symbols for, 147i
System maintenance, 394–95
System management facilities (SMF), 266
System names, 472
System Network Architecture (SNA), 358, 358i
System programmers, 261–62
System residence device, 263
Systems, partitioning of, 140–41, 141i
Systems and programming department, 390
System software, 261i
  types of, 260–62, 262–68, 262i
System software department, 390
System support programs, 261
System support software, 266
System unit, 33–36
System W, 193

Table, 334
TABLETALK, 487
Tabulating machine, 437
Tabulating Machine Company, 437
Tactical decision making, 81, 82t
Tandy Corporation, 45
Technical specialists, 200
Technical support staff, 390
Teleconferencing, 376
Telemarketing, 131
Telephone touch-tone devices, 248, 248i
Terminal phobia, 377
Terminating keywords, 481
Test data, preparation of, 178

Test plan, 176
Third-generation computers, 445–446, 445i, 449t
Third-generation language, 160
Third party, 504
Thrashing, 274
Throughput, 269
Timeliness of information, 86
Timesharing, 274, 446
Timesharing services, 508
Time span, in conventional systems development, 189
Top-down coding, 177
Top-down design, 169
Top-down testing, 177–79, 178i
Track, 295, 297i
Transaction, 78
Transaction processing, 78
Transform, 171
Transform descriptions, 149–50
Transistor, 443
Translation, 463
Translator program, 442
Transmission direction, 353
Transmission mode, 351–52, 352i
Transparent, 273
Tree configuration, for decision data processing, 361, 365i
Tree indexed files, 302–4, 303i
Tree indexes, 296
Tree structures, for data bases, 332, 333i
True binary representation, 288–90
Tuple, 334
Turn-around documents, 247
Turnaround time, 269

United Airlines' Apollo system, 85
UNIVAC computers, 437
UNIVAC-I (Universal Automatic Computer), 441–42, 442i
Universal product code (UPC), 245, 245i, 246i
Unstructured decisions, 83
UPC (universal product code), 245, 245i, 246i
User-billing system, 397
User consultants, 200
User-defined words, 472
User-driven computing, prespecified computing versus, 191–92, 191i
User exits, 194
User-friendliness, 50–51, 377, 447
User interface, 339
Users, 325–26. *See also* End users
Utility programs, 266

Vaccines, 399
Vacuum tubes, 439, 443i
Validation, 193
VDTs (video display terminals), 88
Vendor
  definition of, 498

demonstrations of equipment by, 498
facilities-management, 509
support, 501
Verifiability, of information, 86–87
Very-large-scale integrated (VLSI) circuits, 446
Very large scale integrated (VLSI) semiconductor chips, 213
Video conferencing, 373
Video display terminals (VDTs), 88, 446
Virtual storage, 271–74, 272i, 447
advantages of, 272–73
disadvantages of, 273–74
paging in, 273i
Virtual storage access method (VSAM), 304
Virtual-storage operating systems, 447
VisiCalc, 47, 450
Visual display terminals, 249–50, 249i
VLSI microprocessor, 215i

Voice mail, 372-73
Voice output, 9
Voice-recognition systems, 247–48
Volatile storage, 9, 217
von Leibnitz, Gottfried, 433
von Neumann, John, 441
VP-Planner, 17
VSAM (virtual storage access method), 304

Walkthroughs, 146
WATFIV, 464, 491
Wells Fargo, 412
What-if analysis, with decision-support system, 100–1
Wiler, Maurice, 441
Winchester disk, 39i, 226, 227i
Windows, 49, 50i
Word, 17, 47, 68

WordPerfect, 17, 47, 451
Word processing, 16–17, 47–48, 369–70, 369i
Word size, 33
Work-in-process, 116
Work-in-process inventory system, 117
Workload models, 499–500
Work overload, in conventional application development, 190–91
WORM (write once, read many), 231
Wozniak, Steve, 448
WP/DP (Integrated Word Processing/ Data Processing), 374–75, 375i, 376i
Write Now, 68
WYSIWYG (What You See Is What You Get), 69, 70i

XCON, 106

Photo/Figure Credits—Continued